Can Muslims Think?

Can Muslims Think?

Race, Islam, and the End of Europe

Muneeb Hafiz

ROWMAN & LITTLEFIELD
Lanham • Boulder • New York • London

Published by Rowman & Littlefield
An imprint of The Rowman & Littlefield Publishing Group, Inc.
4501 Forbes Boulevard, Suite 200, Lanham, Maryland 20706
www.rowman.com

86-90 Paul Street, London EC2A 4NE, United Kingdom

British Library Cataloguing in Publication Information Available

Library of Congress Cataloging-in-Publication Data Available

ISBN 9781538165072 (cloth : alk. paper) | ISBN 9781538165089 (epub)

♾™ The paper used in this publication meets the minimum requirements of American National Standard for Information Sciences—Permanence of Paper for Printed Library Materials, ANSI/NISO Z39.48-1992.

For my parents.

Contents

Acknowledgments

In one way or another, I was introduced to many of the ideas explored in this book during my doctoral studies at Lancaster University. I am deeply grateful to have been awarded the faculty's scholarship which made the time and space needed for such an exploration materially possible. My humble thanks also for the early assistance of Garrath Williams, the savvy of my supervisor Mark Lacy, and the generous challenge of my examiners Faisal Devji and Shuruq Naguib.

I have had the privilege, truly, of receiving support and care throughout the process of writing this book, the sources of which have been especially crucial in its completion. The many afternoons and evenings spent with my dear friend David Waines have been a source of joy over the years, even if having me explain and re-explain my half-formed ideas was the opposite for him. I record my particular gratitude to Joshua Entwistle, whose radical hospitality and capacious friendship have taught me so much. Likewise, the unfailing kindness and example of Christina Bodénès have been at once a source of knowledge and sustenance.

To my youngest siblings, Zakee and Ruhee, your borderless creativity and relationship to the question *why* have been a crucial reserve for both my thinking and doing. I have tried to keep my sentences short, though I have no doubt failed overall. To my brother, Ameen, your remarkable wit, words of encouragement, and marvelous laugh have uplifted me immensely. To my father, Aziz, my oldest and wisest interlocutor with whom I have learned how to learn, I am forever indebted and eternally grateful. And, finally, to my mother, Mehrun, a consummate chef, my chief example of strength and greatest source of inspiration, I hope this work makes you proud.

What's in a Question?

What is Enlightenment? Enlightenment is the exodus of humanity by its own effort from the state of guilty immaturity. Laziness and cowardice are the reasons why the greater part of humanity remains pleasurably in this state of immaturity.

—Immanuel Kant, *What is Enlightenment?*

Want of accuracy, which easily degenerates into untruthfulness, is in fact, the main characteristic of the Oriental mind. The mind of the Oriental, like his picturesque streets, is eminently wanting in symmetry. Although the ancient Arabs acquired in a somewhat high degree the science of dialectics, their descendants are singularly deficient in the logical faculty. They are often incapable of drawing the most obvious conclusion from any simple premises of which they may admit the truth. [. . .] The silent Eastern is devoid of energy and initiative, stagnant in mind, wanting in curiosity about matters which are new to him, careless of waste of time and patient under suffering.[. . .] The ways of the Oriental are tortuous; his love of intrigue is inveterate; centuries of despotic government, during which his race has been exposed to the unbridled violence of capricious and headstrong governors, have led him to fall back on the natural defence of the weak against the strong. Look at the high powers of organisation displayed by the European . . . compare these attributes with the feeble organising powers of the Oriental, with his fatalism which accepts the inevitable, and with his submissiveness to all constituted authority.

—Lord Cromer, *Modern Egypt.*

***

The philosopher Achille Mbembe tells us: "Europe is no longer the center of gravity of the world. This is the significant event, the fundamental experience, of our era. And we are only just now beginning the work of measuring its implications and weighing its consequences."[1] Symptomatic of the European idea, Britain goes astray, deeply conflicted about where it is within and with the world, and what it wants to know about, or do, with the racial subject. It is in this context of (white) anxiety that I write Islamophobia. Islamophobia is not only an (il)logical outcome of a constitutive history of raciology, of imposed human hierarchies in European modernity that authorized sophisticated systems of power, knowledge, and governance, with macro and molecular effects in the transatlantic slave trade, (settler) colonialism, and the formation of a global empire. It also, crucially, signals contemporary shifts in the logics of race and racism, that is, important discontinuities with colonial pasts, as they function to discipline, track, engage, celebrate, violate, mobilize, and accumulate "Islam" and "Muslims" in the West and elsewhere today.

Islamophobia is at its core a critique of Muslim reason and life which works according to a logic of racial subjectification and authorizes a range of violations of that same subject-object because s/he does not think or live like "we" do. But this so-called critique is also undergoing a transformation with new technologies, social and economic realities, and the specter of European demotion as the center of gravity in a complexifying world. That is, a world beset by an impulse to separate and balkanize, where anxieties of annihilation impel an atmosphere where the Other must count for nothing. Islamophobia and the phantasm of its racial subject do not then anchor themselves in a politics of identity but in a politics of capture, of life and death.

And yet the racialized subject might also be the best site through which this history and present are read toward a reparatory mode of seeing, listening, telling, and acting, an Other way of living in and with the world. Who is that subject-object upon which race and Islamophobia act and engage? What constraints, dangers, and possibilities are there in being Other within racial formations after empire? What connections do categories of "race," "Islam," and "white" have in our diagnoses and hopes to remedy Islamophobia, also known as the Muslim Problem? These are the guiding questions for my analysis of the twin phantasms of Muslims and Islam in the emergence and (trans)formation of a so-called liberal Europe reeling from an engagement for two decades in a war on "Islamic terrorism" and for the soul of Europe.

In the substantive three parts of the study, each comprised of three chapters, Islamophobia in Britain constitutes a case study as the basis for a kind

---

[1] A. Mbembe. (2017). *Critique of Black Reason*. Durham: Duke University Press, p. 1.

of speculative theory of the racial subject of Islamophobic dehumanization at home in the interior. Race and racism were modern Europe's strategies for orienting a world in which the fundamentally parasitical nature of white freedom and security required and accumulated certain lives as their raw material. At the core of this world-making racist teleology was and is a complex form of violence which works on the Other's perceived ability to reason, to think, and be trusted to live as an autonomous, that is, human subject. Today, the Muslim and his/her Islam are caught up in new technologies and economies of cross-examination, with all their attendant violence, dynamic interplay between hypervisibility and concealment, and processes of exclusion. Everyday practices of Islamophobia in British national life as tied to specific "knowledge" about the Muslim and as practices of power produce myriad phantasms of Muslim moral, social, and ontological alterity to obscure or justify as necessary the lived realities of anti-Muslim racism.

Pursuing a theory of the Muslim as a distinctly racial subject, I locate Islamophobia as the premier manifestation of mutating structural logics of racism pointing to a whole range of transformations occurring in contemporary Western society concerning democracy, rights, feminism, secrecy, integration, surveillance, the body, violence, law, and the future(s) of race. I conceptualize this racist structural arrangement and its matrices of power, knowledge, and governance as one of a variegated form of *interrogation*, a perpetual provocation and anxiety about the relation between (white) self and (Muslim) Other, which participates in racial, gendered, and colonial violence, discursive and material. The substantive three parts of the book theorize three central archetypes of—distinct but inherently interconnected—racist, misogynist, Islamophobic "interrogation": the interrogators and the interrogated, and the dialects, dialectics, and scales of relation through which they function.

This study of Islamophobia pursues an understanding of Britain's international history which signals an alternative mode of, and political ethic for, engaging not simply in an amended history of the present of race, racism, and colonialism but also living in the present itself. I seek to develop an approach within studies of the international—postcolonial or otherwise—which pays close attention to the human subject in his/her raced and gendered distinctions, who must live within an entangled global order and through whom the echoes and effects of the race, racism, and colonialism that birthed the international system operate. Which is to say that I think about Britain's relation to the modern global order from the racial subject outward, from the individual to the international rather than the other way around. In taking the Muslim subject on whose psychic and material presence that same order feeds as my focus, I pay close attention to the details of a racial subject within a society in whose order and impulses we are witness to international histories of race, racism, and colonialism. The racialized subject, however, might also be the best site through which this history and present are read toward a reparatory mode of seeing, listening, telling, and acting, an Other way of living in the world. These are the basic concerns and disciplinary ambitions of the present study.

THE MUSLIM AS POSTCOLONIAL PREDICAMENT

In the contemporary British social and political scene, there appears to be an increasing public consciousness of race and racism, in particular, to its systemic character and effect. Though the expression of this awareness ranges from the critical to the absurd. The twentieth-anniversary reflections on the death of Stephen Lawrence, the problem of institutional racism, and the failed sea change sought by the landmark MacPherson report[2] are in dialogue with the widespread recognition of the continued racist effects of the war on/of terror.[3] The more vehemently xenophobic rhetoric surrounding debates about immigration and notions of the country being full up and whose coffers are spent, gain traction in conjunction with the systemic difficulties faced by Britain's public services which necessitate migrant labor. In fact, migrancy, in general, and the perpetual "migrant crisis," in particular, are a floating presence bracketing most problems of the day. There are also more prosaic but no less revealing issues in the desire and unease for greater representation shown in the unhealthy responses to the possibility of a black James Bond (in Idris Elba),[4] the actuality of a black Hermione Granger (in the theater adaptation of

[2] On October 24, 2018, the Home Affairs Committee announced an inquiry on the 20th anniversary of the Macpherson report, February, 25, 2019. The original report can be found here: https://assets .publishing.service.gov.uk/government/uploads/system/uploads/attachment_data/file/277111/4262 .pdf. See also: Barbara Cohen. (2019). "The Stephen Lawrence Inquiry Report: 20 Years On." *Runnymede Trust*. Available at: https://www.runnymedetrust.org/uploads/StephenLawrence20br iefing.pdf

[3] Z. R. Eisenstein. (2004). *Against Empire: Feminisms, Racism, and the West*. London: Zed Books; Nisha Kapoor and Kasia Narkowicz. (2019). Unmaking citizens: passport removals, pre-emptive policing and the reimagining of colonial governmentalities, *Ethnic and Racial Studies*; Nisha Kapoor. (2017). *Deport, Deprive, Extradite: 21st Century State Extremism*. London: Verso; A. Kundnani. (2014). *The Muslims Are Coming!: Islamophobia, Extremism, and the Domestic War on Terror*. London, UK; New York: Verso; Ruth Blakely, Ben Hayes, Nisha Kapoor, Arun Kundnani, Narzanin Massoumi, David Miller, Tom Mills, Rizwan Sabir, Katy Sian, and Waqas Tufail. (2019). *Leaving the War on Terror: A Progressive Alternative to Counter-Terrorism Policy*. Amsterdam: Transnational Institute.

[4] In particular, the comments of novelist Antony Horowitz who said Elba was "too street" to play OO7. See: Nadia Khomani. (2015). "Idris Elba says he's still smiling after comments by James Bond author." *Guardian*. Available at: https://www.theguardian.com/film/2015/sep/03/idris-elba -still-smiling-comments-james-bond-author-anthony-horowitz.

Harry Potter and the Cursed Child),[5] and the portrayal of Othello as a black Muslim tragic hero in Richard Twyman's English Touring Theatre production of the play.[6]

On the other hand, there continues to be a great deal of ignorance if not altogether repression of the long shadow that imperial racism continues to cast over British politics and society, most notably in the unfolding racial drama of "Brexit," the ongoing and very public racial violence of the police and broader state security apparatus, never-ending "migrant crises," and the widespread fixation with Muslim women, in economic, cultural, and political milieu. There are also new forms of irresponsibility amid contemporary transformations of power, knowledge, and governance at large. And everywhere, a collective of institutions, political as well as cultural, do the work of race in silencing demands for justice, instead casting them in undecipherable terms, rendering them incoherent, and as "problems" that we would much rather not have to face.

In the last sixty years or so, there has also been a historical transformation in racist discourses. While scientific race-thinking and biological racist discourses—raciology—declined, cultural racism became the hegemonic form of racism in the late world system.[7] The signs of culture and religion (specifically Islam) have been close at hand for the neo-fascist resurgence on the contemporary European political scene.[8] As the signs of culture and

---

[5] See: Amelia Butterly. (2015). "Hermione Granger to be played by black actress Noma Dumezweni, sparking fan debate." *BBC Online*. Available at: http://www.bbc.co.uk/newsbeat/article/35150488/hermione-granger-to-be-played-by-black-actress-noma-dumezweni-sparking-fan-debate; and of the angry reaction, see: Rebecca Ratcliffe. (2016). "JK Rowling tells of anger at attacks on casting of black Hermione." *Guardian*. Available at: https://www.theguardian.com/stage/2016/jun/05/harry-potter-jk--rowling-black-hermione

[6] See: Aina Khan. (2018). "A Portrait of Othello as a Black Muslim Tragic Hero." *Al Jazeera*. Available at: https://www.aljazeera.com/indepth/features/portrait-othello-black-muslim-tragic-hero-181019213737799.html

[7] As Ramon Grosfoguel and Eric Mielants argue, cultural racism is a form of racism that does not even mention the word "race." It is focused on the cultural inferiority of a group of people. Usually it is framed in terms of the inferior habits, beliefs, behaviors, or values of a group of people. It is close to biological racism in the sense that cultural racism naturalizes/essentializes the culture of the racialized/inferiorized people. The latter are often represented as fixed in a timeless space. R. Grosfoguel and E. Mielants, "The Long-Durée," pp. 4–5. See also: P. Gilroy. (2000). *Between Camps: Race, Identity and Nationalism at the End of the Colour Line*. London: Allen Lane; A. Lentin and G. Titley. (2011). *The Crises of Multiculturalism: Racism in a Neoliberal Age*. New York: Zed Books; Ramón Grosfoguel. (2003). *Colonial Subject*. Los Angeles: California University Press.

[8] The extermination of the Nazi period has long constituted "the most profound moral and temporal rupture in the history of the twentieth century and the pretensions of its modern civilisation," and while "remembering it has been integral to the politics of 'race' for more than seventy years," its connections to the brutal, quotidian, paradigmatic violence according to *popular* raciological truths as practiced in the colonies is often forgotten. Gilroy, *Between Camps*, p. 25; A. Mbembe. (2001). *On the Postcolony*. Los Angeles: University of California Press, chapter 1; Hannah. Arendt. (1973). *The Origins of Totalitarianism*. New York: Harcourt Brace Jovanovich; Z. Bauman. (2000). *Modernity and the Holocaust*. Ithaca, NY: Cornell University Press.

religion have come to stand in for—or employed simultaneously to—race in discourses of difference and threat, the judgment of racial subjects is all the more pervasive for having accumulated/integrated the cultural and the religious, newer racialized bodies, forms of thought, dress and living, into its field of vision, economies, and practices.[9] Culture comes to be associated, often aggressively, with the nation or the state and thus a rigid historical and identitarian story; this differentiates "us" from "them," almost always with some degree of xenophobia. In this sense, "the trouble with this idea of culture is that it entails not only venerating one's own culture but also thinking of it as somehow divorced from, because transcending, the everyday world. . . . Culture conceived in this way can become a *protective enclosure.*"[10]

Islamophobia, however, is a concept that emerged to name something that was previously unrecognized in categories like racism and, thus, hints at such a silence which needs to be addressed.[11] What it is precisely that needs to be addressed, or rather, the silence which Islamophobia names, along with the

---

[9] Religion as a racialized category, however, is not a postwar phenomenon but has a long history in the modern world: "Race and Religion are conjoined twins. They are offspring of the modern world. Because they share a mutual genealogy, the category of religion is always already a racialized category, even when race is not explicitly under discussion." See: Theodore Vial. (2016). *Modern Religion, Modern Race.* New York: Oxford University Press, p. 1.

[10] Edward Said. (1994). *Culture and Imperialism.* London: Vintage, p. xiv.

[11] Islamophobia—or, anti-Muslim racism—is not a post-9/11 phenomenon, especially in the British context. In fact, the presentism embedded in many post-9/11 studies of anti-Muslim racism is an important element in my decision to depart from a study of blackness and race, and the emergence of a particular racial and racializing economy from early modernity up to the present. While available, critical race approaches with a global vision to Islamophobia are dwarfed by the literature which situates Islamophobia within or as an outcome of the war on terror. A summary of instructive critical race approaches can be found in the following: Y. Morsi. (2017). *Radical Skin, Moderate Masks: De-radicalising the Muslim & Racism in Post-racial Societies.* London: Rowman and Littlefield International; APPG. (2018). *Islamophobia Defined.* London: Home Office; N. Massoumi, T. Mills, and D. Miller, eds. (2017). *What is Islamophobia: Racism, Social Movements and the State.* London: Pluto Press; T. Saeed. (2018). *Islamophobia and Securitization: Religion, Ethnicity and the Female Voice.* Basingstoke: Palgrave MacMillan; R. Grosfoguel. (2006). "The Long-Durée Entanglement Between Islamophobia and Racism in the Modern/Colonial Capitalist/Patriarchal World-System: An Introduction." *Human Architecture: Journal of the Sociology of Self-Knowledge,* 1, 1–12; A. Kundnani. (2014). *The Muslims are Coming! Islamophobia, Extremism and the Domestic War on Terror.* London: Verso; K. Beydoun. (2018). *American Islamophobia: Understanding the Roots and Rise of Fear.* Oakland: University of California Press; Bouteldja, H. (2017). *The Whites, Jews and Us.* Semiotexte; H. Dabashi. (2015). London: Verso; C. Allen. (2010). *Islamophobia.* London: Ashgate; N.J. Doyle (2013). "Islamophobia, European Modernity and Contemporary Illiberalism, Politics," *Religion & Ideology,* 14(2), 167–72; L. Jackson. (2017). *Islamophobia in Britain: The Making of a Muslim Enemy.* Palgrave Macmillan UK; Nazia Kazi, (2018). *Islamophobia, Race, and Global Politics.* London: Rowman and Littlefield; D. Kumar. (2012). *Islamophobia and the Politics of Empire*; Salman Sayyid and AbdoolKarim Vakil. (2010). *Thinking Through Islamophobia: Global Perspectives.* Columbia University Press; Gordon Conway. (1997). *Islamophobia: A Challenge for Us All.* London: The Runnymede Trust. Available at: https://www.runnymedetrust.org/companies/17/74/Islamophobia-A-Challenge-for-Us-All.html; Farah Elahi and Omar Khan. (2017). *Islamophobia: Still a Challenge for Us All.* London: Runnymede. Available at: https://www.runnymedetrust.org/uploads/Islamophobia%20Report%202018%20FINAL.pdf.

strategies, obstacles, and anxieties involved in it remain a matter of dispute across the political spectrum. Yet, everyone appears to have something to say about Islam(ophobia), its meaning, its very existence or not, and the conditions that underpin its pronouncement.

The disputes surrounding the category of Islamophobia derive largely from two sources: philosophical and political. The former concerns a conceptual lack of clarity about the concept and its substantive content. There is now a significant and growing interdisciplinary literature on Islamophobia that is dominated by empirical studies, technical analyses of media and discursive (mis)representations, and a range of sociopsychological approaches to the problem of anti-Muslim feeling. Though instructive, they cannot provide us with the theoretical clarification we might want. Largely, if not by definition, privileging the ontic over the ontological, we are still left unsure about the substance (and measure) of Islamophobia. Alternatively, political disputes concern the contexts within which Islamophobia is at once disputed and plays itself out, most notably in questions of national security, immigration, social cohesion, violence, national culture, identity, and belonging. Here there is a clash, perceived or real, between national majorities and postcolonial, ethnically or racially marked minorities in which the production and consequent critique of Islamophobia can be situated.

Neither of these disputes, philosophical or political, captures in any meaningful sense the intervention I seek to pursue in this project. On the one hand, conceptual clarification, ontologically or otherwise, focuses on definition and language, and the instruments which must enforce a particular standard against a problem to be addressed, risking an impoverished historical, material, and ethical critique. On the other hand, the political theater of Islamophobia, while effectively signaling the fluidity with which it travels, can likewise perpetuate a presentism that isolates Islamophobia in the post–Cold War or post-9/11 world with little regard for the continuities manifested in Islamophobia with longer histories of domination, resistance, violence and experimentation, and perhaps more importantly, the complexities of its imagined subject.

With this in mind, then, what concerns us here are the various modes of being that the Muslim can inhabit within racist structures, institutions, and imaginaries. Which is to say that I take Islamophobia as a given phenomenon insofar as it effects people in the world and is a premier affective tonality of our times. The target of my theorization, therefore, lies elsewhere and is concerned much more with the way in which societies invested in the racial idea act on, against, and through the racial subject—the Muslim as much as his other, the white man—and the "hearts and minds" of all in the era of the terror threat. I wish also to remain cognizant of the figure of "race" as a mutable and holistic phenomenon that structures Islamophobia as a practice of producing and dealing with the Muslim and her Islam (or indeed those in proximity to them) as entities to be kept at bay, under watch and incited to various forms of confession.

Who is that subject-object upon which race and Islamophobia act and engage? What constraints, dangers, and possibilities are there in being Muslim within a racial order such as modern, (post)colonial Britain? What purchase do categories of "race," "nation," and "religion" have in our discussions and hopes to remedy racism and Islamophobia, also known as the Muslim Problem? These are the guiding questions for my analysis of the twin figures of Muslim and Islam in the emergence and formation of a liberal Britain engaged for nearly two decades in a war on Islamic terrorism. Pursuing a theory of the postcolonial subject after empire, I aim for an active negotiation between forms of philosophical speculation and empirical case study, that is, between offering and deploying a range of concepts to clarify our understanding of race, racism, and colonialism in the (post)modern world, and examining closely the realities of the neoliberal, war on terror present. This study is, in sum, an attempt to build an adequate vocabulary for analyzing the complexities of racism today and its potential future(s). I locate Islamophobia as an (il)logical outcome of a constitutive history of raciology, of imposed human hierarchies that authorized sophisticated systems of governance, power, and knowledge with macro and molecular effects in the transatlantic slave trade, (settler) colonialism, and the formation of a global empire with correspondences in the present.

With the colony in view, the entanglements and mutations between race, sovereign violence, war, culture, death, and more complicate assumptions of both colonialism's end and continuity. These entanglements endure but with the new challenges, added complexities, and contradictions of wars with no end, whose human refuse are everywhere seen to intrude, hungry for forms of support and welfare assumed to be at our expense, and to whom no hospitality can be shown. The increasing complexity of technologies of control and coercion (from the drone to biometry), measurement, and (synthetic) reproduction (from the algorithm to genomic manipulation), which have as their target the very fabric of life are all undergirded by the autonomous figure of race. Yet we are also experiencing a revivification of widespread debates about Europe's colonial past outside the academy in popular culture, across art, literature, film, and television.

It is worth, therefore, staying alive to the relations between the local and global, the individual and the international, the subjective and the historical, precisely as it engages memory of colonialism and the volatility of the present. This relational and entangled perspective has generative implications for our orientation toward the future, one in which the decentering of the Euro-American world arrives with simultaneous danger and possibility. A change that is significant for fundamental issues such as the "management" of human mobility; decolonization—whether of race, racism, and coloniality in the world or of the university; bordering and border violence; and crucially our ongoing witness to capitalism's contradictions and humanity's fast-track to ecological collapse. And yet, the struggles for justice and dignity which underpin these concerns are never over and concluded. That there are, there-fore, alternative epistemologies, ways of seeing and being in the world which can point toward liberatory models of radical hospitality, community, and humanity, paths out of the dark night, from which we must learn.

I aim to make my intervention through a detailed though consciously peri-patetic theorization of the problem of race and Islamophobia, and the histo-ries and present that have formed them as our *collective* inheritance. I seek to advance an analysis of the postmetropole, or the postcolonial as it concerns the heart of the empire and the subjects who must wear its names. While lim-ited by an in situ diagnosis insofar as I take (Islamophobia in) Britain as my central case study, the theoretical framework I propose engages Islamophobia as an example of a broader set of techniques which apply in racial orders and processes of racialization, while at the same time taking Islamophobia to pose a specific set of problems, possibilities, and also a subjective site for racism's repair. It is in this sense that Islamophobia is a rich site of analysis; it con-tains within the work it does on human lives and imaginaries an instructive case study with many tributaries, engaging and being engaged by the central problems of/in our world today.

RACE-ING THE EUROPEAN IDEA

It is a strange yet telling silence that explanations of the post-9/11 world, most notably in the discipline of international relations, have predominantly exam-ined the effects that the war on terror has had on the ambivalent relationship between liberalism, security, war, the nation-state, and freedom within one civi-lization: the West.[12] There is now, however, a sustained debate on Islam and the war on terror in general, and Islamic jurisprudence and a "law of minorities"[13] in particular, especially in the imperial centers of Western Europe and the

---

[12] A. Behnke. (2004). "Terrorizing the Political: 9/11 Within the Context of The Globalization of Violence." *Millennium*, 33(2), 279–312; B. Buzan. (2006). "Will the 'Global War on Terrorism' Be the New Cold War?" *International Affairs*, 82(6), 1101–18; R.B.J. Walker, ed. (2006). "Special Section: Theorizing the Liberty-Security Relation: Sovereignty, Liberalism and Exceptionalism." *Security Dialogue*, 37(1), 7–82.

[13] A. Sulayman. (1987). *Towards an Islamic Theory of International Relations: New Directions for Islamic Methodology and Thought.* Herndon, VA: International Institute for Islamic Thought; A. Soroush. (2000). "Tolerance and Governance: A Discourse on Religion and Democracy." In *Rea-son, Freedom and Democracy in Islam: Essential Writings of 'Abdolkarim Soroush,* edited by M.

"new" empire of the United States.[14] There appears nonetheless to be a commitment (eroding though it surely is) to side-lining questions of race, racism
and non-western experiences of modernity[15] in the global order through which
the war on terror and its (racial) logics have been produced and permeated.[16]

Sadri and A. Sadri. Oxford: Oxford University Press, pp. 156–70; R.L. Euben. (2002). "Contingent
Borders, Syncretic Perspectives: Globalization, Political Theory and Islamizing Knowledge."
International Studies Review, 4(1), 23–48; R.L. Euben. (2004). "Travelling Theorists and Translat-
ing Practices." In *What Is Political Theory?*, edited by S.K. White and J.D. Moon. London: Sage
Publications, pp. 145–73.

[14] S. Hashmi. (1998). "Islamic Ethics in International Society." In *International Society: Diverse
Ethical Perspectives*, edited by D. Mapel and T. Nardin. Princeton, NJ: Princeton University Press,
pp. 215–36; P. Mandaville. (2002). "Reading the State from Elsewhere: Towards an Anthropology
of the Post-national." *Review of International Studies*, 28, 199–207; J. Piscatori. (2003). "Order,
Justice and Global Islam." In *Order and Justice in International Relations*, edited by R. foot, J.L.
Gaddis, and A. Hurrell. New York: Oxford University Press, pp. 262–86.

[15] For remedies to this effort, a number of edited collections have been published that emphasize
the importance of non-Western experiences of modernity, see: A. Acharya and B. Buzan. (2007).
"Why is there no Non-Western IR Theory?: Reflections on and from Asia: An Introduction."
International Relations of the Asia-Pacific, 7(3), 1–26.; S. Chan. (1999). "Chinese Perspectives
on World Order." In *International Order and the Future of World Politics*, edited by T. Paul
and J. Hall. Cambridge: Cambridge University Press, pp. 197–212; G. Chowdhry and S. Nair,
eds. (2004). *Power, Post-colonialism and International Relations*. London: Routledge; P. Darby.
(1997). *At the Edge of International Relations: Post-colonialism. Gender and Dependency*. London: Pinter; B. Gruffydd Jones, ed. (2006). *Decolonizing International Relations*. London: Rowman & Littlefield Publishers; S. Neuman. (1998). *International Relations Theory and the Third
World*. London: Palgrave. I. Neumann. (1999). *Uses of the Other: 'The East' in European Identity
Formation*. Minneapolis: Minnesota Press.

[16] For a range of useful studies on the global and local racism of the war on terror, see: Suad Abdul
Khabeer. (2017). *Muslim Cool: Race, Religion, and Hip Hop in the United States*. New York: NYU
Press; Christopher A. Bail. (2015). *Terrified: How Anti-Muslim Fringe Organizations Became
Mainstream*. Princeton, NJ: Princeton University Press; Bakalian, Anny, and Medhi Bozorgmehr.
(2009). *Backlash 9/11: Middle Eastern and Muslim Americans Respond*. Berkeley: University of
California Press; M. Cherif Bassiouni, ed. (1974). *The Civil Rights of Arab Americans: The Spe-
cial Measures*. North Dartmouth, MA: Arab-American University Graduates; Moustafa Bayoumi.
(2008). *How Does It Feel to Be a Problem?* New York: Penguin; Bayoumi, Moustafa. (2015).
This Muslim American Life: Dispatches from the War on Terror. New York: NYU Press; Eduardo
Bonilla-Silva. (2010). *Racism without Racists: Color-Blind Racism and the Persistence of Racial
Inequality in the United States*, 3rd ed. Lanham, MD: Rowman & Littlefield; Louise Cainkar.
(Forthcoming). "Fluid Terror Threat: A Genealogy of the Racialization of Arab, Muslim, and
South Asian Americans." *Amerasia Journal*, 44(1); Louise A. Cainkar. (2009). *Homeland Insecu-
rity: The Arab American and Muslim American Experience after 9/11*. New York: Russell Sage;
Sylvia Chan-Malik. (2011). "'Common Cause': On the Black-immigrant Debate and Constructing
the Muslim American." *Journal of Race, Ethnicity, and Religion*, 2(8), 1–39; Sohail Daulatzai.
(2012). *Black Star, Crescent Moon: The Muslim International and Black Freedom Beyond
America*. Minneapolis: University of Minnesota Press; Chris Earle. (2015). "Good Muslims, Bad
Muslims, and the Nation: The 'Ground Zero Mosque' and the Problem with Tolerance." *Commu-
nication and Critical Cultural Studies*, 12(2), 121–38; Steve Garner and Saher Selod. (2015). "The
Racialization of Muslims: Empirical Studies of Islamophobia." *Critical Sociology*, 41(1), 9–19;
Zareena Grewal. (2014). *Islam Is a Foreign Country*. New York: NYU Press. Ramon Grosfoguel.
(2012). "The Multiple Faces of Islamophobia." *Islamophobia Studies Journal*, 1(1), 9–33. Ramon
Grosfoguel and Mielants, Eric. (2006). "The Long-Durée Entanglement between Islamophobia and
Racism in the Modern/Colonial Capitalist/ Patriarchal World-system: An Introduction." *Human
Architecture*, 5(1), 1; Deepa Kumar. (2012). *Islamophobia and the Politics of Empire*. Chicago:
Haymarket Books; Erik Love. (2017). *Islamophobia and Racism in America*. New York: NYU

Even current debates over Islam and the war on terror are susceptible to constrained analyses limited to macropolitical lenses with impoverished historical detail. Or, rather differently, studies of a singular, as opposed to intersectional, focus of race, racism, and colonialism struggle to account for the complex and contradictory granular effects of (post)imperial politics, and the subjective sites of their operation.[17] Which is to say that the figure of the "human," who it is that experiences the "boomerang effects" most intensely; who it is even that can legitimately "think" and produce valid knowledge of the world and human existence within an international order belied by racial, gendered, and genocidal forms of imperial power in not nearly questioned enough.[18] The theorization of the race-power nexus, their "racial projects,"

Press; Sunaina Maira. (2009). *Missing: Youth, Citizenship, and Empire after 9/11*. Durham, NC: Duke University Press; Sunaina Maira. (2016). *The 9/11 Generation: Youth, Rights, and Solidarity in the War on Terror*. New York: NYU Press; Mahmood Mamdani. (2004). *Good Muslim, Bad Muslim: America, the Cold War, and the Roots of Terror*. New York: Pantheon; Nasar Meer. (2013). "Racialization and Religion: Race, Culture and Difference in the Study of Antisemitism and Islamophobia." *Ethnic and Racial Studies*, 36(3), 385–98; Nasar Meer and Tariq Modood. (2009). "Refutations of Racism in the 'Muslim question.'" *Patterns of Prejudice*, 43(3–4), 335–54; Naber, Nadine. (2006). "The Rules of Forced Engagement: Race, Gender, and the Culture of Fear among Arab Immigrants in San Francisco Post-9/11." *Cultural Dynamics*, 18(3), 235–67; Jasbir Puar. (2007). *Terrorist Assemblages: Homonationalism in Queer Times*. Durham, NC: Duke University Press; Junaid Akram Rana. (2016). "The Racial Infrastructure of the Terror-industrial Complex." *Social Text*, 34(4), 111–38; Runnymede Trust. (1997). *Islamophobia: A Challenge for Us All*. London: Runnymede Trust; Runnymede Trust. (2017). "Islamophobia—20 Years On, Still a Challenge for Us All." Retrieved February 15, 2018 (https://www.runnymedetrust.org/blog/islamo phobia-20-years-on-still-a-challenge-for-us-all); David Tyrer. (2013). *The Politics of Islamophobia: Race, Power and Fantasy*. London: Pluto.

[17] Some exceptions in the discipline of international relations, for example, are: Anna M. Agath-angelou. (2010a). "'Necro-(Neo) Colonizations and Economies of Blackness: Of Slaughters, 'Accidents,' 'Disasters' and Captive Flesh." In *International Relations and States of Exception: Margins, Peripheries, and Excluded Bodies*, edited by Shampa Biswas and Sheila Nair. London: Routledge, pp. 186–209; Anna M. Agathangelou. (2010b). "Bodies of Desire, Terror and the War in Eurasia: Impolite Disruptions of (Neo) Liberal Internationalism, Neoconservatism and the 'New' Imperium." *Millennium-Journal of International Studies*, 38(3), 693–722; Anna M. Agathangelou and L. H. M. Ling. (2004). "The House of IR: From Family Power Politics to the Poisies of Worldism." *International Studies Review*, 6(4), 21–49; Carol Anderson. (2003). *Eyes Off the Prize: The United Nations and the African American Struggle for Human Rights, 1944–1955*. Cambridge: Cambridge University Press; Geeta Chowdhry and Sheila Nair. (2002). *Power, Postcolonialism and International Relations: Reading Race, Gender and Class*. London: Routledge; Hilbourne Watson. (2001). "Theorizing the Racialization of Global Politics and the Caribbean Experience." *Alternatives*, 26(4), 449–83; Sarah White. (2002). "Thinking Race, Thinking Development." *Third World Quarterly*, 23(3), 407–19; Howard Winant. (2001). *The World is a Ghetto: Race and Democracy since World War II*. New York: Basic Books; A. Katherine Wing. (2000). *Global Critical Race Feminism: An International Reader*. New York: New York University Press; R. Shilliam. (2018). *Race and the Undeserving Poor*. Newcastle upon Tyne: Agenda Publishing.

[18] Exceptions include for a succinct overview see F. Dallmayr. (2004). "Beyond Monologue: for A Comparative Political Theory." *Perspectives on Politics*, 2(2), 249–57; G. Larson and E. Deutsch, eds. 1988. *Interpreting Across Boundaries: New Essays in Comparative Philosophy*. Princeton, NJ: Princeton University Press. See also: F. Dallmayr. (1999). *Border Crossings: Towards a Comparative Political Theory*. Boulder, CO: Lexington Books; F. Dallmayr. (2001). "Conversation Across Boundaries: Political Theory and Global Diversity." *Millennium*, 30(2), 331–47; A. Parel and R. Keith, eds. (1992). *Comparative Political Philosophy—Studies Under the Upas Tree*. London:

and the processes by which meaning and value are assigned and distributed based on "racial formations," that is "the sociohistorical process by which racial categories are created, inhabited, transformed, and destroyed"[19] is deeply useful for the study of the global after empire,[20] and is of intellectual and, more importantly, ethical urgency.

Interestingly, issues of race and racism were integral to the birth of international relations as an academic discipline insofar as it was founded to solve the dilemmas posed by empire building—specifically British and American—and colonial administration facing white Western powers[21] in their experimental, expansionist projects of accumulation in the so-called "waste places of the earth"[22] populated by superfluous and instrumental objects, a fungible humanity. At the core of these dilemmas were human subjects who had to be managed, dealt with, disciplined, classified, remade, and, if necessary, killed. Race, racism, and colonialism had a constitutive and not merely instrumental role in forming the international order,[23] dominant theories of it, and the

---

Sage; H. Jung, ed. (2002). *Comparative Political Culture in the Age of Globalization: An Introductory Anthology*. Boulder, CO: Lexington Books. For an insightful critical treatment of the 'multiple modernities' literature, see: G.K. Bhambra. (2007). *Rethinking Modernity: Post-colonialism and the Sociological Imagination*. Basingstoke: Palgrave.

[19] William Omi and Howard Winant. (1994). *Racial Formation in the United States*, 2nd ed. New York: Routledge, p. 55; Howard Winant. (2001). *The World is a Ghetto: Race and Democracy since World War II*. New York: Basic Books. On the modern state as a racial formation, see: D. T. Goldberg. (2002). *The Racial State*. Malden, MA: Blackwell Publishers.

[20] See also: Frank Dikötter. (2008). "The Racialization of the Globe: An Interactive Interpretation." *Ethnic and Racial Studies*, 31(8), 1478–96; M. Duffield. (2010). "The Liberal Way of Development and the Development—Security Impasse: Exploring the Global Life-Chance Divide." *Security Dialogue*, 41(1), 53–76; D. F. Silva. (2007). *Toward a Global Idea of Race*. Minneapolis: University of Minnesota Press; Sarah White. (2002). "Thinking Race, Thinking Development." *Third World Quarterly*, 23(3), 407–19; Howard Winant. (2001). *The World is a Ghetto: Race and Democracy since World War II*. New York: Basic Books; A. Katherine Wing. (2000). Global Critical Race Feminism: An International Reader. New York: New York University Press.

[21] Tarak Barkawi and Mark Laffey. (2006). "The Postcolonial Moment in Security Studies." *Review of International Studies*, 32, 329–52; Robert Vitalis. (2000). "The Graceful and Generous Liberal Gesture: Making Racism Invisible in American International Relations." *Millennium—Journal of International Studies*, 29(2), 331–56.

[22] D. Bell. (2005). "Race and Empire: The Origins of International Relations." *International Studies Review*, 7(4), 633–35; David Long and Brian Schmidt, eds. (2005). *Imperialism and Internationalism in The Discipline of International Relations*. Albany, NY: State University of New York Press and Brian Schmidt. (1998). *The Political Discourse of Anarchy*. Albany, NY: SUNY Press; Robert Vitalis. (2005). "Birth of a Discipline." In *Imperialism and Internationalism in the Discipline of International Relations*, edited by David Long and Brian C. Schmidt. State University of New York Press, pp. 159–82.

[23] A. M. Agathangelou and L. H. M. Ling. (2009). *Transforming world politics: From empire to multiple worlds*. London: Routledge/Taylor & Francis Group; R. B. Persaud and R. B. J. Walker. (2001). "Apertura: Race in International Relations." *Alternatives*, 26(4), 373–76; Siba-N'Zatioula Grovogui. (1996). *Sovereigns, Quasi Sovereigns, and Africans: Race and Self-determination in International Law*. University of Minnesota Press; John M. Hobson. (2012). *The Eurocentric Conception of World Politics: Western International Theory, 1760–2010*. Cambridge: Cambridge University Press; Hilbourne Watson. (2001). "Theorizing the Racialization of Global Politics and the Caribbean Experience." *Alternatives*, 26(4), 449–83; Randolph Persaud and R. B. J. Walker.

paradigmatic principles that populate notions of the international itself: the state,[24] governance, global lines of stratification and development,[25] international law,[26] bureaucracy, human rights,[27] national cultures,[28] among many others. We might nonetheless speak of a "racial aphasia"[29] within mainstream studies of the international, or which war is always fundamental.

I take seriously the inextricable relationship between modernity and coloniality, that is, between modernity and a particular conception of (white) Reason, Human, and Being.[30] Like Europe, Britain also plays out as an "idea" and an ideal subject—white, male, propertied—whose hegemonic understanding is encumbered by the knowledge-power of *modernity* and its

---

(2001). "Apertura: Race in International Relations." *Alternatives*, 26(4), 373–76; Robbie Shilliam. (2006). "What about Marcus Garvey? Race and the Transformation of Sovereignty Debate." *Review of International Studies*, 32, 379–400; Robbie Shilliam. (2009). "The Atlantic as a Vector of Uneven and Combined Development." *Cambridge Review of International Affairs*, 22(1), 69–88; J. Bandopadhyaya. (1977). "Racism and International Relations." *Alternatives*, 3(1), 19–48; Srdjan Vucetic. (2011). "A Racialized Peace? How Britain and the US Made Their Relationship Special." *Foreign Policy Analysis*, 7(4), 403–21.

[24] Benedict Anderson. (1991). *Imagined Communities: Reflections on the Origin and Spread of Nationalism*. London: Verso; Bob Jessop. (1990). *State Theory: Putting the Capitalist State in its Place*. London: Penn State Press; Wael Hallaq. (2013). *The Impossible State: Islam, Politics and Modernity's Moral Predicament*. New York: Columbia University Press.

[25] W. Rodney. (1972). *How Europe Underdeveloped Africa*. London: Bogle-L'Ouverture Publications.

[26] A. Anghie. (1999). "Finding the Peripheries: Sovereignty and Colonialism in Nineteenth-Century International Law." *Harvard International Law Journal*, 40, 1; A. Anghie. (2006). "The Evolution of International Law: Colonial and Postcolonial Realities." *Third World Quarterly*, 27(5), 739–53; A. Anghie. (2007). *Imperialism, Sovereignty and the Making of International Law* (Vol. 37). Cambridge University Press; Barry Buzan and George Lawson. (2013). "The Global Transformation: The Nineteenth Century and the Making of Modern International Relations." *International Studies Quarterly*, 57(3), 622; Carl Schmitt. (2003). *The Nomos of the Earth in the International Law of the Jus Publicum Europaeum*. New York: Telos Press.

[27] Gurminder Bhambra and Robbie Shilliam. (2008). *Silencing Human Rights: Critical Approaches to a Contested Project*. London: Palgrave.

[28] Naeem Inayatullah and David L. Blaney. (2003). *International Relations and the Problem of Difference*. New York: Routledge; M. Koskenniemi, W. Rech, and F. M. Jiménez. (2017). *International Law and Empire: Historical Exploration*; Pinar Bilgin. (2008). "Thinking past 'Western' IR?" *Third World Quarterly*, 29(1), 5–23.

[29] By "racial aphasia" I mean a "calculated forgetting" of racism's constitution of the international order See: Sankaran Krishna. (2001). "Race, Amnesia, and the Education of International Relations." *Alternatives*, 26(4), 373–76; Debra Thompson. (2013). "Through, Against and Beyond the Racial State: The Transnational Stratum of Race." *Cambridge Review of International Affairs*, 26(1), 133–51.

[30] Anibal Quijano. (2000). "Coloniality of Power, Eurocentrism, and Latin America." *Nepantla: Views from South*, 1(3), 533–34; Aníbal Quijano. (2007). "Coloniality and Modernity/Rationality." *Cultural Studies*, 21(2), 168–78; María Lugones. (2007). "Heterosexualism and the Colonial/Modern Gender System." *Hypatia*, 22(1), 186–209; Enrique Dussel. (1993). "Eurocentrism and Modernity" (Introduction to the Frankfurt Lectures). *Boundary 2*, 20(3), 65–76; (1995). *The Invention of the Americas: The Eclipse of the "Other" and the Myth of Modernity*. New York: Continuum; (2000). "Europe, Modernity, and Eurocentrism." *Nepantla: Views from South*, 1(3), 465–78; Walter Mignolo and Catherine Walsh. (2018). *On Decoloniality: Concepts, Analytics, Praxis*. Duke University Press.

nocturnal face, *coloniality*.[31] Crucially, "the codification of the difference between conquerors and conquered in the idea of 'race' . . . the constitutive, founding element of the relations of domination that the conquest imposed"; and "the constitution of a new structure of control of labor and its resources and products" articulated "slavery, serfdom, small independent commodity production and reciprocity, together around and upon the basis of capital and the world market."[32] Coloniality is shorthand for the *coloniality of power*. As Walter Mignolo explains, coloniality of power is "the logic that underlines the differences, manifestations, and enactments of modern imperial/colonial formations (Spanish, Portuguese, Dutch, French, British, German, United States) and all its dimensions: knowledge (epistemic), economic, political (military), aesthetic, ethical, subjective (race, sex), spiritual (religious)."[33]

Coloniality, put simply, is a logic of bordering.[34] The notion of borders has great bearing on the argument within this study for they are not only geographic/territorial. They are also racial, gendered, and sexual. They construct and isolate epistemic and ontological, linguistic, national, and cultural forms. These same borders, however, point to the hegemonic architectures of modernity/coloniality from early, liberal modernity and beyond. Europe's demotion presents a moment to disrupt the force of borders—full of risk and promise—especially epistemic and racial, capitalizing on the deep cracks in the imperial frame toward a new construction of the world.

Enrique Dussel's summary of the core elements of the myth of modernity—propelled and constituted not instrumentally but gratuitously by racist, colonial domination—remains pertinent:

(1) Modern (European) civilization understands itself as the most developed, the superior, civilization. (2) This sense of superiority obliges it, in the form of

---

[31] Coloniality is itself a *de*colonial concept. Naming the (un)intended consequences of the narratives of modernity, coloniality is a reminder, as Aníbal Quijano has told us, of the central axes or patterns of power that were foundational to modernity. As a matrix of power, coloniality came to operate in Abya Yala—broadly understood as the Americas of the South in relation with the Caribbean—and subsequently elsewhere, in multiple spheres of control over humanity, subjectivity, and being. Maldonado-Torres contends, "as modern subjects we breathe coloniality all the time and every day." See: Maldonado-Torres. (2010). "On the Coloniality of Being: Contributions to the Development of a Concept." In *Globalization and the Decolonial Option*, edited by Walter Mignolo and Arturo Escobar. London: Routledge, p. 97.

[32] A. Quijano. (2000). "Coloniality of Power, Eurocentrism, and Latin America." *Nepantla: Views from South*, 1(3), 533–34.

[33] W. Mignolo and C. Walsh. (2018). *On Decoloniality: Concepts, Analytics, Praxis*. Durham: Duke University Press, pp. 140–41.

[34] Gloria Anzaldúa's statement on border culture is useful here: "The U.S-Mexican border *es una herida abierta* where the Third World grates against the first and bleeds. And before a scab forms it hemorrhages again, the lifeblood of two worlds merging to form a third country—*a border culture*." Gloria Anzaldúa. (1987). *Borderlands/La Frontera: The New Mestiza*. San Francisco: Aunt Lute.

a categorical imperative, as it were, to "develop" (civilize, uplift, educate) the more primitive, barbarous, underdeveloped civilizations. (3) The path of such development should be that followed by Europe in its own development out of antiquity and the Middle Ages. (4) Where the barbarian or the primitive opposes the civilizing process, the praxis of modernity must, in the last instance, have recourse to the violence necessary to remove the obstacles to modernization. (5) This violence, which produces, in many different ways, victims, takes on an almost ritualistic character: the civilizing hero invests his victims (the colonized, the slave, the woman, the ecological destruction of the earth, etc.) with the character of being participants in a process of redemptive sacrifice. (6) From the point of view of modernity, the barbarian or primitive is in a state of guilt (for, among other things, opposing the civilizing process). This allows modernity to present itself not only as innocent but also as a force that will emancipate or re- deem its victims from their guilt. (7) Given this "civilizing" and redemptive character of modernity, the suffering and sacrifices (the costs) of modernization imposed on "immature" peoples, enslaved races, the "weaker" sex, et cetera, are inevitable and necessary.[35]

I submit, however, that not enough attention is paid to the abstract(ed) figure of the "human." The national, state, institutional, governmental, or (narrowly political) conflictual arena are all too often the convenient points of departure for analyses in relation to racism and colonialism; an analytical bracket that studies Islam and the war on terror has also internalized to their detriment.[36] Put simply, I am pursuing an analysis of the postmetropole over the postcolony in an attempt to show how a "thick" exploration of race and Islamophobia, or more accurately the (sub)human content of the Muslim as s/he is produced under racial formations, contains within it/him/her the colonial-international flows of power and knowledge. I seek to reverse and enliven critical energies of scholarship as they concern human subjects of race, racism, and colonialism.[37] Propelled by an account of the ethical significance of the contemporary conjuncture, and seeking to clarify and remedy the

---

[35] Dussel, "Eurocentrism and Modernity," p. 75.
[36] For notable exceptions, see: Devji, Faisal. (2005). *Landscapes of the Jihad: Militancy, Morality, Modernity*. London: C. Husrt & Co.; Zillah Eisenstein. (2004). *Against Empire: Feminisms, Racism and the West*. London: Zed Books; Nisha Kapoor. (2018). *Deport, Deprive, Extradite: 21st Century State Extremism*. London: Verso; Hamid Dabashi. (2011). *Post-Orientalism: Knowledge and Power in a Time of Terror*. New Jersey: Transaction Publishers; Yassir Morsi. (2017). *Radical Skin, Moderate Masks: De-radicalising the Muslim and Racism in Post-racial Societies*. New York: Rowman & Littlefield.
[37] G. K. Bhambra. (2007). *Rethinking Modernity: Postcolonialism and the Sociological imagination*. Basingstoke, Hampshire: Palgrave and Gurminder K. Bhambra. (2014). *Connected Sociologies*. London: Bloomsbury Academic; D. Chakrabarty. (2000). *Provincializing Europe: Postcolonial thought and Historical Difference*. Princeton, NJ: Princeton University Press.

often unspecified, undifferentiated subject who ostensibly lives in the (inter) national order, I pay close attention to the names and classifications made to stick on the racial subject's being, as both enemy and disturbing object, within a Britain and Europe in the throes of but the latest war on/of terror.

WRITING RACE INTO THE BIOPOLITICAL

Managing, speaking about, and making claims for the Muslims rely on these borders. They refer also to a way of substituting what *is* with another reality in the service of powerful (imperial) interests through the coming together of epistemic and coercive means. From the outset, liberalism (a foundationalism in modernity) as a philosophical position and ideology was forged in parallel with imperial expansion and has been entangled with the most illiberal of policies: slavery, colonialism, genocide, and racism.[38] It was in relation to expansion in the modern/colonial world

> that liberal political thought in Europe confronted such questions as universalism, individual rights, the freedom of exchange, the relationship between ends and means, the national community and political capacity, international justice, the nature of the relationship between Europe and extra-European worlds, and the relationship between despotic governance beyond national borders and responsible representative governance within them.[39]

In the emergence of this liberal philosophy, it was the black slave, Foucault forgets, who represented this danger, the primary conduit of threat. Foucault's genealogy of biopower cannot fully recognize the black slave for it rests on an unspecified concept of the "human" through whom biopower acts, and an under-theorization of racism.[40]

Foucault locates the origins of liberalism—the essential quest for freedom against sovereign power—in the rise of capitalism which necessitated

---

[38] See: Immanuel Wallerstein. (1995). *After Liberalism*. New York: New Press; D. Losurdo. (2011). *Liberalism: A Counter-History*. London: Verso, 2016; J. Massad. (2015). *Islam in Liberalism*. Chicago and London: University of Chicago Press; F. Devji and Z. In Kazmi (2017). *Islam after Liberalism*. Oxford: Oxford University Press.

[39] Mbembe, *Critique*, p. 55. This is not to acquiesce to the idea that it was only white Europeans who were engaged in these questions, that modernity was exclusively European. But instead to claim that these questions were engaged in the context of an unprecedented colonial expansion and, crucially, subjective penetration and reconstitution. On this, see: Wael Hallaq. (2018). *Restating Orientalism: A Critique of Modern Knowledge*. New York: Columbia University Press; Nelson Maldonado-Torres. (2007). "On the Coloniality of Being." *Cultural Studies*, 21(2–3), 240–70.

[40] Alison Howell and Melanie Richter-Montpetit. (2018). "Racism in Foucauldian Security Studies: Biopolitics, Liberal War, and the Whitewashing of Colonial and Racial Violence." *International Political Sociology*, 13(1), 2–19.

"political investment of the body"[41] in order to "turn peasants into punctual, efficient industrial workers."[42] This meant that through the "extractive-effects" on workers' bodies—the body as a source of labor through which value could be produced and exchanged—modern capitalism sought to produce "governing-effects" on the subject.[43] The formation of an unprecedented sovereign power in the form of the administrative state from the late sixteenth to the nineteenth century required the government focused on "controlling the mass of the population on its territory rather than controlling territoriality as such."[44] Modern sovereign power came to operate and mediate (individual) subjects in a normalizing (homogenized) society[45] at the level of the human body—an "anatomo-politics"—and at the level of the population as a biological species: Foucault's "biopolitics."[46] With the shift to biopower, Foucault explains, "wars are no longer waged in the name of a sovereign who needs to be defended; they are waged on behalf of the existence of everyone; entire populations are mobilized for the purpose of wholesale slaughter in the name of the life necessity, massacres have become vital. It is as managers of life and survival, of bodies and the race, that so many regimes have been able to wage so many wars, causing so many men [sic] to be killed."[47]

There is now a sophisticated and illuminating critique of liberalism's predication on the model of war and the sovereign security state's necessary production of (in)security so as to justify the various biopolitical procedures that aim to transform and improve, that is, make more productive, those spaces and populations constructed as backward within capitalist and (post)colonial

---

[41] Michel Foucault. (1977). *Discipline and Punish: The Birth of the Prison.* New York: Random House, p. 25. See also: Michel Foucault. (1980). *Power/Knowledge: Selected Interviews and Other Writings 1972–1977.* Edited by C. Gordon. New York: Pantheon Books, p. 137.

[42] Claudia Aradau and Tobias Blanke. (2010). "Governing Circulation: A Critique of the Biopolitics of Security." In *Security and Global Governmentality: Globalization, Governance and the State,* edited by Miguel de Larrinaga and Marc G. Doucet. London: Routledge, p. 48. See also: David Scott. (1999). *Refashioning Futures: Criticism after Postcoloniality.* Princeton, NJ: Princeton University Press, pp. 47–48.

[43] Scott, *Refashioning Futures,* pp. 40, 51–52.

[44] Bob Jessop. (2006). "From Micro-Powers to Governmentality: Foucault's Work on Statehood, State Formation, Statecraft and State Power." *Political Geography,* 26(1), 37. In Foucault's original, see: M. Foucault. (2003). "Society Must Be Defended." Lectures at the Collège de France 1975-1976. New York: Picador, pp. 37–39; 249–50. M. Foucault. (2004). *Securité, territoire, population. Cours au Collège de France, 1977-1978.* Paris: Seuil/Gallimard, p. 221.

[45] M. Foucault. (1982). The Subject and Power. *Critical Inquiry,* 8(4), 777–95.

[46] Foucault termed this novel and thoroughly European technology of power, biopower. Foucault (2003: 242–43).

[47] Foucault, *Power/Knowledge,* p. 137.

modernity.[48] Attempts to "theorise with Foucault beyond Foucault"[49] in order to produce biopolitics of security that attends to the martial character of liberal politics and the classification of danger and risk always susceptible to the disciplinary and lethal dimensions of sovereign power,[50] nevertheless suffer from "methodological whiteness": "a way of reflecting on the world that fails to acknowledge the role played by race in the very structuring of that world, and of the ways in which knowledge is constructed and legitimated within it. It fails to recognise the dominance of 'Whiteness' as anything other than the standard state of affairs and treats a limited perspective—that deriving from White experience—as a universal perspective."[51] To be sure, Foucault does pay attention to racism's central place in the operations of liberal power and violence.[52] However, because of the unspecified notion of the "human," or rather because of a reliance on "white humanist notions of man prior to racialization, the racism [he] deals with is a kind of racism-without-colonialism, more an unfortunate cultural artifact than a global system of expropriation fundamental to the conditions of possibility for the liberal way of war and biopolitical security assemblages."[53]

---

[48] Vivienne Jabri. (2006). "War, Security and the Liberal State." *Security Dialogue,* 37(1), 47–64; Vivienne Jabri. (2007). *War and the Transformation of Global Politics.* New York: Palgrave Macmillan; Michael Dillon and Julian Reid. (2009). *The Liberal Way of War: Killing to Make Life Live.* London: Routledge; Colleen Bell and Brad Evans. (2010). "Post-interventionary Societies: An Introduction." *Journal of Intervention and Statebuilding,* 4(4), 363–70; Colleen Bell. (2011). *The Freedom of Security: Governing Canada in the Age of Counter-Terrorism.* Vancouver, Canada: UBC Press; Brad Evans. (2011). "The Liberal War Thesis: Introducing the Ten Key Principles of Twenty-First-Century Biopolitical Warfare." *South Atlantic Quarterly,* 110(3), 747–56; Alison Howell. (2014). "The Global Politics of Medicine: Beyond Global Health, against Securitisation Theory." *Review of International Studies,* 40(5), 961–87; Alison Howell. (2015). "Resilience, War, and Austerity: The Ethics of Military Human Enhancement and the Politics of Data." *Security Dialogue,* 46(1), 15–31.

[49] Michael Dillon and Reid Julian. (2009). *The Liberal Way of War: Killing to Make Life Live.* London: Routledge, p. 36.

[50] Julian Reid. (2006). "Life Struggles War, Discipline, and Biopolitics in The Thought of Michel Foucault." *Social Text,* 24(1.86), 127–52; Michael Dillon and Julian Reid. (2009). *The Liberal Way of War: Killing to Make Life Live.* London: Routledge; Brad Evans. (2010). "Foucault's Legacy: Security, War and Violence in the 21st Century." *Security Dialogue,* 41(4), 413–33.

[51] Gurminder K. Bhambra. (2017a). "Brexit, Trump, and 'Methodological Whiteness': On the Misrecognition of Race and Class." *The British Journal of Sociology,* 68 (S1): S214–32; Gurminder K. Bhambra. 2017b. "Why Are the White Working Classes Still Being Held Responsible for Brexit and Trump?" LSE Brexit, November 10, 2017. Available at: http://blogs.lse.ac.uk/brexit/.

[52] M. Foucault. (2003). *"Society Must Be Defended": Lectures at the Collège de France, 1975–1976.* Edited by Mauro Bertani and Alessandro Fontana. New York: Picador, pp. 255–56; Michael Dillon. (2008). "Security, Race and War." In *Foucault on Politics, Security and War,* edited by Michael Dillon and Andrew W. Neal, 166–96. Basingstoke, UK: Palgrave Macmillan; Vivienne Jabri. (2006). "War, Security and the Liberal State." *Security Dialogue,* 37(1), 47–64; Vivienne Jabri. (2007a). *War and the Transformation of Global Politics.* New York: Palgrave Macmillan; Andrew N. Neal. (2008). "Goodbye War on Terror?" In *Foucault on Politics, Security and War,* 43–64. London: Palgrave Macmillan.

[53] Howell and Richter-Montpetit, "Racism in Foucauldian Security Studies," p. 3. The full implications of Foucault's Eurocentrism and the rich critiques from postcolonial, critical race, Black,

With the compounds of modern/colonial and coloniality/rationality in mind, in contrast, I seek to account for the constitutive and not merely instrumental position of race, racism, and colonialism in the workings of state power. Biopower, sanitized of its colonial dimension, or more accurately the colonial condition of possibility for its emergence, constructs Europe as a self-generating, destructive but ultimately autarkic force which insists on (an undifferentiated) corporeal domination necessary for capitalist and thoroughly modern forms of accumulation, but is ultimately a system in which racism comes after the fact of biopower and the biopolitical. Empire and racism, constitutive of the very liberalism that Foucault critiques, continue to set the terms of the conversation on power, violence, and governance even in its

---

feminist perspectives on war, violence, liberalism and biopolitics have been taken up elsewhere in IR, most notably, however, in war and security studies. See: Tarak Barkawi and Mark Laffey. (1999). "The Imperial Peace: Democracy, Force and Globalization." *European Journal of International Relations*, 5(4), 403–34 and Tarak Barkawi and Mark Laffey. (2006). "The Postcolonial Moment in Security Studies." *Review of International Studies*, 32(2), 329–52; Siba N'Zatioula Grovogui. (1996). *Sovereigns, Quasi Sovereigns, and Africans: Race and Self-Determination in International Law*. Minneapolis: University of Minnesota Press and Siba N'Zatioula Grovogui. (2001). "Come to Africa: A Hermeneutics of Race in International Theory." *Alternatives*, 26(4), 425–48; Himadeep Muppidi. (1999). "Postcoloniality and the Production of International Insecurity: The Persistent Puzzle of US-Indian Relations." In *Cultures of Insecurity: States, Communities, and the Production of Danger*, edited by Jutta Weldes, 119–46. Minneapolis: University of Minnesota Press and Himadeep Muppidi. (2001). "State Identity and Interstate Practices. The Limits of Democratic Peace in South Asia." In *Democracy, Liberalism, and War: Rethinking the Democratic Peace Debate*, edited by Tarak Barkawi and Mark Laffey, 45–66. Boulder, CO: Lynne Rienner; Shampa Biswas. (2001). "'Nuclear Apartheid' as Political Position: Race as a Postcolonial Resource?" *Alternatives*, 26(4), 485–522 and Shampa Biswas. (2014). *Nuclear Desire: Power and the Postcolonial Nuclear Order*. Minneapolis: University of Minnesota Press; Sankaran Krishna. (2001). "Race, Amnesia, and the Education of International Relations." *Alternatives*, 26(4), 401–24; Anna M. Agathangelou and L. H. M. Ling. (2004). "Power, Borders, Security, Wealth: Lessons of Violence and Desire from September 11." *International Studies Quarterly*, 48(3), 517–38; Geeta Chowdhry and Seila Nair, eds. (2004). *Power, Postcolonialism and International Relations: Reading Race, Gender and Class*. New York: Routledge; Naeem Inayatullah and Robin L. Riley. (2006). *Interrogating Imperialism: Conversations on Gender, Race, and War*. New York: Palgrave Macmillan; Vivienne Jabri. (2007b). "Michel Foucault's Analytics of War: The Social, the International, and the Racial." *International Political Sociology*, 1(1), 67–81; Robert Shilliam. (2008). "What the Haitian Revolution Might Tell Us about Development, Security, and the Politics of Race." *Comparative Studies in Society and History*, 50(3), 778–808; Anna M. Agathangelou. (2010a). "Necro-(Neo) Colonizations and Economies of Blackness: Of Slaughters, 'Accidents,' 'Disasters' and Captive Flesh." In *International Relations and States of Exception: Margins, Peripheries, and Excluded Bodies*, edited by Shampa Biswas and Seila Nair, 186–209. London: Routledge; Anna M. Agathangelou. (2010b). "Bodies of Desire, Terror and the War in Eurasia: Impolite Disruptions of (Neo) Liberal Internationalism, Neoconservatism and the 'New' Imperium." *Millennium-Journal of International Studies*, 38(3), 693–722; Anna M. Agathangelou. (2013). "Slavery Remains in Reconstruction and Development." In *Globalization, Difference, and Human Security*, edited by Mustapha Kamal Pasha, 152–65. London: Routledge; Laleh Khalili. (2012). *Time in the Shadows: Confinement in Counterinsurgencies*. Stanford, CA: Stanford University Press; Paul Amar. (2013). *The Security Archipelago: Human-Security States, Sexuality Politics, and the End of Neoliberalism*. Durham, NC: Duke University Press; Meera Sabaratnam. (2013). "Avatars of Eurocentrism in the Critique of the Liberal Peace." *Security Dialogue*, 44(3), 259–78.

subversive modes. Foucault's Eurocentrism is surely well known but remains largely unremedied.[54] Without any serious consideration of "race," racism, and coloniality, we are left confused about those subjects who were never understood to be human in the first place, that is, human enough for biopower to work through them; for those, to extend Foucault's own terminology, without a soul through which power might do its work.

The assumption that Europe and European history is universal history, or in more sophisticated forms, that Other histories are merely preparatory stages for, or accumulated into, European history as History, is widespread in international theory. As Gurminder Bhambra tells us, "Eurocentrism is the belief, implicit or otherwise, in the world-historical significance of events believed to have developed endogenously with the cultural-geographical sphere of Europe."[55] James Blaut explains the impact of the "European miracle" well:

> It is the idea that Europe was more advanced and more progressive than all other regions prior to 1492, prior, that is, to the beginning of the period of colonialism, the period in which Europe and non-Europe came into intense interaction. If one believes this to be the case . . . then it must follow that the economic and social modernization of Europe is fundamentally the result of Europe's internal qualities, not of interactions with the societies of Africa, Asia, and America after 1492. Therefore: the main building-blocks of modernity must be European.

---

[54] For discussion to this effect in IR and security studies, see previous note; See also: Melanie Richter-Montpetit. (2007). "Empire, Desire and Violence: A Queer Transnational Feminist Reading of the Prisoner 'Abuse' in Abu Ghraib and the Question of 'Gender Equality.'" *International Feminist Journal of Politics,* 9(1), 38–59 and Melanie Richter-Montpetit. (2014a). "Beyond the Erotics of Orientalism: Lawfare, Torture and the Racial–Sexual Grammars of Legitimate Suffering." *Security Dialogue,* 45(1), 43–62; Robert Shilliam. (2008). "What the Haitian Revolution Might Tell Us about Development, Security, and the Politics of Race." *Comparative Studies in Society and History,* 50(3), 778–808; Alison Howell. (2018). "Forget 'Militarization': Race, Disability, and the Martial Politics of the Police and of the University." *International Feminist Journal of Politics,* 20(2), 117–36. For Eurocentrism, the installment (and demotion) of Europe as the world's center of gravity, see: Samir Amin. (2010). *Eurocentrism. Modernity, Religion and Democracy: A Critique of Eurocentrism and Culturalism.* Pambazuka Press and (2010). *Global History: A View from the South.* Pambazuka Press; Dipesh Chakrabarty. (2000). *Provincializing Europe: Postcolonial Thought and Historical Difference, Princeton Studies in Culture/Power/History.* Princeton, NJ: Princeton University Press; Jean Comaroff. (2011). *Theory from the South; or, How Euro-America Is Evolving toward Africa.* Boulder, CO: Paradigm; Hamid Dabashi. (2015). *Can Non-Europeans Think.* London: Zed Books; Arjun Appadurai. (2013). *The Future as Cultural Fact: Essays on the Global Condition.* London: Verso Books; Kuan-Hsing Chen. (2010). *Asia as Method: Toward Deimperialization.* Durham, NC: Duke University Press; and Walter Mignolo. (2011). *The Darker Side of Western Modernity: Global Futures, Decolonial Options.* Durham, NC: Duke University Press.

[55] Bhambra, *Rethinking Modernity,* p. 5. Emphasis in the original. Ella Shohat and Robert Stam argue that "contemporary Eurocentrism is the discursive residue or precipitate of colonialism, the process by which the European powers reached positions of economic, military, political, and cultural hegemony in much of Asia, Africa, and the Americas." Ella Shohat and Robert Stam. (1994). *Unthinking Eurocentrism: Multiculturalism and the Media.* London: Routledge, p. 15.

Therefore: colonialism cannot have been really important for Europe's modernization. Therefore: colonialism must mean for the Africans, Asians and Americans, not spoliation and cultural destruction but, rather, the receipt-by-difference of European civilization: modernization.[56]

History becomes "the configuration of the Spirit in the form of becoming. . . . The people that receives such an element as a natural principle . . . is the dominant people at this moment of World History. . . . Against the absolute right that such a people possesses by virtue of being the bearer of the development of the world Spirit, the spirit of other peoples has no rights (rechtlos)."[57] These chosen people (especially, for Hegel, Germany, and England) have "absolute right" emanating from an inner experience as a consequence of the Spirit in Europe's "moment of development" (Entwicklungstuffe).[58] Europe is, thus, legitimately on the search for new consumers in Other lands and must, therefore "occupy" them. Hegel does not appear very much concerned with questions of habitation, nor indeed the humanity of Others who might need to be housed when their lands are put to modern "cultivation."[59] Given the need to occupy and consume, this means these lands "must be seized from other peoples. The periphery of Europe is a "free space" that allows the poor, produced by the contradictions of capitalist development, to become capitalists or property owners themselves in the colonies."[60]

Although thoroughly critical of (the myths of) modernity, Europe, and colonialist violence, my own approach may nonetheless be regarded as

---

[56] James M. Blaut. (1993). *The Colonizer's Model of the World: Geographical Diffusionism and Eurocentric History.* New York: Guilford Press, p. 2. Anibal Quijano further explains that narratives of Eurocentric exceptionalism "[are] based on two principle founding myths: first the idea of the history of human civilization as a trajectory that departed from a state of nature and culminated in Europe; second, a view of the differences between Europe and non-Europe as natural (racial) differences and not consequences of a history of power." Anibal Quijano. (2000) "Coloniality of Power, Eurocentrism and Latin America," *Nepantla: Views from the South,* 1(3), 541.

[57] G. W. F. Hegel. (1969). *Encyklopadie der philosophischen Wissenschaften: im Grundrisse,* edited by F. Nicolin and O. Poggler. Hamburg: F. Meiner. See also: sections 346 and 347, p. 430.

[58] In the face of this, we might have guessed, "no other people can be said to have any rights proper to it, and certainly none that it could pose against Europe. This is one of the clearest definitions not only of Eurocentrism but of the sacralization of the imperial power of the North or the Center over the South, the Periphery, the colonial and dependent world of antiquity." E. Dussel. (1993). "Eurocentrism and Modernity (Introduction to the Frankfurt Lectures)." *Boundary 2,* 20(3), 65–76.

[59] Hegel charges on nonetheless: "Through a dialectical impulse to transcend itself that is proper to it, such a society is, in the first place, driven to seek outside itself new consumers. For this reason it seeks to find ways to move about among other peoples that are inferior to it with respect to the resources that it has in abundance, or, in general, its industry. . . . This development of relations offers also the means of colonization towards which, in either an accidental or systematic way, a completed civil society is impelled. Colonization allows a portion of population to return to the principle of family property in the new territory, and, at the same time, it acquires for itself a new possibility and field of labor." G. W. F. Hegel. (1957). *Philosophy of Right.* Oxford: The Clarendon Press, sections 246 and 248.

[60] Dussel, "Eurocentrism," p. 74.

Eurocentric in that it takes as the center of its analysis European hegemony, for which Britain has long been emblematic (or rather symptomatic). If this is the case, however, then it is a Eurocentrism that deprivileges Europe (and Britain) and instead seeks to analyze the strategies (always precariously) deployed to maintain an imprint on the earth accumulated through imperialism, unspeakable violence, and according to a racial economy of life (colonization) and its necessary elimination (genocide). Foucault influentially claimed that under disciplinary regimes of power, spectacular forms of violence were no longer necessary, or had at least become superfluous to the sovereign in liberal, capitalist modernity. However, state practices of cruelty, even in public, remain indispensable to the production, management, and erasure—symbolic and material—of populations deemed to lie outside the enclosure and "absolute right" of the "human."[61] Thus, the very (sub)human subject at the core of the biopolitical must be interrogated. This is what I seek to do through my study of Islamophobia. The various processes, classifications, practices, intimacies, excesses, that is, forms and degrees of violence, in which the racial figure and sign of Muslim and Islam are ensnared, are always already informed by the privileging of the white(ned), colonialist/capitalist subject; the white "I" as the center of all meaning.

Human life is not, however, undifferentiated in its insecurity vis-à-vis sovereign power as Foucault (and Agamben) ultimately maintain through

---

[61] Joy James. (1996). *Resisting State Violence: Radicalism, Gender, and Race in US Culture.* Minneapolis: University of Minnesota Press, p. 34. See also diverse forms, and studies, of disabled humanity: Dylan Rodrìguez. (2006). "(Non) Scenes of Captivity: The Common Sense of Punishment and Death." *Radical History Review,* 96, 9–32, 160; Liat Ben-Moshe, Chris Chapman, and Allison Carey, eds. (2014). *Disability Incarcerated: Imprisonment and Disability in the United States and Canada.* New York: Palgrave Macmillan; Angela Davis. (2002). "From the Convict Lease System to the Super-Max Prison." In *States of Confinement: Policing, Detention, and Prisons,* edited by Joy James, revised and updated, 60–74. New York: Palgrave Macmillan; James, Joy, ed. (1998). *The Angela Y. Davis Reader.* Malden, MA: Blackwell; Joy James, ed. (2000). *States of Confinement: Policing, Detention and Prisons.* New York: St. Martin's Press; Joy James, ed. (2007). *Warfare in the American Homeland: Policing and Prison in a Penal Democracy.* Durham, NC: Duke University Press; Dylan Rodríguez. (2007). "Forced Passages: Imprisoned Radical Intellectuals and the U.S. Prison Regime." In *Warfare in the American Homeland: Policing and Prison in a Penal Democracy,* edited by Joy James, 35–57. Durham, NC: Duke University Press; Ruth Wilson Gilmore. (2007). *Golden Gulag: Prisons, Surplus, Crisis, and Opposition in Globalizing California.* Berkley: University of California Press; Majia Holmer Nadesan. (2010). *Governmentality, Biopower, and Everyday Life.* London: Routledge; Khalili (2012); Joao Costa Vargas and Jaime Amparo Alves. (2013). "Geographies of Death: An Intersectional Analysis of Police Lethality and the Racialized Regimes of Citizenship in São Paulo." In *New Racial Missions of Policing: International Perspectives on Evolving Law-Enforcement Politics,* edited by Paul Amar, 37–62. London: Routledge; Richter-Montpetit (2014b); Jasbir K. Puar. (2017). *The Right to Maim: Debility, Capacity, Disability.* Durham, MN: Duke University Press; Dinesh Wadiwel. (2017). "Disability and Torture: Exception, Epistemology and 'Black Sites.'" *Continuum,* 31(3), 388–99; Farah Tanis, Dixon Ericka, Leonie Mills, and Melanie Richter-Montpetit. (2018). "Sexualized Violence and Torture in the Afterlife of Slavery: An Interview with Farah Tanis and Ericka Dixon of Black Women's Blueprint." *International Feminist Journal of Politics,* 20(3), 446–61.

their colonial silence. Discriminating between good and bad (modern and nonmodern?) forms of life are not, therefore, merely an effect of biopolitical rule and the practice of discrimination *after* its construction as such, but constitutive of it. Everyone everywhere may well be potentially dangerous, and thus potentially guilty but this is not the point. As Edward Said once said: "I do feel, whether anything is said overtly or not, I feel as if I am a delinquent; sort of, *before anything gets going I am somehow guilty as charged.*"[62] Racist security practices, domestic and foreign, are endemic and not exceptional to the liberal rule that arrived with capitalist modernity in which certain lives are vulnerable to gratuitous violence simply for being.[63] Put differently and against Agamben's Eurocentric terms, one might become the target of "bare life" under "states of exception," except there are particular subjects, namely racial(ized) subject-objects for whom the (white) exception is, in fact, the rule even prior to its very legislation. For the racial subject within racist structures, one's very being is a transgression and is *thus subject to violation in the first instance.*

I take Islamophobia as symptomatic of the irrationality of the violence generated by these myths and practices while paying close attention to the cracks that have long formed in them, and the bandage solutions employed time and again, then as now, in their concealment. An irrationality that is projected outward to the Muslim to produce the summons which names this book.[64] The varying responses to which dictates the levels, forms, and intensities of violation. This study serves as a prolegomenon to a work that pursues further the possibility of retrieving the Other as a site of ethical pedagogy for ethicizing a world made white in its modernity but whose internal contradictions and ecological limits are, quite literally, on fire.

A NOTE ON "RACE": STATE, LABOR, LOGIC

There were and are of course many Europes, real and imagined, though perhaps the contours separating them have always been blurred. Europe here,

---

[62] Said's words were a response to a question about being Palestinian in America and New York in particular. See Christopher Sykes's (1988) documentary on Said as part of the BBC series, Exiles. Available at: https://www.youtube.com/watch?v=7g1ooTNkMQ4&t=1s

[63] Frantz Fanon. (1967). *Black Skin, White Masks.* New York: Grove Press; Hartman, Saidiya V. (1997). *Scenes of Subjection: Terror, Slavery, and Self-Making in Nineteenth-Century America.* Oxford: Oxford University Press; Anna M. Agathangelou. (2010b). "Bodies of Desire, Terror and the War in Eurasia: Impolite Disruptions of (Neo) Liberal Internationalism, Neoconservatism and the 'New' Imperium." *Millennium-Journal of International Studies,* 38(3), 693–722; Frank B. Wilderson, III. (2010). *Red, White & Black: Cinema and the Structure of U.S. Antagonisms.* Durham, NC: Duke University Press.

[64] This provocation in the service of productive critique has allies. See: Hamid Dabashi. (2015). *Can Non-Europeans Think?* London: Zed Books and before him, Kishore Mahbubani. (2001). *Can Asians Think? Understanding the Divide between East and West.* Hanover NH: Steerforth Press.

however, recalling Levi-Strauss's[65] usage of the word, is a founding "myth," "the original home of the modern,"[66] built on a paradigmatic "first in Europe, then elsewhere" historicism. Following Frantz Fanon, Europe is literally the creation of the "Third World," a forgotten but persistent fact which shapes our world today. "Racism," Hamid Dabashi explains, "is not a question of one's blood type (the Christian criterion used in sixteenth-century Spain to distinguish Christians from Moors and Jews in Europe) or the color of one's skin (Africans and the New World civilizations). Racism consists in devaluing the humanity of certain people by dismissing it or playing it down (even when not intentional) at the same time as highlighting and playing up European [liberal] philosophy, assuming it to be universal."[67]

Racism cannot merely be a temporally or spatially bounded phenomenon, something from a bygone past, or only from here or there, but a system of conditions and techniques that live on well beyond the direct functioning of colonial power and the processes of formal decolonization/independence of the twentieth century.[68] Coloniality's law of race is, after all, reflected powerfully everywhere we look, at both macro and molecular levels: the global interstate system; international divisions of labor; (socio)economic paradigms; the subjects and practices of modern warfare; neoliberalism, the industries of Silicon Valley and digital technologies; the algorithm and the algorithmization of white supremacy; genomics and its racial syntax; the

---

[65] Claude Levi-Strauss. (1955). "The Structural Study of Myth." *The Journal of American Folklore,* 68(270), 428–44; Claude Levi-Strauss. (1963). *Structural Anthropology.* New York: Basic Books.

[66] Dipesh Chakrabarty. (2007). *Provincializing Europe: Postcolonial Thought and Historical Difference.* Princeton, NJ: Princeton University Press.

[67] Hamid Dabashi. (2015) *Can Non-Europeans Think?* London: Verso, p. 20.

[68] There is a vast literature on these debates and implications. For an initial literature see the following and their generous bibliographies: Walter D. Mignolo. (2015). "Global Coloniality and the World Disorder." World Public Forum, November 2015, available at: http://wpfdc.org/images/2016_blog/W.Mignolo_Decoloniality_after_Decolonization_Dewesternization_after_the_Cold_War.pdf (last accessed on January 3, 2019); Gloria Anzaldúa. (1987). *Borderlands/La Frontera: The New Mestiza.* San Francisco: Aunt Lute Books; Walter Mignolo. (2011). *The Darker Side of Western Modernity: Global Futures, Decolonial Options.* Durham: Duke University Press; Immanuel Wallerstein. (1995). *After Liberalism.* New York: New Press; Santiago Castro-Gómez. (2007). "The Missing Chapter of Empire: Postmodern Re-organization of Coloniality and Post-Fordist Capitalism." *Cultural Studies,* 21(2–3), 428–48; Walter D. Mignolo. (2007). "Delinking: The Rhetoric of Modernity, the Logic of Coloniality and the Grammar of Decolniality." *Cultural Studies,* 21(2–3), 449–514 and (2007b) "The Decolonial Option and the Meaning of Identity in Politics." *Anales Nueva Epoca (Instituto Iberoamericano Universidad de Goteborg)* 9/10, 43–72; W. Mignolo and C. Walsh. (2018). *On Decoloniality: Concepts, Analytics, Praxis.* Durham: Duke University Press; Kwasi Wiredu. (1992). "Formulating Modern Thoughts in African Languages: Some Theoretical Considerations," in *The Surreptitious Speech: Presence Africaine and the Politics of Otherness, 1947–1987,* edited by V.Y. Mudimbe. Chicago: University of Chicago Press, pp. 301–32 and Kwasi Wiredu. (1998). "Toward Decolonizing African Philosophy and Religion." *African Studies Quarterly. The Online Journal of African Studies,* 1(4); Sylvia Wynter. (2001). "Towards the Sociogenic Principle: Fanon, the Puzzle of Conscious Experience, and What It Is Like to Be 'Black'." In *National Identities and Socio- political Changes in Latin America,* edited by Mercedes F. Duran-Cogan and Antonio Gómez-Moriana. New York: Routledge, pp. 30–66.

transcription of genetic characteristics as a digital imprint; the fluid administration of state violence within new technetronic regimes; reproductive technologies and the general interest in refashioning life along lines defined by
racial determinism, among many others. I do not intend to engage with each
of these by affirming or negating their importance, their logics, and specificities, but will have the occasion to discuss the substance of some of them as
my argument requires and as I proceed. What is worth noting, however, is
that race and racism do not only have a past. They have a future.

Reflection upon these biopolitical procedures and anthropological hierarchies might also fit into the broader project of an amended history of modernity, what Enrique Dussel calls "transmodernity,"[69] which necessitates much
more unstable temporal and entangled spatial dimensions so as to forge a
productive "alienation" from one's own immanent worldly situation. Critical
knowledge of one's own culture and society can only arise from a carefully
cultivated degree of estrangement. Overfamiliarity or taken-for-grantedness
can occlude from view a "vulgar" cosmopolitanism or, worse still, commod-
ify culture as property; some with higher, more worldly ("universal") value
than others. Instead, a proper commitment to multiplicity is a decentring force
which challenges, if not altogether encourages, abandoning the certitude
and comfort of speaking from the "center."[70] Imperialism consolidated the
mixture of cultures and identities on a global scale. But its worst and most
paradoxical gift was to allow people to believe that they were only, mainly,
exclusively, white, or black, or Western, or Oriental.[71] The scale upon which
sameness and difference have been measured must be altered productively
"so that the strangeness of strangers goes out of focus and other dimensions
of a basic sameness can be acknowledged and made significant."[72]

The connections I am attempting to draw between practices of racial orders
(such as Britain), and the flows of power and formulations of knowledge
which underpin them, require a shift in our view of the colony, the metropole,
and how their relations might be mapped. We must first generate a view of
the colony beyond its aims as an extractive commercial operation. As Gilroy
notes, "No longer merely a settlement, an adventure, an opportunity, a place
for self-creation, self-discovery, and a space of death, it can be recognized as

---

[69] E. Dussel. (1995). *The Invention of the Americas: Eclipse of "the other" and the Myth of Modernity.* New York: Continuum; E. Dussel. (2002). *Posmodernidad y transmodernidad: diálogos con
la filosofía de Gianni Vattimo.* Puebla, México: Universidad Iberoamericana/Instituto de Estudios
Superiores de Occidente; E. D. Dussel. (2012). "Transmodernity and Interculturality: An Interpretation from the Perspective of Philosophy of Liberation." *TRANSMODERNITY: Journal of
Peripheral Cultural Production of the Luso-Hispanic World,* 1(3).

[70] Salman Sayyid. (2014) *Recalling the Caliphate, Decolonization and World Order.* London: C.
Hurst & Co, p. 59.

[71] Edward Said. (1993). *Culture and Imperialism.* London: Vintage.

[72] Gilroy, *After Empire,* p. 3.

a laboratory, a location for experiment and innovation that transformed the exercise of governmental powers at home and configured the institutionalization of imperial knowledge to which the idea of 'race' was central."[73] For Gilroy, "race" refers primarily to an "impersonal, discursive arrangement, the brutal result of the raciological ordering of the world, not its cause," and tracking the term directs our "attention toward the manifold structures of a racial nomos—a legal, governmental, and spatial order—that . . . is now reviving the geopolitical habits of the old imperial system in discomforting ways."[74] Racial subjects are, thus, *produced* as a means to justify their infrahuman status and experience of a power tethered to the racial idea.[75]

Race is especially tenacious precisely because it is both fiction and force.[76] The two not only support one another, insofar as fictitiousness propels rather than abets the forceful character of race but both exist in a relation of mutual constitution. The fictions of race—lack, absence, degradation, deviance, violence, excess, pollution, raw matter, licentiousness and so many more—are baked into the violence of racist power which tracks, mocks, violates, and captures the racial subject and make real the false names that stick to him. Which is to say that race must be made real through the practices of institutions which proceed more or less systematically, though this should not give us the impression that race is somehow always coherent or only constructed (in a thin sense). Race is therefore a technology, at once erratic, motile, puncturing, fluid, designed, and redesigned to enable those who wield sovereign power to maintain it.[77]

---

[73] Paul Gilroy. (2004). *Postcolonial Melancholia.* New York: Columbia University Press, p. 46. He continues that "problems like the disappearance of public torture are often understood to identify a significant stage in the development of a new type of power: capillary, biopolitical, and primarily directed toward the management of population. . . . There were different biopowers at work in these colonial histories, and they did not remain sealed off from the mainstream at the distant ends of the imperial system." See also: Paul Gilroy. (2005). "Multiculture, Double Consciousness and the 'war on terror'." *Patterns of Prejudice,* 39(4), 431–43.

[74] Paul Gilro. (2005) *After Empire: Melancholia or Convivial Culture.* London: Routledge, p. 39.

[75] In his lectures at the Collège de France, Michel Foucault puts forward the argument that the appearance of a political language of race and its growing relationship to governmental/disciplinary power were not merely incidental developments. Instead, he draws a strong link between his concept of biopower and racism's inscription as the basic mechanism of state power. He goes on to argue that "the modern State can scarcely function without becoming involved with racism at some point." M. Foucault. (2003). *"Society Must Be Defended": Lectures at the College de France, 1975–1976.* Edited by Mauro Bertani and Alessandro Fontana. New York: Picador, p. 254. The language of that power was addressed to the pragmatic challenges of colonial rule, but the historical currency of race thinking has come to be used in other more implicit, mundane ways than "what must live and what must die."

[76] Karen E. Fields and Barbara J. Fields. (2012). *Racecraft: The Soul of Inequality in American Life.* London: Verso.

[77] H. Jones and N. Jones. (2020). "Race, Technology, and Posthumanism." In *The Bloomsbury Handbook of Posthumanism,* edited by M. Thomsen and J. Wamberg. London: Bloomsbury Academic.

In this sense, race can be split into different aspects, but which come together to consolidate the racial order, even if its particular properties are sometimes in disharmony or disarray. There is first a *state of race*, which amounts to an *ontology*. It refers to the condition of being assigned a "race." To be sure we are confronting, initially at least, processes of assignation as opposed to self-designation. It concerns the subject of race, in this case, the Muslim. The notion of "race" remains fundamental to the negation of cobelonging, that we all inhabit a world which must be shared, instead giving legitimacy to racist notions and practices which are compelled to separate, demarcate, and expel. As is now well known, Kant's universality posited in *Critique of Pure Reason* turns out not to be universal for it does not, nor should it the argument goes, admit certain groups into the enclosure of humans on the very basis that they lack reason.[78] Relations with the subject(s) of race, then, are always already constrained by the correspondence between race and its assigned state, one of absolute or partial defect that is ontological in character and which makes, for example, the widespread representation of non-European peoples, that is, much of the world as being trapped in a lesser form of being.

The state of race points to an inaugural *absence*: the absence of the same and which reminds us that the racial subject's Other, the white man or woman, is its necessary counterpart and one which white Europe has worked hard to universalize. The state of race also contains a *presence*—of fossils and monsters, of history. "If the fossil," as Michel Foucault writes, is "what permits resemblances to subsist throughout all the deviations traversed by nature," and functions primarily "as a distant and approximate form of identity," the monster, in contrast, "provides an account, as though in caricature, of the genesis of differences."[79] The impositions of various states of nonbeing, nonthinking, nonliving to racial subjects was central to the European project formed by cycles of unlimited expenditure and unprecedented accumulation, especially in the Enlightenment colonialism of the eighteenth century and beyond.

But the production of the state of race, one in which the Muslim resides, requires a massive structural, psychic, and economic web of investments and intimacies through which race comes to take its hold on a social order and, as such, must also be a principle of sovereignty over that same order. In that sense, there must be systems of labor which support race's production and

---

[78] On Kant's revealing racism in his lesser-known works, see: Emmanuel Chukwudi Eze. (1997). "The Color of Reason: The Idea of 'Race' in Kant's Anthropology." In *Postcolonial African Philosophy: A Critical Reader*, edited by E.C. Eze. Oxford: Blackwell, pp. 103–31.

[79] Michel Foucault. (1973). *The Order of Things: An Archaeology of the Human Sciences*, ed. and trans. R. D. Laing. New York: Random House, pp. 156–67.

which, sometimes quite literally, employ individuals across a network of institutions trafficking in the phantasms and classifications which constitute the racial subject. The *labor of race* forms a whole *psycho-material complex*: representation, discourse, law, knowledge, and culture combined. Or, put differently, the nation-state.

I want to dwell on the state as a vehicle for power, knowledge, and governance because it is the backdrop for much of my analysis. Race as a technology (of the state) is not completely devoid of the pursuit for truth but functions to codify the conditions, convictions, and behaviors fit for the appearance of the racial subject, a being who has come by many names but whose manifestation everywhere is today known as the Muslim. The labor of race is not, therefore, only ways of speaking but also ways of doing, not simply a structure of the imagination but of the political and economic order, that is, a range of practices and daily work which justify the arithmetic of racial domination.

With the birth of modern Europe, the structure of modern (philosophical and technical) knowledge of the human comes to be in a supportive and entangled relation to the structure of modern power as represented by, among other things, the phenomenon of the nation-state, its colonialist procedures at home in Europe, and abroad in faraway territories of Others-made-subhuman. To discuss either power or knowledge is, in effect, to engage in both, for "it is conceptually impossible," Wael Hallaq notes,

> to view power in the modern and Foucauldian senses as anything other than being organically tied to knowledge. Logically and ontologically, there is no modern power without knowledge, and if this is accepted, as it should be, then our language, in this context at least, is highly redundant. All we need to say is the word "power," and knowledge is automatically included in the very term, just as the word "mother" must include an unadulterated reference to "daughter," "son," or "child," without whom "mother" is inconceivable.[80]

There is little doubt that Enlightenment modernity encompassed intellectual, philosophical, and political movements across a wide spectrum. However, it can also be argued that the Enlightenment as a paradigm, in its totality—and despite its Kierkegaards, Kants, and Herders—featured a shared substrate of assumptions approximating a unified will despite its internal multiplicity. As the political philosopher John Gray has argued, the core project

---

[80] Hallaq, *Restating*, p. 16. Put another way, "virtually every prominent and influential European thinker in the three hundred years before the eighteenth century and nearly the full century after it were either agonistic toward or enthusiastically in favour of imperialism." Sankar Muthu. (2003). *Enlightenment Against Empire*. Princeton: Princeton University Press, p. 1.

of the Enlightenment "was the displacement of local, customary or traditional moralities, and all forms of transcendental faith, by a critical or rational morality, which was projected as the basis of a universal civilisation."[81] A universal civilization invested in and driven by a theology of progress. A theology, in turn, embodied in the very colonialist instruments of governance which sought to dismantle, reconstruct, and fundamentally reconstitute the sociopolitical, not to mention the moral-psycho-epistemic makeup of the colonized, all in the name of forward development, reason, rationality, and human civilization. Ideals that could only ever confirm a teleology written by and for modern Europe in the throes of intense intra-European competition.

Race and racism's relation to the production of the (racial) subject is an active, dynamic principle which (re)constituted social realities, whole "networks of meaning" of those foreign subjects who could/can only ever be incomprehensible problems in the social realm.[82] The human sciences, anthropology, geography, philosophy, economics, and more undertook elaborate work to make the idea of race epistemologically correct.[83] The connection drawn between race and definitions of the human was an ideological formation sustained by the practices and discourses of the colonial state. But also "scientific" theories of race within these modern disciplines of knowledge which could only look at but never recognize the racial multitudes in the colonies with whom something might be shared. Given the mercantilism of imperial extraction and colonial war, the nation-state was always already a racial project. The colonized were subject to the modern state which, as a specific historical product, remade the world and its societies, human and natural, in its own image,[84] completely invested as it was/is in a theology of its own construction, progressing to an endpoint of its own arbitrary will.[85]

---

[81] John Gray. (1995). *Enlightenment's Wake: Politics and Culture at the Close of the Modern Age.* London: Routledge, p. 123.

[82] Du Bois, The Souls of Black Folk and Fanon, Black Skin, White Masks.

[83] Paul Gilroy. (2000). *Between Camps: Race, Identity and Nationalism at the End of the Colour Line.* London: Allen Lane, p. 58.

[84] James Scott. (1998). "Taming Nature: An Agriculture of Legibility and Simplicity." In *Seeing Like a State: How Certain Schemes to Improve the Human Condition Have Failed.* London: Yale University Press. Taking this logic of colonial reproduction further, Edward Said discusses the idea of "ecological imperialism" in which the Europeans, wherever they went, began to change the natural habitat so as to resemble what they left behind in the metropole. Plants, animals, crops, entire building methods were imported wholesale, "complete with new diseases, environmental imbalances, and traumatic dislocations for the overpowered natives." Edward Said. *Culture and Imperialism.* London: Vintage, p. 225. See also: Alfred Crosby. (1966). *Ecological Imperialism: The Biological Expansion of Europe, 900-1900.* Cambridge: Cambridge University Press, pp. 196–216; Neil Smith. (1984). *Uneven Development: Nature, Capital, and the Production of Space.* Oxford: Blackwell, p. 101.

[85] See Bowden. (2011). "Colonialism, Anti-Colonialism, and the Idea of Progress." In *History and Philosophy of Science and Technology, Encyclopedia of Life Support Systems,* edited by UNESCO-EOLS Joint Committee. Oxford: EOLSS, pp. 1–2. For a critique of the residues of this thoroughly modern/colonial doctrine in Critical Theory, see Amy Allen. (2016). *The End*

To speak of the modern state is by necessity to assume a particular conception of sovereignty (also European in origin) constructed around the fictitious concept of will to representation—the idea that the nation embodying the state is the sole author of its own will and destiny.[86] Sovereignty here is in turn also to include perforce *popular* will as the master of one's own *collective* destiny.[87] The modern nation-state is, then, a secularized god of political order whose origin and tributaries all point to Europe.[88] Of course, all premodern societies were ruled according to certain political and ideological structures, no doubt having their own organically constituted ordering apparatuses with their attendant instruments and regimes of discipline. But the conceptual association made between scientific, value-free, that is *reasoned* knowledge with a notoriously equivocal conception of universal morality that would produce universally valid structures, institutions, and, most importantly, laws, gave the unique impersonal character of the modern state its legitimacy. Which is to say, it is the very impersonal nature of sovereignty which makes of the state both an empirical set of institutions, but also a pervasive ideological structure which at once orders and is shaped by the (racial) dynamics of the social and economic matrix.

Engels's insight to the effect that, "the state presents itself to us as the first ideological power over man," or, moreover, the notion presented in *The German Ideology* that the state constitutes the "illusory common interest" of a society is instructive.[89] The state and its sovereignty emerges as *an ideological thing*; it can be understood as the device, or network of devices, in terms of which subjection—whether political or class domination or otherwise[90]— is legitimated. The state is first and foremost an exercise in legitimation and what is being legitimated is something which if seen directly would be illegitimate; unacceptable forms of (sovereign) violence and domination. Indeed, why else all the legitimation work?[91] Politically institutionalized power, its

---

of *Progress: Decolonizing the Normative Foundations of Critical Theory*. New York: Columbia University Press, 2016.

[86] Colin Hay et al., eds. (2006). *The State: Theories and Issues*. New York: Palgrave.

[87] Carl Schmitt. (1985). *Political Theology: Four Chapters on the Concept of Sovereignty*. Trans. George Schwab. Chicago: University of Chicago Press, pp. 25–28. See also: Benedict Anderson. (2006). *Imagined Communities: Reflections on the Origin and Spread of Nationalism*. 2nd ed. London: Verso.

[88] Christopher Dawson. (1956). *The Making of Europe*. New York: Meridian Books.

[89] K. Marx and F. Engels. (1965). *The German Ideology*. London: Lawrence and Wishart, part I, p. 53.

[90] Bob Jessop. (2016). *The State: Past, Present, Future*. Cambridge: Polity, pp. 100–106.

[91] Abrams continues, "The state, in sum, is a bid to elicit support for or tolerance of the insupportable and intolerable by presenting them as something other than themselves, namely, legitimate, disinterested domination. The study of the state, seen thus, would begin with the cardinal activity involved in the serious presentation of the state: the legitimating of the illegitimate. The immediately present institutions of the 'state system'—and in particular their coercive functions—are the principal object of that task. The crux of the task is to over-accredit them as an integrated

simultaneous integration into the very fabric of society and isolation outside and/or above that same fabric, creates for subjects of the state the acceptable conditions for acquiescence. The police, prisons, border forces, armies, and so on are the most overtly coercive instruments of domination. Yet they are but the backup instruments of the burden of legitimacy.[92] But it is their association with the idea of the state along with constituent ideas of national interest/security/order/citizen and intruder that silences protest, excuses force, and convinces almost all of us that the fate of the victims is necessary if not also just.[93] But the state is not the reality which stands behind the mask of political practice. It is itself the mask which prevents our seeing political practice—social subordination, domination, illusory common interest—as it is. The state much like its enemy is, then, in every sense of the term a triumph of concealment.[94]

If there is a theological tone to this work of legitimation, then it is not by accident. In fact, as Paul Kahn reminds us, the sovereign state "is conceived as the efficient agency of its own construction . . . comparable to divine Creation ex nihilo" and "capable of having or expressing such an act of will."[95] Which is to say that the modern state has a metaphysic of sovereignty and attributes akin to monotheism:

> First, it is omnipotent: all political forms are open to its choice. Second, it wholly fills time and space: it is equally present at every moment of the nation's life and in every location within the nation's borders. Third, we know it only by its product. We do not first become aware of the popular sovereign and then ask what it has accomplished. We know that it must exist, because we perceive the state as an expression of its will. We deduce the fact of the subject from the

---

expression of common interest cleanly dissociated from all sectional interests and the structures—class, church, race and so forth—associated with them. The agencies in question, especially administrative and judicial and educational agencies, are made into state agencies as part of some quite historically specific process of subjection; and made precisely as an alternative reading of and cover for that process." Abrams, "Notes," p. 76.

[92] What is legitimated, insofar as it is legitimated, is "real," that is coercive, power: armies, police and prisons, as well as the whole process of fiscal exaction—"the skeleton of the state stripped of all misleading ideologies." Duncan Bell. (1976). *The Cultural Contradictions of Capital.* New York: Basic Books, quoting Rudolph Goldschield, p. 220.

[93] Especially influential critical interventions into the notion of the justifiability, or legitimacy until proven otherwise logic, of state violence can be found in prison abolition literatures. See: Michelle Alexander. (2010). *The New Jim Crow: Mass Incarceration in the Age of Colorblindness.* New York: New Press; Angela Davis. (2003). *Are Prisons Obsolete?* New York: Seven Stories; Angela Y. Davis. (2005). *Abolition Democracy: Beyond Empire, Prisons, and Torture.* New York: Seven Stories Press; Ruth Wilson Gilmore. (2007). *Golden Gulag: Prisons, Surplus, Crisis, and Opposition in Globalizing California.* Los Angeles: University of California Press.

[94] Alan Finlayson and J. Martin. (2006). "Poststructuralism." In *The State: Theories and Issues,* edited by C. Hay et al. New York: Palgrave, pp. 155–71; Abrams, "Notes," p. 77.

[95] Paul Kahn. (2005). *Putting Liberalism in Its Place.* Princeton, NJ: Princeton University Press, p. 267.

experience of its created product. Finally, we cannot be aware of this sovereign without experiencing it as a normative claim that presents itself as an assertion of identity. We understand ourselves as a part, and as a product, of this sovereign. In it, we see ourselves.[96]

In fine, the epistemic and material break from the tyrannies of divine rule, monarchy, church, and tradition, meant European subjects, as enlightened (white, propertied, European) citizens, became sovereign over their own lives and destinies as members of the nation subsumed by the state. Which in turn meant a level of representation through the body politic to the extent that the modern state became sovereign over everything. Put simply, one's own individual identification with the sovereign in its full implication amounts to being conceived and fashioned through the sovereign will.[97] The concept loses none of its force with the *type* of government that a state takes, "for even in the absence of traditional democratic practices, any state comes to expect its sovereign will to be embodied in the acts and speech of its rulers, even when they happen to be a band of devils. That the elision from the democratic will to tyranny and vice versa remains protected by sovereignty is an accurate expression of the historical transitions from absolute monarchies to democratic rule under the trenchant concept of the sovereign state."[98] So profound an idea was modern sovereignty, that it structures a global system in which, internationally, sovereignty means that other states recognize one another's legitimate authority to represent its nation and its authority within its borders, even if, remarkably, its own subjects reject this authority.

An international arrangement was mapped out in the aftermath of the so-called Peace of Westphalia (1648) that was structurally tied to the internal, domestic dimension of sovereignty in which within a nation's borders, there is no higher order than that of the state. The "peace" of Westphalia was in many ways, like a great number of concepts in modernity, a euphemism.[99] While its ostensible referent was the expansion of a recognizable international

---

[96] Ibid., pp. 267–68.

[97] Carl Schmitt summarized the matter incisively when he wrote that "All significant concepts of the modern theory of the state are secularized theological concepts not only because of their historical development—in which they were transferred from theology to the theory of the state, whereby, for example, the omnipotent God became the omnipotent lawgiver—but also because of their systemic structure." Carl Schmitt. (1985). *Political Theology: Four Chapters on the Concept of Sovereignty.* Trans. George Schwab. Chicago: University of Chicago Press, p. 36. On this theme, see also: Samir Amin. (2004). *The Liberal Virus.* New York: Monthly Review Press; Anderson, *Imagined Communities*; Talal Asad. (2003). *Formations of the Secular: Christianity, Islam, Modernity.* Stanford, CA: Stanford University Press.

[98] Hallaq, *Impossible*, p. 26.

[99] For a classic study on the implications of this modern sovereignty outside of Europe, see: Siba-N'Zatioula Grovogui. (1996). *Sovereigns, Quasi Sovereigns, and Africans: Race and Self-determination in International Law.* University of Minnesota Press, pp. 43–76.

society, "Westphalia engendered novel norms of non-interference between sovereigns and neutralized religious conflict from *inter-European state relations*," as distinct from a barbarous World-outside. Westphalia and the form of sovereignty that was its epistemic terrain was a manifestation of decidedly European self-identification.[100] Kayaoglu argues: "European self-identification depended on various European other identifications; the assertion of the complete superiority and exceptionalism of the European political and legal order has necessitated the European willingness to spread it, even if the process of civilizing non-European societies frequently requires some evil."[101]

Thus, the sovereignty inscribed in Westphalia stood for the intensification of the enslavement and colonization of many peoples across the world as the glue of European self-identification; those peoples who on the basis of their non-Europeanness could never really belong to a kindred community of sovereign destiny.[102] Just as the form of modern sovereignty was sacralized in the nation-state and disseminated internationally in the Treaty of 1648, it was equally a global principle upon which lesser peoples were turned into fuel for modern capitalism, development, and governance, with all the genocidal violence that it entailed.

Sovereignty constituted the conceptual vehicle for the instantiation of what W. E. B. Du Bois would call, "the problem of the color-line—the relation of the darker to the lighter races of men in Asia and Africa, in America and the islands of the sea";[103] and what allowed modern imperialism to wear a "democratic face" at home and a "stern and unyielding autocracy" in the colonies. That is, a world designed with two faces, partitioned by the sovereign (democratic) will of European states—a continent comprised of competing imperial units—defined by massive concessionary corporate interest structures, and the human refuse of that same will to dominance.[104] It is a uniquely virulent form of sovereignty which had to do away with almost all forms of constraint, in order to justify the colonial project with all the uninhibited experimentation, exploitation, and death that underpinned it, and for which

---

[100] Alexander Barder. (2015). *Empire Within: International Hierarchy and Its Imperial Laboratories of Governance*. London: Routledge, p. 26.

[101] Turan Kayaoglu. (2010). "Westphalian Eurocentrism in International Relations Theory." *International Studies Review,* 12(2), 193–217, at p. 206.

[102] Presupposed by the modern nation of the sovereign state.

[103] W.E.B. Du Bois. (1961). *The Souls of Black Folk.* New York: Crest Books, p. 23.

[104] See the analysis of Enrique Dussel's *ego cogito* and *ego conquiro* in Ramón's Grosfoguel, (2013). "The Structure of Knowledge in Westernized Universities: Epistemic Racism/Sexism and the Four Genocides/Epistemicides of the Long Sixteenth Century." *Human Architecture: Journal of the Sociology of Self-Knowledge,* 11(1), 73–90, at 78–79. See also: Enrique Dussel. (1995). *The Invention of the Americas: Eclipse of "the Other" and the Myth of Modernity,* trans. Michel D. Barber. New York: Continuum; Nelson Maldonado-Torres. (2008). *Against War: Views from the Underside of Modernity.* Durham: Duke University Press.

the concept of lower races was fundamental.[105] Furthermore, the nation-state as a representation of sovereignty and the expression of the sovereign will, historically and today, appears to know little other than that will. Which is to say that the Aristotelian final cause of the state's existence is nothing more than its own continued existence. The state exists for its own sake. As Paul Kahn says, it is "not an end among others; it is that end for which all others can be sacrificed,"[106] and thus any ethical and moral benchmarks must be instrumental and always provisional.

Benchmarks by definition set limits on what can and cannot be done. Sovereign will being sovereign subsumes all other wills including that of the citizen, never mind that colonial subject whose rational willing and testimony has ab initio been declared void. But that is not all: "the citizen himself is not above being sacrificed for the highest end. Indeed, the citizen is the archetype and fullest manifestation of sacrifice, because there is nothing more precious than life except the nation-state, the sui generis cause that can legitimately demand and receive that ultimate sacrifice."[107] This points to a larger dynamic for which the concept of sovereignty is a manifestation. The modern project, of which the nation-state was a paradigm (in the Schmittian mode of the central domain), did not simply emerge and evolve through a series of economic, political, and material developments that necessitated forms of systematic coercion and discipline. That is, forms which presupposed these same developments. But rather, as Hallaq explains,

> For the European colonists to be able to exploit the Haitians, the Amerindians, and untold others in the manner that they did, to subjugate them as machines rather than as humans (or, for that matter, as human labor), to subject them to unprecedented forms of slavery and to merciless conceptions of property, to develop these experiments into a system of coercion and discipline in a Foucauldian fashion, and to turn all this around and further colonize the world with a view to enriching their coffers and in the process reengineer them as new subjects, to cultivate genocide as a new weapon when all else fails, to do all this, they must have *already* been in possession of, or in the process of possessing, a worldview that did away with that benchmark.[108]

---

[105] Du Bois illuminated this in his discussion of "the crucial significance of race and racism as fundamental organising principles of international politics; axes of hierarchy and oppression structuring the logics of world politics as we know it." Anievas et al. (2014). *Race and Racism in International Relations: Confronting the Global Colour Line.* London: Routledge, p. 2.

[106] Kahn, *Putting Liberalism*, p. 276.

[107] Hallaq, *Impossible*, p. 28.

[108] Hallaq, *Restating*, p. 20.

A worldview without benchmarks, one able to rationalize the exploitation and genocide of untold peoples, that is, to rationalize colonization and extermination in the name of sovereign will, did not and indeed could not have existed without the principle of race. Which is to say that the removal of benchmarks to satisfy the ultimate ends of the sovereign will of the modern state, under which even the citizen can be legitimately sacrificed, did not happen homogenously across the world. Certain benchmarks, if that is even the correct designation given its temporariness, were more straightforwardly removed in certain contexts than others; certain subjects and peoples more easily disposed of. The racial subject in the formation of colonial and capitalist modernity signified, among other things, the absence of moral constraints on white Europe's interactions with its Others. The lives of Others could be spent without limit.

Sovereign will also gives birth to *the law*. The law is "sovereignty's paradigmatic manifestation in the practice of governance."[109] Indeed, the capacity to produce law is, like sovereignty itself, a cognate essence of the state without which no state can be thought of as a state. Law as the premier expression of sovereign will does not exist in a vacuum and is shaped by external, intersecting political, economic, and cultural conditions. But if law is the manifestation of sovereign will and sovereign will itself is unaccountable to any external moral and ethical benchmarks, then everything—legislated against or otherwise—is allowed for, quite simply, sovereign will dictates it. Sovereignty over the colonized—and indeed over pretty much everything else—need not obey any particular rules or constraining principles. This, I think, is sovereignty's very quiddity. So in the early period of the state's formation, it did not really matter that in 1562 Captain John Hawkins had smuggled 300 black subjects out of Portuguese Guinea against the will of the sovereign. To be sure, Queen Elizabeth was furious: "It was detestable and would call down vengeance from heaven upon the undertakers,"[110] she cried. But ultimately, Hawkins told her that in exchange for the slaves he had a cargo of sugar, hides, pearls, and ginger in the Caribbean, and she forgave the pirate and became his business partner.[111]

---

[109] Hallaq, *Impossible*, p. 29.

[110] As quoted in Daniel P. Mannix, in collaboration with Malcolm Cowley. (1962). *Black Cargoes: A History of the Atlantic Slave Trade, 1518-1865*. New York: Viking, p. 22.

[111] "A century later the Duke of York was branding the initials 'DY' on the left buttock or breast of each of the 3,000 blacks his concern annually took to the 'sugar islands.' The Royal African Company, whose shareholders included Charles II, paid 300 percent in dividends, although only 46,000 of the 70,000 slaves it shipped between 1680 and 1688 survived the crossing. On the voyage many Africans died of epidemics or malnutrition; others committed suicide by refusing to eat, hanging themselves by their chains, or throwing themselves into a sea bristling with sharks' fins." Galeano, *Open Veins*, p. 80. See also: Mannix, *Black Cargoes*; Eric Williams. (1944). *Capitalism and Slavery*. Chapel Hill: University of North Carolina Press.

Race as the invention of a human absence, a life lived in the negative, was and continues to be part of a worldview in which, as a fundamental principle, some are worth less, or ontologically and spiritually worthless, and can thus feel the effects of sovereign control, violence, or domination, that is, the labor of race, much more intensely than others. The mutual constitution of the sovereignty of the modern state, and the massive extractive, corporate interests of colonial empires has meant that the state became a global(ized) mechanism for racialized violence and exclusion. In sum, the modern state's very existence as the highest value and end thus licenses sovereign will to be pursued without any ethical and moral constraints which hold firm, and have made the modern European state a racial principle of the modern global order.

Kelsen's argument that the state consists of three interrelated elements: territory, people, and power is surely true, but the three are imbricated in the labor of race, trafficking as they do in the production of racial subjects. Nevertheless, Kelsenian power can be thought of as a state's capacity for a level and type of violence necessary to enforce its law both internally and internationally.[112] If the modern state is constituted by sovereign will and law is the paradigmatic manifestation of that will which presupposes, in turn, sufficient violence to implement and enforce that law, then changes in the quality and instruments of violence also point to shifts in our working notions of sovereignty, sovereign violence, and the bordered territory over which the state is sovereign. And if the *violence of state borders*, designed to keep the stranger out, like the intensity of sovereign will (read: law), is felt differently by different subject groups, then the *borders of violence*, that is, the nature and effects of law, are also differentiated and discriminating in its target populations.

Colonization established many of these border regimes. It was a form of constitutive power, beyond the Kelsenian legal and even the Foucauldian biopolitical, whose interactions with foreign territories and indigenous populations were shaped by race, commerce in a uniquely virulent form, and bureaucracy. Just as sovereignty is the life force of the state, and law is the specific, indeed paradigmatic, expression of sovereignty, bureaucracy is the specific instrument of power, knowledge, and governance designed to fulfill race's internal logic.

The *logic of race* is, in sum, enclosure and erasure combined. Hannah Arendt's words in *The Origins of Totalitarianism* remain lucid. Arendt writes:

---

[112] This distinction being contingent, of course, on a given sovereign state's conception of its territory and its borders over (and through) which it is sovereign. Hans Kelsen. (1961). *General Theory of Law and State.* Trans. A. Wedberg. New York: Russell and Russell.

Of the two main political devices of imperialist rule, race was discovered in South Africa and bureaucracy in Algeria, Egypt, and India; the former was originally the barely conscious reaction to tribes of whose humanity European man was ashamed and frightened, whereas the latter was a consequence of that administration by which Europeans had tried to rule foreign peoples whom they felt to be hopelessly their inferiors and at the same time in need of their special protection. Race, in other words, was an escape into an irresponsibility where nothing human could any longer exist, and bureaucracy was the result of a responsibility that no man can bear for his fellow-man and no people for another people.[113]

In the colonial order, race was at once a core principle of the political body (the nation incorporated by the state), and, philosophically, "the emergency explanation of human beings whom no European or civilized man could understand and whose humanity so frightened and humiliated the immigrants that they no longer cared to belong to the same human species."[114]

There are perhaps few words used by any analyst of the state that have been less controversial and the subject of general consensus than the following statement of Weber:

The primary formal characteristics of the modern state are as follows: it possesses an administrative and legal order subject to change by legislation, to which the organized activities of the administrative staff, which are also controlled by regulations, are oriented. This system of order claims binding authority, not only over the members of the state, the citizens . . . but also to a very large extent over all action taking place in the area of its jurisdiction. It is thus a compulsory organization with territorial basis. Furthermore, today, the use of force is regarded as legitimate only insofar as it is either permitted by the state or prescribed by it. . . . The claim of the modern state to monopolize the use

---

[113] Hannah Arendt. (1976). *The Origins of Totalitarianism*. San Diego, CA: Harcourt, p. 207 and more generally, chapters 6 and 7. Earlier (p. 185) she writes, "Two new devices for political organization and rule over foreign peoples were discovered during the first decades of imperialism. One was race a principle of the body politic, and the other bureaucracy as a principle of foreign domination. Without race as a substitute for the nation, the scramble for Africa and the investment fever might well have remained the purposeless 'dance of death and trade' (Joseph Conrad) of all gold rushes. Without bureaucracy as a substitute for government, the British possession of India might well have been left to the recklessness of the 'breakers of law in India' (Burke) without changing the political climate of an entire era."

[114] Ibid. *Origins*, p. 185. As we will see in the next section on cultural hegemony, the historicity of the modern state, its sovereignty and will, and bureaucracy all interlaced with race and racism, meant that colonization did not begin in the colonies but at home in civilized Europe.

of force is as essential to it as its character of compulsory jurisdiction and of continuous operation.[115]

There is a close interrelationship between actualities of social subordination and bureaucracy in Weber's political sociology. For Weber, the administrative order is both an integral part and an extension of the legal order. In the vernacular of administration, bureaucracies are not merely the "delivery mechanisms" of law and policy, constituted as they are of a wide array of norms, metrics, and unspoken rules, but they also allow a much more robust intervention of the legal order into the social.

The bureaucratic machine exhibits, then, a characteristically *rational* type of domination, the central features of which are the principles of (rationally based) voluntarism and systematization (the administrative order as an empirically measurable and measuring entity). While Weber rightly stresses both the structural and societal aspects of standardization, that "equal treatment" includes both the general populace and the members of the state apparatus, he does not emphasize enough the "irresponsibility" of bureaucracies and their rational forms of exclusion and erasure. As Marx has extensively argued, we would be naïve to think that the structural relationship between a rational bureaucratic order and the disadvantaged subjects of the social (or even global) order is one that cultivates equality. It is instead, like the state, an exploitative and irresponsible institution that would disappear from any future communist world. If the modern state is constituted by an especially dominating form of racial sovereignty of which law—sanctioning resource extraction, tracking, trade, deportation, occupation, settlement, or genocide— was its paradigmatic manifestation, then it was/is the bureaucratic apparatus which brings the full force of the former elements into being.

Bureaucratic structures are surely varied and multifaceted, they form a part of the full gamut of social life, from mental health to the military. In fact, the nature of their jurisdictions means that they often compete—for resources, influence, securing their respective domains, greater portfolios, and so on.[116] Despite this differentiation and competition, they are simultaneously enclosed in a controlling paradigmatic structure—the phenomenon often euphemistically known as *centralization*. Bureaucratic divisions, from the very lowest levels, are supervised and instructed by higher and more powerful unifying administrative units, "which in turn tend to accumulate under their jurisdiction various bureaucratic divisions that exhibit the feature of competition, if

---

[115] Max Weber. (1978). *Economy and Society: An Outline of Interpretive Sociology*. Vol. 1. Berkeley: University of California Press, p. 56.
[116] R. Bendix. (1945). "Bureaucracy and the Problem of Power." *Public Administration Review*, 5(3), 194–209.

not turf protection."[117] The more bureaucracy expands, the more it is at the behest of unified organizational rules,[118] thus creating a hierarchical structure of administration and ordered domination. So, in a top-down pyramidal structure, it is the top that rules, orders, and administers, but it is ultimately the tool or technique of bureaucracy[119] that orders surveillance, discipline, governance, violence, death, and indeed life. Furthermore, the instruments of administration and bureaucracy will likely continue to enjoy progressive growth in complexity, pervasiveness, and regulatory power with the exponential interactions between digitized life and datafication constitutive of the planet as we know it.[120]

Bureaucracy does not merely order the institutional plane and intrude on the private sphere and civil society, but it also orders and sets the standards for the community. It does not only administer, manage, and measure society, but its very measurements become constitutive of our working notions of the social itself and the subjects within it. It is not the human community that creates the state, but bureaucracy that breeds its own community, the community of the state.[121] In this vein, James C. Scott's comments are useful:

> If the natural world, however shaped by human use, is too unwieldy in its "raw" form for administrative manipulation, so too are the actual social patterns of human interaction with nature bureaucratically indigestible in their raw form. No administrative system is capable of representing any existing social community except through a heroic and greatly schematized process of abstraction and simplification. It is not simply a question of capacity, although, like a forest, a human community is surely far too complicated and variable to easily yield its secrets to bureaucratic formulae. It is also a question of purpose. State agents have no interest—nor should they—in describing an entire social reality, any more than the scientific forester has an interest in describing the ecology of a forest in detail. Their abstractions and simplifications are disciplined by a small number of objectives, and until the nineteenth century the most prominent of these were typically taxation, political control, and conscription.[122]

If the state is, at least in part, an ideological power, then race provides the atmosphere for its world of myth. For myth is "a rendering of unobserved

---

[117] Hallaq, *Impossible*, p. 32.

[118] G. Gill. (2003). *The Nature and Development of the Modern State*. New York: Palgrave.

[119] N. Rose and P. Miller. (1992). "Political Power Beyond the State: Problematic of Government." *British Journal of Sociology,* 43(2), 173–205.

[120] Eckard Bolsinger. (2001). *The Autonomy of the Political: Carl Schmitt's and Lenin's Political Realism*. Westport, CT: Greenwood Press.

[121] Ibid., pp. 30–33.

[122] James Scott. (1999). *Seeing Like a State: How Certain Schemes to Improve the Human Condition Have Failed*. London: Yale University Press, pp. 22–23; emphases added.

realities," but "it is not necessarily a correct rendering. It is not just that myth makes the abstract concrete. There are senses in which it also makes the non-existent exist."[123] Again, this ideological dimension posits the modern state, like race, as both fiction and force,[124] its fictitiousness far from undermining or tempering its force actually buoying it.[125] That is, making the nonexistent exist requires the invention of classifications (Scott's abstractions and sim-plifications) which when sanctioned by sovereign will and taking on juridical forms underpinned by the threat of violent enforcement for noncompliance, and delivered through bureaucratic structures, sustain and mystify their inau-gural invention.

The racial order is, thus, nothing without its bureaucracy. And while the premodern state was content with a limited level of intelligence about its subjects sufficient to allow it to keep order, extract taxes, and raise armies, the modern state increasingly aspired to "'take in charge' of the physical and human resources of the nation and make them more productive. These more positive ends of statecraft required a much greater knowledge of the society."[126]

The reason that Marx, like countless other theorists, saw in bureaucracy a rational form of domination was its transformation of detachment into virtue. But a form of racial sovereignty having come to structure the worldview of modern Europe legitimated domination and mastery over inferior races as much as nature, the former being, in effect, brute and inert like the earth.[127] The common sense, bureaucratized habitus of racism allowed for the classi-fication and treatment of human populations as objects, devoid of any value that was not given by white Europe. Highly exploitative and violent in the extreme, race and bureaucracy in the context of the European *commercium* was the penetrative mechanism for the outlook of the sovereign unshackled by benchmarks. Having been classified and structurally positioned as having no value, as human-metal and human-merchandise, the racial subject could be studied and subjected to the full range of the European sovereign's admin-istrative-analytical apparatuses, without them making any moral demands on Enlightened Europe.

Race was the "emergency explanation"[128] which allowed the categorization of entire human populations, cultures, and territories as beyond the pale of

---

[123] Abrams, "Notes," pp. 68–69.

[124] Karen E. Fields and Barbara J. Fields. (2012). *Racecraft: The Soul of Inequality in American Life*. London: Verso.

[125] Alana Lentin. (2018). "Race." In *The Sage Handbook of Political Sociology*, edited by William Outhwaite and Stephen Turner.

[126] Scott, *Seeing*, p. 51.

[127] Jacques Donzelot. (1979). *The Policing of Families*. New York: Pantheon, pp. 21–219, 227.

[128] Hannah Arendt. (1973). *The Origins of Totalitarianism*. New York: Harcourt Brace Jovanovich, p. 185.

full humanity. It cultivated "the emergence of what has been called objective and detached scientific thought, represented across the academic fields of natural science, engineering, economics, business, law, history, and the like—all of which pretend to some sort of objectivity. In all these disciplines, the scholar can study the Other (who is an integral part of nature) dispassionately, without it making any value-laden or moral demands on him."[129] To allow for such demands to be made, however, would contradict the *Weltanschauung*, that is, modern sovereignty in the first place. Race, bureaucracy, and sovereignty, then, speak to broader epistemological changes in the structure of modern power, knowledge, governance, and the relation between them. Yet they all individually and together mobilized the racial signifier, with the interplay between them delineating the limits of the real and the deeply violent processes to keeping certain things, especially the racial subject, alive so that he may be studied but always proximate to expulsion and premature death.

In the relationship between the colonizer and colonized, that is, in the encounter between the logic of bureaucracy within the racial metaphysics of the European order, the reality of the colony was whatever sovereign will dictated and bureaucracy administrated. Equally true, however, is the operation and perspective of a racist structure of administrative vision that becomes the standard for the community, a habitus of which bureaucracy is a crucial part. Which is to say that bureaucracy fashions and refashions that community[130] on the basis of, or in a dialectic with, sovereign will and thus not solely in a top-down movement. Sovereign will, like its law and bureaucracy which work to exclude and erase, must pervade the entire culture.

In setting the standards of the community, state bureaucracy must regulate sub-bureaucratic structures and render them subordinate to its rational imperatives; those imperatives in turn subordinated to the larger imperatives of sovereign will. Whether that is the control or extermination of colonized populations, the extraction of tax from citizens, the plunder of resources, the recording of (un)fulfilled national service, or drone strikes from 30,000 feet. Yet the processes of state power and rule are increasingly molecular, going so far as to *constitute* the subject of the state—the citizen—and regulating civil society and the cultural fabric from the registration of birth to the

---

[129] Wael Hallaq. (2018). *Restating Orientalism: A Critique of Modern Knowledge*. New York: Columbia University Press, p. 96. See also: Akeel Bilgrami. (2008). "Gandhi, Newton, and the Enlightenment." In *Values and Violence*, edited by I. A. Karawan et al. New York: Springer, pp. 15–29. Domenico Losurdo. (2011). *Liberalism: A Counter-History*, trans. Gregory Elliott. London: Verso, pp. 3–4; Sven Beckert and Seth Rockman, eds. (2016). *Slavery's Capitalism: A New History of American Economic Development*. Philadelphia: University of Pennsylvania Press.

[130] For an illuminating set of analyses which contend with and seek to overcome the simplifications of bureaucracy, see: James Scott. (1999). "Thin Simplifications and Practical Knowledge: Mētis." In *Seeing Like a State: How Certain Schemes to Improve the Human Condition Have Failed*. London: Yale University Press.

certification of death and most everything else in between: schooling, further and higher education, surveillance, policing, health, environment, welfare, resource provision, travel, labor, armed forces, safety at work, taxes, public hygiene, parks, leisure, and entertainment.[131] The uniqueness and unprecedented nature of the modern nation-state as a system of order and discipline necessitated equally unique forms of individual subject formation. As Hallaq summarizes, "If the state is a uniquely European product (as is almost universally agreed), and if the state is overarching in its control over its population (and here a few would disagree), then the subjectivities produced by the state systems must also be unique."[132]

On an epistemic level, the various institutions of the state were neither neutral nor distinct from one another, but systemic manifestations of highly specific ways of doing and ordering things.[133] These techniques were intended to discipline the operations of the body, entering the body of the subject into an economy of state power, a highly effective set of techniques explaining their rapid circulation from one institution to the next, and indeed from one European country to another.[134] Nonetheless, they reflected,

> the two major concerns of submission and utility, that is, submission to a regulating technique that engenders docility and, on the other hand, utility as a materially productive performance. From both perspectives, the body was not only a site of empirical analysis but also of intelligibility. It had become colonizable and as such capable of manipulation and analysis, of being shaped according to a particular will so that through it certain desired effects could be produced.[135]

As Foucault has explained, the "human body was entering a machinery of power that explores it, breaks it down and rearranges it. A 'political anatomy,' which was also a 'mechanics of power,' was being born; it defined how one may have a hold over others' bodies, not only so that they may do what one wishes, but so that they may operate as one wishes, with the techniques, the speed and the efficiency that one determines."[136] All of this is to say that

[131] The most productive accounts of such processes remain those of Michel Foucault. See: M. Foucault. (1980). *Power/Knowledge. Selected Interviews and Other Writings 1972-1977*. New York: Pantheon; M. Foucault. (2004a). *Securité, territoire, population. Cours au Collège de France, 1977-1978*. Paris: Seuil/Gallimard; M. Foucault. (2004b). *Naissance de la biopolitique. Cours au Collège de France, 1978-1979*. Paris: Seuil/Gallimard.

[132] Hallaq, *Impossible*, p. 99.

[133] I am invoking Foucault's (1970) arguments in *The Order of Things: An Archeology of the Human Sciences*. Trans. R. D. Lang. New York: Pantheon.

[134] Frank Tallett. (1992). *War and Society in Early Modern Europe, 1495-1715*. London: Routledge, pp. 39–44.

[135] Hallaq, *Impossible*, p. 101.

[136] Michel Foucault. (1995). *Discipline and Punish: The Birth of the Prison*. New York: Vintage, p. 138.

the training of the body of the subject (now, citizen) did not proceed only through coercion, but through the cultural fabric.

The principle of race was central to this "training." The steady habituation to the instruments and imperatives of sovereign will occurred parallel to the process of making common sense the ontological inferiority of the foreigner.[137] The colonial idea and the racist ethos that were its constituent traveled along many byroads including education, advertising, music halls and popular theaters, juvenile literature, and children's extracurricular organizations such as the Boy Scouts and Girl Guides.[138] The transmission and translation of the colonial world, in conjunction with the material policies of the modern European state, nourished fears of depopulation, replacement, disease, immigration, and "racial grafting,"[139] while presenting the African, the Indian, and other Others, not only as children but as stupid children, lying in wait to be brought up to the white European present. Colonization thus became a form of assistance, moral and technical education, and the conduit for the gift of civilization.

Ostensibly democratic discourse was steeped in nationalist and militaristic values underpinned by a racist ethos in which the cultural, educational, and political fabric was equally imbricated.[140] The educational system and military system were in frequent dialogue in the form of teaching manuals and school textbooks, and their popular histories. The work of English historian and political essayist, J. R. Seeley, for one, is of crucial importance and in whose work, read ubiquitously by English schoolchildren, the alleged gloom and pessimism of the late Victorian period is not borne out.[141] History for Seeley was meant to stimulate exertions on behalf of the nation (in certain contexts seen to suffer from a crisis of masculinity and moral purpose), and to

---

[137] See: Sean Quinlan. (1996). "Colonial Bodies, Hygiene and Abolitionist Politics in Eighteenth-Century France," *History Workshop Journal,* 42, 106–25.

[138] Catherine Hall. (2002). *Civilising Subjects: Metropole and Colony in the English Imagination.* Chicago: The University of Chicago Press; Catherine Hall. (2006). *At Home with the Empire: Metropolitan Culture and the Imperial World.* Cambridge: Cambridge University Press; Catherine Hall. (2008). "Making Colonial Subjects: Education in the Age of Empire." *History of Education,* 37(6), 773–87.

[139] Though eventually commonplace across the imperial centers of Europe, the origins of concerns of this kind lie in France. See: Arsène Dumont. (1890). *Dépopulation et civilisation: Étude démographique.* Paris: Lecrosnier et Babé; Rosa Schwartzburg. (2019). "No There Isn't a White Genocide." *Jacobin.* Available at: https://www.jacobinmag.com/2019/09/white-genocide-great-replacement-theory.

[140] J. M. MacKenzie, ed. (1984). *Propaganda and Empire; The Manipulation of British Public Opinion 1880–1960.* Manchester: Manchester University Press; S. Tomlinson. (1981). *Educational Subnormality: A Study in Decision-making.* London: Routledge and Kegan Paul; S. Tomlinson. (1989). "The Origins of the Ethnocentric Curriculum." In *Education for All: A Landmark for Pluralism,* edited by G.K. Verma. London: Falmer, pp. 26–41; S. Tomlinson. (2014). *The Politics of Race, Class and Special Education;* The Selected Works of Sally Tomlinson. London: Routledge.

[141] John Mackenzie. (1984). "Imperialism and the School Textbook." In *Propaganda and Empire: The manipulation of British public opinion, 1880-1960.* Manchester: Manchester University Press.

raise the morale of *all* its (raced and gendered) members.[142] Imperial expansion was, then, to be seen as the moral of British history and acted as the key to the future. Similarly, the phenomenal boom of the music hall in the 1870s often reflected the dominant imperial ethos of the day and, crucially, appealed to all social classes.[143] There were, of course, official attempts to control the sometimes subversive output of the music hall through fire and licensing regulations, the self-censorship of its impresarios, and the outright censorship of anti-establishment songs in favor of royalist, militarist, and imperial nationalist performances.[144] Likewise, the Victorian melodrama was a staple of imperial theater where imperial subjects were a perfect opportunity to externalize villainy: "the corrupt rajah, the ludicrous Chinese or Japanese nobleman, the barbarous 'fuzzy wuzzy' or black" often faced a "cross-class brotherhood of heroism, British officer and ranker together."[145] There was a widespread, quotidian racism and militarism, from products in the home to music halls and theater, in the uniformed youth movements, such as Boy Scouts and Girl Guides, to the churches and missionary societies of the day. All came to embrace (and not unprofitably) the new imperial, racial nationalism.[146]

What might have been an essentially middle-class ethos concerning the empire was transferred to the other social classes through the potent mechanisms of printing, photography, spectacle, and pageant. An ideological formation which was constituted out of the intellectual, national, and global conditions of empire during the late Victorian era, synthesized "a renewed militarism, a devotion to royalty, and identification and worship of national heroes, together with a contemporary cult of personality, and racial ideas associated with Social Darwinism to produce a new type of patriotism derived from Britain's unique imperial mission."[147] It was a common

---

[142] Adam Dighton. (2016). "Race, Masculinity and Imperialism: The British Officer and the Egyptian Army (1882–1899)." *War & Society*, 35(1), 1–18; Catherine Hall. (2010). *Defining the Victorian Nation: Class, Race, Gender and the British Reform Act of 1867*. Cambridge: Cambridge University Press; A. Windholz. (1999). "An Emigrant and a Gentleman: Imperial Masculinity, British Magazines, and the Colony That Got Away." *Victorian Studies*, 42(4), 631–58.

[143] L. Senelick. (1975). "Politics as Entertainment: Victorian Music-Hall Songs." *Victorian Studies*, 19(2), 149–80.

[144] John Mackenzie. (1984). "The Theatre of Empire." In *Propaganda and Empire: The Manipulation of British Public Opinion, 1880-1960*. Manchester: Manchester University Press.

[145] Ibid., p. 45. In the British case, the moral stereotyping of melodrama with a powerful racial twist was on full-display with the popular Eastern themes found in Barrymore's *El Hyder* (1818), Moncrieff's *The Cataract of the Ganges* (1823), *Cetewayo at Last* (1882) and *The Indian Mutiny* (1892).

[146] John M. Mackenzie. (1986). *Imperialism and Popular Culture*. Manchester University Press: Manchester, UK.

[147] Mackenzie, *Propaganda and Empire*, p. 2. Mackenzie's broader work is useful for its analyses of imperial propaganda and the seemingly mundane artifacts of empire, though race and racism, nor the broader structural and epistemic changes occurring in Britain and Europe for which race was paradigmatic are not fundamental to the scope of his work. Nonetheless, see: (1988). *Propaganda and Empire: The Manipulation of British Public Opinion, 1880-1960*. Manchester:

sense—though not uncontested[148]—truth that empire had the power to elevate not only the "backward" world of other races, but to regenerate the British themselves, and to raise them from the apprehension of the later nineteenth century. Creating a national purpose with highly moralized racial and deeply racialized moral content would lead to class conciliation.[149] In sum, there were domestic economic, political, and social advantages of "selling" the empire (of racial hierarchy), literally and figuratively, and in which civic and colonial pedagogy were embedded. Producing oneself as a racist subject in everyday attachments to the empire, its central figures and stolen profits was a cross-class process: rich and poor, old and young alike.

The dictates of governmentality required that the population be educated in the ways of good conduct and social order, which in a thoroughly capitalist system, secured the citizen's ability to work and produce.[150] But for this intricate project of forming the good citizen, crude physical force could never be sufficient. And this much was well understood by European rulers, democratic or otherwise, as needing to begin early in the subject's life, in which sustained discipline into the racial morality of modernity could be legislated to a detail, and for which the school was essential. I quote Hallaq at length here:

> Systemically concomitant with the consolidation of the police apparatus, the school became a standard social institution by the end of the nineteenth century. The laws of education coerced parents to send their children to schools on pain of imprisonment. Primary education forced the great majority of Europe's children into a regimented system, mostly stern and punitive, where certain ideas and ideals were inculcated. This was the culmination of the moment in which

Manchester University Press; and, more usefully, (2010). *Museums and empire: Natural history, human cultures and colonial identities*. Manchester: Manchester University Press. Alternatively, Catherine Hall's studies of imperial Britain are deeply valuable, especially pertinent because of their cognizance of the British involvement in the transatlantic slave trade and its myriad cultural effects. See (2002). *Civilising Subjects: Metropole and Colony in the English Imagination 1830-1867*. Cambridge: Polity Press; (2006). *At Home with Empire: Metropolitan Culture and the Imperial World*. New York: Cambridge University Press; (2010). *Defining the Victorian Nation: Class, Race, Gender and the British Reform Act of 1867*. Cambridge: Cambridge University Press.

[148] Priyamvada Gopal. (2019). *Insurgent Empire: Anticolonial Resistance and British Dissent*. London: Verso.

[149] J.A. Hobson. (1901). *The Psychology of Jingoism*. London.

[150] Michel Foucault's work remains important to these themes. See. Michel Foucault. (1994). "The Subject and Power." In *Power: Essential Works of Foucault, 1954–1984*, edited by James D. Faubion, trans. Robert Hurley et al., vol. 3. New York: New Press, pp. 326–48, at 333. See also Martin L. van Creveld. (1999). *The Rise and Decline of the State*. Cambridge: Cambridge University Press, pp. 168–69, 205–24, 417–18. On the further growth of prisons and its relation to "productivity", see Gary Teeple. (2000). *Globalization and the Decline of Social Reform*. Aurora, Ontario: Garamond, pp. 122–26. See also Christopher Lasch. (1978). *The Culture of Narcissism: American Life in an Age of Diminishing Expectations*. New York: Norton, pp. 125–53.

the citizen was formed, the child of the state, the loyal subject, the lover of the homeland and the nation. And this subject was as unprecedented as the conditions that gave rise to it. Europe was indeed exceptional. . . . It [the body of the citizen] has become colonizable, capable of being manipulated into, and shaped according to, the will of the sovereign, who has now become constituted not by the will of a king or a pope, but by the very diffused and bureaucratized subject that was newly engineered. Colonization did not begin in the distant colonies, but right at home.[151]

Society and the cultural fabric are not to be seen as separate from the state power, for to do so would be to miss the crucial process by which state and culture/society dialectically produce each other, i.e. "governmentalization."[152] European Enlightenment's conception of sovereign will dictates that no autonomous authority can be imputed to any actor within the state. As Bourdieu maintains, the cultural domains are "constituted as such by the actions of the state which, by instituting them in things and in minds, confers upon the cultural arbitrary all the appearances of the natural."[153] State power is not held *over* society only then, but works through, by, and with the cultural order. But the dialectical relationship between the state and culture/society is not merely one of state control. Nor is it myopically enclosed within the myriad processes of ideological legitimation of the illegitimate—the naturalness of the state and its attendant forms of social subordination. State power not only institutes its will in and through culture/society, but both are mutually constituted by one another.[154]

We can, therefore, make the useful distinction between two types of power: "one of which involves the capacity of an agent to force another to do or not do something, thereby reducing the relationship to a unilateral form of coercion. The other generates the reception of, and cooperation with, power on the part of the very subject that is subordinated to that power. Thus, under this second type of power, the state's ability to work through the various units of civil society increases state autonomy by virtue of its success in generating the greatest sum of social and cultural consent."[155] It does not merely seek

---

[151] Hallaq, *Restating Orientalism*, p. 101. Hallaq's analysis is thoroughly Foucauldian though expanded, to account for its colonial effects, and in this essay with the paradigmatic role of race.

[152] M. Foucault. (2007). *Security, Territory, Population: Lectures at the Collège de France, 1977–1978*. Palgrave: Basingstoke, UK, p. 109. See also: P. Miller and N. Rose. (2008). *Governing the Present. Administering Economic, Social and Personal Life*. Polity: Cambridge.

[153] Pierre Bourdieu. (1999). "Rethinking the State: Genesis and Structure of the Bureaucratic Field." In *State/Culture: State Formation After the Cultural Turn*, edited by George Steinmetz. Ithaca, NY: Cornell University Press, pp. 53–75.

[154] Bob Jessop. (2016). "State and Nation." In *The State: Past, Present, Future*. Cambridge: Polity Press, pp. 148–63.

[155] Hallaq, *Impossible*, pp. 33–36.

out but attempts to construct what Sally Falk Moore has appropriately called "ratifying bodies public," giving populist legitimacy to decisions made elsewhere.[156] The state, even in the sense of political institutions, does not provide us with a concretely defined empirical referent because these institutions are only one among a cluster of power centers—corporations, cultural institutions of various sorts, the media, and so on, being others. Yet "it is via the *ensemble of* power centres that functions of the state are executed."[157]

The function of race is, therefore, expressed at multiple planes together—epistemically, conceptually, performatively, structurally. Sovereign power, for which race is a crucial technology, can only represent, manage, dominate, and exterminate any human community insofar as it can simplify, abstract in aggregate. Europe's foundational code of race which structured the modern order according to the sovereign will of the racial state, administrating its territories through a connection forged between race and bureaucratic reason, and penetrating the cultural makeup of imperial societies—colony as well as metropole—has had lasting effects. Any account of politically institutionalized power, therefore, must confront race, racism, their provenance, and essential utility in colonial modernity if it is to be adequate. Their effects are like wounds (re)opening and complexifying in the social, political, economic, and epistemic predicaments of the day. Wounds which result in further effects, human and, crucially, natural.

In this study, the figure and site of the Muslim forms an instructive point of entry to analyze power, its conditions of possibility, and coordinates for a way out of the dark night. Europe may well be experiencing demotion but the place of the racial subject within it shows that this shift will not happen smoothly or swiftly and is full of risk. But a humanity that enlivens a world inhabited in the open is possible. Despite the widespread and "democratized" impulses to denigrate and deport, it is a world to which we are each of us coinheritors and have a responsibility of care.

A NOTE ON METHOD

In many ways, this is a book defined by its discontinuity and rapid movement, from one place, situation, feeling, image, or period to another. I am, consciously or not, quite present in the book and, as such, its form and style attempts to strike a generative balance between theory, reflection, and conversation. The narrative does not hold chronology too dear and the reader

---

[156] Sally Falk Moore. (1986). *Social Facts and Fabrications: "Customary" Law on Kilimanjaro, 1880—1980.* Cambridge: Cambridge University Press, p. 314.

[157] Abrams, "Notes," p. 87.

may wish to engage in its contents along crossed lines rather than proceed straightforwardly from front to back. But it is ultimately an attempt to make sense of a moment and context in which fast truths and fundamental incoherence structure and constitute the premier rationale for how to live or not to live with the Other, with whom I must be a neighbor and who likely does not know my name. Much of it was written in the summer of 2019, in a world before Covid-19, but one all too familiar with fears of contagion, the stranger, intermixture, breath and speech, and no less transfixed by a sacred commitment to the border, the police, the citizen, and the nation. I submit that the racial subject, the Muslim, is an important character in this story, as s/he was yesterday and will likely be tomorrow.

The first part apprehends the first archetype of the racial subject of Islamophobia: *The Muslim Questioned.* The subject here is caught within processes and economies designed to make the Muslim speak, but always already a form of speech which can only ever confirm her inherent difference, disposability, and threatening character. This hostile relation driven by the violence of a molecular kind forces the Muslims to move within shifting scales of relations between three points: Distance, Disclosure, and Secrecy.

The second part analyzes the second archetype: *The Muslim Question.* More liberally, a space is here left open for a possible relation between equals, between white subject and Muslim Other. Yet this mode cannot escape arelation of condescension where the Muslim is called to translate herself through a language of gratitude for having been tolerated by liberalism; a language that is incited at a kind of everywhere-press-conference where her speech is constrained by the autocue which can never fully renege her as a racial subject. The Muslim here is caught within dialects of Proximity, Affirmation, and Publicity.

Finally, the third part concerns the third archetype: *The Muslim Questioner.* The Questioner unravels the dehumanizing irrationality of her, and indeed the social world, being cast as racial. The Muslim might embody an alternative hermeneutic or relation between self and Other that is drawn from an (Islamic) archive outside of the constitutive racist episteme of modern Europe. The Muslim Questioner, thus, names a paradigm of disobedience that seeks to de-link from race as a hegemonic social, political, and economic principle—among Muslims as much as white Europe—just as the idea of white Europe experiences demotion and the world or, more accurately, the earth reckons with its finitude. This final mode is constituted by three dynamics of mutual intersorption: Refusal, Transparency, and Otherwise.

THE MUSLIM QUESTIONED

"WHERE IS YOUR GOD NOW?"

Brain scans give clue to what shapes jihadists—

—The Guardian.

But it makes the immigrant laugh to hear the fears of the nationalist, scared of infection, penetration, miscegenation, when this is small fry, peanuts, compared to what the immigrant fears—dissolution, disappearance.

—Zadie Smith, *White Teeth.*

***

In the early hours of December 2, 2003, Babar Ahmad awoke to a loud sound outside his South London home. It seemed a car had crashed into the front of the house and, when he arose, there was little to suggest that this was anything other than an accident. That is, until his eyes registered a column of around fifteen riot police officers lined up in the front garden. Babar would later recall feeling "reassured" by the police presence. Then came a second bang and the officers rushed through the front door clearing the house. Ahmad stood upstairs with his hands raised in surrender, in the hope that his nonconfrontational pose and visibility would calm the situation and communicate to the officers that they had the wrong house. It did not. And he quickly learned that it was he who was their intended target.

The officers, it would later be revealed, had been led to believe that he was the leader of an Al-Qaeda–linked cell and "were told to prepare to confront a highly proficient terrorist, and accordingly to 'deck and dominate' the suspect in counterinsurgent fashion. Having removed his wife from the bedroom, they beat him with their fists and knees, verbally abusing him as they did so, stamped on his bare feet with boots, rubbed the metal handcuffs against the bones of his forearms, and applied life-threatening neck holds to him until he felt he was about to die."[1] Bloodied, beaten, and separated from his wife, a group of four officers then dragged him downstairs to his prayer room. They proceeded to sexually assault him by pulling, fondling, and cupping his genitals before forcing him into prayer-like prostration. With his pyjama bottoms pulled down and genitals exposed, face and body bruised, hands cuffed tightly behind his back as he was lying on the floor surrounded, one of the officers taunted, "You are in prayer now," while the other officers began to laugh. And, amid the humiliating brutality of the arrest, one of the other officers asked a crucial question: *Where is your God now?*[2]

Babar Ahmad would seek an admission of wrongdoing by the Metropolitan Police having filed a complaint with the Independent Police Complaints Commission[3] against the main arresting officers, Roderick James-Bowen, Mark Jones, Nigel Cowley, and John Donoghue. Readied with unequivocal photographic evidence that Ahmad "was subjected to harrowing physical and psychological assault," and that the ostensible aim of the officers "whilst waving the flag of 'fighting terrorism' was to inflict pain, humiliation and intimidation,"[4] the misconduct trial following Ahmad's complaint cleared the officers of wrongdoing. Later, when civil proceedings were launched against the officers, the Met Police offered settlements of £20,000 and then £60,000 to prevent the case from going to court. Ahmad refused, and in an unprecedented victory, the Met finally admitted full liability for "subjecting Babar to grave abuse tantamount to torture and offered again to pay him £60,000 in damages."[5] The case gained a significant degree of exposure and as a result the then-mayor of London, Boris Johnson, announced an inquiry into the abuse with the Crown Prosecution Service later charging the officers with actual bodily harm. However, when the case finally reached trial, "the jury took only forty-five minutes to decide their verdict of not guilty and some

---

[1] Kapoor, N. (2018: 51–52). *Deport, Deprive, Extradite: 21st Century State Extremism*. London: Verso.
[2] John Fahey. (2011) 'Officers Beat Me, Says Al Qaeda Suspect', *Independent*. Available at: https://www.independent.co.uk/news/uk/crime/officers-beat-me-says-al-qaida-suspect-2279398.html; Khalida Yusuf. (2006). "A Counter-Productive Extradition Policy—The Effect of the Babar Ahmad Case in Radicalising Muslims in Britain", London: Free Babar Ahmad Campaign.
[3] The existence of the Commission was itself a response to mobilizations against, and inquiries into, racial violence of the police and the institutional racism of policing and criminal justice in general. The Lord Scarman Inquiry into the Brixton riots in 1981 and the Stephen Lawrence Inquiry in 1999 into the police response to the murder of Stephen Lawrence were landmark cases in this regard.
[4] Khalida Yusuf, A Counter-Productive Extradition Policy, p. 7–8.
[5] Kapoor, *Deport*, p. 63.

jurors requested to meet the officers to shake their hands. None of the officers faced a disciplinary hearing and all were returned to full duties."[6]

In the story of Babar Ahmad's arrest, abuse, and its context of war (on terror), the first mode of apprehending the Muslim is on display. The mechanisms through which s/he is apprehended, that is, a networked system with global reach and through technologies and economies of Islamophobia, consolidate a decidedly racial formation. I want to think through this incident as one, like many others, that is indicative of the racial logics undergirding practices of power, knowledge, and governance, to arrive at some conclusions about the—technical, legal, political, historic—conditions of possibility for their occurrence. The figure of the Muslim is tracked and captured within a paradigm of hostility; he moves, or is prompted to move, within the shifting scales of relation between three points: distance, disclosure, and secrecy.

Distance maintains the Muslim as a principle of radical exteriority, a figure who is ontologically separated from us by unbridgeable and irreconcilable differences. It becomes important, then, to maintain a sufficient space— physical, institutional, material, cultural—between us and the Muslim; to erect barriers of various kinds so that the Other might be made to progress to a sufficient stage of humanity. Old colonial narratives are resuscitated but also refashioned and repurposed to maintain an epistemology of distance in conjunction with shifting coordinates of friend and enemy, innocence and guilt, truth and falsity.

Disclosure in this paradigm names processes and technologies mobilized to extract an incessant confession from the Muslim, inciting responses to questions concerning their reasons for movement, their location, circulation, intent, and vulnerabilities. Questions armed with juridical weight and whose answers have substantial material effects on their lived, social, and indeed private existence. The twinned economies and technologies of counterterrorism and

---

[6] Ibid. See also: Scott Poynting. (2016). Entitled to be a Radical? Counter-Terrorism and Travesty of Human Rights in the Case of Babar Ahmad. *State Crime Journal*, 5(2), 204–219; Free Babar Ahmad. (2018). "Timeline." *Free Babar Ahmad Campaign*. Available at: https://freebabarahmad .com/timeline/; Fiona Murphy. (2011). "Babar Ahmad's principled stand shames the IPCC." *Guardian*. Available at: https://www.theguardian.com/commentisfree/2011/jun/05/babar-ahmad -metropolitan-police-ipcc; Robert Vekaik. (2016). "The trials of Babar Ahmad: from jihad in Bosnia to a US prison via Met brutality." *Guardian*. Available at: https://www.theguardian.com/ uk-news/2016/mar/12/babar-ahmad-jihad-bosnia-us-police-interview; Dominic Casciani. (2012). "The battle to prosecute Babar Ahmad." *BBC Online*. Available at: https://www.bbc.co.uk/news/uk -17606337; CAGE. (2016). "Babar Ahmad: Outsourced judiciary and betrayal of human dignity." *CAGE*. Available at: https://www.cage.ngo/babar-ahmad-outsourced-judiciary-and-betrayal-human -dignity; Fahad Ansari. (2013). "Babar Ahmad Police Trial: A Verdict Based on Fear, not Fact?" *CAGE*. Available at: https://www.cage.ngo/babar-ahmad-police-trial-verdict-based-fear-not-fact; Islamic Human Rights Commission. (2009). "Stunning victory for Babar Ahmad." *IHRC*. Available at: https://www.ihrc.org.uk/news/articles/4416-stunning-victory-for-babar-ahmad/; British Broadcasting Corporation. (2011). "Babar Ahmad police officers not guilty of assault." *BBC News Online*. Available at: https://www.bbc.co.uk/news/uk-13638164

radicalization become the premier contexts for extracting and inciting disclo-sure from the Muslims. With the simultaneously expansive and intimate char-acter of these institutional frameworks of capture, and their complexly adaptive and productive power, processes of disclosure signify the generalization of the interrogation room as a social condition for the racialized; an interrogation in which the question of guilt, threat, and thus violation is ab initio precluded.

Finally, *secrecy* names a constitutive drive of the Muslim Questioned; the nocturnal face of this otherwise exuberant, well-resourced, solar matrix of objectively, dispassionately, scientifically classifying, marking, surveilling, inciting, and incarcerating the Muslim. There is a concomitant necessity to erase a confrontation with the racial violence involved in this first mode for fear of what it reveals about such a social, political, and material world in which it is routinized. Complex structural mechanisms of criminal justice provide an instructive example of the lengths required for such a project of concealment. Equally important, however, is disguising the public secrets of race and white supremacy. Which is to say that the fundamental illegitimacy of racism, its circulating fictions and phantasms which uphold racial orders are all well known if vehemently denied in old and new ways. The perpetual need within this paradigm to transform these dehumanizing effects into the work of national security, of justice, is intensified by perpetual anxieties of demotion, domination, and replacement of an assumed white national subject, she who also fears the exposure of what this mode of dealing with the Muslim brings on herself.

Chapter 1

Distance

The Muslim Questioned primarily revolves around the concern as to whether it is possible to craft a relationship with Muslims that is anything other than one between unequal partners. It is, therefore, anchored in a fundamental notion of distance: What it is that disallows closeness between my body and that of the Muslim's? What it is that might license strategies of detachment between us and the Other? What it is that maintains the Muslim as a principle of radical exteriority? The concept of distance here refers to an old technique in which the white subject—a premier product of liberal modernity—is placed as the center of all meaning. All there is left to do, then, is to classify differences from its form and Being. In the principle of race, we have a historic technology of distancing, maintaining a necessary separation. For the Muslim and his kind are made of a raw difference and as such are always already matter out of place. But the notion of distance between the white subject and its Others in the history of European colonial modernity emerges as an epistemological category that has in fact constructed the very facts of ontology. The physical distance—historically the space between metropole and colony, or Europe and the World-outside—that the concept of race authorizes impels an entire system of interrogation. Or, a worldview based on an impulse to place the rawness of the Other into an order of things to be classified and the practices that order licenses. That is, objects "out there" to be cataloged but always in relation to that white subject (the human) from whom one is at a distance and who is domiciled in, or rather *as*, white Europe. It is in the fact of distance from the human and his Europe itself that breeds essential differences which can only ever be threatening and must, therefore, be minimized if not altogether extinguished.

The circular motion between distance and difference which simultaneously traps and produces the Muslim Questioned generates a short but powerful form to fill: "Who is he?" "Where does he move?" "What differentiates him from us?" "Of what or whom does he speak?" "How is he to be governed?" Each of these questions are variations on a formula and narrative which name a reality flowing from and oriented toward an "I" considered to be the center of all meaning, an "I" that is under siege from an insurgent abnormality whose name, form, and character are judged as Muslim and thus must be managed and kept under watch.[1] At base, a system of interrogation is only coherent if there is a distance—physical, legal, social—between those with the questions and those who must confess, correctly *and* honestly, with due care but on demand.[2] The relation of interrogation is always one between unequal partners because it is up to us not simply to represent the Muslim's desires, action, and inaction in our own way, but to enact those representations in the social and institutional world. The official record must articulate, or rather, is an articulation of a rationale based on lines of inquiry targeted at an object in order to, where possible, erect barriers of differentiation. For if, when faced with the Muslim bruised and beaten, I was to recognize myself as a subject-the-same-as-he, or constituted of similar differences, then I may be guilty of the same crimes,[3] and could hardly justify my right to interrogate.

How did the officers who beat, sexually assaulted, and wrongfully arrested Babar Ahmad conceptualize this distance and those differences? What does the officer's search for Allah's whereabouts reveal?[4] What conceptual purchase might race, Islamophobia, and a play of unequal subjects have had for this instance of state-sanctioned violation? I think answers are to be found further into our working notion of distance as radical exteriority from humanity, deeper in the void which must separate the white subjects which matter, and the corrosive matter which constitutes the threatening presence of the Muslim.

THE DISTURBING OBJECT

By the time Babar Ahmad reached the police station following his arrest, he had sustained at least seventy-three forensically recorded injuries. He was

---

[1] For useful studies of this discourse in practice, see: Evelyn Baring Cromer. (1908). "The Government of Subject Races." *Edinburg Review*, pp. 1–27; and Evelyn Baring Cromer. (1915). *Modern Egypt*. New York: Macmillan; Catherine Hall. (2012). *Macaulay and Son: Architects of Imperial Britain*. New Haven, CT: Yale University Press.

[2] This is of central concern to the next section on disclosure.

[3] And whether the original suspect did or did not commit the crime is inconsequential within this paradigm for they are always already silent.

[4] For an insightful analysis of another instance of a grotesque "inverted multiculturalism," akin to the abuse of the officers who degraded Ahmad in specifically religious/cultural ways, see Faisal Devji's commentary on the abuses at Abu Ghraib. Faisal Devji. (2008). *The Terrorist in Search of Humanity: Militant Islam and Global Politics*. London: C. Hurst & Co.

bleeding from his ears and blood was found in his urine.[5] Six days later, he was released without charge. During his incarceration, "his house was thoroughly searched, his possessions removed for examination, and his biometric data was sent to US intelligence authorities."[6] Two days after his release, and via the Metropolitan Police, an FBI agent faxed a forty-nine-page document detailing exhibits seized in the operation on December 2 to at least nineteen FBI offices in the United States. Eight months later in July 2004, that is, eight months anchored in the prospects of future incarceration, after a thorough investigation of the exhibits, Babar Ahmad was informed by the Crown Prosecution Service that there was insufficient evidence to charge him with any terrorist or even criminal offense. This message delivered some closure, even if the seventy-three injuries and the morning hours of the 2nd could not be erased. Yet in August 2004, three weeks after the CPS communication, while on his way home from work,

> Babar was re-arrested pursuant to an extradition request from the US in which they alleged that in the 1990s he had been a supporter of terrorism, committing terrorism offences in the USA from 1996 to 2003. The accusations inferred he had tried to solicit support for terrorism in Chechnya and Afghanistan using websites that supported Chechen and Taliban rebel fighters during that time. Babar was, however, a resident in the UK during this entire period. Detained in prison, this time Babar would remain incarcerated without trial in Britain for eight years before being deported to the US in October 2012, where he faced the prospect of a lifetime in solitary confinement.[7]

The Ahmad case is a long and complex one and we do not have the space to analyze it exhaustively. I do, however, want to focus on the element of distance. Not simply was there a fundamental distance assumed between the officers and the suspect Ahmad, which official power can propel and naturalize. The processes of collaboration with, and extradition requests from, the US government have a quite literal aspect of distance. The flow of information, allegedly incriminating, between institutions and sovereign states, quite literally had to cross great distances to put Babar Ahmad behind bars in the United Kingdom. The legal battle that ensued around Ahmad's extradition was, however, much less a contestation about the validity of the charges of terrorist activity, but a negotiation over whether a person named as an "enemy

[5] Verkaik, "The Trials of Babar Ahmad"; Ansari, "Babar Ahmad Police Trial."
[6] Kapoor, *Deport*, p. 52. See also: Yusuf, "A Counter-Productive Extradition Policy."
[7] Ibid.

combatant,"[8] and thus *legitimately* subject to the full excesses of sovereign violence, might have protection under European protocols on human rights. In fact, the possible substantiation of the charges did not matter in the slightest because under terms of the US-UK Extradition Treaty of 2003, later ratified by the United Kingdom in 2004, the United States did not have to provide evidence to support its allegations, regardless of where the suspect ended up being incarcerated.

Ahmad's labeling as an "enemy combatant" did not go unchallenged. It became a key point of contestation in the early stages of his appeal against extradition requests. Ultimately, in response to the arguments of lawyers that doing so "would violate European human rights conventions, US officials agreed that upon extradition Babar, and others also facing extradition under similar circumstances, would not be treated as 'enemy combatants,' but tried in civilian court to face life, and death, in prison."[9] Yet the verifiability of the charges themselves was not under discussion. Judgment had been delivered; debates on innocence or guilt a foregone conclusion. What *was* up for negotiation was the intensity of punishment. The category "enemy combatant" in operation under contemporary security regimes in the war on/of terror allowed the construction of a gulf between the subject and his/her rights. A notion of Europe, and more specifically British democracy, as a community of kindred folk who must, as such, exclude and separate based on perceived conceptions of identity and foreignness, jettisoning those of a surplus or superfluous population who must necessarily be left "completely or partially without rights" is conceived as the natural order of things.[10] That in order to constitute a civilized society in a world divided into nation-states, a politics which clearly distinguishes between its own citizens and those enemies who must be kept at a firm distance is essential.

But the notion that this separation speaks to a strict hospitality-hostility dichotomy, with citizens at one end and their darker enemies on the other, should not be assumed. Both are in fact rooted in a politics propelled by

---

[8] For a useful, historically-sensitive discussion of the subject of such a label and sovereign violence, see: Devji, *Terrorist*, pp. 142–59.

[9] Kapoor, *Deport*, p. 54–55.

[10] Carl Schmitt. (2000). *The Crisis of Parliamentary Democracy*, trans. Ellen Kennedy. Cambridge MA, MIT Press, p. 10. As Freud argued in 1915, history "is essentially a series of murders of peoples." See: Sigmund Freud. (2001: pp. 289–300; p. 292). "Our Attitude Towards Death." In The Standard Edition of the Complete Psychological Works of Sigmund Freud, Volume XIV (1914–1916): On The History of the Psycho-Analytic Movement, Papers on Metapsychology, and Other Works, trans. James Strachey et al. London: Vintage. Lacan went even further in the 1950s: "our civilisation is itself sufficiently one of hatred." Jacques Lacan. (1991). *The Seminar of Jacques Lacan, Book I: Freud's Papers on Technique, 1953–1954*, trans. John Forrester. New York: Norton, p. 277.

a fundamental energy enlisted in sovereign desire, an energy capable of licensing processes of capture, raiding, and manhunts as much as ensuring efficient collection of taxation, registering legible forms of regular employment, and records of a fixed address. This energy, however, proceeds according to differing intensities of violence, varying movement, and speeds of capture depending on its direction and the name given to its target. Islam, the Muslim, the foreigner, the immigrant, the refugee become variants of the intruder who must not be trusted and everywhere disturbs. The Muslim Questioned, then, names a paradigm which situates the Muslim within an epistemology of distance, a human group with whom nothing can be shared and, as such, must reduce in number and presence if not disappear altogether. The restoration of a society's own experience under threat from a disturbing object must involve the recognition that between us and them there is no possibility of kinship.

ORIENTALISM AND ECONOMIES OF ANTONYMY

It is worth briefly recalling Edward Said at this point. The term "Orientalism" has several important and interrelated dimensions for Said. The French and the British—and to a lesser degree the Germans, Russians, Spanish, Portuguese, Italians, and Swiss—have a long tradition of Orientalism which Said meant as "a way of coming to terms with the Orient that is based on the Orient's special place in European Western experience. The Orient is not only adjacent to Europe; it is also the place of Europe's greatest and richest and oldest colonies, the source of its civilizations and languages, its cultural contestant, and one of its deepest and most recurring images of the Other."[11] Perhaps the clearest designation of the term is its academic disciplinary form: "Anyone who teaches, writes about, or researches the Orient—and this applies whether the person is an anthropologist, sociologist, historian, or philologist—either in its specific or its general aspects, is an Orientalist, and what he or she does is Orientalism."[12] Related to this academic tradition is Orientalism as a "style of thought based upon an ontological and epistemological distinction made between "the Orient" and (most of the time) "the Occident."[13] Thus a

---

[11] Said, *Orientalism*, p. 1.
[12] Ibid., p. 2.
[13] Ibid., p. 2. On Orientalism as "Occidentalism", see: I. Buruma, A. Margalit, and Mazal Holocaust Collection. (2004). *Occidentalism: The West in the Eyes of Its Enemies*. London: Penguin; Gilbert Achcar. (2008). "Orientalism in Reverse," *Radical Philosophy*, 151; Sadik Jalal al-'Azm. (2014). "Orientalism and Orientalism in Reverse," *Khamsin: Journal of Revolutionary Socialists of the Middle East* 8, Politics of Religion in the Middle East. Available at: https://libcom.org/library/orientalism-orientalism-reverse-sadik-jalal-al-%E2%80%99azm

very large mass of writers, among whom are poets, novelists, philosophers, political theorists, economists, and imperial administrators, have "accepted the basic distinction between East and West as the starting point for elaborate theories, epics, novels, social descriptions, and political accounts concerning the Orient, its people, customs, 'mind,' destiny, and so on."[14]

The third meaning Said gives to the term is Orientalism as "the corporate institution for dealing with the Orient—dealing with it by making statements about it, authorizing views of it, describing it, by teaching it, settling it, ruling over it: in short, Orientalism as a Western style for dominating, restructuring, and having authority over the Orient."[15] Evoking Michel Foucault,[16] Orientalism is understood as a discourse, a systematic discipline of particular (discursive) investments in and, most importantly, limitations on what might be said or thought about the Orient. That is, how through the enunciative act—speaking the Orient into being—European states and culture(s), especially the British and the French, were able to manage and *produce* the Orient "politically, sociologically, militarily, ideologically, scientifically, and imaginatively during the post-Enlightenment period,"[17] from about the late eighteenth century onward in earnest. All of these meanings together represent a "whole network of interests inevitably brought to bear on (and therefore always involved in) any occasion when that peculiar entity 'the Orient' is in question."[18]

For Said, distance is not just a privileged ontological matrix in which Orientalists found themselves or established for themselves in the pursuit and effects of colonial domination, of "dealing with," dismantling, or reconstituting the Orient. Rather, the distance between the modern West and Oriental East configures the particular facts of their being in the world, Occident and Orient alike. The Orient had to be orientalized after all. Racism before races might be another version of this dynamic. Orientalism as a discourse, or more broadly a whole structure of knowledge and worldview which insisted on the absolute demarcation between "East" and "West," would come to generate "facts" about the Oriental Other, of which the Muslim was central.[19] Simply

---

[14] Ibid., p. 3.

[15] Ibid., p. 3.

[16] Specifically: M. Foucault, A. Sheridan, and M. Foucault. (1972). *The Archaeology of Knowledge.* New York: Pantheon Books; and *Discipline and Punish: The Birth of the Prison.*

[17] Said, *Orientalism*, p. 3.

[18] Ibid., p. 3.

[19] Orientalism and the Oriental do not stand in for Islam and the Muslim, as the rich critical postcolonial literature extending Said's work in different contexts and more specific ways has shown us. Islamophobia, on the other hand, is precisely a form of racism constituted by the presence of Islam and expression of Muslimness or perceived Muslimness. The All Parliamentary Group on British Muslims, a cross party group of parliamentarians, was set up in 2017. A year later they produced a report entitled, "Islamophobia Defined, towards a working definition of Islamophobia / anti-Muslim hatred". The resulting definition was: "Islamophobia is rooted in racism and is a type of racism

put, Islam and the figure of the Muslim are the privileged locus of "management," caught up in structures of meaning, feeling, and action that are premised, within our paradigm of hostility, on an insurmountable distance and, therefore, difference.

This systematic movement of distancing and differentiation has deep roots in European, specifically British modernity with mutated manifestations and newer complexities in our world today. The Eastern Question (or set of questions), which is to say, the rigged examination of the innumerable ways in which the East and Islam lacked "our" qualities was, however, always already the white Western (European) Question. As Joseph Massad notes:

> Thus, *the Eastern Question, against which this nascent Europe measured itself, was always the Western Question*, the question of constituting the West as the West and repudiating the East, which it feared was the point of origin of this West, as its antithesis. This much we have already learned from Edward Said's *Orientalism*. That the Eastern Question would also become the Question of Islam and therefore the Question of (Protestant) Christianity would be germane to the European liberal project, which emerged from the Enlightenment, of presenting the West as a place with important characteristics that are always lacking in its Eastern and Islamic antitheses.[20]

The examples of this are legion. But what binds them all is the principle of distance, difference, and "race" as providing the imperial license to generalize a condition of ontological absence in the Other's being and society, the Muslim and her Islam per se. That race and Islam come together to produce Islam as both antonym—*not* white, Western, European, or British—and metonym—the related process of controlling the slippage of the term "Islam" and its adherents toward particular referents and away from others. To its antonyms: "Christianity," "the West," "liberalism," "individualism," "democracy," "freedom," "citizenship," "secularism," "rationality," "tolerance," "human rights," "women's rights," "sexual rights," and not to others with which Islam is apparently interchangeable or at least connotative: "oppression," "repression," "despotism," "totalitarianism," "subjection," "injustice," "intolerance," "irrationalism," "cruelty," "misogyny," or "homophobia."[21]

---

that targets expressions of Muslimness or perceived Muslimness." See: https://static1.squarespace.com/static/599c3d2febbd1a90cffdd8a9/t/5bfd1ea3352f531a6170ceee/1543315109493/Islamophobia+Defined.pdf

[20] Massad, *Islam*, p. 17.

[21] On the production and circulation of such antonyms, see: Mahmood Mamdani. (2004). *Good Muslim, Bad Muslim: America, the Cold War, and the Roots of Terror*. New York: Pantheon/Random House; Talal Asad. (1993). *Genealogies of Religion: Discipline and Reasons of Power in Christianity and Islam*. Baltimore: Johns Hopkins University Press and Asad, pp. 189–93. (1994) "Ethnographic Representation, Statistics, and Modern Power," *Social Research*, 61(1),

The distance between the two, "us" and Islam, has worked historically and today to produce an Islamic theology, if not a whole "Islam" compatible with an imperial, colonial (modern?) order necessarily propelled by liberal states such as Britain in the name of disseminating those products of modernity above for which Islam is an—if not *the*—antithesis.

What this amounts to is, in sum, the constitution of the Other as various kinds of physical *object*-subjects, into a series of type-images which authorize procedures of separation, interrogation, violence, and exclusion on the basis of a whole epistemology of distance and difference. The game of (re) presentation under colonialism was imbricated in the processes by which the enslaved and, later, the natives were made into images, and thus matter to be discarded and/or ruled without inhibition. The Schmittian conception of the political, the expansive, and the constitutive distinguishing of friend from enemy—citizen from enemy combatant—has long been situated in the context of a necessary completion of Being in Western metaphysics, and the enunciation from Europe of who it is that has access to the enclosure of the ontology of life in universal history. In Heideggerian terminology, "Being" is opposed to "beings," the capitalization signifying an unbridgeable ontological hierarchy, an uncrossable distance, which defined modern Europe. An enclosure constituted by a fundamentalist white supremacy and as the exclusive site of Being's disclosure.[22]

78; Yassir Morsi. (2017). *Radical Skin, Moderate Masks: De-radicalising the Muslim & Racism in Post-racial Societies.* London: Rowman and Littlefield; Jalal-'Azm, "Orientalism"; Achcar, "Orientalism in Reverse."

[22] It is no exaggeration to say that the durability of the colonial experiment was contingent on robust matrices of representational power, of caricatures and type-images such as these, upon which, and this is crucial, the *material* and not merely the discursive work of race was conducted and legitimated. As Edward Said's *Orientalism* (2003) has shown us, the French and the British—and to a lesser degree the Germans, Russians, Spanish, Portuguese, Italians, and Swiss—have a long tradition of Orientalism which Said meant as "a way of coming to terms with the Orient that is based on the Orient's special place in European Western experience. The Orient is not only adjacent to Europe; it is also the place of Europe's greatest and richest and oldest colonies, the source of its civilizations and languages, its cultural contestant, and one of its deepest and most recurring images of the Other." Related to the academic tradition is Orientalism more generally as a "style of thought based upon an ontological and epistemological distinction made between 'the Orient' and (most of the time) 'the Occident.'" Said, *Orientalism*, 1–2. Which is to say, in Orientalism and the exercise of colonial power, there is a fundamental relation of dependence between the constructed self and degenerate Other, that is, the Orient and the Occident, or Islam an Europe. On Orientalism as "Occidentalism," see: I. Buruma, A. Margalit, and Mazal Holocaust Collection. (2004). *Occidentalism: The West in the eyes of its enemies.* London: Penguin; Gilbert Achcar. (2008). "Orientalism in Reverse," *Radical Philosophy*, p. 151; Sadik Jalal al-'Azm. (2014). "Orientalism and Orientalism in Reverse," *Khamsin: Journal of Revolutionary Socialists of the Middle East* 8, Politics of Religion in the Middle East. Available at: https://libcom.org/library/orientalism-orientalism-reverse-sadik-jalal-al-%E2%80%99azm

ISLAM: THE OLD ENEMY MADE NEW

But it is worthwhile remembering that Islam is not merely the Other of liberal Europe, the West, or Britain in this equation. Islam is at the core of an economy of antonymy against the philosophical position and political project of liberalism. It is, put simply, at the very heart of liberalism, at the heart of Europe and Britain. As Joseph Massad reminds us,

> Islam is at the heart of liberalism, at the heart of Europe; it was there at the moment of the birth of liberalism and the birth of Europe. Islam is indeed one of the conditions of their emergence as the identities they claim to be. Islam, as I will show, resides inside liberalism, defining its identity and its very claims of difference. It is an internal constituent of liberalism, not merely an external other, though liberalism often projects it as the latter. Like Europe, liberalism's external other turns out to be internal to it, though the ruse of externalising them as outsiders intends to hide the operation of projecting them as an outside so that liberalism's inside can be defined as their opposite, as their superior.[23]

The association of white Christianity[24] with science and reason, of Protestantism with a capitalist economy, industriousness, and democracy, is coded in liberal ideology. John Locke, the father of liberalism, excluded Islam along with Judaism, Confucianism, and others from the realm of reasonableness. Indeed, Britain's view of itself as a reasonable, tolerant, liberal democracy from the nineteenth century onward was largely undisturbed by its despotic rule over around eight hundred million subjects across the empire, which by 1920 included half of the world's Muslims. The many forms of imperial governmental violence were rationalized by a great many liberal

---

[23] Massad, *Islam*, p. 1. The examples of this are legion. But what binds them all is the principle of distance, difference, and, I would argue, "race" as providing the imperial license to generalize a condition of ontological absence in the Other's being and society; the Muslim and her Islam per se. That race (with its state, work, and logic all at play) and Islam come together to produce Islam as both antonym—*not* Western, or Europe, or British—and metonym—the related process of controlling the slippage of the term "Islam" and its adherents toward particular referents and away from others. On the production and circulation of such antonyms, see: Mahmood Mamdani. (2004). *Good Muslim, Bad Muslim: America, the Cold War, and the Roots of Terror.* New York: Pantheon/Random House; Talal Asad. (1993). *Genealogies of Religion: Discipline and Reasons of Power in Christianity and Islam.* Baltimore: Johns Hopkins University Press and Asad, pp. 189–193. (1994). "Ethnographic Representation, Statistics, and Modern Power." *Social Research,* 61(1), 78; Yassir Morsi. (2017). *Radical Skin, Moderate Masks: De-radicalising the Muslim & Racism in Post-racial Societies.* London: Rowman and Littlefield; Jalal-'Azm, "Orientalism"; Achcar, "Orientalism in Reverse."

[24] For an alternative account, see: G. Heng. (2011). "The Invention of Race in the European Middle Ages I: Race Studies, Modernity, and the Middle Ages." *Literature Compass,* 8, 315–31; G. Heng. (2018). *The Invention of Race in the European Middle Ages.* Cambridge: Cambridge University Press.

thinkers and British statesmen as just and in keeping with the distant natives' own traditions.[25] From the seventeenth century onward more generally, the British, along with the Dutch and the French, conceived of themselves as having "elaborated and integrated into their societies an understanding of political freedom, and yet during this very period they pursued and held vast empires where such freedoms were either absent or severely attenuated for the majority of the native inhabitants."[26] John Stuart Mill's "democrat at home, despot abroad" liberalism, then, was the rule rather than the exception.[27]

Absolute difference—the function of distance—has been a consistent stream of intense argumentation in relation to the "Muslim world," not to mention Muslim citizens of Western democracies for decades. In fact, the dominant approach, referred to as "culturalism," made sense of "Islamic extremism" through the lens of inherent variances in who we, the white West/ Britain are and what Muslims represented. As Arun Kundnani notes,

> Muslim communities are seen as failing to adapt to modernity as a result of their Islamic culture. Islam, they say, fails to separate religion from the state, and to render unto Caesar the things which are Caesar's. Because its founder was a statesman as well as a prophet, they hold, Islamic culture is inherently antithetical to a modern, secular containment of its aspiration to impose itself on society. Further, because the teachings of Islam fail to separate it from the political sphere, the atavisms of religious fanaticism are dangerously introduced into the public realm.[28]

"Islamic extremism" corresponds here with an ancient conflict as exemplified in Bernard Lewis's argument of "clash": "It should by now be clear," writes Lewis, "that we are facing a mood and a movement far transcending the level of issues and policies and the governments that pursue them. This is no less than a clash of civilizations—the perhaps irrational but surely historical reaction of an ancient rival against our Judeo-Christian heritage, our secular present, and the worldwide expansion of both."[29] Lewis's words, by no means exceptional, are saturated by the dominant raciological narratives of the late nineteenth and twentieth centuries based on notions of the incessant struggle

---

[25] Losurdo, *Liberalism*; D. Bell. (2014). "What Is Liberalism?" *Political Theory*, 42(6), 682–715 and D. Bell. (2016). *Reordering the World: Essays on Liberalism and Empire*. Princeton; Oxford: Princeton University Press; Uday Singh Mehta. (1999). *Liberalism and Empire: A Study in Nineteenth-Century British Liberal Thought*. Chicago: University of Chicago Press.
[26] Mehta, *Liberalism*, pp. 7–8.
[27] Losurdo, *Liberalism*, chapter 7.
[28] Kundani, *The Muslims are Coming*, p. 55.
[29] Bernard Lewis. (1990). "The Roots of Muslim Rage." *The Atlantic Monthly,* 266, 60.

between human essences, higher and lower order of beings, haunted by the specter of pollution and degeneration.

The wars on/of terror, as then British Prime Minister Tony Blair confessed, are "not just about changing regimes but changing the values systems governing the nations concerned. The banner was not actually 'regime change'; it was 'values change.'"[30] Consistent with the colonial roots of this distance-difference dialectic, a British *cultural* effort[31] against "Islamic extremism," in which our values and who we are could only ever be on the right side of history, is expressed in Gordon Brown's words later in 2007. He spoke about how there was a renewed requirement for the techniques used "during the cold war in the nineteen-forties, fifties, and sixties, when we had to mount a propaganda effort, if you like, to explain to people that our values represented the best of commitments to individual dignity, to liberty, and to human life."[32] Yet to be Muslim here is to be in a state of race, one of degeneration if not infancy, and hence unaware or incapable of such enlightened commitments. Muslims thus become a privileged group subject to the intense multiplication of interrogation-space designed to suture the anxieties of imperial decline occasioned by the perception of penetration and loss of virile power that frame the attacks on the World Trade Center.

THE EASTERN QUESTION AND/
AS THE WOMAN QUESTION

If there is a discourse that has been saturated by concerns of individual dignity, liberty, and human life; a discourse in a particularly tense relation to Islam and its supposed culture, then it is that of the Woman Question; or, feminism and/in Islam. Doctrines of individualism have been central to dominant, if provincial, conceptions of Man; what it is to be European, British, secular. In sum, what it is to be modern. Or, to be white is to be—or have a relative proximity to—modernity; to be modern is to be white. The coming of an industrial culture, with revolutionary processes and technologies of extraction, production, and manufacture—tied of course to the epistemological, governmental, and disciplinary transformations in Europe—insisted

---

[30] Tony Blair. (2006). *Speech to World Affairs Council*, Los Angeles, August 1.

[31] An effort that invokes a particular construction of British culture and "Fundamental British Values." As the National Security Strategy (2010) notes, "our national interest requires us to stand up for the values our country believes in—the rule of law, democracy, free speech, tolerance and human rights." HM Government. (2010b). "Securing Britain in an Age of Uncertainty." The National Security Strategy, London.

[32] Gordon Brown. (2007). "Terror Alert", interview with Andrew Marr, *BBC News Online*. Available at: http://news.bbc.co.uk/1/hi/programmes/sunday_am/6258416.stm

on the power, duties, and potential value of the individual. The principle of individualism served to distinguish, however,

> Occidental from Oriental culture, since the latter is treated as devoid of individual rights and of individuality. Individualism is the golden thread which weaves together the economic institutions of property, the religious institution of confession of conscience and the moral notion of personal autonomy; it serves to separate "us" from "them." In Orientalism, the absence of civil society in Islam entailed the absence of the autonomous individual exercising conscience and rejecting arbitrary interventions by the state.[33]

It was only in Europe, it was thought, that rational individuality was realized. In this colonial equation, the hive mentality of Muslim subjects—regardless of the remarkable heterogeneity within that category, to say nothing of the unprecedented histories of circulation, philosophical, and theological contestation, and complex social formations of Muslims[34]—was a default assumption. An assumption that justified the conquest of vast territories, the resettlement of the world through the twin processes of social excretion (of the criminal, the poor, the superfluous, the adventurous and entrepreneurial from the metropole), and an unprecedented tipping point, which altered the political and civilizational cosmology of the earth toward Europe and which, for the colonized, came at the cost of new forms of theft, violence, murder, and enslavement.[35] Further still, the myth of modern (white) reason was one which constructed an unbridgeable distance between us (the discoverers) and them (the enunciated).[36] The link between European, specifically British contributions to civilization, Protestantism, and women also relied on this

---

[33] Bryan Turner. (1984). "Orientalism and the Problem of Civil Society in Islam." In *Orientalism, Islam, and Islamists*, edited by Asaf Hussain, Robert Olson, and Jamil Qureshi. Brattleboro, VT: Amana Books, pp. 20–35.

[34] For a remarkable repository of such ambiguity and contradiction within "Islam," see: Shahab Ahmad. (2016). *What is Islam? The Importance of Being Islamic*. Princeton: Princeton University Press; Marshall Hodgson. (1974). *The Venture of Islam: Conscience and History in World Civilization, Volumes 1-3*. Chicago: University of Chicago Press; Fazlur Rahman. (2002). *Islam*. Chicago: University of Chicago Press.

[35] James Belich. (2009). *Replenishing the Earth: The Settler Revolution and the Rise of the Anglo-world*. Oxford: Oxford University Press; Domenico Losurdo. (2011). *Liberalism: A Counter-History*. London: Verso, chapter 3; Dirk Moses, ed. (2008). *Empire, Colony, Genocide: Conquest, Occupation, and Subaltern Resistance in World History*. New York: Berghahn; Patrick Wolfe. (2006). "Settler Colonialism and the Elimination of the Native." *Journal of Genocide Research*, 8(4), 387–409.

[36] Enunciation is an essential feature of coloniality or the colonial matrix of power. The act of enunciation which produces and fixes the enunciated was the preserve of modern reason, or white Europe. See: Walter Mignolo. (2018). "The Conceptual Triad: Modernity/Coloniality/Decoloniality." In *On Decoloniality*, edited by Walter Mignolo and Catherine Walsh. Durham: Duke University Press, pp. 135–52.

gulf between unequal partners. This was the case not only on the part of colonial officials who emphasized the oppressiveness of Oriental (especially Islamic) cultures toward women[37] but also fundamental to the consciousness and political work of white women's and white feminist movements of eighteenth- and nineteenth-century Western Europe.

The case of Mary Wollstonecraft (d.1797) is an instructive one. In her foundational text for Western liberal feminism, Wollstonecraft would deploy the image of the enslaved Muslim woman to castigate white Christian Europeans for the treatment of "their" women, as if to put forward concerns about the phenotypical risk of *Orientalism*—of being like the Muslim Orientals—for modern, white European patriarchy. She would declare "that the books of instruction [for women], written by men of genius, have had the same tendency as more frivolous productions; and that in the true style of Mahometanism, [women] are treated as a kind of subordinate beings, and not as a part of the human species."[38] The gendered despotism of European men could not be allowed to continue for it was understood to be, as Zonana explains, the "defining feature of Eastern life and a perverse corruption of Western values. . . . [Indeed] any aspect of the European treatment of women that Wollstonecraft finds objectionable she labels as Eastern."[39] Wollstonecraft's brand of feminist Orientalism perpetuated the colonially convenient myth that women in Islam have no soul, using it as the cornerstone of her agitation for women's rights in the West. Zonana asserts that "the feminism of Wollstonecraft's *Vindication of the Rights of Woman* ultimately reduces itself to what would have been in her time a relatively noncontroversial plea: that the West rid itself of its oriental ways, becoming as a consequence more Western—that is, more rational, enlightened, reasonable."[40] Discrimination against women, then, was an alien import, an inherently Eastern despotism that traveled to Britain from the Muslim Orient where this same despotism was constitutive and inherent.

The racial principle at work in the gender question becomes clearer when we recognize that Wollstonecraft was following in the tradition of a late-seventeenth century English pamphlet, *An Essay in Defence of the Female Sex . . . Written by a Lady*, which posited the dual despotisms of African slavery in the transatlantic trade and (apparently soulless) Muslim women, as akin to the discrimination suffered by white Christian women under patriarchy.

---

[37] These practices were "most manifest in Chinese foot-binding, Indian widow-burning (sati), and child marriage, and the gender segregation of Muslim societies, their oppressive yet enticing institution of the harem, and most prominently the so-called veil or hijab." Massad, *Islam*, p. 111.
[38] Mary Wollstonecraft. (1996). *A Vindication of the Rights of Woman*. New York: Dover, pp. 6–7.
[39] Joyce Zonana. (1993). "The Sultan and the Slave: Feminist Orientalism and the Structure of Jane Eyre." *Signs*, 18(3), 600.
[40] Zonana, "The Sultan," p. 602.

Bernadette Andrea argues that "when applied to the Islamic as opposed to the transatlantic case [of slavery]," the slave analogy posited as an anti-slavery argument "encapsulate[s] the orientalism associated with emerging liberal feminism, which articulated its goal of expanded property rights for 'freeborn Englishwomen' through the negative foil of those women who 'are born slaves' in the 'Eastern parts of the World.'"[41] The thrust of this early white feminist literature, indebted though it was to a male travel literature which helped to consolidate the colonial, enlightening, framing of interaction with the Muslim world, was therefore constituted by certain projections of Muslims and, specifically, their treatment of women. The larger technique, however, was the analogy drawn between (what is inherent in) colonized and (thus aberrant in) European populations that cut across race and gender. The urban poor, for example, and "the insane were in one way or another con-structed as biological 'races apart' whose differences from the white male, and likeness to each other, 'explained' their different and lower position in the social hierarchy."[42] Or as Edward Said would explain of the case of the Orientals:

> Along with all other peoples variously designated as backward, degenerate, uncivilized, retarded, the Orientals were viewed in a framework constructed out of biological determinism and moral-political admonishment. The Oriental was linked thus to elements in Western society (delinquents, the insane, women, the poor) having in common an identity best described as lamentably alien. Orientals were rarely seen or looked at; they were see through, analyzed not as citizens, or even people, but as problems to be solved or confined or—as the colonial powers openly coveted their territory—taken over.[43]

A specifically white Protestant Christianity as the precondition for the libera-tion of women would thus become the cornerstone of the women's move-ment. Josephine Butler, another prominent English feminist, would place a high value on this (imperial) Christianizing feminism pursued through the work of missionaries and the force of colonial power, especially when it came to the evangelizing effort in British India. It would be the status of Oriental women that formed the reference against which white women in the metro-pole could measure their advance at home. As Tracey Fessenden argues:

---

[41] Bernadette Andrea. (2009). "Islam, Women, and Western Responses: The Contemporary Rel-evance of Early Modern Investigations." *Women's Studies* 38: 273–92.
[42] N. Stepan. (1986). "Race and Gender: The Role of Analogy in Science." *Isis*, 77(2), 261–277.
[43] Said, *Orientalism*, p. 207.

The evangelical Christianity of the emergent white middle class, with its gendered spheres of home and world, proved especially amenable to an alliance between women's rights and imperialism: the assumption that Protestant Christianity was the most advanced religion, one in relation to which others were primitive, allowed evangelical women to take part in the "civilizing" operations of empire, associated with men, without appearing to depart from their appointed sphere, associated with Christianity.[44]

However, this same literature was often deployed in turn as an instrument to limit the rights of white women in Britain, a technique through which these women under patriarchal oppression in the enlightened world, "were depicted as living in a paradise of gender relations, threatening them with the imagined slavery of Muslim women were they to get out of line."[45] Lord Cromer, ruler of colonial Egypt, for example, would champion the unveiling of Egyptian women similarly criticizing Islam's oppression of women in stark contrast to the individual dignity of women under Christianity and Western governance. But Cromer opposed women's suffrage in Britain, obstructing women's education and the training of women doctors, while his "feminism" abroad in the colony codified unveiling as Egyptian Muslim women's liberation and modernization. Leila Ahmed notes, "this champion of unveiling of Egyptian women was, in England, founding member and sometime president of the Men's League of Opposing Women's Suffrage. Feminism on the home front and feminism directed against white men was to be resisted and suppressed; but taken abroad and directed against the cultures of colonised peoples, it could be promoted in ways that admirably served and furthered the project of the dominance of the white man."[46] Which is to say that the alliance made between the early white feminists in Britain and the colonial project propelled by wealthy, white men did little to destabilize the gendered status quo. In fact, "the analogies were used by scientists to justify resistance to efforts at social change on the part of women and 'lower races,' on the grounds that inequality was a 'fact' of nature and not a function of the power relations in a society."[47] The feminist alliance with the imperial racism and Islamophobia

---

[44] Tracey Fessenden. (2008). "Disappearances: Race, Religion, and the Progress Narrative of US Feminism." In *Secularisms*, edited by Janet R. Jakobsen and Ann Pelligrini. Durham, NC: Duke University Press, p. 140.

[45] Massad, *Islam*, p. 114. See also: Bernadette Andrea, "Islam, Women, and Western Responses," pp. 276–80.

[46] Leila Ahmed. (2004). *Women and Gender in Islam: Historical Roots of a Modern Debate*. New Haven, CT: Yale University Press, pp. 374–76.

[47] Stepan, "Race and Gender," p. 275.

of colonial expansion, then, was to the ultimate detriment of the white wom-
en's liberal feminist movement of the eighteenth and nineteenth centuries.[48]

The increasing numbers of women drawn to the rhetoric of ISIS have
brought with it analyses of the group's subversion of the racism and alienation experienced by young women in the West in their day-to-day lives. In
framing their political project as post-national and post-racial in nature, ISIS
market themselves as offering an exit from the violence of patriarchy at home
in the major cities of Britain and Europe.[49] This has demanded a state-led
appropriation of (liberal) feminism as the basis for comprehending, or classifying, Muslim women and their bodies in a context in which Muslim women
are equal in potential for the perpetration of massive violence.[50] The colonial
tradition of casting Muslim women as slaves or submissive subjects under a
God-sponsored patriarchy conjoins with the unfolding complexities of the
war on terror. This has brought with it new techniques of (raced and gendered) distancing in the Muslim Questioned, a context in which it is Muslim
women who are increasingly subjected to the disciplinary mechanisms of
the state but also the racism and Islamophobia sustained by its legislated
violence.

In the early years of the war on terror, military intervention, regime change,
and the reconstitution of "failed states" were largely framed in a way which
recalled the civilizing mission of white men and women intent on saving
brown women. As Nisha Kapoor notes,

> The dominant discourse, and one that continues on some levels, was of sub-
> missive Muslim women oppressed by the barbarism of a pre-modern culture.
> As more women have joined ISIS, hegemonic discourses have veered towards
> representing their sexuality as a lethal weapon. The rhetoric of "jihadi brides"
> invokes a different kind of race-gendered representation of Muslim women as

---

[48] Margaret Hunt argues early feminists like Wollstonecraft "assumed that Western European women
were far better off than women living in Muslim lands." Margaret R. Hunt. (2007). "Women in
Ottoman and Western European Law Courts: Were Western European Women Really the Luckiest Women in the World?" In *Structures and Subjectivities: Attending to Early Modern Women*,
edited by Joan E. Hartman and Adele Seeff. Dover: University of Delaware Press, p. 176. Yet this
early white feminist argument took shape when European Christian married women had no right
to property, who was in face *like* property, until "The Married Women's Property Act" was passed
at the end of the nineteenth century when, under Islamic law, "Muslims cannot be enslaved (hence,
the fallacy of the 'Muslim wife as slave') and Muslim women always had an inalienable right to
own property. However, despite challenges within the feminist camp to the alliance between the
advocacy for English women's rights and their complicity with Orientalism and other imperialist
discourses, the view that Western women—and in the contemporary world, American women—are
the 'freest' women in the world as opposed to inherently oppressed Muslim women is still widespread." See: Andrea, "Islam, Women, and Western Responses," p. 274.

[49] Rafia Zakaria. (2015). "Women and Islamic Militancy." *Dissent*, 62(1), Winter.

[50] Rashid, Naaz. (2016). *Veiled Threats: Representing the Muslim Women in Public Policy Discourses*. Bristol: Policy Press.

oversexed and hypersexualised, with equal potential as Muslim men for being the purveyors of violence. This way of portraying a weaponised sexuality has had material consequences as women increasingly become the target of state violence. The number of women arrested for terrorism-related offences more than doubled in Britain between 2014 and 2015, and there are growing numbers of stories of women, suspected of supporting or engaging in terrorism-related activity in some form, having their children taken from them as part of pre-emptive policing strategies.[51]

The silent subjects of this discourse and policy of war can only exist in the eyes of strangers as an abstraction, an imagined subject cloaked in secret significations which s/he has had no hand in authoring, and which are designed to function as evidence in the interrogation of their irreconcilable difference and threat. This process of creative, if also destructive, license masked as "knowledge" of Muslims, was thrown into great relief with the spatial, psychic, and temporal collapse that came with the end of empire, and social interaction with formerly colonized populations in the metropolitan interiors of Europe. This did not, however, cultivate fundamental reorientations in the whole "epistemology of ignorance"[52] which gave coherence to colonial narratives of difference and barbarism, modernity, and civilization. Instead, the underlying logics of white supremacy, fundamentalist in nature, have been made to do more complex work as Britain has had to confront the undeniable reality of black and brown humanity face to face. A proper confrontation is nonetheless forever deferred, or interrupted, by the work of race, its proliferating abstractions, and the carceral economies sustained by them, which foreclose the possibility of this confrontation as a meeting of equals. The play of abstractions involved in the Woman Question (and the Muslim Questioned) is nonetheless a battle,

> between civilization and barbarism continues to take place on the spectacle of the contained, mutilated, or brutalized bodies of Muslim women, enabling the human/humanist subjects of the empire to save, protect, and kill all at once.

[51] Kapoor, *Deport*, pp. 154–55. Alan Travis. (2015). "UK Terror Arrest at Record Level After Increase in Female Suspects." *Guardian*, December 10.

[52] This is a term borrowed from Stephen Steinberg. (2007). *Race Relations: A Critique*. Stanford: Stanford University Press, p. 41. She quote from Charles Mills that: "As a general rule, the white misunderstanding, misrepresentation, evasion and self-deception on matters relating to race are among the most pervasive mental phenomena of the past few hundred years." See also: L. M. Alcoff. (2007). "Epistemologies of Ignorance: Three Types." In *Race and Epistemologies of Ignorance*, edited by S. Sullivan and N. Tuana. Albany: State University of New York, pp. 39–58; C.-M. Pascale. (2010). "Epistemology and the Politics of Knowledge." *The Sociological Review*, 58(2_suppl), 154–65; S. Sullivan and N. Tuana, eds. (2007). *Race and Epistemologies of Ignorance*. Albany: State University of New York.

These processes point to another moment of compatibility between the empire and the nation as they invest in the supreme power of the state, modern forms of militarism, and the state's right to kill in the nation's name. The mobilization of foundationalist religious or secular meanings as they invest in the timelessness of the female body as the defining evidence of the boundaries of us versus them, here versus there, West versus Islam, civilized versus barbaric, and secularism versus religion is part of this process.[53]

In his classic essay, "Stranger in the Village," James Baldwin bore witness to the experience of existing in another's eyes as a dark abstraction. He wrote: "Everyone in the village knows my name, though they scarcely ever use it, knows that I come from America—though this, apparently, they will never really believe: black men come from Africa—and everybody knows that I am the friend of the son of a woman who was born here, and that I am staying in their chalet. But I remain as much a stranger as I was the first day I arrived, and the children shout *Neger! Neger!* as I walk down the streets."[54] Names and their (dis)associations are fundamental to the Muslim Questioned: a subject who surely has a name though we scarcely ever use it. Or if we do, it only drives the relation of interrogation between us and him, and consolidates his filiation with other men, women, and children similarly suspect. With the function of distance as I have explained it in view, Baldwin's words capture with characteristic clarity the constitutive dynamic of naming in order to erase. The denial of strangers their names and histories, and the possibility of their living and circulation in a *shared* reality, are replaced with investments—psychic, cultural, and militaristic—in those that instead disappear humanity, or name them as its antithesis. A chasm is maintained between the Muslim and I, which in turn structures and provides order to our world which is constantly under attack.

PREEMPTING MUSLIM CRIMINALITY

In this first mode of interrogation, then, everyone may know the name of the Muslim but speaks of, looks at, and hears terrorists. The distance at which she must be kept pervades a wide range of social, political, governmental processes and helps constitute an array of technologies and economies of the wars on/of terror. I want to end this chapter with a related techno-economy likewise subject to the will to distance: preemptive policing strategies.

---

[53] Minoo Moallem. (2008). "Muslim Women and the Politics of Representation." *Journal of Feminist Studies in Religion,* 24(1), 109.

[54] James Baldwin. (1964). *Notes of a Native Son.* London: Michael Joseph, p. 153.

Preemption here speaks to the fixity of the Muslim Other in a *pre-criminal* space, a term which is at once a mode of classifying forms of Muslim culpability, and speaks to a spatial, even geographical, arrangement in which the Muslim is constantly mapped.[55] What ties the two together is that something is known with some certainty, for it is fundamental to her, about Muslims before even they themselves become aware of their criminality. The fact of the Muslim's inherent recalcitrance to the commitments that constitute our way of life, along with the absolute transparency of the source of their (subconscious) motives—God-patriarch, Islam, Islamic culture, and the Qur'an—thus behooves us to remake the Muslim as the means to excise them of their proximity to terrorist violence. We must speak for them, bring them to life in a way which might align with the values which represent the best of humanity.

Muslim pre-criminality frames responsibility for the violence done in Islam's name in relation to the white European victimhood. Abstracted from any context in which the allegiances that people form with groups such as ISIS appear comprehensible,[56] the assumption that "we" would not, indeed could not, do such a thing because ours is a culture of reasoning individuals as opposed to a culture that is symbolic of rationality's collapse, is enough to legitimate perpetual scrutiny of the Muslim Other. Just as in the past, this ostensibly permanent, global, struggle against disturbing (Muslim) objects is framed in metaphysical terms. A necessary war must proceed against these existential enemies, "with whom no agreement is either possible or desirable, [and] thus appear in the form of caricatures, clichés, and stereotypes, granting them a figural sort of presence. In turn, this presence only serves to confirm the type of (ontological) menace we perceive as confronting us."[57] Then as now, distance and difference with the Muslim Questioned opens up the

---

[55] On the pre-criminal in counterterrorism and Muslims, see: C. Baker-Beall, C. Heath-Kelly, and L. Jarvis. (2014). *Counter-Radicalisation: Critical Perspectives*. Abingdon: Routledge, pp. 206–22; D. Goldberg, S. Jadhav, and T. Younis. (2016). "Prevent: What Is Pre-Criminal Space?" *BJPsych Bulletin,* 41, 2; C. Heath-Kelly. (2017). "The Geography of Pre-criminal Space: Epidemiological Imaginations of Radicalisation Risk in the UK Prevent Strategy, 2007–2017." *Critical Studies on Terrorism*, 10(2), 297–319; C. Heath-Kelly. (2012). "Reinventing Prevention or Exposing the Gap? False Positives in UK Terrorism Governance and the Quest for Pre-emption." *Critical Studies on Terrorism*, 5(1), 69–87; J. McCulloch and S. Pickering. (2009). "Pre-Crime and Counter-Terrorism Imagining Future Crime in the 'War on Terror'." *The British Journal of Criminology*, 49(5), 628–45; J. McCulloch and D. Wilson. (2016). *Pre-Crime: Pre-Emption, Precaution and the Future*. Abingdon: Routledge; G. Mythen, S. Walklate, and F. Khan. (2013). "Why Should We Have to Prove We're Alright?': Counter-Terrorism, Risk and Partial Securities." *Sociology*, 47(2), 383–98.

[56] See: Ruth Blakely, Ben Hayes, Nisha Kapoor, Arun Kundnani, Narzanin Massoumi, David Miller, Tom Mills, Rizwan Sabir, Katy Sian, and Waqas Tufail. (2019: chapter 3c). *Leaving the War on Terror: A Progressive Alternative to Counter-Terrorism Policy*. Amsterdam: Transnational Institute; Kapoor, *Deprive*, chapter 1 and 2.

[57] Mbembe, "Society of Enmity," p. 29.

possibility of the deployment of pure means without ends, or more accurately, a whole arsenal of means—institutional, molecular, intimate—for shifting ends which legitimize the deployment of pure means. The distance between us and the Muslim Questioned is ultimately insurmountable. Islamicity and Muslimness—as racial elements—become the basic measures of distance, difference, and, therefore, enmity.

One might well ask: who is this enemy really? Is it a nation, a state, a religion, a civilization, a culture, or an idea? It matters not. Islam and its Muslims are, to their very core, proliferating antonyms for what is taken to define the European community. In this calculus of state power and the imperial politics of the war on/of terror, accuracy is straightforwardly substituted for the law of the sword, or rather the one supports the other given the instrumental nature that knowledge about Muslims has.[58] But it is the enduring persistence of the law of race—the ultimate currency of sanction—and the enduring political consciousness of empire (and new anxieties of European demotion) which consolidate arguments that our powers of persuasion instituted by regime change, values change, cutting-edge weaponry, surveillance, and collateral humanity might begin the process of their conversion/humanization to modernity, the closing of the distance, as it were, if only they were to listen, stands still and answer our questions with smiles on their unveiled faces.

Where is your God now and why does he make you this way? It is through variations on the question and the multiplication of spaces in which it can be asked and answered with the fewest inhibitions—physical, psychic, legal—that we can know, however precariously, the many ways in which the Muslim is a problem to be dealt with, dispatched as the Muslim Questioned are between institutions and questioning agencies. The racial fundamentalism constitutive of the epistemology of distance as I have outlined, the belief that nothing can be owed to the Other or lost in their disappearance, then opens the door to a monumental verdict.[59] A moment of rapture when the wait for the Other—terrorist, foreigner, immigrant, Muslim—to attack is refused and the difficult choice is finally taken to do what is necessary to deal with the Muslim Questioned, those damned of the faith of Western humanism who must be located, marked, codified, and made to answer without pause.

Distance in the Muslim Questioned showed its explicit racial function in the case of Gary McKinnon. Following a national campaign for Babar Ahmad to be put on official trial in the United Kingdom, a backbench parliamentary

---

[58] Carl Schmitt. (2007). *The Concept of the Political*, trans. George Schwab. Chicago: University of Chicago Press, p. 26.

[59] See: Jean Comaroff. (2009). "The Politics of Conviction: Faith on the Neo-liberal Frontier." *Social Analysis*, 53(1), 17–38; Nicola Perugini and Neve Gordon. (2015). *The Human Right to Dominate*. Oxford: Oxford University Press.

debate took place to discuss Britain's extradition arrangements. The issue of extradition was high on the political agenda due in part to the well-known *Daily Mail*-sponsored campaign to save Gary McKinnon—white, British, male—from transfer to the United States. McKinnon was accused of hacking into ninety-seven US military and NASA computers, who after gaining access deleted critical files from their operating systems. As Nisha Kapoor writes,

> Gary's defence was that he was looking for evidence of a state cover up of UFO activity. The Daily Mail had for some time been lobbying against terms of the extradition treaty, namely for what it saw as unjust infractions on British sovereignty and limitations placed on UK law to "protect UK citizens." The reach of its campaign was such that both David Cameron and Nick Clegg had lobbied against Gary's impending extradition in their 2010 election campaigns. A few months after his election, Prime Minister David Cameron went on to raise the issue with President Obama.[60]

The Babar Ahmad case was invoked only to erase altogether its racial and religious specificities. In his opening statement of the debate, Dominic Raab argued that "in taking the fight to the terrorists and the serious criminals after 9/11, the pendulum [had] swung too far the other way."[61] He continued, "Gary McKinnon should not be treated like some gangland mobster or al-Qaeda mastermind."[62] The central concern in the debate was that a number of (white) British citizens such as McKinnon were subjected to inhumane conditions of incarceration and injustice contrary to the principles of "British justice" and values. The arrangements sanctioned by the US-UK Extradition Treaty of 2003 allowed for the convenient sidestepping of safeguards built into the criminal justice system with the potential for "accidentally punishing the innocent or over-punishing those guilty of minor crimes."[63] We are implored, David Davis continues, "[to] keep in mind that the rather draconian process that we have, which was put in place to defend us against terrorism, does not appear to have had much impact in that respect. In practice, the outcome is much more mundane. The truth of the matter is that we will have

---

[60] Kapoor, *Deport*, p. 117. See also: Geoffrey Robertson. (2010) "Cameron and Clegg Must Now Do Their Moral Duty and Save Gary McKinnon." *Daily Mail*, May 27, 2010. Available at: https://www.dailymail.co.uk/debate/article-1281208/Cameron-Clegg-moral-duty--save-Gary-McKinnon.html; Jo Adetunji. (2010). "Gary McKinnon Campaigners Praise PM for Raising Hacker's Case with Obama." *Guardian*, July 21, 2010. Available at: https://www.theguardian.com/world/2010/jul/21/gary-mckinnon-campaigners-pm-hacker-obama.
[61] Dominc Raab. (2011). House of Commons Debate, 5 December 2011, vol. 537, col. 82.
[62] Ibid., col. 84.
[63] David Davis. (2011). House of Commons Debate, 5 December 2011, vol. 537, col. 93.

far more Gary McKinnons extradited than Osama bin Ladens."[64] That Babar Ahmad was also accused of a computer-related crime and yet did not warrant the defense afforded to McKinnon that he "could be prosecuted in this country, given that the acts of unlawful access occurred within our jurisdiction (i.e., from his computer in North London),"[65] was left unacknowledged. The dialect of distance in the Muslim Questioned and its underpinning assumptions foreclosed certain possibilities of defense for racialized suspects such as Babar Ahmad who has a priori been framed as uniquely guilty. McKinnon's crimes were computer-related whereas Ahmad was a terrorist until proven otherwise.

The mental health of Gary McKinnon was also made to do the work of race insofar as an aspect of the debate about his extradition concerned the ethical dimensions of criminalizing an individual with mental health issues. McKinnon had Asperger's Syndrome and it was through this clinical lens that the naivety attributed to Gary's crimes—looking for evidence of a state-sponsored cover-up of UFO activity—was connected to his vulnerability to "the stress of social complexity,"[66] and the harsh conditions of incarceration. McKinnon was understood at numerous institutional levels as an individual suffering from Asperger's who, while guilty of a naive computer crime, was fundamentally harmless and uniquely vulnerable to the difficult environment of incarceration. The mental health condition of the Muslim men involved in extradition arrangements of the kind discussed by Raab and others simply did not have access to the status of vulnerability even when Talha Ahsan—also charged with computer-related offenses conducted from his London home— had Asperger's, or that Haroon Aswat was known to suffer from paranoid schizophrenia. In both cases, their mental health was fodder for their depiction as violent suspects with irrational and barbaric tendencies.

Not only was the guilt of these three Muslim men—Ahmad, Ahsan, and Aswat—as important cases of the Muslim Questioned, a priori precluded by their racialized characteristics and nature, the mobilization of any evidence such as mental health conditions, which might elicit sympathy or humanize to a degree of innocence, was disallowed at multiple structural levels. Racially coded distinctions of the war on terror—innocence and guilt chief among them—that reinforced an ontological distance between the violent terror suspect and the vulnerable, ultimately over-punished (white) British citizens in

---

[64] Ibid., col. 91.

[65] James Slack and Michael Seamark. (2010). "An Affront to British Justice: Gary McKinnon Extradition CAN Be Stopped, Says Lib Dem QC." *Mail Online*, May 31, 2010. Available at: https://www.dailymail.co.uk/news/article-1282765/Gary-McKinnon-extradition-stopped-says-LibDem-QC-Lord-Carlile.html

[66] Gary McKinnon v. Secretary of State for the Home Department, [2009] EWHC 170, HC(Admin), para. 12.

this instantiation of the Muslim Questioned. But the suspension or occlusion of certain legal defenses and admissible evidence for the figure of the Muslim is symptomatic, an unexceptional illustration of liberalism's *constitutive* exceptions and limits: democracy and feminism at home, enlightened despotism, and coerced unveiling abroad. These exceptions, however, are no longer separated by actual distances between metropole and colony. As an epistemology which orders the institutional and social world, distance has a much more motile, stealthy character and a set of technologies. The current modes of war in which the Muslim has become a principal object must simultaneously collapse the space between the target of interrogation and his tracker, while maintaining if not magnifying the ontological chasm between him and us. The older logics of warfare, occupation, and extermination are, then, no longer sufficient but are accompanied by more complex, fluid techniques of sustainable violence. But the law of race remains the fundamental point of departure which sanctions the differing intensities of the exception and the subjects who most experience the mechanisms of force and capture unleashed by states of emergency. The suspensions and double-standards involved in the McKinnon case were therefore fundamentally consistent, against the arguments of state and criminal justice, with British liberal values.[67]

Aimé Césaire saw this clearly in the pseudo-humanism embedded in the Universal Declaration of Human Rights established in 1948 by European colonial powers such as Britain and France. He wrote, "And that is the thing I hold against pseudo-humanism: that for too long it has diminished the rights of man, that its concept of those rights has been—and still is—narrow and fragmentary, incomplete and biased and, all things considered, sordidly racist."[68] Universal human rights laws, paradoxically, mobilized racial distinctions in order to remain coherent. The Colonial Office in Britain would, in fact, contest the extent to which the European Convention on Human Rights applied to the colonies. Human rights and the assumed humanity which gives them meaning have a conditional character for the racial subject. When agreeing on the terms of the Geneva Convention, "European powers and the new superpowers [reluctantly] agreed to certain provisions . . . the British and French did not necessarily see them as applicable to the colonial wars being

---

[67] On these 'consistencies' with sovereign power more generally, see: David Theo Goldberg. (2002). *The Racial State*. Oxford: Wiley Blackwell; Barry Hindess. (2005) "Citizenship and Empire." In *Sovereign Bodies, Citizens, Migrants and States in the Postcolonial World*, edited by Thomas Blom Hansen and Finn Stepputat. Princeton, NJ: Princeton University Press; Barnor Hesse and S. Sayyid. (2006). "The Postcolonial Political and the Immigrant Imaginary." In *A Postcolonial People; South Asians in Britain*, edited by N. Ali, V. S. Kalra, and S. Sayyid. London: Hurst; Katy Sian, Ian Law, and S. Sayyid. (2013). *Racism, Governance and Public Policy: Beyond Human Rights*. Abingdon: Routledge.

[68] Aimé Césaire. (1972). *Discourse on Colonialism*. London: Monthly Review Press, p. 3.

fought in Asia and Africa."[69] When the article for protecting noncombatants was eventually signed, it was implied that it would only be in effect if the sovereign so decided in conjunction with severe limits on the rights of rebel forces.[70] Indeed, the British did not ratify the Conventions until 1957 and, consistent with a colonial will, were not beholden to them in its brutal campaigns in Malaya, Cyprus, and Kenya.

The current state of anxiety—against terror but also forms of penetration, pollution, degeneration, demotion—is based on relations of total war. Relations not only with a World-Outside but which mediate the very separation between the interior under threat and the threatening, disposable subjects who disguise themselves as one of us. It has become an essential relation which functions on a socialized distinction between combatant and noncombatant which, put differently, is a distinction between those for whom categories of innocence and guilt must naturally apply. Mutated structures of criminalization (guilt) in the war on terror and the techniques of dehumanization which propel their violent, racist effects are indebted to the "human" enshrined in the Universal Declaration. The Muslim Questioned names, in sum, a whole paradigm which operates through the banalization of the logic of the (colonial) applications clause and the violation of basic protocols of hospitality when faced with the Muslim.

---

[69] Khalili, *Time in the Shadows*, p. 229.
[70] See also: Barnor Hesse. (2004). "Im/plausible Deniability: Racism's Conceptual Double Bind." *Social Identities*, 10(1), 9–29; Paul Gilroy. (2010). *Darker than Blue: On the Moral Economies of Black Atlantic Culture*. London: The Belknap Press of Harvard University Press; Antony Anghie. (2004). *Imperialism, Sovereignty and the Making of International Law*. Cambridge: Cambridge University Press; A. W. Brian Simpson. (2004). *Human Rights and the End of Empire*. Oxford: Oxford University Press, p. 491.

Chapter 2

Disclosure

Within the paradigm of hostility, the constant will to question is ultimately a demand for Others to have their time completely taken up in answering other's questions and that, ideally, they have little to say for themselves. In sum, to be in a perpetual state of disclosure. Disclosure, in effect, names a technique to manage the distance between white self and Muslim Other. But even this, I think, underestimates how constitutive of disclosure, of confession, is the Other's presumed *silence*. The Muslim Questioned is assumed to have nothing to say that we do not already know. It is the principle of race and the Other's fixity within it which precludes their meaningful speech outside of our questions and in a voice of one's own. Disclosure, in turn, goes hand in hand with the increasing power of the ideology of total security and the simultaneous limits and safeguards of citizenship against the threat of "Islamic terrorism." The manufacture and installation of mechanisms aimed at calculating risk, codifying those who are assumed to embody that risk, and, in turn, accumulating protection into the currency of citizenship become the desired order of the security state. Which is to say that there is an economy—technological, political, cultural, corporate—which propels a mode of hostile power and the intense pressure to question the Muslim today. The Muslim Questioned—the paradigmatic racial subject of this ideology—is further embedded in and classified according to parallel industries of euphemism: radicalization, feminism, law, democracy, terrorism, criminality, among many others.[1]

---

[1] Hasan Azad. (2017). "Thinking About Islam, Politics and Muslim Identity in a Digital Age." *Journal of Islamic and Muslim Studies*, 2(2), 122–34; Nathan Lean. (2017). *The Islamophobia Industry. How the Right Manufactures Hatred of Muslims*. Pluto Press; N. Massoumi, T. Mills, and D. Miller, eds. (2017). *What is Islamophobia: Racism, Social Movements and the State*. London: Pluto Press.

There is a self-assurance in our hostile interactions with the Muslim Questioned on the basis of the ontological distance between us. Given the ever-presence of race as a foundational rule or code and, more specifically, the fantasy of whiteness, self-assurance is equally drawn from "structural violence and the ways in which it contributes on a planetary scale to the profoundly unequal redistribution of the resources of life and the privileges of citizenship. But that assurance comes also from technical and scientific prowess, creations of the mind, forms of political organization that are (or at least seem to be) relatively disciplined, and, when necessary, from cruelty without measure."[2] The common-sense nature of the distance between us and them, and the superior, co-constitutive instruments of violence (war) and political organization (liberal democracy and its white citizen-subject), in turn, naturalizes the notion that the Other, that is, the racial subject, must answer our questions, while at the same time their speech (or protest or claims to protection) is rendered indecipherable or inconsequential. This form of violence operates on the granular level of what one must (not) think, do, or say, and the questions to which one must respond. The principle of race, after all, depends upon an assemblage of practices—disparate but more or less systematic—whose underlying logic is one of division, but whose immanent target is the body (speech, vision, movement) of the marked. A figure caught in processes through which particular human groups are corralled, excluded, and made to speak, with physical destruction or elimination or, as Césaire has it, murders without reason as its extreme manifestation.

Within this assemblage is the systematic incitement to disclose myriad details about the Other's deviance, based on a set of preformulated assumptions—or, phantasms—about those very differences. The Other's speech, protest, answers, behaviors, ways of living and being, therefore, can only ever serve as evidence of their irreconcilability and intractability, and legitimize their persistent interrogation. Made common sense, the racial principle works mask the generalization of the interrogation room as a social condition for the Muslim Questioned. By this, I mean to reflect on the widespread presupposition that between ourselves and those who threaten the dissolution of our enlightened ways of life, social body, and culture, there can be no cessation of hostilities. Not only are all the powers of the nation(-state) at our disposal in the delivery of the verdict to isolate and inoculate the threatening force embodied by the Muslim, but the instruments of securing ourselves against such a threat must equally overwhelm the enemy's capacity to transform themselves endlessly in their permanent plotting and conspiracy. It is for this reason that this assemblage of practices which cohere on the race-terror nexus

---

[2] Mbembe, Achille. (2017). *Critique of Black Reason*. Durham: Duke University Press, pp. 45–46.

must endlessly accumulate more and more spheres of life into its juridical purview, extra-military activities, political and psychic resources, and all their relations of force. This set of resources works to generalize the interrogation room in the name of securing the conditions of possibility for national security, prosperity, and victory. Which is to say that any relation other than hostility toward the Muslim Questioned is to risk our own Being for it would imply the possibility of closing the distance that separates us.

RADICALIZATION AND/IN THE INTERROGATION ROOM

The most obvious manifestation of these dynamics is the actual interrogation of the racial subjecthood of the Muslim, not simply on an individual basis but on the grounds of his possible belonging to a dangerous periphery of a suspicious whole. Indeed, as the recent works of Nisha Kapoor, Arun Kundnani, and others have shown us, Babar Ahmad's case was not unique but symptomatic of an entire social condition cultivated by the policies of state power and, I would add, the international historical culture which underpins dominant relations with racialized Others: Muslim, black, immigrant, poor, or otherwise. It is worth, therefore, analyzing the chief paradigms for the management of threat and (in)security, the premier discourses of inciting disclosure premised on the Other's alien nature: those of counterterrorism, counter-extremism, and in particular the concept of "radicalization" embedded, in Britain, in the expansive "Prevent" strategy.[3]

From the very beginning Prevent insisted on focusing only on Muslims,[4] with the threat of radicalization in particular (and the terror threat in general) portrayed as a problem borne of Islamic practice and Muslim communal life. Radicalization, it was argued, stemmed from individual or group *psychological* or *theological* factors (or a mixture of the two), knowledge of which was assumed to be a reliable foundation for the development of policies to reduce the risk of radicalization and future violence.[5] Bernard Lewis's notion

---

[3] The Contest strategy (2006) is the British government's counterterrorism framework originally devised in 2003 following the 9/11 attacks in the United Stated, of which Prevent is one of the four major work streams. HM Government. (2006). Countering International Terrorism: The United Kingdom's Strategy, Norwich: HMSO.

[4] DCLG (2007a, 2007b).

[5] Indeed, an external, and highly critical, evaluation of activity in Prevent concluded that: "We have been unable . . . to document any practical Prevent work in the community that is not directed in some way at Muslim communities" (cited in Kundnani, 2009: 24). *Spooked: How not to Prevent Violent Extremism.* London: Institute of Race Relations.

of "Muslim Rage"[6] proved to be a central intellectual influence on thinking about the Middle East and Muslims on both sides of the Atlantic. Such a frank state focus on British Muslims per se, on Muslim leadership, and religious interpretations within Muslim communities in particular through Prevent, perpetuated the merging of Islam and threat, which stigmatized entire Muslim communities,[7] and prompted the allegation that Muslims had replaced the Irish as Britain's "suspect community."[8] Implicit in both the theological and psychological approaches is the notion that the "new terrorism"[9] of radical Islamism operates through informal social/communitarian networks. Rather than political propaganda recruiting individuals into a group organized with a clear command structure (as, for example, the Provisional IRA was assumed to function), the suggestion is that individuals are radicalized into supporting an "ideology" as part of an informal social grouping.[10]

Crucially, the utilization of questionable concepts of "conveyer belt" journeys to "radicalization"—that individual radicalization proceeds in a linear movement from indoctrination of the vulnerable subject to particular ideas, culminating in violent terrorist behavior is paradigmatic.[11] After 7/7 there

---

[6] See. Lewis, B. (1990). "The Roots of Muslim Rage." *Atlantic Monthly*, September. Samuel Huntington in his "'clash of civilisations' thesis, went further than Lewis and popularized a 'clash of civilisations' as a general formula for understanding post–Cold War international relations and seeing Islam itself, rather than Islamic fundamentalism, as an underlying problem for the West." Kundnani, *The Muslims*, p. 57.

[7] Y. Birt. (2008). "Governing Muslims after 9/11." In *Thinking through Islamophobia: Symposium Papers*, edited by S. Sayyid and A. Vakil. Leeds: Centre for Ethnicity and Racism Studies, pp. 26–29; Kundnani, *Spooked*; R. Lambert and B. Spalek. (2008). "Muslim Communities, Counter-Terrorism and Counter-Radicalisation: A Critically Reflective Approach to Engagement." *International Journal of Law, Crime and Justice*, 36(4), 257–70; P. Thomas. (2011). *Youth, Multiculturalism and Community Cohesion*. Basingstoke: Palgrave Macmillan.

[8] M. Hickman, L. Thomas, H. Nickels, and S. Silvestri. (2012). "Social Cohesion and the Notion of Communities: A Study of the Experiences and Impact of Being Suspect for Irish Communities and Muslim Communities in Britain." *Critical Studies on Terrorism*, 5, 89–106; C. Pantazis and S. Pemberton. (2009). "From the 'Old 'to the 'New' Suspect Community: Examining the Impacts of Recent UK Counter-Terrorist Legislation." *British Journal of Criminology*, 49, 646–66; P. Thomas. (2012). *Responding to the Threat of Violent Extremism—Failing to Prevent*. London: Bloomsbury Academic.

[9] Walter Laqueur's "new terrorism" thesis distinguished between older, political forms of terrorism, inspired by nationalism, communism or fascism, and the new "Islamic fundamentalist violence" that he saw as "rooted in fanaticism." The so-called "fanatics" and their ideological sympathizers were unreformable and no political or economic change could stem their hatred. Only overwhelming force would be successful against this new enemy. See: W. Laqueur. (1999). *The New Terrorism: Fanaticism and the Arms of Mass Destruction*. New York: Oxford University Press.

[10] A. Kundnani. (2012). "Radicalisation: The Journey of a Concept." *Race and Class*, 54, 3–25; Q. Wiktorowicz. (2005). *Radical Islam Rising: Muslim Extremism in the West*. Oxford: Rowman & Littlefield.

[11] Much of the critical discussion surrounding Prevent, pursued most notably in studies by Mark Sageman, Arun Kundnani, Paul Thomas, and Vicki Coppock and Mark McGovern (2014) exposes well both the problems—conceptual and strategic—and the (political) utility of such "conveyor belt" theories. Other critical, mainly comparative studies include: Sarah Dornhof. (2009). "'Germany: Constructing a Sociology of Islamist Radicalisation." *Race & Class*, 50(4); Aziz Z. Huq.

was a widespread recognition among state policymakers that there needed to be observable mechanisms to progress a more effective preemptive and preventative counterterrorism effort. That is, progression beyond the mass surveillance of—and misplaced/poorly conceived engagement with—British Muslim communities in general and Muslim youth in particular. Therefore, a new priority became the "Channel" project,[12] a scheme whereby young people viewed as "vulnerable" to radicalization would be referred for individual counseling. Channel now forms a key part of the Prevent strategy.[13] In effect, it profiled young people who were not suspected of criminal activity but, based on indicators, were nevertheless regarded as drifting toward extremism. This was to be supported by training through the "Workshop to Raise Awareness of Prevent" (WRAP) for front-line professionals, such as teachers and health workers necessary to "educate against extremism"[14] and for how to spot signs of individual radicalization. The public profile of the Prevent scheme seemed to be reducing until the twin events of the 2013 "Islamist"-inspired murder of a soldier, Lee Rigby, and the "radicalizing" effects of the unfolding Iraq/Syria crisis which provided new challenges. This led to a re-energizing and regrowth of Prevent.[15] The climate of suspicion surrounding Muslims in general and Muslim youth in particular has become further embedded in state engagement with British Muslims and in British society at large.[16]

"Vulnerability to extremism" discourse is given powerful legitimacy via the development and application of positivistic psychological technologies, important to the (guise of) scientific and, as will become clearer, an all too familiar raciologic of radicalization and vulnerability.[17] The UK Home Office

(2010). "Modeling Terrorist Radicalization." *Duke Forum for Law & Social Change*, 2(39); Jonathan Githens-Mazer and Robert Lambert. (2010). "Why Conventional Wisdom on Radicalization Fails: The Persistence of a Failed Discourse." *International Affairs*, 86(4); Faiza Patel. (2011). *Rethinking Radicalization*. New York: Brennan Center for Justice at New York University School of Law.

[12] HM Government. (2012). *Channel: Vulnerability Assessment Frameworks*. London; HM Government. (2015a). *Channel Duty Guidance: Protecting Vulnerable People from Being Drawn into Terrorism*. London.

[13] "The process is a multi-agency approach to identify and provide support to individuals who are at risk of being drawn into terrorism." HMG, *Channel Duty Guidance*, p. 3.

[14] L. Davies. (2008). *Educating Against Extremism*. Trentham: Stoke-on-Trent.

[15] HM Government. (2013). *Tackling Extremism in the UK: Report from the Prime Minister's Task Force on Tackling Radicalisation and Extremism*. London: Author.

[16] V. Coppock and M. McGovern. (2014). "Dangerous Minds? De-constructing Counter-Terrorism Discourse, Radicalisation and the 'Psychological Vulnerability' of Muslim Children and Young People in Britain." *Children and Society*, 28, 242–56; C. Heath-Kelly. (2013). "Counter-Terrorism and the Counter-Factual: Producing the 'Radicalisation' Discourse and the UK Prevent Strategy." *The British Journal of Politics & International Relations*, 15, 394–415; Kundnani, *The Muslims*.

[17] Coppock & McGovern, "Dangerous minds"; Kundnani, "Radicalisation"; Tarek Younis. (2019) "Counter-Radicalization: A Critical Look into a Racist New Industry." *Yaqeen Institute*. Available

introduced the "Vulnerability Assessment Framework" in April 2012 to assess the "vulnerability" of those referred to its Channel program.[18] However, the notion of vulnerability as embodied by a series of indicators—referred to as "psychological hooks" in policy texts—runs the risk of those in authority viewing individuals' vulnerability on the basis of subjective opinion.[19] Official literature on "vulnerability" (and its deployment of "safeguarding" discourse alongside)[20] presents "scientism and naïve realist claims," avoiding "attention to how the knowledge, 'facts,' norms and models are the outcome of specific contextual productions and interactions."[21] Vulnerability, like extremism, is as much a vague catchall construction of counterterrorism policy than a meaningful category or sociopsychological phase through which an individual becomes particularly susceptible to radicalization.[22] "Devoid of meaningful social and political agency, divorced from the structural circumstances of their lived experiences, and problematised in terms of their mental well-being, young British Muslims are thus rendered as appropriate objects for state intervention and surveillance."[23] The particular idea of vulnerability at the heart of Prevent and Channel is framed within specific and deeply problematic conceptions of children's mental health and well-being.

---

at: https://yaqeeninstitute.org/tarekyounis/counter-radicalization-a-critical-look-into-a-racist-new -industry/#.XYC5KJNKg1I

[18] HM Government. (2012). *Channel: Vulnerability Assessment Frameworks*, London.

[19] Ibid., Annex C. The list is revealing: feelings of grievance and injustice; feeling under threat; a need for identity, meaning, and belonging; a desire for status; a desire for excitement and adventure; a need to dominate and control others; susceptibility to indoctrination; a desire for political or moral change; opportunistic involvement; family or friends' involvement in extremism; being at a transitional time of life; being influenced or controlled by a group; relevant mental health issues. The loose nature of these indicators calls into question their use as coherent guidelines for spotting vulnerability and mapping "pathways to terrorism."

[20] Especially in education: See: HM Government. (2015d). *Working Together to Safeguard Children*, London; The Office for Standards in Education, Children's Services and Skills (Ofsted). (2015). *The Common Inspection Framework: Education, Skills and Early Years*, Manchester. See also: Y. Birt. (2015). "Safeguarding Muslim Children from Daesh and Prevent." *The Muslim News*. Available at: http://www.muslimnews.co.uk/newspaper/top-stories/safeguarding-muslim-children-from -daesh-and-prevent/ (accessed 29/08/15) and Paul Thomas. (2016). "Youth, Terrorism and Education: Britain's Prevent Programme." *International Journal of Lifelong Education*, 35(2), 171–87.

[21] E. Burman. (2012). "Deconstructing Neoliberal Childhood: Towards a Feminist Antipsychological Approach." *Childhood*, 19(4), 423–438.

[22] Heath-Kelly, *Counter-Terrorism and the Counter-Factual*; Kundnani, "Radicalisation"; Kundnani, *The Muslims*.

[23] Coppock and McGovern's deconstruction of counterterrorism discourse and challenges to the purported "psychological vulnerability" of Muslim youth is useful here: V. Coppock and M. McGovern. (2014). "Dangerous Minds? De-constructing Counter-Terrorism Discourse, Radicalisation and the 'Psychological Vulnerability' of Muslim Children and Young People in Britain." *Children and Society*, 28, 242–43.

MUSLIM VULNERABILITY, INTERRUPTED

But Muslims are appropriate subjects for such interventionist processes—the *instruments of disclosure*—because of a prior authorization guaranteed by the racial principle. Those charged with the duty of "safeguarding" under Prevent and Channel, then, are potentially on the search for abstract "psychological hooks" for the threat of radicalization to which Muslims, specifically Muslim youth, are especially vulnerable. The pervasiveness of the logics of such policy in all major institutions of public life, with all its (un)intended consequences ranging from the criminal to the absurd,[24] scaffolds the public realm with a kind of mystifying passion and state of insecurity. Insecurity, as we know, is the condition upon which these structures rely, not solely for making available state resources, legal exceptions, and human labor, but for the more profound systemic charge of shaping, licensing, and directing violence toward the Other as a constitutive drive of contemporary human life. The sophisticated mechanisms of disclosure, of which Channel is but one form, must be seen in the global context of a proliferation of the privileged sites of capture and questioning for the (Muslim) Questioned; the intense multiplication of arenas in which the Other is at once made to speak and is the object of neglect, and in which both the rule of law and those subject to it are produced as legal exceptions: "Refugee camps, camps for the displaced, migrant camps, camps for foreigners, waiting areas for people pending status, transit zones, administrative detention centres, identification or expulsion centres, border crossings, welcome centres for asylum-seekers, temporary welcome centres, refugee towns, migrant integration towns, ghettos, jungles, hostels, migrant homes."[25]

---

[24] The new statutory duty for those with safeguarding duties to engage with Prevent after the Counter-Terrorism and Security Act 2015 is, with growing frequency, bordering on the absurd and overreactions are not difficult to find. A Muslim boy who misspelled a word during an English lesson, writing that he lived in a "terrorist house," was reported and interviewed by the police in accordance with the CTSA. See: Kathryn Snowden. (2016). "Muslim Boy's 'Terrorist House' Spelling Error Leads to Lancashire Police Investigation." *Huff Post*. Available at: http://m.huffpost .com/uk/entry/9025336. Similarly, a four-year-old boy at nursery meant "cucumber" not "cooker bomb" and was reported to authorities and said to be on the pathway to radicalization. See: Asian Network Reports. (2016). "Boy at Nursery Meant 'Cucumber' not 'Cooker Bomb'." Available at: http://www.bbc.co.uk/programmes/p03m5jh9. But the point here is that the culture of suspicion promoted by Prevent will likely increase such cases and further deepen the demonizing of Muslims in school and in wider society, despite the fact that 90 percent of referrals lead to no action being taken.

[25] Mbembe, "Society of Enmity," p. 32. See. Michel Agier, ed. (2014). *Un monde de camps, La Découverte*, Paris; L. Mayblin. (2017). *Asylum After Empire: Colonial Legacies in the Politics of Asylum Seeking*. London: Rowman and Littlefield International; L. Mayblin, M. Kazemi, and M. Wake. (2019). "Necropolitics and the Slow Violence of the Everyday: Asylum Seeker Welfare in the Postcolonial Present." *Sociology*.

The war on terror and the prospect of European weakening have together heightened concerns of racial interest, native prosperity, and the Muslim subject as its enemy, and licensed the governmentalization of the camp. That is, the multiplication of emptied spaces simultaneously fenced off to any ethics of democracy and fenced in by its ever-present exception, designed to dump those not of our kind,[26] places of neglect and separation which attempt to disappear the complex questions of migrancy and racism, terror and war, hostility and hospitality, abandonment and radicalization, constructing them instead as an ever-present reality to the point of banality. But as Hannah Arendt has shown, the banal can in effect license the extreme.[27] The brutality and excesses of these sites are no longer shocking but become necessary solutions for "keeping away what disturbs, for containing or rejecting all excess, whether it is human, organic matter or industrial waste."[28]

Vulnerability then has two faces: our constant vulnerability to the violent excesses of the Other and the Other's inherent vulnerability to violent excess. Present discourse about the roots of "Islamic terrorism" and its relation to Islamic texts—namely the Qur'an—from which the Muslim learns how to perpetuate in a more insidious way the racial, ideological edge stipulating a tendency toward violence peculiar among Muslims thus necessitating their encampment and/or legitimate disposability. There are all too often two contradictory assumptions underlying state-sponsored claims of "root causes" of Muslim deviance which populate the lines of expansive national security policy, special military dispositions, and large research grant applications alike, all geared in a relation of mutual constitution toward knowing and mastering the Muslim. As Talal Asad summarizes,

> (a) the Qur'anic text will force Muslims to be guided by it; and (b) that Christians and Jews are free to interpret the Bible as they please. For no good reason, these assumptions take up contradictory positions between text and reader: On the one hand, the religious *text* is held to be determinate, fixed in its sense, and having the power to bring about particular beliefs (that in turn give rise to particular behaviour) among those exposed to it-rendering readers passive. On the other hand, the religious *reader* is taken to be actively engaged in constructing the meaning of texts in accordance with changing social circumstances-so the texts are passive. . . . A magical quality is attributed to Islamic religious texts, for they are said to be both essentially univocal (their meaning *cannot* be subject

---

[26] Alexander Barder. (2015). *Empire Within: International Hierarchy and Its Imperial Laboratories of Governance*. Oxon: Routledge.

[27] Hannah Arendt, 1906–1975. (1994). *Eichmann in Jerusalem : A Report on the Banality of Evil*. New York: Penguin Books.

[28] Barder, *Empire*, p. 11.

to dispute, just as "fundamentalists" insist) and infectious (except in relation to the orientalist, who is, fortunately for him, immune to their dangerous power). In fact in Islam as in Christianity there is a complicated history of shifting interpretations, and the distinction is recognized between the divine text and human approaches to it.[29]

The orientalist, then as now, does not only refer to the individual scholar, or state strategist, or bureaucrat, or policymaker, but the entire *formation*—institutional as well as national—that gives prior legitimacy to these assumptions, the forms of questioning and the attendant violence and neglect that often follow. Which is to say that because "race" has played such an integral conceptual and material function in the formation of the modern national body and subject, and the form of sovereign (security) state power to which it is subject and through which it is reproduced, the contradictions in the above set of assumptions that inform surveillance and interventionist mechanisms do not matter in the least. Though they present conflicting analyses of individual (Muslim) agency, reason and the power of the Text, both ultimately reassert the concomitant aberrant knowability of Muslims and their dangerous surreptitiousness in our towns and cities, schools, and workplaces.

Of course, the concomitance between the threat of Muslim "fanaticism" spread as homogenous group feeling is nothing new. The formation of a united Muslim front against the British Empire influenced by thinkers such as Jamaluddin al-Afghani (d. 1897) and the policies of Abdul Hamid II are precedents for the production of notions of Muslim fanaticism and collective ideology.[30] The "fanatic" and his potential to form a network with other like-minded people as threats to the empire became just another name for "Muslim." Pan-Islamism was always already pan-fanaticism. The racial habitus that formed generations of British subjects by the twentieth century brought with it a whole system of naming and an archive of images[31] and collected taxonomies of the racial body that, in turn, legitimated the full range of policies and material practices which remade the colonized and their

---

[29] Asad, *Formations*, pp. 10–11.
[30] Francis Robinson. (1999). "The British Empire and the Muslim World." In *The Oxford History of the British Empire, Volume IV: The Twentieth Century*, edited by Judith Brown, pp. 405–406.
[31] See especially: John M. (John MacDonald) Mackenzie. (1986). *Imperialism and Popular Culture*. Manchester, UK: Manchester University Press; John Mackenzie. (1999). "The Popular Culture of Empire in Britain." In *The Oxford History of the British Empire*, edited by W. R. Louis, and J. M. Brown. Oxford: Oxford University Press. See also: Muneeb Hafiz. (2018). "Brexit, Propaganda and Empire." *Discover Society*. Available at:https://discoversociety.org/2018/12/04/focus-brexit-propaganda-and-empire/; Bob Bessant. (1994). "British Imperial Propaganda and the Republic." *Journal of Australian Studies*, 18(42), 1–4; J. Coutu. (2006). *Persuasion and Propaganda: Monuments and the Eighteenth-Century British Empire*. McGill-Queen's University Press; M. Stanard. (2009). "Interwar Pro-Empire Propaganda and European Colonial Culture: Toward a Comparative Research Agenda." *Journal of Contemporary History*, 44(1), 27–48.

societies. The anxiogenic character of our times has resuscitated an epistemology of distance and old questions of ontological difference in the service
of the Other's incessant disclosure *and* erasure under the aegis of "radical,"
"Islamic," "ideology," and the peculiar vulnerabilities of the Muslim subject
to its exuberant and civilization-destroying effects.

The auspices of Western wars on/of terror have in many ways, however,
instituted a new era and innovative economies of warfare and slaughter
today with smart bombing, surgical strikes, aerial bombardments, manhunts
at the level of genomic data and biometry, and, crucially, the drone. Or elsewhere we find extrajudicial executions, state-sanctioned murder, and the
sinister intimacies of the technologies and international relations through
which they become possible. But the hard matter constituting technologies and fissile matter of tracking and capture, and the rapid calculation of
machineries of death through which the earth itself becomes transparent
are encased in a resurfacing and comforting idea; the idea of the West as
the chosen province of the world capable of knowing the universal against
Others who cannot or to whom it must be revealed. The advanced character
of war today becomes then the delivery mechanism of this revelation; a
form of war-power whose theater is both internal and external, horizontal
and vertical, solid and livestreamed, which brings with it a scaffold of legal
exceptions and spectacular violence that seeks to mirror in the process
the domesticity of the video game. Crucially, the mutual consolidation of
political, "ordinary" police, immigration, and military spheres through and
with surveillance collection, their transport routes, and special dispensa-
tions—both commercial and legal—has become a premier model of governing the racial subject. It is no longer enough to find the enemy and unmask
him before he is dispatched or disappeared. He must instead be created; he
must first be conceived as the subject of nightmares, a subject whose malign
presence might everywhere infect the body of civilization, in order for him
to be found, drawn out, and confronted in a war-like relation that can have
no limits: moral or legal.

This amounts to a peculiar logic of capture based on twinned conceptions of our simultaneous *victimhood* (besieged as we are by the active
cunning of the Other) in a moment of European demotion and fracture, and
virile power (with a machinery of seizure and death of global reach) in the
service of tracking, enclosing, and classifying the Muslim Questioned and
making him confess. Because security officials are interested in patterns of
(Muslim) belief and behavior that must correlate with terrorist risk, irrespec-
tive of whether they cause terrorism,[32] questions of causality are usually left

---

[32] From the beginning the construction of Muslims as a "suspect community," that the terror threat
originated from within this homogenized grouping, there was a danger of changing the nature of

unaddressed in radicalization discourse, despite its claim to be interested in "root causes."[33] But of course, causality is always secondary in this equation because (Muslim) difference and distance as we have defined them here are foregone conclusions.[34] All that is left to do, therefore, is to maintain a constant vigilance in acquiring "knowledge" about Muslims, their homogenous culture and ideology, that might prompt their slow journey away from suspicion but have the effect of turning the Muslim into aggregated data, a group of racial codes and categories of risk legible to institutions of violence and the juridical methods through which their work is secured. The point of departure must always be guilt, its remedy likewise incessant confession. This circular motion of confirming that which we already know—the Muslim subject is Other and therefore the study of radicalization is in effect the study of that racial Otherness—is an established mode of hostile relation with disciplined population groups in the history of race and state. Yet knowledge produced about the racial subject, here the Muslim, is undergoing rapid transformation in its reach, level of analysis and fields of relation.[35]

---

responsibility in the imaginations of counterterrorism officials. C. Pantazis and S. Pemberton. (2009). "From the 'Old 'to the 'New' Suspect Community: Examining the Impacts of Recent UK counter-terrorist legislation." *British Journal of Criminology* 49: 646–66. British Muslims in society, Muslim young men in particular, were quickly seen not as citizens to whom the state is accountable but as potential recruits to the ideological threat. This perspective utilizes Sederberg's analogy of terrorism as "disease," the *causes* being—more accurately the *conditions* under which—the myriad psychological-theological factors listed in Prevent literature could infect young Muslims. P. Sederberg. (2003). "Global Terrorism: Problems of Challenge and Response." In *The Control of the New Global Terrorism*, edited by C. W. Kegley. New York: Pearson, pp. 267–84.

[33] Kundnani, "Radicalisation," pp. 10–11.

[34] The concept of radicalization became, according to Neumann, a vehicle that allowed discussions of the forces that underpin terrorism to become possible again. In actuality, however, the radicalization discourse inherited a number of assumptions which would come to frame counterterrorism policy. P. Neumann. (2008). *Perspectives on Radicalization and Political Violence: Papers from the First International Conference on Radicalization and Political Violence*. London: International Centre for the Study of Radicalization and Political Violence, p. 4. What is at the center of this new radicalization discourse is the individual and, to an extent, the ideology and group. Thus, wider contexts and declared grievances are often neglected in analyses of radicalization presenting the Islamist as a "rebel without a cause." M. Sedgwick. (2010). "The Concept of Radicalisation as a Source of Confusion." *Terrorism and Political Violence,* 22(4): 48–81. See also: Kundnani, "Radicalisation," p. 5; Kundnani, *The Muslims,* p. 116. Coppock and McGovern, "Dangerous Minds," p. 242.

[35] This is a feature of post-9/11 research. Instead they have tended to focus on approaches which provide state officials with a supposedly scientific basis for assessing "indicators of risk" of "vulnerability to radicalization," the central concern of radicalization discourse/theories. Coppock & McGovern, "Dangerous mind"; Kundnani, *Spooked*; "Radicalisation"; Sedgewick, Mamdani, *Good Muslim*; Zillah Eisentein. (2004). *Against Empire: Feminisms, Racism and the West.* London: Zed Books; Hamid Dabashi. (2009). *Post-Orientalism: Knowledge and Power in a Time of Terror.* New Jersey: Transaction Publishers.

THE SUBJECT OF CONFESSION

We should think about these indicators of threat and measures of vulnerability as a wide array of questions asked of Muslims in the hopes of having them disclose information which must confirm, always inadequately, the passivity of their views and docility of their public/political presence.[36] While, on the one hand, it is understood and frequently repeated that the terrorist threat vis-à-vis Muslims in Britain came from "radicalised individuals who are using a distorted and unrepresentative interpretation of the Islamic faith to justify violence,"[37] and "a tiny minority who oppose tolerance and diversity,"[38] counter-radicalization documents state nonetheless that a "key measure of success will be demonstrable changes in attitudes among Muslims."[39] This in turn legitimizes a quick move from a particular strategic focus on certain ideas to the need for certain identities and practices. Reflecting again on the peculiar logic of capture, "radicalization" and its broader industry should be thought of in the context of desire and appetite. The political economy of radicalization is rooted in the rationalization of phantasms and the circulation of type-images, and regimes of counterterrorism which must continually "invent" the terrorizing object-subject veiled in newer significations: behavior, attitudes, cultural proclivities and tendencies, and inherent vulnerabilities, all of which could never be mine. These invented phantasms of race, of which the everywhere-Muslim is an extreme manifestation, is not a real one, and marks a shadow into which all evils that are not ours can be emptied, but which leave its manufacturers haunted by their own invention. And these significations become sufficient "knowledge" and "evidence" for the intense operation of surveillance, codification, "engagement," in sum, procedures of disclosure

---

[36] Even the more holistic studies of (Al-Qaida) terrorism and its root causes ultimately reinforce such conveyor belt theories of radicalization with a canny "psychologisation of threat" disseminated and embedded within/through informal social networks. Most notably authored by scholar-strategists such as Sageman and Wiktorowicz, both central advisors in the war on terror effort, which begin cogently by situating terrorist violence within their myriad social-political-religious contexts but confirm a tired narrative. M. Sageman. (2004). *Understanding Terror Networks.* Philadelphia: University of Pennsylvania Press; M. Sageman. (2008). *Leaderless Jihad: Terror Networks in the Twenty First Century.* Philadelphia: University of Pennsylvania Press; M. Sageman. (2008). "The Next Generation of Terror." *Foreign Policy* 165: 37–42; Q. Wiktorowicz. (2005). *Radical Islam Rising: Muslim Extremism in the West.* Oxford: Rowman & Littlefield.

[37] HM Government. (2006). *Countering International Terrorism: The United Kingdom's Strategy.* Norwich: HMSO, p. 1.

[38] DCLG, *Preventing Violent Extremism: Guidance,* p. 2. See also: Greg Kennedy and Christopher Tuck. (2014). *British Propaganda and Wars of Empire: Influencing Friend and Foe, 1900-2010.* Oxford: Oxford University Press, p. 225; T. O'Toole, N. Meer, D. N. DeHanas, S. H. Jones, and T. Modood. (2016). "Governing through Prevent? Regulation and Contested Practice in State–Muslim Engagement." *Sociology,* 50(1), 160–77.

[39] DCLG. (2007b). *Preventing Violent Extremism Guidance Note for Government Offices and Local Authorities in England.* London: Author, p. 7.

which in turn reinforce the necessary existence of the Muslim Questioned and the excesses they demand.[40]

Excesses of the kind that authorized Project Champion:[41] a police surveillance operation involving the installation of 216 CCTV cameras in Birmingham's largely Muslim suburbs of Washwood Heath and Sparkbrook, creating a "surveillance ring" around these areas. Importantly, the counter-terrorism purpose of the cameras was concealed from local residents, and the cameras were badged as a "crime safety initiative" with deeply flawed, community consultation. Further still, local councilors were not told that the cameras were paid for with money from the "terrorism and allied matters" fund.[42] Such overt surveillance initiatives as Project Champion "represent a move beyond territorial control to the management of circulations." Where subjects are indeed in/of a place targeted by techniques of security practice but "their mobilities are monitored, delineated and assessed"[43] underpinned and, in turn, legitimized by highly problematic assumptions.[44]

This much is true. However, the tracking of movements, the sponsorship of lucrative state funding in return for the knitting of surveillance mechanisms within seemingly banal community cohesion work, and the changing

---

[40] Excesses such as the mapping of Muslim communities. See: Khalida Khan. (2009). *Preventing Violent Extremism & Prevent: A Response from the Muslim Community*. London: An-Nisa Society, p. 4.

[41] P. Fussey. (2013). "Contested Topologies of UK Counterterrorist Surveillance: The Rise and Fall of Project Champion." *Critical Studies on Terrorism*, 6(3), 351–70; A. Isakjee and C. Allen. (2013). "'A Catastrophic Lack of Inquisitiveness': A Critical Study of the Impact and Narrative of the Project Champion Surveillance Project in Birmingham." *Ethnicities*, 13(6), 751–70; T. O'Toole, N. Meer, D. N. DeHanas, S. H. Jones, and T. Modood. (2016). "Governing through Prevent? Regulation and Contested Practice in State-Muslim Engagement." *Sociology*, 50(1), 160–77.

[42] While not itself a Prevent initiative, Project Champion did much to undermine the implementation of Prevent, if only through the very high levels of suspicion toward the program. Other useful commentaries on Project Champion: A. Akhtar. (2010). "A Muslim Community, Securitised." *Guardian*. Available at: https://www.theguardian.com/commentisfree/belief/2010/jun/20/muslim -birmingham-surveillance; S. Jolly. (2010). "Birmingham's Spy-Cam Scheme Has Had its cover blown." *Guardian*. Available at: https://www.theguardian.com/commentisfree/libertycentral/2010 /jun/23/birmingham-spy-cam-scheme.

[43] Fussey, "Contested Topologies," pp. 351–52. In the throes of a global terror war, or alternatively, imperialism as a global project, there is a "steady replacement of the citizen by the human being, whose biological security now routinely trumps his rights of citizenship in anti-terror measures at home and humanitarian interventions abroad." Devji, *Terrorist*, p.7.

[44] A similarly damaging finding has been the "strategic communications" work of the Home Office's Research, Information and Communications Unit (Ricu). Modelled on the IRD, a propaganda unit set up by the Atlee government in 1948. See: Ruth Blakely, Ben Hayes, Nisha Kapoor, Arun Kundnani, Narzanin Massoumi, David Miller, Tom Mills, Rizwan Sabir, Katy Sian, and Waqas Tufail. (2019: chapter 3c). *Leaving the War on Terror: A Progressive Alternative to Counter-Terrorism Policy*. Amsterdam: Transnational Institute. The aims of Ricu have quite explicitly been "to effect behavioural and attitudinal change" of British Muslims. See. I. Cobain, R. Evans, M. Mahmood, and A. Ross. (2016). "Inside Ricu, the Shadowy Propaganda Unit Inspired by the Cold War." *Guardian*. Available at: https://www.theguardian.com/politics/2016/may/02/inside-ricu-the -shadowy-propaganda-unit-inspired-by-the-cold-war.

of attitudes among Muslims in Britain (to what we are still uncertain) should each be thought of as *instruments of disclosure according to a principle of race*. The extraction of information, both with and without the consent of its sources, is propelled, legitimated, and classified according to the logic of race which underscores a particular population group as necessitating constant marking, tracking, and entrapment within a thoroughly integrated institutional fabric: the interrogation room as a social condition constituted by an assemblage of security practices and new legal norms. The explicit mechanisms of surveillance and state violence, in conjunction with state patronage in the form of public funding for the mapping of Muslim attitudes, all speak to this social condition for the racial subject, his Islam, and the systemic fabric of racism.

In this era of national security and radicalization, "all government departments needed to be plugged in to the machinery of counterterrorism. And the local authority chief executive in East Lancashire was as significant to the government's integrated response as the army commander in Lashkar Gah. The Prevent program pressed staff of the former to see themselves as engaged on an ideological battlefield whose human terrain was Muslim citizens."[45] We can observe the focus on ideological convictions as precursors to radicalization—ideology, that is Islam itself as the "root cause"—along with a parallel expansion and reorganization of the agents tasked with tackling this ideology, as blurring the boundaries of the foreign and the domestic, though the thread connecting the two is the problem of the Muslim.[46] Regardless of the actual pertinence of the massive amount of data disclosed, collected, and flowcharted for stopping terrorist violence, the maybe-maybe not logic of the security state renders the Muslim always potentially criminal, and means that the racism of counterterrorism and counter-radicalization policies is everywhere sustained. The Muslim Questioned must, after all, remain a disturbing object, matter out of place.

Hazel Blears, then communities secretary, would go further and see it fit to argue that, "[t]his country is proud of its tradition of fair play and good manners, welcoming of diversity, tolerant of others. This is a great strength.

---

[45] Kundnani, *The Muslims*, p. 162. State responses to terrorism have, therefore, gone far beyond "exceptional measures" and manifested themselves in a wholesale reorganizing of "everyday 'normal' political and bureaucratic rationalities." L. Mavelli. (2013). "Between Normalisation and Exception: The Securitisation of Islam and the Construction of the Secular Subject." *Millennium: Journal of International Studies,* 41(2), 159–81.

[46] Ironically, however, the gathering of vast quantities of information has meant law enforcement and intelligence agencies—the drivers of Prevent in its securitized nature—are, in fact, less efficient at connecting material to specific criminal acts, which, in turn, means they are less effective at detecting actual terrorist plots, information about which "was somewhere in the government's systems, but its significance was lost amid a morass of useless data." Ibid., *The Muslims*, p. 284.

But the pendulum has swung too far."[47] Rarely is there a mention of the serial, everyday uses and abuses of the names "Muslim" and "Islam" in practices and industries of radicalization and counterterrorism propelled by logics of separation and encampment, these abuses instead being naturalized in ostensibly banal or well-meaning concerns around integration and the health of the democratic civic order that serve as cuts and bruises on the presence of Muslims in Britain. The Muslim Questioned, as the privileged subject of disclosure,

> constantly run[s] the risk of letting themselves be touched in the most intense manner by someone—an institution, a voice, a public or private authority—asking them to justify who they are, why they are here, where they come from, where they are going, why they don't go back to where they came from; in other words, a voice or authority which deliberately seeks to cause them a large or small shock, to irritate them, to hurt them, injure them, to get them to lose their cool and self-composure as a pretext to violate them, to slander and debase without restraint that which is most private, most intimate, and vulnerable, in them.[48]

This is the racial logic of the assemblage that is the Muslim Questioned and its everyday harms that are its fuel. That an aspect of these mechanisms of suspicion and detection under the sponsorship of "radicalization" is to irritate, to hurt, to provoke a loss of the Other's composure is not up for debate here. That slander against the Muslim might lead to a reaction on their part which is, in turn, cast as evidence justifying that slander—the intersorption of guilt and interrogation for the Muslim—is instead obscured by Blears's easy pronouncement of innocence and excessive British tolerance.[49] It is

---

[47] Blears, H. (2009). "Many Voices: Understanding the Debate About Prevent Violent Extremism." *Migration Studies Unit lecture series LSE.* Available at: http://www.lse.ac.uk/publicEvents/events /2008/20081203t1539z001.aspx.

[48] Mbembe, "Society of Enmity," p. 31.

[49] Charles Farr, the head of Prevent, furthers Blears' remarks to rationalize a more focused (and by focused I mean a police/CTU-led) approach to the objective Prevent: "It does seem to me from where I sit entirely appropriate that this Government, and I think probably any other government, will want to challenge aspects of what we might call Islamism which fall short of espousing violence—[. . .] views in some quarters here that western culture is evil and that Muslims living in this country should not engage with western cultural organisations, for want of a better term, with western culture itself. There is nothing violent about that and it is not necessarily going to lead to terrorism, but it does seem to me to be unreal for this or any other government not to say that they are going to challenge that, and that is no more nor less than what this Government is now saying." Farr goes on to contend that the government is saying: "Yes, we will challenge violent extremism and, by the way, we will criminalise it and we will proscribe groups who espouse it, but we want to go a bit further. We are not going to sit on the sidelines and listen without responding to either Islamist extremist views or indeed to the far right." House of Commons Home Affairs Committee. (2009). *Project CONTEST: The Government's Counter-terrorism Strategy: Ninth Report of Session 2009-09.* London: The Stationary Office Limited, Q171. Again, a causal relationship between an extremist ideology and terrorist actions is assumed. The Prevent strategy summarizes this

never really considered that "what governments call extremism is to a large degree a product of their own wars."[50] "Race" and racism have long had the function of erasing all context—at once social and historical—and avoiding questions of motivation that extend beyond the pathological tendencies of unreason of the racialized. It is also on the basis of this erasure, however, that new instruments of disclosure and global networks of data flows and deportation routes through which the disturbing figure of the Muslim travels are legitimized. The paradox here is that the field of vision, for both state agencies and researchers, is at once near-planetary—the everywhere-jihadi— and yet cast as an individual problem of the racial subject and others-of-her-kind. Policies under the auspices of counterterrorism and radicalization are involved in the production and capture of figures and legends. The Muslim and her Islam, whose emptiness can be filled with all our fears and proliferating classifications, leave us with a tale about the Muslim with which we are already familiar.

THE EVENT OF DISCLOSURE

Ultimately, the Muslim Questioned and his/her Islam are *known* entities, subject in the paradigm of hostility to classifications, indices, lists, flowcharts, and other measures of risk. There is, furthermore, a peculiar satisfaction that is gained from the successes (and excesses) of questioning and the work of race in the service of disclosure that was evidenced in the home of Babar Ahmad in 2003. There is a thrill in the paradigm of hostility, constituted as it is by an exuberant desire and economy of capture, that accompanies one's capacity to demonize "enemies" beyond the confines of humanity, beyond all possibility of relations of reciprocity or care. In a permanent war on terror which brings together unbridled impulses of patriotism and militarism, there is a kind of pleasure gained "when a presumed enemy is shot down by special forces or when he is captured alive and subjected to endless interrogations, rendered and tortured in one of the many so-called 'black sites' that stain the

---

neatly: "Central to the development of any movement or group is the construction of an ideological framework. Ideology offers its believers a coherent set of ideas that provide the basis for organised political action, whether it is intended to preserve, modify or overthrow the existing system of power. Ideology may also coordinate activity in the absence of leadership or a command structure. [. . .] Ideology is a central factor in the radicalisation process. People who accept and are motivated by an ideology which states that violence is an acceptable course of action are more likely to engage in terrorism-related activity. People who come to believe in such an ideology may be not only willing to kill but also to sacrifice their own lives. Challenging that ideology is therefore an essential part of a preventative counter-terrorism programme." Home Office. (2011). *Prevent*. London: Home Office, p. 44.

[50] Kundnani, *The Muslims*, p. 15.

surface of our planet."[51] This perverse pleasure, furthermore, is underpinned by massive economic, political, and psychic resources which reproduce so often images of the predatory capacity of special military and police forces, a capacity and preparedness that is increasingly naturalized or integrated into everyday social spheres to the point of ordinariness. One has only to remember the case of Shamima Begum, the sinister delight and the outpouring of callous imagery in the form of "'memes,'"[52] and the use of her deprivation of citizenship as fodder for all manner of intrigue and moronic humor to understand this perverse pleasure.

On Tuesday, February 10, 2015, schoolfriends Shamima Begum, fifteen, Kadiza Sultan, sixteen, and Amira Abase, fifteen, traveled from Bethnal Green in east London to Turkey and then crossed into ISIS-controlled areas of Syria. In February 2019, Shamima Begum, now nineteen, was found heavily pregnant in the Al-Hawl refugee camp in north-eastern Syria pleading for her return to the United Kingdom, hoping that "for the sake of her child" that she be allowed to come back. On February 16, Begum gave birth to a son, Jarrah, her third child after her two other children had died while she had been living in Raqqa and had been "married off" to Yago Riedijk ten days after her arrival in 2015.[53]

Predictably, a national conversation ensued, debating whether and why Shamima Begum, now an adult and mother, should be allowed back home to Britain. Fundamental to a trial by media has been an interview in which "her seeming indifference and her lack of remorse for marrying an ISIS

---

[51] Mbembe, "Society of Enmity," p. 26. See also: Mohamedou Ould Slahi. (2015). *Les Carnets de Guantanamo*. Paris: Michel Lafon.

[52] A Google Search for "Shamima Begum memes" produces over 150,000 results, many of which recast Begum using well-known memetic characters and forms popular across social media/On the "meme" itself, see: Johnson, D. (2007). "Mapping the Meme: A Geographical Approach to Materialist Rhetorical Criticism." *Communication & Critical/Cultural Studies*, 4(1), 27–50; M. Knobel and C. Lankshear. (2007). *A New Literacies Sampler*. New York: Peter Lang; G. M. Jones and B. B. Schieffelin. (2009). "Talking Text and Talking Back: 'My BFF Jill' from Boob Tube to You-Tube." *Journal of Computer Mediated Communication*, 14(4), 1050–79; W. L. Bennett. (2003). "New Media Power: The Internet and Global Activism." In *Contesting Media Power,* edited by N. Couldry and J. Curran. Lanham, MD: Rowman & Littlefield, pp. 17–37; and J. Burgess. (2008). "All Your Chocolate Rain Are Belong to Us? Viral Video, YouTube and the Dynamics of Participatory Culture." In *Video Vortex Reader: Responses to YouTube,* edited by G. Lovink and S. Niederer. Amsterdam, Netherlands: Institute of Network Cultures, pp. 101–109; L. Shifman. (2013). "Memes in a Digital World: Reconciling with a Conceptual Troublemaker." *Journal of Computer Mediated Communication*, 18, 362–77; L. Shifman. (2014). "The Cultural Logic of Photo-Based Meme Genres." *Journal of Visual Culture*, 13(3), 340–58.

[53] Her children, a daughter called Sarayah and son called Jerah, were born before January 2017. "Her son died three months ago, aged eight months, of an unknown illness and malnutrition. She tried to take him to an Isis hospital but there were no drugs available and not enough medical staff. Her daughter then grew sick and died aged one year and nine months." Available at: https://www.thetimes.co.uk/article/isis-bride-shamima-begum-i-regret-everything-please-let-me-start-my-life-again-in-britain-9g0tn08vn

fighter" was used to "confirm her apparent inhumanity and her monstrous tendencies."[54] Then-home secretary Sajid Javid initially indicated that it could prove very difficult to strip Begum of her British citizenship, a decision not normally taken against an individual without another nationality and who was born in Britain. Javid, skirting the specifics of the Begum case in response to a question, said, "if an individual only has one citizenship, then generally the power cannot be used because by definition if you took away their British citizenship, they would be stateless. . . . I certainly haven't done that, and I am not aware that one of my predecessors has done that in a case where they know an individual only has one citizenship, as that would be breaking international law as we understand it."[55]

Nevertheless, on February 19, it emerged that the Home Office had written to Begum's family to inform them that an order was in the process of being made which would enact the home secretary's power of citizenship deprivation, a power legitimated by a clause in the 1981 British Nationality Act where the Secretary is "satisfied that deprivation is conducive to the public good."[56] When asked about his decision, Javid said, "I have not deployed the power on the basis that someone could have citizenship to a second country. I've always applied it on the strict advice of legal advisors in the Home Office and more broadly in the government that when the power is deployed with respect to that individual, they already have more than one citizenship."[57] Begum's family stressed repeatedly that she did not have Bangladeshi citizenship, with the government of Bangladesh also confirming that she did not. Javid curiously confirmed that Begum's third child, Jarrah, would be a UK national stating that British-born mothers like Begum had that right at least. However, he was careful to add that it would be "incredibly difficult" to assist the newborn given the danger of their location, a refugee camp in northern Syria.

Shamima Begum learned of these developments for the first time when asked to read the order given by Sajid Javid live on air as part of an exclusive

[54] Nisha Kapoor. (2019). "Citizenship Deprivation at the Nexus of Race, Gender and Geopolitics." *Verso Blog.* Available at: https://www.versobooks.com/blogs/4250-citizenship-deprivation-at-the-nexus-of-race-gender-and-geopolitics

[55] Peter Walker. (2019). "Sajid Javid: Difficult to Strip Shamima Begum of UK Citizenship." *Guardian.* Available at:https://www.theguardian.com/uk-news/2019/feb/27/sajid-javid-difficult-to-strip-shamima-begum-of-uk-citizenship

[56] HMG. (1981). *British Nationality Act 1981,* Subsection 40[5]. Available at: http://www.legislation.gov.uk/ukpga/1981/61. See the excellent work by legal scholar Nadine El-Enany concerning the imperial inheritance of contemporary British immigration and asylum legislation: Nadine El-Enany. (2019). *(B)Ordering Britain. Law, Race and Empire.* Manchester: Manchester University Press.

[57] Walker, "Sajid Javid."

interview with ITV.[58] Following Begum's reading aloud of the Home Office order, the interviewer asks Begum, "So the Home Secretary has deprived you of your British citizenship?" Begum replies, "Yeah, but I have heard that other people have been sent back to Britain, so I don't know why my case is any different to other people. Or is it just because I was in the news four years ago? It's kind of heart-breaking to read." To which the interviewer replies, "But *you've* done this to your son, I mean this is a consequence of your actions," later asking, "what would your message to the Home Secretary be?" Begum asks for sympathy and understanding and for "a reason why they see me as a threat to the UK." When asking Begum for her message to her family, the interviewer says, "you've destroyed their lives . . . how do you feel about that?" The interview is a deeply invasive spectacle, saturated with extreme close-ups on Begum's confused face and the interviewer's questions barely masking the taunt-like character of their impulse all of which make for uncomfortable viewing. The decision to deprive Shamima Begum of her citizenship appears to be final. On Friday, March 8, the death of Jarrah was confirmed having been buried along with two other children who were burned in a fire on Thursday night.[59]

We are reminded in this case that the Muslim Questioned is precisely and necessarily imaged and imagined fodder to satiate the insatiable appetite of a racial formation which must continually produce the racial subject. The will for the Other's incessant disclosure, regardless of the fact that their speech falls on deaf ears, is ultimately based on an equally unrelenting desire to place a minimal value on the lives of those who do not, or cannot be allowed

---

[58] ITV News. (2019). "Shamima Begum Interview: The Moment IS Bride Learns She's Lost UK Citizenship." *ITV News Online*. Available at: https://www.youtube.com/watch?v=CMFTjKgAWfg

[59] Following the confirmation of the child's death, a government spokesperson said, "The death of any child is tragic and deeply distressing for the family. The Foreign and Commonwealth Office has consistently advised against travel to Syria since April 2011. The government will continue to do whatever we can to prevent people from being drawn into terrorism and travelling to dangerous conflict zones." On March 10, it was reported that two more British women, sisters Reema, thirty, and Zara Iqbal, twenty-eight, with five young children between them, have had their citizenship removed under the same powers enacted in the Begum case. For details of the case's unfolding, see: Josh Halliday, Aisha Gani and Vikram Dodd. (2015). "UK Police Launch Hunt for London Schoolgirls Feared to Have Fled to Syria." *Guardian*. Available at:https://www.theguardian.com /world/2015/feb/20/fears-london-schoolgirls-isis-syria; Mattha Busby and Vikram Dodd. (2019). "London Schoolgirl Who Fled to Join Isis Wants to Return to UK." *Guardian*. Available at: https://www.theguardian.com/world/2019/feb/14/london-schoolgirl-who-fled-to-join-isis-wants-to -return-to-uk; Frances Perraudin and Vikram Dodd. (2019). "Isis Briton Shamima Begum Pleads to Return to UK after Giving Birth." *Guardian*. Available at: https://www.theguardian.com/uk -news/2019/feb/17/shamima-begum-who-fled-uk-to-join-isis-has-given-birth-say-family; Martin Chulov, Nazia Parveen, and Mohammed Rasool. (2019). "Shamima Begum: Baby Son Dies in Syrian Refugee Camp." *Guardian*. Available at: https://www.theguardian.com/uk-news/2019/ mar/08/shamima-begum-confusion-after-reports-newborn-son-may-have-died; Dipesh Gdher and Caroline Wheeler. (2019). "UK Sisters Who Wed Isis Fighters Lose Citizenship." *The Times*. Available at: https://www.thetimes.co.uk/edition/news/uk-sisters-who-wed-isis-fighters-lose-citi- zenship-36sz69fn9

to, belong even with the requisite documentation, proof of citizenship, and entitlement to hospitality. And given the specific historical facts of modern Britain and Europe, the placeless and unbelonging are all too often racialized Others, traveling from parts of the former empire, or from conflicted lands witness to contemporary acts of imperial violence of the British state both of which remain pertinent to Begum's case.[60] The historical echoes of the carceral landscape of the colony and the techno-economies of wars on/of terror instead return home to the heart of empire in the deprivation of Shamima Begum's citizenship.

Begum's profile is one of unconscionable "betrayal." That in traveling to Syria and joining ISIS, Begum had acted against the interests of the nation though symptomatic of the people from which she comes—Muslims—and, therefore, depriving her of her British citizenship is to communicate symbolically that she cannot legitimately belong to the nation. But as Kapoor wrote recently,

> This is its populist appeal. But this is a construction of the British nation that is once again abjectly silent on the matter of Empire. . . . The dramatic rise of ISIS from 2012 is the result of various intersecting factors—"the destructive spread of sectarianism, the devastating repression in Syria and Iraq, and the interests of different regional and international powers in the Middle East." Britain plays here a deep role, both historic and contemporary, in cultivating and reinforcing the conditions that allowed a movement such as ISIS to flourish. The disaffected youth returning to its shores are therefore, in part, a product of its own making. Meanwhile, the total silence by the British government and mainstream media alike on the ongoing air strikes on civilian areas of Idlib should remind us that none of this is about valuing the life of Syria.[61]

The construction of the nation inherently innocent of atrocity and of any implication in the emergence of ISIS and the Syrian conflict more broadly is, of course, nothing new. The constitution of the subject-citizen of the empire was consciously habituated according to a sovereign will to racism and the benevolence of the colonial enterprise from a very young age.[62] Likewise,

[60] Paul Gilroy. (2004). *Postcolonial Melancholia*. New York: Columbia University Press and *After Empire: Melancholia or Convivial Culture*. London: Routledge; Lucy Mayblin. (2018). *Asylum after Empire: Colonial Legacies in the Politics of Asylum Seeking*. London: Rowman & Littlefield; Robbie Shilliam. (2018). *Race and the Undeserving Poor*. London: Agenda Publishing; Kapoor, *Deprive*; Centre for Contemporary Cultural Studies. (1982). *The Empire Strikes Back: Race and Racism in 70s Britain*. London: Hutchinson.

[61] Kapoor, "Citizenship deprivation."

[62] J. M. MacKenzie, ed. (1984). *Propaganda and Empire; The Manipulation of British Public Opinion 1880–1960*. Manchester: Manchester University Press; S. Tomlinson. (1981). *Educational Subnormality: A Study in Decision-making*. London: Routledge and Kegan Paul; S. Tomlinson.

it is racism that allows the explicit judgment of Begum's betrayal, lack of remorse, and apparent indifference to death, while precluding any serious reflection on British and wider Western apathy to violence, death, and murder that surrounds it. To contend with both—Shamima Begum joining ISIS *and* the racist imperialism of Western states—in similar terms, that is, to see both as reality, would make it much more difficult to draw clear distinctions between the nation and Others, or Shamima Begum and/as a citizen due to certain protections. It would complicate the interplay between the logics of capture, expulsion, and exclusion contingent on there being some essence which separates us from them, which in turn authorize strategies of abandonment. In the deprivation of Shamima Begum's citizenship, the normalization of carceral landscapes, and the narrative of siege cast in a racialized language of nationality and legitimate membership to the nation, appear regardless of the liberal pretensions to the sacred nature of citizenship for rights, freedom, and the ability to belong. Though this is an extreme case, in the contemporary pathology of bordering, the systematic generalization of the withdrawal of care in spite of the legal status of the "citizen" might not be so extreme.

In the Begum case, we are witness to the potential generalization of a *migrant existence*, a mode of being in the world inflected with uncertainty and instability cast in racial terms.[63] In depriving Begum of her citizenship on the basis that she has the possibility of citizenship elsewhere, there is a precedent being set which formalizes a two-tier citizenship system—those with migrant parents and, therefore, perpetually Other are at risk of being marked, tracked, and, in the extreme, being removed from the perceived safety and liberty of national citizenship. These are, then, processes of legally produced vulnerability which because of the inbuilt codes of race central to the context of the state's emergence and consolidation affects in more intense ways individuals and families who are marked by birth and, therefore, cannot belong. But this is the paradox. For the abandonment, expulsion, and exclusion of subjects does not signal the end of domination. Instead, in the legal production of vulnerability as shown by the case of Shamima Begum and the

---

(1989). "The Origins of the Ethnocentric Curriculum." In *Education for All: A Landmark for Pluralism*, edited by G.K. Verma. London: Falmer, pp. 26–41; S. Tomlinson. (2014). *The Politics of Race, Class and Special Education; The Selected Works of Sally Tomlinson*. London: Routledge; Danny Dorling and Sally Tomlinson. (2019). *Rule Britannia: Brexit and the End of Empire*. London: Biteback Publishing.

[63] El-Enany Nadine. (2020). *(B)ordering Britain. Law, Race and Empire*. Manchester: Manchester University Press, chapter 5, pp. 175–218. Particularly instructive are broader discussions around the intensification of the control of human mobility in our world today. See also: Luke De Noronha. (2020). *Deporting Black Britons. Portraits of Deportation to Jamaica*. Manchester: Manchester University Press; David Theo Goldberg. (2018). *Are We All Postracial Yet?* London: Polity; M. Richmond and A. Charnley. (2018). "Race, Class and Borders." *Base*. Available at: https://www.basepublication.org/?p=665

hostile environment, there is a practical abdication of responsibility on the part of sovereign power, simultaneous to the broader generalization and, thus, intensification of state or at least state-sponsored control and assemblages of violence. The case of Shamima Begum—Muslim-woman, -traitor, -victim, -agent—might come to allow migrant existence with all its precariousness, bureaucracy, documentation, waiting rooms, identity cards, biometric data collection, and codification, to be an *un*exceptional condition of national membership for those named as racial subjects of which the Muslim is front and center today. There is the dispersal of a paranoid mentality which legitimates the augmentation of state powers of removal (erasure) and forms of administration (disclosure) which, while unfolding all too often along the lines of racial difference, affects the entire society and marks its intensifying exit from relations of reciprocity and care.

In a related case, Jack Abraham Letts who came to be known as the infamous "Jihadi Jack," a man "suspected" of leaving Britain to join ISIS and deprived of his citizenship under the same powers as those employed in Shamima Begum's case, was also interviewed by ITV. But his interview casts a rather different optic, one of genuine remorse and even Letts's productive potential with one headline reading "Free me so I can fight against Islamic radicalisation."[64] His parents would insist that Jack Letts "is still a British citizen" with Letts himself stressing that he still *felt* like a British national. In another interview he said: "I genuinely don't care if they give me a piece of paper saying whether I'm British or not. I'm British because my mother's British and her family have been British for 5000 years. It's not something that comes on a piece of paper and can be taken, at any time."[65] Begum was given no such space. The lengths taken by some to construct Letts's decision to join ISIS as unfathomable given his being *of* Britain, his Britishness being a type of inner experience, is telling having been described thus in *The Telegraph*: "Jihadi Jack: The OCD teenager who took a football to bed with him who grew up to be a terrorist."[66] Mental health (his OCD), minority status (teenager), and love of the national sport (football) are all deployed in Letts's humanization.

[64] Dominic Waghorn. (2019). "Jihadi Jack: 'Free Me So I Can Fight Against Islamic Radicalisation." *Sky News*. Available at: https://news.sky.com/story/jihadi-jack-free-me-so-i-can-fight-against-islamic-radicalisation-11789744

[65] See: PA Media. (2019). 'Isis Suspect Jack Letts Stripped of British Citizenship—Report." *Guardian*. Available at: https://www.theguardian.com/uk-news/2019/aug/17/isis-suspect-jack-letts-stripped-british-citizenship; British Broadcasting Corporation. (2019). "Jihadi Jack: IS Recruit Jack Letts Loses UK Citizenship." *BBC News Online*. Available at: https://www.bbc.co.uk/news/uk-49385376

[66] Josie Ensor. (2019). "Jihadi Jack: The OCD Teenager Who Took a Football to Bed with Him Who Grew Up to Be a Terrorist." *The Telegraph*. Available at: https://www.telegraph.co.uk/news/2019/06/21/jihadi-jack-ocd-teenager-took-football-bed-grew-terrorist/

In the varied construction of Shamima Begum-as-enemy—a dangerous *enemy-agent* to the nation and its protected citizens from whom she must be kept at bay, or a weakened *enemy-absconded* who overestimated the strength of her own convictions, competence, and of her chosen camp who is now rendered the butt of a limp joke, or an *enemy-repentant* who chose the wrong side and who now recognizes her mistake at leaving the enclosure of British civility—we are forced to reflect on her case as a networked *event of disclosure*, the Muslim Questioned live-on-air. But is Begum a figure of essential antagonism as is the Schmittian enemy, the Other who must count for nothing and whose death is the only thing that can spell one's own secure life? Or is she perhaps a subject whose oblivion is necessitated by her denial—through her inaugural escape to ISIS—of the superiority of "our" own Being against her being and Others-of-her-kind? Can we concede the status of victimhood to Begum as is claimed by organized racial power? And how does that status of victimhood differ or overlap with its character latent in state discourses of the impossibility of an Islamic feminism, of Muslim's primordial patriarchy and exceptional oppression of women?[67] The case of Shamima Begum is an intense manifestation of the way in which Muslim voices do not drive our analysis, or if the Muslim speaks, her voice is transcribed as something else, something more incriminating, an interpretation that is made to the measure of a stock image/footage without sound.[68] The Muslim Questioned is one stock image or another made to disclose information with which we are already familiar.[69]

INVENTION OF PRIMARY PHANTASIES

As is the function of the sham interrogation, the increasingly harrowing climate of state-sanctioned Islamophobia has served to severely minimize space available for addressing complex and pressing questions: of radicalization and violence, racialization, imperialism, religion and secularism, law and gender equality. This has impacted not merely the public realm of the street, of work offices, or even community spaces, but has pervaded the most intimate familial spaces. Given the wide range of "behaviors" attached to the *Becoming-Terrorist-of-the-Muslim* couched in euphemisms of safeguarding, expressions of political difference are reconstructed as signifiers of deeper

---

[67] Suhaiymah Manzoor-Khan. (2019). "Notes on Shamima." *The Brown Hijabi.* Available at: https://thebrownhijabi.com/2019/02/18/notes-on-shamima/

[68] Z. Sardar and M. W. Davies. (2010). "Freeze Framing Muslims: Hollywood and the Slideshow of Western Imagination." *Interventions,* 12(2), 239–50.

[69] Yassir Morsi. (2018). "The 'free speech' of the (Un)free." *Continuum,* 32(4), 474–86.

maladies to be disclosed in the intimate spaces of private life. These questions are nonetheless,

> relegated to symptoms of family dysfunction and a failure of parenting, in which, the "status of women and attitudes toward sexuality play a central role in the narrative." The targeted policing of Muslim women involves the scrutiny of motherhood, a strategy that has long been in use against suspect communities, as well as calls on mothers (and wives, sisters and sometimes daughters) to perform duties of surveillance within their families and communities and report signs of extremism and radicalisation, to play their role in counterterrorism policing. Such a practice is a critical element of the tapestry of state violence and illuminates the intricacies of criminalisation which manipulate affective relations as tools of enforcement and simultaneously demonise Muslim women through their relations with Muslim men.[70]

An important measure of European modernity was the force of law and authority of an impersonal state rather than religion and the authority of religious leaders in specifying the identity of that new subject: the modern citizen. Winifred Fallers Sullivan argues that even though, "modern law itself looks deeply self-contained, all-powerful and secular, we know that it was profoundly shaped by religion in its origins and continues to depend in fundamental ways on religious understandings of the nature of the human person and of society."[71] In the interplay between (racial) sovereign power and the broader social fabric, it is too convenient to argue that the demand for disclosure is somehow exclusive to state organs of policing, or the hostile space of the interrogation room. Both European state power and its very meaning

---

[70] Kapoor, *Deprive*, p. 160; Rashid, *Veiled Threats*, especially chapter 5. See also an increasingly prominent literature of the role of gender as well as race, and the possibilities of radical feminism in the interconnected struggles against state-sanctioned racism and Islamophobia: Gargi Bhattacharyya. (2008). *Dangerous Brown Men: Exploiting Sex, Violence and Feminism in the War on Terror*, pp. 56–57; Centre for Contemporary Cultural Studies. (1982). *The Empire Strikes Back. Race and Racism in '70s Britain*. Oxon: Hutchinson & Co.; Priyamvada Gopal. (2013). "Speaking with Difficulty: Feminism and Antiracism in Britain after 9/11." *Feminist Studies*, 39(1), 98–118; Saba Mahmood. (2009). "Feminism, Democracy, and Empire: Islam and the War on Terror." In *Gendering Religion and Politics: Untangling Modernities*, edited by Hanna Herzog and Ann Braude. Basingstoke: Palgrave, 193–215; Suhaiymah Manzoor-Khan, "Intersectional, Radical, Unpalatable and Abrasive." Available at: https://thebrownhijabi.com/2015/08/31/intersectional-radical-unpalatable-and-abrasive-that-is-the-feminism-im-about/; Inspire. (2014). Making a Stand Campaign, Inspire website. The Inspire campaign encouraged Muslim women in the United Kingdom to make a stand against terrorism; it would be revealed, was funded, and supported by the Home Office's Research, Information and Communications Unit, a quasi-propaganda arm of the counterterrorism industry in Britain. See Simon Hooper. (2016). "UK Grassroots Anti-extremism Campaign Produced by Home Office." *Middle East Eye*, June 13.
[71] Winifred Fallers Sullivan. (2006). "Comparing Religions, Legally," *Washington and Lee Law Review*, 63(1): 913.

have been premised on the thematic of racial (as-religious) difference, a thematic that has been normalized through the establishment of pretty much every major institution—from state-public to cultural and archival. What this has produced, following my schema, is an entire *culture of questioning* similarly based on the principle of race. That the suspicion of, and the incitement for, the Muslim to disclose who, or more precisely what and why they are, becomes a holistic effort insofar as the Muslim Questioned are caught up in an imperial cultural matrix which makes demands upon them, represents them, and makes them speak.

The self-assurance systematically cultivated by the colonial policy of ignorance—of not bothering to learn about the native beyond the construction of efficient models for their control—is undergoing mutation today in the form of surveillance data, the pseudo-science of radicalization which passes itself off as knowledge (of the Muslim) and the larger context of white (supremacist) anxiety. Which is to say that it is through connected matrices of power, governance, and knowledge which produce the Muslim Questioned that the Muslim is successfully—and with legal weight—consolidated as an object of the "real." And it is the success of this (global) process which remains undisturbed in this mode by counterevidence and complex shapes more broadly that in turn drives a self-confidence in the fact of the Muslim subject being what is said about her. In the colonial context, the invention of the native was imbricated in a fundamental need for ontology and created, consciously or not, an essential relation of dependence between the colonizers and the colonized.[72] To be sure, this policy of ignorance is of a particular kind that casualizes violence and licenses all manner of abuses. But much more than that, the "civilizational" confidence gained through this policy paradigm, if not whole episteme, was able to take hold *precisely* because of the perceived "successes" in making the native speak, of dismantling the allegedly arcane structures of their societies and, in the process, reconstituting the interrogated subject as one more closely resembling, though never completely, a human being. The objectification of the native and its knowledge was, against Edward Said, not simply for the sovereign Occident but for the native Oriental him/herself.[73]

There is today the fundamental drive of having a (Muslim) enemy at one's disposal, as both political-security practice and everyday logic, in the context of the mimetic rivalry brought on by the war on terror. This is a rivalry that precariously stems the existential crises of the end of the European idea, and which marshals the sophisticated mechanisms of distancing and

---

[72] See Part One of A. Memmi. (2003). *The Colonizer and the Colonized*. London: Earthscan.

[73] Wael Hallaq. (2018). *Restating Orientalism: A Critique of Modern Knowledge*. New York: Columbia University Press, chapter 2.

disclosure.[74] The Muslim Questioned fulfills the role of *the* enemy, at once motile, vulgar, spectacular, and naïve, whose existence is essential to the symbolic and structural order of Britain and the West.[75] To be sure, it was against the background of actual colonial rule, direct or indirect, that British understandings of Muslims were developed. Remarkably consonant with a war on terror Britain, a central image was that of the Muslim "fanatic," a people prone to holy war and therefore irreconcilable with modern reason and rule. As Francis Robinson discusses, this view of Muslim fanaticism "had its origins in the various jihad movements which the British encountered in early-nineteenth-century India,"[76] from Somalia to Egypt to Tipu Sultan. In fact, it was kept alive by the Mutiny rebellion of 1857, which was considered, wrongly, to be a Muslim conspiracy. The British, it seemed, were being inconvenienced by bellicose Muslim extremism from all parts of the empire. In what amounted to a colonial formulation of *can Muslims think?* W. W. Hunter's famous tract *The Indian Musalmans* was written in response to the Viceroy's question, "Are the Indian Muslims bound by their religion to rebel against the Queen?"[77]

---

[74] See this thorough report by the civil-rights group, Cage, on Schedule 7 powers and structural Islamophobia: CAGE. (2019). *Schedule 7: Harassment at Borders The Impact on the Muslim Community*. London: CAGE. Available at: https://www.cage.ngo/product/schedule-7-harassment -at-borders-report. The report reads, "through this evidence-based research, the report concludes that Schedule 7 disregards the norms of due process at every level, and it permits and justifies systematic abuses against individuals including ordinary Muslims, journalists, aid workers, and lawyers. As such, the law is not only ineffective, but it is deeply counterproductive." See also: Dr. Asim Qureshi's article on his experience of being detained, questioned and processes under such powers: Qureshi. (2019). "My Schedule 7 Stop: Power and Coercion Presented as 'choice' and a 'friendly chat'." Available at: https://5pillarsuk.com/2019/07/31/my-schedule-7-stop-power-and -coercion-presented-as-choice-and-a-friendly-chat/; and, more generally, Dan Sabbagh. (2019). "Detention of Muslims at UK Ports and Airports 'structural Islamophobia'." Available at: https:// www.theguardian.com/news/2019/aug/20/detention-of-muslims-at-uk-ports-and-airports-struc- tural-islamophobia

[75] As Fanon and many others have shown us, the daily dilemma of the native was to try and distin- guish between that which they had been forced to interiorize as the necessary remaking of his per- son in the colony, and the part of themselves that was truly theirs before the colonist's arrival. And further still, the colonial order functioned on the continued presence of these psychic, invented, objects taken to be the truth of the colonized. Extending Fanon, the daily dilemma of the Muslim Questioned—a disturbing object to whom only hostility and interrogation can be the rule—is to figure out the degree to which he is guilty and that is all.

[76] Francis Robinson. (1999). "British Empire and the Muslim World." In *The Oxford history of the British Empire*, edited by W. R. Louis and J. M. Brown. Oxford: Oxford University Press, p. 405.

[77] Cited in George Makdisi. (1965). *Arabic and Islamic Studies in Honor of Hamilton A. R. Gibb*. Leiden: Brill. For an insightful discussion of the tract in relation to British confrontation with *jihad* in India, see: Faisal Devji. (2005). *Landscapes of the Jihad: Militancy, Morality, Modernity*. London: C. Hurst & Co., pp. 36–41. Further still, "this understanding of Muslims was translated into Africa in the 1880s in discussions of Arabi Pasha's revolt in Egypt and the Mahdist rising in the Sudan. It was nourished by the jihads which spluttered into existence from time to time in the early decades of the twentieth century in French and Italian as well as British African territories." Robinson, "The British Empire and the Muslim World," p. 405.

There is of course an unfolding connection to be drawn between raciology as the nuclear power plant of modern knowledge about the "human," and the historical construction of the Muslim fanatic in the empire. Yet their racist traces today and the contemporary recruitment drive of the industries of counterterrorism and radicalization conceal mutations in that racism, new intimacies and economies between white self and Muslim Other that can be captured in our notion of disclosure and desire to make the Muslim speak. Yet again, benchmarks, in this case institutional norms of freedom, trust, and confidentiality, can be undermined if not altogether discarded in the management of "threat" and instantiation of national security. In education for example, there seems a clear tension between the imperatives of policing the expression of certain ideas (as "safeguarding") and education as a means to empower students to think critically and learn to express their views in effective ways.[78]

Nonetheless, the bolstering of Prevent as a statutory duty since the Counter-Terrorism and Security Act ([CTSA] 2015),[79] and the reinforcement/enforcement of interventionist processes like Channel by initiatives like WRAP has been the response of the day.[80] Setting limits to acceptable critical debate

---

[78] "If there are specific individuals at risk you would support them anyway out of a duty of care. But the local Prevent Board is asking for a more general map of Muslim communities. I make confidentiality promises to young people, which I shouldn't break unless it is a matter of child protection or a criminal act." Youth Project Manager, cited in Institute of Race Relations. (2010). "Evidence to the UK Parliamentary Select Committee Inquiry on Preventing Violent Extremism." *Race and Class,* 51, 73–80.

[79] The original Counter Terrorism and Security Bill was drafted at a time of heightened threat: "In the context of this heightened threat to our national security, the provisions in this Bill would strengthen the legal powers and capabilities of law enforcement and intelligence agencies to disrupt terrorism and prevent individuals from being radicalised in the first instance." HM Government. (2015b) Counter-Terrorism and Security Act 2015. Part 5 of the explanatory notes for the original Counter-Terrorism and Security Bill through which the PREVENT work stream and ambitions are made *legally* relevant, addresses the risk of being drawn into terrorism. Provisions under the Bill "would create a duty for specified bodies to have due regard, in the exercise of their functions, to the need to prevent people from being drawn into terrorism. It would also give the Secretary of State a power to publish guidance to which specified bodies must have regard when fulfilling this duty. The effect would be to put the existing Prevent programme on a statutory footing." Further, the notes maintain that "Prevent activity in local areas relies on the co-operation of many organisations to be effective. Currently, such co-operation is not consistent across Great Britain. In legislating, the Government's policy intention is to make delivery of such activity a legal requirement for specified authorities and improve the standard of work on the Prevent programme across Great Britain. This is particularly important in areas of Great Britain where terrorism is of the most concern but it is clear that all areas need, at the minimum, to ensure that they understand the local threat, and come to a judgement as to whether activities currently underway are sufficient to meet it." HM Government. (2015b: 3, 34) Counter-Terrorism and Security Act 2015.

[80] This impetus of Channel is showing its alarming results. "Across the UK, between 2007 and 2010, 1120 individuals were identified by the Channel project as potentially travelling on a radicalisation pathway. Of these, 290 were under sixteen years old and fifty-five were under twelve. Over 90 percent were Muslim (the rest were mainly identified for potential involvement in far Right extremism). By the end of 2010 almost 2500 people had been identified by the Channel project as possible risks." Kundnani, *The Muslims,* p. 154. "Since 2012, more than 4,000 people have

within hardening climates of paranoia and suspicion, in schools, for example, is now legally relevant.[81] The duty to protect children against radicalization through the implementation of the Prevent strategy and the teaching of "fundamental British values," is now a legal duty to be actively audited by external bodies such as the Office for Standards in Education, Children's Services and Skills (Ofsted). "The Prevent Duty"[82] is thoroughly couched in the language of safeguarding children: "The Department for Education should ensure that the governing body of every school extend the responsibilities of the teacher designated Child Protection Officer to include Prevent within his/her role."[83] Teachers and other professionals with a duty of care, including doctors and mental health professionals, however, are quickly beginning to feel that, while they may disagree with the increasingly Islamophobic climate Prevent exists within and is shaped by, they will be found out by official bodies like Ofsted inspectors with larger consequences for the institution.[84]

The argument made as to why the Prevent strategy had been unsuccessful prior to the statutory changes of the CTSA 2015 is because of a lack of consistent institutional cooperation.[85] It is the unwillingness of various bodies,

---

been referred, half of them under-18s—with the youngest a three-year-old from London"; Homa Khaleeli. (2015). "'You Worry They Could Take Your Kids': Is the Prevent Strategy Demonising Muslim Schoolchildren?" *Guardian*. Available at: http://www.theguardian.com/uk-news/2015/sep/23/prevent-counter-terrorism-strategy-schools-demonising-muslim-children.

[81] Alex Kenny, a member of the NUT's executive committee, told Al Jazeera that "many teachers and students no longer felt comfortable discussing issues such as the *Charlie Hebdo* shootings in Paris and warned that fears about being labelled extremist were shutting down debate in the classroom." S. Hooper. "UK Teachers See Thin Line Between Spy and Protector." Al Jazeera Online. Available at: http://www.aljazeera.com/indepth/features/2015/04/uk-teachers-thin-line-spy-protector-150412075115174.html; S. Hooper. (2015). "Stifling Freedom of Expression in UK Schools." Al Jazeera Online. Available at: http://www.aljazeera.com/indepth/features/2015/07/stifling-freedom-expression-uk-schools-150721080612049.html.

[82] Department for Education. (2015b). *The Prevent Duty*, London.

[83] Paul Thomas. (2016). "Youth, Terrorism and Education: Britain's Prevent Programme." *International Journal of Lifelong Education*, 35(2), 171–87.

[84] The involvement of external bodies, like Ofsted for example, means that Prevent is a major priority for educational institutions. The emphasis on overtly proving one's institution's engagement with Prevent has "educationalists busily inviting police officers in to schools and Further Education (FE) colleges and asking for more WRAP training to demonstrate Prevent compliance to the external inspectors." Thomas writes, "Anecdotal evidence (private correspondence to author) from a recent OFSTED inspection of a major Further Education college in the north of England suggested that Prevent and its implications for the Muslim (but not white) students was the main focus for the inspection of a college that is crucial to the educational and life chance of many thousands of urban young people." Thomas, "Youth, Terrorism and Education," pp. 11–12. Similarly, educators themselves say "Prevent has already had a chilling effect in schools, and that freedom of speech—itself a British value—is being compromised." Khaleeli, "You worry they could take your kids."

[85] The need for this change is articulated in the CTSA as follows: Prevent activity in local areas relies on the cooperation of many organizations to be effective. Currently, such cooperation is not consistent across Great Britain. In legislating, the Government's policy intention is to make delivery of such activity a legal requirement for specified authorities and improve the standard of work on the Prevent program across Great Britain. This is particularly important in areas of Great Britain where terrorism is of the most concern but it is clear that all areas need, at the minimum, to ensure

schools in particular, to play a role of de facto counterterrorism officials based on racist assumptions that is problematized, and not the motivations behind their supposed failure to cooperate that is the chief obstacle to be addressed by the CTSA. The legal duty on "specified authorities" works to solidify the complex network of cooperation among many actors—safeguarding professionals, public bodies, local councils, police and security/intelligence services—inciting and classifying the products of disclosure. This reflects an important institutional arrangement which under the CTSA monitors and enforces compliance with the rule, that is, doing the work of, race and reproducing the Muslim Questioned.

VEILING THE RACIAL PHANTASM

In the context of the emergence of name *Negro*, Fanon notes that, "the body from then on is an apparently formless form that incites surprise, dread, and terror: 'Look, a Negro! Mama, look, a Negro, I'm scared!'"[86] He exists only through his inspection and assignation within a skein of significations that are beyond him. This drives a situation whereby the Negro subject, who comes to be absolutely defined by significations of the Negro formulated by those who named him such, is responsible for not only the lacks in himself and his body but his race and ancestors. Likewise, using the phrase "Muslim fanatic" today risks speaking tautologically for they are, in the reality produced, funded, researched by the economies of "radicalization"—psychic and actual—one and the same. The fanatic-as-Muslim is a name which licenses injury and authorizes systematic interrogation in the various way outlined above. A figure that is veiled, within this mode at least, by a range of significations that stain in new ways the bodies and lives of Muslims. A set of meanings and implications which *disclose* who the Muslim is, among a prefigured range of possible options provided beyond her own will or admission. Whatever her confession, the Muslim leaves us with incriminating facts with which we are already accustomed. As Houria Bouteldja bluntly puts it:

> Wimps or monsters, servants or executioners, shoe-shiners or kamikazes. These are our only options. We have realized the white prophecy: to become non-beings or barbarians. Our complexities and our nuances have evaporated. We have been diluted, confiscated from ourselves, emptied out of all historical substance. We claim to be what we have been but are nothing but fantasmatic,

---

that they understand the local threat, and come to a judgment as to whether activities currently underway are sufficient to meet it. HMG, *CTSA*, p. 34.
[86] Fanon, Black Skin, White Masks, pp. 91–92.

disarticulated caricatures of ourselves. We cobble together disparate scraps of identity, held in place with bad glue. Our own parents look at us, perplexed. They think, "Who are you?"[87]

We could argue then that the enemy today who is so often named Muslim is a ubiquitous yet obscure figure, a disturbing subject-object whose infectious trace is seen and read everywhere but whose body can never be pinned down once and for all. That s/he is even more dangerous and our potentially falling victim to her much more intensely felt because if she is to have a face then it is a veiled face. Yet this is only a partial picture. In the Muslim Questioned, veiling is itself part of the procedure of constructing the enemy and authorizes the intense and often violent search for her/him. Those who are theorized, pathologized, questioned, the suspects about whom images and narratives are weaved beyond reasonable bounds, connect a series of vicious chains of associations which lock them into the excesses of power and the erasing logics of race. The Muslim Questioned appears as a primary phantasy and, therefore, that the images, codified data, and "particular behaviors" do not match reality becomes irrelevant. Doubt becomes vice; uncertainty and delay become the sole preserve of the Muslim. Which is to say dissimulation would, in this case, be counterproductive. For the enemy certainly has a face, or must be made to have one, even if it is obscured, or if it is quite literally veiled in the niqab then it must be ripped off in the name of (in)security. To be sure, violation, disfigurement, and strangulation are necessary conditions for the forms of disclosure I am analyzing, and which are executed through a contemporary politics of hatred through which the contemporary drives of war-states against Others cohere. Islam and Muslimness are powerful names. They each arrive with their significations that have been integrated into law and that have become the interior routes to the certainty of the unbridgeable chasm between our humanities; satisfying that threshold of legitimacy required for his/her incessant tracking, their questioning at will, and their need to disclose that which we already know plagues their modes of thought, culture, and living.

But the desire for invention, of investments in the invasive techno-economies of securing a population against another, exists simultaneously with a relation absent of any desire for the racial subject's being "here," and within social and political formations which multiply structures of separation, marking, and discrimination, casting the Muslim Questioned as but the "silent remainders of politics."[88] Knowledge and recognition of the Other are not only no longer necessary requirements for the civic realm but are produced as risks in the face of this everywhere-enemy and the specter of Europe and

---

[87] Houria Bouteldja. (2016). *Whites, Jews, and Us*. South Pasadena: Semiotext(e), pp. 102–103.
[88] Michel Foucault. (1994). "Face aux gouvernements, les droits de l'homme." In *Dits et écrits*, vol. 4. Gallimard: Paris, p. 708.

its presumed white subject's demotion as but one province and people among many. The primary phantasy of the Muslim Questioned licenses a *structural abandon*, a formation, as Freud would put it, only "excited by immoderate stimuli. Anyone seeking to move it needs no logical calibration in his arguments, but must paint with the most powerful images, exaggerate, and say the same thing over and over again."[89] The Muslim Questioned describes a hostile system which invents them in order to injure them, an invention that simultaneously authorizes a prohibition on speech and constitutes the Muslim's body as both a target and border to be policed. We already know all we need to, we have access to all the facts and data. All that is left to do is devise measures to confirm that which we already know and to which the Muslim is in constant denial.

With the increasing power of the security state in our contemporary context, the wounds of disclosure propelled by the principle and phantasms of race have only multiplied, operating with shifting degrees of scope and intensity. The administrative grids of modern life have become increasingly propelled by new technologies of surveillance and discipline, not to mention the fissile atmosphere driven by liberal democratic regimes who consider themselves to be struggling in a constant war with not-quite-human enemies with whom no communication is possible that exacerbate forms of racial categorization. The licenses of postcolonial power, underpinned by a kind of *hydraulic racism*, have become more complex with the emergence of the security state and the technologies of governance and discipline at its disposal. But I think that the analogy of the interrogation room, generalized as a social condition for the racialized—the Muslim Questioned—conceptualizes the flows and effects of power and "knowledge"—or covert data—involved in the treatment and tracking of suspect populations. That despite the horrors of the slave trade, Nazism and the Holocaust, all officially recognized as moments with which we have successfully reckoned, race persists as the condition of possibility for security, identity and politics for Britain's engagements with Muslims.[90]

---

[89] Sigmund Freud. (2004). *Mass Psychology and Other Writings*, trans. J.A. Underwood, London: Penguin, p. 26.

[90] Stuart Hall's work on race as such a condition remains insightful. See: S. Hall. (1978). "Racism and Reaction." In *Five Views of Multi-Racial Britain*. London, Commission for Racial Equality; S. Hall. (1980). "Race, Articulation and Societies Structured in Dominance." Reprinted 1996 in *Black British Cultural Studies: A Reader*, edited by H. A. Baker, M. Diawara, and R. H. Lindeborg, Chicago, IL: University of Chicago Press; S. Hall. (1991). "Old and New Identities, Old and New Ethnicities." In *Culture, Globalisation and the World System*, edited by A. King, Basingstoke, Macmillan; S. Hall. (1996e). "When Was the Postcolonial? Thinking at the Limit." In *The Postcolonial Question*, edited by I. Chambers and L. Curti. London: Routledge; S. Hall. (2000a). "The Multicultural Question." In *Un/Settled Multiculturalisms*, edited by B. Hesse. London, Zed Press; S. Hall. (2000b). "Frontlines/Backyards." In *Black British Culture and Society*, edited by K. Owusu. London: Routledge.

However, with the new economies and borders of violence, not to mention the profitable violence of borders themselves, have come technologies in the service of disavowal. That is, modes of concealment through which violations of the Other, her body and much else, can only be discussed euphemistically and are integrated into a recycled narrative of Western liberal democracy's defense in the hopes of deceiving the most gullible constituencies. All of this must be masked, just as the faces of the Muslim Questioned are disfigured and their voices muted or rendered incomprehensible. Which is to say, in sum, that in keeping the little secret of race, or the modern fundamentalism of white supremacy, sophisticated technologies are deployed against but the latest "terror threat."

Chapter 3

Secrecy

Within this paradigm, then, the term "Muslim" designates a fragmented world. A world split between reason and religion, tolerance and fanaticism, innocence and guilt, interrogators and the interrogated. Distance and disclosure work according to a logic whereby surveillance, assault, scrutiny, deviancy, propensities to violence, and tendencies to misogyny are authorized by the names "Islam" and "Muslim," borne of the historic and foundational principle of race. The increasing power and the (un)exceptional generalization of the security state shaped by the wars on/of terror have only further embedded the reasoning that the "Muslim" is not, but constantly disguises itself as, one of us, and must continuously be made to disclose his whereabouts and motivations for moving. He must thus be caught up in a formation which attempts to preclude him from speaking in a voice of his own, and about things which might concern him and Others he might care for or represent. The complex technologies powered under this license are ultimately total in scope and force, oriented toward the management of migration and mobility on a planetary scale, where terrorist threats and the agencies and armies tasked with capturing or destroying them all participate in global flows of data, capital, legal exceptions, and matrices of re- and depopulation across all manner of juridical, intelligence, and social networks.

In order for a population to be secured against the terrorist threat emanating from individuals passing for our neighbors and doctors and the average passerby, everyone must stay at home. The threat is carried by individuals organized in religious networks that circumvent the porous borders which have previously remained open to facilitate a freedom of movement deserved yesterday by the civilized among us. Unfortunately, we learn, those who embody the threat are rooted in the social world just as we, their possible victims, are. The disclosure of identity at any given moment and the collection of exhaustive information on every one of us become essential. But we must remember that the massive expansion of digitized systems holding unfathomable quantities of data, which consolidate as the body's essential identity under these logics of protection and security, are preprogramed to uphold racial formations. While it would be preferable, therefore, for everyone to stay at home and hold extensive proof of identity, movement, and motivation, questions of mobility and character are intensely oriented toward those always already cast as out of place.

Exuberant, well-resourced, and state-sanctioned projects of distancing and disclosure for public record and national security are simultaneously, however, schemes of concealment. The hostile paradigm of the Muslim Questioned necessitates a foundational effort toward secrecy just as everything that might threaten us is stripped bare and emptied of its contents. The phantasms of race—proliferating but usual suspects—have always been caught up in a public secret.[1] A secret so blatant in its falsehood and effects that the strategies of concealment have had to increase in sophistication, molecular violence, and jurisdiction in order to sustain the lie of racial difference. A form of deceit that is so fundamental, to Europe and to Britain, that it is absent, a secret which quilts social, economic, and political relations with the trauma of defeat, loss of impotence, and anxieties of pollution and degradation. Secrecy is disclosure's necessary counterpart in a racial order which must keep the Muslim at a distance and under constant watch, but which must also suppress an intense autophobia and confrontation with the murder sanctioned in its name.

THE REMOVAL OF WITNESSES: TRANSGRESSIVE LIFE IN THE DELIVERY OF SECRET JUSTICE

The various strategies, technologies, and legal arrangements I have discussed thus far rest upon a perverse ethics: *the removal of witnesses*. Those from, or of, the darker parts of the world cannot be allowed to testify in their defense, but only confess varying aspects of their guilt which we already knew. Secrecy as I mean it here must suppress, as much as is possible, its opposite: the ethics of bearing witness. In one such example,

---

[1] In the opening lecture of the series *The Genealogy of Race*, Patricia Williams discusses the power of race, and the histories of enslavement and imperialism that birthed racism as public secrets. Patricia Williams. (1997). "The Emperor's New Clothes." *Reith Lectures*. For an ethnography of the public secret, see also: Michael Taussig. (1997). *The Magic of the State*. New York: Routledge; Michael Taussig. (1999). *Defacement*. Stanford: Stanford University Press.

in 2011, in the course of negotiations with former Kenyan detainees, the British government announced that it had in its possession some secret files outside the regular classification system. Thus started the disclosure of previously non-existent documents, and by November 2013 some 20,000 files had been declassified. They came from 37 colonies worldwide, from Malta, Nigeria and Kenya to Aden, Malaya and the Bahamas. These documents are sometimes called the "migrated archives" and they are available at the National Archives (previously known as the Public Record Office) in Kew, UK. In addition, a large number of papers are believed to have been totally destroyed, either burnt or sunk at sea. Hence what we can see now is only a tiny family of survivors from an entire group that faced extermination. The whole policy was eventually entitled "Operation Legacy."[2]

There is a peculiar consonance, however, between the systematic dumping of colonial records (apparently inadmissible evidence), and the intense contemporary pressures of documentation felt by Muslim subjects, between Operation Legacy out at sea and Operation Champion on Birmingham streets. That is, between *disclosure and erasure*. Both allow the nation(-state) to construct itself as a victim having to deal with unwanted threats and "problems," which cannot be allowed to occupy public space and who can be dispatched in secret.[3] Both underpin a will to secrecy which evidence the shifting scales of violence through which various techniques of material and symbolic erasure remind those who cannot be from here of their always-conditional residency as guests.

Crucial to disguising the effects of racism available to sovereign power is a generalized system of secret justice. In the colonial matrix of white supremacy

---

[2] Shohei Sato. (2017). "'Operation Legacy': Britain's Destruction and Concealment of Colonial Records Worldwide." *The Journal of Imperial and Commonwealth History*, 45(4), 697–719. See also, Caroline Elkins. (2011). "Alchemy of Evidence: Mau Mau, the British Empire, and the High Court of Justice." *The Journal of Imperial and Commonwealth History*, 39(5), 731–48. Caroline Elkins. (2015). "Looking beyond Mau Mau: Archiving Violence in the Era of Decolonization." *The American Historical Review*, 120 (June), 852–68; Huw Bennett. (2011). "Soldiers in the Court Room: The British Army's Part in the Kenya Emergency under the Legal Spotlight." *The Journal of Imperial and Commonwealth History*, 39(5): 717–30; Ian Cobain. (2013). "Revealed: The Bonfire of Papers at the End of Empire." *Guardian*. Available at: https://www.theguardian.com/uk-news/2013/nov/29/revealed-bonfire-papers-empire. Sato also goes on to show that "The FCO holds another approximately 600,000 files of what it used to call the 'special collections' (now renamed the 'non-standard files'), which are currently in the process of being transferred from a repository in Hanslope Park, Milton Keynes, to the archives in Kew. Whereas many of these eventually turned out to be of a different nature from the 'migrated archives', the FCO also discovered in August some '170,000 files in legacy records series held outside the FCO main archive.'"

[3] In fact, a paranoid fantasy in which Britain is always a threatened or defeated nation has long been a staple of the "dark imagination of English reactionaries." See Fintan O' Toole. (2018). "The Paranoid Fantasy behind Brexit." *Guardian*. Available here: https://www.theguardian.com/politics/2018/nov/16/brexit-paranoid-fantasy-fintan-otoole

and British power,[4] as much as in our contemporary moment of the security state racism, "justice" delivered in secret is essential, if not paradigmatic. It is the nocturnal face of liberal democracy and its cultural values.[5] Central to the systematic delivery of secret justice has been the proliferation of technologies of surveillance and repression in which the citizen is at once entangled and its beneficiary. The citizen can never truly know what the data collected about them will be mobilized for. The transcription of everything from biological, genetic, and behavioral characteristics packaged and delivered as a digital imprint is a privileged mechanism for the modern security state and in which racialized populations feel its effects most intensely. Our current moment in the story of race is a hypochondriac one where entire categories of the population are subject to mutable forms of racial categorization which can attach themselves to almost anything its target allegedly is, says, or does— culture, ritual, forms of living, language, dress, and much else. Already a migrant being of raw difference and defined by their radical exteriority, the Muslim is an intruder in whom all types of incriminating evidence is inscribed, on visible, affective, filial, physiognomic, and even genetic levels.

In the context of the unfolding wars on/of terror and the instruments of violence and surveillance—mechanisms of constructing and measuring distance, of extracting disclosure and confession—the migrant subject is not only a formal, descriptive category. In the generalization of migrant existence, the

---

[4] The Morant Bay Rebellion is an instructive case study where the principle of race and the technique of removing witnesses come together. When the rebellion quickly spread throughout the eastern part of the island, Edward Eyre promptly declared martial law allowing him to send troops and militiamen throughout the island to suppress the rebellion and, crucially, to justify on legal grounds the convenient instrument of impromptu court-martials which very often resulted in the punishment of hanging. The capture of Paul Bogle, the assumed mastermind of the commotion, was summarily hung under martial law. Further still, the (extra)ordinary execution of Assemblyman George William Gordon, who had no evidenced connection to the rebellion. Also accused of instigating the rebellion (his suspicion likely framed within his well-known support of black rights), Gordon, having surrendered himself to the authorities, was put on a boat and transferred from an area operating under civil law to a different location where martial rules were in force. This precisely so that he, like Bogle and their allies revolting against the British colonial subjugation, and for a more just stake in Jamaican land and labor, could be put to death without the slightest of governmental inconvenience. Gordon was tried under martial law and hung on October 23, 1865. See: John Bigelow. (2006). *Jamaica in 1850, or, the Effects of Sixteen Years of Freedom on a Slave Colony.* Champaign, IL: University of Illinois Press; G. Heuman. (1991). 1865: prologue to the Morant Bay Rebellion in Jamaica In: New West Indian Guide/ Nieuwe West-Indische Gids 65(3/4), Leiden, 107–27; A. Erickson. (1959). "Empire or Anarchy: The Jamaica Rebellion of 1865." *The Journal of Negro History,* 44(2), 99–122; Christine Chivallon and David Howard SLAVERY & ABOLITION, 2017, 38(3), 534–558. See also a narration of radical transnational solidarities at the time of the rebellion: Priyamvada Gopal. (2019). *Insurgent Empire: Anticolonial Resistance and British Dissent.* London: Verso, especially chapter 2.

[5] Fundamental British values of the rule of law, human rights, free speech, and tolerance. Department for Education. (2014). *Promoting Fundamental British Values as Part of SMSC in Schools*; Department for Education. (2015a). *Keeping Children Safe in Education: Statutory Guidance for Schools and Colleges.* London; Department for Education. (2015b). *The Prevent Duty,* London.

conditional nature of citizenship and, therefore, basic rights for all those embedded within an essential category of difference and, thus, who must be kept at a distance are potentially migrant. Detention, deportation, deprivation, and the normalization of desertion which they authorize, necessitate the institutionalization of such abdication. In this paradigm of hostility, Islam and Muslimness are perhaps the premier markers of that difference, a difference that is measured, flowcharted, predicted, and used as material evidence in the form of removal that define the delivery of secret justice.

On this point of secrecy, witness, and erasure, it should be remembered that the colony, especially the Indian colonial state, was a theater for experimentation, "where historiography, documentation, certification, and representation were all state modalities that transformed knowledge into power."[6] Knowledge of the world and its inhabitants was/is not simply a collection of functional data, but information that was collected precisely for refining mechanisms to "deal with" the native populations in relation to a set of informing assumptions and prejudices that filled the (British) orientalist canon. In the late nineteenth century, the first census was completed under the British Raj. *The Imperial Gazetteer of India* (1881), which had been in the works for Sir William Hunter since 1869, along with the Statistical Survey, gathered an unprecedented amount of fieldwork-based material to produce, in conjunction with the census, a rich work of historical reference comprising "114 volumes and 54,000 pages, the ethnographic studies of 'tribes and castes,' and the distinct 'histories' compiled by energetic officials." The Civilian Raj, thus, "extended and codified its administrative knowledge and imposed its categories on an untidy social reality."[7]

The ethnographic material enhanced the ability of the Raj to exert authority over aggregated native populations but did not overcome the vexing issue of being unable to identify individual Indian subjects in both civil and criminal matters. In spite of the impressive reach and centralized bureaucratic power and knowledge of the colonial state, British civil servants struggled "to concretely ascertain the identity of specific individuals."[8] "Establishing the identities of individual Indians," Chandak Sengoopta argues, "was important not only to avert conceptual chaos or to improve administrative efficiency in a largely illiterate environment—the prime motive was to counter what virtually

[6] Nicholas B. Dirks. (1996). "Foreword." In *Colonialism and Its Forms of Knowledge*, edited by Bernard S. Cohn. Princeton, NJ: Princeton University Press, p. xi.
[7] John Darwin. (2009). *The Empire Project: The Rise and Fall of The British World-System, 1830–1970*. Cambridge: Cambridge University Press, p. 187.
[8] Barder, *Empire Within*, p. 84. This impulse to specificity of modern sovereign power is discussed well by James Scott under the concepts of "legibility." See: J. C. Scott. (1998). *Seeing Like a State: How Certain Schemes to Improve the Human Condition Have Failed*. New Haven: Yale University Press.

every British official considered intrinsic to Indians: the propensity to lie, deceive, cheat and defraud."[9] British colonial administrative rule required, therefore, a new technology of individual identification, discriminate enough to isolate the individual native body and identity according to tribe, caste, and religion.

Enter William Herschel. Herschel, an official with the Indian Civil Service in Bengal, began to take individual handprints to verify that a local contractor would not renege on a contract. The practice was later refined with Herschel's speculation that fingerprints, their markings, and grooves were unique to each individual and could, thus, serve as that new technology of individuation. Though the practice began as a civil-corporate rather than criminal technique of administrative isolation—precontract not pre-crime so to speak—it emerged nonetheless in a specifically discriminatory, colonial, and racial context in which "inferiority of the ruled and their attendant deceptions and frauds provoked the search for greater and more efficient social control and identification."[10] The native deceptions, the colonists would miss, were actually techniques of the colonized that aimed at, among other things, disturbing relations of power in the colony.[11] Fingerprints nonetheless became a technology of marking individual identity propelled by a whole range of assumptions that informed their collection, and processes of interpretation away from the cunning eyes and native "problems" of colonial India.[12]

A century on, the processes of technical experimentation and technological methods involved in the administration of state surveillance, violence, and criminal justice have been refined through, among other instruments, the massive growth of DNA databases. The key provision deployed in processes of intelligence gathering in the name of fighting terrorism has largely been Schedule 7 of the Terrorism Act 2000,[13] which specifically allowed unrestricted stop and question procedures at ports. This power drew from the emergency legislation contained in the Prevention of Terrorism (Temporary

---

[9] Chandak Sengoopta. (2003). *Imprint of the Raj: How Fingerprinting Was Born in Colonial India.* London: Macmillan, pp. 47–48.

[10] Simon A. Cole. (2002). *Suspect Identities: A History of Fingerprinting and Criminal Identification.* Cambridge, MA: Harvard University Press, p. 65.

[11] On such "deceptions", see: J. C. Scott. (1985). *Weapons of the Weak: Everyday Forms of Peasant Resistance.* New Haven: Yale University Press; J. C. Scott. (1990). *Domination and the Arts of Resistance: Hidden Transcripts.* New Haven: Yale University Press. On techniques of disturbing even the most extreme forms of domination, James Scott's work remains authoritative. See: Scott, *Weapons of the Weak*; Scott, *Domination and the Arts of Resistance.*

[12] As Christian Parenti writes, "Among dactyloscopy's chief advantages—or so believed white colonial administrators, police, and bureaucrats—was its ability to compensate for the homogenizing effects of racist perceptions." Christian Parenti. (2003). *The Soft Cage: Surveillance in America from Slavery to the War on Terror.* New York: Basic Books, p. 49.

[13] HM Government. (2000). "Schedule 7: Port and Border Controls." *Terrorism Act 2000.* London: Home Office. Available at: http://www.legislation.gov.uk/ukpga/2000/11/schedule/7

Provisions) Act 1974 in response to the threat of Irish Republican terrorism and the surveillance of the Irish population in the 1970s.[14] Although renewed every six months since 1974, the provisions under emergency legislation were made permanent through the Act of 2000, and advanced the addition of DNA collection and the creation of a robust database. The recording and retention of DNA for policing crime, has become standard practice since the 1990s. In particular, the Criminal Justice and Public Order Act 1994 set in motion processes of building a repository formally linking genetics and criminality, a repository that by 2009 would be the biggest in the world with around five million profiles stored with few signs of uninhibited growth.[15] The expansion of these powers and institutional processes under the patronage of counterterrorism strategy have legislated that DNA samples can be taken by the police without consent from anyone arrested on suspicion of any recordable offense and retained indefinitely. Put otherwise, this amounts to the codification of race and criminality at the genomic level. As Nisha Kapoor explains,

Pressures to expand the recording and retention of the DNA of terrorism suspects led to the creation of an adjunct Counter-Terrorism DNA Database in July 2006, also administered by London's Metropolitan Police Service on behalf of the Counter-Terrorism Unit. By building on these established infrastructures for fighting crime more broadly, Britain's counterterrorism database has operated under similar powers, recording the DNA of mass numbers of individuals whose genetic traces happen to be found in spaces—homes, places of work, public venues—that are targeted in counterterrorism operations. The framing of counterterrorism in terms of national and global security, however, has raised the stakes, extending the scope of the practice beyond that which has been more formally legislated. Now, DNA obtained for counterterrorism purposes, such as Babar Ahmad's, can be shared internationally with partner states with which the British government is working in cooperation. *DNA collected for such purposes is also much more likely to be collected covertly, without the suspect's knowledge, and DNA records have been obtained from discarded cigarettes or drink*

---

[14] Schedule 7 has a predictably large discrepancy between the number of people stopped and those actually detained and charged. See: Paddy Hillyard. (2000). Suspect Community; Graham Ellison and Jim Smyth, The Crowned Harp: Policing Northern Ireland, London: Pluto Press. It is estimated that only 0.2 per cent of those stopped in 2015 were arrested. Benjamin Politowski. (2016). "Terrorism in Great Britain: The Statistics", House of Commons Briefing Paper, no. 7613, 9 June 2016. This repository is a system that depends upon racial profiling, or rather, is symptomatic of the modus operandi of the racial power with its procedures felt most intensely by the young black male population of the United Kingdom. In 2007, it was revealed that the DNA of an astonishing three-quarter of this demographic was on the national database. See: The Home Affairs Committee, Select Committee on Home Affairs—Second Report 2006–07, London: House of Commons, 2007.

[15] Helen Wallace. (2013). "The UK National DNA Database: Balancing Crime Detection, Human Rights and Privacy." EMBO Reports, July 2006, s26–s30; Home Office, National DNA Database Strategy Board Annual Report 2012–13, London: Home Office.

containers, during surveillance operations or when a suspect visits the home of an informant.[16]

Of course, next to nothing is known about how this data is recorded or codified and what it means for its subjects with respect to travel, employment, surveillance, and so on, for the institutional network involved in counterterrorism strategy is massive. This is to say nothing of the equally worrying factor of the social consequences of the extreme overrepresentation of black men in these databases, which have, under regimes of counterterrorism and radicalization strategies, become increasingly populated by Muslim men. In the present and future tense of race, the samples collected, and profiles constructed could be plugged into commercial structures in which biometric data is sold to private companies carrying out research linking crime and genetics which in turn refines the militarized extraction of this data. The search for the elixir of the "criminogenic gene" is overwhelmingly tied to race and, under Islamophobia, to religion and Muslimness all of which may have a life yet to come.

The secrecy of the conditions under which DNA is collected, and the ambiguity of how this data will be used is essential to the delivery of secret justice. Race, genomics, criminality, and the biometric database further consolidate an entire economy—these companies often have substantial research funds at their disposal—for the legitimation of state violence and cultures of suspicion vis-à-vis the figure of the Muslim. The covert sophistication of "criminogenetics" functions in conjunction with overt mechanisms for racial slurring. At the General Election of 1964, Peter Griffiths, a Conservative parliamentary candidate had his ultimately successful campaign in Smethwick buoyed by unofficial leaflets bearing the slogan: "If you want a Nigger for a neighbour—vote Labour!" The later immigration policies of the Conservative British government such as the Home Office's *Operation Vaken*, under then Home Secretary Theresa May, who was also at the forefront of the counterterrorism strategy, were reminiscent of the Smethwick strategy. *Vaken* deployed "Go Home" immigration vans, bearing the slogan "Go home or face arrest," driven around areas in six London boroughs with high ethnic minority populations to demonstrate the government's tough stance on immigration.[17] The

---

[16] Kapoor, *Deport*, p. 64. Emphases added.

[17] See: V. Lowndes and R. Madziva. (2016). "'When I Look at This Van, It's Not Only a Van': Symbolic Objects in the Policing of Migration." *Critical Social Policy*, 36(4), 672–92; Alan Travis. (2013). "'Go Home' Vans Resulted in 11 People Leaving Britain, Says Report." *Guardian*. Available at: https://www.theguardian.com/uk-news/2013/oct/31/go-home-vans-11-leave-britain; and Jeremy Bernhaut. (2014). "One Year on from the 'Go Home Vans' Flop: Has the Home Office Learned Anything?" *openDemocracy*. Available at: https://www.opendemocracy.net/en/5050/one-year-on-from-go-home-vans-flop-has-home-office-learned-anything/

immigration question has always been one asked in bad faith, and a question to which immigrants, always already racially coded, can never provide the correct answer. The Muslim, under formations of Islamophobia sponsored and legitimated by the terror threat, and in a deeper sense the foundational principle of "race," is more and more constructed as a premier *figure of migrancy* regardless of citizenship status, a subject who must go to a home that is anywhere but here.

Babar Ahmad and many others[18] have been at the receiving end of such secret justice in which the kind of violence of December 2003 has been constitutive. With charges initially dropped and "release" from prison after a short spell, often no more than two weeks, these suspects were rearrested and handed over to the Border Agency on the grounds that they were not conducive to the "public good," a legally relevant category. Most importantly, however, is the agency responsible for hearing the inevitable appeals to deportation and extradition orders: the Special Immigration Appeal Commission (SIAC), a court set up to deal with immigration cases where national security concerns were also raised. Nisha Kapoor explains,

> Modelled on a colonial administrative system, decisions are made by three selected judges and no jury. The court hears evidence in a mixture of open and closed sessions, and decisions can largely be set out in closed judgements. In the closed sessions, appellants and their lawyers are not allowed to see the evidence against them but instead they are assigned a (security-cleared) special advocate to represent them, and with whom they are not permitted to communicate once the advocate has been privy to the evidence against them.[19]

Within SIAC, through which the vast majority of individuals suspected of terrorism offenses are managed with very few dealt with through the criminal justice system, suspicion alone is enough for the authorization of state power and violence. The closed, secret processes of SIAC's judicial processes are designed to preserve the sanctity of executive power. The court is in effect and designs a colonial administrative system which supplements the official criminal justice system, in which state-appointed, security-cleared judges legitimate the routine use of closed evidence and secret justice. With much lower evidentiary standards than "normal" criminal court proceedings, SIAC provides the government with great latitude in the rationalizations and decision-making processes that inform its judgments. But perhaps the biggest impact of SIAC is that it has "established a cultural precedent and fine-tuned

---

[18] Most notably are the cases examined in Nisha Kapoor's important book, *Deport, Deprive, Extradite* (2018) and the broader work of the Deport, Deprive, Extradite Project. See: http://dde.org.uk/

[19] Kapoor, *Deport*, p. 73.

operational capacity for the use of closed courts and secret evidence."[20] It has normalized the mode of secret justice and generalized the category "public good" as a measure to discard, or to make secret, highly complex issues.

In 2005, when control orders[21] became a substitute for the indefinite detention of foreign nationals suspected of terrorism-related offenses, the appeals against such orders were heard at the High Court which functioned under the same conditions as in SIAC. The exceptional measures of SIAC were moved wholesale to the High Court. Moreover, the normalization of these procedures has been so successful in fact that, "they have been used in employment tribunals, in mental health review tribunals, and in immigration cases that are not marked as national security–related cases, but where individuals have been refused naturalised citizenship on grounds of 'bad character' because of suspected association with others deemed to be suspicious."[22] SIAC-like proceedings and base evidentiary standards have been employed in myriad justice-related fora: from parole board hearings, antisocial behavior orders, criminal hearings on police shootings, and gang and drug-related operations.

Justice that must be kept secret is not justice at all. But in the heady atmosphere of war and its paranoia, blatant contradictions are disappeared by their simultaneous repetition and disavowal, what amounts to simply looking the other way. The unreason of superior "races" must be suppressed, paradoxically, by extravagant processes of overcompensation and complexity with their acronyms, cartoonish titles, and immense funding. The racist effects of statecraft, culture, science, and much else must remain unrecognized and illegible for then they would otherwise become fundamentally illegitimate and criminal.[23] Put simply, the illegitimacy of the Muslim Questioned cannot be recognized as existing at all. The truth that we do not wish to be treated

---

[20] Ibid. p. 78.

[21] Established in the Prevention of Terrorism Act (2005), a Control Order is an order given by the Home Secretary to restrict the liberty of, and impose any obligations to, any individual for the purpose of "protecting members of the public from the risk of terrorism." See: https://publications .parliament.uk/pa/cm200405/cmbills/061/05061.1-7.html. The instrument of Control Orders has since been repealed under the Terrorism Prevention and Investigation Measures Act (2011), though the CTSA of 2015 made other counterterrorism measures, namely cooperating with Prevent and Channel a statutory duty across all public institutions.

[22] Kapoor, *Deport*, p. 78. Further challenges for the acknowledgment of unlawful state violence has been met by a doubling-down of such processes of secret justice: "With challenges brought by former Guantanamo Bay detainees against the British government's complicity in torture, the Justice and Security Act 2013 was passed which permitted closed proceedings in civil courts for any case in which the government decides that the disclosure of sensitive material would be 'harmful to the public interest'." (Ibid.)

[23] And recognized as such *within* Britain even, or especially, at the height of empire as Priyamvada Gopal's detailed study shows us, in fact, metropolitan notions of freedom and justice were significantly shaped by indigenous forms of anticolonial resistance in the colonies themselves. Priyamvada Gopal. (2019). *Insurgent Empire: Anticolonial Resistance and British Dissent*. London: Verso.

the way that the Muslim is must remain unacknowledged. In this sense, the Muslim Questioned is always already a question of race and its brittle character. For the subject, or the imagined national citizen, assumed to be endangered by the Muslim, is also the one whose worst nightmare is to wake up in the skin, dress, and name of that being who we call Muslim. This pathological angst is not simply the preserve of narrow-minded "white people" who occupy the lower classes, but is a general condition of individuals who in fact hate their own condition and whose dignity is secured in their whiteness which at its core is an identity lived in the negative. I am white *because* I am not Muslim. She is Muslim *because* she is not white. The nightmare of this war is not to wake up as a Muslim in the backward home to which they must be made to return, but to be named Muslim right here at home in what is supposed to be the familiar streets of their own country.

An interrogator who is thoroughly implicated in *producing* the guilty suspect as guilty must do all he can to erect barriers between his assumed innocence and assured status of questioner, and the marginalized and marked classifications of the guilty.[24] The image of the despotic Muslim, who is saturated in a kind of cosmic guilt which precedes him and the God whom he worships, has long functioned in the process of self-definition by projection. As Bryan Turner has noted, underlying the liberal theory of the individual was,

> a profound anxiety about the problem of social order in the West. . . . . Bourgeois individualism—in the theories of Locke and Mill—was challenged by the mob, the mass and the working class which was excluded from citizenship by a franchise based on property. The debate about Oriental Despotism took place in the context of uncertainty about Enlightened Despotism and monarchy in Europe. The Orientalist discourse of the absence of civil society in Islam was thus a reflection of basic political anxieties about the state of political freedom in the West. In this sense the problem of Orientalism was not the Orient but the Occident. These problems and anxieties were consequently transformed [sic] onto the Orient which became, not a representation of the East, but a caricature of the West. Oriental Despotism was simply Western monarchy writ large.[25]

---

[24] This should be thought as a form of discipline that worked on and through bodies which had only just become white. In Losurdo's analysis of relations between slaves and slave owners/buyers/exporters, the delineation of liberal identity and freedom necessitated forms of separation which, in fact, curtailed the freedoms of white, propertied subjects. Any disruption of the sacred separation been black and white could not be tolerated. See: Losurdo, *Liberalism*, chapters 2, 7 and 8. See especially his comments on the "SomersettCase," pp. 47–49. See also: Seymour Drescher. (1987). *Capitalism and Antislavery*. Oxford and New York: Oxford University Press, p. 37; David B. Davis. (1975). *The Problem of Slavery in the Age of Revolution*. Ithaca: Cornell University Press, pp. 231, 472, 495–96.

[25] Turner, "Orientalism and the Problem of Civil Society in Islam," p. 26.

The explicit racism of discourses of Oriental despotism, and its present war on terror mutations in discussions about Islam's troubling, if not antithetical relationship with democracy, human rights (especially for women)[26] and rational free willing, hides, in fact, secrets of specifically western problems of order, freedom, and justice. That everywhere she appears, the figure of the Muslim must produce and unleash structures of feeling and force which consolidate her guilt, not only for the terror that her people threaten but the disorder that defines the society we once had but have since lost. To behave otherwise when faced with the Muslim would be to question the racist underpinnings of our entire system of reality, to render suspect all the ways the Other has been systematically mistreated and all obligations to them renounced. "Terrorist," "fanatic," "extremist," and "Muslim" are names within this paradigm that license such behavior. Yet, the incoherence of this system must be known, for how else do the actions of a fraction of one-tenth of a percent of a population group *reasonably* stand in for an entire section of society, if not according to the principle of race? And why else insist on the secrecy of justice? There is, in sum, a widespread will and set of juridical methods designed to look at the Muslim but never see him and what we tell ourselves we must do to him. The Muslim Questioned is a theater of secrecy where everyone knows the lie but where the liar simply looks the other way.

SEEKING THE STATUS OF VICTIMHOOD

On a deeper level, the outpouring of Islamophobia today relates to the founding but repressed secret of the illegitimacy—but structuring role—of racism, the concealment of absurdity's centrality to our understanding of the world and the material policies which bring it into being. It is a kind of delirium caused by the fact of not knowing what else to think (of oneself) or how else to behave in the absence of race's phantasms. It is, in sum, a delirium caused by the fact that no one—not those who invented him, not those who named him thus—would want to be a Muslim or to be treated as one. To harmonize the unreason which structures the society (white supremacy) while concealing the very existence of its racist effects, we must instead perceive ourselves to be in a state of permanent threat from the racial subject. Daily life under regimes of permanent threat, governed by technologies of states of insecurity comes to be experienced as a long series of small shocks: a night raid here, a hostage situation there, finally, a shoot-out, and, preferably nearby a site of national memory, the killing of an enemy.

---

[26] Rashid, *Veiled Threats*; Bhattacharyya, *Dangerous Brown Men*; Eisenstein, *Against Empire*.

Secrecy under contemporary matrices of power licensed by the threat of terrorism[27] have mobilized a whole range of new technologies for the deeper invasion of trauma into the quotidian life of citizens, whereby we expect footage of the next attack, and have routinized the intense access that authorities—state as much as corporate—have to the private lives of individuals.[28] The violent tendencies of the Muslim propel a politics of resentment and hatred, a politics that authorizes the deployment of all powers of the nation to neutralize him, to compartmentalize, if not incarcerate, the contagion he is perceived to bring. But this is a politics in which we also burden ourselves with the Muslim we have created insofar as it behooves us, bearers of European civilization and the promises of modernity, to rectify them by any means necessary, suppressing the inevitable criminality involved in that same rectification. (Il)legal techniques of surveillance and tracking crucial to this project heighten the grip of fear over, and exit from, liberal democracy and manufacture variations on the monster or the ghost, all designed to reproduce and renew that same fear. No more 9/11s we say.

In the heady atmosphere of the war on those who terrorize us and who must, therefore, be terrorized, some of whom might be "saved," the violence of racism is reproduced via the enclosure of the status of victimhood. For such a status is unequivocal; as a victim it is you who have been wronged. Resolution and justice, therefore, come to be measured on terms set by the victimized. Economies of secrecy are essential to keeping some coherence to this longstanding narrative of the national body as that which seeks to civilize, as hospitable and always innocent though constantly under attack, confronting ingratitude and a lack of cooperation. Recognition of the basic fact of criminality as an essential scaffold of national and institutional life cannot be entertained without seriously disrupting the fundamentalism of Muslim pre-criminality, preemptive national security, discourses of loyalty, and the necessity to choose a side.

In the Muslim Questioned, where relations of interrogation and the kill become a social condition, we are excited only by immoderate stimuli, and "must paint with the most powerful images, exaggerate, and say the same thing over and over again."[29] It is this same work of pathological repetition and material reproduction that has given race such a firm grip on the

---

[27] A threat that is conceived as truly global and globalized integrating formerly peripheral regions into and within an American/British dominated security and, crucially, media regimes. See: Devji, *Landscapes*, pp. viii–xii.

[28] Zuboff, Shoshana. (2018). *The Age of Surveillance Capitalism: The Fight for a Human Future at the New Frontier of Power*. London: Profile Books. For an analysis of the globally networked and molecular quality of these practices, see: Jeff Halper. (2014). *War Against the People: Israel, Palestinians and Global Pacification*. London: Pluto Press.

[29] Sigmund Freud. (2004). *Mass Psychology and Other Writings*, trans. J.A. Underwood. London: Penguin, 6.

national(ist) imaginary in Britain.[30] In the widespread impulse to secrecy, against the sacred Enlightenment principle of individualism, this is a time of *mass morality*. Contemporary psychic modes under regimes of counterterrorism, "radicalization" and war—at once expansive and intimate—are constituted by a fundamental desire for mythology and the hunt, where we exist in relation to an ever-present threat which gnaws at the national body and who must everywhere be exposed.

The fundamentalisms involved in the dialects of distance, the mechanisms of exacting disclosure, and the processes of making-secret involved in the Muslim Questioned are not considered antithetical to rational thinking. As Joseph Massad notes,

> In some ways it seems that if religion was a causal factor in economics, modes of thought, and political systems from the sixteenth century onwards, and culture and later civilisation (and their relationship to climate and geography and later to race and genetics) became the heir to this system of causality in the nineteenth and much of the twentieth century, today we find that it is religion as culture, or culture as religion, that defines Islam as a causal factor determining certain political systems and not others.[31]

The arithmetic of the wars on/of terror, propelled by distinctly racial principles and its discourses of civilization and its twin, degeneration, are buttressed by the increasing expansion of algorithmic reason and the imprint of social media.[32] (Re)presentations of the war on terror *produce* the threat

---

[30] See: Sivamohan Valluvan. (2019). *The Clamour of Nationalism: Race and Nation in Twenty-First-Century Britain*. Manchester: Manchester University Press.

[31] Massad, *Liberalism*, p. 42.

[32] There is now a rich and growing literature on "race" after the internet and especially technologies of social media. See: Syed Mustafa Ali. (2013). "Race: The Difference that Makes a Difference." *TripleC*, 11(1), 93–106; Syed Mustafa Ali. (2016). "A Brief Introduction to Decolonial Computing." *XRDS*, 22(4), 16–21; S.M. Ali. (2017). Decolonizing Information Narratives: Entangled Apocalyptics, Algorithmic Racism and the Myths of History." Proceedings, 1, 50; Les Back. (2002). "Aryans Reading Adorno: Cyber-Culture and Twenty-First Century Racism." *Ethnic and Racial Studies*, 25(4), 628–51; J. Daniels. (2015). "'My Brain Database Doesn't See Skin Color': Color-Blind Racism in the Technology Industry and in Theorizing the Web." *American Behavioral Scientist*, 59(11), 1377–93; Lisa Nakamura and Peter A. Chow-White, eds. (2012). *Race after The Internet*. New York: Routledge; Safiya Umoja Noble. (2018). *Algorithms of Oppression: How Search Engines Reinforce Racism*. New York University Press. On the broader trend of the (neoliberal) collusion between the economic and the biological, see: Grégoire Chamayou's (2013) philosophy of the drone is particularly pertinent to these issues. See his, *Théorie du drone*. Paris: La Fabrique. See also: Peter M. Asaro. (2013). "The Labor of Surveillance and Bureaucratized Killing: New Subjectivities of Military Drone Operators." *Social Semiotics,* 23(2), 196–224; Alain Badiou. (2012). "La Grèce, les nouvelles pratiques impériales et la ré-invention de la politique." *Lignes*, 39, 39–47; Jeff Halper. (2014). *War Against the People: Israel, Palestinians and Global Pacification*. London: Pluto Press; Naomi Klein. (2007). *The Shock Doctrine: The Rise of Disaster Capitalism*. New York: Metropolitan Books; Adi Ophir, Michal Givoni, and Sari Ḥanafi. (2009).

of Muslims, Islamic terrorism, and the struggle against them through the deployment and live footage of everything—surgical strikes, searches, raids, precision bombing, drone warfare, the loss of national citizenship, and all its collateral damage—as a visceral experience, climaxes with metronomic regularity which rest upon a kind of communion of martyrs—militant jihadi, decorated soldier, innocent bystander together. The primary phantasy of Muslim violence is accompanied by representations of benevolent sacrifice endured by the nation in a unity of fundamentalisms; ours (racism) and theirs (terrorism).[33]

That liberal democracies incorporate a heavy dose of criminality into that same national body under attack by the contagion of Muslimness further draws a relation of dependence between us and the Muslim.[34] Hatred and suspicion of the Other do not simply have a vertical dimension but also a horizontal one which orders social links according to a logic of separation and differentiation—one fundamentally shaped by the racist impulse and thus various forms of distance. We should know very well that much of the colonial world (especially its paradigmatic site of the plantation) was characterized by such an order of segmented forms of distrust and ambivalence. An order, however, that is plagued by the pathological anxiety about the reversibility of positions at once denied—*"we could never be like they are"*— and repressed—*"they might take our dominant position."* The fear of being Muslim (for we know what Muslimness authorizes or else why the fear of both the Muslim and becoming his kin), and the psychic affliction concerning the walls separating us from the Muslim not being high or sturdy enough,

The Power of Inclusive Exclusion: Anatomy of Israeli Rule in the Occupied Palestinian Territories. New York: Zone Books; and Eyal Weizman. (2017). *Hollow Land.* London: Verso; David H. Ucko. (2009). *The New Counterinsurgency Era: Transforming the U.S. Military for Modern Wars.* Washington, DC: Georgetown University Press; Jeremy Scahill. (2007). *Blackwater: The Rise of the World's Most Powerful Mercenary Army.* New York: Nation Books; John A. Nagl. (2005). *Learning to Eat Soup with a Knife: Counterinsurgency Lessons from Malaya and Vietnam.* Chicago: University of Chicago Press.

[33] Speaking of the *jihad*, Devji notes that "Martyrdom creates a global community because it is collectively witnessed in mass media. These witnesses are therefore part of the jihad's struggle either as friends or enemies." In the communion of martyrs as I have described, this witnessing is as true for state violence of liberal democracies as Britain and "martyrdom," producing competing "global communities." See: Devji, *Landscapes*, p. 99; Devji, *Terrorist*, pp. 38–40.

[34] As Joseph Massad notes, in some ways it seems that if religion was a causal factor in economics, modes of thought, and political systems from the sixteenth century onward, and culture and later civilization (and their relationship to climate and geography and later to race and genetics) became the heir to this system of causality in the nineteenth and much of the twentieth century, today we find that it is religion as culture, or culture as religion, that defines Islam as a causal factor determining certain political systems and not others. Here it is not a juxtaposition of civilization and democracy in a temporal comparison that is being staged, but rather civilization, culture, and religion as anterior to and productive of political systems of rule, including democracy, Islam as a religious tradition that survives in modernity and continues to promote or suppress democracy. Massad, *Islam in Liberalism*, p. 42.

is another dimension of the secret as I mean it here. These are the facts: it is we who are burdened with the threat of the Muslim, but we would never ourselves want to be treated as he and his kin are. Therefore, while objects given the name Muslim must be tracked and to which are attached all manner of degraded and suspicious inclinations by virtue of their phenotypical constitution, it is we who are haunted by the specter of replacement despite our assumed primordial supremacy and democratic nature.

None of this is strictly new of course and must be kept fairly mundane. The expulsion of Muslims and Jews from Europe in the fourteen to seventeenth centuries in an attempt to manage the tension between a hyper-secular materialist industrialism and a changing Christian character, and to consolidate the racial configuration of both, relates to the later intense forms of "marking" and problematization of "the Turkish subject in Europe whereby anti-Turkish and anti-Ottoman sentiments were used to rally populations into supporting all types of egregious racist policies."[35] In the late 1990s, the idea of the Islamization of Europe received much attention and gave birth to the Stop the Islamization of Europe campaign, mainstreaming the overt racism and xenophobia of what were considered fringe parties. More recently, we have multiple expressions of "The Great Replacement"—a theory of the "dilution" and minoritization of white majorities across Euro-America—caused by immigration and miscegenation which centers around, and in the context of the outgrowth of the war on terror and the threat of "Islamic terrorism," is made coherent via the figure of the Muslim as the Other par excellence. This anxiety of displacement from what is assumed to be one's own, a fear based on a principle of race and logic of property, finds echoes in the colonial context in which the myriad efforts of separation and differentiation were necessary means to shield the numerical inferiority (and perceived racial, civilizational superiority) of the colonizers who imagined themselves to be surrounded on all sides by things threatening their survival and the march of modern progress. The powerful means of destruction may well have been effective in their genocidal and suppressive effects but did little to assuage the anxieties felt by the colonizers of their immanent extinction despite, paradoxically, seeking to uplift the humanity of the darker races.

At the core of the lie that must be concealed here is the absolute avoidance of questions of *why* nations colonize, segregate, and differentiate in this way; why people move; the motivations and root causes of fanatical violence; of

---

[35] Hatem Bazian. (2019). "Islamophobia, Racism and the 'Great Replacement'." *Daily Sabah.* Available at: https://www.dailysabah.com/columns/hatem-bazian/2019/05/08/islamophobia-racism-and-the-great-replacement. The "Turk" is a well-known "orientalist" trope, particularly in association with forms of "despotism." For one such view, see: Alexis De Tocqueville. (1838). *Democracy in America.* New York: Adlard and Saunders, 2 vols., especially vol. 1, chap. 3, pp. 28–35.

what must be the conditions of possibility for a fifteen-year-old girl finding purpose and meaning with enemies of an Islamic state; and crucially for our purposes, the complicity of race in producing these problems and anxieties together. Notions of white replacement and the return of bogus eugenics and race science in the corridors of the academy can only be obtained if the mirrored illusions of white superiority (entitlement) and white victimhood (annihilation) are simultaneously taken as reality. Being deprived of an absolute enemy who has an inherent hatred for our way of life—with no mechanism of division more absolute than race—is to be deprived of a necessary condition of identity and nation in the British context. But with a war without end as our common context, to be deprived of the existence of the Muslim as we have imagined her is to be deprived of a "that demon without which almost nothing is allowed."[36] The techniques of invention and consolidation, however, become more sophisticated and networked when it is believed that the fiercest enemy is he who has lodged himself into the deepest pores of the nation, participates in the labor market as a doctor or engineer, consumes as we consume, but who works nonetheless to destroy the nation's fundamental values *from within*. But the secret is that it suffices to create this Muslim enemy in order to track them, bring them out into the open, and neutralize them as part of a politics of hatred which sanctions the freeing of all inhibitions.[37]

THE DESIRE FOR MYTH

The Muslim Questioned, then, speaks of structures, relations, and processes which capture certain subjects and name particular impulses as Muslim in order to mask them. Masking was fundamental to modes of classification as they arose in the colonial world and though they mutate during their long decomposition, they continue to maintain certain secrets: chiefly, the racist and extractive mentality of liberal modernity's central commitments. The Muslim, then, cannot be allowed to answer freely, or if they do then it must be "we," at once their guarantors and guards, who decide the truth of their speech and the substance of their confession. It is so often the confessions of Others that preserve and are constitutive of Europe, Britain, and the white supremacy central to their illusions in which we must all live. These illusions are not opposed to reality but actually empower the (re)production of appearances, behaviors, and vulnerabilities that stitch together the hollow

---

[36] Mbembe, "Society of Enmity," p. 26.

[37] David Theo Goldberg discusses some of these processes as a contemporary age of civil war. David Theo Goldberg. (2017). "Violence." *HKW*. Available at: https://www.youtube.com/watch?v=FTA4aR8qBR4

but disturbing figure of the Muslim. Her presence is overwhelming. All the threats and fears she embodies become the very motor of the real in which to show hospitality is either to admit defeat or spell doom on a civilizational scale.

Where the production of this reality was once administered by traditional centers of authority, it should be clear from the foregoing that it is increasingly delegated to, or networked through, objects and technologies trafficking in large quantities of data and capital. There can be no salvation for our enemies who must simply be kept away or be made to submit, while the violence and violation of democracy must be concealed or integrated into its ordinary functioning. Appeals are made by white men and women—but not only them—to the great nation, to good old law and order, to virility and the ecstasy of victory. Calls are made for the Muslim to "to take responsibility for oneself," or elsewhere "to tear off one's chains and unveil" and "to shatter all taboos which your unjust God places on you." Our current moment of encounter and reckoning in which the Muslim is fundamental mobilizes him as a figure who appears to petrify and taunt white people, none more than the male chauvinist: "They veil their wives. They can have four of them. The bastards!"[38]

Secrecy and the structural removal of witnesses at once obscures and propels an anxiety which captures the Muslim's Other—the white subject—who fears replacement and is only partially comforted by the violence involved in her name. But in seeing the Muslim as being at an absolute distance, insisting they be tracked, coded, and made to speak while being silenced, in "seeing the other man as *an animal*, accustoms himself to treating him like an animal, tends objectively to transform *himself* into an animal."[39] The secret of race and racism when faced with the Muslim Questioned—pants down, abused, and mocked—is itself an accursed share, whereby security becomes possible only through war without end.

In the story of Babar Ahmad, we are simultaneously transported back to the colony and reminded of the racial violence constitutive of sovereignty, and projected forward into complex matrices of racial marking, listing, coding

---

[38] Houria Bouteldja. (2017). *Whites, Jews and Us: Towards a Politics of Revolutionary Love*. London: Semiotext(e), p. 83; Nacira Guénif-Souilamas and Éric Macé. (2004). *Les Féministes et le garçon arabe, Éditions de L'Aube*. Paris; Joan Wallach Scott. (2009). *The Politics of the Veil*, Princeton, NJ: Princeton University Press.

[39] Aime Césaire. (2000). *Discourse on Colonialism*, trans. Joan Pinkham. New York: Monthly Review Press, p. 33, 41. Fanon speaks, in turn, of "this Europe where they are never done talking of Man, yet murder men everywhere they find them, at the corner of every one of their own streets, in all the corners of the globe." Or, again, "that same Europe where they were never done talking of Man, and where they never stopped proclaiming that they were only anxious for the welfare of Man: today we know with what sufferings humanity has paid for every one of their triumphs of the mind." Frantz Fanon. (2001). *Wretched of the Earth*, London: Penguin.

where new forms of molecular violence is a floating presence constitutive of the social life of the marked or the immigrant. The constant background of racist effects expressed in moral terms against the Muslim terror threat unleashes all powers of the nation which are mobilized simultaneous to the adjournment, if not wholesale suspension, of moral reflection. The Muslim Questioned may live among us but can never become, nor were they ever, one of us. If they cannot be expelled then they must constantly disclose their location or enter into relations of interrogation always undergirded by the hope of being led back beyond our borders. It is only under these conditions that the abdication of responsibility and relations of care to the Muslim can take on an aspect of gratifying pleasure, a form of desire which licenses all forms of absolute and irresponsible power, and the widespread acceptance of the most incoherent arguments as the basis for criminality in the name of justice.

For in the problem of how to separate the national body from the cist which gnaws at it, while also shielding it from threats who live among us and need not be the true authors of evil but merely resemble them in name, skin color, or dress, lies the possibility that there is in fact not much at all which separates us. The Barbadian novelist, George Lamming, wrote about this paradox:

> The British West Indian writer confuses [the critic] because, for a variety of reasons, he seems so perilously near to the Other whose judgment begins with the unconscious premis[e] that he is, in fact, different. The novels which have come from these territories in the last few years seem to betray the anxieties, desires, and illusions that appear identical with those of his English equivalent. His conception of what a novel is appears to be the same. . . . He does really speak English. It is not his second language. And even when it makes embarrassing demands on his tongue, or emerges in strangely hybrid forms, it does not seem to cause any surprise.[40]

In the dark realities of surveillance and (pre-)crime, judgment, and interrogation, the Muslim Questioned is protected, however precariously, by the illusions produced through classifications designed to injure, functioning as the proliferating agents of the Muslim's fundamental differences. The Muslim is a name that simultaneously frightens and confuses the white subject who is assumed to be his Other and superior, one who is split between imaginings of a white European past whose primary meanings derive from myths of benevolence and absolute power, and the immanence of Europe's disintegration and fracture. The figure of the Muslim is rooted in this history

---

[40] George Lamming. (1956). "The Negro Writer and His World." *Presence Africaine*, 8-9-10: 318–25.

of race but is given an urgency through the reality of the Muslim as citizen,[41] a subject who was surely born and raised here, who works and consumes as we do but who was never really one of us. The unparalleled violence and sophistication of systems of illusion under the aegis of combating Muslim terror are showing their cracks. The status of victim under siege despite our attempts to modernize the Muslim threat is permeated by a brittle but distinctly racial logic. It is everywhere under question but must beget greater violence in its sustenance and the multiplication of spaces where it is we who ask the questions and the Muslim who confesses.

---

[41] As Nisha Kapoor explains, ultimately, state violence has depended again "on criminalised bodies, racialised criminalised bodies. It produced these bodies and disciplined them. In this disciplining we were (re)learning that the struggle for full rights and recognition had not yet been won. Not only this, but that the goal posts were moving further away. Citizenship did not guarantee rights to a fair trial. It did not guarantee due process. It was itself not guaranteed. It had to be earned by brown and black subjects, continuously. In an instant, it could now be taken away." Kapoor, *Deport*, pp. 172–73.

THE MUSLIM QUESTION

"WHICH LANGUAGE IS THE BEST WORTH KNOWING?"

The function, the very serious function of racism is distraction. It keeps you from doing your work. It keeps you explaining, over and over again, your reason for being. Somebody says you have no language and you spend twenty years proving that you do. Somebody says your head isn't shaped properly so you have scientists working on the fact that it is. Somebody says you have no art, so you dredge that up. Somebody says you have no kingdoms, so you dredge that up. None of this is necessary. There will always be one more thing.

—Toni Morrison, "A Humanist View".

I mean longer prison sentences, I mean making it easier to deport foreign terrorist suspects back to their own country and I mean doing more to restrict the freedom and movement of terrorist suspects when we have enough evidence to know they are a threat but not enough evidence to prosecute them in full in court. And if our human rights laws stop us from doing it, we'll change the laws so we can do it.

—Theresa May.

***

The British did not gain effective military and state control over India until 1757. Though the British Royal Charter under Queen Elizabeth I formed the British East India Trading Company in 1600 after the defeat of the Spanish

Armada, engagement with, management of, and resource extraction from India had been conducted overwhelmingly through expensive methods and political economies of (corporate) military control.[1] After the British defeat of Nawab Siraj-ud-Daula under Robert Clive to become rulers of Bengal, the richest province in India, it was only then that a systematic—and unprecedented—campaign to draw out the resources of the country through cheaper though no less violent juridical methods of control could proceed. The immediate and most obvious motivation was of course profit: accumulating and integrating the country into the open market, thus becoming subject to the logics of bureaucracy and *commercium*.[2] The Charter Act of 1813 is noteworthy: it renewed the license issued (though on different terms) to the British East India Company and continued the company's rule in India; it also ended the company's monopoly over the major goods drawn out of Indian land.[3] Further still, the Crown's sovereignty was asserted, the permission for Christian missionaries to preach their religion and propagate English was granted, and, interestingly, Rs.100,000 was allotted to promote education in Indian literature. The sovereignty of the Crown and the Company's continued corporate presence meant the growth of British power and constituted a thoroughly mercantile force in the country.

The triumph of the market and accumulation of profit, however, were not enough. A more substantial reconfiguration of India, its subjects, and their

---

[1] On the imperial political economy of the Company, see: John Keay. (1993). *The Honourable Company: A History of the English East India Company*. London: HarperCollins Publishers; Philip J. Stern. (2012) *The Company-State: Corporate Sovereignty And The Early Modern Foundations Of The British Empire In India*. Oxford: Oxford University Press; William Dalrymple. (2019). *The Anarchy: The Relentless Rise of the East India Company*. London: Bloomsbury Publishing. See also, the political aspirations of the Company as itself a polity: Philip J. Stern. (2007). "Politics and Ideology in the Early East India Company-State: The Case of St Helena," 1673–1709, *The Journal of Imperial and Commonwealth History*, 35:1, 1–23.

[2] Colonization that brought together the three logics of race, commerce, and bureaucracy was unique in human history. Hannah Arendt's words in *The Origins of Totalitarianism* remain lucid. Arendt writes: "Of the two main political devices of imperialist rule, race was discovered in South Africa and bureaucracy in Algeria, Egypt, and India; the former was originally the barely conscious reaction to tribes of whose humanity European man was ashamed and frightened, whereas the latter was a consequence of that administration by which Europeans had tried to rule foreign peoples whom they felt to be hopelessly their inferiors and at the same time in need of their special protection. Race, in other words, was an escape into an irresponsibility where nothing human could any longer exist, and bureaucracy was the result of a responsibility that no man can bear for his fellow-man and no people for another people." Arendt, *Origins*, p. 207 and chapters 6 and 7. Earlier (p. 185) she writes, "Two new devices for political organization and rule over foreign peoples were discovered during the first decades of imperialism. One was race as a principle of the body politic, and the other bureaucracy as a principle of foreign domination. Without race as a substitute for the nation, the scramble for Africa and the investment fever might well have remained the purposeless "dance of death and trade" (Joseph Conrad) of all gold rushes. Without bureaucracy as a substitute for government, the British possession of India might well have been left to the recklessness of the "breakers of law in India" (Burke) without changing the political climate of an entire era."

[3] Though the death knell of the company's monopoly would not come until the Charter Act for India in 1833.

exterior and interior lives was needed. The ultimate goal was to refashion India, to civilize it in the image of its modern colonizers, and to civilize its peoples just short of changing their blood and color. This was an extravagant and intrusive project, but a project based on the contention that the ontological gap which was assumed to have separated the British (as members of the Anglo-Saxon family) from the Indians, the white from the nonwhite, was not absolute. That there may, after all, come to be an affinity and measure of proximity between us and them. The conditions of possibility for our mutual benefit is contingent, nonetheless, on the Other's (newfound) recognition of who they are and should aim to be, a price to be paid in the coin of tradition to make way for progress into modernity with major implications for what the Indian should be, how s/he should live, what is and is not worth knowing.

The ultimate goal was, as Thomas Babington Macaulay's "Minute on Indian Education" (1835)[4] testifies, to remake the Indian subject herself.[5] The first child of Zachary Macaulay, prominent governor of Sierra Leone, and Selina Mills, favored protégé of the famed Evangelical writer and protagonist of the manners-and-morals reform movement, Hannah More, Macaulay soon became secretary of the Board of Control for India. In office, he played a crucial part in drafting the new Charter Act of 1833. Catherine Hall writes,

> He was an extraordinarily gifted child from his earliest years, amazing adults with his feats of reading and writing. His years in Cambridge were followed by an attempt at a career in law but it soon became apparent that writing was his metier. As a young essayist for the *Edinburgh Review* in the 1820s, he dazzled with the brilliance of his rhetoric and became the toast of the Whigs for his polemical critique of James Mill's *Essay on Government*. His oratorical triumphs in the Commons in the cause of a limited measure of reform were rewarded with a seat on the Board of Control for India. He was soon to become the Secretary and play a crucial part in drafting the new Charter Act of 1833. . . . He left England for India in 1834 and stayed for three and a half years.[6]

It is at this time that the management of India, and the question of what to do with its Muslim and Hindu inhabitants, loomed large in his thinking and policies of reform. An important point of entry for this project was the indigenous

---

[4] Bureau of Education. Selections from Educational Records, Part I (1781-1839). Edited by H. Sharp. Calcutta: Superintendent, Government Printing, 1920. Reprint. Delhi: National Archives of India, 1965, 107–117. Available at: http://www.columbia.edu/itc/mealac/pritchett/00generallinks/macaulay/txt_minute_education_1835.html

[5] For biographical information see George Otto Trevelyan. (1881). *The Life and Letters of Lord Macaulay* (London: Longman, Green); John Clive. (1973). *Thomas Babington Macaulay: The Shaping of the Historian* (London: Secker & Warburg); Catherine Hall. (2012). *Macaulay and Son: Architects of Imperial Britain* (New Haven, CT: Yale University Press).

[6] Catherine Hall. (2008: 782–83). "Making colonial subjects: education in the age of empire." *History of Education*, 37:6, 773–787.

institutions of learning whose value would be judged in relation to imperial Britain, its mercantile and extractive aims, and the presumed rationality of the conquering subject. Says Macaulay:

> It is said that Sanscrit and Arabic are the languages in which the sacred books of a hundred millions of people are written, and that they are on that account entitled to peculiar encouragement. Assuredly it is the duty of the British Government in India to be not only tolerant but neutral on all religious questions. But to encourage the study of a literature, admitted to be of small intrinsic value, only because that literature inculcated the most serious errors on the most important subjects, is a course hardly reconcilable with reason, with morality, or even with that very neutrality which ought, as we all agree, to be sacredly preserved.
>
> [C]an we reasonably or decently bribe men, out of the revenues of the State, to waste their youth in learning how they are to purify themselves after touching an ass or what texts of the Vedas they are to repeat to expiate the crime of killing a goat? I think it clear that we . . . are free to employ our funds as we choose, that we ought to employ them in teaching what is best worth knowing, that English is better worth knowing than Sanscrit or Arabic, that the natives are desirous to be taught English.

The hundreds of millions of people with some worldly and immanent, if immensely heterogenous, attachment to sacred books written in Arabic and Sanskrit were quite simply misguided. These were subjects who found meaning in things of little intrinsic value and who asked all the wrong questions and provided even worse answers. In fact, the natives have admitted it to us, Macaulay appears to be saying; they no longer want the dead languages of Arabic and Sanskrit and their cultures of knowledge which are likewise stuck in the past. No, the Indians want to be English. Macaulay's "Minute" should be read as an honest expression for how to remake the Indian subject by dismantling Sanskrit and Arabic centers of learning, whose knowledge amounted to folly and myth in the face of the modern, industrial, and colonizing force of reason. These longstanding processes of learning, rooted in a social fabric to which they were organic and coherent, would instead be replaced with English as the sole medium of instruction and a "modern" curricula of classics in order to produce Indians as fit intermediaries between the colonists and the colonized. And the remaking of the Indian subject, just as the formation of the modern British subject, would have to begin as early as possible in the subject's life.

Macaulay was also canny enough to set the reformation of Muslim and Hindu traditions of learning into its necessary economic and political context of imperial austerity when he argues that "[It] is impossible for us, with our limited means, to attempt to educate the body of the people."[7] Sacrifices, therefore, had to be made in order for the sheet to balance, and the project of bringing the Indians up to and into modern life was finite in the resources that could be allotted to it.[8] The limited means of the empire to educate the people of India, however, speaks to a paradox which brings together two conflicting, if condescending, ideas when faced with the Indian native: resignation and trust. While the Muslim of India could not be us—modern, rational, moral— she could be entrusted to fulfil aspects of our reforming project and by doing so bring himself and others of his kind closer to us:

We must at present do our best to form a class who may be interpreters between us and the millions whom we govern—a class of persons Indian in blood and colour, but English in tastes, in opinions, in morals and in intellect. To that class we may leave it to refine the vernacular dialects of the country, to enrich those dialects with terms of science borrowed from the Western nomenclature, and to render them by degrees fit vehicles for conveying knowledge to the great mass of the population.

I believe that the present system tends not to accelerate the progress of truth but to delay the natural death of expiring errors. . . . We are a Board for wasting the public money, for printing books which are of less value than the paper on which they are printed was while it was blank—for giving artificial encourage-ment to absurd history, absurd metaphysics, absurd physics, absurd theology— for raising up a breed of scholars who find their scholarship an incumbrance and blemish, who live on the public while they are receiving their education, and whose education is so utterly useless to them that, when they have received it, they must either starve or live on the public all the rest of their lives.[9]

---

[7] Macaulay's argument here would not be out of place in austerity Britain and the (racial) drama of Brexit given the intersections of institutional racism and cuts to public services, including educa-tion. See: Emejulu, A., &Bassel, L. (2015). "Minority women, austerity and activism." *Race & Class*, 57(2), 86–95; Laleh Khalili. (2017). "After Brexit: Reckoning With Britain's Racism And Xenophobia," Poem, 5:2–3, 253–265; Sian, K., Law, I., Sayyid, S. (2013). *Racism, Governance, and Public Policy.* New York: Routledge; Satnam Virdee & Brendan McGeever. (2018). "Racism, Crisis, Brexit, Ethnic and Racial Studies," 41:10, 1802–1819.

[8] Macaulay would explain: "If the Benares and Delhi Colleges should be retained, I would at least recommend that no stipends shall be given to any students who may hereafter repair thither, but that the people shall be left to make their own choice between the rival systems of education without being bribed by us to learn what they have no desire to know . . . Benares is the great seat of Brahminical learning; Delhi of Arabic learning. If we retain the Sanscrit College at Benares and the Mahometan College at Delhi we do enough and much more than enough in my opinion, for the Eastern languages." Thus, redirected investment into the teaching of English was needed: "The funds which would thus be placed at our disposal would enable us to give larger encouragement to the Hindoo College at Calcutta, and establish in the principal cities throughout the Presidencies of Fort William and Agra schools in which the English language might be well and thoroughly taught."

[9] Bureau of Education. Selections from Educational Records, Part I (1781–1839). Edited by H. Sharp. Calcutta: Superintendent, Government Printing, 1920. Reprint. Delhi: National Archives of India, 1965, 107-117. Emphases added. Available at: http://www.columbia.edu/itc/mealac/pritchett /00generallinks/macaulay/txt_minute_education_1835.html

Macaulay's words above have real pertinence for the Muslim Question as I mean it: our second mode of "knowing," relating to, and living with the Muslim. I think it worth asking what Macaulay's ambitious attitude in his prescriptions and proscriptions for Indian education under British colonial rule represents for British (post)colonial consciousness of what to do with our Muslim neighbors. Were his ambitions exceptional? Did they depart from some other mode of encounter with India, its Hindus and Mahometans? Do they exhibit a particular paradigm of governance, of state-making and discipline that are exclusive to the colonial laboratory of early nineteenth-century India? Of what utility is the concept of "race"? Finally, where is Islam and the figure of the Muslim in Macaulay's attitude to reason, good public spending, and the moral, useful individual?

With these questions and others as our context, in this second mode the Muslim is caught within the fluid character of relations between dialects of proximity, affirmation, and publicity. *Proximity* proceeds according to the possibility that there might exist associations of familiarity, of reciprocity even, between us and the Muslim Other. This possibility is, however, contingent on the Muslim's willingness to be improved and to work on themselves. I argue that Macaulay's pronouncements captured what was a massive project to reconstitutee Indian education and forms of sociality which, together with the work of chief Orientalist Sir William Jones to re-from the law in India, sought to remake the Indian subject himself.

Affirmation, secondly, supports such technologies of integration manifested in the regular demand for the Other to corroborate the supremacy of the values that we are assumed to hold, to attest to the desirability of sameness in the first place, and to condemn those who do not agree. The analogy of translation, of reproducing alien words and concepts in a language with which we are familiar, but which necessitates certain elisions captures the core of this idea. It is as if the figure of the Muslim must always be prepared to *attend the everywhere press conference and read from the autocue* of the Muslim Question, its "translated" terms, intimacies, and desires. The reproduction and dissemination of racial fictions in the language of (multi)culture and religion within regimes of cohesion and integration (per)form useful sites for our analyses here.

Publicity, finally, is the open (un)certainty about the nature and location of our Muslim enemy, the turning of racism into the pretense of a patchwork, liberal multiculture attested to from within and without, by us—white Britain—and Muslims alike, in and through the *public* presence of the Muslim speaker. I contend also with the new possibilities and coalitions occasioned by the newfound publicity of Muslims after the fall of the twin towers invoking Miriam Cooke's notion of "The Muslimwoman," and analyzing the media(ted) circulation of the racial and gendered subject, a figure that is not easily reneged by the racial formation of (post)colonial Britain. Instead, we are surrounded by racism-made culture, a culture in which to ask the Muslim Question is its mundane aspect and which is manifest from processes of national mourning to the historical figures who quite literally scatter the streets of the capital. The three together form this second paradigm, enticingly tolerant but deeply condescending, borne of a colonial matrix of power with effects—peculiar, familiar, absurd, and contradictory—put to new forms of work in the British postcolonial predicament.

Chapter 4

Proximity

From a particular vantage point and with a great deal of good faith, part of what comes out of Macaulay's "Minute" is a concern about the extent to which anything could be shared between the British colonists and the Hindu and Muslim subjects of empire who (against their own desires it would seem) are taught and are invested in traditions of Sanskrit and Arabic learning. What are the conditions of possibility and contours of sociality in which proximity, friendship, and trusteeship between us and them become coherent? As far as Macaulay was concerned, the very possibility, hope even, for future amities rested on reconstitution of the Indian subject from a young age so that when they grow to working age, they have been properly formed by, and have come to recognize, what counts as "useful learning." That is, what the Indians under British colonial sovereignty *really* desire to know is that which would bring them—a class of Indian persons in blood and skin pigmentation—up to the level of the English "in tastes, opinions, morals and intellect." The possibility of proximity—linguistically, ontologically, and epistemologically—at once exhibits a paradigmatic liberal move which posits genuine care for progressive change in/for Others, but on terms forcefully and necessarily set by the modern colonizers themselves. This is a friendship under the pain of punishment and regimes of theft. No friendship at all.

Whereas the Muslim Questioned is constituted by an inherent logic of separation and insists on a fundamental distance between the white subject and the Muslim, the Muslim Question signals the possibility of proximity between the two based on a logic of *integration*. Whereas the paradigm of hostility is one which (de)humanizes and seeks to maintain the walls (always too thin) separating us and the racial Other, this second mode has an impulse to *progress*, to *make-them-like-us*, which is in truth what they, the Muslims, want. Though the forms and intensity of the violence involved in the first

paradigm were not seen as a contradiction to the liberal and democratic credentials of colonial Britain,[1] this second paradigm seeks more legitimately,
that is, less contradictorily, to buttress British claims to its professed fundamental values of democracy, the rule of law, liberty, the rights of man, and
tolerance. In sum, to modernity's essential promises.[2]

The Muslim Question, then, is the simultaneity of separation and intimacy.
In the colonial desire to bring English instruction and intellect to the Indians,
and by doing so bringing them toward the border of modernity as consistent
with the actual will of the colonized,[3] numerous technologies constituting a
regime of separation are put to work. But their functioning depends quite fundamentally on proximity with those subjects who are separated. The Muslim
Question in the nineteenth-century Indian context concerns the production
of future intermediaries who, prior to the means of our rational medium of
instruction, exist as disturbing objects who have survived natural decline,
initial destruction, or have had the audacity to refuse to disappear, but who
cannot be thought of as completely exterior from the (English) self and are

---

[1] As Uday Singh Mehta writes, "Already by the eighteenth and certainly following the Reform Bills
of the nineteenth century Britain, in its self-image, was a democracy, yet it held a vast empire that
was, at least ostensibly, undemocratic in its acquisition and governance; following Locke, there was
a broad consensus that linked the exercise of political power with the rights of citizens, and yet the
existence of the empire meant that British power was overwhelmingly exercised over subjects rather
than citizens; again following Locke, and in the aftermath of the Glorious Revolution (168), the idea
of the power of the state being limited and checked by the separation of the branches of government
had taken hold, and yet imperial power, as George I and his ministers emphasized and as later liberals such as both the Mils concurred (at least with respect to India), had no such constraints placed on
its exercise; similarly, by the mid-nineteenth century among radicals and liberals, the conditions for
good government had been recognized as intimately linked with the conditions of self-government,
and yet in someone like John Stuart Mill, who most forcefully articulated this argument, it applied
only to the Anglo-Saxon parts of the empire." Mehta, *Liberalism and Empire*, p. 7.

[2] The regular abandonment of ethical benchmarks in the formation, worldview, and actual practices
of British and "Western" matrices of power, in the name of modernity and the sovereignty of its
Reason is an essential facet, and not merely an instrumental aspect, of European modernity. It is
only in this way that the logics of "race" and colonialism, of war and limitless expenditure could
be justified as being in the service of "progress." The absence of benchmarks allows a principle of
absolute arbitrariness to make common-sense consistency of outright contradiction. Thus, slavery
and democracy, new rights of the citizen at home, and the dismantling of indigenous life and rights
abroad, exist in harmony according to the arithmetic of modern, sovereign colonial power. See:
Amy Allen. (2017). *The End of Progress: Decolonizing the Normative Foundations of Critical
Theory*. New York: Columbia University Press; Wael Hallaq. (2018). *Restating Orientalism: A
Critique of Modern Knowledge*. New York: Columbia University Press; Utsa Patnaik and Prabhat
Patnaik. (2017). *A Theory of Imperialism*. New York: Columbia University Press; Utsa Patnaik.
(2017). "Revisiting the Drain, or Transfers from India to Britain in the Context of Global Diffusion
of Capitalism." In *Agrarian and other histories: Essays for Binay Bhushan Chaudhuri*, edited by
B. B. Chaudhuri, S. Chakrabarti, and U. Patnaik.

[3] As Macaulay said: "we ought to employ them in teaching what is best worth knowing, that English
is better worth knowing than Sanscrit or Arabic, that the natives are desirous to be taught English,
and are not desirous to be taught Sanscrit or Arabic, that neither as the languages of law nor as the
languages of religion have the Sanscrit and Arabic any peculiar claim to our encouragement, that
it is possible to make natives of this country thoroughly good English scholars, and that to this end
our efforts ought to be directed."

important to the sovereign designs s/he pursues in the name of queen, country, and civilization.

In pronouncements of proximity and of the conditional possibility of mutuality, the Muslim who is b(r)ought into the enclosure of "we" becomes the privileged site in a racial logic of suspicion (as Muslim) and accumulation (as potentially one of us). Under such conditions, everything that the Muslim does or says, or is assumed to believe, becomes coded as involved in a larger plot or conspiracy, and must instead be superseded by the project of their internalization of useful knowledge, their learning English, their training as competent intermediaries, secretaries, chauffeurs, and, ultimately, wards of a modernity that is ours but might be theirs.[4] Reading Macaulay in this way opens up lines of communication—overlapping, contradictory, circular, broken—with contemporary modes of racial power, the pronouncements made in its name, and the policies sanctioned by its worldview. Macaulay, then, is a *type*, a peculiar model of engaging with the Muslim Question that has not left us. A model which has in fact come to perform newer but also distinct functions undergirded by a set of "promises" that recalls its opposite—the ruse, the lie. In sum, the "swindle of liberalism."[5]

IMPROVING THE NATIVE

In the expansion and consolidation of the multifarious project of the empire, encountering new peoples and societies, the imperatives of effective management over territory and, more importantly, human lives had to confront complex questions. A key problem, Catherine Hall notes,

> emerged as to how to rule these new subjects of empire—whether enslaved or free Africans, or indigenous peoples of North America, Australia, or India. What would it mean to make these peoples into colonial subjects? What was their status? How should they be ruled? Might they eventually have the same

---

[4] Macaulay was skeptical of the possibilities of useful learning within Islamic and Hindu traditions of Arabic and Sanskrit: "But to encourage the study of a literature, admitted to be of small intrinsic value, only because that literature inculcated the most serious errors on the most important subjects, is a course hardly reconcilable with reason, with morality, or even with that very neutrality which ought, as we all agree, to be sacredly preserved. It is confirmed that a language is barren of useful knowledge. We are to teach it because it is fruitful of monstrous superstitions. We are to teach false history, false astronomy, false medicine, because we find them in company with a false religion."

[5] G. Khiabany and M. Williamson. (2015). "Free Speech and the Market State: Race, Media and Democracy in New Liberal Times." *European Journal of Communication,* 30(6), 583. Provocatively, in the history of modern Islam, "Al-Qaeda has assumed the role that had been assigned to Muslim liberals or modernists, as they are often known, of whom so much continues to be expected to this day. The holy grail of Islamic liberalism has been pursued relentlessly for some two hundred years now, but with little success." This is the other side of the swindle. Devji, *Landscapes*, p. 162.

rights as British subjects? Once empire was no longer primarily about trade, extracting as much as possible from commercial relations, and became about the governance of territories and peoples, the question of how to rule became central. In a system of slavery, authority could be maintained with the sword and the whip. But by the late eighteenth and early nineteenth centuries huge numbers of people living in what had become British territories were not enslaved.[6]

The colonial question of rule takes shape in a unidirectional form: "How do we rule *them*?" It is for this reason, in part at least, that the function of proximity is to construct a measure of filiality but which must remain similarly unidirectional: "Ultimately, it must be us who rules them so how might they become *more like us*?" The core of this dynamic of differentiation proceeds like the critic John Berger's lighthouse perspective:

> The convention of perspective . . . centers everything in the eye of the beholder. It is like a beam from a lighthouse—only instead of travelling outward, appearances travel in. The conventions called those appearances reality. Perspective makes the single eye the center of the visible world. Everything converges on the eye as to the vanishing point of infinity. The visible world is arranged for the spectator as the universe was once thought to be arranged for God.[7]

In the relationship between the colonizer and colonized, the reality of the colony was whatever sovereign will dictated and bureaucracy administrated, a reality which flowed from fundamental ideas of primitive language, "absurd history," and modern reason. To be sure, those cast as primitive in one way or another are impervious to rational experience and to our ways of thinking but they can be molded in the hands of a superior race, can be convinced of, and might come to inherit a life which possesses a will that need not be delegated from the heavens nor consumed by ancestral hatreds nor a law that had to be revealed rather than discovered by powers of the mind.[8] An essential "prelogical" essence of the racial Other appears tenaciously paradigmatic

---

[6] Hall, "Making Colonial Subjects," pp. 773–74.

[7] John Berger. (1992). *Ways of Seeing*. London: Penguin, p. 16. See also David Michael Levin, ed. (1993). *Modernity and the Hegemony of Vision*. Berkeley: University of California Press; and more recently, Sheldon Wolin. (2016). *Politics and Vision: Continuity and Innovation in Western Political Thought*. New Jersey: Princeton University Press.

[8] On historical expressions of the fungible humanity of Others subject to this process of "moulding," see: Said, *Orientalism*, es. chapter 2. See also: Lucien Lévy-Bruhl. (1910). *Les fonctions mentales dans les sociétés inférieures*. Paris: F. Alcan. See also Lévy-Bruhl. (1922). *La mentalité primitive*. Paris: Presses Universitaires de France; and Lévy-Bruhl. (1928). *L'âme primitive*. Paris: Presses Universitaires de France; Arthur Gobineau. (1983). "Essai sur l'inégalité des races humaines." In *Œuvres complètes*. Paris: Gallimard, 1, p. 623, 1146; R. van der Veer. (2003). "Primitive Mentality Reconsidered." *Culture & Psychology*, 9(2), 179–84.

within British regimes of fundamentalist white supremacy. In the colonial laboratory, race functioned as the privileged *language* not only of conflict and of history but of law. It was the principal substance from which reason and thus power flowed and came to recast various forms of elimination and segregation as the necessary route to redemption.

It is, therefore, important to draw connections, given our view of the colony and the postcolonial subject, between Macaulay's arguments for the *Becoming-English-of-the-Indians*, and his expression, minimal though it may have been, of a (re)cognizable Indian humanity. Macaulay's "Minute" was clear that religion (or "absurd theology") was complicit in the perpetuation of the unreason of the Muslim (and Hindu) population. Again, the name "Islam" licensed certain practices of violation in the highly charged (racio-*logical*) atmosphere of both the colony and metropole. It was assumed that the sanctuaries of white Europe, including the Board of Public Instruction, birthed the rights of Man and the contents of human civilization. And while the colony was a space and genealogy apart from that civilization, it could not simply be represented as a free zone of lawlessness under British rule but a place to be tamed and made useful. Only then could it be pillaged in good conscience, give free reign to the children of empire to carry forward the assumption that there could be no principles, no social forms, no sanctuaries that one could not, a priori, violate.[9]

But in Macaulay's pronouncements on, or *for*, the Muslims of India, he signals to the potential incorporation of these foreign subjects into (the service of) European civilization. As a liberal technique, there was indeed a search for a specific measure of difference and enmity that licenses the major reconstructive project that was British colonial modernity in India, but a measure always already framed by the blood and color of the Indians. The result was a system of tutelage and training in English that might allow the natives to see reason. Though not *of* Britain, that is, not *of us*, there are aspects of them which might at least make of them "fit vehicles for conveying knowledge" to those Others-of-their-kind otherwise beyond the pale. In a sense, then, the project of "progress-from-above" in India was a search for an insight into an Other world waiting to be rehabilitated.

But this would be a colossal engineering project, at the forefront of which was "local" law as a juridical realm that was "disorderly" and "confused" to British tastes and reason. Thus came the Hastings Plan, named after Warren Hastings—the corrupt British governor of the Bengal—through which the Indian legal order, with particular emphasis on the "chaotic" nature of Islamic (and Hindu) law, would be modernized. The plan, as Hallaq notes,

---

[9] Arendt, *Origins of Totalitarianism*, p. 189.

conceived a multitiered system that required exclusively British administrators at the top, seconded by a tier of British judges who would consult with on-the-ground Muslim legal experts with regard to issues governed by the Shari'a. At the lowest rung of judicial administration stood the run-of-the-mill Muslim judges who administered law in the civil courts of Bengal, Madras, and Bombay. The plan was designed to absorb local customs and norms into a British institutional structure of justice and to streamline them in accordance with "universal" ideals of justice.[10]

The alleged chaos of indigenous Islamic law spoke to its ambiguous, pliable, and casuistic nature understood as a mass of juristic opinion that did not resemble the modern codices of British law that had, it was thought, progressed beyond the "disorder" and "primitive experience" of Islamic and Hindu legal structures.[11] The preeminent classicist and Orientalist Sir William Jones (1746–1794) was to be the chief architect of the "resolution" of the "Indian problem" through the production of a "complete digest of Hindu and Mussulman law."[12] This was nothing short of a social, moral, and structural revolution in India, licensed and authorized by a colonial matrix of power in which British law and industrial modernity were the only legitimate modes of being, and through which the former glory of India might be brought up to date. It did not occur to either Macaulay, Hastings, or Jones that it was in fact they who required greater training and better education before the declaration of their inherently destructive plans.[13]

---

[10] Hallaq, *Restating Orientalism*, p. 131.

[11] Werner Menski. (2003). *Hindu Law: Beyond Tradition and Modernity*. Oxford: Oxford University Press, pp. 164–65.

[12] Cited in Bernard Cohn. (1996). *Colonialism and Its Forms of Knowledge: The British in India*. Princeton: Princeton University Press, p. 69. See also Scott A. Kugle. (2001). "Framed, Blamed and Renamed: The Recasting of Islamic Jurisprudence in Colonial South India." *Modern Asian Studies*, 35(2), 257–313. And more generally, see: Siraj Ahmed. (2012). *The Stillbirth of Capital: Enlightenment Writing and Colonial India*. Stanford: Stanford University Press; Garland Cannon and Kevin Brine, eds. (1995). *Objects of Enquiry: The Life, Contributions, and Influence of Sir William Jones, 1746–1794*. New York: New York University Press; Michael J. Franklin. (2011). *Orientalist Jones: Sir William Jones, Poet, Lawyer, and Linguist, 1746–1794*. Oxford: Oxford University Press; John Strawson. (1995). "Islamic Law and English Texts." *Law and Critique*, 6(1): 21–38.

[13] But developing knowledge of the Muslims and Hindus was not a worthwhile pursuit for the colonists for the Indian subjects were already transparent in their lack of value. As Macaulay's famous words attest: "I have no knowledge of either Sanscrit or Arabic. But I have done what I could to form a correct estimate of their value. I have read translations of the most celebrated Arabic and Sanscrit works. I have conversed, both here and at home, with men distinguished by their proficiency in the Eastern tongues. I am quite ready to take the oriental learning at the valuation of the orientalists themselves. I have never found one among them who could deny that a single shelf of a good European library was worth the whole native literature of India and Arabia. The intrinsic superiority of the Western literature is indeed fully admitted by those members of the committee who support the oriental plan of education."

Instead, the future India, its Muslim and Hindu subjects, could only ever be dictated on British colonial and modern terms. The Muslim (and Hindu) Question was enunciated and it was so. As Siraj Ahmed notes,

> The point of [Jones's] translation was . . . to provide the 1793 Permanent Settlement with its legal architecture. Jones considered the legal codes on which he labored . . . to be his most valuable contributions to history, not his many other Orientalist works nor the Indo-Aryan thesis, for which he is much more famous: he aspired to be "the Justinian . . . of the East." Jones wanted orientalism, in other words, to serve the demands of colonial property. . . . Jones's Orientalism gave the East India company's revolutionary rule of property the appearance of an ancient origin, folding it into the "Sakuntala Era," at least as far as his European reading public was concerned. The Laws of Manu simultaneously authorized the Permanent Settlement and drew attention away from its material context and consequences. Its logic seemed to be dictated by immemorial traditions.[14]

The massive project of translation of the Hastings-Jones nexus was to alter the very sociology of legal-moral knowledge of the Muslims, simultaneous to putting in place "a complete check on the native interpreters of the several codes."[15] Codification and classification were and still are central mechanisms of sovereign power, precisely and not coincidentally contingent on the thorough reconstitution of indigenous forms of living and being, and their replacement with alien, if not altogether antithetical, legal, social, economic, and epistemic orders. The Shari'ah in India and its attendant legal-moral structures was one such experiment of translation, codification, and classification which resulted in the suppression of customary law, the jettisoning of human, lived and living complexities of Shari'ah jurists toward an "Anglo-Muhammadan" law.

The order of this phrasing is no coincidence; it refers to a system and culture of imposed hierarchy. The hyphen between the Anglo/modern and Muhammadan/unmodern is, in sum, a representation of the meaning and form of proximity in the colonial consciousness and economic order of the British. It is at once a link and a break, both of which are in the service of furthering mercantile, "civilizational" imperatives of Britain and Europe. The colossal projects of the "Indian problem," the Muslim (and Hindu) Question, was not

---

[14] Ahmed, *Stillbirth of Capital*, pp. 176–77.
[15] Cited in B. Cohn, *Colonialism and its Forms of Knowledge*, p. 69. See also Michael Anderson. (1999). "Legal Scholarship and the Politics of Islam in British India." In *Perspectives on Islamic Law, Justice, and Society*, edited by R. S. Khare. Lanham, MD: Rowman & Littlefield, p. 74; Wael Hallaq. (2009). *An Introduction to Islamic Law*. Cambridge: Cambridge University Press, especially chapter 7.

merely an expression of Macaulay's and Jones's individual ambition, erudition, or talent, but was supported by the culture of valuation that proceeded according to the racial principle: whiteness and Englishness as particular markers of full humanity and actual presence in the world and in history (whose violence was salvific and always justified), Indianness, especially in its Muslim form, and its "color" as a matter to be discarded and made anew, molded in the hands of a superior race. The border zone between "Europe" and the "World-outside" is at once blurred and bolstered. It is precariously obscured insofar as the possibility of "their" incorporation into the realm of reason is one that might exist, yet hardened through the reassertion of the walls that separate us from them: blood, color, language, and reason.

In the contemporary postcolonial scene, with its mutations in constitutive relations of imperialism, arguments for the proximity of us and the Other in a similarly Macaulayite fashion remain au courant. As we will see, there are such continuities with the Muslim Question as Macaulay and his kin spoke it specifically because it has a real function—discursive, imaginary, political, and material—in official state and wider cultural interactions with the Muslim. But central to the settler-colonial equation were questions surrounding occupation and the taking of land, livelihood, and other resources of life from the natives which cannot be so brazen in contemporary Britain.[16] Yet while this remains the case in settler-colonial societies, from Brazil to Palestine to the United States to contemporary India (and the connections between then), modes of violation sanctioned by their racial logics in the management of certain population groups are still with us. Fundamentally, in the questions, *What are they? Can they be like us?* which plagues the European exit from any semblance of democracy, the character of responsibility, or rather its limits, is brought into view. What is it that we owe the Other?

---

[16] A distinction between native conceptions and use of property, and the modern notion of property, deriving from the higher distinction between the soil of Britain and that of the natives, in turn borne of the spatial, temporal, and ultimately ontological division between the human and sub/nonhuman could be legitimately made according to the law of race. As Carl Schmitt has told us, "Just as in international law the land-appropriating state could treat the public property (*imperium*) of appropriated colonial territory as leaderless, so it could treat private property (*dominium*) as leaderless. It could ignore native property rights and declare itself to be the sole owner of the land; it could appropriate indigenous chieftains' rights and could do so whether or not that was a true legal succession; it could create private government property, while continuing to recognize certain native use rights; it could initiate public trustee-ownership of the state; and it also could allow native use rights to remain unchanged, and could rule over indigenous peoples through a kind of *dominium eminens* [eminent domain]. All these various possibilities were undertaken in the praxis of the 19th and 20th century colonial land appropriations." Carl Schmitt. (2003). *The Nomos of the Earth in the International Law of the Jus Publicum Europaeum,* trans. G. L. Ulmen. New York: Telos, 199. See also, Brenna Bhandar. (2018). *Colonial Lives of Property: Law, Land and Racial Regimes of Ownership.* Durham: Duke University Press.

INTEGRATING THE MUSLIM

While the wounds of empire remain open and festering in our war on terror times, proximity in the Muslim Question maintains a peculiar relationship to the responsibility that finds developments in the *Casey Review* (2016),[17] an important commission on the state of cohesion, integration, and opportunity in contemporary Britain. In the report that resulted, there was an overwhelming focus on Muslims and Islam, with both terms mentioned dozens of times. The Muslim appears simultaneously as the target *and* outer limit of integration and (in)tolerance, integrated into the enclosure of Britishness and British values, tolerated in their Muslimness. The report notes,

> While there has been a range of polling that suggests British Muslims feel positive about Britishness and life in Britain, polls also highlight differences in attitudes, with some Muslims and some other minority faith groups or indeed other minority sections of society expressing less progressive views, for example towards women's equality, sexuality and freedom of speech . . . Polling in 2015 also showed that more than 55% of the general public agreed that there was a fundamental clash between Islam and the values of British society, while 46% of British Muslims felt that being a Muslim in Britain was difficult due to prejudice against Islam. We found a growing sense of grievance among sections of the Muslim population, and a stronger sense of identification with the plight of the "Ummah," or global Muslim community.[18]

Ethnic minority subjectivity, coded as Muslim, becomes the measure of enmity insofar as it is these population groups who have failed to integrate. British Muslims, especially British Muslim women, are betrayed not by systemic neglect and institutional racism, but by the real "key to success": the will to integrate. The strong sense of identification with the global Muslim community, the *ummah*, that is, a form of belonging that far extends the nation or the citizen, is constructed as a barrier to belonging and to learning fundamental British values.[19] The report also goes on to suggest that the United Kingdom requires a major new strategy for social cohesion that focuses on the promotion of the English language in the context of austerity Britain in which the very same language proficiency classes are being widely defunded,[20] and shifts in the structure of social benefits which overwhelmingly affect black women and women of color.

---

[17] Dame Louise Casey. (2016). *The Casey Review A Review into Opportunity and Integration*. London: DCLG.
[18] Ibid., pp. 12–13.
[19] Ibid., pp. 66–72.
[20] Ibid., p. 97.

The deep ambivalence in the report is the idea that the answer to the Muslim Question rests on processes of "improvement" and overcoming that which remains an inherent barrier to progressive movement forward into modern national life.[21] Talk of "the emancipation of marginalized groups of women"[22] is discussed with little acknowledgment of structural and material factors which might foreclose emancipatory projects. Bradford, which comprises a frequent case study in the report due to its high ethic minority and Muslim population, is not situated in the reality of its being the fourth poorest constituency in the country and one of the hardest hit by austerity policies.[23] Nor is there recognition of the 326 percent rise in Islamophobic attacks in the year prior to the report.[24] Instead, the report

---

[21] Interestingly, the reports cites Professor Eric Kaufmann who promotes a concept of "multivocalism": "something qualitatively distinct from both multiculturalism and the current policy of civic nationalism. This recognises that in allowing diverse people to attach to Britain in their own way, we strengthen, rather than weaken, British identity." This is, however, the same scholar who authored *Whiteshift*, a book which argues that white-majority democracies in Europe are under threat from increasing immigration, ethnic-minority presence and, even, miscegenation. Kaufman would also have his book, *Whiteshift*, published, arguing that "western politics is being remade through demographic changes and 'the tug of war between white ethno-traditionalism and anti-racist moralism.' White identity is under threat from nonwhite immigration, creating a sense of resentment that is fueling rightwing populism. White people, Kaufmann argues, should be able to assert their own 'racial self-interest' like any ethnic group. Dignity lies in the ability to control demographic change." Eric Kaufmann. (2018). *Whiteshift: Populism, Immigration and the Future of White Majorities*. London: Allen Lane. See also: Kenan Malik. (2018). "White Identity is Meaningless. Real Dignity Is Found in Shared Hopes." *Guardian*. Available at: https://www.theguardian.com/commentisfree/2018/oct/21/white-identity-is-meaningless-dignity-is-found-in-shared-hopes. And on the broader academic trend of populist academia, Martin Shaw. (2018). "Going native: Populist academics normalise the anti-immigrant right." *Politics*. Available at: https://www.politics.co.uk/comment-analysis/2018/10/31/going-native-populist-academics-normalise-the-anti-immigrant.

[22] Casey, *Casey Review*, p. 167. See also: Rashid, *Veiled Threats*, especially chapter 2.

[23] Kate Karban. (2015). "The Impact of Austerity on Bradford. Or, Poverty, Inequality and Mental Well-being: The Double0Whammy Effect." *University of Bradford*. Available at: https://www.bradford.ac.uk/news/archive/2015/the-impact-of-austerity-on-bradford.php; Socialist Worker. (2017). "Anger as Labour Council in Bradford Plans Huge 'ideological' Cuts to Children's Services." Available at: https://socialistworker.co.uk/art/45735/Anger+as+Labour+council+in+Bradford+plans+huge+ideological+cuts+to+childrens+services

[24] Tell MAMA. (2016). *The Geography of Anti-Muslim Hatred. Tell MAMA Annual Report 2015*. London: Faith Matters. Available at: https://tellmamauk.org/geography-anti-muslim-hatred-2015-tell-mama-annual-report/; Harriet Sherwood. (2016). "Incidents of anti-Muslim abuse up by 326% in 2015, says Tell MAMA." *Guardian*. Available at: https://www.theguardian.com/society/2016/jun/29/incidents-of-anti-muslim-abuse-up-by-326-in-2015-says-tell-mama; Ted Jeory. (2016). "UK Entering 'unchartered territory' of Islamophobia after Brexit Vote." *Independent*. Available at: https://www.independent.co.uk/news/uk/home-news/brexit-muslim-racism-hate-crime-islamophobia-eu-referendum-leave-latest-a7106326.html. Likewise, Bradford, which comprises a frequent case study in the report due to its high ethic minority and Muslim population, is not situated in the reality of its being the fourth poorest constituency in the country and one of the hardest hit by austerity policies. See: Kate Karban. (2015). "The Impact of Austerity on Bradford. Or, Poverty, Inequality and Mental Well-being: The Double0Whammy Effect." *University of Bradford*. Available at: https://www.bradford.ac.uk/news/archive/2015/the-impact-of-austerity-on-bradford.php; Socialist Worker. (2017). "Anger as Labour council in Bradford plans huge 'ideological' cuts to children's services". Available at: https://socialistworker.co.uk/art/45735/Anger+as+Labour+council+in+Bradford+plans+huge+ideological+cuts+to+childrens+services

constructs Muslims as needing yet failing to do the hard work of integration, of working on themselves, though requiring tutelage through the increased promotion of the English language, boosting social mixing and a more explicit focus on British values and Muslims' problematic attitudes toward them.[25] In short, there is both a literal and conceptual proximity between them and us: "they"—the Muslim Question—live nearby, play the same sports, maybe even work in the same offices, though live segregated lives, resist our "universal" values and do not have a proper grasp of our language or customs. Britishness, like the function of race, comes to take on the form of an "inner experience" that can only be shared by those who profess the same faith (in one's citizenship as much as religious tradition), who are assumed to obey the same laws (as opposed to prioritizing an insidious local Shari'ah system), authorities, commandments, and commitments. In sum, those who in the nature of their being belong to, and legitimately in, the same community. Entrance into this community, like the subjects who have unquestioned access to the inner experience of Britishness, is always already coded white.

Responsibilities to, and the demands of, the Muslim Question work in tandem with its opposite. There is a dialectic between responsibility, on the one hand, and its thorough abdication on the other couched in a liberal dialect of proximity. The simultaneous ambiguity and certainty about what and who constitutes the community and, therefore, who it is that is tasked with the responsibility of integration, produces a state-sponsored and wider cultural investment in a type of mytho-religious thinking, a form of thought that is assumed to be the preserve of those who we struggle against—the Islamic terrorist cell burrowed into the pores of national life—but is only slightly attenuated in their (moderate) neighbors who must also answer the Muslim Question. The threat of terrorism which colors innumerable discourses and strategies such as integration, internalizes Islamophobia which precludes the necessity to actually engage with Muslims. The heady mix of militarism and romanticism has meant that a civilizational hierarchy must be made to (re)exist in which Britain and Europe are assumed to sit at the top. This is maintained because Muslims are a numerical minority and can, therefore, have their concerns discarded. However, the liberal move of proximity is also disrupted by Muslims' undeniable bodily presence and citizenship in Britain which problematizes a coherent sense of the racial, civilizational order baked into the so-called integration.[26]

---

[25] Casey, *Casey Review*, chapter 4, pp. 53–58.
[26] A. Lentin and G. Titley. (2011). *The Crises of Multiculturalism: Racism in a Neoliberal Age*. New York: Zed Books.

Proximity and condescension work productively together in this second paradigm to produce a dialectic of (ir)responsibility. The recognition of proximity—the idea that there exists something to be shared between us and the Other—demands that we fulfill certain responsibilities. In this paradigm, these are masked under the aegis of responsibility of improvement, or rather presenting Muslim with the opportunity to improve. However, because proximity is conceived in unidirectional terms according to a hegemonic raciology, proximity simultaneously authorizes the abdication of any obligations to the Other, obligations of dialogue, of debt, of care, of rights, of life. In the arithmetic of the civilizing process and the management of problem populations which frame its techniques, responsibility and recklessness are not opposed but dialectically fused.

The paradox is thus: obligations to the Other can be abandoned in the very name of obligations to the Other. In the colonial situation as presented by Macaulay and all those who submit themselves to his language, the cultivation of an enlightened class of Indians and the codification of indigenous (Islamic) culture, as demanded by our higher station—in tastes, morals, intellect, blood, and color—is contingent on our ability to discard other, that is, false duties that we have overburdened ourselves with. The result is thus: education can be reformed, foreign system of law and forms of sociality imposed, subjects reconstituted as "modern," while existing social, legal, and familial structures can be razed to the ground streamlining the extraction of resources then sold back to the native Indian population for a large profit. Elsewhere, unprecedented famines can be caused as a consequence of wartime policies of rationing in the very same war in which Indian colonial soldiers were dispensed to the most deadly frontiers. Yet there are no contradictions to be seen here, no ethical benchmarks to be upheld. Arbitrariness, not consistency, is the mode by which rules are followed and values are lived. It is the sovereign, after all, who gets to decide on the exception.

PECULIAR COALITIONS IN THE MUSLIM QUESTION

In this liberal mode of condescension, it is worth understanding how certain social ills are prioritized over others. Or even the various investments in what is to constitute a social ill in the first place. In the Muslim Questioned, we spent some time unpacking the utility of the concept and economy of "radicalization" for legitimating certain forms of engagement with the figure of the Muslim. Most notably was the exclusivity of Muslim vulnerabilities to certain modes of thought which necessitate a policy framework that is preemptive in nature which locates, constantly, Muslim men, women, and youth in a pre-criminal space.[27] But if it is public safety, or more specifically the lives, freedom, and dignity of women that is a priority, then it is worth asking why there hasn't been a concomitant focus, nationwide and as a statutory duty for public workers with safeguarding duties, on "vulnerabilities towards domestic homicide" when overwhelmingly the victims are female, often partners or former partners of the perpetrators. Nor "have individuals working in public bodies like schools and hospitals not been given hour-long training sessions to 'identify' and 'report' pre-domestic homicide perpetrators, and why has a similar construct to 'radicalization' not yet been developed to describe individuals who might kill their partners or family members in the future."[28] Might the lack of pre-criminal identification as a nationwide strategy across major institutions have something to do with the fact that most of such perpetrators are white males, conceived of as aberrations of an otherwise culture of tolerance, equality, and respect for all?[29] In fact, services for women suffering from domestic abuse under regimes of austerity have been subject to or at risk of facing crippling budget cuts across the United Kingdom.[30] It is, therefore, "important to bear in mind that the academic and financial investments in counter-terrorism and all its sub-strands (now including hate crimes, etc.) reflect specific political interests—not just public safety. It is unsurprising, then, why many believe the War on Terror and the prioritization of Muslim-perpetrated violence, above other forms of violence, are derived from wider structures of

---

[27] Mohammed Elshimi. (2015). "Prevent 2011 and Counter-Radicalisation: What Is De-radicalisation?" In C. Baker-Beall, C. Heath-Kelly, and L. Jarvis (eds.) *Counter-Radicalisation: Critical Perspectives*. Abingdon: Routledge, pp. 206–22; D. Goldberg, S. Jadhav, and T. Younis. (2016). "Prevent: What Is Pre-Criminal Space?" *Bjpsych Bulletin* 41(2); C. Heath-Kelly. (2017). "The Geography of Pre-criminal Space: Epidemiological Imaginations of Radicalisation Risk in the UK Prevent Strategy, 2007–2017." *Critical Studies on Terrorism*, 10(2), 297–319; C. Heath-Kelly. (2012). "Reinventing Prevention or Exposing the Gap? False Positives in UK Terrorism Governance and the Quest for Pre-emption." *Critical Studies on Terrorism*, 5(1), 69–87; J. McCulloch and S. Pickering. (2009). "Pre-Crime and Counter-Terrorism Imagining Future Crime in the 'War on Terror'." *The British Journal of Criminology*, 49(5), 628–45; J. McCulloch and D. Wilson. (2016). *Pre-Crime: Pre-Emption, Precaution and the Future*. Abingdon: Routledge; G. Mythen, S. Walklate, and F. Khan. (2013). "'Why Should We Have to Prove We're Alright?': Counter-Terrorism, Risk and Partial Securities." *Sociology*, 47(2), 383–98.

[28] Tarek Younis. (2019). "Counter-Radicalization: A Critical Look into a Racist New Industry." *Yaqeen Institute*, p. 7. Available at: https://yaqeeninstitute.org/tarekyounis/counter-radicalization-a-critical-look-into-a-racist-new-industry/#.XYC5KJNKg1I

[29] Violence Policy Center. (2018). "More Than 1,800 Women Murdered by Men in One Year, New Study Finds." *VPC*. Available at: http://vpc.org/press/more-than-1800-women-murdered-by-men-in-one-year-new-study-finds/

[30] Jones, O. (2014). "Britain Is Going Backwards on Violence Against Women." *The Guardian*. Available at: https://www.theguardian.com/commentisfree/2014/mar/30/britain-violence-against-women-domestic-abuse-funding-cuts

Islamophobia."[31] We must be vigilant to arguments of proximity and integration and improvement when inconvenient facts like domestic homicide are made invisible through projections of the Muslim Other's exceptional problem with violence and misogyny, with arrested development, untapped potential, and patriarchy.

In fact the liberal feminist mission of the Woman Question exists in relation to the dominance of the Muslim Question. Rosalind Morris astutely summarizes this mission in the wake of 2001:

> To understand the current moment as one in which the Woman Question dominates, constituting as it does the justificatory rationale for both Islamist and anti-Islamist policy, requires a recognition that this question is not interior to Islamism, but that it is perhaps the most important site of complicity and mutual entailment in a war that encompasses us all. The Woman Question is, in fact, the hinge or point at which a politics of the nation become that of international relations. It is there that absolute freedom and absolute lack of freedom turn on each other. Which is to say, the Woman Question is also always the Eastern Question.[32]

The (Muslim) Woman Question, like the Muslim Question, is also, extending Morris's formulation, the Western Question. The colonial discourse of the position of women inside Christianity has been updated to the position and relative freedom of women in the West, in Europe, in Britain, and that violations of such equality, "rare" as they are, are always already noncultural and nonreligious aberrations. Part of the ongoing self-making of Euro-America today is its projection of itself on account of the (fictional) equal position of its women with its men, which must always be contrasted primarily with the position of Muslim women.[33] Further still, the European and British obsession with the Muslim Question as the Woman Question pervades not simply domestic debates about the labor activity of ethnic minority women[34] but also invokes a politics of Muslim women's migrant labor. Sara Farris discusses European "femonationalism" to describe the mobilization of feminist ideas in the service of nationalist agendas. Farris writes,

---

[31] Younis, "Counter-Radicalization," p. 7. See also, R. Sabir. (2017). "Blurred Lines and False Dichotomies: Integrating Counterinsurgency into the UK's Domestic 'War on Terror'." *Critical Social Policy*, 37(2), 202–24.

[32] Rosalind C. Morris. (2002). "Theses on the Question of War: History, Media, Terror." *Social Text* 72, 20(3), 154. The gap between Islamism and Islam per se given the closing of the domestic and foreign realms in discourses and policies in response to threats from "Islamic terrorism" is often blurred. The threat of Islamism, therefore, also implicates domestic Muslim minorities in Britain as elsewhere.

[33] Massad, *Islam in Liberalism*, p. 123 and chapter 2 more broadly.

[34] Incidentally, this is also a specific concern for the *Casey Review*, pp. 89–94.

The image of the immigrant as male Gastarbeiter (guest worker) that was diffused in the 1950s and 1960s, when Europe received the first significant flows of foreigners from all over the world, has not been replaced by the figure of the migrant as female maid. Rather, when women migrants are mentioned at all, they are portrayed as veiled and oppressed Orientalist objects. The public debate on the role of migrations and contemporary Europe's status as a multicultural laboratory has indeed been dominated by an insidious discursive strategy that tends to obscure the importance of those women as care and domestic workers and instead represents them as victims of their own culture.[35]

These discursive strategies and material policies mask deeper European anxieties about identity and economics. Farris explains:

Recent discourses about multiculturalism and migrants' integration, particularly in the case of Muslims, have been strongly marked by demands for migrants to adapt to Western culture and values. We should note that one of the essential items in such a list of values is gender equality. The mobilization, or rather instrumentalization, of the notion of women's equality both by nationalist and xenophobic parties and by neoliberal governments constitutes one of the most important characteristics of the current political conjuncture, particularly in Europe.[36]

Recent discourses about multiculturalism's many failures and the integration of migrants, and the reintegration of a newly recognized Muslim threat, at home as well as abroad, has been marked by demands to adapt to "Western" or "British" cultural values. The postcolonial and decolonizing world is of course not the colonial situation as such. At the same time, however, techniques such as Macaulay's, Hasting's, and Jones's among many others are tenacious and are made to serve newer, more complex functions today in the heart of empire implicit in the "liberating" policy reforms of Dame Louise Casey. Notions such as feminism, integration, vulnerability, tolerance which pretend to a communal concern all too often mask a distinctly racial politics. The "femonationalist" insurgence is all too often consolidated by the glue of European anti-Islam feeling and structural Islamophobia. The figure of the Muslim, specifically the Muslim woman, within such discourses and policies of state is embedded in a kind of primordial condition of stasis. In the call to "emancipate" Muslim women from others-of-their-kind, we are directed to

---

[35] Sarah R. Farris. (2012). "Femonationalism and the 'Regular' Army of Labor called Migrant Women." *History of the Present* 2(2), 184.

[36] Ibid., p. 185.

policies which function on a simultaneous abdication of responsibility and legitimation of intrusion, violence, and reconstitution.

HOW SHOULD THE NATION MOURN?

Returning to the grand mythological schema that upholds such regimes of (racial) integration, whether from the vantage point of a secretary of state or a feminist activist, arguments of proximity and a potential friendship in and with the national body are entwined in "diffuse psychic structures and generic passionate forces" that are responsible for the "dominant affective tonality of our times and serve to sharpen many contemporary struggles and mobilizations."[37] This dynamic is thrown into great relief when an attack takes place on British soil that results in casualties, and that licenses a kind of tailor-made mourning, a prepackaged summons to prove the resilience, if not virility, of the national body made more affective via neoliberal technologies of social media and rolling news coverage. These outpourings of national grief are often accompanied by images symbolizing the failures of integration: the minaret, the hijab, groups of men in Islamic dress. These images (and characters) are at once anchored in the idea of national mourning as an opportunity to bring people in their differences together, while reminding us of the need to keep in place a logic of marked separation which feeds on a threatening, siege-like, anxiogenic vision of the world in which the burden of proof of allegiance always lies with the marked.

In the first year anniversary of the attack at Westminster, when Khalid Masood drove a car into pedestrians on Westminster Bridge and fatally stabbed a police officer guarding the Palace of Westminster, the five casualties were remembered in a ceremony at Westminster Hall followed by a silent vigil on Westminster Bridge. As if to capture in a single frame, the dialect of proximity as we have been discussing it in the Muslim Question, the dominant image disseminated of the vigil was of the "human chain"[38] formed by Muslim women wearing blue hijabs symbolizing peace (Figure 4.1).

---

[37] Mbembe, "Society of Enmity," p. 26.

[38] For reports of the event, see: Sara Kamouni and Aine Fox. (2017). "Muslim Women Gather to Form Human Chain on Westminster Bridge in Honour of Victims Killed in London Terror Attack." *Mirror Online*. Available at: https://www.mirror.co.uk/news/uk-news/women-gather-form-human -chain-10105637; Daily Sabah. (2017). "Muslim Women Form Human Chain on Westminster Bridge in London as Symbol of Unity." Available at: https://www.dailysabah.com/europe/2017 /03/27/muslim-women-form-human-chain-on-westminster-bridge-in-london-as-symbol-of-unity; Middle East Eye. (2017). "Muslim women form human chain along Westminster Bridge after London attack". Available at:https://www.middleeasteye.net/news/muslim-women-form-human -chain-along-westminster-bridge-after-london-attack; James Rodger. (2017). "Muslim women form human chain on Westminster Bridge after London terror attack." *Birmingham Live*. Available

Figure 4.1   A Group of Women Linked Hands on Westminster Bridge on Sunday to Pay Tribute to the Victims. *Source:* Courtesy of PA/BBC (Press Association Media Group).

Akeela Ahmed, an activist and campaigner who helped organize the gathering in collaboration with the Women's March, argued that the vigil was a move toward "reclaiming" the Bridge from the act of terrorism. "It's important," Ahmed goes on to argue, "that we say terror will not defeat and divide us and pay respects to those that died," she said. "Keith Palmer is a hero and we are marking our respect for him and all the emergency services who protect us."[39] Perhaps this gesture and optic might well do the work of reclamation. The regularity with which this series of events occurs, the attack-mourning-interview-analysis structure of the aftermath of Muslim terrorist violence would suggest that this gesture must have some function. For, as Yassir Morsi reminds us, "Someone always arrives on set to speak about Islam and Muslims. We have all played that role, played it from the beginning. A black or brown face brought to condemn another black or brown man's act, as an act done against his religion and our collective decency. For white anxieties about the threat of terror need someone who looks like me to say, 'not all of us.'"[40]

at: https://www.birminghammail.co.uk/news/midlands-news/muslim-women-form-human-chain-12801580

[39] Quoted in Alexandra Topping. (2017). "Women Link Hands on Westminster Bridge to Remember Victims." *Guardian*. Available at: https://www.theguardian.com/uk-news/2017/mar/26/women-westminster-bridge-london-womens-march-solidarity-attack-victims

[40] Yassir Morsi (2018). "The "free speech" of the Unfree' Continuum." *Journal of Media & Cultural Studies*, 4.

What do moments of solidarity, or proximity, such as these do for the work of recovery, of reclamation? Indeed, what is being reclaimed and answered? Why does the optic of Muslim women in hijabs play such a central role in the communication of the myth of (anti)nationhood?[41] What is done, if anything, to recover a genuine human presence that is not burdened or marked by the specter of racial difference, by an Otherness that need not require surveillance or emancipation? Is the Muslim Question answered?

The thread that I have sought to draw from Macaulay and the question of Indian education, through Casey and (Muslim) integration, and the event of the Westminster Bridge vigil, elucidates the tenacity of techniques involved in the simultaneous gestures of solidarity and separation toward the figure of the Muslim (woman). The directives of integration, present in regimes of counterterrorism, (scientific) models of radicalization, and frameworks of integration on the contemporary British scene, even if followed through to the letter, can never satisfy the demands of the Muslim Question. For it is a question asked in bad faith which, paradoxically, further authorizes its legitimacy in a historical moment where spaces of the interview and debrief are multiplying within and beyond the racist, Islamophobic formation of modern Britain.

In the context of the terrorist attack and its aftermath, "the nation is summoned to shed its tears of rancor in public and show its defiance against the enemy. And with each tear, a shining path is traced. Clothed in the rags of international law, human rights, democracy, or, simply put, 'civilization,' militarism no longer needs a disguise. To relight the flame of hatred, old allies are suddenly transformed into 'enemies of humanity as a whole,' while might becomes right."[42] The image of the Muslim in solidarity with "us" is remarkable precisely for its situatedness within a racial imaginary and politics in which the Islamic terrorist stands in for the chief enemy of humanity, and the Islam (and Muslim) from which he springs forth constitutes a terrain

---

[41] On this optic, see: S. Yaqoob. (2008). "Muslim Women and War on Terror." *Feminist Review*, 88(1), 150–61; L. Amoore. (2007). "Vigilant Visualities: The Watchful Politics of the War on Terror." *Security Dialogue*, 38(2), 215–32; R. Lentin. (2012). "Turbans, Hijabs and Other Differences: 'Integration from Below' and Irish Interculturalism." *European Journal of Cultural Studies*, 15(2), 226–42. On subversions of such a framing, see: Rashid, *Veiled Threats*, chapter 7; N. Massoum. (2015). "'The Muslim Woman Activist': Solidarity Across Difference in the Movement Against the 'War on Terror." *Ethnicities*, 15(5), 715–74.

[42] Mbembe, "Society of Enmity," p. 28. There is a peculiar intermixture of logics of might and a kind of militaristic voyeurism in this instance given the matrices of power that connect such acts of "reclamation" and the Muslim Question. See, Devji's "A community of spectators" for a perspective on the soldier as photographer. Faisal Devji. (2008). *The Terrorist in Search of Humanity: Militant Islam and Global Politics*. London: C. Hurst & Co., pp. 151–58. On the contemporary logic of might more broadly, see: Jean Comaroff. (2009). "The Politics of Conviction: Faith on the Neo-liberal Frontier." *Social Analysis*, 53(1), 17–38; Nicola Perugini and Neve Gordon. (2015). *The Human Right to Dominate*. Oxford: Oxford University Press.

of interrogation and force implicating all who wear its names. Some of the damned might be made fit intermediaries between a white Britain under attack and their kin whose violent and resentful desires might be tamed. Yet proximity in the Muslim Question is, in the final analysis, friendship, condescension, judgment, intimacy, and incarceration, in equal measure.

Chapter 5

Affirmation

It should be clear by now that there are both profound disjuncture and undeniable similarities between our first two paradigms—hostility and condescension—and its constituent narratives of distance in the former and proximity in the latter. Nevertheless, race and its functions of damnation of varying degrees, separation, and erasure remain crucial as a principle of differentiation even when making pronouncements about the value, potential, and *utility* of the Other. White subjects and institutions remain the center of all meaning, and notions of proximity, sameness, responsibility have inscribed within them the thematic of racial difference and hierarchy. What seems initially as, a distinct paradigm of engagement with the Other, can actually affirm the systemic prejudices, processes of extraction, and violence of the Muslim Questioned; a violence which aims for the Other's reconstitution in whatever form required by—and most legible to—the contemporary play of racial narratives underpining the nation and its attendant anxieties of demotion. We should recall that the will for Other's perpetual *disclosure*—of motivations, location, confession—in the first paradigm is ultimately not at all concerned with what the Muslim has to say. Disclosure, based on a racial epistemology of ignorance, is an exuberant display of power.

Affirmation, on the other hand, is the regular demand for the Muslim to corroborate the vision we have of them and, most importantly, of ourselves but *in their own voices*. A space must be left open in this second paradigm for Muslims to represent themselves, to articulate and pursue visions of the future in which the Muslim is understood to be an ostensible protagonist. Yet affirmation is also a form of avowal, a whole process—institutional, extractive, cultural, state-sponsored—of *confirmation* where the unidirectional pathway from them to us, from Islam to liberal (and colonial) modernity remains the only legitimate route. A route that is unthinkable without a *theology of progress.*[1] As a doctrine of European modernity, "progress"—the forward movement of time, the natural evolution, and resolution of human societal contradictions, leading to a more rational and better world—was a concept essential to Thomas Babington Macaulay's worldview and structured his policy recommendations in India. As a principle, one that is often universalized in academic knowledge as much as in the practices of state, the theology of progress is the belief, conscious or otherwise, that the world moves along a linear trajectory to a destination in common; one literally *progresses* from an earlier stage of development toward civilization leaving behind the follies of irrational faith, its blood and color.

THE TRANSLATION OF DIFFERENCE

Affirmation and the theology of progress are, at base, the submission of Others to a single language with which to think, to be, and live in the world. As Paul Leroy-Beaulieu explains, at the beginning of the twentieth century, colonization "was the expansion power of a people, its power of reproduction, its expansion and multiplication across space; it is the submission of the universe or a vast portion of it to its language, its customs, its ideas and its

---

[1] The literature challenging such notions of "progress" and its inherently destructive, indeed genocidal effects is significant. Brett Bowden, however, summarizes the basic features of the doctrine of progress: "The idea of progress has two related components. The first is that the human species universally progresses, albeit at different rates and to different degrees, from an original primitive or child-like condition, referred to as savagery, through to barbarism, and culminates at the apex of progress in the status of civilization. The second component of the idea of progress holds that human experience, both individual and collective, is cumulative and future-directed, with the specific objective being the ongoing improvement of the individual, the society in which the individual lives, and the world in which the society must survive. For some thinkers it seems logical that what follows from the general idea of progress is the notion that progress is directed in a particular direction, or that history is moving forward along a particular path toward a specific end. History, in this conception, is not merely the cataloguing of events, but a universal history of all humankind, a cumulative and collective history of civilization, that is, History. The notion that different peoples or cultural groups are at different stages of development along the path of universal progress has led some to deem it necessary to try to ameliorate the condition of those thought to be less civilized. This enterprise has variously been known as the 'white man's burden,' the 'burden of civilization,' or the 'sacred trust of civilization.' The general aim of these often violent and overly-zealous 'civilizing missions' was to ameliorate the state of the 'uncivilized' through tutelage, training, and conversion to Christianity. With European expansion, wherever 'civilized' and 'uncivilized' peoples existed side by side, there soon developed an unequal treaty system of capitulations, also known as extraterritorial rights. In much of the uncivilized world this system of capitulations incrementally escalated to the point that it became full-blown colonialism." See Bowden. (2011). "Colonialism, Anti-Colonialism, and the Idea of Progress." In *History and Philosophy of Science and Technology, Encyclopedia of Life Support Systems*, edited by UNESCO-EOLS Joint Committee. Oxford: EOLSS, pp. 1–2. For a critique of the residues of this thoroughly modern/colonial doctrine in Critical Theory, see Amy Allen. (2016). *The End of Progress: Decolonizing the Normative Foundations of Critical Theory*. New York: Columbia University Press.

laws."[2] Affirmation as a logic has the propensity to ratify certain relations of power through which species and subspecies can be classed hierarchically and whose hierarchy comes in turn to structure the spatial arrangements of the social realm. Affirmation also refers to the gap, the cursed invitation, left open for the Other to claim a genuine stake in the present, and even future, of the social and political world always contingent on this theology of progress and submission to translation. As the eminent feminist philosopher, Judith Butler, notes that "translation by itself can also work in full complicity with the logic of colonial expansion, when translation becomes the instrument through which dominant values are transposed into the language of the subordinated, and the subordinated run the risk of coming to know and understand them as tokens of their 'liberation.'"[3]

Macaulay, Hastings, Jones and the economies of knowledge and colonization which authorized their audacious plans insisted on the necessity of translating Islam and Muslim life into English and European modernity, the remaking of Muslim life and social structures in the image of British Protestant Christianity and later secularist formations.[4] Translating Islam from which the terrorist arrives requires the task of presenting his world which may come into contact with ours as an extreme or lesser developed form of being lying in wait for transformation by our commitments to reason, democracy, feminism, sexual liberation, tolerance, and the rule of law, commitments that do not, or perhaps cannot, exist for the Muslim's epistemic and ontological enclosure within weaker languages of Arabic, Urdu, Bangla, and others. Translation as a technique of the security state and technology of domination in the war on terror is no less prominent shown in US and UK governmental sanction, in conjunction with subsidiary economies of nongovernmental organizations and private foundations' lucrative sponsorship of all manner of translation projects from English to Arabic and Arabic to English in the wake of September 11. Muslim and Qur'anic terminology such as "Shari'ah," "Jihad," "Islam," and likewise "Woman," "Gender," "Law" and many others have felt the effects of translation from at least the nineteenth

---

[2] Leroy-Beaulieu, *De la colonisation*, pp. 605–606.
[3] Judith Butler. (2000). "Restaging the Universal: Hegemony and the Limits of Formalism." In *Contingency, Hegemony, Universality: Contemporary Dialogues on the Left*, edited by Judith Butler, Ernesto Laclau, and Slavoj Žižek. London: Verso, p. 35.
[4] On the secular and the colonial constitution of normative secularity, see: Talal Asad. (2003). *Formations of the Secular: Christianity, Islam, Modernity*. Stanford: Stanford University Press; Talal Asad. (2018). *Secular Translations: Nation-State, Modern Self, and Calculative Reason*. New York: Columbia University Press. See also: the collection of essays on critique, power and the secular: T. Asad, W. Brown, J. Butler, and S. Mahmood. (2013). Is *Critique Secular?: Blasphemy, Injury, and Free Speech*. New York: Fordham University; and a useful lecture concerning the loaded study of the secular, Wael Hallaq. (2014). "Beyond Secularism and Islamism." *VIDC*. Available at: https://www.youtube.com/watch?v=WFAqQiIVsF8&t=5518s

century onward.[5] The commitment to neoliberalism and the huge industries of "rights" and "radicalization" seeking to accumulate (non-)Euro-American Arabs and Muslims into the global market and the post–Cold War international community has brought translation as a technique into collusion with various corporate imperatives. As Massad explains:

> While this would begin in the 1980s with the International Monetary Fund's push to dismantle the welfare state in the Third World more generally, it would get another strong push following the events of September 11 and the US invasion of Iraq in 2003. It was in that context that large public relations campaigns were launched in Egypt, Jordan, Lebanon, and the Gulf states, among others, to transform Arab and Muslim cultures into cultures that can advance the neoliberal agenda.[6]

Ultimately, we are reminded of Spivak's important caveat that the racially configured subject must be made to emerge as a subject *for* Europe in terms that liberalism and the modernity that houses it can recognize, in order to affirm the supremacy of that same system. It is not that the subaltern cannot speak, it is that they cannot speak in terms comprehensible to the white Britain and Europe that colonialism birthed. The act of translation, in sum, "is enmeshed in a web of linguistic, political, social, economic, 'cultural,' in short, *power* contexts that determine that act itself, its structures, its imperatives, its effects, and its publics. In a colonial world of unequal power, languages are not equal."[7] Which is to say, languages and the forms of life that they cultivate are also unequal in the calculus of empire and the politics they

---

[5] Massad, *Islam*, especially chapters 1 and 2. See also: Asad, Talal. (1993). "Cultural Translation in British Social Anthropology." In *Genealogies of Religion: Discipline and Reasons for Power in Christianity and Islam.* Baltimore: Johns Hopkins University Press, pp. 171–99; Kathryn Babayan and Afsaneh Najmabadi. (2008). *Islamicate Sexualities: Translations across Temporal Geographies of Desire.* Cambridge, MA: Harvard Center for Middle East Studies; Richard Jacquemond. (2009). "Translation Policies in the Arab World: Representations, Discourse, and Realities." *Translator,* 15(1): 15–35. And more generally, see, Gayatri Chakravorty Spivak. (1993). "The Politics of Translation." In *Outside in the Teaching Machine.* New York: Routledge, pp. 200–225.

[6] Massad, *Islam*, p. 167. Prominent examples of these have been the "Culture of Hope" campaign in Jordan simultaneous to the dismantling of the welfare state and mass privatization; the "I Love Life" campaign under the Hariri financial empire in Lebanon; and the "Culture of Optimism" campaign in Egypt with a pan-Arab edge. All three would stress the (translation/supremacy of) "the liberal value system of individualism, free enterprise, markets, personal responsibility, privatization, human rights, etc., and aimed at transforming 'Arab culture,' which was posited as responsible for Arab 'failures' in development, into one that could advance neoliberal success." See: Mayssoun Sukarieh. (2012). "The Hope Crusades: Culturalism and Reform in the Arab World." *Political and Legal Anthropology Review,* 35(1), 115.

[7] Massad, *Islam*, p.7.

have engendered. Indeed, as Talal Asad has shown us, they are so "unequal" that some languages are "stronger" than others.[8]

Regardless of the unequalness of languages and the cultures that live in them, once the entwining of different racial "segments" became a principle of governance, translation also became necessary. But most peculiar, albeit essential, to this model of integration and accumulation, which is of course always already a robust model of separation and differentiation, is "that it can be tailored to the demands of occupation (or abandonment, if need be). It can also, when required, transform itself into an instrument of strangulation."[9] The colonial enterprise, in the final analysis, could not afford to be inhibited by principles, norms, legal standards that might halt the mercantile imperatives that sustained it, which is to say, anything that might stall the inevitable forward march of progress.[10] The perverse ethics of the colonial enterprise were matched only by their perverse pleasures and kleptomania. If anything or anyone of the colonial world was to be lost or damaged, the assumption was that it could easily be replaced. There could be no taboos, no concern with embarrassment or disgust.

Anxieties about Britain and Europe's demotion within and with the world have resuscitated similar relations with Others, both at home and abroad, in order to maintain the faith of Britain's power that translation—just as in Casey and the Westminster vigil—presupposes. Emancipation (especially of Muslim women) and solidarity with the nation (especially when it is wounded by Islamic terror) are the terms upon which the Muslim can be one of us. To be sure, an epistemology of ignorance can still obtain when translation, however sensitive and accurate, is put into the service of forms of erasure or separation. Translation can quite easily become a mode by which the suspension

---

[8] On "unequal" languages, see: Talal Asad. (1993). *Genealogies of Religion: Discipline and Reasons of Power in Christianity and Islam*. Baltimore: Johns Hopkins University Press, pp. 189–93. On "strong" languages, see also Talal Asad. (1994). "Ethnographic Representation, Statistics, and Modern Power." *Social Research,* 61(1), 78.

[9] Mbembe, "Society of Enmity," p. 24.

[10] Perhaps the premier contemporary example of such strangulation and the sophisticated technologies involved in the dialectic between physical proximity, distance, and control of a subject population is that of the occupation of Palestine by Israel. Particular focus is given to the management of population registers, issuing of identity cards that confer certain differential rights, mapping and signage as mechanisms of erasure, militarized architectures, cutting-edge technologies of urban pacification and surveillance, and much more. The literature unpacking these processes and economies is massive but for a sufficient overview of the central dynamics see also: Jeff Halper. (2015). *War Against the People: Israel, Palestinians and Global Pacification*; Eyal Weizman. (2017). *Hollow Land: Israel's Architecture of Occupation*; Helga Tawil-Souri. (2012). "Digital Occupation: Gaza's High-Tech Enclosure." *Journal of Palestine Studies,* 41(2), 27–43; Ian Slesinger. (2018). "A Cartography of the Unknowable: Technology, Territory and Subterranean Agencies in Israel's Management of the Gaza Tunnels." *Geopolitics*; Jess Bier. (2017). "Palestinian State Maps and Imperial Technologies of Staying Put." *Public Culture,* 29(1(81)), 53–78; Alexandra Rijke and Claudia Minke. (2019). "Inside Checkpoint 300: Checkpoint Regimes as Spatial Political Technologies in the Occupied Palestinian Territories." *Antipode,* 51(3), 968–88.

of moral reflection is sanctioned. In one such contemporary example, Lisa Stampnitzky, in her seminal book, *Disciplining Terror*,[11] has examined how the study of terrorism (and academic sub-discipline it birthed) has consolidated itself through the work of many scholars and self-described experts and what they have spoken and written about in papers, at conferences, often supported by generous research grants and, in many cases, state-sponsorship. The term terrorism itself is, therefore, contingent on *political* rhetoric, a rhetoric that has fundamental debts to historical matrices of imperial power. It is through this lens that it is decided whose violence should be considered "terrorism" and whose wars of terror are in the service of "security," "rights," "liberation," and therefore, "legitimate."[12] As Tarek Younis notes, "the aggregation of data based on politically-loaded, pre-defined parameters paints a particular picture of who terrorists are, what terrorist objectives appear to be, and where terrorists are likely to be found."[13]

And as a facet and dominant tonality of our time, it becomes a principle of necessary separation. For even though we may argue against the total fusion of the terrorist with the Muslim familiar among us, for we are tolerant and celebrate diversity, they are both figures with whom I can never be at ease or be with in silence, never completely allow myself to engage in relations of mutual implication. I must constantly be affirmed in my tolerance of the Muslim and s/he should speak of it publicly.

THE EVERYWHERE PRESS CONFERENCE

This situation can nonetheless produce a degree of mutuality. If the Muslim Question offers a different politics to the interrogation room, then it is one founded on the idea that the gap between me and the Muslim can be closed and that she may indeed have a political dimension of her own that can be heard. Friendship with the Muslim, however, arises as a particular form of intimacy contingent on her ability to express white Europe's own self-image in a voice of her own. If disclosure is the generalization of the interrogation room in which the Muslim's guilt, or more favorably, the severe limit of their innocence is precluded, then affirmation is *the normalization of the press conference and the autocue.* Constantly answering other people's questions weighed down by the racism of its purpose, a friendship of quotation has

---

[11] L. Stampnitzky. (2013). *Disciplining Terror: How Experts Invented "Terrorism"*. Cambridge: Cambridge University Press.

[12] For example, in the 1980s, an Israeli attack on Palestinian soil was not recorded as an incident of international terrorism, while a Palestinian attack on Israeli soil was. See: L. Stampnitzky. (2013). *Disciplining Terror: How Experts Invented 'Terrorism'*. Cambridge: Cambridge University Press.

[13] Younis, "Counter-Radicalization," p. 6.

proven to be an effective way of dispersing the thematic of racial difference while ostensibly encouraging the Muslim to speak of herself and others.

Within our moment of radicalization and the terror attack, Muslims are everywhere expected to have an opinion on this or that Muslim atrocity, this or that instance of state violence: to condemn, celebrate, explain, or affirm as required. This is to reassure those asking the Muslim Question that terrorism is not Islamic, despite what these groups might argue; that Islam is a religion of peace; that Muslims are guided by the Qur'anic tenet: "Whoever kills an innocent life it is as if he has killed all of humanity."[14] It is, in sum, to vouch for the humanity of Muslims contingent on the sub-humanity of the terrorist hordes fronting as Muslims. That Muslims are *on the whole* unthreatening, have fully integrated, and have learned British values. Please let us continue to live among you. There are, however, *some* who cannot be saved. The actor and rapper Riz Ahmed encapsulates this dynamic in the opening of his spoken word poem, *In These Sour Times*:

In these sour times
Please allow me to vouch for mine
Bitter taste in my mouth
Spit it out with a rhyme
I'm losing my religion to tomorrow's headlines
Forrest Gate
Sorry mate?
Nah nothing—it's fine.[15]

However, the solicitation of confession according to popular and institutional desires often requires that responses to the Muslim Question be phrased in certain ways, and the material policies formulated on the basis of those answers directed toward inciting similar speech in the future. It is not confession as it is in the Muslim Questioned, but a circular system of affirmation. "*Forest Gate—Sorry Mate—Nah nothing—it's fine*" articulates the quotidian interaction of invoking uncomfortable facts as the Forest Gate raid[16] and, later

---

[14] Q.5:32.

[15] Find Riz Ahmed's most recent performance of the poem here: Riz Ahmed. (2017). "Riz Ahmed's Moving Performance of 'Sour Times'." *The Tonight Show Starring Jimmy Fallon*. Available at: https://www.youtube.com/watch?v=M9tUEhgExPM. Ahmed would perform it on one of America's most popular later-night talk shows, after the attack in Charlottesville by neo-Nazi James Alex Fields Jr.

[16] This line refers to the Forest Gate, east London raid, known as Operation Volga, in 2006 which saw the arrests of Mohammed Abdul Kahar, 23, and Abdul Koyair, 20, who were suspected terrorists in possession of a chemical bomb. No chemical materials were found and both were later released. Kahar would be shot in the shoulder (or chest depending on the report) during the raid which found nothing and cost the taxpayer approximately £2.2 million.

in the poem, Abu Ghraib and Guantanamo Bay,[17] unsettling in their violent, inhumane, supposed contradictions with the impulse to liberate that is baked into Britain, only to be cut off mid-question. Affirmation is a sleight of hand and speech able to maintain a fundamental inequality between us and the Muslim, which sustains a matrix of power inscribed with the self-assurance, policies of ignorance, and irresponsibility authorized by the law and power of race in white Britain and Europe more broadly.

We can take this further. Discourses of tolerance and policies of modernization, reformation, and reconstruction—at times in direct and critical confrontation with institutions of slavery and colonization—did much more to consolidate racism as a habitus and popular culture in the colony and metropole alike. Again, the case of a Macaulay on education, this time Thomas Babington's father, Zachary, serves as an instructive example. From the beginning of his governorship of Sierra Leone in the 1790s, Macaulay saw education as crucial to the success of the settlement and the civilizing of the natives.[18] Through his connections with the Clapham Sect, a movement of Church of England social reformers active in the eighteenth and nineteenth century, Macaulay would become close with the famed Evangelical writer and reformer, Hannah More. For More, it was a religious responsibility to train children properly: "to be deeply impressed with a few fundamental truths, to digest them thoroughly, to meditate on them seriously, to get them deeply rooted in the heart."[19] The Evangelicals, including Macaulay, like many of the Clapham reformers, believed that all human beings were descendants of Adam and Eve, belonging to the same human family. The differences between peoples encountered in the British colonial project were much more to do with accidental circumstances of life (to which I would add industry

---

[17] "What happens in Guantanamo is a historical embarrassment to America and its values, and it screams in your faces—you hypocrites, 'what is the value of your signature on any agreement or treaty.'" These are the words of Osama Bin Laden in his famous "Letter to America" of November 2002. Quotes in Devji, *Landscapes*, pp. 128–29.

[18] There have been a number of accounts of this period in the history of Sierra Leone and treatments of Macaulay's time there as narrated in his journal and letters. See particularly Viscountess Knutsford. (1900). *Life and Letters of Zachary Macaulay*. E. Arnold; Christopher Fyfe. (1962). *A History of Sierra Leone*. Oxford: Oxford University Press; Ellen Gibson Wilson. (1976). *The Loyal Blacks*. Ontario: Capricorn Books; Suzanne Schwarz and Zachary Macaulay. 1768–1838 (2000). *Zachary Macaulay and the development of the Sierra Leone Company, 1793–4*. Leipzig: Institut für Afrikanistik, Universität Leipzig; James St. G. Walker. (1976). *The Black Loyalists: The Search for a Promised Land in Nova Scotia and Sierra Leone*. London: Longman; Cassandra Pybus. (2006). *Epic Journies of Freedom: Runaway Slaves of the American Revolution and their Global Quest for Liberty*. Boston: Beacon and (2007). "'A Less Favourable Specimen': The Abolitionist Response to Self-Emancipated Slaves in Sierra Leone." *Parliamentary History Supplement*, 98–113; Deirdre Coleman. (2005). *Romantic Colonization and British Anti-Slavery*. Cambridge: Cambridge University Press; Simon Schama. (2005). *Rough Crossings: Britain, the Slaves and the American Revolution*. London: BBC Books.

[19] Cited in Christopher Tolley. (1997). *Domestic Biography: The Legacy of Evangelicalism in Four Nineteenth- Century Families*. Oxford: Clarendon, p. 27.

and modernity) rather than any "original faults in moral character" or "natural inferiority in understanding,"[20] a perspective at odds with the widespread eugenicist philosophies in support of the slave trade and settler-colonial rule.

At the same time, however, Macaulay and the Evangelicals believed in natural order and hierarchy, that it was possible for all peoples to be civilized.[21] Macaulay's colonial pedagogy, therefore, detailed the "barbarisms" of Black Africa and Black Africans in the colonial sites on which they worked, simultaneous to the profession of his belief in the conjoined humanity of all humans through an inaugural divine conception. The critique of the institution of slavery based on a progressive Evangelicalism simultaneously "succeeded in fixing representations of African difference and inferiority and disseminating them more widely than ever before. They claimed universalism but practised the making of racial hierarchies, always alongside those of class and gender: this was a rule of difference."[22]

In the civilizing project under Zachary Macaulay, however, the effects of the actual encounter and its educational processes with Black people in Africa did not go according to plan. As Catherine Hall continues, "Evangelicals thought enslaved Africans were victims of the 'circumstances' of slavery. Once freed they would become new Christian subjects—grateful, obedient, industrious, and domesticated. On the contrary, they found them full of demands and claims, and subscribing to dissenting practices which were almost as bad as African barbarisms."[23] Those demands were for rights to life, property, and justice, for claims of equality and mutuality.[24] In a single motion, differences between us and the Other are explained as circumstantial and accidents of the inevitable (that is, *progressive*) colonial encounter with Other peoples of the world, while representation of the Other's essence *as*

---

[20] Cited in Schwarz, ed., *Journal of Zachary Macaulay*, Part 2, xxiv.

[21] A popular reference to this was the rescue of Scottish Highlanders from their "barbarism." See: Margaret Holland, Viscountess Knutsford. (1900). *Life and Letters of Zachary Macaulay*. London: Edward Arnold, p. 13.

[22] Hall, "Making Colonial Subjects," p. 778. Hall's articulation of a "rule of difference" invokes Partha Chatterjee's "rule of colonial difference." On the rule of difference, see Catherine Hall. (2000). "The Rule of Difference: Gender, Class and Empire in the Making of the 1832 Reform Act." In *Gendered Nations. Nationalisms and Gender Order in the Long Nineteenth Century*, edited by Ida Blom, Karen Hagemann, and Catherine Hall. Oxford: Berg, pp. 107–36. On the colonial "grammar of difference" see Ann Laura Stoler and Frederick Cooper. eds. (1997). *Tensions of Empire: Colonial Cultures in a Bourgeois World*. Berkeley: University of California Press, especially Introduction. The historian Thomas Metcalf makes this argument in relation to the colonization of India. See: Thomas R. Metcalf. (1994). *Ideologies of the Raj, New Cambridge History of India*, vol III.4. Cambridge: Cambridge University Press.

[23] Hall, 'Making colonial subjects, p. 779. For a more exhaustive case study of this colonizing vision see Catherine Hall. (2002). *Civilising Subjects. Metropole and Colony in the English Imagination, 1830–1867*. Cambridge: Polity.

[24] On the shock and resentment that white abolitionism experienced when faced with Black struggles for freedom, see "Anglo-Saxon Empire and the Residuum" in: Robbie Shilliam. (2018). *Race and the Undeserving Poor*. London: Agenda Publishing.

Other becomes fixed in its racial and thus degenerative character toward a *rule of colonial difference.*[25] This motion sustains white (male, propertied) subjectivity as colorless normativity, against which difference is measured, in Sierra Leone in the 1790s as much as in India in the nineteenth century.

Tony Blair, prime minister of Britain, in the wake of September 11 would say "It cannot be said too often: this atrocity appalled decent Muslims everywhere and is wholly contrary to the true teaching of Islam."[26] That,

> It is that out of the shadow of this evil, should emerge lasting good: destruction of the machinery of terrorism wherever it is found; hope amongst all nations of a new beginning where we seek to resolve differences in a calm and ordered way; greater understanding between nations and between faiths; and above all justice and prosperity for the poor and dispossessed, so that people everywhere can see the chance of a better future through the hard work and creative power of the free citizen, not the violence and savagery of the fanatic.[27]

Against intensifying accusations of the war on terror as a war on Islam, he would later say, "It is not a clash of civilisations—all civilised people, Muslim or other, feel revulsion at it. But it is a global struggle and it is a battle of ideas, hearts and minds, both within Islam and outside it. This is the battle that must be won, a battle not just about the terrorist methods but their views. Not just their barbaric acts, but their barbaric ideas. Not only what they do but what they think and the thinking they would impose on others."[28] Muslims can, therefore, be civilized *like us*. And yet, national security requires an expansive and sophisticated, not to mention intrusive and violent, set of industries because counterterrorism and the war on terror

---

[25] This phrase was popularized in: P. Chatterjee. (1994). *The Nation and its Fragments.* Princeton, NJ: Princeton University Press. See also: Guido Abbattista. (2006). "Empire, Liberty and the Rule of Difference: European Debates on British Colonialism in Asia at the End of the Eighteenth Century." *European Review of History: Revue européenne d'histoire,* 13(3), 473–98; E. Kolsky. (2005). "Codification and the Rule of Colonial Difference: Criminal Procedure in British India." *Law and History Review,* 23(3), 631–83; Kim A. Wagner. (2018). "Savage Warfare: Violence and the Rule of Colonial Difference in Early British Counterinsurgency." *History Workshop Journal,* 85, 217–37.

[26] T. Blair. (2001). "Tony Blair's speech to the Commons." *The Guardian* Online. Available at: http://www.theguardian.com/world/2001/oct/04/september11.usa3

[27] T. Blair. (2001). "Tony Blair at the Labour Party Conference." *The Guardian* Online. Available at: http://www.theguardian.com/politics/2001/oct/02/labourconference.labour6. There is a remarkable competition between pretensions to humanisms at play here: the militant humanism of the War on Terror and the ethics of forgiveness of Al-Qaeda discourse. As Devji notes, "Unlike the rhetoric used in the War on Terror, which is determined to punish Islamic militants for crimes committed, that used in Al-Qaeda's jihad would forgive President Bush and Britain's former Prime Minister Blair for crimes as great if only they were to repent. However preposterous, Al-Qaeda's rhetoric is more Christian than that of its Western enemies." Devji, *Terrorist,* p. 32.

[28] T. Blair. "Prime Minister Blair's Speech." *The New York Times.* Available at: https://www.nytimes.com/2005/07/16/international/europe/prime-minister-blairs-speech.html

function on the de facto *and* de jure assumption of Muslim threat—domestic and foreign—against which we must maintain a constant vigilance, and in which most social and public institutions must be invested.[29]

"The allocation of government resources and funding for 'multicultural' projects in the service of 'integration' and 'social cohesion,' often supplemented by counterterrorism policy funding, has thus helped to "cement fixed and often reductive identities that inhibit recognition of complex, and thus 'fully human,' subjects, instead reifying notions that certain cultural behaviors and tendencies belong to particular ethnic and racial groups. In the 1980s and 1990s, these state-managed approaches to multiculturalism surfaced, at times, to pacify anti-racist struggles and move attention away from the material problems of racism and injustice."[30] This remains central to state policy rationales founded on uncritical cultural stereotypes and the vague assumption that emphasizing certain (shifting) values in opposition to prevailing notions of other, that is, problematic ideologies to which Muslims are exceptionally vulnerable, would cultivate a more "resilient" society and a more cohesive recognition of a shared British identity.[31]

---

[29] I am invoking the statutory changes merging from and enforced under the CTSA (2015).

[30] Kapoor, *Deprive*, p. 158. See also: J. Narayan. (2019). "British Black Power: The Anti-imperialism of Political Blackness and the Problem of Nativist Socialism." *The Sociological Review*, 67(5), 945–67. On the (colonial) technique of cementing reductive identities through projects of ostensible liberation, see: Pragna Patel. (2002). "Back to the Future: Avoiding Déjà Vu in Resisting Racism." In *Rethinking Anti-Racisms: From Theory to Practice*, edited by Floya Anthias and Cathie Lloyd. London: Routledge, pp. 128–48. In her infamous book Susan Moller Okin poses a similar question but ultimately perpetuates the type of "colonial" feminism critiqued by scholars such as Lila Abu-Lughod, Leila Ahmed, Inderpal Grewal, Anne Norton and Wendy Brown. Okin. (1999). *Is Multiculturalism Bad for Women?* Princeton, NJ: Princeton University Press. As an introduction to a critique of colonial feminism and its trenchant racism, see: Leila Ahmed. (1982). "Western Ethnocentrism and Perceptions of the Harem." *Feminist Studies*, 8(3), 521–34; Leila Ahmed. (1992). *Women and Gender in Islam*. New Haven, CT: Yale University Press, pp. 121–22; Wendy Brown. (2012). "Civilizational Delusions: Secularism, Tolerance, Equality." *Theory and Event* 15(2); Zillah Eisenstein. (2007). *Sexual Decoys: Gender, Race and War in Imperial Democracy*. London: Zed Books, p. 171; Inderpal Grewal. (2013). "Outsourcing Patriarchy: Feminist Encounters, Transnational Mediations and the Crime of 'Honor Killings,'" *International Feminist Journal of Politics*, 15(1), 11; Rema Hamami and Martina Reiker. (1988). "Feminist Orientalism and Orientalist Marxism." *New Left Review*, 170, (July–August).

[31] In a prominent case of resistance to the sponsorship of counterterrorism funding for a cultural cohesion event, the refusal of several high-profile speakers to attend the 2019 Bradford Literature Festival that was partially funded by counter-extremism money is instructive. See the poet and writer Suhaiymah Manzoor-Khan's statement of withdrawal here: Suhaiymah Manzoor-Khan. (2019). "Statement of Explanation for Withdrawal from Bradford Literature Festival 2019—Suhaiymah Manzoor-Khan." Available at: https://twitter.com/thebrownhijabi/status/1141327385901617152. See also: Suhaiymah Manzoor-Khan and Saima Mir. (2019). "Does Bradford Festival's Counter-Extremism Funding Warrant a Boycott?" *Guardian*. Available at: https://www.theguardian.com/commentisfree/2019/jun/24/bradford-literary-festival-counter-extremism-funding-boycott; Selina Bakkar. (2019). "Suhaiymah Manzoor-Khan, Malia Bouattia, Lauren Booth, Sahar Al Faifi and More Pull Out of BLF Over Counter-Extremism Funding." *Amaliah*. Available at: https://www.amaliah.com/post/56146/bradford-literature-festival-2018; and Yahya Birt's excellent analysis of the situation can be found here: Yahya Birt. (2019). "British Muslims, Cultural Freedom, and

The withdrawal of several prominent speakers and performers at the recent Bradford Literature Festival is an instance of resistance to such a rationale. It was revealed that the festival was a beneficiary of a fund called *Building a Stronger Britain Together*[32] which is inextricably tied to the government's 2015 counter-extremism strategy.[33] In the broader context of securitized engagement infrastructures and the focus on "ideology" (the roots of which unquestionably derived from communal practices and thinking of an essentialized Muslim community), Muslim "stakeholders" become an important instrumental resource in the industries of radicalization and counterterrorism.[34] This rationale has equally impacted multiculturalist programs—with clear emphases on Muslim women—whose underlying assumption is that conservative religious leaders identified by the state determine parameters of what constitutes *the* religio-cultural tradition. Thus "women's demands for freedom and equality are seen as being outside 'cultural traditions' . . . and therefore not legitimate."[35] Nira Yuval-Davis

---

the Counter-Extremism Industry." *Medium*. Available at: https://medium.com/@yahyabirt/british -muslims-cultural-freedom-and-the-counter-extremism-industry-d41d1faf96b9. Ultimately, those who withdrew from the Festival on the grounds of funding would successfully organize a separate event in Bradord.

[32] Find the government report on the program here: HMG. (2016). *Building a Stronger Britain Together*. Available at: https://www.gov.uk/guidance/building-a-stronger-britain-together

[33] This is the same strategy under which it became a statutory duty for those with "safeguarding" roles—expansively defined—to cooperate with such a strategy and its interventionist mechanisms. See: HM Government. (2015b). Counter-Terrorism and Security Act 2015; HM Government. (2015c). Counter-Terrorism and Security Bill: Explanatory Notes, These notes refer to the Counter-Terrorism and Security Bill as brought from the House of Commons on January 7, 2015; HM Government. (2015d). *Working Together to Safeguard Children*. London: The Office for Standards in Education, Children's Services and Skills (Ofsted). (2015). *The Common Inspection Framework: Education, Skills and Early Years*, Manchester.

[34] Ruth Blakely et al. *Leaving the War on Terror*; R. Lambert and B. Spalek. (2008). "Muslim Communities, Counter-Terrorism and Counter-Radicalisation: A Critically Reflective Approach to Engagement." *International Journal of Law, Crime and Justice*, 36(4), 257–70; P. Thomas. (2012). *Responding to the Threat of Violent Extremism—Failing to Prevent*. London: Bloomsbury Academic. Asma Jahangir argues, against this rationale that "it Is no the Government's role to look for the 'true voices of Islam' or of any other religion or belief. Since religions or communities of belief are not homogenous entities it seems advisable to acknowledge and take into account the diversity of voices [. . .] The contents of a religion or belief should be defined by the worshippers themselves." A. Jahangir. (2008). Report of the Special Rapporteur on Freedom of Religion or Belief: Mission to the United Kingdom' United Nations, p. 21. As Birt notes, "Even if the most commonly stated objective was 'increasing resilience' in nearly two-thirds of projects, only 20 per cent worked with individuals defined to be 'at risk' and—most shockingly—only 3 per cent with those 'glorifying or justifying violent extremism'. Financially, therefore, very little PVE money was directed at those who might have needed it most, and politically it is significant as tangible proof that many statutory and community partners have been uncomfortable with direct counter-terrorism work and have sought to employ the funds for other ends." Birt, "Promoting Virulent Envy," p. 55. See also: Karen Kellard, Leighton Mitchell and David Godfrey. (2008). *Preventing Violent Extremism Pathfinder Fund: Mapping of Project Activities 2007/08*. London: CLG, pp. 5–10.

[35] Nira Yuval-Davis. (1992). "Fundamentalism, Multiculturalism and Women in Britain." In *"Race", Culture, Difference*, edited by J. Donald and Ali Rattansi. London: Sage, p. 284.

notes how multiculturalist programs have provided an increase in funding for religious schools simultaneous to a decrease in funding for women's services such as refugees. Yuval-Davis's view, however, echoes popular conceptions of Islamic culture and Muslim social mores, embedded in state counterterrorism policy, arguing that a "structure and curriculum similar to those of a mixed school do not apply because their 'purpose is clearly to bring up girls to be dutiful wives and mothers."[36] As Nisha Kapoor explains,

> this kind of assertion is premised on the same sorts of racial/religious stereo-types of Muslim communities that are in continuous circulation, particularly as they relate to depictions of Muslim women as pathologically submissive and without agency, in need of rescue. Since her claim is, indeed, contradicted by statistics that show some Muslim girls schools rank among the highest achieving in the country, its credibility is called into doubt while the question of how to struggle against the intricate relationship of race and gender oppression remains insufficiently addressed. This type of secularist anti-racist feminist politics fails to speak to the gendered forms of oppression experienced by Muslim women through the interplay among race, religion, gender and imperialism in contem-porary global politics.[37]

It must remain the case, therefore, that following an attack, someone, preferably an *imam*, always arrives to deliver a statement constrained by the "not of us" scripting. That is, not of *all* Muslims, just some. And which, therefore, should dispel our fears of Muslims and Islam, and dampen the desire to deport or discount their presence in Britain. The statement strives to answer the Muslim Question, even as there is the concomitant fear of retaliation the following day: a van plowing into—on this occasion—innocent worshippers after Friday prayers. It is a statement often neatly sandwiched between images of the mosque, the minaret, dozens of vaguely confused

---

[36] Ibid., p. 286.

[37] Kapoor, *Deport*, pp. 159–60. It should go without saying that a (feminist) politics underpinned by rationales of cultural essentialism, blind to the intersorption of race, religion, gender, and imperial-ism has had many Euro-American feminist, anti-racist critics, never mind scholars from the "Third World." This literature and their bibliographies are massive, but for some notable works, see: Angela Davis. (1984). *Women, Race, & Class*. New York: Vintage, and (1984). *Women, Culture, and Politics*. New York: Random House; bell hooks. (1981). *Ain't I A Woman: Black Women and Feminism*. Boston: South End Press, and (1984). *Feminist Theory: From Margin to Center*. Boston: South End Press. See also Kumari Jayawardena. (1986). *Feminism and Nationalism in the Third World*. London: Zed Books, and Chandra Talpade Mohanty, Ann Russo, and Lourdes Torres, eds. (1991). *Third World Women and the Politics of Feminism*. Bloomington: Indiana University Press; Lydia Sargent, ed. (1981). *Women and Revolution: A Discussion of the Unhappy Marriage of Marxism and Feminism*. Boston: South End Press; Annette Kuhn and AnnMarie Wolpe, eds. (1978). *Feminism and Materialism: Women and Modes of Production*. London: Routledge and Kegan Paul; Juliet Mitchell. (1974). *Psychoanalysis and Feminism*. New York: Pantheon Books.

Muslims in their peculiar dress, their women covered. I am reminded here of Michel Foucault's "tactical polyvalence of discourses"[38] wherein liberal discourses (and material policies) of democracy, equality, and tolerance make possible the appearance of a "reverse discourse," wherein Muslim resistance to the actual effects of such discourses is reconstructed as obstinacy and ingratitude that is endemic to the Muslim minority. As the respondent to the Muslim Question, one disagrees only after one fundamentally agrees: "We must repeat our belief in society's democratic 'promises.'"[39] The everywhere press conference is, nevertheless, occasions a way of speaking so that someone does not get her hijab ripped off her head, even as the Muslim Question insists that the emancipation of Muslim women from Islamic dress is the order of the day.

THE MUSLIM QUESTION OF DEMOCRACY

In many ways, then, the Muslim Question is constituted by a will to non-sense where principles and their violation require one another. If the hostile relation of interrogation detailed in the first part of the book necessitates various forms of confession from the Muslim, this second mode requires forms of corroboration. But the modes through which corroboration is extracted or enacted must remain open to all possibilities. Should contradictions arise between the view we have of ourselves (liberal, tolerant, democratic) and the contexts in which the Muslim must corroborate its truth—at the press conference or otherwise—they cannot be admitted as such. There must always remain order to what amounts to narcissistic outpourings following an Islamic terror attack as much as an instance of Muslim violation.

On the important question of democracy, British colonial policy in the postwar period indeed remained open to all possibilities. There had been a significant shift in popular political vocabularies in which certain ideas of empire, the civilizing mission, and the white man's burden had all but been expunged. The British diplomat, Mark Sykes,[40] clearly understood this well. In the context of the British conquest of Mesopotamia and Palestine, he wrote that "If Britishers are to run Mesopotamia we must find up to date reasons for their doing so and up to date formulae for them to work the country on. We shall have to convince our own Democracy that Britishers ought to do

---

[38] Michel Foucault. (1979). *The History of Sexuality, vol. 1: An Introduction.* Translated by Robert Hurley. London: Allen Lane.

[39] Morsi, "Free Speech," p. 6.

[40] Michael D. Berdine. (2018). *Redrawing the Middle East: Sir Mark Sykes, Imperialism and the Sykes–Picot Agreement.* I.B. Tauris.

the work and the Democracies of the world as well."[41] The search for up-to-date formulae is an incessant one because the rule, putting subjects to work, and the profits that are their product can have no limits. But democracy in the context of the Muslim Question "would be the 'up to date reason' and 'formulae' that colonialism sought in order to justify itself to the colonised was hardly obscure to the latter, but that the so-called British democracy and other democracies had to be 'convinced' of the colonial project and deceived into believing it was one of democratisation has been a successful deception for so many of the natives of Western democracies."[42] The deceit, in sum, is for the subjects of white democracy and not for the Muslim that is its supposed Other.

It did not matter, for example, that "Islam" had been mobilized both for and against democratic flourishing. It would be the lightning rod to suppress the mobilizations of secular, anti-imperialist nationalists in Egypt via the alliances forged between the British and the Egyptian Society of the Muslim Brothers since the early 1940s. The Society would come to infiltrate the communist movement in 1944 and would pass "intelligence" obtained after the end of the Second World War to the "friendly" Egyptian government aiding the capture of communist agitators in the universities and unions. Soon after the 1952 coup that brought Abdel Nasser and the Free Officers to power, the Society would again sit down for meetings with the British to challenge 'Abd al-Nasir's ambitious land reform and broader nationalization efforts.[43]

In contrast, the British in the mid-nineteenth century would obtain a proclamation from the caliph 'Abd-al-Majid I enjoining Indian Muslims not to join anti-British rebellions and to remain loyal to the caliph's "allies." This deployment of caliphal authority would later be taken up by sultan Abdul Hamid II against European encroachments in the region. Interestingly, Napoleon had earlier appealed to Islamic theological legitimacy for his colonial campaign and in the context of Napoleon's threat to British rule in India, British diplomats had interceded with the Ottoman caliph to urge Indian Muslims to be vigilant of the "false promises of the French."[44] Following the so-called Mutiny of 1857 and its brutal suppression, the removal of Mughals from

---

[41] Cited in Helmut Mejcher. (1976). *Imperial Quest for Oil: Iraq 1910–1928*. London: Ithaca Press, p. 53.

[42] Massad, *Islam*, p. 94.

[43] Massad, *Islam*, pp. 76–84. See also: Richard P. Mitchell. (1969). *The Society of the Muslim Brothers*. Oxford: Oxford University Press, p. 28; Joel Beinin and Zachary Lockman. (1987). *Workers on the Nile: Nationalism, Communism, Islam and the Egyptian Working Class, 1882–1954*. Princeton, NJ: Princeton University Press, p. 372.

[44] On the political context of the proclamation, see Aziz Ahmad. (1967). *Islamic Modernism in India and Pakistan, 1857–1964*. Oxford: Oxford University Press, pp. 123–24; Hamid Enayat. (1982). *Modern Islamic Political Thought*. Austin: University of Texas Press, p. 58, and Jacob M. Landau. (1990). *The Politics of Pan-Islam: Ideology and Organization*. Oxford: Clarendon Press, p. 185.

power was met with the further reconstitution/erasure of Islamic legal-moral structures, displacing further the "middle-stage" of Anglo-Muhammadan law. These colonial state processes in the 1860s and 1870s would progress so much so that "by the end of the century, and with the exception of family law and certain elements of property transactions, all indigenous laws were supplanted by British law."[45]

The rebellion of 1857 was a wake-up call to the British that signaled the need for direct administrative structures designed and managed by the British state. That is, a series of reforms designed to settle (or make legible)[46] Indian governance in conjunction with its subjects to the wills of colonial rule. As John Darwin argues, "Their [the civilians] authority was enhanced by the new emphasis on administrative and financial stability rather than the force-able annexation of princely states—a practice that had given the Company rule its aggressive, militaristic character."[47] The "emergency" situation of the rebellion became an opportunity to govern on the basis of "scientific" knowledge of the native population. Yet such knowledge, largely ethnographically produced, as a way of understanding, locating, and governing what was an immensely complex social fabric, also uncovered and reified certain hierarchies among the Indian population: Muslim and Hindu. "Caste" in India, for example, and "tribe" in Africa "were in part colonial constructs, efforts to render fluid and confusing social and political relationships into categories sufficiently static and reified and thereby useful to colonial understanding and control."[48]

The scientific turn in colonial administration was predicated upon a racial principle and "anthropological interest in charting the physical and cultural characteristics—all of them lumped together as racial characteristics—of the population."[49] Racial science and its classifications, then, did not simply manage an extremely diverse population, but in large part constituted their social and material reality in regimented and systematically impoverished forms. Such an ambitious program of modernizing reform was of course challenged by the cultural and linguistic heterogeneity of India. That is, plagued by the fact of the Muslim and Hindu natives' ways of being human and being in

---

[45] Wael Hallaq, (2009). *Shari'a: Theory, Practice, Transformations.* Cambridge: Cambridge University Press, p. 383.

[46] On the idea of legibility as it pertains to (imperial) governance, see: Scott, *Seeing Like a State,* Part 1.

[47] John Darwin. (2009). *The Empire Project: The Rise and Fall of the British World- System, 1830–1970.* Cambridge: Cambridge University Press, p. 187.

[48] Ann Laura Stoler and Frederick Cooper. (2014). "Between Metropole and Colony: Rethinking a Research Agenda." In *Tensions of Empire: Colonial Cultures in a Bourgeois World.* Berkeley: University of California Press, p. 11.

[49] Chandak Sengoopta. (2003). *Imprint of the Raj: How Fingerprinting Was Born in Colonial India.* London: Macmillan, p. 42.

the world with Other complex humans. Hence, the colonists would argue, the need for such ambitious reforms including Macaulay's pronouncements of the Indians' uniform desire to learn English and leave behind Arabic and Sanskrit. Education, commerce, and law were, therefore, interwoven as sites of reconstitution, informed if not licensed by the racial principle.[50]

It is according to a similar license that the very concept of Islamophobia is constructed as a subversive mechanism to restrict our free speech, to shield Muslims and constrain the inquiry into difficult aspects of the Muslim Question concerning violence, gender, sexuality, and all the rest.[51] It can then be asserted that, in truth, Muslims are, after all, fundamentally happy with life in Britain, content with having to do the learning and improvement that is asked of them. As the famous 2014 video, "Happy British Muslims,"[52] attests, Muslims' diverse forms of expression, dress, and race, communicates that they are not (always) a threatening presence. Or, in another familiar argument taken up by Muslims themselves, Islamic versions of democracy are perfectly compatible, that is, translatable with the ideal type of its (white) European superior.[53] Translation can indeed have a "counter-colonialist possibility"

---

[50] The British occupation of Egypt in 1882 equally came with a concerted and systematic effort to produce new (theological) understandings of governance and sociality. Lord Cromer, British strongman and ardent anti-feminist was on good terms with a well-known reformist thinker of the nineteenth century, Muhammad ʿAbduh, who would be appointed by the British occupation authorities as the Chief Mufti of Egypt in 1899. Cromer would lavish praise on ʿAbduh's reforms on a number of occasions, notably in the Annual Report in 1905, the year of ʿAbduh's death. Cromer would, however, criticize him harshly in later years. In the maintenance of these (imperial) matrices of power, thoroughly contradictory in its arguments though sustained by a narcissism of fundamentalist white supremacy, there can be no benchmarks, no promises that cannot be broken at a given moment, sometimes without explanation. On Cromer and Abduh, see: Roger Owen. (2005). *Lord Cromer: Victorian Imperialist, Edwardian Proconsul.* Oxford: Oxford University Press, p. 361.

[51] For a resurgent debate on the struggle to define Islamophobia as an affront to free speech, see: Melanie Phillips. (2018). "Islamophobia Is a Fiction to Shut Down Debate." *The Times.* Available at: https://www.thetimes.co.uk/article/islamophobia-is-a-fiction-to-shut-down-debate-wwtzggnc7; Peter Tatchell. (2019). "Free Speech Is Under Threat Over Islamophobia." *The Times.* Available at: https://www.thetimes.co.uk/article/free-speech-is-under-threat-over-islamophobia-85r6h8czr; Barry Duke. (2019). "'Islamophobia' Definition Poses a Threat to Free Speech in the UK." *The Free Thinker.* Available at: https://www.patheos.com/blogs/thefreethinker/2019/05/islamophobia -definition-poses-a-threat-to-free-speech-in-the-uk/; Hardeep Singh. (2019). "We Must Be Free to Criticise Islam." *Spiked.* Available at: https://www.spiked-online.com/2019/01/04/we-must -be-free-to-criticise-islam/; Adam Milstein. (2019). "Islamophobia—The 21st Century Weapon to Silence Our Freedom of Speech." *JPost.* Available at: https://www.jpost.com/Opinion/ Islamophobia-the-21st-century-weapon-to-silence-our-freedom-of-speech-588988

[52] BENI. (2014). "Pharrell - Happy British Muslims! #HAPPYDAY." Find the video at: https://www .youtube.com/watch?v=gVDIXqILqSM

[53] See for example Mahmud ʿAbbas al-ʿAqqad. (1964: 43, 47) al-Dimuqratiyyah fi al-Islam. Cairo: Dar al-Maʿarif bi-Misr. Al-ʿAqqad reproduces the liberal concept of democracy where for him: "Islamic democracy as such is based on four foundations that no extant democracy can be established without, namely, (1) individual responsibility, (2) universal equal rights, (3) the imperative on rulers to seek [the people's] counsel, (4) solidarity among subjects regardless of sects or classes." Islamic democracy "deserves to be called human democracy [al-dimuqratiyyah

through exposing "the limits of what the dominant language can handle" by altering its meaning as it is being repeated, iterated, and *mimed*.[54] Alas, this is not frequently the case. Instead, affirmation is the rule and regular attendance at the press conference(s) of liberal tolerance is where the Muslim must arrive on time. Any violence or inequality involved in this relation between the Muslim and her questioner is justified by the need to work the Muslim on and keep the country safe. This is an old trick.[55]

The racial subsidies involved in the Muslim Question, with its institutional, juridical, democratic arrangement, amount to an ambitious effort at arranging the world according to a logic of one's own liking so as to make it more amenable to being put to work, as Sykes once phrased it. In the colonial world, this had a literal dimension and a thoroughly aesthetic edge.[56] But at their core, the codification of "custom," the dismantling of Islamic institutions of learning and the mobilization of democracy for contradictory purposes authorized and maximized the efficiency of extraction and theft, with the murder and social death which constituted its processes propelled by the need for Muslim reform that was its up-to-date formula. But while the efficient extraction of raw material and the bloody labor which connected metropole to the colony was once the project for which all formulae were oriented, the empire is no longer what it once was. Yet the impulse to capture and question, or solicit the corroborating statement from the Muslim remain, but now with much more contradictory, incoherent, frenzied movements. Nonetheless, the Muslim Question has as its target a subject whose lifeworld is imaged and articulated, in law as much as in culture, as one constituted by a list of beliefs,

al-insaniyyah] as it established freedom based on the right of humans who had no rights or power before [Islam]."

[54] Butler, "Restaging the Universal," p. 37.

[55] A trick that the British were especially effective at. The most developed institutional form has been the apartheid regime in which hierarchies were of a biological order, though heavily indebted to forms of British indirect rule in the South Africa. See: Lucy P. Mair. (1936). *Native Policies in Africa*. London: Routledge and Kegan Paul; Frederick D. Lugard. (1980). *The Dual Mandate in British Tropical Africa*. London: W. Blackwood and Sons.

[56] The planting of trees, the organization of city streets, the use of certain forms of architecture in the construction of colonial state buildings, archways and museums, many of which still exist, as signifiers in marble, bronze, and stone of the supremacy and power of the colonists is well known. We can also find impulses to conflate race and geography, presupposed in the social reproduction of "home" in the colonies, in the racist writings of white colonists in South Africa. See: Coetzee, John M. (1988). *White Writing: On the Culture of Letters in South Africa*. New Haven, CT: Yale University Press. Taking this logic of colonial reproduction further, Edward Said discusses the idea of "ecological imperialism" in which the Europeans, wherever they went, began to change the natural habitat so as to resemble what they left behind in the metropole. Plants, animals, crops, entire building methods were imported wholesale, "complete with new diseases, environmental imbalances, and traumatic dislocations for the overpowered natives." Said, *Culture and Imperialism*, p. 225. See also: Alfred Crosby. (1966). *Ecological Imperialism: The Biological Expansion of Europe, 900-1900*. Cambridge: Cambridge University Press, 196–1116; Neil Smith. (1984). *Uneven Development: Nature, Capital, and the Production of Space*. Oxford: Blackwell, p. 101.

behaviors, convictions, and modes of living which must, in the final analysis, become irrelevant to modern life: inessential to reason and its supposedly democratic, feminist, English-speaking subject.

NARCISSISM OF THE INESSENTIAL

There is something fundamentally narcissistic about these racist arrangements which call on the Muslim who, following an attack on its modern ways of life and the political, social, and sexual freedoms, afforded under its democracy, to attest to its validity and rightful hegemony. A heavy dose of narcissism supported the colonial potentate and various forms of knowledge it produced about the colonized, simply waiting to be molded, desirous to be put to worthwhile work.[57] But the symptoms of disorder and its pervasive patterns continue to have a racial referent, for it is the Muslim, the foreigner, the intruder that must be confronted, led beyond our borders, or be willing to improve outside of his blood and color. In this relation to the Muslim, which the white subject experiences as aggression and philanthropy simultaneously, both the white subject and his Other become obscured. By virtue of this narcissism, in which I accommodate the Muslim and she is grateful and motivated to show why she should be, a foundational policy of ignorance is

---

57 Interestingly, the (colonial) desire for affirmation in the context of liberal, capitalist, colonial modernity fulfils all of the major clinical criteria for the diagnosis of narcissistic personality disorder. According to the *Diagnostic and Statistical Manual of Mental Disorders (DSM-V)*, the criteria for the mental affliction are as follows:
Significant impairments in personality functioning manifest by:
Impairments in self functioning (a or b):
a. Identity: Excessive reference to others for self-definition and self-esteem regulation; exaggerated self-appraisal may be inflated or deflated, or vacillate between extremes; emotional regulation mirrors fluctuations in self-esteem.
b. Self-direction: Goal-setting is based on gaining approval from others; personal standards are unreasonably high in order to see oneself as exceptional, or too low based on a sense of entitlement; often unaware of own motivations. AND
Impairments in interpersonal functioning (a or b):
a. Empathy: Impaired ability to recognize or identify with the feelings and needs of others; excessively attuned to reactions of others, but only if perceived as relevant to self; over- or underestimate of own effect on others.
b. Intimacy: Relationships largely superficial and exist to serve self-esteem regulation; mutuality constrained by little genuine interest in others' experiences and predominance of a need for personal gain
Pathological personality traits in the following domain:
Antagonism, characterized by:
a. Grandiosity: Feelings of entitlement, either overt or covert; self-centeredness; firmly holding to the belief that one is better than others; condescending toward others.
b. Attention seeking: Excessive attempts to attract and be the focus of the attention of others; admiration seeking. American Psychiatric Association. (2012). "Narcissistic Personality Disorder." *Diagnostic and statistical manual of mental disorders (DSM-5)*. Naklada Slap, Jastrebarsko, Croatia.

rationalized away as the true version of things. The white subject is caught in a kind of mass somnolence—with others of her kind—when confronted with the Muslim, despite the sheer volume of information and the number of academic studies at our disposal.

In our world that is still reeling from wars on/of terror, this age-old disposition is frequently the default. Truth need only have superficial verifiability; "knowledge" and thus the truth of the Muslim are produced in the act of our reasoned (scientific even) pronouncements about her. When it came to Africa, for example, Jean-Baptiste Labat in 1728 concisely summarized this idea of myopic truth: "I have seen Africa, but I have never set foot there."[58] What Labat says about Africa and the Western imagination remains apt about Islam decades after the publication of Edward Said's *Orientalism*. Islam is not a place but it might as well be, for there is a kind of primordial quality to the subject it produces, some of whom are ready to enter modernity and affirm the supremacy of its values. The Muslim Question becomes a ubiquitous move for the working out of white Europe's own subjectivity. This narcissism is thus an entire worldview, a whole condescending paradigm of knowing and speaking about, acting on, through and with Others. Pronouncements and policies made about this or that aspect of Islam and the Muslim need only bring into view that which confirms the systemic and systematically impaired ways of seeing that racial power and racist impulse, and their institutions of knowledge and power required.

Affirmation produces a situation in which the Muslim is caught up somewhere between forgetting and abandonment. The Muslim Question is a play of opposites: proximity brings with it a will to segregate and self-expression is contingent on a type of renunciation. Answering the Muslim Question *correctly*, thus, requires the de-essentialization of Islam and any active commitments to it. It is this that then allows for the integration and accumulation of those constructed as non-European peoples into European, Western civilization, in which Britain has long played a key role in its definition. In popular, if condescending, discourses of the need for stability in, and (economic) friendship with the Muslim world and minority Muslim communities in Western democracies, the de-essentialization of Islam is,

paradigmatic for all thinking about assimilation of non-European peoples to European civilisation. The idea that people's historical experience is inessential

---

[58] Likewise, the eminent English orientalist and translator of Rumi, Reynold A. Nicholson, never set foot in the Muslim world, nor did he have any interest in meeting Muslims for fear that it would complicate the process of translation. For Labat on Africa, see: (1728) *Nouvelle relation de l'Afrique occidentale*, vol. 1. Paris: G. Cavalier, quoted in Andrew Curran. (2005). "Imaginer l'Afrique au siècle des lumières." *Cromohs: Cyber Review of Modern Historiography* 10.

to them, that it can be shed at will, makes it possible to argue more strongly for the Enlightenment's claim to universality: Muslims . . . can be assimilated or . . . "translated" into a global ("European") civilisation once they have divested themselves of what many of them regard (mistakenly) as essential to themselves. The belief that human beings can be separated from their histories and traditions makes it possible to urge a Europeanisation of the Islamic world.[59]

This is a de-essentialization that affirms the fundamentally *imagined* nature of faith and the *truth* of modern reason (with all its racist contents) that normative secularity demands.[60] The everywhere press conference and the Muslim who always appears is a situation borne of the type of ambitious reforms that Macaulay and Jones brought to the colonial world, but which find parallels in the politics and economy of the war on terror. In both cases, it is the Qur'an upon which the full intensity of such a worldview is enacted. In the liberal paradigm of condescension, the Muslim Question is ultimately answered through the public death of Allah, the suppression of religious selves into whispers expressed privately within the walls of the prayer room. Saba Mahmood discusses this process of de-essentialization as essential to the discourses and politics of "Islamic reformation" so familiar today. Mahmood writes,

> Once religious doctrine is shorn of its manifest forms, and divinity of its worldly presence, scripture can then be read for its symbolic significance. In the words of an influential anthropologist, "religion *is* a system of symbols"[61] that affirms for the believers a general order of existence and provides them with a certain order of meaning. For many modern liberals and progressives, such a formulation is not only commonsensical but necessary for the realization of a liberal democratic polity. The fact that this understanding of religion and scripture as a system of signs and symbols, ready for a cultured individual to interpret according to her poetic resources, enjoys such broad appeal is in part what the term *normative secularity* captures.[62]

[59] Asad, *Formations of the Secular*, pp. 169–70.

[60] On the notion of normative secularity and its demands of this type of renunciation, see: Ibid., chapters 5 and 6; Saba Mahmood. (2006). "Secularism, Hermeneutics, and Empire: The Politics of the Islamic Reformation." *Public Culture*, 18(2), 342–43; Saba Mahmood. (2016). *Religious Difference in a Secular Age: A Minority Report*. Princeton: Princeton University Press, chapter 5.

[61] Clifford Geertz. (1973). "Religion as a Cultural System." In *The Interpretation of Culture*. New York: Basic; emphasis added. Geertz's formulation is widely embraced within the social sciences. For a critique of this conception and recognition of its genealogy, see Talal Asad. (1993). *Genealogies of Religion: Disciplines and Reasons of Power in Christianity and Islam*. Baltimore: Johns Hopkins Press, pp. 27–55.

[62] Saba Mahmood. (2006). "Secularism, Hermeneutics, and Empire: The Politics of the Islamic Reformation." *Public Culture*, 18(2), 342–43. An instructive parallel is to be drawn between this "normative secularity" and the popularity of images of the Prophet Muhammad in the nineteenth

Discourses about the veil, its supposed Qur'anic provenance, and its meaning in liberal, democratic, secular societies are a ubiquitous manifestation of
the type of politics Mahmood discusses found in the full range of academic,
popular, and official writing. In whatever context, the hijab is marked as a
symbol of something, dependent upon either the woman's intentions for its
adornment or the context within which it is worn. Whether the veil is understood to be a symbol of religious or cultural identity, or a symbol of women's
oppression under patriarchal structures of Islam (as do many feminists), the
veil should, either argument agrees, be read as a symbol. As is all too often
the case, "Women who contend that the veil is part of a religious doctrine,
a divine edict, or a form of ethical practice and that it therefore has nothing
to do with 'identity' are usually judged to be victims of false consciousness,
mired in a traditionalism that leads them to mistakenly internalize the opinions of misogynist jurists whom they should resist. Such is the fate that must
befall the veil in a secular imaginary."[63] But this imaginary of the veil is a
product of a larger symbolic system in which the very belief in God, in Allah,
with all that it presupposes in "being Muslim," must also be understood
symbolically, for how could a human, the Muslim Question asks, *reason*ably
agree to this voluntarily?[64]

LICENSING THE REMOVAL OF LIMITS

Old certainties about the self and Other in this contemporary racial drama and
its relation to the Muslim are resurrected and held again as genuine truths.
To set limits to the Muslim Question, and the varying forms of violence and
insult licensed by it, would be to introduce doubt into a febrile atmosphere
in which the worst crime becomes hesitation. Where processes of marking
aspects of the Muslim's life as inessential structures the relation between him
and us, there is no need for pause, even as the Muslim must always be ready
to appear, and affirm, on cue. In a society and worldview gripped by anxieties
of demotion and racial terrors, it becomes simple enough to surrender itself,
without the possibility of collective deliberation, to the law of race. We are
witnessing in new ways the limitlessly proliferating dynamics of marking

---

century in places like British India under regimes of colonial, Islamic reform or purification, as a
human being stripped of all miracle and instead a model of civic virtue, thus, as human, making
him more vulnerable to insult and attack. See: Devji, *Terrorist*, p. 169. See also, Devji's broader
discussion in the same work of Islam's historical and contemporary relationship to/in liberalism.
Terrorist, pp. 169–79.

[63] Ibid., p. 343.

[64] In what remains one of the best critiques of these narratives and demands, see: Saba Mahmood.
(2005). *Politics of Piety: The Islamic Revival and the Feminist Subject*. Princeton, NJ: Princeton
University Press.

certain peoples out for capture between two loveless places:[65] one that the Other has been tasked to abandon and another that does not wish to know her. Constant repetition of the Muslim's belief in society's democratic promises or self-deportation appears to contain the only possibility of respite.

This is, however, a game already lost. The libertine, uninhibited racism of the Muslim Questioned finds its counterpart in the *nanoracism* of the Muslim Question under its many nicknames—"liberalism," "feminism," "integration," "British values"—all of which smuggle in phantasms of the racial subject even as they invite him to speak. Houria Bouteldja brilliantly articulates:

> We are losers. [. . .] We are fugitives and we love the fables that prolong our flight. We hang on to glorious pasts. Pasts that we idealize and that artificially raise our self-esteem, so much so that we sometimes ape our masters and remain condemned to being nothing but pale copies. We are convincing neither in our cultural refinement nor in our crime. We seek the proof of ourselves in the past. We seek it in the mythical Andalusian-Arabic civilization, the only one capable of rivalling the supposed grandeur of Western civilization, when in fact we are nothing but the children of the *fellahs*. . . . Or, we seek it in the pharaohs' Egypt . . . Those very pretentious Qatari skyscrapers, which rival New York's, are more gracious to our eyes than the ancestral skyscrapers of Sanaa in Yemen. And you really have to see it, this pathetic pride, when we brandish a verse from the Koran in which the atom is invoked. Because without the atom, there would be no atomic bomb, and without the atomic bomb, there would be no Hiroshima . . . Hiroshima, mon amour.[66]

The Muslim Question is now an everyday quilt of racism through which the (un)spoken codes of white supremacy and the toxic mix of narcissism and fear of empire can be sustained. The straightforward, if unreal, connection drawn between Britain, and Euro-America more broadly, and values of freedom, the rule of law, tolerance, and democracy—all of which have and continue to be mobilized in the violations of racist power, knowledge, and governance—can exist undisturbed. James Baldwin captured the ruse by which the symbolic and material erasure of racism's effects is unthought in Europe: "I doubt that the villagers think of the devil when they face a cathedral because they have

---

[65] On the "loveless place" of Muslims in Britain, see: Amaliah Voices Podcast. (2019). "The Dehumanisation of Muslims and Why Islamophobia Isn't a Phobia" | Small Talk Ep.2 in With Suhaiymah M. Khan' *Amaliah*. Available at: https://www.amaliah.com/post/54957/the-dehumanisation-of-muslims-and-why-islamophobia-isnt-a-phobia-small-talk-ep-2-in-with-suhaiymah-m-khan

[66] Houria Bouteldja. (2016). *Whites, Jews, and Us. Towards a Politics of Revolutionary Love*. South Pasadena: Semiotext(e), pp. 103–104. A fellah is a farmer or agricultural laborer in the Middle East and North Africa.

never been identified with the devil."[67] Affirmation in the Muslim's voice, everywhere he participates in friendships of quotation, keeps the devil at a distance and instead always casts him as our Other—Muslim, immigrant, intruder. The white man, Baldwin continue, is thus able "to preserve his simplicity and avoid being called to account for crimes committed by his forefathers, or his neighbours."[68] The virile power of Europe and Britain exists, then, undisturbed in its racial myths even as the spatial distance between the white nation and its nonwhite subjects is closed following decades of postcolonial migration, European demotion, and the necessity for, albeit denied, migrant labor.[69]

Perhaps no longer subhuman or completely beyond the pale, the Muslim might escape the interrogation room but must instead be persuasive in their reasons for being (here). Without a confrontation with reality—with history, the histories of Others, wealth, constitutive processes of re- and depopulation—under regimes of the Muslim Question, the white world becomes full of innumerable Others who are seen as always being at the edge of revolt. It is not, however, just the Muslim who is stuck between places for which he does not have the correct documentation, and elsewhere that do not wish to know or care for him. But *all* those who submit themselves to the phantasms of race, whether in the mode of hostility or condescension, are wracked with a phobia of intimacy, entanglement, complex shapes, and words which surely comprise the world. The white subject who, under the aegis of the Muslim Question, is told that Britain is his, will constantly be disturbed by his simultaneous inability to disappear the Muslim nor understand him. Whether we wish to know nothing about the Muslim because she exists at an absolute ontological distance, or whether, alternatively, our engagements with her are constrained by her ability to corroborate our fragile "reality" of things, we ultimately have no defensible memory of the very country we claim as "ours," as "white," as democratic.

If there is to be a future for the Muslim Question, for the incessant need and (constantly produced) desire for affirmation, then it is one that will be exacerbated by technologies of the internet and social media. Already an era of mass morality, the mechanisms of affective life which function according to an almost total interconnection between individuals, made possible by the hegemony of neoliberalism and the supremacy of the technologies of Silicon Valley, we may be entering an era of *virtual hordes*.[70] The immoderate

---

[67] James Baldwin. (1964). *Notes of a Native Son*. London: Michael Joseph, p. 164.

[68] Ibid., p. 157.

[69] Shilliam, *Race and the Undeserving Poor*; Gilroy, *After Empire*; J. Solomos. (1993). *Race and Racism in Britain*. Macmillan International Higher Education; Valluvan, *The Clamour of Nationalism*.

[70] See: Adam Curtis. (2016). *HyperNormalisation*. British Broadcasting Corporation; Karim Amer and Jehane Noujaim. (2019). *The Great Hack*. Netflix. On the connections between internet and

stimuli of racism and Islamophobia, in which notions of Muslim threat and ingratitude are central, are propelled by a narcotic economy of "likes" and "retweets,"[71] supported by an algorithmic reason which functions according to the same logics of erasure.[72] It is no coincidence that the techniques of secrecy as much as publicity depend upon the more opaque corners of the digitized and algorithmic world.

The allure of certainty and displacement of responsibility provided by racial ideas will continue to proliferate not only among the "working classes," as we are often told—those subalterns among the whites—but as an essential part of mass culture and within the so-called "polite society." Affirmation in the Muslim Question may well perform defensive functions, which obscure the offensive effects of racism and Islamophobia through discourses of tolerance and public performances of solidarity. But this creates a social and political world that is as brittle as it is subtly violent, a white world constantly on the edge of inward collapse or violent outward expansion because it does not know how to be still and live with others. And yet the voice of the Other which comforts the white world about its democratic promises and the work Islam has yet to do on itself is, in the final analysis, a necessary balm for sustaining the public secret of race, which can more powerfully be kept by its object of condescension. "Yes, unfortunately, we have got some things wrong too," the white world says. "Come, let us explain our fallibility and how good we are for recognising it."

---

morality, see: John Sullins. (2018). "Information Technology and Moral Values." *Stanford Encyclopedia of Philosophy.* Available at: https://plato.stanford.edu/entries/it-moral-values/

[71] There is much fanfare around Donald Trump's idiosyncratic use of social media using Twitter, for example, to make policy announcements, offer commentaries on state leaders and international events, and even to publicize the hiring and firing of senior staff. On Trump and social media, see: Pablo Boczkowski. (2018). *Trump and the Media.* Boston: MIT Press.

[72] On the intersections of racism and algorithm, see the notion of "platformed racism" in Ariadna Matamoros-Fernández. (2017). "Platformed Racism: The Mediation and Circulation of an Australian Race-based Controversy on Twitter, Facebook and YouTube, Information." *Communication & Society,* 20(6), 930–46. See also: J. Daniels. (2015). "'My Brain Database Doesn't See Skin Color': Color-Blind Racism in the Technology Industry and in Theorizing the Web." *American Behavioral Scientist,* 59(11), 1377–93; Lisa Nakamura and Peter A. Chow-White eds. (2012). *Race after the Internet.* New York: Routledge; Safiya Umoja Noble. (2018). *Algorithms of Oppression: How Search Engines Reinforce Racism.* New York University Press. On "techno-racism" and facial recognition, see: Clare Garvie, Alvaro Bedoya, Jonathan Frankle. (2016). *The Perpetual Line-Up: Unregulated Police Face Recognition in America.* Georgetown Law: Center on Privacy & Technology. Available at: https://www.perpetuallineup.org/findings/racial-bias; Daniel Cossins. (2018). "Discriminating Algorithms: 5 Times AI Showed Prejudice." *New Scientist.* Available at: https://www.newscientist.com/article/2166207-discriminating-algorithms-5-times-ai-showed-prejudice/; Sahil Chinoy. (2019). "The Racist History behind Facial Recognition." *New York Times.* Available at: https://www.nytimes.com/2019/07/10/opinion/facial-recognition-race.html

Chapter 6

Publicity

I find Macaulay's "Minute" especially pertinent to our analysis of the Muslim Question precisely because of the *substance* of his words. They contained within them the consolidation of a particular worldview, publicly, honestly, and confidently expressed, as the basis for an ambitious project on Indian education and the Muslim subject of India. His speech consolidated notions of proximity and affirmation as pillars of colonization in the light of day, sanctioned by sovereign power and European modernity's self-assurance. It would seem, therefore, that there were no secrets to be kept, only progress to be had. However, I propose that we think more carefully about the idea of the public secret: what I understand as rendering true or accurate or valuable, a set of deep-rooted fantasies which become so via the mechanisms of publicity, the podium and the autocue.

The hostility which characterizes the Muslim Questioned also had a necessary public dimension, a kind of exuberant and repeated public performance of racism to quiet the anxieties of the white subject taken as the center of all meaning. Publicity and its relation to the secret are, however, somewhat different here. Publicity is the performance of recognition, critique even, of the status quo, while still making pronouncements about that which one knows next to nothing, has not witnessed, or has refused to witness, or has witnessed but then swiftly disavowed. The Muslim Question thrives because of its public dimension. Publicity here is the performance of solidarity and critique of racist effects in ways which never relinquish the haunting figure of the racial subject. That is, an individual and people whose content consists of founding experiences and the labors of victory which constitute white civilization that took place in the past to which one was not a witness but must be its benefactor. What authorizes certain pronouncements, structures of thought, desire, and action is much less rooted in their truth than in the circulation of symbols and powerful systems of representation, of which official memory, memorialization, and collective remembrance are symptomatic. These representations only have meaning, or more accurately, a material, lived environment in which they are embedded because they exist in relation to a history and present that one refuses to admit, and a worldview which cannot see otherwise.

I have stressed the memorial, psychic, nostalgic dimensions of apprehending colonial pasts and putting them to good use. But equally, and more importantly, I have sought to analyze the actual policies of reconstruction and reconstitution, forgetting and keeping secret, which had physical as well as human matter as their objects of design. The public dimension of the Muslim Question requires a display of critique in order to defer actual obligations of hospitality and justice. It maintains also the appearance that the Muslim Question was never asked, that consistent with our values of tolerance and equality, " *'they' are of course one of 'us.'* " As we have seen from the foregoing, however, there is a relation of mutual implication between difference and similarity, contradictory impulses that fuse in the narcissistic outpouring and relations of power that constitute a social and physical world coded white. That while the particular zone(s) in which the Muslim lives is not complementary to the zone in which we live, we are nonetheless entangled and derive a sense of our identities negatively.

The colonial context in which Macaulay's Minute was heard and felt, in both its people and land, was of course divided into compartments: chiefly the zone where the natives lived, and the zone inhabited by settlers. Fanon described this spatial logic as one based on the "principle of reciprocal exclusivity" where "no conciliation is possible, for of the two terms, one is superfluous." All communication in one way or another reaffirmed the sacrificial relation between settler and native, white Man and his Other, and instituted a form of white community in which imitation was desired while it was disallowed as a legal, political, and fundamentally economic reality. Naturally, this base desire for imitation revolves around not the actual practices of white civilization but its fantasies. Only then does the desire and its prohibition make sense. Only then can a latent belief in white supremacy and fear of white replacement together remain coherent. If this spatial division, always already a racial split, has a desire for imitation on one side, then envy is on the other:

> The look that the native turns on the settler's town is a look of lust, a look of envy; it expresses his dreams of possession—all manner of possession: to sit at the settler's table, to sleep in the settler's bed, with his wife if possible. The colonized man is an envious man. And this the settler knows very well; when

their glances meet he ascertains bitterly, always on the defensive, "They want to take our place."[1]

Envy and the violent impulses that it licenses are diffused by having the native speak in public, in a recognizable tongue, and in recognition of her desire to be put to work. The Muslim Question is one asked within a situation of reciprocal exclusivity, intensified by the technical and social complexities of our present. Defined by the extent to which the Other can "improve" into the white settler whose zone of living is everywhere but who experiences life as a constant fight against the insurgent native, the Muslim is here and there filled with pieces of an apprentice identity—sometimes criminal, sometimes useful—leaving open responses only to notions of remedial "improvement," "progress," and "work," to which s/he has been reduced. As a result, instead of inspiring empathy and genuine solidarity, the experiences and criticisms of Others—even if in pursuit of hegemonic modes of integration and/or assimilation—arouses only further disgust and judgment.[2]

Race is at work not only in simple appearance. Surface simulacra of skin pigmentation or dress and the transformation of the name "Muslim" into an insult and the symbol of terror are too explicit in their racism to be considered in the liberalism of the Muslim Question. Yet racism also authorizes the abdication as much as the charge of responsibility for the terrors of the world. High walls and barbed wire, identity cards, security cameras, and the interrogation room are complimented by well-funded community projects, prime-time television series, sharp videos by this or that public figure on an "ethnic" holiday, so as to reinforce the one-way street to hospitality in the white world and its institutions, in sum, various technologies of the podium and the autocue of the Muslim Question. As Nietzsche would say, "appearance is reality," not its opposite.[3] Therefore, discourses (and the economies which underpin them) of integration, reform, counter-extremism, immigration, culture, Europe to which the Muslim Question is associated are not

---

[1] Fanon, *Wretched of the Earth*, p. 39, 61. Frantz Fanon often expressed the impossibility of community in in the colonial situation: "Colonialism is not a thinking machine, nor a body with reasoning faculties. It is violence in its natural state and it will only yield when confronted with an even greater violence." Or: "For the native, life can only spring up again out of the rotting corpse of the settler"; See also: Fanon, *Black Skin, White Masks*, p. 220; Fanon, *Wretched of the Earth*, chap. 5; and Frantz Fanon. (1965). *A Dying Colonialism*. New York: Grove, chap. 4.

[2] Leonard Binder argues "from the time of the Napoleonic invasion, from the time of the Janissaries, from the time of the Sepoy mutiny, at least, the West has been trying to tell Islam what must be the price of progress in the coin of tradition which is to be surrendered. And from those times, despite the increasing numbers of responsive Muslims, there remains a substantial number that steadfastly argue that it is possible to progress without paying such a heavy cultural price." Leonard Binder. (1988). *Islamic Liberalism*. Chicago: University of Chicago Press, p. 293.

[3] Friedrich Nietzsche. (1935). *The Will to Power*. London: Penguin, vol. 3, p. 484.

simply condescending. They seek to further consolidate a racialized matrix of power in more complex and public ways.

HAVE YOU HEARD? APPARENTLY, WE'RE RACIST

In a detailed and well-circulated series of investigative reporting, the *Guardian's* "Bias in Britain" project[4] professed in its headline: "Revealed: the stark evidence of everyday racial bias in Britain."[5] The research covered a wide range of areas in which bias and discrimination were faced by black, Asian, and minority ethnic people: online dating apps; football coaching; teaching in schools and headteachers; student dropout rates in universities; exclusion rates in schools; representation in television and publishing industries (especially children's books); cancer care; mental health services; and homeownership. We do not have the space here for too detailed an analysis of the findings but some brief details will suffice. The publicity generated by the series of reports was based on a poll asking black and minority ethnic (BAME) people "about their experiences of what you might call 'unconscious bias.' It was the first major piece of public polling of its kind. People were asked whether they had experienced a range of scenarios, such as being refused entry to a restaurant for no good reason or being treated like a potential shoplifter. The poll also surveyed 1,000 white British people, so comparisons could be made."[6] Later came a "major" piece of research into bias in the flat and house share market. As the authors write,

> In a snapshot survey of the market, expressions of interest were sent from "Muhammad" and "David" to almost 1,000 online advertisements for rooms across the UK.

---

[4] The methodology of the project: "ICM interviewed a representative sample of 1,000 minority ethnic people aged 18+ living in Great Britain online between 17 and 22 October 2018. The data is based on 2011 census data collected by the Office for National Statistics (ONS). In addition to this sample, ICM interviewed 1,797 white people aged 18+ between 19 and 22 October 2018, drawn from a nationally representative sample achieved using its omnibus service. This survey was also conducted online. The figures are drawn from the same data set as the news story but may vary where they have been represented over a different time period." Robert Booth, Aamna Mohdi, Cath Levett. (2018). "Bias in Britain: Explore the Poll Results." *Guardian.* Available at: https://www.theguardian.com/uk-news/ng-interactive/2018/dec/02/bias-in-britain-explore-the-poll-results

[5] Robert Booth and Aamna Mohdin. "Revealed: the stark evidence of everyday racial bias in Britain." *Guardian.* Available at: https://www.theguardian.com/uk-news/2018/dec/02/revealed-the-stark-evidence-of-everyday-racial-bias-in-britain

[6] Aamna Mohdin. (2018). "Racism in Britain: How We Revealed the Shocking Impact of Unconscious Bias." *Guardian.* Available at: https://www.theguardian.com/membership/2019/jan/26/racism-in-britain-how-we-revealed-the-shocking-impact-of-unconscious-bias

The Guardian found that for every 10 positive replies David received, Muhammad received only eight.

Muhammad was doubly disadvantaged compared with David as he was more likely not to receive a response (44% of the time compared with 36%), and when he did receive a response it was more likely to be negative (25% of the time compared with 18%).

While the survey gives only a momentary view of the situation across five areas in the UK, charities, pressure groups and the Residential Landlords Association (RLA) all said the findings were illustrative of persistent bias in the housing market—whether conscious or unconscious. The RLA described the findings as "disturbing" and said a government requirement on landlords to check tenants' immigration status was compounding the problem.

Minority ethnic groups have long faced discrimination in the housing market: in the 1950s, some adverts for properties specified "no blacks, no Irish, no dogs." Such explicit discrimination is largely in the past, although last year a landlord was taken to court after he barred people from south Asian backgrounds from renting his properties because of "curry smells."[7]

The "Bias in Britain" project was a useful and timely record of racial bias and its admittedly systemic nature. What is more pertinent here, however, is the extent to which the research was "revelatory" or "shocking" and if so of what and to whom. Put differently, the findings would only be "revelations" for those who benefit from the current ordering of imposed hierarchy and social/political benefit. The historic and actual lived experiences, the complaints and grievances filed, the cases opened and settled of racial Others—Muslims and other Others—are "discovered" anew as stark evidence again and again. What gives these revealed experiences meaning, then, is their packaging as a source of shock in an otherwise banal situation where racism and Islamophobia is assumed not to exist, or only exist at the fringes among the aberrant that do not represent British, or white "culture," but individuals.

"Bias in Britain" recalls Paul Gilroy's argument that "the nation's intermittent racial tragedies punctuate the chronic boredom of national decline with

---

[7] Muslims in general reported having more negative experiences than BAME people of other religious backgrounds. For a selection of the most important findings of the series, see: Booth and Mohdin, "Revealed"; Haroon Siddique. (2018). "Flatshare Bias: Room-Seekers with Muslim Name Get Fewer Replies." *Guardian.* Available at: https://www.theguardian.com/uk-news/2018/dec/03/flatshare-bias-room-seekers-with-muslim-name-get-fewer-replies; Mona Chalabi and Sarah Marsh. (2018). "Revealed: Bias Faced by Minorities in UK Driving Tests." *Guardian.* Available at: https://www.theguardian.com/uk-news/2018/dec/03/black-women-far-less-likely-than-white-men-to-pass-driving-tests

a functional anguish":[8] a functional shock, functional revelations, functional publicity. The paradigm of condescension allows facile arguments of proximity and affirmation—that "we" do in fact care about *your* experiences—which seek to sustain, if not further consolidate, the raciological core of the social, national, economic, and institutional realm. It remains a self-congratulatory anguish that continues to pose the Muslim Question and other questions derived from "race," maintaining race-based measures of sameness and difference, while insisting that the Other submit more housing and job applications with fewer responses, accept greater rates of exclusion and surveillance, not to mention the often-gendered violence of everyday life. Publicity here is the performance of shock at racism and Islamophobia, however well documented across decades, in order to bracket these social (civilizational) products as surprises. This produces, in turn, a strained performance of solidarity with the maintenance of white innocence in its dialects of shock and guilt.[9]

Even in the broadcasted (and celebrated) documentation of the discriminatory effects of racial bias, the systemic and systematic denial of humanity (or inferior status) of certain population groups, such discourse is itself inscribed from the very beginning in a tautology: "We are also human beings" the Other is made to say. Or better yet: "We also have a glorious past that proves our humanity and right to commune as equals."[10] That Muslims might also be due a share of the world. It is a discourse that is a natural extension of: "Is theirs a generic humanity?" "Are they like us?" "How, then, should they be treated?" The fiction of the racial subject is in each case maintained. "It" or "they" remain desirous of entry into the enclosure of citizens and thus ward off white Britain, affirming the ultimately innocent and hospitable

---

[8] Gilroy, *There Ain't No*, p. xxiii. See also: P. Gilroy. (2003). "Race is Ordinary: Britain's Post-Colonial Melancholia." *Philosophia Africana,* 6(1), 31–34 and Gilroy, *Postcolonial Melancholia,* chapter 3.

[9] The inaugural formula of white freedom contingent on certain lives as "raw material" is maintained even in the profession of shock and guilt. Sara Salem. (2018). "White Innocence as a Feminist Discourse: Race, Empire and Gender in Performances of 'shock' in Contemporary Politics." *Working Paper.* Available at: https://www.academia.edu/37735749/White_Innocence_as_a_Feminist_Discourse_Race_empire_and_gender_in_performances_of_shock_in_contemporary_politics. More generally, see: C. T. Mohanty. (1988). "Under Western eyes: Feminist Scholarship and Colonial Discourses." *Feminist Review,* 1(30), 61–88; C. Rottenberg. (2014). "The Rise of Neoliberal Feminism." *Cultural Studies,* 28(3), 418–37. On the ignorance of (white) shock, see Gary Younge's recent articles: (2019). "Shocked by the Rise of the Right? Then You Weren't Paying Attention." *Guardian.* Available at https://www.theguardian.com/commentisfree/2019/may/24/country-racist-elections-liberals-anti-racism-movement and (2019). "Our Glorious Past Is What We Remember. The Brutality Behind It We've Forgotten." *Guardian.* Available at: https://www.theguardian.com/commentisfree/2019/may/31/glorious-past-remember-brutality-forgotten.

[10] The centrality—and the trap—of this racist tautology, of proving one's humanity as a *response* rather than a given fact is best elucidated in the work of Sylvia Wynter, Fanon, Audre Lorde Césaire, and, in a general sense, the poetry of Léopold Sédar Senghor. See also: W. E. B. Du Bois. (1946). *The World and Africa: An Inquiry into the Part Which Africa Has Played in World History.* New York: International Publishers.

constitution of "here." The fact of race as a foundational code is, then, perpetuated *through* the periodic publicity of its effects, silencing the haunting
presence of history and authenticating the performance of shock at our racism
and Islamophobia.

When the apologies and shock arrive, they must do so with the perpetual
rediscovery at our racism in order to enter the public world comprehensibly.
Race has surely become a habitus, racism a kind of culture when, even in
its "exposure" as shocking, structural discrimination is shown to have been
practiced without one being conscious of it.[11] As the always-innocent, we are
shocked when those who suffer within the racial formation draw our attention to the reality of what we do. When the racist sees the Muslim, she cannot
comprehend that the Muslim as she sees him is not actually there, does not
exist, but is a product and site of a complex within the white subject herself.
These periodic "revelations" erase as much as they expose. That even as the
severity and violence of racism is discovered in our relations with the Other,

> We pretend that it is just a matter of harmless acts that do not possess all the
> meanings some would like to assign to them. We take offence when the police
> of another country deprive us of our right to laugh, of the right to a humour
> that is never directed against ourselves (self-derision) or against the powerful
> (satire), but always against those weaker than ourselves—the right to laugh at
> the expense of those we wish to stigmatize. A kind of hilarious, utterly moronic,
> almost dishevelled form of nanoracism that takes pleasure in wallowing in
> ignorance and that claims a right to stupidity and to the violence it serves to
> sanction—herein lies the spirit of our times.[12]

As is the base logic of race and racism, the white "I" claims a right to stupidity and ignorance, a right that is simply not there for those who must respond
to the Muslim Question and who must all be historians, social scientists, and
theologians to be taken even minimally seriously.[13] Even this, however, is not

---

[11] The Bias in Britain project, after all, revealed "unconscious bias" despite its institutional, historic
and, crucially for our purposes, constitutive force.

[12] Mbembe, "Society of Enmity," p. 33.

[13] The legal scholar Patricia Williams makes a similar argument in the context of refuting the seemingly inevitable resurgence of racial science every couple of decades as a technique of justifying
"un-deservingness." She said: "One of the great difficulties with pseudoscience is that it is so hard
to refute just by saying it isn't so. The logical structure (if not substance) of pseudoscience posits
what purports to be fact. It requires counter-fact to make counter-argument. Black people find
themselves responding endlessly to such studies before we can be heard on any other subject. We
must credentialise ourselves as number-crunching social scientists quickly in order to be seen as
even minimally intelligent. There's the catch: racial science makes anyone who agrees with it intelligent, enhanced, informed and empowered. Real numbers, real science; it's what school teaches
us to revere. And it makes anyone who knows the great, messy, un-provable contrary, who knows
the indecipherable complexity of black or white people, who knows the reality and potential of

enough. For the revelations of *The Guardian* would not be so shocking given the massive literature by actual social scientists, historians, and theologians on the structural iniquities of racism and Islamophobia in Britain. Instead, there remains a strange "hostility to the proposition that racist violence and institutional indifference are normal and recurrent features of British social and political life" which get "intermingled with absolute and sincere surprise at the nastiness of racism and the extent of anger and resentment it can cause."[14] A kind of surprise that cannot, of course, accommodate the anger and resentment of racially marked Others who, in the face of this violence, are asked to be satisfied by performances of shock and guilt which are built upon the repression of the memories and lived experiences of those same Others.

It can be admitted openly and in deeply offensive ways that Britain does not like Muslims, sees in them the only difference, and "wants to get rid of them but then becomes uncomfortable because it does not like the things it learns about itself when it gives vent to feelings of hostility and hatred."[15] The Bajan novelist, George Lamming, in his assessment of West Indian life in 1960s Britain, contended that "race ceased to be a liberal speculation about life in the United States or South Africa and became, instead, a fact like the milk on your door-step. People who were ashamed of the conduct of their army in Kenya or the Caribbean found themselves unprepared for a black stranger, whose skin made class irrelevant, and who had read that there was a room within which he would like to rent."[16] What Stuart Hall has described as the "profound historical forgetfulness . . . which has overtaken the British

---

all humanity—us silly egalitarians, it makes us unintelligent, uninformed, powerless and naïve." Patricia Williams. (1997). "An Ordinary Brilliance: Parting the Waters, Chasing the Wounds." *The Genealogy of Race, Reith Lectures.* BBC Radio 4.

[14] Gilroy, *Postcolonial Melancholia*, p. 105.

[15] Gilroy, *After Empire*, p. 114. A brutal irony abounds with the ongoing "Windrush scandal." See: Luke De Noronha. (2018). "The Mobility of Deservingness: Race, Class and Citizenship in the Wake of the 'Windrush Scandal'." *The Disorder of Things.* Available at: https://thedisorderofthings.com/2018/07/03/the-mobility-of-deservingness-race-class-and-citizenship-in-the-wake-of-the-windrush-scandal/; Akala. (2018). *Natives: Race and Class in the Ruins of Empire.* London: Two Roads; Sundeep Lidher. (2018). "British Citizenship and the Windrush Generation." *Runnymede.* Available at: https://www.runnymedetrust.org/blog/british-citizenship-and-the-windrush-generation; For details on how the situation has unfolded see: Amelia Gentleman. (2018). "The Children of Windrush: 'I'm Here Legally, But They're Asking Me to Prove I'm British'." *Guardian.* Available at: https://www.theguardian.com/uk-news/2018/apr/15/why-the-children-of-windrush-demand-an-immigration-amnesty. This situation does not speak to an administrative/bureaucratic oversight, but how the imperial logic which instantiated a racialized scale of infrahumanity continues to work and has a place in the very structures of the organized power. Moreover, this logic travels. See: Robert Wright. (2018). "Windrush scandal Spreads to Other Commonwealth Countries." *Financial Times.* Available at: https://www.ft.com/content/ddbdf02e-47c8-11e8-8ee8-cae73aab7ccb

[16] George Lamming. (1962). "After a Decade." *West Indian Gazette* (February), p. 9.

people about race and Empire since the 1950s,"[17] is also, if not more so, a denial of the *present*, or put differently, *the presentness of the past*,[18] the way in which people situate themselves in the past *for* the present and vice versa. There is then the "tendency to pull race out from the internal dynamic of British society, and repress its history,"[19] only for "revelations" of its effects to be registered anew, as facts that shock some but are lived by Others.

PRONOUNCING (WHITE) INNOCENCE

In the summer of 2020, the Metropolitan Police commissioner Cressida Dick and the head of human resources Clare Davies were called upon to reflect on the progress made twenty years on from the publication of the landmark Macpherson Report, following the murder of Stephen Lawrence, which found the Met to be institutionally racist. That summer was marked globally by protests against racist state violence following the murders of Breonna Taylor and George Floyd in Louisville and Minneapolis, respectively. In their briefing to Parliament, Dick and Davis decided that the Met was no longer institutionally racist. The disproportionate number of deaths of black people while in custody, the disproportionate use of force during stop and search, the police's complicity in the economies of surveillance, detention, and DNA collection under the sponsorship of counterterrorism policies underpinned by racist and Islamophobic assumptions, the fact that the Met Police itself will be disproportionately white for at least another hundred years at the current rate of progress, none of these matters. Instead, "it's just unfair to think the police force hasn't changed,"[20] a statement and plaint at once licensed by the right to ignorance and absolute knowledge. The order and truth of things can simply be enunciated.

Who is it that gets to deem the critique of institutional racism "unhelpful" and outdated terms? Cressida Dick told the Home Affairs Select Committee: "The label now does more harm than good, it is something that is immediately interpreted by anyone who hears it as not institutional but racist—full of racists full stop, which we are not. It is a label that puts people off from engaging with the police. It stops people *wanting* to give us intelligence,

[17] Stuart Hall. (1978). "Racism and Reaction." Five Views on Multi-Racial Britain: Talks on Race Relations Broadcast by BBC TV. London: Commission for Racial Equality, pp. 24–25.

[18] James Baldwin. (1985). *"White Man's Guilt." The Price of the Ticket: Collected Nonfiction, 1948-1985.* London: Michael Joseph, pp. 409–14.

[19] Hall, "Racism and Reaction," p. 25.

[20] For the Parliamentary session at which Dick gave this response to a question about the Metropolitan Police's institutional racism specifically in response to stop-and-search procedures, see: Home Affairs Committee. (2019). "The Macpherson Report: Twenty Years On." Available at: https://www.parliamentlive.tv/Event/Index/cd010bb3-558c-4575-9a23-ec4a5070a3cb

evidence, come and join us, work with us."[21] With the ostensible aim of confronting the problem of institutional racism given a name twenty years earlier with the murder of Stephen Lawrence and the ineffectual investigation that followed, Dick's public statements to the country's journalists contains the argument that those who experience racism at the hands of the police do not quite understand what is happening: "we're not all racist at the Met so how could the police be institutionally racist?" she seems to ask. Yet again, the theology of progress safeguards the tolerant core of well-meaning liberal society, with the racism and (institutional) licenses of its rogue racists shielded against the exposure of its fundamental violence, a violence known by all, but felt most intensely among the racialized and poor, explained away in the name of "improvement." Fallibility and the unfounded criticisms of the Met, not the experience of the policed, intervene in its relation of care and the will that people have for working with (if not for) the police.

It is in this way that criticisms of the Met's institutional racism are deemed unfair. *"A better day is coming. Sit still, be patient. We make mistakes, we are human too."* The logic of having, needing even, an audience to witness the innocence of white institutions despite their violence is important to their functioning. And further still, it is a reality into which everyone must be translated, the vision of a world which necessarily becomes the ultimate measure of what must be *everyone's* reality.[22] Evidence of the Met's racial violence is legion, historic, and constitutive but the argument of complexity, echoes of which can be heard in Dick's plea, is a commonplace refrain in its defense. When faced with the finding, Metropolitan Police officers are four times more likely to use force against black people compared with the white

---

[21] Rebecca Camber. (2019). "Scotland Yard Chief Cressida Dick Insists the Met Police Is No Longer Riddled with Racism 20 Years after the Macpherson Report Branded It 'institutionally' Prejudiced." *Daily Mail.* Available at: https://www.dailymail.co.uk/news/article-7234417/Scotland -Yard-chief-Cressida-Dick-insists-Met-Police-no-longer-riddled-racism.html.

[22] Cressida Dick's comments would be based on the work of the committee examining the progress made since the publication of the Macpherson Report in 1999 and the implementation of its recommendations. See: Home Affairs Committee. (2019). "The Macpherson Report: Twenty Years On inquiry." Available at: https://www.parliament.uk/business/committees/committees-a-z/commons-select/home-affairs-committee/inquiries/parliament-2017/macpherson-report-twenty-years -on-inquiry-17-19/; Common Select Committee. (2019). "Cressida Dick Questioned on Progress in Implementing Recommendations of Macpherson Report." Available at: https://www.parliament .uk/business/committees/committees-a-z/commons-select/home-affairs-committee/news-parlia- ment-2017/macpherson-report-evidence-17-191/; For analysis of Dick's comments see: Kevin Maxwell. (2019). "Sorry Cressida Dick, but as a Black Former Detective I Know Just How Racist the Met Still Is." *Independent.* Available at: https://www.independent.co.uk/voices/met-police -cressida-dick-no-longer-institutionally-racist-racism-black-officer-a9001176.html; Vikram Dodd. (2019). "Met Disproportionately White for Another 100 Years—Police Leaders." *Guardian.* Available at: https://www.theguardian.com/uk-news/2019/feb/19/met-police-disproportionately -white-for-another-100-years; Neelam Tailor. (2019). "This Week Saw Police Attack Migrants in Paris While the Met Police Say Their Institutional Racism Is Over." *gal-dem.* Available at: https://gal-dem.com/this-week-saw-police-attack-migrants-in-paris-while-the-met-police-say-their -institutional-racism-is-over/; and this excellent Twitter "thread" from the actress Kelechi Okafor (2019). Available at: https://twitter.com/kelechnekoff/status/1149226175581032448

population, Scotland Yard said predictably, "the causes of disproportionality are not straightforward."

But a serving officer, speaking on condition of anonymity, would say: "As far as they [the Met] are concerned black people are more aggressive." "You should calm them down but instead they are keen to put hands on first because it's flight or fight." Between Cressida Dick and the native informant above, we have a complex situation but one whose resolution is always already on the side of state power and those accused of racism. The unhelpful charge of institutional racism becomes an obstacle for a society where citizens and police exist in banal relations of information exchange and recruitment drives—Dick's "come and join us, work with us." And yet there is the view that black people are more aggressive and therefore necessitate greater levels of vigilance and force in their policing. And those instances where a suspect is injured or killed because of this increased and often preemptive force—a suspect who is disproportionately black and male—are rationalized on the basis, not of his blackness the police are keen to stress, but his congenital aggressiveness. The charges of institutional racism and systematic state murder which follow—and with detailed evidence in hand—are then read back into the vision of society enunciated by the likes of Cressida Dick, where the charge of racism is the problem, not the public and repeated acts of violence licensed by it.

In a society structured by race-thinking, racism is simultaneously the cause of irritation and the balm that soothes it. The presence of the racial subject, a figure who is tasked with being a ward of the nation and its families, is nevertheless a discomfiting presence, especially when she does not arrive on cue or speaks too freely of the nation's broken promises, words that are in turn cast as ingratitude. This then propels all manner of slights against that subject who has shown her true colors: she could never, in truth, be made to be one of us, and her experience of condescension and abuse is altogether justified. White institutions, often pervaded by carceral mentalities, can then maintain that we are fair and tolerant and maintain support for all. Mistakes will be made, a black or brown person regrettably killed or detained here and there, but we are right to remain vigilant to the sins and nature of the Other.

REPORTING FOR DUTY

Boris Johnson's official Eid message on August 12, 2019,[23] displayed a similar mixture of condescension, kinship, repression, and innocence. Johnson begins his message wishing "Eid Mubarak" to Muslims "whether you're

---

[23] Boris Johnson. (2019). "Wishing Everyone Celebrating the Joyous Festival of Eid al-Adha a Very Peaceful and Prosperous Time."– PM' *10 Downing Street.* Available at: https://twitter.com/10DowningStreet/status/1160476648896114689

one of Britain's 3.3 million Muslims, or one of more than a billion people worldwide celebrating Eid-al-Adha."[24] He goes on to say that the story of Eid is one of sacrifice, "about doing your duty and doing what's right. And that is something we see daily from Muslims right across the UK . . . who make such a huge contribution to modern British life." Whether it is "in business, in our public services, culture, the media, at the highest levels of government, and of course in England's world cup-winning cricket team, British Muslims are helping to make this country the success it is today." Johnson's urging of "our"—non-Muslim—celebration of the contributions of British Muslims is saddled with several conditions for making such celebration legitimate, or desirable even. The message is exceptionally unoriginal. Of course, Muslims in Britain contribute a great deal to the industries Johnson lists, and they do give huge amounts to charity, as if to legitimize thinking otherwise: *"Do Muslim, in fact, have jobs and support just causes?"* It turns out, the Prime Minister confirms, for we should always wait for confirmation from a reliable witness, that they do. Indicative of the racial principles of governance—especially as it relates to the border and the racial subject within and without—the economic, labor, and consumptive contributions of Muslims rationalize their presence,[25] on our streets, in our houses, in our workplaces, and in our shopping centers. The figure who answers the Muslim Question is above all a figure captured in pound sterling.

The language of celebration and recognition is deployed, as the shocking statistics of *The Guardian* reveal, at a time when violent racist attacks are disturbingly high, with Islamophobic incidents going up, alarmingly, by 600 percent following the attack by white supremacist Brenton Tarrant on two Christchurch mosques killing fifty-one people,[26] and the fundamentalism

---

[24] Interestingly this number is exaggerated in the British public mind: "we hugely overestimate the proportion of Muslims in the British population—we think that 1 in 6 Britons are Muslim, when actually fewer than 1 in 20 are. The findings show we think 15% of the population are Muslim, when actually only 4.8% are, less than a third of our guess." In fact, the trend of overestimating Muslim populations was a general trend across the forty countries surveyed. See: Ipsos MORI. (2016). "Perils of Perception." Available at: https://www.ipsos.com/ipsos-mori/en-uk/perceptions -are-not-reality-what-world-gets-wrong

[25] Luke de Noronha. (2018). "There Is No Such Thing as a 'Left' Case for Borders." *Red Pepper*. Available at: https://www.redpepper.org.uk/there-is-no-such-thing-as-a-left-case-for-borders/

[26] Jacinda Ardern, prime minister of New Zealand, became a globally adored figure of dignified leadership in the aftermath of a terrorist attack. Predictably, however, the many words and videos attesting to Ardern's sensitivity and immense kindness, true though they were, eventually worked to silence the speech of Muslim themselves, substituting Muslim death, grief and vulnerability for Ardern's leadership as a teaching-moment for other leaders of state all while allowing the all-too-familiar construction of Tarrant as not "of us." On this sleight of hand, see: Sahar Ghumkhor. (2019). "The hypocrisy of New Zealand's 'this is not us' claim." *Al Jazeera*. Available at: https:// www.aljazeera.com/indepth/opinion/hypocrisy-zealand-claim-190319104526942.html. For a general overview of the attacks see: BBC News. (2019). "Christchurch shootings: Mosque attacker charged with terrorism." *BBC News Online*. Available at: https://www.bbc.co.uk/news/world-asia -48346786?intlink_from_url=https://www.bbc.co.uk/news/topics/c966094wvmqt/christchurch

of white supremacy expressed in polite society, in the halls of government and the academy is consonant with rational thinking and legitimate debate.[27] That Brenton Tarrant would capitalize on the same technologies of social media to livestream his murders like footage from a video game,[28] technologies that play such a crucial role in disseminating and globalizing regimes of Islamophobia,[29] is a connection that is unthinkable to Johnson and the conditions which produce him.

-mosque-shootings&link_location=live-reporting-story; See also: For the political context of the attacks, namely a global Islamophobia, See: H.A. Hellyer. (2019). "The Islamophobia that Led to the Christchurch Shooting Must Be Confronted." *Guardian*. Available at: https://www.theguardian .com/commentisfree/2019/mar/15/islamophobia-christchurch-shooting-anti-muslim-bigotry-new -zealand; Jonathan Freedland. (2019). "To Prevent Another Christchurch We Must Confront the Right's Hate Preachers." *Guardian*. Available at: https://www.theguardian.com/commentisfree /2019/mar/15/prevent-another-christchurch-confront-right-hate-preachers; Imam Gamal Fouda. (2019). "'Broken-Hearted But Not Broken': Al Noor imam's Christchurch Speech in Full." *Guardian*. Available at: https://www.theguardian.com/world/2019/mar/22/broken-hearted-but-not -broken-al-noor-imams-christchurch-speech-in-full; Hamid Dabashi. (2019). "When It Comes to Islamophobia, We Need to Name Names." *Al Jazeera*. Available at: https://www.aljazeera.com/ indepth/opinion/islamophobia-names-190329125123813.html; Ibrahim Al-Marashi. (2019). "The New Zealand Massacre and the Weaponisation of History." *Al Jazeera*. Available at: https://www .aljazeera.com/indepth/opinion/zealand-massacre-weaponisation-history-190322062222288.html.

[27] In another pertinent case of early 2018, an investigation was launched by University College London into a series of conferences held on eugenics and intelligence attended by notorious speakers including known white supremacists. See: Lisa Tilley. (2018). "Populist Academics, Colonial Demography, and Far-Right Discursive Ecologies." *Discover Society*. Available at: https:// discoversociety.org/2018/12/04/populist-academics-colonial-demography-and-far-right-discursive -ecologies/. In what could turn out to be a productive response to the inquiry, a separate project has been launched investigating the history of eugenics and eugenicists at UCL, led by an independent chair, Professor Iyiola Soyinka. See: Kirsty Walker. (2018). "Inquiry Launches into History of Eugenics at UCL." Available at: https://www.ucl.ac.uk/news/2018/dec/inquiry-launches-history -eugenics-ucl.Similarly, Noah Carl, who was appointed to a prestigious research fellowship at Cambridge University's St. Edmund's College, has pursued the colonial lines of enquiry drawing connections between race, genes, intelligence, and criminality. See: Richard Adams. (2018). "Cambridge Gives Role to Academic Accused of Racist Stereotyping." *Guardian*. Available at: https://www.theguardian.com/world/2018/dec/07/cambridge-gives-role-to-academic-accused-of -racist-stereotyping. See also: A. Saini. (2017). *Inferior: How Science Got Women Wrong and the New Research that's Rewriting the Story*. London: Fourth Estate Books and Saini. (2019). *Superior: The Return of Race Science*. London: Fourth Estate Books; and the useful essay Gavin Evans on the revival of "racial science": Gavin Evans. (2018). "The Unwelcome Revival of 'race science'." *Guardian*. Available at: https://www.theguardian.com/news/2018/mar/02/the-unwelcome -revival-of-race-science.

[28] Toby Manhire. (2019). "Mark Zuckerberg, Four Days on, Your Silence on Christchurch Is Deafening." *Guardian*. Available at: https://www.theguardian.com/commentisfree/2019/mar/20/mark -zuckerberg-four-days-on-your-silence-on-christchurch-is-deafening.

[29] Hasan Azad. (2017). "Thinking about Islam, Politics and Muslim Identity in a Digital Age." *Journal of Islamic and Muslim Studies*, 2(2), 122–34; Nathan Lean. (2017). *The Islamophobia Industry. How the Right Manufactures Hatred of Muslims*. Pluto Press. For an alternative take on the funding of orientalist research on Islam, See: Hamid Dabashi. (2015). "The Arabs and Their Flying Shoes." In *Can Non-Europeans Think?* London: Verso.

That Johnson himself had likened Muslim women in niqabs to "letter-boxes" and "bank robbers,"[30] which led to a spike in hate crimes committed by men and women against Muslim women who in some cases were called "letterboxes" by their attackers, is ignored.[31] There is little mention in Johnson's message to the fact that Muslim communities in the United Kingdom score highly in deprivation factors, with nearly half (46%) of the Muslim population residing in the bottom 10 percent of the most deprived Local Authority Districts in England,[32] and yet have played a crucial role in healing wounds, quite literally, caused by the violence of austerity and racial capitalism at Grenfell.[33] Nor, crucially, was there recognition of the privileging of Muslim men, women, and children in the intrusive and violent industries of counterterrorism and radicalization.

Small slights, turns of phrase, and racist jokes that are explained away as gestures of wit and devil's advocacy become a source of entertainment, minor

[30] For Johnson's column, see: Boris Johnson. (2018). "Denmark has got it wrong. Yes, the burka is oppressive and ridiculous—but that's still no reason to ban it." *The Telegraph*. Available at: https://www.telegraph.co.uk/news/2018/08/05/denmark-has-got-wrong-yes-burka-oppressive-ridiculous-still/.

[31] Nevertheless, Johnson would go on to defend his comments as being in the service of a "strong, liberal defence of the right of women to wear the burqa." It is Muslims and specifically Muslim women, it turns out, who have misunderstood Johnson's intentions. See: Reuters. (2019). "Boris Johnson: I Compared Muslim Women to Letterboxes to 'Defend Their Right to Wear Burqas'." *Guardian*. Available at: https://www.theguardian.com/politics/video/2019/jul/06/boris-johnson-i-compared-muslim-women-to-letterboxes-to-defend-their-right-to-wear-burqas-video. For news reports on the spike following his comments, see: Tell MAMA. (2018). Pensioners loudly echo Boris Johnson's niqab comments in doctor's surgery. Available at: https://tellmamauk.org/pensioners-loudly-echo-boris-johnsons-niqab-comments-in-doctors-surgery/; Anoosh Chakelian. (2019). "'We Should Be Fearful': Muslim Women on the Prospect of Boris Johnson as Prime Minister." *New Statesman*. Available at: https://www.newstatesman.com/politics/uk/2019/06/we-should-be-fearful-muslim-women-prospect-boris-johnson-prime-minister; Lizzie Dearden. (2018). "'Letterbox' Insults Against Muslim Women Spike in Wake of Boris Johnson Comments." *Independent*. Available at: https://www.independent.co.uk/news/uk/home-news/boris-johnson-burqa-muslim-women-veil-attacks-islamophobia-letterboxes-rise-a8488651.html.

[32] See. "British Muslims in Numbers." *Muslim Council of Britain*. Available at: https://www.youtube.com/watch?v=mQlM4w15s2E

[33] On the intersections of racism, capitalism and the logics of empire, see: I. Danewid. (2020). "The Fire This Time: Grenfell, Racial Capitalism and the Urbanisation of Empire." *European Journal of International Relations*, 26(1), 289–313. On Muslim aid following the disaster, see: Konathan Gornall. (2017). "The Grenfell Disaster Has Highlighted Muslim Contributions to Community." *The National*. Available at: https://www.thenational.ae/opinion/the-grenfell-disaster-has-highlighted-muslim-contributions-to-community-1.92231; Joseph Downing and Richard Dron. (2018). "Grenfell Tower: How Twitter Users Fought Off Fake News to Honour Muslim Heroes." *The Conversation*. Available at: https://theconversation.com/grenfell-tower-how-twitter-users-fought-off-fake-news-to-honour-muslim-heroes-98059; Helena Horton. (2017). "Grenfell Tower Fire: Muslims Awake for Ramadan among Heroes Who Helped Save Lives." *The Telegraph*. Available at: https://www.telegraph.co.uk/news/2017/06/14/local-heroes-saved-lives-helped-residents-grenfell-tower-fire/; James Rippingale. (2018). "The Toll of Burying Grenfell's Dead: London's Muslim Undertakers." *Al Jazeera*. Available at: https://www.aljazeera.com/indepth/features/toll-burying-grenfell-dead-180926072155075.html; Anna Scheverien. (2018). "For Mosque at Heart of Grenfell Tragedy, a Bittersweet Anniversary." *New York Times*. Available at: https://www.nytimes.com/2018/06/14/world/europe/mosque-grenfell-ramadan.html

releases of national energy, just as they did during the Shamima Begum case. As a form of "narcotherapy," simultaneously intoxicant and treatment, these slights that wound (Others) and empower (whites), mask the diminishing returns of the greatness (and whiteness) of Britain and Europe in the world today. Johnson's words are symptomatic of a proprietary mentality, a brand of prejudice based on a sense of ownership, over prosperity and culture alike. A range of acts, names, and unspoken codes—suspicion, skepticism, long stares, puzzlement, slips of the tongue—are distinct but related to the hydraulic racism of the state and the beast of institutional racism, as Fanon calls it.[34] With race as a foundational rule, even public expressions of friendship and welcome arrive with a profound desire to stigmatize. The press conference, real or imagined, rests on this type of framing.

Where harsher logics of seizure and expulsion constitute the Muslim Questioned, narratives of care and capture fuse in this second mode. The public profession of care is underpinned by more "liberal" forms of capture. In one such example, the creation of Vulnerability Support Hubs (VSHs), a mental health-related project piloted by UK counterterrorism police between April 2016 and October 2017, is the product of this toxic mix. VSHs are

> partnership services between NHS Forensic mental health teams and Policing, commissioned by Counter Terrorism Policing Headquarters (CTPHQ) in 2016. The aim of the VSHs is to improve the health and criminal justice outcomes for individuals referred into PREVENT and, by doing so, help mitigate the risk of terrorism to communities. The hubs work on the NHS principle that "there is no wrong door"; individuals with poor mental health that are identified via a Prevent referral (i.e. they have displayed behaviour that gives rise to a concern they are vulnerable to radicalisation) should have the same rights and opportunities to access help and support as individuals that are identified by G.Ps, schools or criminal justice services.[35]

In 2016, CTPHQ commissioned research which suggested that around half the people referred to Prevent had "vulnerabilities related to mental health."[36] We saw earlier how broad and vague the signs of radicalization are, those "psychological hooks" which cover anything from the "need for identity"

---

[34] David Theo Goldberg and Taiye Salasi draw similar connections between the hydraulic work of race the state does and the interpersonal manifestations of hatred. Selasi discusses the notion of "the stare" to capture such a racist dialectic. See: https://www.hkw.de/en/programm/projekte/veranstaltung/p_131635.php

[35] National Police Chiefs' Council. (2020). "Report Published into the Functioning of Vulnerability Support Hubs." *NPCC*. Available at: https://news.npcc.police.uk/releases/report-published-into-the-functioning-of-vulnerability-support-hubs

[36] V. Dodd. (2016). "Police Study Links Radicalisation to Mental Health Problems." *Guardian*, May 20. Available at: https://www.theguardian.com/uk-news/2016/may/20/police-study-radicalisation-mental-health-problems

to "comradeship or adventure." VSHs are significant because they uniquely embed NHS mental health professionals within counterterrorism police operations.[37] Each hub would include a range of mental health professionals and be colocated within "core Counter Terrorism Unit environments [London, Birmingham, Manchester] and work in partnership with frontline CT and Prevent Officers, with strategic and operational oversight provided by a senior CT Officer. This," official guidance would suggest, "will ensure that cultural change and learning is achieved across the system to improve clinical and risk outcomes."[38] However, case responsibility was retained by the host CTU with mental health teams acting in a consultancy capacity. The mental health professionals would also undergo a high degree of police vetting to obtain security clearance and the so-called "STRAP" accreditation, a system used to restrict access to highly sensitive intelligence.

Consistent with the Muslim Question, there is a fusion—both discursive and institutional—of care and militarized power. Earlier we discussed the "Prevent Duty" where in 2015 the counter-extremism program was made a statutory duty for a range of public bodies. This meant that, among others, NHS trusts were legally bound to "have due regard to the need to prevent people from being drawn into terrorism."[39] The vast majority of the people assessed at VSHs are people who have been referred to Prevent whom the police suspect may have mental health conditions. An interim evaluation report would go further and claim that the Hubs assist vulnerable people, and have been "especially beneficial . . . for those who may have struggled to access mainstream health services due to homelessness or immigration status."[40] It is for this reason that the final evaluation report of the pilot would conclude that "all three hubs have evidenced the benefits of mental health practitioners being embedded into CTU environments with both qualitative and quantitative evidence to demonstrate the added value to both safeguarding

---

[37] Joint police/mental health projects are not exceptional in the United Kingdom. One example is the Fixed Threat Assessment Centre (FTAC) based at Barnet, Enfield and Haringey, a joint police/mental health unit set up in October 2006 by the Home Office, the Department of Health and Metropolitan Police Service. Barnet was one of the NHS Trusts involved in Vulnerability Support Hubs. FTAC exists to "assess and manage the risk to politicians, members of the British Royal Family, and other public figures from obsessive individuals."

[38] National Counter Terrorism Policing. (2017). "Prevent Mental Health Hubs: Final Evaluation Report." Available at: https://www.counterterrorism.police.uk/wp-content/uploads/2020/11/PMH HFinalReportDec171-Redacted.pdf

[39] Home Office. (2021). "Revised Prevent Duty Guidance: For England and Wales." *HM Government.* Available at: https://www.gov.uk/government/publications/prevent-duty-guidance/revised-prevent-duty-guidance-for-england-and-wales

[40] H. Aked, T. Younis, and C. Heath-Kelly. (2021) "Racism, Mental Health and Pre-crime Policing—the Ethics of Vulnerability Support Hubs." *Medact.* London, p. 42.

and CT risk management functions. Confirmation of recurrent funding will reduce delays in recruitment and enhance continuity of hub personnel."[41]

But rarely are those referred to the Hubs assessed directly by mental health professionals. Acting in a consultancy capacity, staff would instead operate at an arms-length from the matrix of counterterrorism officials—whether Prevent referees or the police—whose questionable idea of the meaningful association between mental health and terrorism was the founding and driving logic. Or rather, the premise connecting mental health/vulnerability to radicalization and terrorism was the public line. They would, according to the police, "improve the understanding of both police and health professionals of the associations between mental health conditions and vulnerability to radicalisation."[42] In addition, it was claimed the hubs would "increase access to mainstream services for vulnerable individuals and—as a result of early intervention—improve health outcomes, achieve cost efficiency savings and reduce risk to the public."[43] The VSH system, in sum, constitutes a system of mutual benefit: those with mental health issues and thus vulnerable to radicalization, if not already extremist, would receive help, and the wider population is protected by the public health intervention which has as its target the preemption of terrorist violence of which poor mental health is a risk factor.

However, while no standardized data collection techniques were used during the pilot, documents show that many of those referred are children. Concerningly, those referred to the Central Hub during the pilot were mostly teenagers. The youngest was just six years old.[44] This is consistent with the wider Prevent program (in which most referrals come from the education sector),[45] and render suspicious, if not outright threatening, otherwise banal aspect of adolescence, especially where the young person concerned is Muslim. When accounting for population demographics, referral statistics to VSHs reveal a grossly disproportionate Muslim presence. Overall, a racialized Muslim is at least twenty-three times more likely to be referred to a mental health hub for "Islamism" than a white British individual is for "Far Right extremism"[46]—that white subaltern figure who cannot represent others of his kind. Again, the fusion of care and counterterrorism in the VSH system thus connects the medical psychiatric environment to the economies and impulses of warfare, with all its juridical and carceral implications.

---

[41] National Counter Terrorism Policing, *Prevent Mental Health Hubs*, p. 5.
[42] National Police Chiefs Council. (n.d). "Mental Health Pilot Hubs." Available at: https://www.npcc.police.uk/NPCCBusinessAreas/TAM/MentalHealthPilotHubs.aspx
[43] Ibid.
[44] Aked et al., *Racism*, p. 14.
[45] Home Office. (2020). "Individuals Referred to and Supported through the Prevent Programme, April 2019 to March 2020." Available at: https://www.gov.uk/government/statistics/individuals-referred-to-and-supported-through-the-prevent-programme-april-2019-to-march-2020
[46] Aked et al., *Racism*, p. 20.

Like the Muslim Question itself, the VSH system also connects care and criminality. We saw earlier the disproportionate Muslim presence in the economies of Prevent and the pre-criminal space—a set of arrangements made possible through all manner of special dispositions—which simultaneously collapsed the planetary distances between allies in the war on terror and magnified the distance at which the Muslim must be kept from the rest of us. It seems the economies of care read similarly:

> At the North Hub for example, while 41.7% of referrals were white, the combined total of referrals from different racialised groups was almost equal, at 41.2% . . . At the South Hub, the most referrals during the period analysed were of Asian ethnicity (102), followed by white Europeans (90), Black people (56) and Arabs (26)—again, figures indicative of racialised groups' over-representation. Unsurprisingly, migrants are also massively overrepresented: at the North Hub, an astounding 48% of those referred were not UK-born.[47]

Likewise, the fetish of migrancy which pervades the relation between the Muslim and his white Other also plays out. Hub reports "contain frequent references to asylum seekers and migrants, including unaccompanied asylum-seeking children ('UASC'), and even people undergoing deportation proceedings, some of whom appear to have fled war and conflict." People with precarious socioeconomic and immigration status are further pathologized in an atmosphere where criminality and threat are floating presences next to their names.

Taking a broader view, then, the toxic intimacies of the VSH—vulnerability, care, war, and terror—are undergirded by the racism of the criminal justice system. Muslims make up around 5 percent of the population but 17 percent of UK prisoners, only 1 percent of whom have been incarcerated for "terrorism-related offenses".[48] The logic of preemption, now standard across all public institutions, is never far from the Muslim, a logic further embedded insofar as it empowers health workers, teachers, and the police alike to perform their duty to the nation against terrorism. But the public expression of concern for the mental health and justice outcomes for those suspected of radicalization is this logic's liberal face which consolidates the threat of the racial subject just as it expresses care for him. It also obscures the very real mental health challenges that impact society in general and Muslims in particular. Muslims have recovery rates that are much lower than the national

---

[47] Ibid., p. 19.
[48] R. Mohammed. (2021). "Muslims in Prison—Time for a Wake-Up Call." *Prospect*, April 13. Available at: https://www.prospectmagazine.co.uk/society-and-culture/theway-muslim-prisoners -are-treated-should-be-taken-much-more-seriously-byprison-authorities.

Preliminary analysis of the quantitative and qualitative data presented in this interim report is suggestive of a positive impact within all three mental health hubs in relation to the following outcomes:-

   ✓ Improved detection of mental health vulnerabilities
   ✓ Significantly reducing the time it takes to get health information and has thus markedly saving police time and resources.
   ✓ Increased confidence in Police assessment of risk / vulnerability, and facilitated access to appropriate services
   ✓ Enabling more efficient use of interventions, including use of mentors and disruptions, which are now more targeted to assessed need with improved outcomes and reduced costs.

Figure 6.1 First interim evaluation of the three mental health hubs—page 5

average for psychological therapies (3% versus 8%), and mental health settings all too often reflect the racism of wider society and institutions, such as anxiety around women wearing the headscarf.[49]

The racism of counterterrorism and criminal justice, which produce and consolidate VSHs as spaces for the Muslim Question, occurs in twin contexts of managed deprivation: austerity policies and the concerted underfunding of mainstream mental healthcare and social services on the one hand, and policies of the hostile environment which severely restrict access to healthcare for migrants on the other. The disproportionately racial and Muslim character of the hubs comes together with the central concern for (and benefit of) efficiency and cost saving explicitly expressed in its evaluation reports.[50] While referral to Prevent could license immigration enforcement, potentially leading to detention or deportation for those with insecure immigration status, is less a direct cost-saving mechanism than expelling that which disturbs.

Consonant with Cressida Dick's public plea for fairness, then, the VSH system is likewise concerned with time as Figures 6.1 attests—*give us more time,* white institutions and their proliferating outposts say. In the first part of the book, we considered the way in which racial anxieties as a tonality of our time has meant that to express doubt in the face of an Other is to admit defeat; no hospitality can be conceded for it is always assumed to be at our disbenefit. In the Muslim Question, however, some nuance, the possibility of mutuality between the Muslim subject and white "I," is an important feature of its toxic liberalism and the publicity it sanctions. Ultimately, publicity— guilt, shock, promises of progress—in this second mode can acknowledge the

---

[49] G. Mir, R. Ghani, S. Meer, and G. Hussain. (2019). "Delivering a Culturally Adapted Therapy for Muslim Clients with Depression." The Cognitive Behaviour Therapist, 12, e26.51. T. Younis and S. Jadhav. (2020). "Islamophobia in the National Health Service: An Ethnography of Institutional Racism in Prevent's Counter-Radicalisation Policy." *Sociology of Health & Illness,* 42(3), 610–26.
[50] Aked et al., *Racism,* p. 43, 46.

```
(iv)   Cost

Quantifiable economic benefits of all three mental health hub pilots are undergoing evaluation and will
be reported on more substantially in the final report. Initial consideration suggests that the following
may all contribute to financial efficiency:-

    •   Reduced police time spent in trying to source information
    •   Fewer but more productive and informed contacts with cases
    •   Reduced wastage in utilising ineffective channel and social care interventions
    •   moving referrals through the prevent pathway more rapidly,
    •   reducing the likelihood of re-referrals to Prevent
```

Figure 6.2   First interim evaluation—page 6

"mistakes" of racism, but cannot cognize the very basis of society as racist. Those empowered by the Muslim Question, therefore, never stop to ask why the same mistakes keep getting made.

It becomes simply sufficient to ask for more time and for the racial subject/critic to be less unfair and more forthcoming with their secrets (see Figure 6.2). *"The Met metes out less racial violence now, the vulnerability and mental health of foreigners deserves support, the Prime Minister says Eid Mubarak!"* Interestingly, Boris Johnson's Eid message invokes Sara Khan and Sajid Javid, two prominent Muslim figures, as Muslims who contribute to British political life.

Khan is best known as the lead for the latest Commission for Countering Extremism and cheerleader of the Prevent strategy.[51] In a telling case, a Prevent-sponsored project launched in 2014, #MakingAStand, supported by Khan and whose focus was the radicalization of Muslim women, the central image of the campaign was a Muslim woman adorned in a union jack hijab, a clearer representation of the Muslim Question as I am using it, with all its proximity-defending, affirmation-inciting publicity, is surely impossible. Yet the fact that this was not detected or taken seriously prior to the project's launch, signals its normalization and the many press conferences it must organize to render its insulting effects banal.[52]

---

[51] See: Bushra Wasty. (2018). "Why We're Concerned about Sara Khan, the New Anti-extremism Chief." *Guardian.* Available at: https://www.theguardian.com/commentisfree/2018/jan/25/concerned-sara-khan-anti-extremism-british-muslims; Jamie Grierson. (2018). "Choice of New UK Anti-extremism Chief Criticised as 'Alarming'." *Guardian.* Available at: https://www.theguardian.com/politics/2018/jan/24/leading-muslim-campaigner-sara-khan-head-anti-extremism-drive; MEE Staff. (2018). "Anger Over Sara Khan Appointment to Lead UK Counter-Extremism Commission." Available at: https://www.middleeasteye.net/fr/news/sara-khan-counter-extremism-commissioner-2047397586

[52] Later it was uncovered that the project was listed in a catalogue of Prevent projects as a "RICU Product." In another important case, a social media network launched around the term "woke"—taken to mean socially and politically conscious/progressive—is equally if not more so involved in the work of Prevent and Britain's counterterrorism industry, again as a product of RICU. This Is Woke describes itself as a "news/media company" engaging "in critical discussions around Muslim identity, tradition and reform." Issues as a far-ranging as climate action, the hijab, fake news, veganism, terrorism and much more are presented on the platform, with numerous images of smiling

Figure 6.3 Image from the RICU-Produced #MakingAStand Campaign. *Source:* Courtesy of Getty/Julian Case.

women in hijabs. The content of the company's Instagram feed features quotes from famous activists for justice including Martin Luther King Jr. and Nelson Mandela. In one curious choice, the feed features Umar ibn-al Khattab, the second caliph of Islam, alongside the quote: "sometimes the people with the worst past, create the best future." When approached for more information about the project under the terms of the UK's Freedom of Information Act, the Home Office refused to disclose any, citing the section concerning national security. For an instructive overview of such processes of deception, see Yahya Birt. (2019). "Astroturfing and the Rise of the Secular Security State in Britain." *Medium.* Available at: https://medium.com/@yahyabirt/astroturfing-and-the-rise -of-the-secular-security-state-in-britain-cd21c5005d43. For further details on #MakingAStand, see: Ian Cobain. (2019). "Revealed: The 'woke' Media Outfit That's Actually a UK Counterterror Programme." *Middle East Eye.* Available at: https://www.middleeasteye.net/news/revealed -woke-media-outfit-thats-actually-uk-counterterror-programme; Tara John and Vasco Cotovio. (2019). "'Woke' News Platform Aimed at Young Muslims Is Actually a Secret UK Counter-Terror Program." *CNN World.* Available at: https://edition.cnn.com/2019/08/16/uk/woke-counter -terrorism-facebook-intl-gbr/index.html; Asim Qureshi. (2019). "The Excellent Investigation by @IanCobain into the Way RICU and the Home Office Have Been Directly Responsible for Messaging for a 'woke' Muslim Project Requires Further Lines of Inquiry." Available at: https://twitter .com/AsimCP/status/1162388047062798336. For the Facebook page of the platform: https://www .facebook.com/thisiswoke/ and its Instagram feed: https://www.instagram.com/thisiswoke/. The Research Information and Communications Unit is said to be the Home Office's propaganda arm (note 108). See more specifically: Madeline Sophie-Abbas. (2018). "The Detrimental Effects of Current Counter-Extremism Measures on British Muslim Families." *LSE.* Available at: https:// blogs.lse.ac.uk/politicsandpolicy/the-detrimental-effects-of-current-counter-extremism-measures -on-british-muslim-families/; Simon Hooper. (2016). "Exclusive: UK 'grassroots' Anti-extremism Campaign Produced by Home Office." *Middle East Eye.* Available at: https://www.middleeasteye .net/news/exclusive-uk-grassroots-anti-extremism-campaign-produced-home-office.

Sajid Javid, then Chancellor of the Exchequer, oversaw as Home Secretary the deprivation of Shamima Begum's citizenship,[53] and whose Thatcherism[54] confirms for him the existence of the "British Dream"[55] and whose position as Home Secretary was evidence enough to dismiss the Conservative Party's institutional Islamophobia.[56] The glad tidings sent to Muslims at home and abroad, Johnson's phrasing underpinned by the desperate hope for Britain's global power and reach after Brexit, are cleansed of the facts of Muslim (or Muslim-imagined) casualty and death, the obscene collateral damage of the wars of terror, and globalized regimes of racism and Islamophobia. In a ninety-second Eid message, Boris Johnson encapsulates the Muslim Question in all its condescending benevolence.

Publicity in the Muslim Question, therefore, operates on the basis of a mute genealogy: white institutions, their matrices of racial power, knowledge, and governance do not have a history, or if they do it can only be one that always already culminates in the fulfillment of its duties, promises, and the best of values. It is the racial subject who is burdened rather than emancipated by history; there is altogether too much historical evidence of his delayed entrance into modernity and the need for us to put him and his kin to work. It is only on this basis that the systemic but constantly mutating nature of racism as the very fabric of white society can be revealed over and again. The Muslim Question is formed in—and licensed by—the historic anxieties of what the racial subject might say and ask. Instead, we presume that truthful speech and action on her part is only that which coheres with our sense of self and worldview, a sense that is fundamentally impoverished and consciously partial.

---

[53] See: Azizah Kanji. (2019). "Denationalisation: A Punishment Reserved for Muslims." *Al Jazeera.* Available at: https://www.aljazeera.com/indepth/opinion/denationalisation-punishment-reserved -muslims-190109164026878.html; Charles Hymas. (2019). "Sajid Javid's Decision to Strip Shamima Begum of Her Citizenship Questioned by One of UK's Most Senior Judges." *The Telegraph.* Available at: https://www.telegraph.co.uk/news/2019/06/09/sajid-javids-decision-strip -begum-citizenship-questioned/; Patrick Greenfield. (2019). "Sajid Javid Accused of 'Human Fly-Tipping' in Shamima Begum Case." *Guardian.* Available at: https://www.theguardian.com/uk -news/2019/may/31/sajid-javid-accused-shamima-begum-case-syria.

[54] Christopher Hope. (2014). "Sajid Javid: The Millionaire Bus Conductor's Son with a Portrait of Margaret Thatcher on His Wall." *The Telegraph.* Available at: https://www.telegraph.co.uk/news /politics/10755497/Sajid-Javid-the-millionaire-bus-conductors-son-with-a-portrait-of-Margaret -Thatcher-on-his-wall.html

[55] BBC. (2017). "PM Vows to Renew the 'British Dream' - But What Is It?" *BBC News Online.* Available at: https://www.bbc.co.uk/news/uk-politics-41506032

[56] Parveen Akhtar. (2019). "Sajid Javid and the Complex Life of a Muslim Conservative Leadership Hopeful." *The Conversation.* Available at: https://theconversation.com/sajid-javid-and-the-com-plex-life-of-a-muslim-conservative-leadership-hopeful-118849

ENGAGING "THE MUSLIMWOMAN"

The possibility of racism's critique, especially as a principle of liberal democratic societies, does indeed signal new possibilities of expression and claims for justice, claims that can in fact be made in conjunction with the condescension of the Muslim Question. The increased public profile of Muslim women, if not the diverse project of Islamic feminism, is one of the most intense fronts of these intersections. I want to borrow Miriam Cooke's notion of "The Muslimwoman,"[57] which clarifies the ways in which condescension and phantasms of the racial subject can creep into discourses and practices which ostensibly pursue liberation and justice. The circulation of fundamental and fundamentalist identities actually becomes an important support for the public admonition of racism. While racism and Islamophobia are certainly nothing new, the figure of the Muslim qua Muslim as a subject with an essential public presence is today an intense, and lucrative, source of anxiety seemingly everywhere. In narratives and imaginaries of Europe, of Britain and its nation, the figure of the veiled Muslim woman occupies a "privileged" (antithetical) position in relation to such a nation and its white, male subject.[58]

Yet this position also affords original avenues of critique and solidarity. For even if we write against the global wars on/of terror, our writing and its content, if not also its form, is made possible by it.[59] Ultimately, for Cooke, the neologism Muslimwoman "draws attention to the emergence of a newly entwined religious and gendered identification that overlays national, ethnic, cultural, historical, and even philosophical diversity. A recent phenomenon tied to a growing global Islamophobia, this identification is created for Muslim women by outside forces, whether non-Muslims or Islamist men."[60] While the veil, real or imagined, functions like "race" insofar as it marks an essential difference: "it is no longer necessary for a woman to be veiled for her to be marked a 'Muslim woman.' This identification is all-encompassing; it erases individual identity and differences."[61] The Muslimwoman speaks to an ascription, a delegated name that helps circulate, if it is not also definitive of, the Muslim Question. It is, initially at least, an imposed identification which sticks to the racial subject in the guise of appreciating her specificity. It proceeds, then, according to an "equal but different" logic which grants

---

[57] Miriam Cooke. (2007). "The Muslimwoman." *Contemporary Islam* 1, 139–54. See also the deeply instructive roundtable discussion between Cooke and others: Cooke et al. (2008). "Religion, Gender and the Muslimwoman." *Journal of Feminist Studies in Religion,* 24(1), 91–119.

[58] On the publicity of the figure of the Muslim after 9/11, see: Salman Sayyid. (2018). "Islamophobia Conference 2017: Salman Sayyid on the Contradictions of Islamophobia." *IHRCtv.* Available at: https://www.youtube.com/watch?v=BeP3u094ln4

[59] Morsi, *Radical Skin, Moderate Masks.*

[60] Ibid., p. 140.

[61] Ibid.

Muslims and Muslim women a genuine speaking position, though never lets go of the conscious and benevolent act that we have indeed granted "them" somewhere to speak from. Never mind that they often speak in relation to— even if it is against—the peculiarities of women's problems with/in Islam.

An instructive case of the Muslimwoman, of publicity in the Muslim Question is "The Straw Affair,"[62] when the then leader of the British House of Commons and former foreign secretary, Jack Straw, had demanded that women visiting his Blackburn office remove the face veil. In his defense, he argued that the *niqab* made "better, positive relations between two communities [Britain being ostensibly split between Muslim and the rest, an all-too familiar binary] more difficult," adding that the face veil was "a visible statement of separation and of difference."[63] Speaking as the sensitive cultural theorist, Straw explained, "Communities are bound together partly by informal chance relations between strangers—people being able to acknowledge each other in the street or being able to pass the time of day. That's made more difficult if people are wearing a veil. That's just a fact of life."[64] He said elsewhere, "This is an issue that needs to be discussed because, in our society, we are able to relate particularly to strangers by being able to read their faces and if you can't read people's faces, that does provide some separation," he told a local radio station. "Those people who do wear the veil should think about the implications for community relations."[65]

Others in the commentariat agreed maintaining that "the veil becomes more than a garment sanctioned by custom: it turns into a hostile statement about the society in which the wearer lives."[66] Straw would find support for

---

[62] For instructive studies of the Affair, see: J. A. Everett, F. M. Schellhaas, B. D. Earp, V. Ando, J. Memarzia, C. V. Parise, B. Fell, and M. Hewstone. (2015). Covered in Stigma? The Impact of Differing Levels of Islamic Head Covering on Explicit and Implicit Biases toward Muslim Women. *Journal of Applied Social Psychology*, 45, 90–104; M. Malik. (2008). "Complex Equality: Muslim Women and the 'Headscarf'." *Droit et société*, 68(1), 127–152. Available at: https://www .cairn.info/revue-droit-et-societe1-2008-1-page-127.htm; N. Meer, C. Dwyer, and T. Modood. (2010). "Embodying Nationhood? Conceptions of British National Identity, Citizenship, and Gender in the 'Veil Affair'." *The Sociological Review*, 58(1), 84–111.

[63] Matthew Taylor. (2006). "Take Off the Veil, Says Straw - To Immediate Anger from Muslims." *Guardian*. Available at: https://www.theguardian.com/politics/2006/oct/06/immigrationpolicy .labour

[64] Alan Cowell. (2006). "Jack Straw Ignites A Debate over Muslim Veil - Europe - International Herald Tribune." *New York Times*. Available at: https://www.nytimes.com/2006/10/06/world/ europe/06iht-london.3061419.html

[65] BBC. (2006). "In Quotes: Jack Straw on the Veil." *BBC News Online*. Available at: http://news.bbc .co.uk/1/hi/uk_politics/5413470.stm. For a similar argument made by a Muslim feminist, see Mona Eltahawy's comments in a debate on her view regarding the status of women in Arab states. Al Jazeera. (2016). "Do Arab Men Hate Women?" *Head to Head*. Available at: https://www.youtube .com/watch?v=cTvuPYKBtks&t=1238s, at 20:00.

[66] Charles Moore. (2006). "My Straw Poll: Extremists Must Be Seen for What They Are." The Telegraph. Available at: https://www.telegraph.co.uk/comment/personal-view/3632947/My-Straw -poll-extremists-must-be-seen-for-what-they-are.html

his comments within his own party. At the launch of the Commission on Integration and Cohesion—those two axioms of the Muslim Question—Ruth Kelly, then communities secretary, "admitted" to the government's failure of multiculturalism arguing that it encouraged segregation and communities living in isolation.[67] Then Home Secretary John Reid would insist that Britain would not be bullied by Muslim fanatics nor tolerate "no-go" neighborhoods in British society, comments that were consistent with his self-assurance in telling Muslim parents in east London to monitor their children: "There is no nice way of saying this," he said. "These fanatics are looking to groom and brainwash children, including your children, for suicide bombings. Grooming them to kill themselves in order to murder others. Look for the tell-tale signs now and talk to them before their hatred grows and you risk losing them forever. In protecting our families, we are protecting our community."[68]

There was of course criticism of Straw's comments and the broader discourses and policies—both sanctioned by the terror threat and the production of insecurity—that licensed them. Reefat Bravu, chair of the Muslim Council for Britain's social and family affairs committee, said Straw's plaint exacerbated existing tensions: "We had John Reid first and now we have Jack Straw . . . This is going to do great damage to the Muslim community, again we are being singled out by this government as the problem. Women have a right to wear a veil and this is just another example of blatant Muslim-bashing by this government."[69] Mussoud Shadrajeh, chair of the Islamic Human Rights Commission, was concerned by a potential double-standard: "Would he say to the Jewish people living in Stamford Hill [in London] that they shouldn't dress like Orthodox Jews?"[70] Likewise, Khalid Mahmood, Labor MP for Birmingham Perry Barr, said, "I think Jack is at risk of providing succour to people who hold anti-Muslim prejudices. Someone of his stature and

---

[67] Evening Standard. (2006). "Kelly Condemns Multiculturalism." Available at: https://www.standard.co.uk/testnewsheadlines/kelly-condemns-multiculturalism-7083995.html

[68] David Batty. (2006). "Reid Barracked During Speech to Muslim Parents." *Guardian*. Available at: https://www.theguardian.com/world/2006/sep/20/terrorism.immigrationpolicy. There was of course criticism of Straw's comments and the broader discourses and policies—both sanctioned by the terror threat and the production of insecurity—that licensed them. Mussoud Shadrajeh, chair of the Islamic Human Rights Commission was concerned by a potential double-standard: "Would he say to the Jewish people living in Stamford Hill [in London] that they shouldn't dress like Orthodox Jews?" Likewise, Khalid Mahmood, Labor MP for Birmingham Perry Barr said, "I think Jack is at risk of providing succour to people who hold anti-Muslim prejudices. Someone of his stature and understanding of the community, he needs to look at this a bit more in depth and not stereotype a small minority in the Muslim community." The Muslim peer Lady Uddin, however, would defend Jack Straw's decision to raise the issue: "I think there needs to be a debate," she said. "He should have the right to raise this question and people should have a right to disagree. I think the Muslim community needs to address this, not just throw its hands up." Taylor and Dodd, "Take off the veil."

[69] Taylor and Dodd, "Take off the veil."

[70] Ibid.

understanding of the community, he needs to look at this a bit more in-depth
and not stereotype a small minority in the Muslim community."[71] The Muslim
peer Lady Uddin, however, would defend Jack Straw's decision to raise the
issue: "I think there needs to be a debate," she said. "He should have the right
to raise this question and people should have a right to disagree. I think the
Muslim community needs to address this, not just throw its hands up."[72]

The Straw affair should be understood within the moral economy of
the war on terror, of the Muslim Question in which the Muslimwoman,
"veiled or unveiled, has become the cultural standard for the Umma, or
global Muslim society. The religious and gendered exemplar confirms and
highlights the morality of the Umma, a God-fearing patriarchy where men
protect and women are protected,"[73] and also "erases for non-Muslims the
diversity among Muslim women and, indeed, among all Muslims."[74] Such
an economy recalls arguments and anxieties that go back to the nineteenth-
century colonial era, to the Woman Question, the orientalist imaginary and
actual policies of unveiling. As a necessarily public and publicized figure,
the Muslimwoman is invoked to uphold a moral regime which centers on the
inherent foreignness of the racial and gendered subject, and the perception of
Britain and Europe as a land which houses the freest people and women in the
world. As the Iranian cultural theorist, Minoo Moallem argues, "it is under
the sign of a veiled woman that we increasingly come to recognize ourselves
not only as gendered and hetero-normative subjects but also as located in the
free West, where women are not imprisoned . . . Am I a Muslim woman?
Even to answer this question is to enter the discursive spaces of race and
gender in the conditions of postcoloniality."[75]

The Muslim Question leaves open a space for a self-conscious assertion
of identity in response. The ascription of Muslimwoman, however, is also
a technique to sustain the racism of the Muslim Question. On the one hand,
the Muslimwoman is *the* primary identity in the moral economy of the war
on terror, and the terrain upon which that same identity is "deconstructed
and opened to contestation from within,"[76] in the process of transforming
the Muslimwoman label. The hope is that by consequence perceptions of
Muslims generally change for whom Muslim women are constructed as
border markers. As such, there are many opportunities for commercial success

---

[71] Ibid.
[72] Ibid.
[73] Cooke, "The Muslimwoman", p. 141.
[74] Ibid., p. 142.
[75] Moallem, M. (2005: 52–53). "Am I a Muslim woman? Nationalist reactions and postcolonial transgressions." In Afzal-Khan (Ed.) (2005). *Shattering the stereotypes. Muslim women speak out.* Northampton MA: Olive Branch Press.
[76] Cooke, "The Muslimwoman", p. 143.

through, indeed because of, the label at a time (in the postcolony, post-9/11) and context (counterterrorism and radicalization in the racial formation) when an insider's exposure of Islam's alleged inherent misogyny is a bestseller, in conjunction with the integration of Muslims' and Muslim women's counter-stories to right/write the record.[77] The simultaneous publicity of the Muslim Question and the Muslimwoman, not to mention the possibilities of commercial gain, forges a positive correlation between the level of intimate coverage of the Muslimwoman and the literary value of her life. In the popular genre of Muslim misogyny/violence/extremism, the range of stories articulates the "perceived singularity of the Muslimwoman identification even while their authors present themselves as the exception that proves the rule: I am a Muslim woman, therefore I know the Muslimwoman."[78] In the critique of such a genre, those counter-stories that constitute its Muslim diversity/filiality/banality analogue, the overall commonality of Muslims and Muslim women in all the diversity of their individual lives is written.

What we might call the neoliberal wing of this moral economy is further supported by the internet and technologies of social media—what Cooke calls the *virtual veil*. The fall of the twin towers, therefore, becomes an inaugural event. The war on terror as a phenomenon composed of myriad globalized political, cultural, economic, and indeed historical conditions that enabled and continue to enable it has engendered an intensely interconnected world

---

[77] On the former, in 2003, Ayaan Hirsi Ali collaborated with filmmaker Theo van Gogh to produce Submission, a film "dramatizing what she saw as Islamic abuse of women by projecting quotations from the Koran onto the naked bodies of several young women. . . . For many Muslims, this was a deliberate provocation." I. Buruma. (2006). *Murder in Amsterdam. The Death of Theo van Gogh and the Limits of Tolerance*. New York: Penguin, p. 176. Hirsi Ali has gone on to publish two insider books that reveal all. In *Caged Virgin* (2006), she includes the screen script of "Submission" pp. 143–150, and an interview with prominent ex-Muslim (a popular category that marks the epiphanic leaving behind of Islam) Irshad Manji, in which both attack Islam, pp. 89–93. As Cooke (p. 144) notes, "what is more persuasive than two Muslim women agreeing on the alleged inherent misogyny of their religion? She has been awarded numerous prizes, including the Swedish Democracy Prize, the Moral Courage Award." In another case, Kola Boof enthralled many audiences with wild stories about her relationship with Osama Bin Laden, and had herself photographed bare-breasted in her insider tales of African Muslims and their prurient peculiarities. On counter-stories see the popular anthologies: Nouraie-Simone's (2005). *On Shifting Ground: Muslim Women in the Global Era*. New York: Feminist; Afzal-Khan's (2005). *Shattering the Stereotypes: Muslims Women Speak Out*. Northampton, MA: Olive Branch Press; Sarah Husain. (2006). *Voices of Resistance: Muslim Women on War, Faith and Sexuality*. Emeryvill, CA.: Seal; Miriam Khan. (2019). *It's Not About the Burqa: Muslim Women on Faith, Feminism, Sexuality and Race*. London: Picador; and a book that plays with genre, form and content in its anthology, Sabrina Mahfouz. (2017). *The Things I Would Tell You: British Muslim Women Write*. London: Saqi. In fashion, there is the growing prominence of "modest fashion" or "hijab fashion." See: Noor in Indonesia and Azizah in the U.S. (launched in 2002) "target a middle class Muslim woman readership with high-fashion ads, cooking sections and health and beauty tips." Cooke, p. 146. See also: the global campaigns by leading sports brands such as Nike and Adidas in their modest sports fashion ranges.

[78] Cooke, "The Muslimwoman," p. 145.

in which the Muslimwoman speaks and the Muslim Question is answered. As Miriam Cooke summarizes,

> *First*, whether they like it or not Muslim women are feeling compelled to take their religion more seriously than ever before in their identification of self. *Second*, since the creation of the Internet, Muslim women qua Muslimwoman have been forging virtual relationships across continents and creating transnational communities in which information can be pooled, problems can be aired and coalitions built to "define and seek a world in which we can all flourish." *Third*, and again whether they like it or not, they are functioning in terms of a new complex primary identity: Muslimwoman.[79]

Nevertheless, we must be alive to the intersorption of the lucrative economies of the Muslimwoman—publishing, art, theater, film—in broader economies of surveillance, governance, and insult. Publicity in the Muslim Question is, therefore, a double-edged sword. When it comes to the Muslim subject, where is the boundary of the tolerable and what marks its transgression? How might the sorts of Muslim Question(s) posed *through* the prism of the Muslimwoman—in their ascribed and subversive modes together—relate to the contemporary explosion of prime-time dramas depicting Muslim life?[80]

TELEVISING THE MUSLIM QUESTION

The record-breaking, Bafta award-winning show, *Bodyguard*,[81] is situated within this economy—psychic and moral—and mix of racial and gendered intimacies. Promisingly, Jed Mercurio, heavyweight BBC runner and writer,

---

[79] Ibid., p. 150.

[80] Just a quick search of the questions, "Does Islam . . ." or "Do Muslims . . ." produces thousands of results—articles, academic or otherwise, news stories, videos—covering the age-old themes of violence, terrorism, gender, and democracy, largely along two lines: from the perspective of certain "Western values" or Enlightenment modernity's inheritance used as counter-premises of Islam, that is, what Islam is perceived to lack. The second, a refutation, argue that Islam and Muslims are fully, if uncomfortably, reconcilable with such values and, therefore, not threatening to their coherence. A whole popular culture of the Muslim(woman) Question is nonetheless thriving. See: *Muslims Like Us*; *Islam, Women and Me*; *Lost Boys*.

[81] *Bodyguard* tells the fictional story of David Budd, "a heroic but volatile war veteran now working as a Specialist Protection Officer for the Royalty and Specialist Protection Branch of London's Metropolitan Police Service. When he is assigned to protect the ambitious and powerful Home Secretary Julia Montague, whose politics stand for everything he despises, Budd finds himself torn between his duty and beliefs. Responsible for her safety, is he actually her biggest threat?" IMDb. (2018). "Storyline." Available at: https://www.imdb.com/title/tt7493974/?ref_=nv_sr_1?ref_=nv _sr_1. The show's profile page can be found at: https://www.bbc.co.uk/programmes/p06crngy

wanted "twists in the show to completely alter the dynamic."[82] What dynamic? Though the very first episode features a Muslim suicide bomber, Mercurio "dismissed concerns that the decision to show a Muslim suicide bomber risked perpetuating stereotypes, insisting viewers would have to watch to the end of the series to fully understand who is 'plotting to do harm'."[83] In fact, the suicide bomber in the show's opening, a South Asian Muslim woman, turns out to be a victim, frightened and vulnerable to the violence and abuse of her husband, while the hero, David Budd—war veteran, white man— steps in to save the day. Muslim-as-terrorist, Muslimwoman-as-oppressed, and white, male savior all in the first twenty minutes. The narrative flow does, however, gain in complexity to uncover a multilayered plot within the Specialist Protection Branch of the Met, which Budd seeks to protect and gives his postwar life some semblance of order. Ultimately, the series ends with the same Muslim woman from the opening episode who is revealed to be the terrorist mastermind, not her male handler from the show's opening. As the character says herself, no one suspected her precisely because they had been taken in by the "vulnerable Muslim woman as a victim scenario."[84]

How to make sense of this? What do we learn in the show's creator palpably excited as to the narrative innovations of the series shifting the dynamic on the one hand, and the Muslim woman as a terrorist mastermind climactic event, on the other? I am alive to the risks of isolating manifestations of racism to the question of culture. Yet documenting the overwhelming presence of the Muslim Question in popular culture is worthwhile because it has race and racism as its conditions of possibility. (Re)presenting the racial subject— white as much as Muslim—is lucrative and implicated in wider matrices of racial power, knowledge, and governance which propel and are propelled by systematic efforts of expulsion as the dominant tonality of our times.

In the context of the Muslim Question, right on cue, imagination of the Muslim woman can only go so far. That despite the opportunities for proximity and the demand to affirm, having been saved and trusted to stay saved by David Budd, the Muslim Question is an incessant burden for the nation.

---

[82] Jed Mercurio. (2018). "Writer Jed Mercurio introduces 'Bodyguard'." *BBC Writers Room.* Available at: https://www.bbc.co.uk/blogs/writersroom/entries/f5c09a37-a04d-4238-b4b3 -0ba8f23a9a5d

[83] "The other thing," he said, "is that, unfortunately, the reality of our situation is that the principal terror threats in the UK do originate from Islamist sympathisers. I do understand that's different from the religion of Islam, but it's the reality of who the perpetrators are of the majority of the offences. If the show were set in the recent British past, the attackers might be Irish Republicans." See: Jim Waterson. (2018). "Bodyguard Creator Wanted Twist to 'Completely Alter Dynamic'." *Guardian.* Available at: https://www.theguardian.com/tv-and-radio/2018/sep/11/bodyguard-cre- ator-jed-mercurio-bbc-twist-completely-alter-dynamic

[84] Tasnim Nazeer. (2018). "Memo to Bodyguard Writers: Muslim Women Are More than Victims or Terrorists." *Guardian.* Available at: https://www.theguardian.com/commentisfree/2018/sep/24/ bodyguard-muslim-islamophobic-attacks-muslim-terrorist-stereotype

There are always doubts as to their intentions, motivations, and cunning; there remains the possibility of being subjected to the falsifications of Others. As a strategy for dealing with such ambivalence, one that is simultaneously defensive and offensive, *Bodyguard's* degenerate feminism,[85] is invoked to alter the banal and well-critiqued dynamic of white men saving Muslim women from Muslim men. But within the terms set by the Muslim Question, this dynamic progressive incarnation conceives instead of a Muslim woman who demands a fatal equality, a *terrorist feminism*, like those *istishhadiyat*,[86] the Iraqi women kamikaze whose role is no less than that of her brother, son or husband *mujahid*. In the moral economy of scripting the Muslim woman (or the Muslimwoman), holy violence becomes a means of self-expression while, in the minds of the show's writers at least, proof that Muslim women do indeed have agency. Does the Muslim (woman) really need that much help?[87]

The Muslim Question surely increases the Muslim's public presence in a number of conflicting, even contradictory ways. But with the anxieties of war and terror as this haunting figure's subtext, it also seeks to trap those who must answer it, those who wear the names of Islam and Muslim, in a double bind. As Morsi summarizes,

---

[85] Nacira Guénif-Souilamas and Éric Macé. (2004). *Les Féministes et le garçonarabe*. *Éditions de L'Aube*. Paris; Joan Wallach Scott. (2009). *The Politics of the Veil*. Princeton, NJ: Princeton University Press.

[86] There is an already significant but growing literature on the role of women in the violent jihad of Al-Qaeda and ISIS; a genre of work that we might call a feminist terrorism. On December 12, 2005, *Newsweek* magazine put together an extensive article on Women of Al-Qaeda: "The widows of slain guerrillas commonly wed one of their late husband's jihadist relatives. Although these networks appear isolated, they could form the enduring core of Al Qaeda in the future, or a new incarnation of it. And some of the women among them are now more than ready to take up arms, or to carry bombs, whenever the organization needs them. Or whenever the men are gone, or get out of the way." Christopher Dickey. (2005). "Women of Al-Qaeda." *Newsweek*. Available at: https://www.newsweek.com/women-al-qaeda-113757. See also: Murad Batal al-Shistani. (2010). "Is the Role of Women in al-Qaeda increasing?" *BBC News Online*. Available at: https://www.bbc.co.uk/news/world-middle-east-11484672; Julius Cavendish. (2011). "Al-Qa'ida Glossy Advises Women to Cover Up and Marry a Martyr." *Independent*. Available at:https://www.independent.co.uk/news/world/asia/al-qaida-glossy-advises-women-to-cover-up-and-marry-a-martyr-2240992.html. For a select and interdisciplinary bibliography within such a literature see the following and their generous bibliographies: Islah Jad. (2005). "Between Religion and Secularism: Islamist Women of Hamas." In *On Shifting Ground: Muslim Women in the Global Era*, edited by F. Nouraie-Simone. New York: Feminist; Jennifer Philippa Eggert. (2016). "Women Fighters in the "Islamic State" and Al-Qaeda in Iraq: A Comparative Analysis." *Journal of International Peace and Organization*, special issue on the "Islamic State", 90(3–4), 363–80; Katharina Von Knop. (2007). "The Female Jihad: Al Qaeda's Women." *Studies in Conflict & Terrorism*, 30(5), 397–414; Lauren R. Shapiro and Marie-Helen Maras. (2019). "Women's Radicalization to Religious Terrorism: An Examination of ISIS Cases in the United States." *Studies in Conflict & Terrorism*, 42(1–2), 88–119. See also: Emilio C. Viano. (2018). "Special Issue on Female Migration to ISIS." *International Annals of Criminology*, 56(1–2), 1–226.

[87] Sadia Abbas. (2013). "The Echo Chamber of Freedom: The Muslim Woman and the Pretext of Agency." *Boundary 2*, 40(1), 155–189.

The anger and the revulsion in the West towards Islamist violence foregrounds Muslims only to erase us. It frames the debate. We as Muslims are seen to be unseen. We speak not to speak because there is always a compulsion for us to conceal that which reveal us: terrorism. And I am left with a "choice" (one within scare quotes). Either speak to confirm or deny what I am not, I can only contemplate the indeterminacy of my "thrownness" into this War. Its methods, battles, delusions, intimidations, and fabrications shape my subjectivity within its quotes. For, I can only speak freely after its paradigm decides me to be of unfree. That is to say, the content of who I am and what I wish to say is always dictated by the existing form of the conversation.[88]

Islamophobia (and its racial subject), then, mobilizes publicity to translate human differences just as it erases them; incites open speech just as it stifles; invites the Muslim(woman)'s story of freedom and agency just as she is constantly rendered proximate to terror; and organizes press conferences just as it insists on the autocue. There is an insistent call in liberal societies for Muslims to condemn, justify, explain, defend, but also to take up the role of the "therapist,"[89] employed to ease white anxieties of terrorism's foreignness, reminding us all of the need for the Muslim Question.

LISTENING TO STATUES THAT SPEAK

Publicity in the Muslim Question has another dimension, one that is less concerned with performance than *entrapment*, one that is more literally structural and haunts, if not altogether constitutes, public space. That is, spaces full of reminders of the racial principle and the nation's great founding upon it, when it was once purified of the complex shapes and incomprehensibility of the racial subject who could be more straightforwardly dispatched. Whereas the kind of publicity described above is transmitted through visual cultures which depict the Muslim, the type that entraps is the monument, the gallery, the silent statue that once spoke of the Muslim and his kin. It concerns a social world comprised of objects saturated with the traces, assurances, and paraphernalia of empire. The Muslim Question, then, can be asked by inscription, image, memorial as much as by official and unofficial pronouncements of sovereign power. One has only to walk the streets of the country's former industrial centers to have these objects made from all sorts

---

[88] Yassir Morsi. (2018). "The Free Speech of the (Un)free." *Continuum: Journal of Media and Cultural Studies*, 7. See also Morsi's excellent (2017) *Autoethnographic Work, Radical Skin, Moderate Masks: De-radicalising the Muslim & Racism in Post-racial Societies*. London: Rowman and Littlefield.

[89] S. Sayyid. 2014. "A Measure of Islamophobia." *Islamophobia Studies Journal,* 2(1), 10–25.

Figure 6.4 The Sculptor William Behnes's Bronze Statue of Henry Havelock, Which Occupies One of the Four Plinths in Trafalgar Square, to the Southeast of Nelson's Column. *Source*: Photograph by Flickr user Peter 2010.

of materials—marble, granite, steel, bronze, limestone, and so forth—scatter one's field of vision. In fact, the city's geography is unthinkable without these reminders, often orienting one's very navigation of its streets. In this context, these monuments do not serve as merely aesthetic artifacts designed to embellish the grounds of Europe's capitals, but should be read in relation to a style of power and domination constitutive of (post)colonial consciousness and its ever-present anxieties.

Just on the outer limit of the site of the National Portrait Gallery at Saint Martin's Place, off Trafalgar Square, stands tall a statue of Major General Sir Henry Havelock.[90] A monument designed to commemorate the great soldier and military leader "and his brave companions in arms during the campaign in India, 1857."[91] This campaign refers to the unsuccessful, and euphemistically termed, "Sepoy Mutiny," the bloody eighteen-month-long conflict better understood as a war of independence. A soldier would describe the violence in Delhi as,

---

[90] The image depicts the bronze statue of Henry Havelock by the sculptor William Behnes. It occupies one of the four plinths in Trafalgar Square, the one to the southeast of Nelson's Column.

[91] So reads the inscription on the statue.

a war of extermination, in which no prisoners were taken and no mercy shown—
in short one of the most cruel and vindictive wars this world has seen . . . Dead
bodies lay thick in the streets and open spaces, and numbers were killed in their
houses . . . Many non-combatants lost their lives, our men, mad and excited,
making no distinction. There is no more terrible spectacle than a city taken by
storm.[92]

Many texts published in the subcontinent on the place of the uprising in the
long struggle for independence, on the emergence of an Indian nationalism,
and on movements of Muslim separatism, underline the struggle of 1857 as
being crucial. Sayyid Ahmad Khan, perhaps the foremost Muslim thinker
and post-1857 modernist puts forward the argument in his famous work, *The
Causes of the Mutiny 1858*, that the revolt was the end product of accumulated wrongs of East India Company rule. Interestingly, a major source of
dissatisfaction for the Muslims was the proselytizing activities of Christian
missionaries and the widespread belief that the colonial administration sought
slowly but surely to convert everyone to (a specifically English) Christianity.
This idea was later reinforced by the many children made orphans by the
famine of 1837 given to the missionaries to be brought up as Christians.
In 1856 there was a letter issued from the Governor-General's house in
Calcutta that urged the Company's Indian employees to ponder the truths of
Christianity. The new, Macaulayite education system allowed only European
history, Western philosophy, and the natural sciences as conceived in Europe
to be taught, along with the English language as the only medium of instruction, in conjunction with the flourishing of missionary schools sustained and
expanded through substantial government grants.[93] The constant conflict
fomented by the spread of British colonial power, the steady razing of indigenous forms of education, governance, and social life, also met the declining
structures of Muslim empires that,

had revived the old ideal of the crusader spirit in Britain. Popular heroes like
Gordon and Kitchener were presented by the media as chosen instruments to

---

[92] William Dalrymple. (2006). *The Last Mughal: The Fall of a Dynasty, Delhi, 1857*. New York:
Knopf, p. 336.

[93] Esme Cleall. (2017). "From Divine Judgement to Colonial Courts: Missionary 'Justice' in British
India, c. 1840–1914." *Cultural and Social History*, 14(4), 447–61; I. Copland. (2006). "Christian-
ity as an Arm of Empire: The Ambiguous Case of India under the Company, C. 1813-1858." *The
Historical Journal*, 49(4), 1025–54; Tomila Lankina and Lullit Getachew. (2012). "Mission or
Empire?: The Impact of Christian Missionaries on India's Democratic Development." *LSE*. Avail-
able at: https://blogs.lse.ac.uk/southasia/2012/09/07/mission-or-empire/; D. W. Savage. (1997).
"Missionaries and the Development of a Colonial Ideology of Female Education in India." *Gender
& History*, 9, 201–21; Clive Whitehead. (1999). "The Contribution of the Christian Missions to
British Colonial Education." *Paedagogica Historica*, 35(sup1), 321–37.

destroy the Sudanese Mahdi, the false prophet. The traditional image of Islam was resurrected of a violent, fanatical people beyond the reach of reason, who must be suppressed at all costs. At the same time, the decline of Muslim power had highlighted a crucial inner tension within Islam; the tension between the ideal and the real.[94]

Nevertheless, the brutal suppression of the revolt ushered in the official establishment of Crown rule in India, replacing the (corporate) sovereignty of the East India Company in the name of the Crown. Ilyse Morgenstein Fuerst analyzes the revolt's transformative impact on the institutional forms of imperial rule but also pays close attention to the ways in which its popular commemoration contributed to colonial hierarchies of race and gender. Debates among the occupying force about whether the revolt became a religious obligation for the Muslims in 1857 directly informed "the minoritisation and racialisation of Muslims,"[95] as part of the long history in which British narratives have within them the "oft-repeated (and deeply problematic) formulation that Islam and Muslims are inherently tied to ideas of violence."[96] It is in this context of crusader spirit, not to mention the preexisting racialist atmosphere of imposed hierarchy in the colony, that Havelock led the campaign to crush the rebellion, his martyrdom later memorialized through the statue at Saint Martin's Place.

Remarkably, the lives and fates of Macaulay and Havelock, both of whom confronted the Muslim Question in their own ways, are tied not only historically through the rebellion of 1857, but physically. Just to the rear of Havelock's monument, at the entrance of the National Portrait Gallery, are three busts commemorating the people largely responsible for the founding of the Gallery. At the center is the historian Philip Henry Stanhope, and to either side are his major supporters: Thomas Carlyle to Stanhope's right, and to the left, Thomas Babington Macaulay looking out across Saint Martin's Place.

The Muslim Question which fills the physical public space and psychic national atmosphere seems to propel a prophetic or predictive strain. Discussions and policies regarding Islam and its followers are often underpinned by various terms of labor and the future, the ways in which Muslims need to "work" on themselves as the basis for their right to be tolerated and rationale for our distrust. The nineteenth-century Arabist, Edmond Douttée, well versed in threats of Muslim fanaticism and intolerance in Morocco, would argue that the task before Europeans needed to be a *productive* one:

---

[94] R. Greaves. (1996). "India 1857: A Mutiny or a War of Independence? The Muslim Perspective." *Islamic Studies*, 35(1), 25–44.

[95] I. M. Fuerst. (2017). *Indian Muslim Minorities and the 1857 Rebellion: Religion, Rebels and Jihad.* London: I.B. Tauris & Co., p. 5.

[96] Ibid., p. 3.

"we could, on the contrary, favour the birth of a new Islam more inclined towards compromise and tolerance of Europe; to encourage the young generation of *ulama* who are working in that direction, and to increase the number of mosques, madrasas, and Muslim universities, ensuring that we staff them with adherents of new theories."[97] Douttée's comments would not be out of place in a social and institutional world dominated by notions of Muslim radicalization and the future possibilities for Islam's entrance into modernity. As Massad asks: "From where do these commentators suggest their authority derives for such predictive (prophetic?) powers? Is it prophecy, determinism, causality, speculation, theology, or imperial strategy that justifies speaking of the 'future'—the future *in* Islam, *for* Islam, *of* Islam?"[98] Imperial strategies for which stock images of the mosque and the Muslim are spliced together with commentaries of both the extreme and banal, always nonetheless have white anxiety and Muslim intrusion as their subtext.

The racial principle—always lined with anxieties of replacement, disempowerment, and vengeance—is displaced while being confirmed in absentia. Mutating forms of imperial nostalgia, which write the Muslim character, erase the racial/colonial foundations of the nation and yet reproduce heroes and martyrs along racial axes. The whiteness of the country is confirmed in code, but the distinct racism of that equation always takes the racist by surprise. The "human weight"[99] of the Muslim Question must always be erased. In this postimperial village, the denial or suspicion of the Muslim's humanity "is contrasted with, even contingent on, the untroubled and secure identity of the villagers, paradoxically achieved through their existence as unquestionably white subjects, and their simultaneous displacement of this racial identity, despite its centrality, in their own understanding of themselves. Racial identity, for the villagers, is displaced through far more mundane and apparently benign sources,"[100] whether the anthem, the statue, or memorial. In all these cases above, there is an ambivalent knowledge of things and people, a knowing and not knowing simultaneously. In the Muslim Question, the politics of publicity and memorialization, remembrance, and forgetting are never far apart.

---

[97] Enmond Douttee. In Edmond Fazy, ed. (1901). "L'Avenir de l'islam." *Questions diplômatiques et coloniales,* no. 112, p. 396.

[98] Massad, *Islam,* p. 73.

[99] I am invoking James Baldwin's phrase from his essay, "Stranger in the Village", in *Notes of a Native Son.* (1964). London: Michael Joseph, pp. 153–154.

[100] Rob Waters. (2013). "'Britain Is No Longer White': James Baldwin as a Witness to Postcolonial Britain." *African American Review,* 46(4), 722.

VOUCHING FOR MUSLIM HUMANITY

In the first mode of dealing with the Muslim, his future is always already conceived in relation to the interrogation room. The violence and forms of judgment licensed by Islamophobia are deemed a suitable response to a domestic minority (but a soon-to-be global majority) whose presence brings with it anxieties of dilution and chaos. The Muslim Question also has a temporal dimension, a futurology which assumes a monopoly on the racial subject's horizon of being.[101] Mutuality, reconciliation, and solidarity are indeed possible, but the racial fact of the Muslim is nevertheless sustained. The very same commitment to progress—a whole racial mythology—which underpins the best of democratic promises, is perpetually deferred.

Publicity as a technique is a last-gasp resistance to the deeper confrontations occasioned by Europe's demotion and inability to recognize how its foundational rule of race at once structures and haunts it.[102] If not an insult, the Muslim Question makes of "Islam" and "Muslim" names laced with condescension, figures in need of improvement with little recognition of the pathological fixations and impulses to violence which constitute them as figures to be integrated. Much here turns on psychic and material transactions between former and newer colonies, new modes of knowledge and representation, and postcolonial narratives of crisis, pollution, and impotence which constitute and propel the wars on/of terror. Wars which simultaneously order and intensify anxieties of European and British demotion.

The name "Muslim" surely continues to play a central role in the racial drama of Britain's contemporary existence, haunted by the loss of its imperial virility in a world that is at once balkanizing, with new centers of power, wealth, and knowledge being formed and reformed elsewhere.[103] The Muslim Questioned

---

[101] For an insightful study of European colonialism's temporal dimension, see: See: Amy Allen. (2017). *The End of Progress: Decolonizing the Normative Foundations of Critical Theory.* New York: Columbia University Press. On the recurring English technique of future projections of national prosperity contingent on the nation's racial simplification, see: Robbie Shilliam. (2018). *Race and the Undeserving Poor.* London: Agenda Publishing; Sivamohan Valluvan. (2019). *The Clamour of Nationalism: Race and Nation in Twenty-First-Century Britain.* Manchester: Manchester University Press.

[102] A 2014 YouGov poll revealed that 59% of respondents thought the British Empire was "something to be proud of," and only 19% were "ashamed" of its misdeeds; with almost half agreeing that the countries "were better off" for having been colonized speaks to this image of Empire. Again in 2016, the respondents who thought the Empire was a source of pride outnumbered those for whom it was a source of shame by three to one; that the Empire tended to leave its colonies better off than worse off by more than three to one; and with over a third responding they would "like it if Britain still had an Empire." Will Dahlgreen. (2014). "The British Empire Is 'Something to Be Proud of.'" *YouGov.* Available at: https://yougov.co.uk/topics/politics/articles-reports/2014/07/26/britain-proud-its-empire

[103] S. Nuttall and A. Mbembe. (2015). "Secrecy's Software' Current Anthropology." 56(12), 318–24. See also: Jean Comaroff. (2011). *Theory from the South; or, How Euro-America Is Evolving toward Africa.* Boulder, CO: Paradigm.

identifies the racial subject as interrogated suspect and criminal phantasm, as distance, as Other absolutely. The Muslim Question, rather differently and deftly, is the interplay between the summons, *Who are you?* and the required response, *What is it you need me to be?* White subjects and institutions can only cognize Muslim life in forms which require improvement or translation for the liberal world. Houria Bouteldja summarizes this deep condescension:

> Who is this human who persists in prostrating himself five times a day in degrading positions, fasts for a month in often sweltering weather, protects his body and hair from leering eyes, and contributes month after month, year after year, to a fund to build a mosque in the city where his children will grow up, rather than transfer his offerings to the Restos du Cœur? Who is this foolish creature to whom we have delivered Enlightenment on a silver platter, and who persists in turning towards Mecca, like a sunflower that only the sun can subjugate?[104]

It is in the deferral, or rather *referral*, as institutional arrangements of counterterrorism and immigration would have it that the Muslim Question is repeatedly asked, a question always asked in bad faith. The racial subject is the necessary target of such an adjournment. Attachments to the Muslim who may one day become friend, should he deserve it, obscures the otherwise obvious "democratized" violence and deep internal fissures of a Europe imagined and legislated white. The poet Suhaiymah Manzoor-Khan captures the demands of the Muslim Question well:

Some poems force you to write them
the way sirens force their way through window panes in the night
and you can't shut out the news even when you try

"write a humanising poem"
my pen and paper goad me
show them how wrong their preconceptions are

Be relatable,
write something upbeat for a change, crack a smile
tell them how you also cry at the end of Toy Story 3
and you're just as capable of bantering about the weather in the post office queue
    like everyone, you have no idea how to make the perfect amount of pasta, still.

Feed them stories of stoic humour,
make a reference to childhood,
tell an anecdote about being frugal
mention the X factor

---

[104] Bouteldja, *Whites*, p. 128.

Be domestic,
successful
add layers

Tell them you know brown boys who cry
about the sides of Asad's, Amir's and Hassan's they don't know
the complex inner worlds of Summaiyah's and Ayesha's
tell them comedies, as well as tragedies
how full of *life* we are
how full of *love*

But no

I put my pen down
I will not let this poem force me to write it
because it is not the poem I want to write
It is the poem I have been reduced to.[105]

Relations with the Muslim are conditioned by various forms of constraint, impelled by state, economic, juridical, carceral, and discursive arrangements. The Muslim Questioned is interrogation, hostility, and the order of silence combined. The Muslim Question combines the condescension of "tolerance" with the order of the autocue. The racial subject—Muslim and white—is everywhere reproduced while we insist on equality's fundamental nature to our civilizational order. The order to be quiet, to sit still and remain unseen, or at other times to speak on time, to condemn or be condemned, produces a world of anxiety and a politics of hate which authorizes the death or expulsion of those who are not seen to belong. Indeed, the Muslim Question as a paradigm is sustained by its ability to appropriate and incorporate ideals that would deny the existence of the paradigm itself: alleged investments in anti-racist ideals, commitments to multiculturalism, religious tolerance, democracy, and the freedom of the individual. In the 1950s, Britain wrestling with its mounting racism and tortured histories, the American South and the exuberance of the racial principle across the Atlantic was deployed as a

---

[105] Manzoor-Khan's words would receive acclaim in her performance at the 2017 Last Word Festival at which she would be a runner-up in the Poetry Slam final. The poem, in my view, puts words to the lived realities and everyday interactions of the Muslim Question; that the will to humanize oneself within and through structures of racism, Islamophobia, and dehumanization has certain costs, one of which is being reduced to anecdotes of relatability, explaining the inner lives of Asad's and Amir's which signal proximity to, and affirm the normativity of, whiteness. It is a poem written in radical refusal of the summoned response to a question asked in bad faith that the racialized must answer in a certain relatable ways. Suhaiymah Manzoor-Khan. (2017). "The Last Word Festival 2017 - Poetry Slam Final – Suhaiymah Manzoor-Khan." *Roundhouse*. Available at: https://www.youtube.com/watch?v=G9Sz2BQdMF8&t=7s

counterpoint "[against which] to define the virtues of the British nation . . . and appeal to the imagined antiracist ideals tethered to notions of what it meant to be British."[106] But in this state of insecurity and profound anxiety which defines the Muslim Question as the spirit of our time, societies such as Britain witness an increase in the acceptable levels of violence inflicted on the weak, or on those living on the inside but assumed to be from an elsewhere to which they can always be made to return.

In the Muslim Question, proximity, affirmation, and publicity are techniques for the total instrumentalization of social relations. Friendships of quotation, appropriation, translation, and corroboration (in absentia or otherwise) maintain an essential reliance on the fiction of racial subjects, locked in an eternal struggle of accumulation, "collecting" and integrating different population groups, and spheres of economic and political life, in order to make inessential that which confuses us and is perceived to define them. Constituted by a range of tenacious racial codes and relations of force, the Muslim Question functions precisely through the Muslim's public presence, of hearing the Muslim(woman) on television, on bookshelves, at the press conference. We must engage with the Muslim, but our encounter is constrained by the demulcent work of clearing our consciences, for better days are coming and progress will inevitably be made. This is a world which requires a "fugitive communication"[107] that masks the Islamophobia of white institutions, propelled by sterile, contradictory, algorithmic and ever-disposable data about Islam and Muslims.[108]

Returning to Riz Ahmed:

So all the man's that wanna say
That my religion has to change
That we're stuck in a bygone age

---

[106] Kennetta Hammond Perry. (2012). "'Little Rock' in Britain: Jim Crow's Transatlantic Topographies." *Journal of British Studies,* 51(1), 158.

[107] D. Conquergood. (2000). "Rethinking Elocution: The Trope of the Talking Book and Other Figures of Speech." *Text and Performance Quarterly,* 20(4), 325–41; D. Conquergood. (2002). "Performance Studies: Interventions and Radical Research." *The Drama Review,* 46(2), 1–12.

[108] Hamid Dabashi discusses this degenerative epistemic relation with Islam and Muslims as entering the phase of "epistemic endosmosis," that is a form of knowledge that is no longer predicated on any enduring episteme. It is an ad hoc knowledge that can be retracted at any moment with little recognition. See: Hamid Dabashi. (2008). *Post-Orientalism: Knowledge and Power in Time of Terror.* Transaction Publishers. Elsewhere, discussing an instantiation of such an endosmosis in the American and British invasion of Afghanistan and Iraq, he writes: "This is 'fast knowledge' produced on the model of 'fast food,' with plastic cups, plastic knives, plastic forks, bad nutrition, false satisfaction. The US invades Afghanistan and these think tanks produce a knowledge conducive to that project; then the US leads another invasion of Iraq and these think tanks begin producing knowledge about Iraq, with little or no connection with what they had said about Afghanistan, or what they might say about Iran. There is little or no epistemic consistency among the three." See: Hamid Dabashi. (2015). *Can Non-Europeans Think.* London: Zed Books, p. 18.

It's time to set the vinyl straight
Don't you think it's kinda strange
That all this terror outrage
These last gasp castaways
These bastards that will blast away
Just turned up in the last decade?
When Islam has been the way
For millions from back in the day
Instead of thinking that were crazed
Investigate just what it says
Fast, help the poor, and pray
Go Mecca, be steadfast in faith
That's the basics that's the base
So how did we get here today?[109]

"So how did we get here today?" Or, more productively, how might we "go beyond the liberal (white) 'I' and thus liberate the Muslim's Islamic eye. To speak and not be spoken for, to look at, and not only be looked at. To speak within the coordinates of our fantasies and beyond the lines colonialism drew."[110]A drawing that continues. The affirmations of Riz Ahmed's lines that Muslims as private individuals deprive themselves of food and water, and pray in all their peculiarity, do little in societies built according to the foundational rule of race, and its proliferating economies of violent desires. The work of corroboration, argumentation, and attestation it demands, often in public, is, as Toni Morrison says in the epigraph to this chapter, mere distraction. We are in need, therefore, of new questions and, more to the point, Other questioners. I want to explore how it is the Muslim Questioner, who, "knows something that escapes white Reason. Instinctually, because he too recognizes the stars, he has no confidence in the myth of Modernity, which makes promises that it does not keep. His scars, once blessed by the colonies, are still bleeding. He knows better than anyone else the fragility of the modern and the solidity of the archaic. And when he invests, he does not mobilize abstractly universal reason, but his own, which proceeds from his experience and his condition."[111] Instead, we must ask what function racism and Islamophobia as the nation's narcotherapy perform for its beneficiaries. Or do they even, in fact, serve this subaltern figure of the white subject? Is s/he safer, happier, more assured in access to the resources of life through her whiteness? I think not.

---

[109] Find the words to Riz Ahmed's poem, "In These Sour Times" here: https://lyrics.fandom.com/wiki/Riz_MC:Sour_Times
[110] Morsi, "Free Speech," p. 3.
[111] Bouteldja, *Whites*, pp. 128–29.

THE MUSLIM QUESTIONER

"WHERE IS YOUR GOD NOW?"

A feminism which fights simultaneously for a society free of slut-shaming and victim-blaming; as well as for a society wherein wearing the hijab or burka or any form of covering or religious covering by choice would not make you a target or marginalise you. A feminism which fights against rape being used as a weapon of war; but also fights for a world wherein we do not war. A feminism which fights against the sexualisation of female bodies but also for greater space for female sexuality. A feminism for all people, but a flexible and active feminism. A critical and radical feminism.

—Suhaiymah Manzoor-Khan, *The Brown Hijabi*

***

On April 8, 2017, the English Defence League (EDL), the British far-right group, held a demonstration in the city center of Birmingham. After a low turnout at a similar march in London the week prior, West Midlands Police said that they did not expect numbers to reach three figures. Typical of the EDL, the protest was oriented around a defense of Englishness against the rise of radical Islam, Islamic terrorism, and the Islamization of Birmingham, Britain's most "diverse" city. During the protest, a photograph showing a young Asian woman confronting one of the protestors went "viral," the image being widely shared on social media with dozens of articles and news segments discussing the picture.[1] In this image was the leader of the Birmingham

---

[1] Frances Perraudin. (2017). "Photo of Saffiyah Khan defying EDL protester in Birmingham goes viral", *Guardian*. Available at: https://www.theguardian.com/uk-news/2017/apr/09/birmingham -woman-standing-in-defiance-of-edl-protester-goes-viral

Figure 7.1   Viral Photo of Saffiyah Khan Defying EDL Protester in Birmingham. *Source:*
Courtesy of Joe Giddens/Press Association.

EDL protests, Ian Crossland, staring into the eyes and shouting in the face
of Saffiyah Khan. Elsewhere in the foreground, a custodian-helmeted liaison
officer nearby appears to be restraining Crossland. In the background on
the right, another EDL protestor—left arm raised, mouth wide open mid-
exclamation, with his thumb pointing behind him—gestures an expulsion of
some kind.

Saffiyah Khan, a British-born, half-Pakistani half-Bosnian woman, had
no initial intentions that day to get involved in the sporadic counter-protests
mobilizing in the city center; she was merely there to observe. She said, "I was
there with a few friends to look after people—because Muslims and people
of colour are often abused."[2] Khan had got involved to defend Saira Zafar, a
Muslim woman in hijab, who carried a placard reading "No to Islamophobia.
No to War" toward the back of what was by then becoming a more cohesive
counter-demonstration, and who, having shouted "Islamophobes" and "racists" at the EDL, became surrounded by a large group of EDL protestors; predictably, all white men. Saffiyah Khan would explain, "When I realised that

[2] Seth Millstein. (2017). "Who Is Saffiyah Khan? Her Reaction To An EDL Protester Is Captivating",
Bustle. Available at: https://www.bustle.com/p/who-is-saffiyah-khan-her-reaction-to-edl-protester
-is-captivating-50072

nothing was being done [by police] and she was 360 [degree] surrounded, I stepped forward and identified myself as someone who supported her [Zafar] and contradicted them."[3] It was after Khan stepped forward that the protestors gathered around her instead, which is what led to the confrontation with Crossland. Saira Zafar summarized the response to her resistance to the racism of the EDL:

> People [were] shouting all sorts of racist abuse, saying "you don't belong in this country," saying "this is a Christian country," "you're not English." Saying "go back to where you came from." There was one guy who put an Islamophobia banner on top of my head which said that Muslim communities should be investigated, and then put it over my face. And then someone else was putting an EDL flag all over my face, and someone else with a pig mask on who was shouting abuse at me as well.[4]

In fact, another photograph which captured the abuse Zafar describes shows an EDL protestor thrusting a placard on her head which read: "Muslim communities, stop covering up rape." In a joint interview with both Khan and Zafar, Khan recalls, "I wasn't going to let someone who was speaking the truth and being replied to aggressively be put in that position. You didn't look like you [Zafar] wanted to be there and I have an intrinsic problem with that. It was complete chaos,"[5] said Khan. "Can you vouch for me [to Zafar] as well that they were 360 [degrees] around you? They were closing in." Zafar agreed.[6]

EDL "activists" would later claim that scuffles broke out at the protest after counter-protesters shouting "Nazi scum" disrupted a silence being held at the rally for victims of ISIS-claimed attacks in Stockholm and Westminster. Writing on Facebook, Ian Crossland, the group's leader, described Khan as a "dirty unwashed leftwing scrubber." He added: "The disrespectful witch chose the minute's silence for the victims of the terror attack in Stockholm and Westminster. She's lucky she's got any teeth left."[7] It would turn out that

---

[3] Andy Jehring. (2017). "Brummie Saffiyah Khan who SMILED at EDL protesters says: 'I wasn't scared in slightest'", *Birmingham Mail*. Available at: https://www.birminghammail.co.uk/news/midlands-news/brummie-saffiyah-khan-who-smiled-12871182; https://www.theguardian.com/world/video/2017/apr/10/saffiyah-khan-the-woman-who-defied-the-edl-speaks-out-video

[4] Iman Amrani and Mat Heywood. (2017). "'Solidarity is so important': Saffiyah Khan meets woman she stood up for at EDL demo—video", *Guardian*. Available at: https://www.theguardian.com/uk-news/video/2017/apr/11/saffiyah-khan-meets-woman-stood-up-for-edl-demo-video

[5] Frances Perraudin, Iman Amrani and Mat Heywood. (2017). "Saffiyah Khan meets woman she defended at EDL demo", *Guardian*. Available at: https://www.theguardian.com/uk-news/2017/apr/11/saffiyah-khan-meets-woman-she-defended-at-edl-demo

[6] Ibid.

[7] Tim Hobbs. (2017). "Checking in with Saffiyah Khan, the Woman Who Faced Down the EDL", *VICE*. Available at: https://www.vice.com/en_uk/article/z49jn8/checking-in-with-saffiyah-khan-the-woman-who-faced-down-the-edl

there was video evidence that contradicted Crossland's claims, admitted to no less than by Stephen Yaxley-Lennon, more commonly known as Tommy Robinson, the EDL's former leader.[8] Speaking of the incident and the larger importance of solidarity, Zafar said, "Their aim was to silence me, and I was not silenced. Throughout, when they were surrounding me, I was not silent, and I did continue to call them racist. The stance that we both [Khan and Zafar] took in that rally shows that Muslim women are not how, unfortunately, the narrative is nowadays. We are not oppressed; do you know what I mean? We are not easily intimidated. We are quite strong in who we are."[9] Khan would close the interview saying, "You'd expect adult men to realise that was inappropriate whether or not she looked intimidated or said she was intimidated."[10] Ultimately, and as the image shows, they did not come to any such realization.

I think there is much to be learned from this image and the words of these two (Muslim) women for analyzing both racism and its confrontation. A form of opposition which need not take the form of refutation or debate or confession (as the foregoing has analyzed), but instead as something more active, at once imaginative and mundane.[11] The image above captures a whole collection of dynamics—subversive, imaginative, ethical—which signal the possibility of an alternative mode of being *with* an Other. I must be clear, however, that I am not necessarily making the case for proclamations of Muslimness in the face of those who seek to denigrate or minimize this aspect of his fellow subject. In confrontations with an Islamophobia which aims to expel or flatten, I recognize the risk of insisting on the right to one's full Muslimness as the premier facet of their being simply replicating the confessional, interrogative character and effect of racism. The form of knowledge (always already sovereign power) which produces the Muslim as I have analyzed in the foregoing is simply too provincial, anxiogenic, violent to comprehend both the Muslim and her white Other as they actually exist. However, this is

---

[8] Tommy Robinson tweeted that the picture was embarrassing. "OK, just had confirmed by a friend who was at EDL demo, this lady was defending a woman in a navy hijab as she said to the papers," he wrote. "[And] I don't care how many people don't like me saying that, the truth is the truth. [And] the picture is embarrassing." Perraudin, "Photo of Saffiyah Khan".

[9] Perraudin, Amrani, and Heywood, at 2:45.

[10] Ibid., at 2:50.

[11] I am not simply referring to physical confrontations with racists, fascists and their bedfellows, liberal, feminist or otherwise, though this is essential. In May 2019, there were several "Milkshake attacks" on right-wing politicians such as Nigel Farage and Tommy Robinson. When in Kent, with security having noticed a number of people in the town centre carrying milkshakes, Farage would take shelter on the campaign bus. On the trend of milkshakes and right-wing politicians, see: Iliana Magra. (2019). "Why Are Milkshakes Being Thrown at Right-Wing Politicians Like Nigel Farage?", *New York Times*. Available at: https://www.nytimes.com/2019/05/21/world/europe/milkshake-nigel-farage.html. On Farage in Kent, see: Amy Walker. (2019). "Nigel Farage shelters on campaign bus to avoid milkshake attack", *Guardian*. Available at: https://www.theguardian.com/politics/2019/may/22/nigel-farage-shelters-on-campaign-bus-to-avoid-milkshake-attack

the point: these are problems of Europe, gasping and frightened in the face of its exposure and demotion.

Returning to the image, Saffiyah Khan, casually dressed, her hands deep in her pockets, is in close proximity to an EDL agitator—those "Keep Britain White" provocateurs—in the all-black of the League's (sports)[12] uniform. Ian Crossland appears to be screaming at her, at her very existence, her being visible at all on the streets of his Birmingham, his Christian England. Despite his assertions of Khan's non-belonging in the (white)space of Crossland's world(view), Saffiyah Khan exudes a quiet confidence in the basic *fact* of her place in the world, amused at the foolishness of this man and his other white, male, "friends." The contrast in their stances is telling. Crossland seems ready to fight, almost at the beginning of a lunge forward, Khan in relaxed bemusement. Crossland is foaming at the mouth in a white rage, like those men around him, in opposition to the half-smiling face and silence of Khan.

The photograph above is a remarkable (political) image of "race," of "whiteness" (in its peculiar masculinity), and its subjectification. Khan appears to be saying without words: "this problem and anxiety of yours, of me the Muslim, is *all* yours." In her calm dignity and quiet self-assertion, Saffiyah Khan knows herself to Be, to fully belong, living in and being of this place, this being her world, completely seeing through the exuberant performance of white, English, European anxieties that contend otherwise. Crossland and his handful of EDL interlocutors, on the other hand, appearing as a group of red-faced Crusaders seeking to stem the tide of rampant Islamization and reclaim the streets of Britain ostensibly in the name of something much larger than themselves, are in fact not at home at all. Instead, they feel the need to justify why it—Birmingham, Britain, Europe—must surely be theirs.

Theirs is a drama of racial (un)certainties, assurances granted by the decaying property of whiteness,[13] disguising a deep fear of the narrowness of their own being. Whereas Crossland's febrility represents a shrinking of being— white, male, English—Saffiyah Khan, in her very being and presence, opens up, enlarges, makes worldly an otherwise parochial set of (political) desires. Ultimately Khan, and to be sure Zafar, can speak authoritatively about Ian Crossland's world; he is utterly clueless about theirs. Saffiyah Khan's very

---

[12] On the British scene, there has long been an Imperial politics of sport as a scaffold for white British nationalism. See: Gilroy's section in *After Empire*, "Two World Wars and One World Cup", pp. 116–125; Ben Carrington and Ian McDonald. (2001). *Race, Sport and British Society.* London: Routledge and Ben Carrington. (2010). *Race, Sport and Politics: The Sporting Black Diaspora.* London: SAGE Publications Ltd.

[13] Cheryl Harris. (1993). Whiteness as Property. *Harvard Law Review, 106*(8), 1707-1791; Peggy McIntosh. (1989). White privilege: Unpacking the invisible knapsack. Peace and Freedom, July/August, 10–12. Philadelphia, PA: Women's International League for Peace and Freedom; Peggy McIntosh (2015). Extending the Knapsack: Using the White Privilege Analysis to Examine Conferred Advantage and Disadvantage, *Women & Therapy*, 38:3–4, 232–245.

person poses a set of questions too complex for Crossland and his ilk, a very broad church indeed. All those who cling to race as an existential crutch and the seductive phantasms of the Muslim that are its products know some form of his anger and anxiety very well. Khan's questions are posed in a different register, a different dialect, if not a different language altogether, one of the silences, of refusals to speak and confess, of half-smiles and bemusement.

I contend that the image above communicates a set of relations instructive for our third mode of the racial subject, *the Muslim Questioner*, constituted as it is by three dynamics of mutual intersorption: refusal, transparency, and difference. The Muslim Questioner, a speculative archetype to be sure, signals a whole range of possibilities and responsibilities that seek to leave behind, or rather, work through the brittle and violent impulses of a world in which race continues to be a foundational rule, toward the possibility of a world more humane and hospitable. Through a sustained reading of the image above, and mobilizing a wide range of interlocutors, or questioners, not all of them Muslim, I want to close the book with an attempt to generate some principles for an alternative and disobedient ethic in the face of the degeneracy—political, cultural, ecological—that racism and Islamophobia require, and the widespread desires for vengeance that they license.

Inscriptions, intimacies, and economies of Islamophobia produce deep cuts in the social, political, and intimate world(s) of contemporary Europe. With the weight of colonialism, its discomforting associations, and present mutations in view, I have sought to analyze the violence, paranoia, anxiety, non-sense, and institutional arrangements with which irresponsible forms and practices of racial violence, power, governance, and knowledge are essentially associated. I have conceptualized this system as one of an intense questioning, whether of the interrogation room in which guilt has ab initio been precluded, or that of the press conference with answers convincingly read from the autocue. Racism and Islamophobia ultimately construct chains of dependence between the white subject and his Muslim Other constituted by varying degrees of dehumanization. It is in this systemic equation in which Muslims, and specifically Muslim women, are a privileged site of its operation. It is in this context that the photograph of Saffiyah Khan and Ian Crossland was taken and should be read.

In the face of such a system and culture, the first dynamic signaling its dismantling is the act of *refusal*. From the triangular trade of Transatlantic slavery and the plantation complex, to the continued settler colonial domination of indigenous populations through forms of genocide and war, not to mention legal, structural, and subjective reconstitution of native peoples and traditions, varying chains of dehumanization and imposed hierarchy have been essential. Equally fundamental, however, have been the modes and processes of refusal; the outright rejection of the terms and taxidermy—social, epistemic, ontological—of empire and their transformation in the postcolonial turns of Islamophobia and the wars on/of terror. In the opening chapter, I analyze a negative mode of racism's confrontation, the rejection to shoulder the burdens of "race" and the fiction of the racial subject which rely on processes of despoliation and sustain imperial matrices of power. The Muslim subject is fundamental to the coherence of such a formation, but which is nonetheless always on the cusp of collapse.

Transparency describes the discomfort that the opening of the little secret of race causes in white Europe, a discomfort occasioned by the everyday presence of the Muslim. A secret nonetheless which formed modern Europe, its frenzied power, shallow knowledge, and contradictory governmental practice, and which is today coming apart at the seams. The narrowness of national citizenship is exposed as the inadequate guarantor of protection and hospitality that in many ways it was designed to be. In fact, quite basic limits to the category of citizen become apparent when viewed from the perspective of those assumed not to belong. The Muslim Questioner points toward a post-national possibility and a denationalization of the imagination. In a brief discussion of the basic concept of the *ummah*, the ethical and cosmological purpose of travel, translocation and direction, the iniquities and rigged markets of Europe, nation, and citizen are shown to perform distinct functions in upholding severe racial limits to hospitality. A set of functions that seek to cage in an increasingly proliferating multiplicity and intermixture at the expense of racial subjects, in which there is a peculiar interplay between remembrance, memorialization, and amnesia to keep history out.

This brings us, finally, to *Otherwise* which, by way of conclusion, pursues a positive mode of self-conscious assertion of dissimilarities, sometimes irreconcilable but never dehumanizing, within an inherently heterogeneous social and natural world as pregnant with possibilities for pointing toward an *otherwise* without racism. I mobilize a range of specifically Muslim resources for (re)thinking in time and alternative temporal regimes which force us to think nonlinearly; of and with spaces that are saturated in value of the kind incomprehensible to colonial-capitalist extraction and datafication; and of the subject herself within more expansive notions of humanity that can account for the life of the natural world and the reciprocal nature of our shared finitude. Which is to say that in delving into not simply the Muslim archive of scripture but of Muslim life—heterogeneous, contradictory, in flux—the basic parameters of being in the world can be rethought providing preliminary resources which might be utilized in the struggle against racism and Islamophobia, a struggle which must implicate us all.

Chapter 7

Refusal

Memories of the revolt, insurrection, mutiny, the anticolonial revolution, and the breaking chains of dependence have always haunted the crimes of colonial power, modern reason, and the never-ending crises produced by racial difference. At base, the dynamic of refusal as I mean it here is to declare that human beings as human beings have an uneliminable aspect. The refusal to accept the (colonial) terms of dehumanization that are racism and Islamophobia is to assume that in one's very being alive, regardless of color, religion, "tastes," and "intellect," is necessarily to be fully human.[1] There can be no half or partial humanity according to the world(view) and social relations this refusal gives rise to. Refusal does not aim at humanization because there is simply no need, or rather, impulses to question its existence in an Other it is rendered incoherent. Humanization of the Muslim Questioned—who only enters the enclosure of humanity, however partially, through confession—and of the Muslim Question—whose full humanity is contingent on the desire and willingness to be improved and put to work—is rendered invalid because both rest on the fungibility of, or ambiguity about, the Other's humanity. Which is to say, both are questions not worth asking. Or, further still, questions inconceivable in the first place, for the terms upon which they are given meaning—the law of race—are rejected outright. This is the conceptual meaning of refusal as I employ it here. As Achille Mbembe says,

---

[1] Though not pursuing a philosophical argument of uneliminable surplus, for one such study on resistance in even extreme cases of domination such as slavery and serfdom, see: James C. Scott. (1990). *Domination and the Arts of Resistance. Hidden Transcripts*. London: Yale University Press. For an instructive historical account of transnational solidarities in anticolonial resistance, see: Priyamvada Gopal. (2019). *Insurgent Empire: Anticolonial Resistance and British Dissent*. London: Verso.

I am a human being, and that is all. The Other can dispute this quality, but they can never rob me of it ontologically. The fact of being a slave or of being colonized—of being the object of discrimination and bullying, privation and humiliation, because of the color of my skin—changes absolutely nothing. I remain a complete human being no matter how violent are the efforts aimed at making me think that I am not one. This *uneliminable surplus* escapes all attempts at capture and fixation within a particular social or legal status. Even death cannot interrupt it.[2]

This outlook does not give rise to an acquiescent secession from the world. It is not simply a resistance to confession but its outright refusal. *Confess what?* When principles of the uneliminable surplus of all living beings—human and nonhuman—are apprehended through knowledge that is necessarily partisan in nature, the deep fissures in the white world become apparent.

In the two paradigms that we have thus far analyzed, speech/translation, in both the plaints of the Muslim and the industrial reconfiguration of the (post) colony, is always constrained. In the hostility of the interrogation room, there is little the Muslim can say, though must be made to nonetheless, to "prove" an innocence always deferred as a code for their lesser humanity. Likewise, the condescension of the press conference and the autocue demands certain admissions and affirmations. That some among you, Muslims, are indeed criminal and, therefore, you were never really of us and that we, Muslims, all desire to be one of you. These social, political, and economic relations, undergirded by juridical processes, produce an order in which the impulses of exclusion, marking, tracking, and judgment are never satiated. Both paradigms, generalized as social conditions, require innumerable forms of condemnation, which is to say, systems which authorize exclusion and the jettisoning of difficult cases and their uncomfortable associations.[3] All of this assumes that there is always someplace else for the Muslim to go, a place that is always already defined by its not being here.

Refusal, however, is the insistence that there is in fact nowhere else to go. That, as Sivanadan has put it, "we are here because you were there."[4] Taking

---

[2] Mbembe, *Critique*, p. 46.

[3] The mechanisms of deportation and deprivation, and the sophisticated mechanisms of secret justice, integration and publicity should be understood in this context. Within racial formations, they are processes by which the perceived coherence of the formation itself can be maintained, the imagined (white) subject at its center sustained, and the heavy costs exacted for their development explained away, incarcerated or dumped at sea. Recall Operation Legacy, or Shamima Begum and its highly instructive analogical value. In the deep-seated will to ignorance, the British state authorized the literal dumping at sea of incriminating evidence of abuse in Kenya and elsewhere.

[4] "Myths and stereotypes reinforce each other. The myth sets out the story, the stereotype fits in the characters. It was said, for instance, that the post-war 'influx' of West Indian and Asian immigrants to this country was due to 'push-and-pull' factors. Poverty pushed us out of our countries, and

the uneliminable surplus of humanity as an incontrovertible aspect of being in the world, extravagant technologies of exclusion, secrecy, affirmation, and violence can only ever do the work of death and accumulation. Which is to say that the essential relation of dependence constructed between the sub- or instrumental humanity of the Other, and the assumption of full or universal humanity as inherent in who "we" are—the latent philosophy of Europe—inculcates a set of borders beyond which there is no real escape. They are, the Questioner says, structures—legal, political, cultural—of *your* making, products of modern reason, borne of a history most repressed by, but nonetheless mostly concerns, the same white subjects and institutions.

There may well (technically) be other places for uncomfortable subjects to be sent, made to stay, left to die or to disappear.[5] But this leaves unanswered the question of *why* they came in the first place and *who* they are at all. It is popular to cast postcolonial citizens as evidence of "the empire come home."[6] But even this postcolonial move is too heavily invested in colonially cast notions of interior and exterior. Malcolm X, visiting the same Marshall Street witness to the racist slogan of the Peter Griffiths campaign, would refer to the town's black community as one denied its citizenship rights because they were understood within, and legislated through, categories of "immigrant"

---

prosperity pulled us into Britain. Hence the stereotype that we were lazy, feckless people who were on the make. But what wasn't said was that it was colonialism that both impoverished us and enriched Britain. So that when, after the war, Britain needed all the labour it could lay its hands on for the reconstruction of a war-damaged economy, it turned to the reserves of labour that it had piled up in the colonies. That's why it passed the Nationality Act of 1948 making us colonials British nationals. (Equally, when, after 1962, it did not need that labour, it brought in a series of restrictive and racist immigration acts.) Quite simply we came to Britain (and not to Germany for instance) because we were occupied by Britain. Colonialism and immigration are part of the same continuum—we are here because you were there." Ambalavaner Sivanandan. (2008). "The Speech by the IRR's Director, A. Sivanandan, at the IRR's Fiftieth Celebration Conference on 1 November 2008." *Institute of Race Relations.* Available at: http://www.irr.org.uk/news/catching-history-on-the-wing/. See also: Sivanandan. (2008). *Catching History on the Wing.* London: Pluto Books, Part II.

[5] Kapoor, "Citizenship Deprivation." See also the numerous reports of deaths and disappearances as a result of Windrush deportations: Kevin Rawlinson. (2018). "Windrush: 11 people wrongly deported from UK have died—Javid", *Guardian.* Available at: https://www.theguardian.com/uk -news/2018/nov/12/windrush-11-people-wrongly-deported-from-uk-have-died-sajid-javid; Diane Taylor. (2019). "Revealed: Five Men Killed in Past Year After Being Deported from UK to Jamaica." *Guardian.* Available at: https://www.theguardian.com/uk-news/2019/may/09/revealed -five-men-killed-since-being-deported-uk-jamaica-home-office; Gracie Bradley. (2019). "From Grenfell to Windrush, State Racism Kills—Sometimes Quickly, Sometimes Slowly." *openDemocracy.* Available at: https://www.opendemocracy.net/en/opendemocracyuk/from-grenfell-to -windrush-state-racism-kills-sometimes-quickly-sometimes-slowly/; Diane Abbott. (2018). "We Still Do Not Know the True Scale of the Windrush Generation Scandal." *New Statesman.* Available at: https://www.newstatesman.com/politics/staggers/2018/11/we-still-do-not-know-true-scale -windrush-generation-scandal

[6] E. Bleich. (2005). "The Legacies of History? Colonization and Immigrant Integration in Britain and France." *Theory and Society,* 34(2), 171–95.

and "native," categories that he would vehemently refuse.[7] Colonization, in a rather straightforward sense, was to be made an immigrant in one's own home. It was to be told, regardless of all evidence to the contrary, that one had no history, some culture, but whose house was never theirs. The empire-come-home teleology does little to interrogate the status of the subject created by such notions of "home" and "away," and in fact places the postcolonial subject conveniently in a theology of progress, distinct from, but related to, Macaulay's "Minute," or the kind that Cressida Dick is invested in her reading of the Met as no longer being institutionally racist. Or elsewhere, the placing of anticolonial movements and decolonization as somehow inevitable "improvements" to colonization and freedom, without questioning the provenance of, and need for, never mind the ethics of, empire.[8] The question, "why are you here?" that is asked in innumerable ways, and according to which the figure of the Muslim is "interviewed repeatedly [and] harried for quotes, accusations, [and] dark promises of vengeance,"[9] is deeply revealing in its very asking. Suhaiymah Manzoor-Khan's poem insists on a mode of refusing the summons authorized by this familiar question, instead putting the challenge to those upholding the iniquities of the racial formation, those with deep investments in the enclosure of race. She says:

So this will not be a 'Muslims are like us' poem
I refuse to be respectable

Instead
Love us when we're lazy
Love us when we're poor

---

[7] The unofficial leaflets bearing the slogan "If you want a Nigger for a neighbour—vote Labour!," buoyed support for Griffiths in Smethwick and ultimately contributed heavily to his win of the seat in the West Midlands on a swing of 7.5 percent. He would later lend support "to a local council proposal to buy up property in Smethwick's Marshall Street for occupancy by white residents only." See: Rob Waters, "Britain is no longer white," p. 725.

[8] There is a temptation in studies of/from the postcolonial to inflate claims of agency without serious regard for that overwhelming and recurrent failures of anticolonial resistance before they finally won out. This amounts to accumulating "emancipatory" anticolonial movements into a theology of progress wherein these movements that we now celebrate could not have existed without colonialism. The conversation, therefore, remains on the terms of racism, modern progress, and the teleology of white Europe. On these themes, see: Hallaq, *Restating*, p. 307n135; Allen, *End of Progress*. For an account of agency's inflation in the specific case of Islam under colonial rule, see the excellent study by Leonard Wood. (2016: 262). *Islamic Legal Revival: Reception of European Law and Transformations in Islamic Legal Thought in Egypt, 1875–1952*. Oxford: Oxford University Press.

[9] James Campbell. (1991). *Talking at the Gates: A Life of James Baldwin*. London: Faber and Faber, p. 208. James Baldwin says, elsewhere: "[T]he question of controlled immigration is a question asked essentially in bad faith. The English people, after all, English history, has created these Black Englishmen, who have as much right to the capital as any White Englishman. They've paid quite as much for it as any White Englishman." Quoted in James Mossman. (1965). "Race, Hate, Sex, and Colour: A Conversation with James Baldwin and Colin MacInnes." Baldwin, *Conversations* 46–58.

Love us in our back-to-backs, council estates, depressed, unwashed and weeping,
Love us high as kites, unemployed, joy-riding, time-wasting, failing at school,
Love us filthy, without the right colour passports, without the right sounding English,

Love us silent, unapologizing, shopping in Poundland,
skiving off school, homeless, unsure, sometimes violent
Love us when we aren't athletes, when we don't bake cakes
when we don't offer our homes, or free taxi rides after the event,
When we're wretched, suicidal, naked and contributing nothing
Love us then

Because if you need me to prove my humanity I'm not the one that's not human.[10]

REFUSING THE STATUS OF VICTIMHOOD

Crossland, as a signifier of "race" in the "thick" sense we have been analyzing, has already made up his mind. This element of foreclosure is as true in the Muslim Questioned as it is in the Muslim Question. What is particularly interesting, however, is that Crossland and his people, in their protest and attempts to reclaim the Streetspace in England's defense, to stamp it white and make it great, are framed, in their own minds at least, as the victims of siege.[11] Saffiyah Khan, on the other hand, has escaped the status of victimhood altogether in refusing to play the role of those who—or *that* which—must confess and affirm. In her quiet, half-smiling bemusement, it is not Khan but the EDL, the defenders of whiteness, who are out of place, the liabilities, thoroughly (self-)saturated in the burdens of victim status. This signals a break from "good conscience" and the denial of responsibility toward that which we must collectively strive for: not having to speak an other's "language." Hegemonic discourses and policies of The Muslim Question(ed) are an attempt to cage in an uncomfortable multiplicity and to be shielded from those jarring moments of reality where the attempt to interpolate the (insulting or condescending) names of the Muslim fail, that when "she [Muslim, Muslim woman, Muslimwoman] refuses to be

---

[10] Suhaiymah Manzoor-Khan, *This Is Not a Humanising Poem*, Roundhouse.

[11] There is a significant literature on the politics of white victimhood and white innocence; a crude reversal which simultaneously erases the political, cultural, economic, and material inequalities in society along racial lines white maintaining the white "I" as the center of all meaning. See: Robin DiAngelo. (2011). "White Fragility." *International Journal of Critical Pedagogy*, 3(3), 54–70 and (2019). *White Fragility: Why It's So Hard for White People to Talk About Racism*. London: Penguin; Gloria Wekker. (2016). *White Innocence: Paradoxes of Colonialism and Race*. Durham: Duke University Press; Paul Gilroy. (2004). Postcolonial Melancholia; Williams, "The Pantomime of Race" in *The Genealogy of Race*, especially her discussion of the black church tourism/fetish.

constituted as a subject by those who hail her, she undermines their control and the reproduction of their ideology."[12]

In this world of wars on terror, the name "Muslim" has been made to do much work; it forms the nodal point of a racially cast psychological profile, or as the basis of a license (to violation), or to put it more broadly, to form a name that comes to carry an entire destiny and generalized condition. To pose the question instead, *who are we?* acknowledges the historical and present conditions which speak to the impossibility of dividing a society, formed by such close historical relationships and that have been constituted through the collective labor that the colony was made to do, into convenient abstracted categories of white native and Muslim intruder. What do we mean by one's own people in a world, Europe, Britain, that is no longer and, in truth, never was white?

In this sense, refusal is concerned as much with the present as with the future of this uneliminable surplus.[13] "I am Muslim," therefore, is a break toward another future because, in the Questioner's *refusal to move*, one has to confront her, which in truth is the white subject's confrontation with itself.[14] There is no road, Saffiyah Khan's very presence shows, that will lead white Britain back to the simplicity of that European village "where white men still have the luxury of looking on [her] as a stranger."[15] If the Muslim Questioner offers a form of knowledge, it does not pretend to a (scientific) objectivity, which sits at the very core of modern reason and the racial fatalisms it produces. On the contrary, refusal indicates the impossibility of objectivity or neutrality, that presumed speaking/seeing/thinking position of policymakers and institutions that deal with Muslims and make pronouncements about them and their future. The Muslim Questioner, in that sense, is self-consciously and openly partisan insofar as there can never be any legitimate concessions given to a racist order. As Frantz Fanon said: "I have not wished to be objective. Besides, that would be dishonest: It is not possible for me to be objective."[16]

Cooke, "The Muslimwoman," p. 153.

[13] In the modern/colonial matrices of power, we should remember, there can be no benchmarks. See Hallaq's instructive discussion of the notion of benchmarks in chapter 2 of *Restating*. See also: Kwame Anthony Appiah. (2010). *Cosmopolitanism: Ethics in a World of Strangers*. London: W. W. Norton & Company. The contingency of benchmarks, which is no benchmark at all, is only worsening under regimes of neoliberal "disinhibition".

[14] Bouteldja, *Whites*, p. 124. What has long been assumed to be the gift of whiteness—for no one wants to be the Muslim Question(ed)—is cast as the burden which "white people" who live in their whiteness as an essential mark of separation between them and Others, have not begun to do the work of divestment from a force that has been defined by its power to erase; that is, the "salary of whiteness."

[15] Baldwin, "Stranger in the Village," p. 165.

[16] Fanon, *Black Skin, White Masks*, p. 86.

Crossland, indicative of all those individuals and institutions who derive meaning from the rules of race, does not, indeed cannot bring themselves to think this way. They are ever-bound by the narcissism of colonial consciousness which was, obliquely, captured by US filmmaker, Woody Allen, in a syllogism to end all syllogisms: *God is good. I am good. Therefore, I am God.* This form of thought is a kind of trance, a mantra of a white, secular Europe which defend it from its own contradictions.[17] There are everywhere traces of such contradictions, those who perceive themselves to be victim defenders while locked into a system of reality in which it must be they who derive most benefits. The racism of empire has come home in a peculiar form in which it is the defenders of Englishness who are stuck in the status of victimhood. Surely this was not the plan.

THE RECURRING TERROR OF RACIST FUTUROLOGY

The refusal of this structure of thought is to question who it is that has the monopoly on the future.[18] The Muslim Questioner refuses this monopoly and its delegated/deferred future(s) to be received as a gift, by a subject who views herself as a citizen above all else. Refusal here is a rejection of the wait for "progress," as James Baldwin speaks of it: "What is it you want me to reconcile myself to? I was born here almost sixty years ago. I'm not going to live another sixty years. You always told me it takes time. It has taken my father's time, my mother's time. My uncle's time. My brother's and sister's time. My niece's and my nephew's time. How much time do you want for your 'progress'?"[19] Baldwin is querying the impoverished visions of the future constituted by race, a deficient and defunct futurology conceived and delegated from a position of, following Aimé Césaire, "European reductionism."[20]

---

[17] It is worth remembering that the styles of power and domination in colonialism and its foundational rule of race aimed at a deep inscription not merely on the bodies of the enslaved in the Caribbean, or later the colonized native the world over, Muslim or otherwise, but to leave imprints "on the spaces that they inhabit as indelible traces on the imaginary. Domination must envelop the subjugated and maintain them in a more or less permanent state of trance, intoxication, and convulsion so that they are incapable of thinking lucidly for themselves" (127).

[18] I use "monopoly" here as a conscious invocation of the colonial matrices of corporate, economic power essential to Britain's former greatness, especially monopolies on industrial production, trade routes, and with the Royal African Company, of human-metal, human-merchandise.

[19] Karen Thorsen. (1989). *James Baldwin: The Price of the Ticket.* Available at: https://www.kanopy.com/product/james-baldwin-price-ticket

[20] What Césaire defines as: "that system of thought, or rather instinctive tendency, on the part of an eminent and prestigious civilization to take advantage of its prestige by creating a vacuum around it that abusively reduces the notion of the universal to its own dimensions, that is to think the universal only on the basis of its own postulations and through its own categories." The result, he explains, is to "amputate man from the human and isolate him, permanently, in a suicidal

But refusal is not a form of rejection that, in one's experience of exclusion, of confession, and of judgment, leads to a secession from the world. This negative mode of refusal is alive to the fact that its reversal, ultimately hatred and isolation, opens the door to an eternal and disastrous reciprocity, a "pendulum motion of terror and counterterror."[21] The killer who kills himself or kills others according to mythological schema—political, national, or theological—discharges himself of the responsibilities that, as a Being in the world fundamentally conjoined to others within it, were once his to attend.[22] Refusal is, in fact, thoroughly worldly in that it claims responsibility for a world which we must all ultimately share, a form of militancy which aims to make heterogeneity thrive. Europe is not the world but only a small part of it. It is a mode of engagement that remains fully cognizant of the multifarious and interconnected oppressions of the day, acutely aware that old feuds and new apartheids are propelled by global processes of accumulation, occupation, and insecurity. The strategy, therefore, "should be not only to confront empire" but, as Arundhati Roy reminds us, "to lay siege to it. To deprive it of oxygen. To shame it. To mock it. With our art, our music, our literature, our stubbornness, our joy, our brilliance, our sheer relentlessness—and our ability to tell our own stories. Stories that are different from the ones we're being brainwashed to believe."[23] The fundamentalisms of race calls for secession or closure, which is why the border is always fundamental, and beyond which there must be a denial of responsibility for and in an increasingly impoverished world.

Refusal here is, in turn, a call to take the full measure of one's life, one that is necessarily lived in concert, in and as part of a larger world of other lives and ways of living.[24] Refusal requires a thinking and doing that is unthinkable, undoable without it being lived with others, human and nonhuman alike. It is, further, an experience that is always in progress, unstable, changing, even contradictory. It is a call to be taken up by and with the messiness of being in the world,[25] not above it as delegators or occupiers. The Muslim Questioner's experience is, then, one full of risk but which is rooted in recognition of her historical situation, the obligations that are occasioned by her filiations, to others here and now, as well as those yet to come. The world becomes a site

---

pride if not in a rational and scientific form of barbarism." Aimé Césaire. (1987). "Discours sur la négritude," speech, University of Florida, February 26, 1987. Available at: http://www .humaniteinenglish.com/spip.php?article898

[21] Fanon, *Wretched*, p. 47.

[22] Talal Asad. (2007). *On Suicide Bombing*. New York: Columbia University Press. See also: Devji, *Terrorist*, pp. 57–78.

[23] Arundhati Roy. (2005). *An Ordinary Person's Guide to Empire*. London: HarperCollins UK, p. 86.

[24] Fanon, *Dying Colonialism*, p. 32.

[25] Appiah, A. (2006). *Cosmopolitanism* and Appiah. (2018). *The Lies that Bind: Rethinking Identity : Creed, Country, Color, Class, Culture*. 1st edition. New York: Liveright Publishing.

of unending creation and struggle where, as I hope it has become clear, the modes of thinking and living that racism and white supremacy license are fundamentally sterile, brittle, and whose relations of fraternity are thoroughly mediated by violence. While present at—and as—the nuclear power plant of western reason, race is unable to comprehend a world that is necessarily in motion, a common world in which Europe is not its center but its burden. Refusal in a world borne of imperial compulsion distinctly racial in nature is one which attempts to puncture and transform the hostile, poisonous membrane that is the legacy of colonialism.[26]

The world of the Muslim question is based upon a principle of unequal shares: as human, as right-holder, as a being due to certain debts. To be sure, each racial order has its own historical, systemic, and cultural dependencies and associations. However, the principle of shares is everywhere essential. Whether the Muslim is called to live either as historical minorities (in the modern period at least) whose existence is systematically extinguished (the case of China); or whose presence is not denied per se, but whose entire belonging to the community is increasingly precarious (the case of India); or as minorities that society chooses neither to see, nor recognize, nor listen to as such (the case of Britain and Europe), the horizons of struggle and the sound of refusal remains the same: silence. We see everywhere white Europe's fundamental inability to be quiet, instead making this or that claim about racial hordes and intruders who must be denied. When all manner of processes, structures, events ask of the racial subject: "And you, why are you Muslim?" she smiles and says nothing at all.

Refusal thus asserts a principle of equal shares, affirming the fundamentally creative impulse that is at the core of struggling for a hospitable world, one that can obtain everywhere, regardless of the seismic racial, Islamophobic formulations whose "profound historical forgetfulness"[27] masks this fact. To affirm the reason of Others is to take on their questions of justice, expression, ethics, history, violence, responsibility, and debt that are never over and concluded. Questions that relate to the possibility of standing and moving and writing with one's own bodies, hands, and feet toward and in a world that we must all share.[28] Saffiyah Khan's refusal in the image above enjoins us to refuse the retreat which denies this possibility. It is a sign, in fact, that the

---

[26] For an elaboration of such an interpretation of Fanon, see: Miguel Mellino. (2011). "Frantz Fanon, un classique pour le présent." *Il Manifesto*, May 19. See also: Miguel Mellino. (2013). The *Langue* of the Damned: Fanon and the Remnants of Europe." *South Atlantic Quarterly* 1 January; 112(1), 79–89.

[27] Stuart Hall. (1978). "Racism and Reaction." *Five Views on Multi-Racial Britain: Talks on Race Relations Broadcast by BBC TV*. London: Commission for Racial Equality.

[28] Fanon's words: "I am a man, and I have to rework the world's past from the very beginning." Fanon, Black Skin, White Masks, p. 201.

retreat is incomplete, is always contested. And as long as this is the case, the conditions are there for the possibility of reparation.[29]

It is not a form of refusal, however, which foregrounds Muslimness as racism's antidote, for this would again produce a hostile dialog which affirms rather than destabilizes the European idea, its racial contents and impulse to separate. Refusal must also create space for silence, for the right to stay *and* to move, for Islamicity as an aspect of the private, political, and social life of Britain and Europe, while not defining its adherent, the Muslim, as a problem to be solved and a more or less disturbing or intruding figure to be dealt with. While Islam and the Muslim are often cast in racial terms, I think they can be invoked in ways, both philosophical and practical, which make plain the incoherencies constitutive of the widespread will to retreat, to deny hospitality and instead create multiplying spheres of abandonment for those who are not one of us. The need for an enemy, for the racial subject against whom we stand on guard as a condition for rooting oneself in the world, at once produces the very phantasms whom we constantly fear, but can never truly recognize fusion and assembly as inherent facts of being in the world, as Muslim or otherwise. If to be Muslim is to be an intruder, or requires his being marked and vulnerable to slight or injury licensed by his less-than-human status, then that is because our definition and "knowledge" of the human is fundamentally inadequate. And yet, the Muslim and Islam, in the mode of refusal, are also sites through which we might expand notions of humanity—both the human and nature together—not as a marker of their superiority, but as legitimate sources of knowledge for how to be in and with the world and all its occupants, and to whose fates we are all of us tied.

Britain is not a white country and, as Baldwin tells us, "this world is white no longer, and it will never be white again."[30] Any society that has become accustomed to thinking of itself as exclusively white—supported by technologies which constantly mark the colored stranger in reference to this whiteness—comes to classify human, demographic, and cultural intermixture, as epidemiological threats to an always vulnerable white immune system.[31] But

---

[29] In his Discourse on Colonialism, Aimé Césaire asked: "What is the principle of colonialism?" He replied, it is "neither evangelization, nor a philanthropic enterprise, nor a desire to push back the frontiers of ignorance, disease, and tyranny, nor a project undertaken for the greater glory of God, nor an attempt to extend the rule of law." It is for this reason that "no one colonizes innocently, that no one colonizes with impunity; that a nation which colonizes, that a civilization which justifies colonization—and therefore force—is already a sick civilization, a civilization which is morally diseased, which irresistibly, progressing from one consequence to another, one denial to another, calls for its Hitler." Césaire, *Discourse*, p. 32, 36, 39, 41.

[30] James Baldwin, *Stranger in the Village*, p. 165.

[31] On this phrase coined by Bouteldja, *Whites*, p. 42. See also: Jared Sexton. (2018). "The World Love Love Jam." *The Immanent Frame*. Available at: https://tif.ssrc.org/2018/06/20/the-world-love -jam/; Islamic Human Rights Commission. (2018). "Houria Bouteldja on 'Whites, Jews and Us: Toward a Politics of Revolutionary Love'." *IHRC*. Available at: https://www.ihrc.org.uk/activities

these fusions are irreversible and always leave liberal societies that wish to be white in a paradox. For this is a society whose liberalism cannot resolve its internal tension of wishing to be hospitable but whose fetish for domination is constituted by old and new forms of exclusion and massacre. In this equation, racism and Islamophobia become, paradoxically, antibodies against a historical disease of Europe's own making, a disease whose remedy is equally, if not more toxic.

History is literally present in all that we do and yet the past is a past for which Britain and Europe seek at once to be adored and from which to escape. The past then comes to take on a tyrannical power. But a "creature despised by history finds history a questionable matter."[32] Those with uncomfortable, marginalized places in this history bring with them their own historical memories against the narratives that have tried but cannot, in the final analysis, suppress or deny their presence. Refusal is, then, the effort to "think in color"[33] against the monochromatic vision of "race," and the search for new terms upon which relations to the neighbor can be reconfigured.

/event-reports/18514-houria-bouteldja-on-whites-jews-and-us-toward-a-politics-of-revolutionary-love/;Houria Bouteldja. (2012). "Pierre, Djemila, Dominique. . . and Mohamed." *The Culture Craft*. Available at: https://theculturecraft.wordpress.com/comments/critical-reflections-by-houria-bouteldja/; Houria Bouteldja. (2013). "Decolonising France—An Evening with Houria Bouteldja." *IHRCtv*. Available at: https://www.youtube.com/watch?v=CszbqynuZ4I. For a sustained critique of Bouteldja's blind-spots in *Whites*, see: Ivan Segre and Ross Wolfe. (2018). "A Native with a Pale Face." *Los Angeles Review of Books*. Available at: https://lareviewofbooks.org/article/a-native-with-a-pale-face/#!

[32] Baldwin, "White Man's Guilt," p. 410.

[33] I am invoking the advice given by the great Trinidadian historian, C. L.R. James to the then budding writer, James Baldwin. See the work of James's biographer on the association between the two writers: James D Young. (1999). *The World of C. L. R. James: His Unfragmented Vision*. Glasgow: Clydeside, p. 242, 251.

Chapter 8

Transparency

As a kind of perverse tax, Islamophobia is always *expropriatory* in nature; it is the humanization and freedom of a portion of humanity, tortured though it is, which is contingent on the dehumanization and exclusion, that is, *questioning* of the Muslim's very being. George Bataille has noted that racism as a phenomenon, as the phobia of Others, requires a high degree of baseness and stupidity. It is a form of cowardice of a man or woman who "attributes to some external sign a value that has no meaning other than his own fears, his guilty conscience and his need to burden others, through hatred, with the deadweight of horror inherent in our condition"; he added that men "hate, it would seem, to the same extent that they are themselves to be hated."[1] This high tolerance for baseness and stupidity that has been constitutive of the ideas of Europe and Britain is of historic proportions.

The often racialized, invidiously technical and mutating distinction made between one's being here and being *of* here is a technique to preserve the colonial coherence of a society that does not know what it is, where it is, nor how to be without a racial subject to be deported or put to work. The warped economies of intimacy—psychic and material—which produce and are produced by the Muslim problem, traffic in their own opacity. The constant play of sealed categories such as terror, freedom, security, radicalization, immigration, integration, war, history, vulnerability, man, woman, and child is encased in the phantasms of Islam in order to separate what is said about and done to the Muslim from the larger complexities and complicities of the world. Instead, the Muslim must be an object which disturbs, and orders a politics of hatred in which the inflexibility of the designations attached to the

---

[1] Georges Bataille and Michel Leiris. (2008). *Correspondence*, ed. Louis Yvert, trans. Liz Heron. London: Seagull Books, p. 73.

Muslim, against all evidence to the contrary, becomes a source of national strength: "We know who they truly are, and never again will we be violated by their deceptions."

And yet from the position of the Questioner, the function of this opacity when it comes to how others see and judge him becomes transparent as the crutch which racist societies require in order to keep themselves whole. Put simply, the fixities of the deep but ultimately brittle classifications which name the Muslim serve to keep the notion of white Europe safe from its own contradictions and violence. This high degree of baseness is transparent not through some Archimedean plateau on which the Muslim sits, but simply by being in and with the world, which the base racial categories—if not race itself—always already disallows. The policy of ignorance that configured the historic and contemporary confusions of Europe and Britain (imagined white) with "civilization" per se[2] is made plain as a constitutive perversion, however fortified it may be by constant talk of the border—that most opaque of ideas— and bodies which violate its sacred line. The refusal of the Muslim Questioner is an opening up, an enlarging of the social world. Transparency, as I use it, is an exposure, of opening the European province up to the world. Race as a principle of both civil and international society, extraction, surveillance, and all the rest, on the other hand, is a principle of foreclosure, opacity, of shutting down, of restriction, and burying one's proverbial head in the dirt.[3]

The many signs that mark the mutation (and generalization) of colonialism and its principles, or more accurately, their reproduction in contemporary logics—of war, stigmatization, extraction, digitization, and much more—arrive with widespread efforts in Britain of revisionism, to justify, retroactively, the colonial experiment and the venal and arbitrary forms of rule which set its terms. But whatever the mode of confrontation—institutional or cultural, on government white paper, in museums, inscribed on the plinth or the statue— a genuine engagement with this history requires a *denationalization of the imagination*. It is the emancipatory potential—indeed a profound mechanism of survival—of denationalization that the Muslim Questioner also posits in the making-transparent of the racial, but also national, cultural, and power formation.

---

[2] That is, those "Christian nations" of Europe that defined themselves as "creators and representatives of an order applicable to the whole earth." Carl Schmitt. (2003). *The Nomos of the Earth in the International Law of the Jus Publicum Europaeum*, trans. G. L. Ulmen. New York: Telos, p. 86.

[3] Bill Schwarz. (2011). *Memories of Empire Trilogy*. New York: Oxford University Press; Bill Schwarz. (2003). "Claudia Jones and the West Indian Gazette Reflections on the Emergence of Post-Colonial Britain." *Twentieth Century British History*, 14(3), 264–85; Gilroy, *After Empire*; Stuart Ward, ed. (2001). *British Culture and the End of Empire*. Manchester: Manchester University Press.

DENATIONALIZATION OF THE IMAGINATION

In Muslim reference to the Qur'anic concept of the "ummah," we might learn something about denationalization, an imaginary that forges a community of belonging that is not, indeed cannot be constrained by the various forms of bordering which seek to keep subjects in or out, in both literal and epistemic ways. Islam, as the theorist Salman Sayyid notes, "interrupts the logic of the nation by highlighting the problem of integration; that is, how to include various populations within the boundaries of a nation, while at the same time focusing on the problem of their loyalties to an edifice larger than the nation."[4] The *ummah*, therefore, cannot easily be a nation (accumulated by the state) that insists, as it does in the British case, on an exclusionary force that functions through deep investments in a "common market" inaugurally forged in the cauldron of empire. Nor does it conceive a common way of life in unified, that is, homogenized terms. This Muslim community, as Shahab Ahmad notes, "is constituted in the self-consciousness of each Muslim by the held and experienced the fact that all of its members share a somehow or a something called Islam—whatever that may be or mean to each one of them. In the self-consciousness and self-identity of every Muslim *qua* Muslim is the sense that s/he is a part of an isolable and bounded domain of meaningful phenomena—and, one would add, an isolable and bounded domain of persons and spaces—that is Islam; no matter how vast, differentiated or contested that domain of meaning might be."

Through the ummah, Muslims can think transnationally, while living and acting locally, while situating themselves in a tradition for which travel (and cosmopolitanism) are a necessary part of Muslim's spiritual and also material identity: As Eickelman and Piscatori explain:

> Muslim doctrine explicitly enjoins or encourages certain forms of travel. One is the express obligation to undertake the pilgrimage to Mecca (*hajj*). Another, *hijra*, is the obligation to migrate from lands where the practice of Islam is constrained to those where in principle no such constraints exist. Visits to local or regional shrines (*ziyaras*) and travel in search of knowledge (*rihla*) provide

---

[4] Salman Sayyid, Recalling the Caliphate, p. 103. For Sayyid, the project of Islamism, problematically, heralds the decolonization of the ummah. He writes: "Thus, Muslims often find themselves in a situation in which the dominant descriptions of the world conducted in 'Westernese' are no longer adequate and the project of speaking through Islam is, as yet, not fully developed. Thus, Muslims have to muddle through, bilingually starting in one language but trying to develop another language, as yet unrecognised, a language considered at best a dialect. The effect of this is to maintain Islam and Muslims within a colonial framework from which it is impossible to generate enduring solutions to the many problems and difficulties that confront the ummah. Ways forward require the decolonisation of the ummah, not only in terms of its cultural, economic and political subordination but also in terms of the states of knowledge that enable such subordination." *Recalling*, p. 10.

further examples of religiously inspired travel. Yet other forms of travel unrecognized in doctrine can have equal or even greater significance. For example,
Muslims have often mixed travel for trade purposes with religiously motivated
travel.[5]

Travel and the Muslim (Questioner) as forging a denationalization of the
imagination comes through an apparently contradictory relationship with
territory, place, and direction. The Islamic feminist scholar Miriam Cooke
summarizes this incisively:

> The first [Muslim relationship to territory] is transnational and deterritorialized.
> Pointing *forward*, it narrates social fragmentation and occasional consociations.
> Muslims are scattered throughout most countries of the world; they are not
> members of a single nation. At least once in the lifetime of each Muslim there
> is awareness of this radical internationalism, when the individual performs the
> sacred duty of pilgrimage to Mecca. During the month of the *hajj*, Muslim
> pilgrims from all corners of the world, each national group in its national
> delegation, converge on two Saudi Arabian cities. Mecca and Medina become
> microcosms of the multicultural Muslim world.
>
> The second Muslim story is national and, looking *backward*, it roots itself in
> a specific territory. Despite the fact that they are citizens of most countries of the
> world, Muslims can invoke the unifying politics of *umma*, known in the modern
> period as pan-Islamism. In so doing, they link the transnational with the national
> story by projecting themselves as the "diaspora" of a seventh-century bedouin
> tribe in the Arabian Peninsula.[6]

This double consciousness of place and direction is instructive for the volatility of the present in which we are witness to the denationalization of true
centers of decision-making and the paradigmatic principle of offshoring, of
wealth as much as of violence, debt, and bodies. The recurring terror of the
global wars on/of terror, the racist *anxiogenics* of Euro-America, especially
to the presence of Muslims, masks, however inadequately, their dread that is

---

[5] Dale Eickelman and James Piscatori, eds. (1990). *Muslim Travellers: Pilgrimage, Migration, and the Religious Imagination*. Berkeley: University of California Press, p. 5.
[6] Miriam Cooke. (2000). *Multiple Critique: Islamic Feminist Rhetorical Straegies*. Nepantla: Views from the South 1(1), p. 98. It is also important to note, however, that an Arabocentrism, given the geography of the holy sites, is also unsustainable given the inherent heterogeneity across time and place of Muslims, their loci of belonging, pilgrimage, and self-definition. Indeed, the very definition of "Islam" is an unstable one. On this point, see Shahab Ahmad. (2018). *What is Islam? The Importance of Being Islamic*. Princeton: Princeton University Press. Especially pertinent is the Balkans-Bengal complex Ahmed presents as an alternative topography in the post-formative centuries of Islam.

felt for the return of the law of the sword.[7] The logic of the nation has long been interrupted by the movements of bodies, labor, goods, and wealth which constituted its colonial boundaries, but the spatial and political concept of the *ummah* is also a call for Britain and Europe, to reckon with their own finitude. This is a train of thought that it has never had to follow, or has at least refused to acknowledge precisely because it would necessitate an actual accounting of its source.

The supreme and distinctly racial ideas of the "British race" and, more broadly, Europe have always been posited on their inevitability. These are notions that have been defined by their *excess*, the infinitude of their Being against lesser beings. Instead, the fractures of our present condition, whether evidenced in the resurrection of *lex talionis* or the apparently global Muslim problem, or both together, make plain that there will no longer be, if there ever was, a unique center of the world. And this opening-up is irreversible. The forces of history do not end at (ever-shifting) national borders. The cycles of movement and war tie the global battle against terrorism to migrant crises in which people seek escape and asylum from the violent technologies of "democracy": the surgical strike, the regime change, the drone. The history of colonialism that binds Britain, for example, to the Commonwealth from which migrants have previously arrived is erased in pronouncements of the same colonial transnational grouping as the core of new market growth after Britain's exit from the European Union.[8]

---

[7] Frantz Fanon's articulation of the colonial project and its violence is one underpinned by a logic of retaliation and of vengeance. See: *Wretched of the Earth* and *Black Skin, White Masks*; Frantz Fanon. (2011). "Pourquoi nous employons la violence." In *Œuvres*, edited by Magali Bessone and Achille Mbembe. Paris: La Découverte. See also: I. Wallerstein. (1970). "Frantz Fanon: Reason and Violence." *Berkeley Journal of Sociology*; S. Chan. (2007). "Fanon: The Octogenarian of International Revenge and the Suicide Bomber of Today." *Cooperation and Conflict*, 42(2), 151–68.

[8] Often invoking "a shared history and cultural ties," plans for the vast African continent (in which British companies control more than $1 trillion worth of Africa's key resources) and the Commonwealth (a good number of members of which are attempting to sue the British government for reparations for four centuries of slavery) as sources of post-Brexit enrichment are presented matter-of-factly. These shared ties bespeak, of course, a brutal imperial past of theft, violence, and death. The dream of "Empire 2.0," as it has been labeled is remarkable in its ignorance of history, but also to our contemporary realities in which black and brown people are regarded with contempt and with racism and its attendant violence on the rise. These potential trade projects also speak to the re-racialization of the Commonwealth and former British colonies in "emerging market" terms, occluding from view the historical circumstances which allow these very projected trade deals. On this history and racial economism in "Brexit" idea see: Sivamohan Valluvan. (2019). *The Clamour of Nationalism: Race and Nation in Twenty-First-Century Britain*. Manchester: Manchester University Press; Shilliam, *Race and the Undeserving Poor* and Lisa Tilley's piece on the broader trend of (re)racialization in economic terms, here: Lisa Tilley. (2018). "Recasting and Re-Racialising the 'Third World' in 'Emerging Market' Terms: Understanding Market Emergence in Historical Colonial Perspective." *Discover Society*. Available at: https://discoversociety.org/2018/09/04/recasting -and-re-racialising-the-third-world-in-emerging-market-terms-understanding-market-emergence-in -historical-colonial-perspective/. On these themes in the racialized context of Brexit, see also: Financial Times. (2018). "A British illusion of Commonwealth trade after Brexit." *Financial Times*.

"I don't believe in nations anymore," James Baldwin told *Essence*'s Ida Lewis: "Those passports, those borders are as outworn and useless as war. No one can afford them anymore. We're such a conglomerate of things. Look at the US black man, all that blood in a single stream. Look at the history of anybody you might know. He may have been born in Yugoslavia, raised in Germany, exiled to Casablanca, killed in Spain. That's our century."[9] This has only intensified in our own century. Elsewhere when asked about London, he would say, "I like London. I like the space, I like the sky," yet "he could never forget that London was the capital of the slavers, which was 'the backbone of European affluence.' It was true that African warriors had handed over the Negroes to the British ships. 'But the black slavers didn't build a city called London. Your tribe did.'"[10] The Muslim Questioner, in his very presence on the Streetspace of Britain, recognizes that he is engaged in a kind of competition with these associations that many wishes were hidden or simply not there, but which are nonetheless everywhere visible and, in some cases, quite literally make the city.

THE QUESTIONS OF (ISLAMIC) FEMINISM

Again, the struggle(s) and the questions of Islamic feminism(s)[11] are deeply instructive, especially in relation to historical attempts to denationalize political

---

Available at: https://www.ft.com/content/2761fc62-42eb-11e8-93cf-67ac3a6482fd; https://theconversation.com/why-brexit-cant-transform-commonwealth-trade-94919; Andrew Dilley. (2018). "Why Brexit Can't Transform Commonwealth Trade." *The Conversation*. Available at: https://www.theguardian.com/news/2018/apr/10/commonwealth-uk-brexit-leaving-eu; Ian Jack. (2018). "Britain Sees the Commonwealth as Its Trading Empire. It Is Sadly Deluded." *Guardian*. Available at: https://www.theguardian.com/commentisfree/2018/apr/07/britain-commonwealth-trading-empire-brexit-eu-trade; Afua Hirsch. (2018). "The Scramble for Africa Has Moved on, but Britain Hasn't." *Guardian*. Available at: https://www.theguardian.com/commentisfree/2018/sep/04/africa-britain-trade-theresa-may-brexit. On "Empire 2.0" see: Annabelle Dickson. (2018). "Ex-colonies to UK: Forget Brexit 'Empire 2.0'." *Politico*. Available at: https://www.politico.eu/article/commonwealth-summit-wont-be-empire-2-0-for-brexit-uk/; David Olusoga. (2017). "Empire 2.0 Is Dangerous Nostalgia for Something that Never Existed." *Guardian*. Available at: https://www.theguardian.com/commentisfree/2017/mar/19/empire-20-is-dangerous-nostalgia-for-something-that-never-existed; James Blitz. (2017). "Post-Brexit Delusions about Empire 2.0." *Financial Times*. Available at: https://www.ft.com/content/bc29987e-034e-11e7-ace0-1ce02ef0def9; Julianne Schultz. (2018). "Why the Dream of Empire 2.0 Is Still 'cobblers'." *Guardian*. Available at: https://www.theguardian.com/world/2018/feb/11/ties-that-still-bind-the-enduring-tendrils-of-empire

[9] Quoted in Ida Lewis. "Conversation: Ida Lewis and James Baldwin." Baldwin, *Conversations*, 83–92.

[10] Daily Mail. (1965). "If this Man Didn't Exist He'd have to be Invented." *Daily Mail*, February 22, p. 8.

[11] I am alive to the inherent internal multiplicity of the project that might be called "Islamic feminism." Asma Barlas, for example, resists the identification of her work as "feminist" citing feminism's hegemonic subsumption/accumulation of all efforts toward women's equality, that is, the imposition of the "language" of feminism on all efforts toward equality which "flatten out

imaginations, and prompt us to ask ourselves the different questions. Speaking of the geopolitics of feminist consciousness, Houria Bouteldja asks us:

> Do white women really have an instinctive, feminist consciousness? What are the historical conditions that have *enabled* feminism? It's impossible not to relocate the basis of the *possibility* of feminism within a specific geopolitical moment: that of capitalist and colonial expansion, made possible by the "discovery of America" and by another foundational moment: the French Revolution, itself a condition of the emergence of the rule of law and of the individual citizen. The French Revolution became a promise—the promise of the recognition of complete and total universal citizenship—which was obviously not kept since this citizenship was at first reserved to men. It later became a possible horizon for women because, from then on, thanks to the principles of the revolution, they would be able to solve the equation: if the individual is a citizen, and woman is an individual, then woman is a citizen in full right. . . . Feminism would take a long time to develop (it reached its apogee in the 1970s) but would always be contained within the framework of liberal democracies, founded on the idea of

---

important differences" between (Muslim) women. That "when we call something Islamic feminism we close off the possibility of seeing it as anything else and it is this closure that I [Barlas] find problematic." There is, for Barlas, a dimension of epistemic violence when all efforts of Muslim women's equality and struggles against sexist dehumanization are labeled feminist. Asma Barlas. (2007). "Engaging Feminism: Provincializing Feminism as a Master Narrative." Paper presented at Tempere Peach Research Institute. Finland. August 31. http://www.asmabarlas.com/TALKS /Finland_07.pdf. In my use of the terms Islamic feminism, however, I follow Margot Badran and Sa'diyyah Shaikh usage, and Aisha Hidayatullah's synthetical approach insofar as Islamic feminism speaks to a set of commitments and strategies against sexism and male domination which arises out of a faith commitment. It is a collective epistemological project, modes of critical thought, and an inclusive language employed to challenge the abuse of male power in society, in the interpretation of the Qur'an and much more. See: Margot Badran. (2009). *Feminism in Islam: Secular and Religious Convergences*. Oxford: Oneworld and (1999). "Toward Islamic Feminisms: A Look at the Middle East." In *Hermeneutics and Honor: Negotiating Female "Public" Space in Islamic/ate Societies*, edited by Asma Afsaruddin. Cambridge: Harvard University Press, pp. 159–88; Sa'diyyah Shaikh. (2003). "Transforming Feminisms: Islam, Women and Gender Justice." In *Progressive Muslims: On Justice, gender and Pluralism*, edited by Omid Safi. Oxford: Oneworld, pp. 147–62; Aysha A. Hidayatullah. (2014). *Feminist Edges of the Qur'an*. Oxford: Oxford University Press. For sources which account for the political and historical developments pertinent to the issue of women in Islam outside the purview of this study, see: Yvonne Yazbeck Haddad and John L. Esposito, eds. (1998). *Islam, Gender, and Social Change*. New York: Oxford University Press; Leila Ahmed. (1992). *Women and Gender in Islam: Historical Roots of a Modern Debate*. New Haven: Yale University Press; Nadal-Ali. (2000). *Secularism, Gender, and the State in the Middle East: The Egyptian Women's Movement*. Cambridge: Cambridge University Press; Margot Badran. (1995). *Feminists, Islam, and Nation: Gender and the Making of Modern Egypt*. Princeton: Princeton University Press; Margot Badran. (2009). *Feminism in Islam: Secular and Religious Convergences*. Oxford: Oneworld; Margot Badran ed. (2011). *Gender and Islam in Africa: Rights, Sexuality, and Law*. Stanford: Stanford University Press; Deniz Kandiyoti, ed. (1991). *Women, Islam, and the State*. Philadelphia: Temple University Press; and Nilufer Gole. (1996). *The Forbidden Modern: Civilization and Veiling*. Ann Arbor: University of Michigan Press.

the equality of citizens, and in which white women obtained rights, because of their own struggle, of course, but *also* thanks to imperial domination.[12]

The imperial conditions of possibility for the emergence and integration of "women" as a political and economic category are but one of the numerous techniques to maintain, if not further expand (through the accumulation of bodies and labor at home), racial logics elsewhere.

Put simply, then as now, questions of gender (and more recently, sexuality)[13] are instrumentalized for racist and Islamophobic ends.[14] In highlighting the specifically Muslim and Islamic investments in forms and practices of masculine domination, sanctioned by some male authorities and thus, it is assumed, by Allah himself, what is often obscured is the existence, not to mention fatal effects, of phallocracy at home. The overinvestment in virility—of the nation, of the army and border regime, of our markets, of our global reach—is an important social and political ingredient in which the increase in speed and force becomes a hegemonic symbolic principle and necessary effect of the *Becoming-Great-of-Britain*. This much we should know. But I think there is much to be learned from the ambivalent location of "Muslim women" (as Cooke and others speak of them) for our awareness of the possibility and indeed the reality of multiple belongings and speaking positions of *all* people while maintaining a vigilance toward the "potential for conformist pressures within the community celebrated by pluralists."[15]

Denationalization is also a call to denaturalization. The question of who is from here and who is not; what should be done to those who are "here" but are actually from "there"; and also, the fundamental(ist) entities of "here" and "there" that have long been colored by race. New information technologies have disrupted old certainties—of identity, yes, but also economy, security, governance, and much else—while compelling new coalitions. Phallocracies,

---

[12] Buteldja, *Whites*, pp. 89–90.

[13] See the increasingly popular notion and critique of homonationalism. See: J. Puar. (2013). "Rethinking Homonationalism." *International Journal of Middle East Studies*, 45(2), 336–39; J. K. Puar. (2015). "Homonationalism as Assemblage: Viral Travels, Affective Sexualities." *Revista Lusófona de Estudos Culturais*, 3(1), 319–37; J. K. Puar. (2007). *Terrorist Assemblages: Homonationalism in Queer Times*. Duke University Press. Sara Farris's engagement with the political economy of homonationalism is also useful: Sara Farris. (2018). "The Political Economy of Homonationalism." *Social Text*. Available at:https://socialtextjournal.org/periscope_article/the-political-economy-of-homonationalism/

[14] On the Sexuality Question and/in Islam, see: Puar, *Terrorist Assemblages*; Massad, *Islam in Liberalism*, especially the chapter 'Pre-Positional Conjunctions: Sexuality and/in "Islam"'; Joseph Massad. (2002). "Re-Orienting Desire: The Gay International and the Arab World." *Public Culture*, Spring; Abdelwahab Bouhdiba. (1975). *La sexualité en Islam*. Paris: Presses universitaires de France; Khaled El-Rouayheb. (2005). *Before Homosexuality in the Arab-Islamic World, 1500-1800*. Chicago: University of Chicago Press.

[15] Hollinger, D. (1995). *Postethnic America: Beyond Multiculturalism*. New York: Basic Books, pp. 84–86.

led by strongmen who are part dictator, part buffoon, often work on crude racial and gendered axes, always undone by the denationalized imagination, body, and memory which necessarily opens up the world for conjugation in the plural. For the religious, it can be argued that "meaning is organized around a primary identity (that is an identity that frames the others), that is self-sustaining across time and space. . . . The search for meaning takes place then in the reconstruction of defensive identities around communal principles[,] . . . religion provides a collective identity under the identification of individual behavior and society's institutions to the norms derived from God's law, interpreted by a definite authority that intermediates between God and humanity."[16] The radical connectivity of networked societies such as Britain have fostered a kind of cosmopolitanism marked by religion, especially in the context of regimes of global Islamophobia, that is guided, in my view, most radically and constructively by transnational Muslim (anti-racist, anti-imperial) feminist struggles in which I locate the Muslim Questioner.

I am alive to the inherent internal heterogeneity of "Islamic feminism,"[17] as well as the categories "Muslim" and "woman."[18] However, I am less concerned here with an analysis of the neoliberal technologies of the self that can be subverted by the Muslimwoman than with the fact that "race" and its economies of abstraction, which mark certain bodies and authorize certain modes of behavior toward them, are transparently inadequate. "Primary identities," whether occasioned or propelled by network societies, are limited by definition because they leave no breathing room for those who do not relate to that "primary identity." Racism and Islamophobia, I contend, are systems and gestures—hydraulic, state-sponsored, molecular—that maintain investments in "white" and "nonwhite," which are experiencing both processes of erosion and last-gasp rationalization. What was once understood by some to be *the*

---

[16] Manuel Castells. (1997). *The Power of Identity.* Oxford: Blackwell, p. 7, 11, 13.

[17] For a range of positions on Islam and feminism, see: Fatima Mernissi. (1991). *The Veil and the Male Elite: A Feminist Interpretation of Women's Rights in Islam,* trans. Mary Jo Lakeland. Reading, MA: Addison-Wesley, and (1987). *The Fundamentalist Obsession with Women: A Current Articulation of Class Conflict in Modern Muslim Societies.* Lahore, Pakistan: Simorgh/Women's Resource and Publication Centre; and Amina Wadud. (2006). *Inside the Gender Jihad: Women's Reform in Islam.* Oxford: Oneworld. For more critical assessments, see: Ghada Karmi. (1996). "Women, Islam and Patriarchalism." In *Feminism and Islam: Legal and Literary Perspectives,* edited by Mai Yamani. New York: New York University Press, pp. 69–85. For a general overview of pertinent issues, see: Miriam Cooke. (2000). "Women, Religion, and the Postcolonial Arab World." *Cultural Critique* (45), 150–84; and Leila Ahmed, *Women and Gender in Islam*; Aisha Hidayatullah, *Feminist Edges of the Quran*; "Islamic Feminism: What's in a Name?" Al-Ahram Weekly online, no. 569 (January 17–23, 2002) http://weekly.ahram.org.eg/2002/569/ cul.htm; "Between Secular and Islamic Feminism: Reflections on the Middle East and Beyond." *Journal of Middle East Women's Studies,* 1(1), 6–28; and M. Badran. (2010). "Où en est le féminisme islamique ?" *Critique internationale,* 46(1), 25–44.

[18] See: Castelli, ed. (2001). *Women, Gender, and Religion: A Reader.* New York: Palgrave, p. 4.

human—white, male, propertied, Christian—has now become the subaltern subject who requires his/her whiteness in order to speak.

On the contrary, Muslim women everywhere are seriously challenging the primary identity of the Muslimwoman whether fabricated by the disciplinary regimes of the "neo-Orientalists" or Muslims themselves. In the recurring terror of the world after 9/11, the racism, Orientalism, and Islamophobia that is *of* Britain (and *of* the "West") are, ironically, "doing the work of the Islamists in relaunching the Muslimwoman at precisely the moment when the West is intent upon containing Islamists. Could such Western embrace of the Muslimwoman be the gendered equivalent of a penchant for backing repressive (patriarchal) regimes?"[19] The useful figure of the Muslimwoman plays a twin and contradictory role in authorizing judgment of Muslims at home and abroad, simultaneous to constituting an Other form of license to lend support to repressive patriarchal regimes, who become fodder for legitimizing racial narratives and exclusionary state practices in relation to Muslims at home.

When the twin towers fell and Britain and the West riveted their attention to the Muslim world and the Muslim minority in its domestic population, "Islamophobia raged and the religion and its adherents were feared and denigrated. In the West, the Muslimwoman was conjured as the symbol of degradation in this demonizing frenzy. September 11 laid bare what many really thought and what they "knew" about Islam and Muslims, which they typically rolled into one."[20] Yet despite the mobilization of the Muslimwoman as the designer icon of Islamic oppression (and the Mussel*man* as its exclusive source), Muslim women globally, in Britain and across the Muslim world, continue to struggle for and exhibit "a woman-sensitive and gender-egalitarian version of Islam through their literary and artistic production . . . as well as through their hermeneutic production and sharia activism, otherwise known as Islamic feminism."[21] The politics of the Muslimwoman, like those who fabricate and hail her, depends on the nation-state, its modus operandi vis-à-vis race, gender and nation, and lives in, or rather above, a world of circulating abstractions. Indeed, the Muslimwoman even in its cosmopolitan garb can be quite straightforwardly "integrated into either the neoliberal forms of globalization and consumerism or as the target of a militarized gaze

---

[19] Margot Badran. (2008). "Between Muslim Women and the Muslimwoman." *Journal of Feminist Studies in Religion,* 24(1), 102.
[20] Ibid., p. 103.
[21] Ibid., p. 104.

to be saved from her barbaric cultural and religious traditions"[22] not simply through practices of state but also strategies of self-identification.[23]

The politics of the Muslim Questioner is always one in progress, unstable and shifting. On the contrary, the "mass morality" of racism—those fundamentalist formulations posed in the Muslim Question(ed)—are stagnated, against all arguments and projections to the contrary, by its need to keep alive "primary identities" of white Britishness and the Muslim alike. This also holds true, we should remember, in work to ameliorate the conditions of life for those who wear the "correct" names of "white"—working class or otherwise—and thus fully human/ist.[24] The transparency of Britain's deficient civilizational thinking and invidious hermeneutic that it authorizes, can never really serve but a few. What I have attempted to show in this study is that in the productive power to name Muslims, and specifically Muslim women, as abject subjects (whose abjection can be classified and flowcharted) simultaneously constitutes the subjective location of those doing the naming. In the calculus of (post-)colonial nomenclature, "Orientalists gain positional superiority and become constituted as "civilized subjects"; Islamists shore up patriarchal male authority as a dominant religious subject; politicians become the so-called guardians of secularism and democracy; NGOs become benevolent saviors; and academics are produced as authoritative interlocutors in our narratives. Dissident Muslim women become "good Muslim women" as they claim the authority to define other, "bad Muslims."[25]

---

[22] Minoo Moallem. (2008). "Muslim Women and the Politics of Representation." *Journal of Feminist Studies in Religion,* 24(1), 108.

[23] Inderpal Grewal. (2005). *Transnational America: Feminisms, Diasporas, Neoliberalisms.* Durham, NC: Duke University Press, p. 20.

[24] A caveat is necessary here. Obsession with the category of the white working class, especially after the result of the EU referendum in 2016, is showing itself to fuel a racialized inequality in the north of England. Researchers of a report by the Runnymede Trust and the University of Leeds have argued that the "mystical" demographic of the white working class as embedded in the Norther Powerhouse Agenda, leaves "very little space for ethnic or racial diversity" and engages "very little thinking about these places that are not cosmopolitan like Manchester or Leeds." The report is available here: Roxana Barbulescu, Adrian Favell, Omar Khan, Claudia Paraschivescu, Rosie Samuel, and Albert Varela. (2019). "Class, Race and Inequality in Northern Towns." *Runnymede Trust.* Available at:https://www.runnymedetrust.org/projects-and-publications/employment-3/class-race-and-inequality-in-northern-towns.html. See also: Robbie Shilliam, *Race and the Undeserving Poor*; Valluvan, *The Clamour of Nationalism*; Dorling and Tomlinson, *Rule Britannia*; Maya Wolfe. (2019). "Obsession with White Working Class Fuels Inequality in North, Study Warns." *Guardian.* Available at: https://www.theguardian.com/uk-news/2019/aug/15/white-working-class-fuels-inequality-north; Ian Taylor. (2009). "Myths of the White Working Class." *Socialist Review,* 336. Available at: http://socialistreview.org.uk/336/myths-white-working-class; Gargi Bhattacharyya. (2017). "The Myth of the 'white working class' Stops Us Seeing the Working Class as It Really Is." *Red Pepper.* Available at: https://www.redpepper.org.uk/the-myth-of-the-white-working-class/.

[25] Jasmin Zine. (2008). "Lost in Translation: Writing Back from the Margins." *Journal of Feminist Studies of Religion,* 24(1), 111–12. See also: Mamdani, *Good Muslim, Bad Muslim*; and Morsi (2017). *Radical Skin, Moderate Masks.*

The Muslim Questioner aims to release oneself and society from the circulation of abject subjects (which are really objects) to produce a more just location whose foundational principle becomes one of hospitality regardless of travel, movement, and documentation. This is unsettling work. The principle "we are human beings, and that is all" is one which exposes the narrowness of our own being. Not in the abstracted forms demanded by racism, Islamophobia, and dehumanization, but as an affirmation of the inherent and inescapable heterogeneity of the world, the only one we have and that must be shared by all. I am not arguing that we can leave behind processes of naming—whether psychic or institutional—according to some person-less futurity, one that is equally invested in convenient claims to objectivity. We might argue, returning to Cooke's *Muslimwoman*, that even with her recognition of the politics of "caging" proliferating identities accounting also for processes of transnational feminist engagement, in the category of the Muslimwoman itself there may be an inadvertent reproduction of the cage in its critique. That the Muslimwoman as an archetype places Muslim women— and, thus, all Muslims—into a new discourse and category which asserts the neologism as an ontological status. That whatever a Muslim woman's individual experience, politics, and memories, whether moving with, challenging or unaware of, the cage, she is Muslimwoman nonetheless.

Perhaps this is a discursive imposition, and thus imaginative limitation, that I am equally guilty of in my archetype of the Muslim Questioner. That the Muslim Questioner is a mere ventriloquism of an imagined warrior-subject who cannot exist. The process of naming is fraught. My express purpose for the Muslim Questioner at this stage, located within the notion of transparency and a series of refusals, is to signal a set of disruptive commitments, and argue that in simply living and surviving, Muslims challenge the economies and economics of abstraction, of naming through "race." Around the world "in their demeanor, lives, and work, Muslim women are acting out and displaying the diversity that is theirs and the umma's, and indeed the strengths of both. The Muslimwoman as a construction has limited utility and limited credibility—as Muslim women prove."[26] The October 2007 edition of *Agenda Intercultural* captured this in an excellent cartoon. It featured three very different-looking women, one of whom was wearing a hijab, and an exasperated man who says, "And we know the Muslim woman is, ah, zut! *Why does the Muslim woman always refuse to be what I think she is?*"[27] The demand for the Muslim to be that which is familiar to those who produce her

---

[26] M. Badran. (2008). "Between Muslim Women and the Muslimwoman." *Journal of Feminist Studies in Religion*, 24(1), 101–106. Indiana University Press

[27] Yacine. (2007) "Cartoon." *Agenda Intercultural*, (256), p. 3.

as such always compromises the racist and the cage of race from which he himself cannot escape.

THE CAGE OF CITIZENSHIP

Citizenship might also be thought of a cage. It is a technique and a matrix of power which seeks to incorporate enough subjects—made citizens—to pursue its primary imperatives of extraction, territorial control, and managing the movement of populations. Sovereign power has always found it necessary to integrate certain layers of the proletariat and, crucially, of women into the social, political, and economic spheres of its national economy to compete in the increasingly sophisticated international political system of colonization and underdevelopment. Race and normative/condemned racial subjects were central to these processes, a fundamentalism that was the glue that gave what amounted to a state of nature some semblance of order, and which allowed the balancing act of despotism and misogyny at home, democracy and feminist unveiling abroad to proceed uninterrupted if not celebrated. European societies, as we know, "were horribly unjust toward women (several thousand 'witches' were immolated there), but also that women, thanks to capitalist and colonial expansion, largely improved their condition on the backs of the colonized."[28] The modern nation-state, the citizen, the project of feminism pursued within these historical parameters are a set of political phenomena birthed, sponsored, and exported in order to resolve *internal*, that is, its own, contradictions. The enlightening of the world and integration of (no longer) faraway subjects, of different complexions and customs, are transparent mechanisms of such ad hoc contradiction management. A denationalization of the imagination, which allows us to track the historical birth and movement of concepts and categories—woman, Muslim, veil, feminist—provokes a constant disturbance in this racial order's coherence.[29]

The racial subject—citizen or otherwise—is one that is necessarily made to exist at a limit: of distance, of reconciliation, of ("our") tolerance. Toward this denationalization, citizenship itself can be a constraining factor and an

---

[28] Bouteldja, *Whites*, p. 91.

[29] Saffiyah Khan's bemusement signifies, in my reading, the profound forgetfulness in Crossland's anger and allegiance to a Defence League and an Englishness whose pretensions to representing the white working class is belied by these historical truths of hypocrisy and contradiction. See: Losurdo, *Liberalism*, chapter 2 and 6. The case of post-Brexit Commonwealth prosperity is interesting. Of the fifty-three countries of the Commonwealth, thirty-one have populations of fewer than three million people. A market nowhere near as substantial as illusions of Empire 2.0 would argue, no matter how rigged the system of exchange. Fourteen countries, however, are tax havens. See: Sally Tomlinson. (2019). "Inequality, Brexit and the End of Empire." *LSE Public Lectures and Events*. Available at: http://www.lse.ac.uk/Events/2019/03/20190329t1830vOT/inequality

essentializing instrument. That citizenship is a currency worth more on the "free" market for those who have been racialized as white, or more accurately, the wealthy (and male) among them.[30] That if Islamophobia has become so insidious, "it is also because it has now become a part of the constitutive drives and economic subjectivity of our times. It has not only become a product to be consumed alongside other goods, objects and commodities,"[31] but it is something one allows—if indeed it is even registered as a choice—because it installs a cage of presumed safety which locks the Muslim but also white people into their assumed primordial origins, in a never-ending struggle of what can only be surrender or death. Citizenship, being British, is brandished in a "society of spectacle,"[32] mired as it is in the phantasms and uninhibited Islamophobia of the war on terror. Racism and Islamophobia, however, are commodities that we can no longer, if we ever could, afford. They demand a set of investments in which racialized (and gendered) subjects become the medium of exchange in the currencies of nation, progress, security, and power. And yet, the Muslim Questioner recognizes that she can never truly be what "race" demands of her, never loyal, still grateful enough. Following Gayatri Spivak, we are called to a feminist internationalism in the mode of the group, *Women Living Under Islamic Law*.[33] Says Spivak,

> For it is against the grain of this responsibility of the national in the international that we feminist internationalists strain. I am thinking now of the worldwide group called Women Living under Islamic Law, extending all the way from North Africa to Indonesia with members from immigrant communities in the First World. These feminist internationalists must keep up their precarious position within a divided loyalty: being a woman and being in the nation, without allowing the West to save them. Their project, menaced yet alive, takes me back to my beginning. It is in their example that I look at myself as a woman, at my history of womaning. Women can be ventriloquists, but they have an immense historical potential of not being (allowed to remain) nationalists; of knowing, in their gendering, that nation and identity are commodities in the strictest sense: something made for exchange. And that they are the medium of that exchange.
>
> When we mobilize that secret ontic intimate knowledge, we lose it, but I see no other way. We have never, to quote *Glas*, been virgin enough to be the

---

[30] Of course, this cage of citizenship and its denial to a section of the population is not only the case in a Europe imagined white but plagues the innumerable techniques of caging travel. See Devji's discussion of citizenship status denied to the significant population of foreigners in the Gulf. Devji, *Landscapes*, pp. 72–73.

[31] Mbembe, 'Society of Enmity', p. 33.

[32] Debord, G. (1994). *The Society of the Spectacle*. New York: Zone Book.

[33] A introduction to the transnational solidarity network can be found here: "About WLUML". Available at: http://www.wluml.org/node/5408

Other. . . . Cultures are built violently on the enforced coercion that they are. War is its most extreme signature, and, like all signatures, patriarchal. Our lesson is to act in the fractures of identities in struggle.[34]

The denationalization of the imagination makes plain the racial province that citizenship all too often consolidates. Migrancy, on the other hand, is necessarily (imaginatively and materially) denationalized insofar as it points to a community of belonging more capacious, more worldly than a social and cultural imaginary which submits itself to the figure of the citizen and the father of the nation-state as the only centers of meaning and living.

The specifically Muslim diasporic condition of the ummah, but without a single "motherland," is an instructive denationalized mode of imagining and "sense of connectedness"[35] with the world and to others. It insists on overlapping histories, geographies, obligations that the sacralization of a "citizen" and by consequence the border, obscures, if not altogether erases. Further, the particular denationalizing resources offered by the disobedience of (Muslim) feminist consciousness brings into view the essential gendered effects of constituting the ideal subject of the nation, of white Europe. An interaction between James Baldwin and Audre Lorde is instructive. Baldwin says "A woman does know much more than a man." Audre Lorde in response: "And why? For the same reason Black people know what white people are thinking: because we had to do it for our survival."[36] There must be, I read Lorde to tell us, a commitment to a transnationalism that remains rooted in specific places and identities, perhaps more accurately captured by "translocalism" that invites the postnational as a condition of being, one that is embedded in the messiness of the world, in the impossibility of knowing much and the necessary struggle to learn, and a mode of being which militates for making heterogeneity thrive. Says Audre Lorde, "It's vital for me to be able to listen to you, to hear what it is that defined you and for you to listen to me, to hear what it is that defines me—because so long as we are operating in that old pattern, it doesn't serve anybody, and it certainly hasn't served us."[37] Transparency as I am employing it here is the exposure of the Faustian patterns that racism and Islamophobia surely are. But in the basic fact of his being, the Muslim Questioner poses a series of embarrassing questions for the tale of liberalism, and the hostility which he experiences, whether in the

---

[34] Gayatri Chakravorty Spivak. (1992). "Acting Bits/Identity Talk." Critical Inquiry, 18(4), 770–803.
[35] William A. Graham. (1993). "Traditionalism in Islam: An Essay in Interpretation." *Journal of Interdisciplinary History*, 23, 495–522, at 501, and 521.
[36] The interview between Baldwin and Lorde is available at: James Baldwin and Audre Lorde. (1984). "The Pro-Black Perspective," on KWAZ Radio, with your host Pan-African Nationalist Author Onitaset Kumat. Available at: https://www.youtube.com/watch?v=3_590duLjkw
[37] Ibid.

interrogation room or at the press conference is all evidence which incriminates not him but his investigators.

Domenico Losurdo's work[38] has shown us that the shared contempt for the indigenous of the colonies but also the domestic (and white) working class unified many of Britain's greatest thinkers. That many of Britain's national heroes participated in the practical enslavement and genocide of such peoples *and* respected the utility of deploying the most repressive measures at home among the poor. The workhouse, child labor, and systematic neglect of subjects (white but not yet recognized as such) parallel to the commitments to black enslavement, the slave trade, and the massive project of empire did not precede liberalism but engendered its development. "Race" was not previously inherent in, but became essential to, the formation of liberal, capitalist, and colonial modernity in which the working classes were also disturbing objects until it was convenient. The rebel colonists during their war of independence understood this well when they shouted "we will not be your Negroes" in their fight for liberty and self-determination against the British.[39] The rebels bought into the necessary entanglement of emancipation and de-emancipation, my freedom must come at the expense of another. When does the accumulation of bodies, hearts, and minds—white, white-enough, nonwhite—end? There can only be mutations in, not emancipation from, the propensities of white institutions to elicit violent and vengeful responses to the racial subjects. Impulses which define a natural order built on practices that work to exclude Others from experience, politics, and speech,[40] but leave white people constantly agitated and confused.

THE ALLURE OF DEHUMANIZATION

But the Muslim Questioner realizes, further, that racism and sexism are norms that we have all been born into;[41] distortions which can take root among Muslims as much as "white majorities." An increasingly prominent

---

[38] (2004). *Hegel and the Freedom of the Moderns.* Durham: Duke University Press; (2014). *Liberalism: A Counter-History.* London: Verso; (2015). *War and Revolution: Rethinking the Twentieth Century.* London: Verso; and (2018). *Class Struggle: A Political and Philosophical History.* London: Palgrave Macmillan.

[39] Khiabany and Williamson, "Free Speech and the Market State," p. 576.

[40] Losurdo, *Liberalism*, p. 309.

[41] Audre Lorde has spoken of this self-reflexivity: "It's vital that we deal constantly with racism, and with white racism among black people—that we recognize this as a legitimate area of inquiry. We must also examine the ways that we have absorbed sexism and heterosexism. These are the norms in this dragon we have been born into—and we need to examine these distortions with the same kind of openness and dedication that we examine racism." Cited in: M. Boyd. (2019). "Baldwin and the Black Arts Movement." In *James Baldwin in Context* (Literature in Context), edited by D. Miller. Cambridge: Cambridge University Press, pp. 211–20.

case in point is the phenomenon of anti-black racism among Muslims in Euro-America, in conjunction with an Islamophobic *misogynoir*[42] in wider society. Race has a simultaneously stable and shifting referent, with Muslims in Britain as mostly of South Asian descent complicating the black-white divide, while the consistency of Black Muslim women's experiences of marginalization within the inherently heterogenous Muslim community in Britain and the United States remains in place.

In an interesting case of such absorption, top London Mayoral candidate, Shaun Bailey, has argued that the accommodation of Muslims and Hindus "robs Britain of its community." Bailey is of Jamaican descent and the example of his Islamophobia serves as a good example of the uncertainties of race but also to the unstable character of those who can ask the Muslim Question, despite the realities of institutional racism. In a pamphlet written for the Centre for Young Policy Studies entitled "no man's land," Bailey maintained: "You bring your children to school and they learn far more about Diwali than Christmas. I speak to the people who are from Brent and they've been having Muslim and Hindi days off. What it does is rob Britain of its community. Without our community, we slip into a crime-riddled cess pool."[43] He continued: "There are a lot of really good things about Britain as a place and British people as a body. But by removing the religion that British people generally take to, by removing the ethics that generally go with it, we've allowed people to come to Britain and bring their culture, their country and any problems they might have, with them."[44] The familiar nationalist epidemiology of counterterrorism and integration discourses—of the British nation and culture as a body—is again deployed in relation to the Muslim.

But, for Bailey, this is not the case with the British black community because they do share certain ethical values with British society: "Within the black community, it is not such a bad thing, because we've shared a religion and in many cases a language. It's far easier for black people to integrate,"[45] he said. Without the sense of community Bailey argues for—Christian, non-Muslim, non-Hindu, ethical—Bailey suggests that Britain would have a significant proportion of its population that "would not fight for their country."[46]

---

[42] The term refers to the specific oppression and hatred of black women. See: Moya Bailey and Trudy. (2018). "On Misogynoir: Citation, Erasure, and Plagiarism." *Feminist Media Studies*, 18(4), 762–68; Eliza Anyangwe. (2015). "Misogynoir: Where Racism and Sexism Meet." *Guardian*. Available at:https://www.theguardian.com/lifeandstyle/2015/oct/05/what-is-misogynoir

[43] Shaun Bailey. (2005). *No Man's Land: How Britain's Inner City Young Are Being Failed*. London: Centre for Young Policy Studies, p. 32.

[44] Ibid.

[45] Ibid.

[46] Ibid. Find Shaun Bailey's 2005 report here: https://www.cps.org.uk/files/reports/original/111028105425-NoMansLand.pdf. See also his recent defence of his comments in an interview with the columnist Owen Jones here: Owen Jones and Shaun Bailey. (2019). "Owen Jones Meets

Theresa May later endorsed Bailey as Mayoral candidate at the Conservative Party conference. Mere hours after the revelations about Bailey's report surfaced, May cited Shaun Bailey's prospects as London Mayor as indicative of the Conservative Party's commitment to equality of opportunity. Bailey was, Theresa May said, a man whose "grandparents came to our shores as part of the Windrush generation . . . could be the next mayor of London." The irony of the crime of the Windrush scandal under a Theresa May-led "hostile environment," and the ongoing effects of institutional racism faced by both black and Muslim boys and men, especially with the police, in the context of this self-congratulation likely escaped both Theresa May and Shaun Bailey.

Racism's function and effect toward a retreat from humanity is no less the case with racism *within* Muslim communities also structured by degrees of racial violence and expropriation, whether in the relation to the disposable migrant worker in the beams of Emirati metropolises or black Muslimhood in European metropoles.[47] The unelimibable surplus of humanity, a humanness that cannot be destroyed, even in death, can only form a part of the Muslim Questioner's *denationalism*—via the *ummah*—if it is central to the meaningfulness of one's experience of the idea of the universal community (of Islam) in her conceptualization of Islam and thus herself as Muslim. Simply, Muslims have "a sense of universal human solidarity" across geographical space which forges a mutual implication among peoples regardless of the

---

Shaun Bailey: 'Do You Stand by Your Degrading Comments about Women and Minorities?'" *Owen Jones.* Available at: https://www.youtube.com/watch?v=XSVwQ5LcMLo

[47] Literature which deals with the double bind of being black and Muslim in racial formations, as well as the historic black presence in Islamic history is becoming increasingly prominent. See: Kayla Renée Wheeler's *Black Islam Syllabus.* Available at: https://docs.google.com/document/d/1av hgPrW30AFjegzV9X5aPqkZUA3uGd0-BZr9_zhArtQ/edit and her forthcoming book, *Fashioning Black Islam: Race, Gender and Belonging in the Ummah.* See also: Sherman Jackson. (2014). *Islam and the Problem of Black Suffering.* Oxford: Oxford University Press; Ousmane Oumar Kane. (2016). *Beyond Timbuktu: An Intellectual History of Muslim West Africa.* Cambridge: Harvard University Press; Ahmad Mubarak and Dawud Walid. (2017). *Centering Black Narrative: Black Muslim Nobles Among the Early Pious Muslims.* Illinois: Itrah Press Publishing. See also: Khadeeja Saleem. (2018). "How Should Anti-black Racism in the Muslim Community Be Tackled?" *The Muslim Vibe.* Available at: https://themuslimvibe.com/social-issues/how-should-anti-black-racism-in-the-muslim-community-be-tackled; Emmanuel Mauleon. (2018). "Black Twice: Policing Black Muslim Identities." *UCLA Law Review,* 1326, 1326–90; Emma Green. (2017). "Muslim Americans Are United by Trump—and Divided by Race." *The Atlantic.* Available at: https://www.theatlantic.com/politics/archive/2017/03/muslim-americans-race/519282/; On the triple-bind of being Black, Muslim and woman, see: K. McGuire, S. Casanova, and C. Davis. (2016). "'I'm a Black female who happens to be Muslim': Multiple Marginalities of an Immigrant Black Muslim Woman on a Predominantly White Campus." *The Journal of Negro Education,* 85(3), 316–29; Jamillah A. Karim. (2006). "To Be Black, Female, and Muslim: A Candid Conversation about Race in the American Ummah." *Journal of Muslim Minority Affairs,* 26(2), 225–33; Fahima Hersi. (2019). "On Being Somali: Not Black Enough, Not Muslim Enough." *Amaliah.* Available at: https://www.amaliah.com/post/21386/there-is-no-racism-in-islam-but-there-is-racism-in-the-muslim-community-being-somali. See also the work of *Poetic Pilgrimage,* Britain's first female Muslim hip-hop duo: https://www.aljazeera.com/programmes/witness/2015/03/hip-hop-hijabis-150305091541022.html.

currencies of language, nation, or citizenship. As simultaneous conviction and point of departure, the incoherence of race to any meaningful conceptualization of the ummah constructs a more capacious mode of being in the world which disturbs the contemporary thirst for homogeneity, and the call to vengeance that it licenses, of Muslim and non-Muslim neo-Orientalists, religious extremists, and liberal apologists alike.

IS THIS WORLD WHITE?

An expansive geographical and historical frame is therefore essential. Fanon was convinced that colonialism was at its core a necropolitical force propelled by genocidal impulses. In the myriad contexts that we have thus far analyzed, genocide can be seen to work in ways other than the murder of specific population groups. In fact, genocide often proceeds much more as exposure to slow death, exhaustion, and forms of social eviction. Colonialism and with it the modernity it co-constituted were purified of, and distanced from, the necessary vagaries of the colonial experience and the reality of its projects termed civilization rather than genocide. European centers of progress could thus become and today remain spaces sanctified as civil, democratic, free, and equal regardless of the atrocities continually committed in its name. Instead, the remarkable consistency with which the effects of Europe's "democratic" impulses proceed across the planet, in wars on terror as much as corporate arrangements point to a civilization that is *structurally* genocidal to its very (epistemic) core.[48]

The empire is forever gone and never to return. The critique of suffering, of fear and desire, of law, intimacies, and representation is, in the final analysis, a critique of life, a project that necessitates a critique of codes and categories

---

[48] Fanon, *Dying Colonialism*, pp. 28–29; and Fanon. "Pourquoi nous employons la violence." In *Œuvres*, 413ff.; *Wretched of the Earth*, p. 92; Nelson Maldonado-Torres. (2008). *Against War: Views from the Underside of Modernity*. Durham: Duke University Press, p. 95, 100; Patrick Wolfe. (2006). "Settler Colonialism and the Elimination of the Native." *Journal of Genocide Research*, 8(4), 387–409; Hallaq, *Restating Orientalism*, especially chapter 5; James M. Mooney. (1900). *Historical Sketch of the Cherokee*. Chicago: Aldine Transaction, p. 124. See also A. Dirk Moses. (2017). "Empire, Resistance, and Security: International Law and the Transformative Occupation of Palestine." *Humanity: An International Journal of Human Rights, Humanitarianism, and Development*, 8(2), 379–408; Ilan Pappe. (2014). *The Idea of Israel: A History of Power and Knowledge*. London: Verso; Gershon Shafir. (1996). "Zionism and Colonialism: A Comparative Approach." In *Israel in Comparative Perspective*, edited by Michael N. Barnett. New York: State University of New York Press, 227–42. On the British case specifically, see: Kim A. Wagner. (2018). "Savage Warfare: Violence and the Rule of Colonial Difference in Early British Counterinsurgency." *History Workshop Journal*, 85, 217–37; Caroline Elkins. (2004). *Imperial Reckoning: The Untold Story of Britain's Gulag in Kenya*. New York: Henry Holt & Company and (2005). *Britain's Gulag: The Brutal End of Empire in Kenya*. London: Jonathan Cape; Michelle Gordon. (2015). "Colonial Violence and Holocaust Studies." *Holocaust Studies*, 21(4), 272–91.

which root life as a thing to which various meanings, characteristics, and predispositions can be attached. Muslim life is central to contemporary processes of measurement (classifying, codifying, administrating) and valuation (marking, listing, flowcharting). The logics of older instruments of measurement, such as "the calipers, cephalometers, craniometers, craniophores, craniostats, and parietal goniometers,"[49] mix with the newer imperial conditions of biometric data collection, surveillance, and tracking which are forceful constituents in the politics of hate that racism and Islamophobia empower. As I see it, notions of "here" and "there"; citizen, resident, immigrant; moderate and extremist; traditional and liberal; guilty and innocent are all imbricated in these processes of valuation. Ultimately, they outline what it is we can abdicate and unleash in relations with that subject (or community) who has been found wanting.

The Muslim Questioner is less interested in measurement and value than s/he is with transforming if not overturning historical processes of "translation," legibility, and comprehensibility. It is not, then, the British or any other white people who have to accept the Muslim; *it is the Muslim who has to accept them* for "they are, in effect, still trapped in a history which they do not understand; and until they understand it, they cannot be released from it."[50] In discussing the lack of recognition of the colonial contribution to the war effort, the writer Colin McInnes wrote "for generations they had been nurtured on the idea of England . . . whose history they knew far more intimately than most of us have ever known theirs, and whose language they spoke . . . with the intimacy . . . of a cherished mother tongue."[51] This much remains true. But having built London, that is, drawing the material connections between histories, not simply of celebration but of slavery and colonization, there is the possibility of more just regimes of measurement and value, and, more importantly, a thorough accounting of what has been lost in a world made "white," and what is owed to it.

Transparency names the recognition of the brutalizing demands and insatiable economies propelled and made coherent by racial violence. We must dismantle the obfuscating effects of racism and Islamophobia which sanction an age of war without end, in whose techniques of violence and their public justification we find the echoes of colonialism and mythological feuds with an absolute enemy. This is a kind of dismantling whose creative impulse is a movement toward an alternative set of hopes wherein living among different peoples and cultures is both the creation of the in-common and a form of separation. This impulse becomes the substance of community rather than the

---

[49] Stepan, "Race and Gender: The Role of Analogy in Science," p. 266.
[50] James Baldwin. (1964). *The Fire Next Time.* London: Penguin, p. 8.
[51] MacInnes, Colin. (1961). "Britain's Mixed Half-Million." *Africa South in Exile,* 5(2), 107–115.

border wall which can only understand capture, the stranger and dark intruders for its very existence depends on it.

The integration, assimilation, or dissolution demanded by extractive regimes of imposed hierarchy and its attendant culture of racism serves no meaningful function that might work to produce a freer, more hospitable or just world. It can only ever produce violence of a molecular quality and a politics of hate. But also, the paranoiac, fearful, fidgety condition of the white subject who sees in the Muslim only his Other. As if to speak directly to this world made white, however, Houria Bouteldja reminds us that:

> Everything has an end. Your immune system is weakening. The lacquer is fading. Your social status is weakening. Capitalism, in its neoliberal form, continues to carry out its relentless task. It chips away at your social benefits, or, more accurately, at your privileges. Up until now, to save social democracy, in other words, to save your white middle class interests, you have exploited us. You ordered us to vote tactically. We obeyed. To vote socialist. We obeyed. Then to defend republican values. We obeyed. And above all not to play into the game of the National Front. We obeyed. In other words, we sacrificed ourselves to save you. Two terrible world wars left you with painful memories. "Never again!" You continue to squall this wishful thinking like a broken record, but these psalms have no more impact than the chirping of birds. You no longer want to feed the belly of the beast because, in the past, it devoured you, except it is this beast that feeds you and with which you will devour the world. So, you support the status quo. We pay the bill.[52]

THE ABSURD WAIT/WEIGHT OF RACE

It can be argued that the Muslim does not have the privilege of explicitness, an uninhibited speech that is free from punishment and, in some cases, violence and the call to erase.[53] In the production of Islam and the Muslim as a "thing" from "out there," a blank cartography is continually produced which always invites the enlightened pen, the lucid cognition of "experts," men of letters, policymakers, terror experts, scientists of radicalization who produce a kind of anti-knowledge. In these extremely well-funded industries of insecurity, white Britain has been trained to look outward in order to see itself. As Morsi reminds us, "The almost mythical traits of Islam helped make

[52] Bouteldja, *Whites*, p. 47.
[53] See the excellent essay on context of state-sanctioned attacks on not only speech but respiratory breathing and, therefore, of the radical calling of the breath: Marijn Nieuwenhuis. (2014). "The terror in the air", *openDemocracy*. Available at: https://www.opendemocracy.net/en/terror-in-air/

the West home to the West. Islam's otherness centred Europe as the cultural and rational core of the world. And, it helped legitimate a claim to Europe's universality because it was not this thing, Islam."[54] The dehumanizing "web of racism"[55] that we have sought to excavate here is always already a trap in which its spinners have also been caught. White Europe, in its demotion and fracture, is having to face not only its finitude but the prospect of living with itself. Its disempowerment unleashes a disgust at itself which can no longer be so straightforwardly projected abroad.

In a case not dissimilar to Babar Ahmad's, the incarceration of Talha Ahsan mobilized a massive campaign for his freedom. The Free Talha Ahsan Campaign was able to bring Talha's voice and written words—Ahsan was an accomplished poet—to discussions and debates, strategizing and organizing for justice. In a poem entitled, "This Be the Answer," Ahsan would offer a poetic response to the officer who would ask a bloodied, humiliated, sexually assaulted Babar Ahmad, "Where is your God now?" His response:

A Prisoner on his knees
scrubs around a toilet bowl
and the bristles of the brush
scuttle to and fro
as a guard swaggers over
to yell rather than ask

Where is your God now?

And the prisoner still on his knees
his brush still cleaning answers:

He is with me now, gov.

My God is with me now
hearing and seeing,
whilst your superiors
when they see you, do not look at you
and when they hear you, do not listen to you.[56]

---

[54] Morsi, "Free Speech," p. 11.
[55] Said, *Orientalism*, p. 29.
[56] Talha Ahsan. (2011). "This Be the Answer." In *This Be the Answer: Poems from Prison*. Edinburgh: Radio Ramadan Edinburgh.

Ahsan's words are an incisive critique of our contemporary moment's deep carceral character which generalizes degradation in perpetuity. While its effects are not equally distributed, for the racial subject remains its historic and privileged target, racism's central conceit is that all are touched by, and made complicit in, its numerous deprivations: insecurity, insult, fear, erosions of freedom, stupidity, domination, and various exits from democracy.

It also produces a futurology of the absurd. On August 16, 2019, it was revealed that *SuperSisters*, an online magazine and "a global media platform for young Muslimahs in East London and beyond to share and create inspiring and empowering content with positivity at its core,"[57] was a project that the Home Office had funded and delivered as part of a messaging approach seeking to effect behavioral and attitudinal change among what RICU terms "Prevent audiences,"[58] explicitly defined as British Muslims and specifically Muslim males aged fifteen to thirty. Breakthrough Media, an RICU-favored private sector contractor have stated, privately in internal papers, that its work on behalf of the unit is intended to "promote a reconciled British Muslim identity."[59] All quite familiar.

It turns out, however, that there was only one Muslim woman writing content for the page,[60] the rest of the "content producers" were middle-aged white men also responsible for running the online project, who were masquerading as Muslim women sanctioned by counterterrorism and under the guise of empowerment:[61] the *Becoming-Muslimwoman-of-white-man*. And yet the transparency of this project of concealment is an instructive instance highlighting the lengths those invested in racism's (in)coherence must go in

[57] SuperSisters. "About." Available at: https://www.supersisters.co.uk/about/
[58] On the Cold War roots of the unit, see: Ian Cobain, Bob Evans, Mona Mahmood. (2016). "Inside Ricu, the Shadowy Propaganda Unit Inspired by the Cold War." *Guardian*. Available at: https://www.theguardian.com/politics/2016/may/02/inside-ricu-the-shadowy-propaganda-unit-inspired-by-the-cold-war
[59] Ian Cobain. (2019). "Revealed: The 'woke' Media Outfit that's Actually a UK Counterterror Programme." *Middle East Eye*. Available at: https://www.middleeasteye.net/news/revealed-woke-media-outfit-thats-actually-uk-counterterror-programme
[60] What was presented as a grassroots organization by and for Muslimahs was delivered by two non-Muslims, Jon Hems and Jan Bros, for the Home Office in the name of Muslim women's empowerment. See: Birt, "Astroturfing".
[61] For instructive analyses of the case, see: Asim Qureshi. (2019). "Thread." Available at: https://twitter.com/AsimCP/status/1162462296448352257; Suhaiymah Manzoor-Khan. (2019). "Thread." Available at: https://twitter.com/thebrownhijabi/status/1162616522088599552. The platform has since released a statement: Part One can be found here: https://twitter.com/SuperSistersMag/status/1163829729859919872; Part Two here: https://twitter.com/SuperSistersMag/status/1163829839385829376; and Part Three here: https://twitter.com/SuperSistersMag/status/1163829898038992896. Testimony from former employees of the platform, however, continue to maintain that only a single Muslim woman produced content on the page since its launch in 2016. The rest were middle-aged white men. Further still, a former project manager, Sabah Ismail, experienced direct censorship having been prevented from posting prophetic quotes and references to the Qur'an.

order to do their work. The sinister and deeply worrying character of this case is matched only by its unsettling absurdity. The secrecy of the Muslim Questioned has been further complicated by the neoliberal technologies that dominate our lives, the virtual veil which simultaneously empowers and deceives. Both, however, along racial (and gendered) lines. Yet the transparency of the charade and the exuberant performance demanded from those involved in the labor of white institutions is known to its targets even as it is unknowingly performed by the white "I."

The case of Shamima Begum was apparently one of the reasons the platform was started;[62] how and why? Might the ridicule and moronic, albeit remorseless, cruelty of Begum's treatment in the coverage of her "case" (i.e., *her life*) be connected to the optic of a group of white, suited, middle-aged men hunched over laptops, pretending to be empowered Muslim women in the name of empowering Muslim women, and sanctioned by narratives of, and policies attesting to, Muslims' fundamental inability to emancipate "their" own women? The threat of terror *and* the terrors of the walls separating the racial subject and his Other become floating conditions for the empowerment—through white men—of Muslim women, recalling the muscular feminism of that celebrated British strongman, Lord Cromer and his feminist project of unveiling in colonial Egypt.

Through the Muslim Questioner, I have sought to take up the challenge summarized by Iranian cultural theorist Minoo Moallem:

> it is crucial to interrogate the process of racialization and the articulation of race and religion through gender difference and cultural otherness in the formation and reaffirmation of Muslimwoman in the context of colonial modernity, where Islam as religion and social practice was depicted as the other of the Christian West through gender tropes and gender meanings, as well as through the racialization of the masses of Muslim diasporas and immigrants (mostly from the old colonies in Europe and the United States) and the instigation of such discourses as Islamophobia, Orientalism, and what I have elsewhere called civilizational thinking as they invested in discourses of religious and cultural difference, gender, and binary notions of the West and the rest.[63]

The hallucinogenic work of racism and the abstractions that uphold it goes unnoticed by these men, and others before them, playing *SuperSisters*, the contradictions of their orders and their own debasement surely passing them

---

[62] SuperSisters. (2019). "Status." *Facebook Page*. Available at: https://www.facebook.com/Super-SistersMag/posts/shamima-begum-was-one-of-four-young-british-women-who-fled-to-syria-to-join-isis/2027181044248956/

[63] Moallem, "Muslim Women." p. 108.

by, while their superiors do not look them in the eye. Are there similar processes in place for white feminist platforms in the name of countering white supremacist and patriarchal violence and under the guise of empowerment? Does the banality of "Fundamental British Values" (another Prevent "product") or the events held in their name across, in one example, primary schools in which children dress in the colors of the union jack[64] have in mind their absurdity given the industrial scale of racism and insecurity that is perpetuated by such myths as FBV? Instead, the Muslim Questioner calls for an "attitude of the listener:"[65] an attitude aimed at dismantling the regime of knowledge—the Muslim Question(ed)—predicated on processes of exchange whose mixing, interlacing, and democratizing effects cannot be undone, not on account of "anyone in particular willing it, but by virtue of the historical fact of living it."[66]

The brutality, freneticism, and cynicism that shape encounters between (warring) peoples and nations are mirrored in those peoples' and nations' relationship to the world itself, a world pushed to its limit and that forces us to think about the finitude of not simply provincial notions of the "West," or "Europe" or "Britain," but the earth that is to be inherited and shared. The charge of (neo)liberalism, its racist and Islamophobic effects, and the sophisticated technological vehicles—whether military, corporate, or governmental—become the means by which this absurdity both travels and is propelled.

None of these, however, can hide the fact of the earth's approaching limit and the place of the modern (racial) subject within it. The *SuperSisters* case, therefore, should be seen in connection with the excesses of algorithmic reason, with the "digital-cognitive turn" and the steady fusion of the microchip and biological tissue. Each calls into question the very status of the modern subject but in less productive ways than reckoning with the question of the earth, our place within it, and the unconditional relationship to others who have also inherited it. This is a reckoning which must travel through the history of "race" to be even partially complete. It seems, therefore, that the basic parameters of life need to be (re)thought. By way of a conclusion, I seek to outline the tentative coordinates from which to engage such a pressing project, and in which the Muslim is surely involved.

---

[64] As reported to me by my primary school-aged siblings of nine and seven. Blackburn, our hometown, has long been of particular interest to government integration projects. A cursory search of "British Values Day" results in innumerable primary schools celebrating similar initiatives as the red, white, and blue of the day's fancy dress.

[65] R. White. (2017). "Walter Benjamin: 'The Storyteller' and the Possibility of Wisdom." *The Journal of Aesthetic Education,* 51(1), 1–15.

[66] Dabashi, *Can Non-Europeans Think?*, p. 291.

Chapter 9

Otherwise. Or, Coordinates for an Other World

Various gestures of self-determination, ways of being present with and to oneself, looking both inward and outward, at history, at the world's reception to one's racialized differences, of being Muslim, are pursued here as a form of utopian critique. It is more than a declaration of identity, of Muslimness in response to a world in which the name Muslim provokes insult and alarm, and where white institutions look for him in order to extract a confession or an alibi. The Muslim qua Muslim cannot be thought in white Europe, a civilization filled with chronic dread, and yet this critique is not solely about the fact that s/he might in fact exist where s/he is *not* thought. It is less a question of imagination, then, than it is of praxis. The myriad violations, codices, contracts, legal exceptions, interrogation rooms, and press conferences discussed earlier constitute a social life for the racial subject in which there can be no genuine concern for what might be owed to the Other. Instead, a kind of summoning, in harsher and softer forms, is democratized in liberal societies yearning for a departure from the shadows of history, of the migrant and the Muslim. Europe, in its angst and victimhood, also seeks an outlet for its own confusion and for which the Muslim has become a premier target.

And you, why are you Muslim? *"I promise you all, I am not a threat. We respect the law and treasure our women. We have our peculiarities which I can explain, yes, but I am human, just the same as you."*

The endless reinvention and reproduction of the racial subject as a target of humiliation and discipline should, however, be recognized as the terminal illness of Europe, of its modernity and which forces us to reckon with the fact that her humanity should never be, and, this is the point, indeed never was, in question. Which is to say, I, the white subject's Other, the Muslim, could never have been, in truth, what they say she is, what she appears to be, and what people see her as and say of her within the context of a racial, social, economic, and political order whose sustenance is contingent precisely on the minimization of the Muslim's social status, material presence, and history. It is not that the Muslim exists in an elsewhere, somewhere other than where they are looking for her, or even in fact where she is not thought. The mode of the Muslim Questioner understands that she is pathologically *unable to be thought*. This inability to think the Muslim, and Others of her kind, is integral to the maintenance of the racial order. It is, in fact, *constitutive* of what is able to be thought. This inability to think the racial subject outside of her inherent antagonism to white self is integral to the proliferating programs designed in the name of national security and racial power, knowledge, and governance, which insists on the narcissism of a white-Muslim, core-periphery dynamic, the Woody Allen syllogism—*"God is good, I am good, therefore, I am God"*—bedeviling lucid thought at every turn.

WHAT IS AN ORDER OF TIME?

The Muslim Questioner's refusal of the constant play of "unequal" languages—of democracy, national culture, integration, equality, feminism, private religion, public reason, and much else versus anything the Muslim might say—opens the way to a positive mode of being based on an ideology of equal shares. An order which is no less oriented toward the future, but which treats the past—noble and ignoble—with the epistemic respect that it is surely due.[1] This technique of differentiation without dehumanization "points not to an apologia but to the recognition of what each person, as a human, contributes to the work of the constitution of the world. In any case, the attempt to destroy difference and the dream of imposing a single language on all are both doomed to failure. Unity is always just another name for multiplicity, and the positive difference can only be a difference that is lively and interpenetrating. It is *fundamentally* an orientation toward the future."[2]

This is an orientation that recognizes the wicked inducements, which fill the Muslim Question(ed) and that mediate relations between self and Other. That in the process of excavating history, white Britain, for example, becomes part of the history of India, of Kenya, and of Palestine and its new colonies as much they become a part of it. And as such, one has got to find the terms expansive enough to deal with such a deep cartography, blurred temporality, and planetary scale. Which is to say that the very concept of

---

[1] I am borrowing the title of the excellent review essay by Abdelmajid Hannoum. See: A. Hannoum. (2008). "What Is an Order of Time?" *History and Theory,* 47(3), 458–471.
[2] Mbembe, *Critique*, p. 94.

time and its function as the anchor for psychic events, that is, its fundamental place in the interior structure of subjectivity and the political and economic orders premised on this subject, must be called into question. We must ask questions, therefore, about the role of time and history as reliable anchors.

"Appeals to the past are among the most common of strategies in interpretations of the present," Edward Said has said. "What animates such appeals is not only disagreement about what happened in the past and what the past was, but uncertainty about whether the past really is past, over and concluded, or whether it continues, albeit in different forms."[3] This problem, as I have attempted to show, animates all sorts of discussions—about influence, about blame, and judgment, about the built environment and stolen treasures, about present actualities and future priorities. History is, therefore, present in all that we do, not merely discursively but *materially*.

European modernity as the unfolding of universal history, of homogenous time, is itself the illusion created by the narratives and concept of modernity. "Time" here is not universal but is instead shown to be the provincial European way of naming movement along an invented assembly line of historical transformations and repetitions. Allied with the multiple heads of empire, Western modernity sacrificed Other structures of time and their consequential needs/demands, absolutely and indefinitely, according to a common-sense logic in the name of universal history, homogenous time, Man's improvement, and of civilization's unfolding.[4] It remains, therefore, unable to account for the coexistence of temporalities, of time as simultaneous and nonlinear, of time that is neither nonmodern, premodern, nor postmodern, in faraway alien cultures which must be kept beyond our border, as much as for racial subjects on Europe's metropolitan streets. Interestingly, the rich literary traditions, the worlds of fiction among Blacks and many Others, have always been much more skeptical. In fact, they have often depended to a large degree on a critique of time. Everything in the Black novel, for example, "seems to indicate that time is not a process that one can simply register as what we might call a 'succession of the present'. In other words, there is no time in itself. Time is born out of the contingent, ambiguous, and contradictory relationship that we maintain with things, with the world, or with the body and its doubles." Time thus emerges in "the gaze directed toward oneself and toward the Other, the gaze that one casts on the world and the invisible. It emerges

---

[3] Said, *Culture and Imperialism*, p. 1.
[4] Recognizing the geological turn in critiques of European colonialism, Walter Mignolo goes so far as to argue that "The new recently defined era, the anthropocene, is nothing other than a scientific narrative fiction of the unilineal universal 'history' of humankind. Hence, derived from the imaginary created around the concept of modernity." Mignolo and Walsh, *On Decoloniality*, p. 117. See also: Sylvia Wynter. (2003). "Unsettling the Coloniality of Being/Power/Truth/Freedom: Towards the Human, after Man, Its Overrepresentation. An Argument." *New Centennial Review,* 3(3), 257–337.

out of a certain presence of all these realities taken together."[5] But race inter-
venes in this gaze, or wider *episteme*, for it locks the Other in her supposed
primordial nonmodern origins waiting to be brought up to our, or *the* present.

This European modern "time" is a code that stands for a particular formation of modern/colonial consciousness into which Other notions of time
had to be translated/supplanted. It is here that the many (secular) narratives
recorded of tribal primitive humans and savage Others which arose in the
sixteenth century are rooted. It is worth remembering that the noun *primitive*
was derived from the Latin adjective *primitivus* and became a noun to refer
to aboriginal people in a land visited by Europeans.[6] The code of Eurocentric
time becomes not only a measure of progress through history but also of
humanness.[7] The first element calling for demolition in the system of the
racial subject, of incitement, provocation, and violation, of interrogation
and press conferences is this dwarfing notion of time (assumed in earnest by
the nineteenth-century heights of the empire) which insists that all happens
homogeneously, in one timeline and in an abstract and undifferentiated space.
The avowed secularism of modernity comes the Enlightenment relied upon
the trope of moving forward, of *progress*, which was a Christian teleology.[8]
Ultimately, this historical trajectory, this forward movement of time, universalized the narcissistic celebration of the inward history of Europe as History
per se.[9] Even in times of absolute rupture, this temporal regime held firm.

---

[5] Mbembe, *Critique*, p. 121. Mbembe is engaging Merleau-Ponty here. See: Merleau-Ponty. (2013).
Phenomenology of Perception. Paris: Gallimard, p. 469.

[6] Walter Mignolo. (2000b). "Coloniality at Large: Time and the Colonial Difference." In *Time in the
Making and Possible Futures*, edited by Enrique Larreta. Rio de Janeiro: UNESCO, 237–72. See
also (2011). *The Darker Side of Western Modernity: Global Futures, Decolonial Options*. Durham,
NC: Duke University Press, chapter 4. A summary of the chapter can be found here, http://ucritical
.org/time-and -the-colonial-difference/; Mignolo and Walsh, *On Decoloniality*, p. 215.

[7] Interestingly, the transformation of the word *primitivus* coincides with the advent of the word
civilization to measure and determine uncivilized Anthropos. Meaning: "before a vowel, anthrop-,
word-forming element meaning 'pertaining to man or human beings,' from Greek anthropos 'man;
human being' (including women), as opposed to the gods, from andra (genitive andros), Attic form
of Greek aner 'man' (as opposed to a woman, a god, or a boy), from PIE root *ner-(2) 'man,' also
'vigorous, vital, strong.' Latin humanus was the translation of Greek Anthropos." See: https://www
.etymonline.com/word/anthropo-

[8] It reformed and emerged out of the secular orientation of the European Renaissance to mature three
centuries later in the Enlightenment, and entered Western vocabulary as we have come to know
the word. Etymologically, progress in its figurative sense came to mean "growth, development and
advancement to higher stages" from around 1600.

[9] Wael Hallaq. (2017). "Seventeen Theses on History." In *Manifestos for World Thought*, edited by
Lucian Stone and Jason Bahbak Mohaghegh. Lanham, MD: Rowman and Littlefield, pp. 199–208;
Samir Amin. (2010). *Eurocentrism. Modernity, Religion and Democracy: A Critique of Euro-
centrism and Culturalism*. Pambazuka Press and (2010). *Global History: A View from the South*.
Pambazuka Press; Dipesh Chakrabarty. (2000). *Provincializing Europe: Postcolonial Thought
and Historical Difference, Princeton Studies in Culture/Power/History*. Princeton, NJ: Princeton
University Press; Jean Comaroff. (2011). *Theory from the South; or, How Euro-America Is Evolv-
ing toward Africa*. Boulder, CO: Paradigm; Hamid Dabashi. (2015). *Can Non-Europeans Think*.
London: Zed Books; Arjun Appadurai. (2013). *The Future as Cultural Fact: Essays on the Global*

In her pioneering work, *The Origins of Totalitarianism*,[10] Hannah Arendt notes that after the Second World War, "Western" historical time came to a halt. That "Western culture's innermost structure, with all its beliefs, had collapsed about our ears."[11] In Hitler's emergence and defeat, there was an experience of a disorientation in time which implicated much of the world, for indeed this was a war between new and old empires. But this moment of a loss of faith in time, where total war provoked a stillness and reckoning in Europe, whose genocidal thinking was endemic, was quickly and more ardently forgotten, displaced with capitalist *progress* (another category connoting a unidirectional movement) as the world's necessary motor. Europe became again "an agent moving to overturn the present."[12] Despite the overwhelming experience of disorientation, there was still an assumed universal "present," instituted in (white) Western Europe, that constituted the very self-assurance of European agency to overturn it.

Yet the continuous flow of universal historical time within the rhetoric of modernity does not belong to nature any more than notions of progress or development are the same everywhere.[13] On the Qur'anic critique of pre-Islamic pagan conceptions of time, it is written: "They say, 'There is nothing but our life here below. We live and we die, and only Time destroys us.' But they have no knowledge of this; it is only what they presume. And when Our clear revelations are recited to them, their only argument is: 'Bring us back our fathers, if what you say is true!' Tell them, 'It is God who gives you life and causes you to die, and who will gather you on the day of resurrection, of which there is no doubt. Yet most men know it not'."[14] Time is not understood to signify a tragic sense of absolute fate in which one does not have a meaningful stake or horizon of action. There is, in fact, an entire cosmology underlying Muslim juristic theology or legal theory (*uṣūl al-fiqh*), which enables the reader to bridge the discursive and temporal divide between the empirical and transcendental realms. The *ḥukm* proper—the Divine rule, or

---

Condition. London: Verso Books; Kuan-Hsing Chen. (2010). *Asia as Method: Toward Deimperialization*. Durham, NC: Duke University Press; and Walter Mignolo. (2011). *The Darker Side of Western Modernity: Global Futures, Decolonial Options*. Durham, NC: Duke University Press; Walter Benjamin. (1982). *"Theses on the Philosophy of History" in his Illuminations*, translated by Harry Zohn. New York: Fontana/Collins, p. 263; Walter D. Mignolo. (2002). "The Enduring Enchantment (Or the Epistemic Privilege of Modernity and Where to Go From Here)." *South Atlantic Quarterly*, 101(4), 928–54. For a critique of anti-chronology and why chronologies retain their significance for historians, see Siegfried Kracauer. (1995). *History: The Last Things before the Last*. Princeton: Markus Wiener, chapter 6 in particular.

[10] Hannah Arendt. (1951). *The Origins of Totalitarianism*. New York: Harcourt Brace Jovanovich.

[11] Ibid.

[12] Hartog, Francois. (2015). *Regimes of Historicity: Presentism and Experiences of Time*. Trans. Saskia Brown. New York: Columbia University Press, p. 5.

[13] Ibid.

[14] Q45:24.

value, or judgment—is a transcendental norm, of which the empirical *ḥukm* is but a temporal manifestation. As Ebrahim Moosa notes, "For the classical and medieval jurists, the term *ḥukm* was the locus for an amalgam of the eternal and temporal dimensions . . . [the jurist] exerts him/herself to unveil the already existing rule by 'dis-covering' the empirical indicators that signify the transcendent rule."[15]

"Muslim time" is presented as being a precarious and inherently ambiguous moral span of history with judgment at one pole and creation at the other. The Muslim is entered into a cosmogony of creation in which nature becomes the crucible of (moral) choice. As Lenn Goodman notes, "Here [in nature] we act and choose and are tested, with results that endure through eternity."[16] But the driving force of time does not have a tangible forward, certainly not "progressive" movement to which the subject has true or even partial cognition. We might argue that in the calculus of Muslim cosmogony, salvation, judgment, or condemnation are "endpoints" to an Islamic teleology in which human life, and time in—and stewardship of—nature are but stages in "history." But even if we accept the inevitability of the world's (physical) end, which it surely must, in the very fact of creation's dependence upon a principle that lies beyond human grasp, time becomes a force for moral instruction precisely because of its ambiguity, unknowability, and the ripple effect of human moral (in)action in nonlinear forms and movement.

After all, Europe's position as the modern world's center of gravity was not merely geopolitical. It was and, in many ways, continues to be profoundly cosmological insofar as modernity names a set of narratives which cohere around certain principles: the Western Christian version of humanity, complemented by secular disenchanted narratives of science, economic progress, political democracy, and lately globalization: it is Reason that has displaced God.[17] Europe's decline, that is, our awareness of Other more capacious principles in light of the myriad crises we are facing, presents an opportunity to disrupt the deep forces of the border which constitute the wall, yes, and also pervade the school, the hospital, mental health clinic, interrogation room. But it is a bordering which is necessarily epistemic in nature, rooting subjects in a particular time in which they are in better or worse relation and proximity, with important racial and sexual dimensions. An Other temporal imaginary is—recalling Sylvia Wynter's argument for correlation and Emma Perez's decolonial imaginary—a call to capitalize on the deep cracks in the imperial

---

[15] Ebrahim Moosa. (1998). "Allegory of the Rule (Ḥukm): Law as Simulacrum in Islam?" *History of Religions,* 38, 2, 7, 16, 19.

[16] L. E. Goodman. (1992). "Time in Islam." *Asian Philosophy,* 2(1), 3–19.

[17] Nelson Maldonado-Torres discusses this secular de-Goding of "humanity" in his notion of metaphysical catastrophe (see Maldonado-Torres, 2016). More generally, see Maldonado-Torres (2007, 2008).

frame toward a new construction of the world.[18] Time, then, is constitutive of a particular mode of seeing the world, self, and Other that reproduces the not-so-old constructions of infrahumanity—that carceral spectrum of human value, indebted to the colony, which reproduces its deep structural divisions, inequalities, and violence. The Muslim, as prefigured by our wars on/of terror, is thus also a temporal phenomenon.

In our world of limitless data and fast knowledge, it is no longer sufficient to disrupt "time" in order to document (subaltern) pasts, which may in fact consolidate further the theology of progress simply accumulating more and more pasts into the present. Instead, this critical venture into the temporal must also be tied to a larger material effort to make the world more socially just and hospitable. Edward Said has said that the problem of what constitutes the past, over and concluded, "animates all sorts of discussions—about influence, about blame and judgement, about present actualities and future priorities."[19] Communal memory as a malleable fabric of social life, as a result of human interaction and exchange between lives and bodies, is fertile ground as a point of departure for challenging notions of "then" and "now," "here" and "there."[20] The point is that the history of all cultures is the history of borrowings. The world, however, harshly bordered, is not impermeable. Just as with the Enlightenment's early massive indebtedness to the Islamic sciences, Muslims had borrowed from India and Greece. The enclosures of "races," nations, states, civilizations, and cultures enunciated and instituted by a Europe and Britain fixated with its whiteness cannot deny this universal norm of exchange.

From the position of the Stranger, the intruder, in our case the Muslim, there is an intuitive comprehension of the possibility of coexisting temporalities, of an orientation toward both past and future together. And within this temporal system, time is *enchanted* insofar as its regulating principle is recognized as residing in an *elsewhere*, not necessarily divine but certainly not empty or homogeneous. Time is unpredictable and inaccessible. There must be an ethics to its regulation, therefore, and the violence of our contemporary moment

---

[18] Grosfoguel (2003). On this, see also Jones (2006); Shilliam (2011); Capan (2017); Ling (forthcoming).

[19] Said, *Culture and Imperialism*, p. 1.

[20] Disrupting the Eurocentric narratives of the Orient, the Third World, of Africa, of Islam, of the self and other, replacing them with either a more playful or a more powerful new narrative style which does not simply incorporate but centres Others, is a major component in the process of dismantling (decolonising?) the racial formations and formulations. This kind of work has been carried out by dozens of scholars, critics, and intellectuals in the "peripheral" world. This effort has been called *the voyage in* and insists on an integrative view of human community and liberation. See: Kwame Anthony Appiah. (1992). *In My Father's House: Africa in the Philosophy of Culture.* New York: Oxford University Press; Said, *Culture and Imperialism*, pp. 259–62; B. Robbins. (1994). "Secularism, Elitism, Progress, and Other Transgressions: On Edward Said's 'Voyage in'." *Social Text*, (40), 25–37.

where wars of terror span the entire planet should also be viewed temporally. All this does not mean that there is no distinction between before and after or that the attempt to construct them is meaningless. It is instead to argue for the predominance of a paradoxical time, one that is never fully or with empirical certainty rooted in the present, nor is it ever completely isolated from the past or the future. Free of the hostage situation that the Western idea of time and the belief that there is one single temporality (Western-imagined fictional temporality) has imposed on the world, we are presented with the opportunity to advance a more hospitable, and borderless world. There is the possibility of time(s) of differential duration, disjuncture, and simultaneity.

RETRIEVING THE OTHER

We should of course be alive to the fact that a universal concept such as history carries within it traces of what Hans Georg Gadamer would call "prejudice."[21] Prejudice in this sense is not a conscious bias but "is a sign that we think out of particular accretions of histories that are not always transparent to us."[22] But at the heart of Europe during the many decades of imperial expansion lay an undeterred and unrelenting forward movement which always departed from its shores. This accumulated experiences, territories, peoples, histories; it studied them, it classified them, it verified them, and it allowed "European men of business" the power "to scheme grandly."[23] But it also subordinated them by banishing their identities, turned them into the stuff of nightmares, where they existed as both a lower order of being and potential master should any ground be conceded.

During the last three decades or so, there is an increasing call for heuristic retrieval of premodern tradition and religion not simply to diagnose the various sicknesses of modernity[24]—of which racism and progress have been front

---

[21] Gadamer shows how prejudice as a pejorative was a product of the Enlightenment. He writes: "And there is one prejudice of the Enlightenment that defines its essence: the fundamental prejudice of the Enlightenment is the prejudice against prejudice itself." For Gadamer, the prejudices of the finite, historical individual constitute the historical reality of his being and, crucially, as the inaugural condition of understanding. See Hans Georg Gadamer. (2004). *Truth and Method.* London: Continuum, pp. 272–77.

[22] Dipesh Chakrabarty. (2007). *Provincializing Europe: Postcolonial Thought and Historical Difference.* Princeton, NJ: Princeton University Press, p. xiv.

[23] Angus Calder. (1981). *Revolutionary Empire: The Rise of the English Speaking Empires from the Eighteenth Century to the 1780's.* London: Cape, p. 14.

[24] For diagnoses of such crises, see, for instance, Pransenjit Duara. (2015). *The Crisis of Global Modernity.* Cambridge: Cambridge University Press; Sudipta Kaviraj. (1995). "The Reversal of Orientalism: Bhudev Mukhopadhyay and the Project of Indigenist Social Theory." In *Representing Hinduism: The Construction of Religious Traditions and National Identity,* edited by Vasudha Dalmia and H. von. Stietencron. New Delhi: Sage, pp. 253–79; Kaviraj. "The Idea of Europe: Bhudev Mukhopadhyay and the Critique of Western Modernity" (unpublished paper); Zhao

and center—but also as a call to moral reflection against and beyond (post) modernity as the inevitable endpoint of humanity per se, a movement through history which has brought with it untold destruction of human societies and unprecedented deterioration of natural habitats. These traditions—most prominently from India and China—have rejected the modern Western attitude toward the earth, nature, and the environment,

> especially its nonorganicist and mechanical view that has denuded nature of value as well as of any brand of metaphysics. . . . They have also rejected the exclusivity of a linear concept of history, having stressed the need to expand the concept to include what has been called circulatory history, a rich and fertile notion that converts the modernistic view of history from a nationalist and thus ideological project into an ethical conception that treats the Other, now and in history, with appropriate epistemic respect.[25]

This growing impulse to analyze and reconstruct ways of thinking, being, and living at their most fundamental levels, make absurd and rather superficial investments in unbridgeable racial differences, an inaugural differentiation which formed and licensed the excesses of Europe's own becoming. History, therefore, is no longer a long series of connected events that move horizontally toward us for us to discover its meaning, but become myriad sites for ethical instruction in which myth, magic, and miracle are principles through which anthropocentrism—which has long centered on the white, male, productive, extractive body—is made a rather dubious, if not altogether unethical proposition. And further still, that the Other in these histories can and should be understood through *their own* structure of reason and rationality. Put simply, "if the Other, human and nonhuman, has been the means to, and instrument of, the formation of imperialist and colonialist modernity, then it is this Other that must be retrieved as the critical center in the project of transcending modernity."[26]

Further still, this project—epistemic and material—seeks an orientation that has some commitment to consistency, that being a subject haunted by the terrors and phantasms of race, racism, and Islamophobia prohibits, as all the inconsistencies and irrational rationalities of the Muslim Question(ed) attest.

Tingyang. (2009). "A Political World Philosophy in Terms of All-Under-Heaven (Tian-xia)." *Diogenes,* 56(5), 5–18; Xiang Shiling. (2008). "Theory of 'Returning to the Original' and 'Recovering Nature' in Chinese Philosophy." *Frontiers of Philosophy in China,* 3(4), 502–19; Mukul Sharma. (2012). *Green and Saffron: Hindu Nationalism and Indian Environmental Politics.* Ranikhet: Permanent Black; Vandana Shiva. (1997). *Biopiracy: The Plunder of Nature and Knowledge.* New Delhi: Natraj.

[25] Hallaq, *Restating Orientalism,* p. 244.

[26] Ibid., p. 239.

Study of, and engagement with, the Other must be informed by a principle of self-critique in which understanding is not a means by which to confirm our higher station but is a site of learning for the researcher him/herself.[27] This approach is essential and most urgent for those invested in a world of "race"—liberal, feminist, nationalist, or otherwise—for they need it more than anyone else. Which is to say that the search for, and reflection upon, the terms on which to live, having engaged a thorough excavation of our actual history, is to find in Other archives of thought and praxis resources for engaging the ethical state of the modern subject. What has become the Other of things is no longer, if it ever was, sustainable. In the phantasmatic world of race, those seeking to keep their walls up, their lights on, barbed wire fences and checkpoints in place, can only be *schizophrenic subjects*. Gilles Deleuze and Félix Guattari write,

> It might be said that the schizophrenic passes from one code to another, that he deliberately *scrambles all the codes*, by quickly shifting from one to another, according to the questions asked of him, never giving the same explanation from one day to the next, never invoking the same genealogy, never recording the same event in the same way. When he is more or less forced into it and is not in a touchy mood, he may even accept the banal Oedipal code, so long as he can stuff it full of all the disjunctions that his code was designed to help eliminate.[28]

Separation, schizophrenia, scrambling, all have associations of freneticism, never still, nor quite present to oneself, never mind to Others. Instead, we are called toward a new search in which difference and even opposition are not simplified. Césaire's examination of the Black condition expressed similar concerns: "Who are we in this white world? What can we hope for, and what should we do?" He would offer an unambiguous response: "We are Black."[29] Those differences that could not find expression without questioning, slights, judgment, marginalization, or even elimination were only ever incomprehensible "problems" in the social world—recalling Fanon and Du Bois[30]—because of an epistemic, structural, and economic commitment to

---

[27] Appiah, *Cosmopolitanism.*
[28] Deleuze and Guattari. (1983). *Anti-Oedipus: Capitalism and Schizophrenia*, trans. Robert Hurley, Mark Seem, and Helen R. Lane. Minneapolis: University of Minnesota Press, p. 7, 15.
[29] Césaire, *Discours sur la négritude.*
[30] Du Bois, *The Souls of Black Folk* and Fanon, *Black Skin, White Masks.* On the mutations of what amount to structures of hate, see: David Theo Goldberg. (2002). *The Racial State.* Malden, MA: Blackwell. On the fiction of the racial subject as the premier obstacle to the co-belonging of all humans, see the critique of the texts of W. E. B. Du Bois in Kwame Anthony Appiah. (1992). *In My Father's House: Africa in the Philosophy of Culture.* New York: Oxford University Press, chapters 1 and 2. See also Kwame Anthony Appiah. (1987). "Racism and Moral Pollution." *Philosophical Forum,* 18(2–3), 185–202.

a racial ordering. The Muslim Questioner's Otherwise, instead, enjoins us toward an exacting critique of the weight of history, its burdens and implication for the fundamental questions of our time, that of hospitality, of the common and collective struggles beyond the racial paradigms of interrogation and violation, whether defined by hostility or condescension, or both. As I have attempted to show in this study of race and Islamophobia, we have continued to produce what it is the white world has made and forced as our inheritance, a whole roster of perverse techniques and psychic economies and intimacies of the postcolony and the postmetropole alike. And yet I contend that in the project to retrieve the Other—captured in the Muslim Questioner—we have also inherited innumerable ethical sociologies,[31] techniques toward expansive horizons with potential to repair racism's gaping wounds which scar the earth's poor and marked inhabitants as much as the earth itself.

AN ETHICS OF THE WITNESS

In the rhetoric of modernity, homogeneous, linear calendrical time was met with the concept of worldly[32] "space" working to mediate and obliterate "the changing energies of the seasons, the circulation of the Sun and the Moon, and their impact in our daily living."[33] Time became empty, nature became "brute" and "stupid"; both were disenchanted and, ultimately, under the sovereign will of a small province of the planet, if not a select community within that province. Both time and space become "ours," so to speak, to be mastered and possessed. Consistent with the policy of ignorance in the material and epistemic modes of empire, indigenous notions of time and space were systematically dismantled. Those spatial and temporal systems which rooted the conquered's narrative of events that preceded the very (colonized) "present" in which they were telling their stories were also sacrificed for the salvific project of imperialism. The non-Europeans classified and divided

---

[31] I used the terms sociologies precisely because of the sociality and interconnected nature of the parties recognized by the Qurān as "incurring or provoking distinctive moral attitudes and behaviours. The corporate bodies recognized in qurānic ethics are: Muslims (and mu'mins, 'believers'), scriptuaries (i.e. Peoples of the Book), hypocrites, and rejectors." Kevin. A. Reinhart. "Ethics and the Qur'ān." In *Encyclopaedia of the Qur'ān*, edited by Jane Dammen McAuliffe. Washington, DC: Georgetown University, p. 71.

[32] The notion of "world" is also a revealing projection. An example can be drawn from Hannah Arendt's work (echoing Locke, Hegel, and Marx) in the distinction she makes between "tribe" and a genuine "people," and explicitly links the difference to the "world." Genuine "people" have toiled on nature to create "a human world, a human reality" and therefore have histories. Prehistoric "tribes," on the other hand, live in and on nature, like animals, without building a "human reality" (see Arendt, *Origins*, ch. 7).

[33] Walter Mignolo and Catherine Walsh. (2018). *On Decoloniality: Concepts, Analytics, Praxis.* Durham, NC: Duke University Press, p. 212.

were confronted with a praxis of living and understanding that was not theirs for centuries, but which according to modernity became the measure of humanity.

Yet these imperial encounters, however ignorant and self-referential, did not simply "mark" the invaded. Partly because of empire, all cultures are involved with and, more importantly, in one another; "none is single and pure, all are hybrid, heterogeneous, extraordinarily differentiated, and unmonolithic."[34] This, I think, is as true of contemporary Europe as it is of India or Brazil, despite so much being made of the threat of un-patriotism, and perpetual calls to venerate rigidly contoured national cultures, often at the expense of others. Our notion of "space," place, and home, therefore, must introduce a sense of scale allowing for a commitment to new orders of valuation, to the idea of coexisting temporalities and overlapping geographies in the relation and exchange between myriad local histories, subjectivities, territories.

Ultimately, everything about human history is rooted in the earth, which means that we must think, first and foremost, about habitation. But we must also be cognizant of the fact that some people have always planned to have more territory and therefore must do something about its natives, and the forms of sovereignty which have for generations tied them to the land of later, modern, imperial desire. The colonization of space (and time) was of course military, corporate, and state-political activities accompanied by unspeakable forms of violence, pillage, rape, and death. But they were also conceptual, that is, epistemic endeavors in dialogic motion with the stark materiality of colonial law. Hegel, for example, could not have philosophized space (notions of interiority and the margins of universal humanity) and time (unilinear, Eurocentric) as he did without the actual colonization of time and space in Germany's African possessions.

To be sure, new structures and routes of circulation which made the modern world required colossal capital, transfer of metals, agricultural products, and manufactures. Equally crucial, however, was the dissemination of knowledge of the human sciences/philosophy which disavowed the humanity of the human-merchandise, the indentured, transferred on ships, instantly excluding them from access to the universal and to history, fixing their superfluous humanity in a timeless space. Moving otherwise from the space of modernity requires us to confront the snare that the formal and informal relations of empire made of human sisterhood and brotherhood (Du Bois, 2007: 179).[35] Foregrounding the planetary, rather than the worldly or

---

[34] Said, *Culture*, p. xxix.
[35] W. E. B. Du Bois. (2007). *The Souls of Black Folk*. Oxford: Oxford University Press, p. 179. See also Gilroy (2004: 38–39).

the global, introduces a sense of movement and scale which alerts us to the contingency of the racialized divisions and structure of the world in which institutions, states, and societies are heavily invested. It prompts us to speak of connections within space as opposed to monopolistic claims to it. And it bespeaks the difficulties and dangers of isolating races, nations, and cultures from one another in the name of self-constitution and/or judgment of the Other. As Fanon would say, humanity can only be recovered by would-be postcolonial subjects through a new relation to the land that "will bring . . . bread and, above all, dignity."[36]

So strongly felt and perceived, however, is the ontological distinction between West and non-West due to race/culture/religion, that these boundaries are considered absolute. With the supremacy of the distinction, at their core variations on the distinction between civilization and savagery,[37] there goes what Johannes Fabian calls a denial of "coevalness"[38] in time, and a radical discontinuity in human space. Edward Said was, as he rightly said, always slightly out of place, "but that only brought out what was wrong with that place that could not completely accommodate him in the entirety of his character."[39] The harsh reception and treatment of the migrant, and those turned into him, a political figure between domains, between forms, between homes, between languages, and between space and time, is our measure for making the earth habitable. Retrieving the Other necessitates an ethicizing impulse *for the self*, precisely because of the immoral and demoralizing forces of racism, misogyny, and Islamophobia—deeply unethical formations and formulations—that have taken on a common-sense quality in our world today.

With the refusals of racism's inherited debt and the transparency of such a system which demands it in view, the struggle for a different world requires us to think carefully about ethical and moral responsibility. In a society so heavily constituted from the law of race, where is the locus of such a responsibility? The Qur'an, the text that the politics of Islamic "reformation," intensified by the war on terror, works to produce as a site of thorough de-contestation, has much to contribute as a moral resource. Here the locus of moral responsibility is the individual who is constituted as a (moral) subject faced with a series of problems as an individual within a larger social, political, economic, and cosmological order. The nature of one's moral responsibilities are to a large extent shaped by, and to be understood within

---

[36] Frantz Fanon. (2001). *Wretched of the Earth*. London: Penguin, p. 54.
[37] See Domenico Losurdo. (2014). *Liberalism: A Counter-History*. London: Verso, chapter 2.
[38] Johannes Fabian. (2014). *Time and the Other: How Anthropology Makes Its Object*. New York: Columbia University Press.
[39] Hamid Dabashi. (2015). *Can Non-Europeans Think?* London: Zed Books, p. 53.

the context of one's belonging, which draws a correlative relation between (social) role and (moral) responsibility. The group is key, moreover, because there is also a sense in which the community (of believers) as a whole is viewed as a moral agent.[40] The quintessential moral Qur'anic refrain ordaining that Muslims "command the good and forbid the reprehensible"[41] (with no gendered distinction)[42] presupposes one party exhorting another, thus thoroughly situating the moral agent *in a system* of obligation and debt, through a set of "moral technologies of the self."[43] An Other system of measurement and value, moral connection, and spatial arrangements.

It is here that the well-known and oft-pacified five pillars of Islam should be located, and which constitute the subject and function dialectically to form a moral community, each pillar and moral individual unthinkable in any meaningful sense without that ethical community and larger cosmology. Each individual moral agent is the protégé of another.[44] In sum, the willingness to sacrifice money, or *zakat*, and purify one's wealth through a mandated charity to the poor and downtrodden; yearly fasting, or *sawm*, as an ethical empathy-building practice which requires the sacrifice of sustenance and self-discipline in behavior, thought, word, and deed as a complex system of gratitude; and daily prayers, or *salah*, which affirm and reaffirm (through transcendental dialogue) a metaphysic of care and mercy are all aspects of an Islamic moral system which is a proactive, self- and Other-conscious realm of moral agency, beauty, accountability, and growth.[45] "Piety," after all, "does not consist of merely turning your face to the east or to the west. Rather, the pious person is someone who believes in God, the last day, the angels, the book, and the prophets and who out of his love gives his property to his relatives, orphans, the needy, travelers, supplicants, and slaves; and who performs the required prayers and pays the *zakāt*."[46]

These practices and processes of subjectification are not defensive modes by which the humanity of Muslims is vouched for when interviewed by white

---

[40] This notion of communal moral agency would be articulated in later legal thought as the concept of fard al-kifāya. See: J. Esposito, ed. (1995). *Oxford encyclopedia of the modern Islamic world, s.v. far al-kifāyah*. Oxford: Oxford University Press.

[41] Q3:104, Q3:110; Q31:17; Q22:40–41.

[42] Lamrabet, Asma. (2015). "An Egalitarian Reading of the Concepts of *Khilafah, Wilayah* and *Qiwamah*." In *Men in Charge: Rethinking Authority in Muslim Legal Tradition*, edited by Ziba Mir-Hosseini, Mulki Al-Sharmani, and Jana Rumminger. London: Oneworld.

[43] Wael Hallaq. (2013). *The Impossible State: Islam, Politics and Modernity's Moral Predicament.* New York: Columbia University Press, especially chapter 5.

[44] cf. Q9:71, Q8:72

[45] El Fadl, Khaled. (2005). *The Search for Beauty in Islam: A Conference of the Books.* London: Rowman & Littlefield. The very word *zakat*, for example, is etymologically linked to *zakā* (to be pure) but has the literal meaning of growth. The Qur'an embeds this primary act of belief with others showing the interconnected, mutual intersorption of these moral technologies of the Muslim (Questioner) that do not end at national borders.

[46] Q2:177.

institutions, as the strategic yet perverse optic of Muslim women linking arms on Westminster Bridge strove to communicate. These practices that mobilize the body but which engage in an extra-material form of dialogue are, on the contrary, a positive affirmation of human moral character that is built through ethical (and sacrificial) conduct, to a principle and set of obligations outside of the self, and in concert with others. This is the meaning of power, made possible by a knowledge of the self not as sovereign individual, never mind a racial one, but as part of an ethical community within a wider cosmogony and complex temporal regime. Building moral character is, therefore, accomplished through training (*riyada*), "a thoroughgoing process of subjecting the self to repeated exercises that shape and form the soul. The process might begin with cumbersome effort, which tends to evolve gradually into a sort of normal conduct, ultimately becoming a second nature (*tab'*)."[47]

But it is also a thoroughgoing ethico-political form of training that is as self-reflexive in gratitude as it is vigilant in critique. Gratitude must exist with its counterpart, the call for forgiveness, that is, the recognition of oneself as an actor and shaper of one's worldly situation. The liberation theologian, Farid Esack, asks the question: "What do men owe women?" In pursuing an intimate analysis of Islam and gender justice beyond both apologia and fundamentalism, what appears essential for Esack is a call for forgiveness once having borne witness to the ways in which he has himself benefited from structures and processes of (women's) erasure. He says:

> Each adherent of a religious tradition is simultaneously a shaper of that tradition and while one cannot assume personal responsibility for all the crimes or achievements of that tradition, there is nevertheless a sense in which each adherent shares in the shame or glory. In Islam, as in most all other world religions, males are the key managers and interpreters of the sacred. As a male Muslim theologian committed to gender justice I thus have two reasons to ask for forgiveness. First as part of privileged gender that has consistently denied the full humanity of the gendered other even as I was being nurtured and sustained by it. Secondly, for my own role in—even if only by identification—in a theological tradition which fosters and sustains images of women and practices by men that denies women their full worth as human beings created by God and as carriers of the spirit of God. This call for forgiveness is what the totality of Islamic traditions have done, failed to do and for our inability and/or unwillingness to effectively challenge and eliminate the misogynist traits within our tradition.[48]

[47] Hallaq, *The Impossible State*, p. 132.
[48] Farid Esack. (2001). "What Do Men Owe Women? Islam and Gender Justice: Beyond Simplistic Apolgia." Available at: http://www.oocities.org/faridesack/fewhatdomenowe.html. See also: Farid Esack. (2013). *On Being a Muslim: Finding a Religious Path in the World Today*, especially

To center liberation, justice, and fairness is to insist on a critical solidarity that faces head-on the difficult questions of the day. Esack's argument calls for internal scrutiny, in this case on the question of gender justice, subject to a host of hermeneutical devices that must aim at serving the ends of justice, a form of justice which renders dehumanization as deeply immoral violations, not to mention incoherent to value inherent in life itself. The Muslim Questioner militates for this surplus within *and* without one's "tradition" in full knowledge and confidence that none of the devices, hermeneutical or otherwise, which center justice in relation to the Text are unknown to the world of traditional Islam.[49] The call for repentance, for the work of forgiveness and self-reflection, is, in my view, just as applicable in striving against the iniquities of racial orders requiring a form of witnessing and testimony as moral action, in order to rid a shared planet of racism, Islamophobia, misogyny, all forms of dehumanization and wills to mastery (including over nature).

In Qur'anic ethical epistemology, moreover, there remains a principle of debt owed by the individual toward fairness and justice which transcend the boundaries of social grouping and kinship:[50] "O you who are faithful! Be upright in justice (*qist*), witnesses to God though it be against yourselves or the two parents or kin if he is rich or poor."[51] In the exhortations of uprightness in justice, there is the necessary accompanying (and presupposed) ethical act of bearing witness, a witnessing that pervades the five pillars as daily praxis and in which a specifically national (state) commitment which all too easily lends itself to degrees of dehumanization are made cosmologically unsustainable. To bear witness is to agitate for fairness and justice in spite of the site of one's social (and political) belonging. To be able to bear witness is not a straightforward task. It is in fact a struggle. Human beings are at once fickle, covetous of ease and convenience, while also containing within them

---

chapter 5; F. Esack. (2013). "Redeeming Islam: Constructing the Good Muslim Subject in the Contemporary Study of Religion." *Alternation Journal*, (11), 36–60.

[49] Esack goes one step further and argues that even if hermeneutical devices which challenge the text or subvert "orthodoxy" is construed as a form of violence to the Qur'an, is justified: "If a choice has to be made between violence towards the text and textual legitimization of violence against real people then I would be comfortable to plead guilty to charges of violence against the text." Esack, "What do Men Owe Women." This is a view I agree with though, again, maintaining that we should be alive to rich hermeneutical resources from within the Muslim archive that can serve these strivings for (gender) justice.

[50] The distinction between Muslims and non-Muslim Peoples of the Book is fundamental to qurānic behavioral norms, but a common ethics of monotheism of the members of these traditions seems to underlie more superficial distinctions.

[51] Q4:135; cf. Q31:15. Reinhart notes that "Given this corporatism in qurānic ethical thought, it is not surprising that in later times some believed Muslims were assured salvation by being Muslim. This was, however, a mistake—at least from the Qurān's perspective. While roles and responsibilities are determined by membership in one group or another, ethical responsibility lies solely with individuals. It is individuals who are enjoined to act, and it is individuals who are promised requital according to how they have acted." Reinhart, "Ethics and the Qur'an," p. 76.

the propensity for ethical action without the need for supernatural grace or redemptive sacrifice in its original doing.

We have therefore the full gamut of verses such as: "If harm touches a human he calls to his lord, inclining towards him; then if granted a favour from God he forgets that for which he pleaded before";[52] "They are attentive to God and upright in conduct when in jeopardy or when suffering, but heedless when secure";[53] and "They seek evil as much as good,"[54] "they are prone to oppression and ingratitude,"[55] they are hasty,"[56] "weak,"[57] and "they are oppressive and ignorant."[58] The verses of the Qur'an depict human nature as also inclined to recognize the good (as appropriate to the moral agent's time) through reflection, reason, or instinct. For without these faculties as presupposed in the moral agent-reader of the Qur'an, being enjoined to bear witness would make little sense. Indeed, if ethical action is unattainable, chief among which is the struggle to bear witness—following the Prophetic precedent—then the entire Qur'anic ethical kerygma has no human basis as a text for all times, spaces, and peoples. The Qur'anic description of human nature within its ethical epistemology is, in sum, one that maintains "an artful tension between the possibility of human perfection and the reality of human moral deficiency."[59]

In the struggle (*jihad*) to bear witness, there are profound worldly consequences to being enjoined and fulfilling the role of witness: punishment, marginalization, violence, social death, the list goes on. However, the Qur'an insists:

Thus We have appointed you a middle nation, that ye may be witnesses against mankind, and that the messenger may be a witness against you. And We appointed the qiblah which ye formerly observed only that We might know him who followeth the messenger, from him who turneth on his heels. In truth it was a hard (test) save for those whom Allah guided. But it was not Allah's purpose that your faith should be in vain, for Allah is Full of Pity, Merciful toward mankind.[60]

---

[52] cf. Q39:49
[53] Q17:83; Q41:51; Q70:19–21.
[54] Ibid.
[55] cf. Q13:34; Q22:26
[56] Q17:11; 21:37.
[57] Q4:28
[58] Q33:72.
[59] Reinhart, "Ethics and the Qur'ān," p. 57. See also: H. G. Coward. (2008). *The Perfectibility of Human Nature in Eastern and Western Thought.* Albany: State University of New York Press, chapter 5.
[60] Q2:43

A thorough accounting of such violations against mankind itself is resisted, if not legislated against in numerous ways: outright ignorance; systematic erasure of evidence; legal exceptions; the casting aside or elimination of the witness herself; the familiar transmutation of the witness's testimony as an incriminating tale about the witness with which the accused power is always already familiar. All are supported and propelled by the force of law; all are common techniques of narcissistic power and knowledge to which the foundational rule of race is crucial. The ethical epistemology I am outlining understands acutely that the moral act of bearing witness is a thorn in the side of what might be the chief corrupting source of the reprehensible in human existence: (sovereign) power.[61] Much of what I have analyzed in this study has sought to outline the sophisticated strategies employed by organized power in the service of having uncomfortable testimony swept under the rug. Bearing witness (for the victim *and* for Allah) is costly and is, therefore, to use a Qur'anic motif, *haraj*, a hardship. To bear witness is to be at once fully cognizant of the difficulties of escaping structural, that is, fickle, covetous, human power, and the sophistication of the technologies fueled by the hardship of Others, and the unavoidable ethical exhortation of still doing so as a measure of being on earth as a moral agent in an ethical community and a middle nation.

Witnessing is also, however, a call to a kind of theology of perception which overturns the theology of phantasm (or with its more familiar names of racism and progress) that the witness inevitably confronts, regardless of the political or theological makeup of power and society.[62] Bearing witness "here" and "there," "then" and "now," for "us" and for "them" is to disrupt the axiom of (white) might over right as a hegemonic spirit of our time. It is to recall and add an ethical dimension to what Miriam Cooke describes as the Islamic feminist strategy of "multiple critique":[63] "a multilayered discourse

---

[61] See Dr. Khaled Abou el Fadl's words to this effect: Khaled Abou El Fadl. (2019). "Usuli Institute Khutbah: "From Bearing Witness to Becoming the Opiate of the Masses," 8.23.19," *Usuli Institute*. Available at: https://www.youtube.com/watch?v=qsS7l_vtgEM&t=863s

[62] Witnessing in this sense is an act of reclamation of truth, even if against one's kin, society or religious grouping. See: Khaled El Fadl. (2014). *Reasoning with God: Reclaiming Shari'ah in the Modern Age*. London: Rowman & Littlefield.

[63] Miriam Cooke explains its origins: "I have coined [multiple critique] to describe Islamic feminists' critical rhetorical strategies. First, women who have been consistently marked as victims and who have only recently started to speak for themselves may be able to situate themselves transnationally because of the global nature of the institutions with which they have had to contend. Second, women who have learned as feminists to form principled and strategic alliances which allow them to balance their religious, specifically Islamic loyalties with national, local, class, ethnic, or any other allegiances may be able to invent a contestatory, but also enabling, discourse within the global context that will not be easily coopted. They may thus initiate new forms of conversations across what were previously thought to be unbridgeable chasms." Miriam Cooke. (2000). *Multiple Critique: Islamic Feminist Rhetorical Strategies*. Nepantla: Views from South, Vol. 1, Issue 1, p. 99. See also: Angela Davis. (1995). "Reflections on the Black Woman's Role in the Community

that allows them [Muslim women] to engage with and criticize the various individuals, institutions, and systems that limit and oppress them while making sure that they are not caught in their own rhetoric."[64] To bear witness is to assume, and speak from, a marginality—something Cooke locates in Muslim women's experiences under colonialism *and* in their relationship to global capital—in which it becomes possible to invent a (de)nationalism capable "of holding on to communal, national, and international belonging that do not entail charges of treachery, complicity, or self-sacrifice."[65] Bearing witness from the margins, from the site of the racial subject who is always already human and always already enmeshed in a temporal, moral, and cosmological system beyond the limits of body and human reason, is to expose and exploit the various forms of decentering that bring forth new dangers but also possibilities. As Stuart Hall wrote, though I doubt with Islamic feminists in mind:

[The] most profound cultural revolution in this part of the twentieth century has come about as a consequence of the margins coming into representation—in art, in painting, in film, in music, in literature, in the modern arts everywhere, in politics, and in social life generally. . . . Paradoxically, marginality has become a powerful space. . . . New subjects, new genders, new ethnicities, new regions, and new communities—all hitherto excluded as decentered or subaltern—have emerged and have acquired through struggle, sometimes in very marginalized ways, the means to speak for themselves for the first time. And the dis- courses of power in our society, the discourses of the dominant regimes, have been certainly threatened by this decentered cultural empowerment of the marginal and the local.[66]

In the history and codices of race that we have recounted here, I am reminded of the form of witnessing that constitutes the range of (Muslim) racial life I have sought to record. I am reminded of Shamima Begum and James Baldwin, of Babar Ahmed and the "Sepoy mutineers," of Talha Ahsan, Saffiyah Khan, and Frantz Fanon. Witnessing is both a moral duty and a testimonial activity which is not beholden to notions of time which bracket uncomfortable pasts as over and concluded, nor notions of space that are constrained by precarious national borders, extractive regimes, and

---

of Slaves." In *Words of Fire: An Anthology of African-American Feminist Thought*, edited by Guy-Sheftall. New York: New Press; Abdelkebir Khatibi. (1983). *Maghreb Pluriel*. Paris: Denoel; Deborah King. (1995). "Multiple Jeopardy, Multiple Consciousness: The Context of a Black Feminist Ideology." In Guy-Sheftall 1995; C. Mohanty. (1984). "Under Western Eyes: Feminist Scholarship and Colonial Discourse," *Boundary 2*, 12, 3; Chandra Talpade Mohanty, Ann Russo, and Lourdes Torres, eds. (1991). *Third World Women and the Politics of Feminism*. Indiana University Press.

[64] Ibid., "Multiple Critique," p. 100.

[65] Ibid., p. 102.

[66] Stuart Hall. ([1991] 1997: 183). "The Local and the Global." In *Dangerous Liaisons: Gender, Nation, and Postcolonial Perspectives*, edited by Anne McClintock, Aamir Mufti, and Ella Shohat. Minneapolis: University of Minnesota Press.

the massive techno-economies that uphold their fatal effects. All the figures above in their own ways testified against the nations to which they claimed (and were deprived of) membership. They are not only engaging questions of belonging and protections under law, but life, death, and the possibility of a hospitable earth.

"It was not dreamed, during the Second World War," Baldwin bore witness, "that Churchill's ringing words to the English were overheard by the English slaves—who, now, coming in their thousands to the mainland, menace the English in their sleep."[67] The Muslim Questioner is such a witness, a figure who, as the licentious racism and Islamophobia of contemporary Britain attests, menaces many an English(wo)man in their sleep, but who equally apprehends the poisoned comforts and incentives they provide, as much as the brutalizing effects of structures of dehumanization. The temporal and spatial movements of racism—forward, outward—an inevitable historical progression that we need not accept, especially given our current planetary predicament. It is worth quoting Ashis Nandy at length:

> Why should we adopt the priorities and the hierarchies of the West? Are your 20th century successes so brilliant? World War Two, genocides, the destruction of the environment, what's next? Here are the effects of a "modern" civilization which has privileged the individual over metaphysics, History over eternity, progress over tradition, manly values over sensitivity.[68]

Elsewhere he says,

> Many many decades later, in the aftermath of that marvel of modern technology called the Second World War and perhaps that modern encounter of cultures called Vietnam, it has become obvious that the drive for mastery over men is not merely a byproduct of a faulty political economy but also of a world view which believes in the absolute superiority of the human over the nonhuman and the subhuman, the masculine over the feminine, the adult over the child, the historical over the ahistorical, and the modern or progressive over the traditional or the savage. It has become more and more apparent that genocides, ecodisasters and ethnocides are but the underside of corrupt sciences and psychopathic technologies wedded to new secular hierarchies, which have reduced major civilizations to the status of a set of empty rituals. The ancient forces of human greed and violence, one recognizes, have merely found a new legitimacy in anthropocentric doctrines of secular salvation, in the ideologies of progress,

---

[67] James Baldwin. (1964). *Nobody Knows My Name: More Notes of a Native Son*. London: Michael Joseph, p. 174.

[68] Ashis Nandy, quoted in Houria Bouteldja, *Whites*, pp. 129–30.

normality and hypermasculinity, and in theories of cumulative growth of science and technology.[69]

The earth is a planet saturated with uneliminable, incontrovertible meaning and value but much of which is lost under old and new forms of extraction—data, mineral, biological matter—and their nocturnal techno-economies which support a necropolitics of bordering, surveillance, and death. That peculiar interplay between sovereign will to make live and the systematic impulse to murder, for which race is both litmus test and rationale, characterizes today's overwhelming impulse to expel.

According to my coordinates for an Otherwise, the question is not "what is human and humanity" but rather recognizing who invented and defined themselves as human in their praxis of living, sensing, thinking, doing, and believing, and applied their self-definition universally to distinguish and classify and rank lesser humans. In short, white imperial subjects bequeathed to themselves and their descendants the status of full humanity, the superior subspecies across time and space, fundamentally distinct from (i) a notion of nature—the life-energies of the biosphere—as "brute," "inert," and "stupid";[70] and (ii) those defined as lesser or nonhuman, as Other absolutely, through the mechanisms of racism and sexism (for which religion, particularly Islam, was crucial). The local and self-promoted emergence of the model human—white, Christian, male, in sum, European—from the Renaissance and later the Enlightenment onward exploited, indeed produced, spheres of meaning to demarcate absolute difference and the justification for abdication.

In bearing witness to that which has been stolen and forgotten, however, cracks have long been forming in the house of modernity. It is worth remembering the words of the Insurgent Subcomandante Galeano when he said: *"basta con hacerle una grieta" "([it is] enough to make a crack in it)"*.[71] Earlier than him, Aimé Césaire and later Frantz Fanon referred to "the cracks in Western Christian civilization as spaces, places, and possibilities of and for decolonization."[72] The stories, cultures, and histories of those despised by history which are told and exist in alternative temporal and spatial registers are important for advancing these cracks in (the rhetoric of) modernity and must

---

[69] Ashis Nandy. (1983). Preface to *The Intimate Enemy: Loss and Recovery of Self under Colonialism*. New Delhi: Oxford University Press, pp. ix–x.

[70] These are some of the famous Anglo-Irish chemist Robert Boyle's descriptors for nature.

[71] SupGaleano. (2015). "The Crack in the Wall. First Note on Zapatista Method." May 3. Available at: http://enlacezapatista.ezln.org.mx/2015/05/10/the-crack-in-the-wall-first-note-on-zapatista-method/

[72] See Césaire, *Aimé Discourse on Colonialism* and Frantz Fanon. (1967). *Black Skin, White Masks*. See also: Catherine Walsh. (2014). "Pedagogical Notes from the Decolonial Cracks." *e-misférica* 11(1), http://archive.hemisphericinstitute.org/hemi/en/emisferica-111-decolonial-gesture/walsh.

accompany Europe's end.[73] Merely to insist on one's own identity, history, tradition, uniqueness, as is fashionable today, may initially get to name some basic requirements for the right to an assured, decently humane existence. But it is a planetary consciousness of human(e) differences that is part of the horizon as I am attempting to articulate it. This—the planetary—"is consciousness of the tragedy, fragility, and brevity of indivisible human existence that is all the more valuable as a result of its openness to the damage done by racisms,"[74] which not only constitute our racial discourses of difference and opposition, but also the politics of interrogation and death which characterize racism's contemporary drives.

To speak of connections within time and space—evident in the figure of the racial subject—is to conjure fragile images of self and other which historical time (as progress) has no right to destroy. There is only one world, it belongs to all of us, equally, and we are all its coinheritors. Coinheritance being attached, in my reading, to the essential twinned concepts of privilege and burden. We are coinheritors of a planet that was/is not of our making and whose regulating principle lies *elsewhere*. We are privileged with sentient life and burdened by a constrained *relation*, ethically and morally, in our relationship to the earth and to others.[75] Concepts such as "race," "nature," "human," "woman," "man," "culture" are conceptual consequences of creative and, as we have seen, destructive human effort. In European (Western) vocabulary, the word human emerges as a negative identity, based on an absence of the Other, an insistence on a fundamental non-similarity with those people without the correct god, or a soul, or with dark skin of the night. The figure of the Muslim as I have analyzed him, an intense source of white Europe's anxiety concerning its end, is indebted to this provincial emergence of the human.

The Muslim Questioner's entire ethical pedagogy is one where "external performative acts (like prayer) are understood to create corresponding inward dispositions."[76] The Muslim Questioner, in spite of racist and Islamophobic formations and formulations which can only invent him as an object of capture, engages a spectrum of training, or *riyada*, in which life and living in and of themselves are training. This training is a path on the journey of *akhlaq* (the corridor for acquiring a foundational ethics) to be sure. But more broadly, it is a training of vision and memory in recognition of the precarious and heavy (moral) situatedness of the human in a fractured and fracturing world whose privations are most intensely felt by the racialized and poor. What might

---

[73] Gloria Anzaldúa also found resonance in the cracks for a nepantla perspective. See: Gloria Anzaldúa. (1987). *Borderlands/La Frontera: The New Mestiza*. San Francisco: Aunt Lute, pp. 82–83.

[74] Gilroy, *After Empire*, p. 75.

[75] See: Hallaq, *Restating Orientalism*, especially chapter 5.

[76] Hallaq, *The Impossible State*, p. 207n134.

the external performative acts that correspond to an inward anti-racist, anti-imperialist disposition look like? What sacrifices can be brought in to replace the multiplying abdications authorized by racism and Islamophobia and fears of white replacement and Europe's end?

But we must remember that each language and civilization have their own ways of naming the human self, the moral agent, standing on two legs, using their hands (to create worlds) and engaging in communicative action with those around them in the long and perpetual process of forming cultures and multiple, simultaneous identities. An ethics of the witness, in fine, calls for an ethics and politics premised upon an agonistic, planetary idea of space, capable of comprehending the universality of our elemental vulnerability to the wrongs we visit upon each other, the ultimate indivisibility of the *in-common*, the fundamental ephemerality of human divisions—whether state, national, cultural—and, in the final analysis, of the human her/himself.

ETHICAL VOCABULARIES OF THE MUSLIM QUESTIONER

In the formation of the moral individual through the technologies of the five pillars, the trained behaviors of the body, once second nature for having confronted its ethicizing effects, in turn enhances the heart's predilections. It is at this point that intellectual and bodily performances begin to run in harmony, involving a circular motion (*dawr*).[77] Ethical acts beget certain obligations which beget ethical acts. There is, then, a hope of bringing together what Kwame Anthony Appiah defined as the two strands that intertwine in the notion of cosmopolitanism: "One is the idea that we have obligations to others. . . . The other is that we take seriously the value not just of human life but of particular human lives, which means taking an interest in the practices and beliefs that lend them significance . . . no local loyalty can ever justify forgetting that each human being has responsibilities to every other . . . we need to develop habits of coexistence."[78]

Refusal and resistance, therefore, must come with new obligations to self and to Others. Obligations that transcend the national border which increasingly represent a camp or fortress, in turn producing degrees of the human and nonhuman. This is a striving for the collapse of the two into one another, just as "here" and "there" can only ever have limited utility in a world that is deeply and materially interconnected. As Wael Hallaq writes,

---

[77] Hallaq explains that "This reciprocity in turn produces mutual corroboration as well as progressive and exponential effects." Hallaq, *The Impossible State*, p. 132:

[78] Appiah, *Cosmopolitanism*, p. xv, xvi, xix.

As of the early nineteenth century, Orientalists too made it their business to study what they perceived as "Islam"; but the manuscripts, archives, and artifacts of that world were patently not deciphered within an Islamic cultural context, or within a profoundly ethicized framework or habitus, a crucial absence in their enterprise. For the first time in the history of Islam, its cultural production, especially its text-based traditions (now narrowly conceived and stripped of their cultural and psychological surrounds), was to be subjected to an entirely foreign, but also hegemonic and *transformative*, hermeneutic. This was not only an enterprise intent on organizing Europe's "scholarly curiosity," but one that effectively appropriated, refracted, and redefined the ways Muslims themselves thought of, and about, the world.[79]

This transformative hermeneutic that was the "handmaiden" of European colonialism has not left us and is undergoing mutation as the founding idea of white Europe experiences the crises of both its whiteness and displacement as the earth's center of gravity. A planet on which it becomes more difficult to offshore its wars, technological and juridical experiments, environmental degradation, and the (non)human subjects that were once its discarded refuse. And yet, in the archetype of the Muslim Questioner and the analysis of Islamophobia as a holistic phenomenon with political, cultural, imaginary, economic tributaries, the very sites of degradation, insult, and confusion can serve as a repository for another transformative hermeneutic that seeks to repair the wounds of the former. The present study is of course limited by its in situ diagnosis and brief attention for the development of such a hermeneutic. But in drawing international, transnational, and transhistorical connections, mobilizing a wide range of genres, I have sought to question a fragmentary view of reality which all too easily brackets or jettisons the uncomfortable (and its racialized bodies) drunk on a principle of offshoring; that is, an overwhelmingly unsustainable will *not to know*, of which race was and is an extreme product.

Returning to the Muslim archive, *'Adl*, or justice (literally, "equity") and *qist* as "giving fair measure" is recurrently enjoined throughout the Qur'an. As both a legal principle[80] and quotidian measure of the good, *'adl* takes on simple meanings of "being fair" or "fairness."[81] The exact scope of "good" and "bad" is not spelled out in the Qur'an but appeals to the shifting sense of virtue of its readers and listeners. *'Adl* is a concept that is alive to context, historicity, and the mutable imperatives of time(s). The Qur'an itself is not merely God speaking to Muhammad in seventh-century Arabia, but is a form

---

[79] Hallaq, *Restating Orientalism*, p. 230.
[80] cf. Q2:282; 4:58.
[81] cf. Q4:3, 129; Q16:76, 90.

of dialogue occasioned by social, political, and ethical plaints of the community, and sustained for all eternity and to all humankind. It represents, as Cantwell Smith says it, "the eternal breaking through time; the knowable disclosed; the transcendent entering history and remaining here, available to mortals to handle and to appropriate; the divine become apparent."[82] Farid Esack, says of the Qur'an:

> The principle of progressive revelation reflects the notion of the presence of a Divine Entity who manifests His will in terms of the circumstances of His people, who speaks to them in terms of their reality and whose word is shaped by those realities. This word of God thus remains alive because its universality is recognized in the middle of an ongoing struggle to re-discover meaning in it. The challenge for every generation of believers is to discover their own moment of revelation, their own intermission in revelation, their own frustrations with God, joy with His consoling grace, and their own being guided by the principle of progressive revelation.[83]

The interpretation of progressive revelation, of simply living with it as a believer itself requires the ethical act of *sabr*, or endurance, which is among the most commonly cited virtues in the Qur'an. It takes on the meaning of something akin to the ability to maintain commitment despite difficult circumstances, of perseverance.[84] The moral subject is to show fortitude, and do good deeds,[85] to struggle and be steadfast.[86] Endurance, commitment, patience, and *sabr* recall the processes which the Muslim Question(ed) seek to test and violate. The interrogation and the press conference as social conditions, progressively unliveable for the migrant or the intruder, work precisely to provoke a loss of composure in Others, a depletion of one's capacity to endure so as to confirm their exhaustion as a threat in order to license their deportation.

Yet *sabr* in the face of racism and Islamophobia is not a fatalism that these orders of deprivation will disappear (only) as a sudden act of divine will, but rather that they necessitate unsettling and difficult work, hence, the enduring quality required of those who engage in it. It is after all not the Islamophobe or racist or sexist—of whatever political hue—who has to be careful with their words, but their adversaries. Those who believe in words and who resist

---

[82] W. Smith. (1980). "The True Meaning of Scripture: An Empirical Historian's Nonreductionist Interpretation of the Qur'an." *International Journal of Middle East Studies*, 11(4), 487–505.

[83] Farid Esack. (2001). "What Do Men Owe Women? Islam & Gender Justice: Beyond Simplistic Apologia." Available at: http://www.oocities.org/faridesack/fewhatdomenowe.html

[84] Q2:177.

[85] Ar. *sālihāt*, Q11:11; or to be persistent and rely upon [the] lord, Q16:42.

[86] Q16:110.

the emptying out of language brought on by economies and classifications of war, and the bureaucracies that uphold them.[87] As symptomatic of this impoverishment, notions of radicalization (or that orientalist fascination of inherent Muslim fanaticism) as deployed in the techno-economies of the war on terror surely rest on hollow words, diagrams, databases, ultimately base, contradictory, and designed to sting. *Sidq*, as "telling the truth," or more broadly something like "integrity" or "being true to," calls, on the contrary, for a correspondence between reality and speech, behavior, and worldly living. It calls for some consistency with what we say and what we do. It means fulfilling promises (*sādiqīn*).[88]

In addition to the faith-based conceptual context of *sidq*, the root of the word also implies a public dimension, the proclaiming of one's allegiance, in the root concept of *sadīq*, or "friend,"[89] that far transcends the politics of hatred oriented on the Muslim. Even more so when taken in the context of this larger moral vocabulary (and cosmology) and the concrete practices—*zakat*, *salah*, and *sawm*—which give them a performative and planetary dimension of universal solidarity. A vocabulary and dimension which is only coherent because of the fact of one's inherent value that cannot be contingent on what others might say of me, or do to me even in the event of my incarceration, death, or murder. For the soul, or *ruh*, is a subtle form or substance infused within the body by the very fact of being alive and is "that which makes a creature animate, and to which individuality is attributed."[90] The moral agent is only so because s/he is unequivocally a being that has within them a soul that makes them so, but which must be trained and takes stock of its deeper temporal and spatial location(s). Orders which invented the white race, produce the racial subject, and license degradation, can give no time to the fact of one's sheer accident of being on this earth, the only one that

---

[87] I am recalling Sartre's words on language and the anti-Semite. p. 13: "Never believe that anti-Semites are completely unaware of the absurdity of their replies. They know that their remarks are frivolous, open to challenge. But they are amusing themselves, for it is their adversary who is obliged to use words responsibly, since he believes in words. The anti-Semites have the right to play. They even like to play with discourse for, by giving ridiculous reasons, they discredit the seriousness of their interlocutors. They delight in acting in bad faith, since they seek not to persuade by sound argument but to intimidate and disconcert. If you press them too closely, they will abruptly fall silent, loftily indicating by some phrase that the time for argument is past. It is not that they are afraid of being convinced. They fear only to appear ridiculous or to prejudice by their embarrassment their hope of winning over some third person to their side." Jean-Paul Sartre. (1995). *Anti-Semite and Jew: An Exploration of the Etiology of Hate*. New York: Shocken. On the "systematic looting" of racist and sexist language, see also: Toni Morrison. (1975). "A Humanist View." *Black Studies Center Public Dialogue*. Available at: https://soundcloud.com/portland-state-library/portland-state-black-studies-1. and Toni Morrison. (1993). "Nobel Lecture." *The Nobel Prize*. Available at: https://www.nobelprize.org/prizes/literature/1993/morrison/lecture/
[88] Q34:29.
[89] Q26:101.
[90] Homerin. "Soul," p. 80.

we have, and occupying a certain body, colored a certain shade, with certain documentation. That this becomes the basis of one's perceived human and, thus, sociopolitical status to be projected/colonized into the future indefinitely is absurd when put in the context of *ruh*, through which an uneliminable surplus is presupposed.

On the precarious invention of the white race (in the US case) and the present responsibility of those who are burdened by it, Bouteldja writes:

> I will readily concede this to you: you didn't choose to be white. You're not really guilty. Just responsible. If there is a burden that deserves to be borne, it's this one. The white race was invented to fulfil the needs of what would soon become your bourgeois class, because any alliance between slaves who were not yet black and proles who were not yet white was becoming a threat. Within the context of the American conquest, nothing predestined your ancestors to become white. On the contrary, all the conditions for the alliance between slaves and proletarians were present. It was a close one. In the face of this threat, those who would become the American bourgeoisie offered you a *deal*: to give you a stake in the trafficking of black people and make you ally yourselves with the exploitation of slaves. This is how the bourgeoisie invented common interests between itself and you, or your ancestors, if you prefer. This is how, progressively, by institutionalizing itself, the white race was invented. In fact, race, in the hands of the white bourgeois, is an instrument of management; in your hands, it is a salary, a distinction. Since then, what has separated us is neither more nor less than a conflict of interest between races, a conflict which is as powerful and structured as class conflict.[91]

Has this salary of whiteness made those wearing the name "white" any safer? Any less engaged in fatal conflicts? Less anxious of the stranger and more hospitable even to the wretched or poor of their own kind? In the fatal modes of the racial subject, those housing her in the interrogation room or at the press conference, for whom and for what are questions being asked?

Beginning from a principle of the *ruh* as a sufficient condition for being owed and owing obligations of care, hospitality, fairness, witnessing, and justice in which *sabr* is essential, in conjunction with the work of thinking in time(s) of ambiguous direction, and space(s), interconnected and saturated with inherent value, there are, paradoxically, limits to the questions that can be asked. What I mean by the limits of questioning is that the intrinsic value of all human subjects (and indeed animals and non-sentient life) is rationally posited (if inconsistently practiced) rather than necessitating "rational" proof.

---

[91] Bouteldja, *Whites*, pp. 45–46.

The legal principle of the presumption of innocence has not, for example, required the development of an entire legal-philosophical field to prove the rationality of this proposition.

But a basis for assessing what the ethical credentials of our questions, of knowledge cultivation itself, need not be adjudicated on grounds of meta-physics. We can in fact judge the decisive structures of modern life and their utility according to the ways in which they serve their "consumers," white or otherwise. Not only is this a move against a crude relativism (that so often plague postcolonial moves towards cosmopolitanism) in which each and every worldview is fair game to be left unchallenged as the exclusive pre-serve of some peoples' individual lives. But what in the transformations and investments that have shaped our world, industrialism, technology, capital-ism, bureaucracy, nation-state, and the autonomous (white) figure of "reason" (Man) which haunts them all, has served the earth and the life that populates it?[92] Have they not, in the final analysis, failed all consumers, including those who took their lands to be the center of gravity of the world? This is to say nothing of the decimation of animal and insentient life who are nonetheless also witnessing to the deterioration of the earth and its resources of life, and which while having differential effects according to geography and, more importantly, wealth also implicated in histories I have recounted, ultimately involves us all. For, the survival of the human species and other forms of life is surely at stake:

> Colossal environmental destruction; massive colonialist and imperialist atroci-ties and dehumanization; unprecedented forms of political and social violence; the construction of lethal political identities; the poisoning of food and water; the extermination of alarming numbers of species; increasingly worrying health threats; indecent disparity between rich and poor; social and communal disin-tegration; the rise of narcissistic sovereign individualism and sociopathology; a dramatic increase in individual and corporate psychopathologies; an alarming spread of mental health disorders; a "growing epidemic" of suicide, and much more (the list is long enough to require, literally, an entire ledger)—all of which aggregately constituting a phenomenon that calls attention to a revaluation of modernist, industrial, capitalist, and chiefly (though not exclusively) liberal values.[93]

---

[92] See. Losurdo, *Liberalism*; Sven Beckert and Seth Rockman, eds. (2016). *Slavery's Capitalism: A New History of American Economic Development*. Philadelphia: University of Pennsylvania Press; Lisa Lowe. (2015). *The Intimacies of Four Continents*. Durham: Duke University Press; the use-ful review essay by Panjak Mishra. (2015). "Bland Fanatics," London Review of Books, 37(23), 37–40; and Elisabeth Anker. (2014). "The Liberalism of Horror." *Social Research*, 81(4), 795–823.

[93] Hallaq, *Restating Orientalism*, pp. 232–33. On the urgency of the climate question and knowledge, see also: Naomi Oreskes. (2007). "The Scientific Consensus on Climate Change: How Do We

The questions of "race" and Islamophobia are, however, part and parcel of the finitude of the earth and how it is to be shared. The question of people's self-determination and self-recognition may have moved to new locations and peoples but it remains fundamental to a world that is everywhere closing in on itself.

To the liberal mind, perhaps many of my remarks concerning witnessing, sharing, and the status of the human subject are alarming. There have been in my concluding remarks tentative prescriptions and proscriptions, talk of the limit, echoes of that irrational concept of "tradition," or worse, "submission."[94] But what is racism and Islamophobia if not an expression of submission to fiction and phantasm on a civilizational scale? Submission for the Muslim Questioner, however, takes on a different and deeply instructive meaning. Lenn Goodman put the matter thus:

> Islam may be interpreted to mean resignation to the will of God; but if that will remains no longer other, but is accepted by the consciousness as self, then the I can expect of itself the ability to move mountains. . . . This was the meaning of Islam: the progressive assimilation of self to God (so far as it lies in human power). This entails acceptance of the divine will, but not as something alien. The transmuting of selfish purpose to the will of God need not imply a surrender of will because the assimilation of self to God does not imply a surrender to self. On the contrary . . . this assimilation is the meaning of man's fulfilment qua man, the substance of Plato's answer to the cryptic challenge of the oracle, "Know thyself!" To know oneself was to see in oneself affinities to the divine and to accept the obligation implied by such recognition to develop these affinities—to become, in as much as was in human power, like God.[95]

Goodman's words have great value, I contend, beyond the Muslim and can be translated into the problems of witnessing, sharing, and ethics in our time. Submission should not (only) be understood as an absolute surrender or secession from the world to a suprahuman agency (which include time and space also). It is the recognition of some essential principle outside of the self which must bind him to other things and people. What concerns us here is the reconstructive project of thinking about the human, of life and death,

---

Know We Are Not Wrong?" In *Climate Change: What It Means for Us, Our Children, and Our Grandchildren*, ed. Joseph F. C. DiMento and Pamela Doughman. Cambridge, MA: MIT Press, 65–99; Thesis 3 in Dipesh Chakrabarty. (2009). "The Climate of History: Four Theses." *Critical Inquiry*, 35(2), 197–222, at 215–17. Sanjay Seth. (2013). "'Once Was Blind but Now Can See': Modernity and the Social Sciences." *International Political Sociology*, 7, 136–151.

[94] Submission being the literal meaning of "Islam."

[95] Lenn Evan Goodman. (2003). *Ibn Tufayl's Hayy Ibn Yaqzān: A Philosophical Tale*. Chicago: University of Chicago Press, pp. 17–18.

its mechanization and despoilment, beyond the racism and sexism constitutive of our conceptual universe vis-à-vis human differences, and which have invented the racial subject and the Muslim today as an extreme figure.

How are we to think self and Other that no longer hide and silence the cursed inheritance of modernity while also pointing to an otherwise? A notion of "time" that is a principle of ethical formation, and mapping connections across "spaces" saturated with inherent (not instrumental) value are, I have argued, instructive for this effort. But also, finally, to think about the self, "grounded on cosmologies of *complementary dualities* (and/and) rather than on *dichotomies* or *contradictory dualities* (either/or)."[96] To heed Audre Lorde's timeless insight that "the master's tools will never dismantle the master's house. They may allow us temporarily to beat him at his own game, but they will never enable us to bring about genuine change."[97] It is, in essence, a call to go back to basics and to recognize what some Andean Indigenous thinkers call *vincularidad*—an integral relation and interdependence among all living organisms.[98]

But "there is a reason," James Baldwin reminds us, "after all, that some people wish to colonise the moon, and others dance before it as an ancient friend."[99] On the level of the body, those archaic gestures in the colonial world (to kill, rape, pillage, brainwash, etc.) constituted the *accursed share* of the colony.[100] Aimé Césaire for one struggled his entire life to place racism and colonialism, with all its false names on trial in order to cultivate a place of permanence where the indestructible core of the human being would be made manifest. A place in which a new "we" could reside and which could bear witness to *the rise of humanity* (expansively defined in my schema to include,

---

[96] Mignolo, *On Decoloniality*, p. 155.

[97] Audre Lorde. (2007). "The Master's Tools Will Never Dismantle the Master's House." In *Sister Outsider*. New York: Ten Speed Press, p. 112.

[98] On the concept's place in decolonial Indigenous philosophy, see the argument by the Aymara thinker Fernando Huanacuni Mamani. ([2010] 2015). *Vivir Bien/Buen Vivir: Filosofía, políticas, estrategias y experiencias de los pueblos ancestrales*, 6th ed. La Paz: Instituto International de Integración, pp. 115–68; See also: Rolando Vázquez. (2012). "Towards a Decolonial Critique of Modernity: Buen Vivir, Relationality and the Task of Listening." In *Capital, Poverty, Development: Denktraditionen im Dialog: Studien zur Befreiung und Interkultalitat 33*, edited by Raul Fornet-Betancourt. Wissenschaftsverlag Mainz, Germany: Achen, pp. 241–52; Pérez, Emma. (1999). *The Decolonial Imaginary: Writing Chicanas into History*. Bloomington: Indiana University Press.

[99] James Baldwin. (2007). "To Be Baptised." In *No Name in the Street*. London: Vintage International, p. 128.

[100] Césaire—and later Fanon—have explained that the beneficiaries of imperial raciology amputated their own humanity in the process of excluding the Other; that the coloniser who insists on "seeing the other man as *an animal*, accustoms himself to treating him like an animal, tends objectively to transform *himself* into an animal." Césaire, *Discourse on Colonialism*, p. 33, 41.

so to speak, the nonhuman), and to the deeply held conviction that "humans, no matter where they are, have rights as human beings."[101]

While what we all sure share are our differences, there is no relation to the stranger or neighbor which does not also impact more fundamental issues of habitation, freedom, and hospitality. Thinking this way means to make absurd notions of self, alterity, and identity obstinately rooted in debates about mind/body, masculine/feminine, moderate/extreme, and above all nature/culture dichotomies, conveniently bracketing uncomfortable difference on the losing side in the hope of maintaining some level of coherence in self-definition. Instead, it is to exploit structural closure to insist that *we are each of us guarantors for the Other's share* as part of a collective body that has moral agency. Being in the world with all its natural and human multiplicity does not even begin with the subject. Time, space, and self all fundamentally implicate the Other *and* nature: in Other presents, connected geographies and cosmologies, with a share of the world mutually guaranteed. The archetype of the Muslim Questioner makes a demand for *re-existence*, recognizing the principle of *vincularidad* in our unconditional relationship to humanity and to an increasingly precarious planet.

EXILE

The desire for difference, the assertion of it as embodied in Saffiyah Khan's dignified, half-smiled bemusement captured above, is not one opposed to the project of the *in-common* or against a principle of equal shares. We must take this critique of race, that inaugural code which foreclosed access to the in-common for the majority of the world, forward toward a critical reimagining of modern life without the racial contents with which it seems inseparable. "We must," as Gilroy tells us, "find new courage to reflect on the history of political nationalism that has been entangled with the ideas of race, culture, and civilisation and to understand how Europe's imperial and colonial dominance brought racisms and nationalisms together in ways that still affect present conditions."[102] This contrasts with the tenacious impulses in the world to analyze, engage, and search for evidence in support of policies of hunting, incarceration, murder.[103]

---

[101] Césaire, Discourse, p. 69.

[102] Gilroy, *After Empire*, p. 162.

[103] An impulse that most intensely manifests in debates about Other women. It was never argued, for example, even among the most ardent feminists of the nineteenth century that, "European women could liberate themselves from the oppressiveness of Victorian dress (designed to compel the female figure to the ideal of frailty and helplessness by means of suffocating, rib-cracking stays, it must surely rank among the most constrictive fashions of relatively recent times) only by adopting

This approach, however, even in its liberal mode never bothers to question the unidirectionality of solidarity. Consistent with the policy of ignorance, in this case within feminist activism and scholarship,

> white women have "well-meaning concerns" about brown and black women, or Christian and Jewish American and European women (secular and religious alike) having "well-meaning concerns" about Muslim women of all nationalities. Why is it that there is no international solidarity projects and transnational feminism among Asian and African women, Muslim or otherwise, that express "well-meaning concerns" about their white and non-white American and European sisters who continue to suffer under legal, political, social, and economic regimes of discrimination is a question that is not asked.[104]

This is an approach that is buttressed by state, international, and corporate structures of "solidarity," patronage, sponsorship, lucrative funding, commissions, taskforces, and increasingly complex layers of bureaucracy. The Muslim Question(ed)—the racial subject caught between hostility and condescension—places the burden of being tolerable on the Muslim through the demands for his customs, traditions, forms of sociality, governance, communication, and all the rest to fall in line.[105] There is a pressing need for an expansive vocabulary capable of reflecting the earth's most pressing issues (ecological collapse chief among them), and for which we can mobilize Islamic resources. Which is to say, then, that this vocabulary already

---

the dress of some other culture. nor has it ever been argued, whether in Mary Wollestonecraft's day, when European women had no rights, or in our own day and even by the most radical feminists, that because male domination and injustice to women have existed throughout the West's recorded history, the only recourse for Western women is to abandon Western cultures and find themselves some other culture. the idea seems absurd, and yet this is routinely how the matter of improving the status of women is posed with respect to women in Arab and other non-Western societies" Leila Ahmed. (1992). *Women and Gender in Islam: Historical Roots of a Modern Debate*. New Haven, CT: Yale University Press, p. 244.

[104] Massad, *Islam in Liberalism*, p. 176.

[105] In a rather crude but instructive reversal, Wendy Brown writes, "Decades after Euro-Atlantic women rose up against the sexual codes that bound them to roles of subservience, unpaid and unrecognized labor, sexual availability and decorative objectification, what is to be made of these New York women teetering on the balls of their feet on stilts? Imagine walking for an hour in such shoes, let alone running for a bus, chasing after children, navigating inclement weather, standing all day at work or even for just two hours at a cocktail party in them. In Islamic female religious dress, one would surely be more comfortable, far less likely to sprain an ankle, slip on ice, trip on an uneven sidewalk, permanently damage one's feet, or succumb to chronic sciatica or other back injuries. One might also have better concentration, a wider subjective imaginary, and more versatility in greeting the various episodes and possibilities of a day. In short, if shoes nearly impossible to stand let alone walk in are freely chosen, that does not make them shoes of freedom, something of course that can be said of hijab or niqab as well. Yet to my knowledge, no one, anywhere in the Western world, has ever seriously considered passing legislation to outlaw such shoes, their making or their wearing, including in schools or state offices." Wendy Brown. (2012). "Civilizational Delusions: Secularism, Tolerance, Equality." *Theory and Event* 15(2).

exists—across the "chaotic" multicultural streets of urban centers as much as in the Qur'an; in mass cultural forms as music, film, and art and also the rich traditions of poetry and philosophy of Muslims. It provides a well of alternative, more capacious images of memory, self-understanding, of place.

We must take seriously the multicultural future "prefigured everywhere in the ordinary experiences of contact, cooperation, and conflict across the supposedly impermeable boundaries of race, culture, identity, and ethnicity."[106] The ordinary forms of cohabitation and interaction which constitute an alternative repository of imaginative resources for revising, and in the process expanding a futurology far beyond the fundamentalisms of "race" and the unsustainable yet comforting notion of white civilization that it birthed.[107] In its place, the Muslim Questioner engages a more difficult "reification" that requires a certain level of estrangement from one's immanent locale proposing more open affiliations. I follow Hamid Dabashi in arguing that "we need to change our whole architectonics of this interlocution altogether, and address the only interlocutor that has been left to all of us: a fractured and self-destructing world. [. . .] We must dismantle the fact that we are each other's figment of the imagination. Here the will is not to power; it is to resist power. Once that negative dialectic is posited, we will see alternative worlds emerge beyond 'the West and the Rest.'"[108] I find myself returning often to a passage by Hugo of St. Victor, a twelfth-century monk from Saxony:

> It is therefore, a source of great virtue for the practiced mind to learn, bit by bit, first to change about in visible and transitory things, so that afterwards it may be able to leave them behind altogether. The person, who finds his homeland sweet is still a tender beginner; he to whom every soil is as his native one is already strong; but he is perfect to whom the entire world is as a foreign place. The tender soul has fixed his love on one spot in the world; the strong person has extended his love to all places; the perfect man [and woman] has extinguished his.[109]

---

[106] Gilroy, *Postcolonial Melancholia*, p. xii.

[107] The obstacles for this effort have multiplied where, "the idea of culture has been abused by being simplified, instrumentalised, or trivialised, and particularly through being coupled with notions of identity and belonging that are overly fixed or too easily naturalised as exclusively national phenomena. Recalibrating approaches to culture and identity so that they are less easily reified and consequently less amenable to these misappropriations seems a worthwhile short-term ambition that is compatible with the long-term aims of a reworked and politicised multiculturalism. Indeed, it is doubly welcome because it requires the renunciation of the cheap appeals to absolute national and ethnic difference that are currently fashionable." Gilroy, *After Empire*, p. 6.

[108] Dabashi, *Can Non-Europeans Think?*, pp. 22–23.

[109] Hugo of St. Victor. (1961). *Didascalicon, trans. Jerome Taylor.* New York: Columbia University Press, p. 101.

Erich Auerbach, the great German philologist, argues that Hugo is calling for "exile," what I understand to be a deeply ethical practice in a world that is experiencing intense forms of blockade, of the separation wall, the checkpoint, the garrison, or the (privately-run) detention center as a definitive logic of entire nations, foolishly denying the decimation of the planet which has little time for national borders. Hugo twice makes it clear that the "strong" or "perfect" "man" achieves independence and detachment by working *through* attachments, not by rejecting them, not a secession from the world but a commitment to making it, in all its uncomfortable difference, thrive. Exile, according to Edward Said's reading, "is predicated on the existence of, love for, and a real bond with one's native place; the universal truth of exile is not that one has lost that love or home, but that inherent in each is an unexpected, unwelcome loss. Regard experiences then as if they were about to disappear: what is it about them that anchors or roots them in reality? What would you save of them, what would you give up, what would you recover?"[110]

Exilic possibilities are only ever possible, however, absent the grip of the racism and Islamophobia that has surely gripped Britain and Europe in historical, pathological, imaginary, and also material ways. The worldly associations embodied by the Muslim Questioner who enjoins the difficult struggles of refusal, of denationalization, of struggles that insist on the right to our differences that we must form, are essential and urgent. Muslims, the racialized, can surely think, speak, see, and be in ways that are surely incomprehensible to the inherent reductionism of "race" and its disturbing subject-objects of violation. But we can wait no longer for those who sustain them to catch up. In the face of whiteness's decay and Europe's perceived demotion to but one small part of the world among others, we are living through a moment in which the durability of the world itself, never mind the beings who seek to rule it, is in question. This world's, this planet's, limits are manifesting themselves everywhere; whether in the destruction of homes—human and natural—or the outright disappearance of the resources of life. Ultimately, Arundhati Roy insists, "another world is not only possible, she is on her way. On a quiet day, I can hear her breathing."[111] This is not the reclamation of great pasts, of the attempt to reinstall colonially dismantled structures and borders; for this is impossible. In the Muslim Questioner's refusals, for example, it is not enough to reverse the fundamentalisms of white supremacy and of ISIS with an "Islam is the answer" type essentialization. Nor even is it adequate to pursue "a politics of no worse than" in which the iniquities of

---

[110] Said, *Culture and Imperialism*, p. 406.

[111] Arundhati Roy. (2003). "Confronting Empire." World Social Forum, Porto Alegre. Roy's speech is available at: https://www.youtube.com/watch?v=uu3t8Z-kavA (quote at 20:30). A transcript of the speech can be found at: https://www.thenation.com/article/confronting-empire/

conflicting systems of belief, thought, and practice are relativized so as to erase the deeply moral-ethical quandaries that plague both, and which lock the two (or more) in a never-ending struggle against being "the worse."

It is to treat with epistemic respect what has gone before us, what we have inherited, what it is that we owe to others, the past and future, and, above all, retrieving the Other—human and nonhuman—for ethicizing the self. That in societies and cultures formed from the nuclear power plant of "race," racism, and Islamophobia, the instruments for comprehending such a formation before seeking to dismantle it are to be found precisely in those who experience its effects most intensely. And further still, that in the very fact of living, the attempts made to cage in the inherent heterogeneity of being in the world—of being human and that is all—whether authorized from within or without Islam, are all made inadequate. There is no escape, for the analyst or otherwise, from attending "to the social and economic factors, to the geographic and historical factors and *actors*, to culture as a dynamic entity that produces and is produced by social, economic, historic, and geographic factors and actors, analysts." Massad continues, only then "whether Asian or African or European or American, will [we] be able to begin to understand and analyse social phenomena based on terms and methods that the local situation on hand itself determines, rather than script them *a priori* with research agendas that are connected to imperial policies";[112] imperial policies that have been masked by the names of civilization, security, reform, progress, science, reason, and all the rest. Names that are constitutive of the violent world of racism—with the construction of ever-newer Others as Questions—that has plagued the earth as a force of limitless expenditure and genocide. It is all of this that I have sought to research, fully cognizant of the ways in which "research" itself is a "dirty" word[113] that has strong ties to power and to "race." There is, however, much to be done, much to be thought, to bring this world to fruition. But it begins, I think, from the ethical struggles to listen, to remember, and to ask the right questions.

---

[112] Massad, *Islam in Liberalism*, pp. 211–12.
[113] L. T. Smith. (1999). *Decolonizing Methodologies: Research and Indigenous Peoples*. New York: Zed Books, p. xi.

Bibliography

Abbas, S. (2013). The echo chamber of freedom: The Muslim woman and the pretext of agency. *Boundary 2, 40*(1), 155–189.

Abbattista, G. (2006). Empire, liberty and the rule of difference: European debates on British colonialism in Asia at the end of the eighteenth century. *European Review of History: Revue européenned'histoire, 13*(3), 473–498.

Abbott, D. (2018). We still do not know the true scale of the Windrush generation scandal. *New Statesman.* https://www.newstatesman.com/politics/staggers/2018 /11/we-still-do-not-know-true-scale-windrush-generation-scandal

Abdul Khabeer, S. (2017). *Muslim cool: Race, religion, and Hip Hop in the United States.* New York: New York University Press.

Acharya, A. (2011). Dialogue and discovery: In search of international relations theories beyond the West. *Millennium—Journal of International Studies, 39*(3), 619–637.

Acharya, A., & Buzan, B. (2007). Why is there no non-Western IR theory?: Reflections on and from Asia: An introduction. *International Relations of the Asia-Pacific, 7*(3), 1–26.

Acharya, A., & Buzan, B. (2010). *Non-Western international relations theory: Perspectives on and beyond Asia.* London: Routledge.

Achcar, G. (2008). *Orientalism in reverse.* London: Radical Philosophy, p. 151.

Aching, G. (2011). On colonial modernity: Civilization versus sovereignty in Cuba, c. 1840. In R. Shilliam (Ed.), *International relations and Non-Western thought: Imperialism, colonialism and investigations of global modernity* (pp. 29–46). London: Routledge.

Adams, R. (2018). Cambridge gives role to academic accused of racist stereotyping. *Guardian.* https://www.theguardian.com/world/2018/dec/07/cambridge-gives-role -to-academic-accused-of-racist-stereotyping

Adetunji, J. (2010, July 21). Gary McKinnon campaigners praise PM for raising hacker's case with Obama. *Guardian.* https://www.theguardian.com/world/2010/ jul/21/gary-mckinnon-campaigners-pm-hacker-obama

Afzal-Khan. (2005). *Shattering the stereotypes: Muslims women speak out.* North Hampton, MA: Olive Branch Press.

Agathangelou, A. M. (2010a). Necro-(Neo) colonizations and economies of Blackness: Of slaughters, "accidents," "disasters" and captive flesh. In S. Biswas & S. Nair (Eds.), *International relations and states of exception: Margins, peripheries, and excluded bodies* (pp. 186–209). London: Routledge.

Agathangelou, A. M. (2010b). Bodies of desire, terror and the war in Eurasia: Impolite disruptions of (Neo) liberal internationalism, neoconservatism and the 'new' imperium. *Millennium-Journal of International Studies, 38*(3), 693–722.

Agathangelou, A. M. (2013). Slavery remains in reconstruction and development. In M. K. Pasha (Ed.), *Globalization, difference, and human security* (pp. 152–165). London: Routledge.

Agathangelou, A. M., & Ling, L. H. M. (2004a). Power, borders, security, wealth: Lessons of violence and desire from September 11. *International Studies Quarterly, 48*(3), 517–538.

Agathangelou, A. M., & Ling, L. H. M. (2004b). The house of IR: From family power politics to the poisies of worldism. *International Studies Review, 6*(4), 21–49.

Agathangelou, A. M., & Ling, L. H. M. (2009). *Transforming world politics: From empire to multiple worlds.* London: Routledge/Taylor & Francis Group.

Agier, M. (Ed.). (2014). *Un monde de camps.* Paris: La Découverte.

Ahmad, A. (1967). *Islamic modernism in India and Pakistan, 1857–1964.* Oxford: Oxford University Press.

Ahmad, I. (2013). Islamophobia, European modernity and contemporary illiberalism, politics. *Religion & Ideology, 14*(2), 167–172.

Ahmad, S. (2018). *What is Islam? The importance of being Islamic.* Princeton: Princeton University Press.

Ahmed, L. (1982). Western ethnocentrism and perceptions of the harem. *Feminist Studies, 8*(3) (Fall), 521–534.

Ahmed, L. (1992). *Women and gender in Islam: Historical roots of a modern debate.* New Haven, CT: Yale University Press.

Ahmed, R. (2017). Riz Ahmed's moving performance of "sour times." *The Tonight Show Starring Jimmy Fallon.* https://www.youtube.com/watch?v=M9tUEhgExPM

Ahmed, S. (2004). *The cultural politics of emotion.* Edinburgh: Edinburgh University Press.

Ahmed, S. (2012). *The stillbirth of capital: Enlightenment writing and colonial India.* Stanford: Stanford University Press.

Ahsan, T. (2011). This be the answer. In *This be the answer: Poems from prison.* Edinburgh: Radio Ramadan Edinburgh.

Akala. (2018). *Natives: Race and class in the ruins of empire.* London: Two Roads.

Akhtar, A. (2010). A Muslim community, securitised. *Guardian.* https://www.theguardian.com/commentisfree/belief/2010/jun/20/muslim-birmingham-surveillance

Akhtar, P. (2019). Sajid Javid and the complex life of a Muslim conservative leadership hopeful. *The Conversation.* https://theconversation.com/sajid-javid-and-the-complex-life-of-a-muslim-conservative-leadership-hopeful-118849

al-Ali, N. (2000). *Secularism, gender, and the state in the Middle East: The Egyptian women's movement.* Cambridge: Cambridge University Press.

Al-Marashi, I. (2019). The New Zealand massacre and the weaponisation of history. *Al Jazeera.* https://www.aljazeera.com/indepth/opinion/zealand-massacre-weaponisation-history-190322062222288.html

al-Shistani, M. B. (2010). Is the role of women in Al-Qaeda increasing? *BBC News Online.* https://www.bbc.co.uk/news/world-middle-east-11484672

al-'Aqqad, M. 'A. (1964). *al-Dimuqratiyyah fi al-Islam.* Cairo: Dar al-Ma'arif bi-Misr.

Alcoff, L. M. (2007). Epistemologies of ignorance: Three types. In S. Sullivan & N. Tuana (Eds.), *Race and epistemologies of ignorance* (pp. 39–58). Albany: State University of New York.

Ali, S. M. (2013). Race: The difference that makes a difference. *TripleC, 11*(1), 93–106.

Ali, S. M. (2016). A brief introduction to decolonial computing. *XRDS, 22*(4) (June 2016), 16–21.

Ali, S. M. (2017). Decolonizing information narratives: Entangled apocalyptics, algorithmic racism and the myths of history. *Proceedings, 1*, 50.

All-Party Parliamentary Group. (2018). *Islamophobia defined.* London: Home Office.

Allen, A. (2017). *The end of progress: Decolonizing the normative foundations of critical theory.* New York: Columbia University Press.

Allen, C. (2010). *Islamophobia.* London: Ashgate.

Allen, K. (2018). Whose crisis counts? Intersectionality, austerity and the politics of survival. *Ethnic and Racial Studies, 41*(13), 2301–2309.

Amaliah Voices Podcast. (2019). The dehumanisation of Muslims and why Islamophobia isn't a phobia | small talk Ep. 2 with Suhaiymah M. Khan. *Amaliah.* https://www.amaliah.com/post/54957/the-dehumanisation-of-muslims-and-why-islamophobia-isnt-a-phobia-small-talk-ep-2-in-with-suhaiymah-m-khan

Amar, P. (2013). *The security archipelago: Human-security states, sexuality politics, and the end of neoliberalism.* Durham, NC: Duke University Press.

Amer, K., & Noujaim, J. (2019). *The great hack.* Netflix.

American Psychiatric Association. (2012). Narcissistic personality disorder. In *Diagnostic and Statistical Manual of Mental Disorders (DSM-5)* Naklada Slap, Jastrebarsko, Croatia.

Amin, S. (1989). *Eurocentrism.* New York: Monthly Review Press.

Amin, S. (2010a). Eurocentrism. In *Modernity, religion and democracy: A critique of Eurocentrism and culturalism.* Oxford: Pambazuka Press.

Amin, S. (2010b). *Global history: A view from the South.* Oxford: Pambazuka Press.

Amrani, I., & Heywood, M. (2017). "Solidarity is so important": Saffiyah Khan meets woman she stood up for at EDL demo – Video. *Guardian.* https://www.theguardian.com/uk-news/video/2017/apr/11/saffiyah-khan-meets-woman-stood-up-for-edl-demo-video

Andersen, M. L., & Hill, C. P. (2004). *Race, class, and gender: An anthology.* Belmont, CA: Wadsworth/Thomson Learning.

Anderson, B. (1991). *Imagined communities: Reflections on the origin and spread of nationalism.* London: Verso.

Anderson, C. (2003). *Eyes off the prize: The United Nations and the African American struggle for human rights, 1944–1955.* Cambridge: Cambridge University Press.

Anderson, M. (1999). Legal scholarship and the politics of Islam in British India. In R. S. Khare (Ed.), *Perspectives on Islamic law, justice, and society.* Lanham, MD: Rowman & Littlefield.

Anghie, A. (1999). Finding the peripheries: Sovereignty and colonialism in nineteenth-century international law. *Harvard International Law Journal, 40*(1), 32–114.

Anghie, A. (2006). The evolution of international law: Colonial and postcolonial realities. *Third World Quarterly, 27*(5), 739–753.

Anghie, A. (2007). *Imperialism, sovereignty and the making of international law* (Vol. 37). Cambridge: Cambridge University Press.

Anievas, A., Manchanda, N., & Shilliam, R. (2015). *Race and racism in international relations.* London: Routledge.

Anker, E. (2014). The liberalism of horror. *Social Research, 81*(4) (Winter), 795–823.

Ansari, F. (2013). Babar Ahmad police trial: A verdict based on fear, not fact? *CAGE.* https://www.cage.ngo/babar-ahmad-police-trial-verdict-based-fear-not-fact

Anyangwe, E. (2015). Misogynoir: Where racism and sexism meet. *Guardian.* https://www.theguardian.com/lifeandstyle/2015/oct/05/what-is-misogynoir

Anzaldúa, G. (1987). *Borderlands/La Frontera: The new mestiza.* San Francisco: Aunt Lute.

Appadurai, A. (2013). *The future as cultural fact: Essays on the global condition.* London: Verso Books.

Appiah, A. (2018). *The lies that bind: Rethinking identity: Creed, country, color, class, culture* (1st ed.). New York, NY: Liveright Publishing.

Appiah, K. A. (1987). Racism and moral pollution. *Philosophical Forum, 18*(2–3), 185–202.

Appiah, K. A. (1992). *In my father's house: Africa in the philosophy of culture.* New York: Oxford University Press.

Appiah, K. A. (2010). *Cosmopolitanism: Ethics in a world of strangers.* London: W. W. Norton & Company.

Aradau, C., & Blanke, T. (2010). Governing circulation: A critique of the biopolitics of security. In M. de Larrinaga and M. G. Doucet (Eds.), *Security and global governmentality: Globalization, governance and the state.* London: Routledge.

Arendt, H. (1973). *The origins of totalitarianism.* New York: Harcourt Brace Jovanovich.

Asad, T. (1973). *Anthropology and the colonial encounter.* New York, NY: Humanities Press.

Asad, T. (1993). *Genealogies of religion: Discipline and reasons of power in Christianity and Islam.* Baltimore: Johns Hopkins University Press.

Asad, T. (1994). Ethnographic representation, statistics, and modern power. *Social Research, 61*(1), 55–88.

Asad, T. (2003). *Formations of the secular: Christianity, Islam, modernity.* Stanford: Stanford University Press.

Asad, T. (2007). *On suicide bombing.* New York: Columbia University Press.

Asad, T. (2018). *Secular translations: Nation-state, modern self, and calculative reason.* New York: Columbia University Press.

Asad, T., Brown, W., Butler, J., & Mahmood, S. (2013). *Is critique secular?: Blasphemy, injury, and free speech.* New York: Fordham University.

Asaro, P. M. (2013). The labor of surveillance and bureaucratized killing: New subjectivities of military drone operators. *Social Semiotics, 23*(2), 196–224.

Asian Network Reports. (2016). Boy at nursery meant "cucumber" not "cooker bomb." http://www.bbc.co.uk/programmes/p03m5jh9

Ayoob, M. (1998). Subaltern realism: International relations theory meets the third world. In S. G. Neuman (Ed.), *International relations theory and the third world* (pp. 31–54). New York: St. Martin's.

Ayoob, M. (2002). Inequality and theorizing in international relations: The case for subaltern realism. *International Studies Review, 4*(3), 27–48.

Azad, H. (2017). Thinking about Islam, politics and Muslim identity in a digital age. *Journal of Islamic and Muslim Studies, 2*(2), 122–134.

Babayan, K., & Najmabadi, A. (2008). *Islamicate sexualities: Translations across temporal geographies of desire.* Cambridge, MA: Harvard Center for Middle East Studies.

Back, L. (2002). Aryans reading adorno: Cyber-culture and twenty-first century racism. *Ethnic and Racial Studies, 25*(4), 628–651.

Badiou, A. (2012). La Grèce, les nouvelles pratiques impériales et la ré-invention de la politique. *Lignes, 39,* 39–47.

Badran, M. (1995). *Feminists, Islam, and nation: Gender and the making of modern Egypt.* Princeton: Princeton University Press.

Badran, M. (1999). Toward Islamic feminisms: A look at the Middle East. In A. Afsaruddin (Ed.), *Hermeneutics and honor: Negotiating female "public" space in Islamic/ate societies.* Cambridge: Harvard University Press.

Badran, M. (2008). Between Muslim women and the Muslimwoman. *Journal of Feminist Studies in Religion, 24*(1), 101–106.

Badran, M. (2009). *Feminism in Islam: Secular and religious convergences.* Oxford: Oneworld.

Badran, M. (2010). Oùenest le féminisme islamique? *Critique internationale, 46*(1), 25–44.

Badran, M. (Ed.). (2011). *Gender and Islam in Africa: Rights, sexuality, and law.* Stanford: Stanford University Press.

Bail, C. A. (2015). *Terrified: How anti-Muslim fringe organizations became mainstream.* Princeton, NJ: Princeton University Press.

Bailey, M., & Trudy. (2018). On Misogynoir: Citation, erasure, and plagiarism. *Feminist Media Studies, 18*(4), 762–768.

Bailey, S. (2005). *No man's land: How Britain's inner city young are being failed.* London: Centre for Young Policy Studies.

Bakalian, A., & Bozorgmehr, M. (2009). *Backlash 9/11: Middle Eastern and Muslim Americans respond.* Berkeley, CA: University of California Press.

Baker, L. D. (1998). *From savage to Negro: Anthropology and the construction of race, 1896–1954.* Berkeley, CA: University of California Press.

Baker-Beall, C., Heath-Kelly, C., & Jarvis, L. (2014). *Counter-radicalisation: Critical perspectives.* Abingdon: Routledge.

Bakkar, S. (2019). Suhaiymah Manzoor-Khan, Malia Bouattia, Lauren Booth, Sahar Al Faifi and more pull out of BLF over counter-extremism funding. *Amaliah.* https://www.amaliah.com/post/56146/bradford-literature-festival-2018

Baldwin, J. (1964a). *Nobody knows my name: More notes of a native son.* London: Michael Joseph.

Baldwin, J. (1964b). *Notes of a native son.* London: Michael Joseph.

Baldwin, J. (1964c). *The fire next time.* London: Penguin.

Baldwin, J. (1985a). *Price of a ticket.* New York: St. Martin's Press.

Baldwin, J. (1985b). *"White man's guilt." The price of the ticket: Collected nonfiction, 1948–1985.* London: Michael Joseph.

Baldwin, J. (1993). *Nobody knows my name.* New York: First Vintage International.

Baldwin, J. (2007). To be baptised. In *No name in the street.* London: Vintage International.

Baldwin, J., & Lorde, A. (1984). "The pro-Black perspective," on KWAZ radio, with your host pan-African nationalist author Onitaset Kumat. https://www.youtube.com/watch?v=3_590duLjkw

Ballard, R. (1996). Islam and the construction of Europe. In W. A. R. Shadid & P. S. van Koningsveld (Eds.), *Muslims in the margin: Political responses to the presence of Islam in Western Europe.* Kampen: Kok Pharos, 15–51.

Bandopadhyaya, J. (1977). Racism and international relations. *Alternatives, 3*(1), 19–48.

Barbulescu, R., Favell, A., Khan, O., Paraschivescu, C., Samuel, R., & Varela, A. (2019). Class, race and inequality in Northern towns. *Runnymede Trust.* https://www.runnymedetrust.org/projects-and-publications/employment-3/class-race-and-inequality-in-northern-towns.html

Barder, A. (2015). *Empire within: International hierarchy and its imperial laboratories of governance.* London: Routledge.

Barkawi, T., & Laffey, M. (1999). The imperial peace: Democracy, force and globalization. *European Journal of International Relations, 5*(4), 403–434.

Barkawi, T., & Laffey, M. (2006). The postcolonial moment in security studies. *Review of International Studies, 32,* 329–352.

Barlas, A. (2007). Engaging feminism: Provincializing feminism as a master narrative. Paper Presented at Tempere Peach Research Institute, Finland, August 31, 2007. http://www.asmabarlas.com/TALKS/Finland_07.pdf

Bassiouni, M. C. (Ed.). (1974). *The civil rights of Arab Americans: The special measures.* North Dartmouth, MA: Arab-American University Graduates.

Bataille, G., & Leiris, M. (2008). *Correspondence.* Edited by L. Yvert & Translated by L. Heron. London: Seagull Books.

Batty, D. (2006). Reid barracked during speech to Muslim parents. *Guardian.* https://www.theguardian.com/world/2006/sep/20/terrorism.immigrationpolicy

Bauman, Z. (2000). *Modernity and the holocaust.* Ithaca, NY: Cornell University Press.

Bayoumi, M. (2008). *How does it feel to be a problem?* New York: Penguin.

Bayoumi, M. (2015). *This Muslim American life: Dispatches from the war on terror.* New York: New York University Press.

Bazian, H. (2019). Islamophobia, racism and the "great replacement". *Daily Sabah.* https://www.dailysabah.com/columns/hatem-bazian/2019/05/08/islamophobia-racism-and-the-great-replacement

BBC News. (2019). Christchurch shootings: Mosque attacker charged with terrorism. *BBC News Online.* https://www.bbc.co.uk/news/world-asia-48346786?intlink_from_url=https://www.bbc.co.uk/news/topics/c966094wvmqt/christchurch-mosque-shootings&link_location=live-reporting-story

BBC One. (2018). Bodyguard. https://www.bbc.co.uk/programmes/p06crngy

Beckert, S., & Rockman, S. (Eds.). (2016). *Slavery's capitalism: A new history of American economic development.* Philadelphia, PA: University of Pennsylvania Press.

Behnke, A. (2004). Terrorizing the political: 9/11 within the context of the globalization of violence. *Millennium, 33*(2), 279–312.

Beier, M. (2009). *International relations in uncommon places: Indigeneity, cosmology and the limits of international theory.* New York: Palgrave Macmillan.

Beinin, J., & Lockman, Z. (1987). *Workers on the Nile: Nationalism, communism, Islam and the Egyptian working class, 1882–1954.* Princeton, NJ: Princeton University Press.

Belich, J. (2009). *Replenishing the earth: The settler revolution and the rise of the Angloworld.* Oxford: Oxford University Press.

Bell, C. (2011). *The freedom of security: Governing Canada in the age of counter-terrorism.* Vancouver: UBC Press.

Bell, C., & Evans, B. (2010). Post-interventionary societies: An introduction. *Journal of Intervention and Statebuilding, 4*(4), 363–370.

Bell, D. (2005). Race and empire: The origins of international relations. *International Studies Review, 7*(4), 633–635.

Bell, D. (2013). Race and international relations: Introduction. *Cambridge Review of International Affairs, 26*(1), 1–4.

Bell, D. (2014). What is liberalism? *Political Theory, 42*(6), 682–715.

Bell, D. (2016). *Reordering the world: Essays on liberalism and empire.* Princeton, Oxford: Princeton University Press.

Ben-Moshe, L., Chapman, C., & Carey, Allison (Eds). (2014). *Disability incarcerated: Imprisonment and disability in the United States and Canada.* New York: Palgrave Macmillan.

BENI. (2014). Pharrell – Happy British Muslims! #HAPPYDAY. https://www.youtube.com/watch?v=gVDIXqILqSM

Benjamin, W. (1982). *"Theses on the philosophy of history" in his illuminations.* Translated by H. Zohn. New York: Fontana/Collins.

Bennett, H. (2011). Soldiers in the court room: The British Army's part in the Kenya emergency under the legal spotlight. *The Journal of Imperial and Commonwealth History, 39*(5), 717–730.

Bennett, W. L. (2003). New media power: The internet and global activism. In N. Couldry & J. Curran (Eds.), *Contesting media power* (pp. 17–37). Lanham, MD: Rowman & Littlefield.

Berdine, M. D. (2018). *Redrawing the Middle East: Sir Mark Sykes, imperialism and the Sykes–Picot agreement.* I.B. Tauris.

Berger, J. (1992). *Ways of seeing.* London: Penguin.

Berlin, I. (1998). *Many thousands gone: The first two centuries of slavery in North America.* Cambridge, MA: Harvard University Press.

Bernadette, A. (2009). Islam, women, and Western responses: The contemporary relevance of early modern investigations. *Women's Studies, 38,* 273–292.

Bernhaut, J. (2014). One year on from the "go home vans" flop: Has the home office learned anything? *openDemocracy.* https://www.opendemocracy.net/en/5050/one-year-on-from-go-home-vans-flop-has-home-office-learned-anything/

Bessant, B. (1994). British imperial propaganda and the republic. *Journal of Australian Studies, 18*(42), 1–4.

Beydoun, K. (2018). *American Islamophobia: Understanding the roots and rise of fear.* Oakland: University of California Press.

Bhabha, H. K. (1994). *The location of culture.* London: Routledge.

Bhambra, G. K. (2007). *Rethinking modernity: Postcolonialism and the sociological imagination.* Basingstoke, UK: Palgrave Macmillan.

Bhambra, G. K. (2014). *Connected sociologies.* London: Bloomsbury Academic.

Bhambra, G. K. (2014). Postcolonial and decolonial dialogues. *Postcolonial Studies, 17*(2), 115–121.

Bhambra, G. K. (2017a). Brexit, Trump, and "methodological Whiteness": On the misrecognition of race and class. *The British Journal of Sociology, 68*(S1): S214–S232.

Bhambra, G. K. (2017b, November 10). Why are the White working classes still being held responsible for Brexit and Trump? *LSE Brexit.* http://blogs.lse.ac.uk/brexit/

Bhambra, G., Gebrial, D., & Nisancioglu, K. (2018). *Decolonising the university.* London: Pluto Press.

Bhambra, G., & Shilliam, R. (2008). *Silencing human rights: Critical approaches to a contested project.* London: Palgrave.

Bhattacharyya, G. (2008). *Dangerous brown men: Exploiting sex, violence and feminism in the war on terror.* London: Zed Books.

Bhattacharyya, G. (2017). The myth of the "White working class" stops us seeing the working class as it really is. *Red Pepper.* https://www.redpepper.org.uk/the-myth-of-the-white-working-class/

Bhopal, K. (2018). *White privilege: The myth of a post-racial society.* Bristol: Policy Press.

Bier, J. (2017). Palestinian state maps and imperial technologies of staying put. *Public Culture, 29*(1(81)), 53–78.

Bigelow, J. (2006). *Jamaica in 1850, or, the effects of sixteen years of freedom on a slave colony.* Champaign, IL: University of Illinois Press.

Bilgin, P. (2008). Thinking past "Western" IR? *Third World Quarterly, 29*(1), 5–23.

Binder, L. (1988). *Islamic liberalism.* Chicago: University of Chicago Press.

Birt, Y. (2008). Governing Muslims after 9/11. In S. Sayyid & A. Vakil (Eds.), *Thinking through Islamophobia: Symposium papers* (pp. 26–29). Leeds: Centre for Ethnicity and Racism Studies.

Birt, Y. (2009). Promoting virulent envy – Reconsidering the UK's terrorist prevention strategy. *Royal United Services Institute (RUSI) Journal, 154*, 52–58.

Birt, Y. (2015). Safeguarding Muslim children from Daesh and prevent. *The Muslim News.* http://www.muslimnews.co.uk/newspaper/top-stories/safeguarding-muslim -children-from-daesh-and-prevent/

Birt, Y. (2019a). Astroturfing and the rise of the secular security state in Britain. *Medium.* https://medium.com/@yahyabirt/astroturfing-and-the-rise-of-the-secular -security-state-in-britain-cd21c5005d43

Birt, Y. (2019b). British Muslims, cultural freedom, and the counter-extremism industry. *Medium.* https://medium.com/@yahyabirt/british-muslims-cultural-free-dom-and-the-counter-extremism-industry-d41d1faf96b9

Biswas, S. (2001). "Nuclear apartheid" as political position: Race as a postcolonial resource? *Alternatives, 26*(4), 485–522.

Biswas, S. (2014). *Nuclear desire: Power and the postcolonial nuclear order.* Minneapolis, MN: University of Minnesota Press.

Blair, T. (2001a). Tony Blair at the labour party conference. *The Guardian Online.* http://www.theguardian.com/politics/2001/oct/02/labourconference.labour6

Blair, T. (2001b). Tony Blair's speech to the commons. *The Guardian Online.* http://www.theguardian.com/world/2001/oct/04/september11.usa3

Blair, T. (2006). *Speech to world affairs council.* Los Angeles, August 1.

Blakely, R., Hayes, B., Kapoor, N., Kundnani, A., Massoumi, N., Miller, D., Mills, T., Sabir, R., Sian, K., & Tufail, W. (2019). *Leaving the war on terror: A progressive alternative to counter-terrorism policy.* Amsterdam: Transnational Institute.

Blaut, J. M. (1993). *The colonizer's model of the world: Geographical diffusionism and Eurocentric history.* New York: Guilford Press.

Blears, H. (2009). Many voices: Understanding the debate about prevent violent extremism. *Migration Studies Unit Lecture Series LSE.* http://www.lse.ac.uk/pub-licEvents/events/2008/20081203t1539z001.aspx

Bleich, E. (2005). The legacies of history? Colonization and immigrant integration in Britain and France. *Theory and Society, 34*(2), 171–195.

Blitz, J. (2017). Post-Brexit delusions about empire 2.0. *Financial Times.* https://www.ft.com/content/bc29987e-034e-11e7-ace0-1ce02ef0def9

Boas, F. (1938). *The mind of primitive man.* New York, NY: Macmillan.

Boczkowski, P. (2018). *Trump and the media.* Boston: MIT Press.

Bonilla-Silva, E. (2010). *Racism without racists: Color-blind racism and the persistence of racial inequality in the United States* (3rd ed.). Lanham, MD: Rowman & Littlefield.

Booth, R., & Mohdin, A. (2018). Revealed: The stark evidence of everyday racial bias in Britain. *Guardian.* https://www.theguardian.com/uk-news/2018/dec/02/revealed -the-stark-evidence-of-everyday-racial-bias-in-britain

Booth, R., Mohdin, A., & Levett, C. (2018). Bias in Britain: Explore the poll results. *Guardian.* https://www.theguardian.com/uk-news/ng-interactive/2018/dec/02/bias -in-britain-explore-the-poll-results

Bouhdiba, A. (1975). *La sexualitéen Islam.* Paris: Presses universitaires de France.

Boulaga, F. E. (1977). *La crise du Muntu: Authenticité africaine et philosophie.* Paris: PrésenceAfricaine.

Bouteldja, H. (2012). Pierre, Djemila, Dominique…and Mohamed. *The Culture Craft.* https://theculturecraft.wordpress.com/comments/critical-reflections-by-hou-ria-bouteldja/

Bouteldja, H. (2013). Decolonising France – An evening with Houria Bouteldja. *IHRCtv.* https://www.youtube.com/watch?v=CszbqynuZ4I

Bouteldja, H. (2016). *Whites, Jews, and us: Towards a politics of revolutionary love.* South Pasadena, CA: Semiotext(e).

Bouteldja, H. (2017). *The Whites, Jews and us.* South Pasadena, CA: Semiotexte.

Bowden, B. (2011). Colonialism, anti-colonialism, and the idea of progress. In UNESCO-EOLS Joint Committee (Ed.), *History and philosophy of science and technology, encyclopaedia of life support systems.* Oxford: EOLSS.

Boyd, M. (2019). Baldwin and the Black arts movement. In D. Miller (Ed.), *James Baldwin in context* (Literature in Context, pp. 211–220). Cambridge: Cambridge University Press.

Bradley, G. (2019). From Grenfell to Windrush, state racism kills – Sometimes quickly, sometimes slowly. *openDemocracy.* https://www.opendemocracy.net /en/opendemocracyuk/from-grenfell-to-windrush-state-racism-kills-sometimes -quickly-sometimes-slowly/

Brennan, T. (2014). Subaltern stakes. *New Left Review, 89*(September–October), 67–87.

Breton, A. (1973). *Entretiens, 1913–1952.* Paris: Gallimard.

British Broadcasting Corporation. (2006). In quotes: Jack Straw on the veil. *BBC News Online.* http://news.bbc.co.uk/1/hi/uk_politics/5413470.stm

British Broadcasting Corporation. (2011). Babar Ahmad police officers not guilty of assault. *BBC News Online.* https://www.bbc.co.uk/news/uk-13638164

British Broadcasting Corporation. (2017). PM vows to renew the "British dream" – But what is it? *BBC News Online.* https://www.bbc.co.uk/news/uk-politics -41506032

British Broadcasting Corporation. (2019). Jihadi Jack: IS recruit Jack Letts loses UK citizenship. *BBC News Online.* https://www.bbc.co.uk/news/uk-49385376

Britton, C. (2017). *Race and the unconscious: Freudianism in French Caribbean thought.* Oxon: Routledge.

Brown, C. (1994). "Turtles all the way down": Anti-foundationalism, critical theory and international relations. *Millennium–Journal of International Studies, 23*(2), 213–236.

Brown, G. (2007). "Terror alert", interview with Andrew Marr. *BBC News Online*. http://news.bbc.co.uk/1/hi/programmes/sunday_am/6258416.stm

Brown, W. (2012). Civilizational delusions: Secularism, tolerance, equality. *Theory and Event, 15*(2).

Bureau of Education. (1965). Selections from educational records, part I (1781–1839). Edited by H. Sharp. Calcutta: Superintendent, Government Printing, 1920. Reprint. Delhi: National Archives of India, pp. 107–117. Emphases Added. http://www.columbia.edu/itc/mealac/pritchett/00generallinks/macaulay/txt_minute_education_1835.html

Burgess, J. (2008). All your chocolate rain are belong to us? Viral video, YouTube and the dynamics of participatory culture. In G. Lovink & S. Niederer (Eds.), *Video vortex reader: Responses to YouTube* (pp. 101–109). Amsterdam, Netherlands: Institute of Network Cultures.

Burman, E. (2012). Deconstructing neoliberal childhood: Towards a feminist antipsychological approach. *Childhood, 19*(4), 423–438.

Buruma, I. (2006). *Murder in Amsterdam: The death of Theo van Gogh and the limits of tolerance*. New York: Penguin.

Buruma, I., Margalit, A., & Mazal Holocaust Collection. (2004). *Occidentalism: The West in the eyes of its enemies*. London: Penguin.

Busby, M., & Dodd, V. (2019). London schoolgirl who fled to join Isis wants to return to UK. *Guardian*. https://www.theguardian.com/world/2019/feb/14/london-schoolgirl-who-fled-to-join-isis-wants-to-return-to-uk

Butler, J. (2000). Restaging the universal: Hegemony and the limits of formalism. In J. Butler, E. Laclau, & S. Žižek (Eds.), *Contingency, hegemony, universality: Contemporary dialogues on the left*. London: Verso.

Butterly, A. (2015). Hermione granger to be played by Black actress Noma Dumezweni, sparking fan debate. *BBC Online*. http://www.bbc.co.uk/newsbeat/article/35150488/hermione-granger-to-be-played-by-black-actress-noma-dumezweni-sparking-fan-debate

Buzan, B. (2006). Will the "global war on terrorism" be the new Cold War? *International Affairs, 82*(6), 1101–1118.

Buzan, B., & Lawson, G. (2015). *The global transformation: History, modernity and the making of international relations*. Cambridge: Cambridge University Press.

Buzan, B., & Lawson, G. (2013). The global transformation: The nineteenth century and the making of modern international relations. *International Studies Quarterly, 57*(3), 622.

CAGE. (2016). Babar Ahmad: Outsourced judiciary and betrayal of human dignity. *CAGE*. https://www.cage.ngo/babar-ahmad-outsourced-judiciary-and-betrayal-human-dignity

CAGE. (2019). *Schedule 7: Harassment at borders the impact on the Muslim community*. London: CAGE. https://www.cage.ngo/product/schedule-7-harassment-at-borders-report

Cainkar, L. (Forthcoming). Fluid terror threat: A genealogy of the racialization of Arab, Muslim, and South Asian Americans. *Amerasia Journal, 44*(1), 27–59.

Cainkar, L. A. (2009). *Homeland insecurity: The Arab American and Muslim American experience after 9/11.* New York: Russell Sage.

Camber, R. (2019). Scotland Yard chief Cressida Dick insists the met police is no longer riddled with racism 20 years after the Macpherson report branded it 'institutionally' prejudiced. *Daily Mail.* https://www.dailymail.co.uk/news/article-7234417 /Scotland-Yard-chief-Cressida-Dick-insists-Met-Police-no-longer-riddled-racism .html

Campbell, J. (1991). *Talking at the gates: A life of James Baldwin.* London: Faber and Faber.

Campbell, S., Chandler, D., & Sabaratnam, M. (Eds.). (2011). *A liberal peace?: The problems and practices of peacebuilding.* London: Zed Books Ltd.

Cannon, G., & Brine, K. (Eds.). (1995). *Objects of enquiry: The life, contributions, and influence of Sir William Jones, 1746–1794.* New York: New York University Press.

Cantle, T. (2001). *Community cohesion – A report of the independent review team.* London: Home Office.

Carrington, B. (2010). *Race, sport and politics: The sporting black diaspora.* London: SAGE Publications Ltd.

Carrington, B., & McDonald, I. (2001). *Race, sport and British society.* London: Routledge.

Casciani, D. (2012). The battle to prosecute Babar Ahmad. *BBC Online.* https://www .bbc.co.uk/news/uk-17606337

Casey, D. L. (2016). *The Casey review: A review into opportunity and integration.* London: DCLG.

Castelli, E. (Ed.). (2001). *Women, gender, and religion: A reader.* New York: Palgrave.

Castells, M. (1997). *The power of identity.* Oxford: Blackwell.

Castro-Gómez, S. (2007). The missing chapter of empire: Postmodern re-organization of coloniality and post-fordist capitalism. *Cultural Studies, 21*(2–3), 428–448.

Cavendish, J. (2011). Al-Qa'ida glossy advises women to cover up and marry a Martyr. *Independent.* https://www.independent.co.uk/news/world/asia/al-qaida -glossy-advises-women-to-cover-up-and-marry-a-martyr-2240992.html

Centre for Contemporary Cultural Studies. (1982). *The empire strikes back. Race and racism in '70s Britain.* Oxon: Hutchinson & Co.

Césaire, A. (1972). *Discourse on colonialism.* London: Monthly Review Press.

Césaire, A. (1987, February 26). "Discours sur la négritude," speech, University of Florida. http://www.humaniteinenglish.com/spip.php?article898

Césaire, A. (2000). *Discourse on colonialism.* Translated by J. Pinkham. New York: Monthly Review Press.

Chakelian, A. (2019). "We should be fearful": Muslim women on the prospect of Boris Johnson as prime minister. *New Statesman.* https://www.newstatesman.com /politics/uk/2019/06/we-should-be-fearful-muslim-women-prospect-boris-johnson -prime-minister

Chakrabarty, D. (2000). *Provincializing Europe: Postcolonial thought and historical difference*. Princeton, NJ: Princeton University Press.

Chakrabarty, D. (2009). The climate of history: Four theses. *Critical Inquiry, 35*(2), 197–222, at 215–217.

Chalabi, M., & Marsh, S. (2018). Revealed: Bias faced by minorities in UK driving tests. *Guardian*. https://www.theguardian.com/uk-news/2018/dec/03/black-women -far-less-likely-than-white-men-to-pass-driving-tests

Chamayou, G. (2013). *Théorie du drone*. Paris: La Fabrique.

Chan, S. (1999). Chinese perspectives on world order. In T. Paul & J. Hall (Eds.), *International order and the future of world politics* (pp. 197–212). Cambridge: Cambridge University Press.

Chan, S. (2007). Fanon: The octogenarian of international revenge and the suicide bomber of today. *Cooperation and Conflict, 42*(2), 151–168.

Chan, S., & Moore, C. (Eds.). (2009). *Approaches to international relations: Vol. 4. Non-Western approaches to international relations*. London: SAGE.

Chan-Malik, S. (2011). "Common cause": On the Black-immigrant debate and constructing the Muslim American. *Journal of Race, Ethnicity, and Religion, 2*(8), 1–39.

Chatterjee, P. (1994). *The nation and its fragments*. Princeton, NJ: Princeton University Press.

Chaturvedi, V. (Ed.). (2012). *Mapping subaltern studies and the postcolonial*. London: Verso.

Chen, K.-H. (2010). *Asia as method: Toward deimperialization*. Durham, NC: Duke University Press.

Chinoy, S. (2019). The racist history behind facial recognition. *New York Times*. https://www.nytimes.com/2019/07/10/opinion/facial-recognition-race.html

Chivallon, C., & David, H. (2017). Colonial violence and civilising Utopias in the French and British Empires: The Morant Bay rebellion (1865) and the insurrection of the South (1870). *Slavery & Abolition, 38*(3), 534–558.

Chowdhry, G. (2007). Edward Said and contrapuntal reading: Implications for critical interventions in international relations. *Millennium, 36*(1), 101–116.

Chowdhry, G., & Nair, S. (Eds.). (2004). *Power, post-colonialism and international relations*. London: Routledge.

Chulov, M., Parveen, N., & Rasool, M. (2019). Shamima Begum: Baby son dies in Syrian refugee camp. *Guardian*. https://www.theguardian.com/uk-news/2019/mar /08/shamima-begum-confusion-after-reports-newborn-son-may-have-died

Cleall, E. (2017). From divine judgement to colonial courts: Missionary "justice" in British India, c. 1840–1914. *Cultural and Social History, 14*(4), 447–461.

Clive, J., & Macaulay, T. B. (1973). *The shaping of the historian*. London: Secker & Warburg.

Cobain, I. (2013). Revealed: The bonfire of papers at the end of empire. *Guardian*. https://www.theguardian.com/uk-news/2013/nov/29/revealed-bonfire-papers -empire

Cobain, I. (2019). Revealed: The "woke" media outfit that's actually a UK counter-terror programme. *Middle East Eye*. https://www.middleeasteye.net/news/revealed -woke-media-outfit-thats-actually-uk-counterterror-programme

Cobain, I., Evans, B., & Mahmood, M. (2016). Inside Ricu, the shadowy propaganda unit inspired by the Cold War. *Guardian.* https://www.theguardian.com /politics/2016/may/02/inside-ricu-the-shadowy-propaganda-unit-inspired-by-the -cold-war

Coetzee, J. M. (1988). *White writing: On the culture of letters in South Africa.* New Haven, CT: Yale University Press.

Cohen, B. (2019). The Stephen Lawrence inquiry report: 20 years on. *Runnymede Trust.* https://www.runnymedetrust.org/uploads/StephenLawrence20briefing .pdf

Cohn, B. (1996). *Colonialism and its forms of knowledge: The British in India.* Princeton: Princeton University Press.

Cole, S. A. (2002). *Suspect identities: A history of fingerprinting and criminal identification.* Cambridge, MA: Harvard University Press.

Coleman, D. (2005). *Romantic colonization and British anti-slavery.* Cambridge: Cambridge University Press.

Comaroff, J. (2009). The politics of conviction: Faith on the neo-liberal frontier. *Social Analysis, 53*(1), 17–38.

Comaroff, J. (2011). *Theory from the South; or, how Euro-America is evolving toward Africa.* Boulder, CO: Paradigm.

Comaroff, J. L., & Comaroff, J. (1991). *Of revelation and revolution, vol. 2, the dialectics of modernity on a South African frontier.* Chicago: University of Chicago Press.

Commons Select Committee. (2019). Cressida Dick questioned on progress in implementing recommendations of Macpherson Report. https://www.parliament .uk/business/committees/committees-a-z/commons-select/home-affairs-committee /news-parliament-2017/macpherson-report-evidence-17-191/

Conquergood, D. (2000). Rethinking elocution: The trope of the talking book and other figures of speech. *Text and Performance Quarterly, 20*(4), 325–341.

Conquergood, D. (2002). Performance studies: Interventions and radical research. *The Drama Review, 46*(2), 1–12.

Conway, G. (1997). *Islamophobia: A challenge for us all.* London: The Runnymede Trust. https://www.runnymedetrust.org/companies/17/74/Islamophobia-A -Challenge-for-Us-All.html

Cooke, M. (2000a). Multiple critique: Islamic feminist rhetorical strategies. *Nepantla: Views From the South, 1*(1), 91–110.

Cooke, M. (2000b). Women, religion, and the postcolonial Arab world. *Cultural Critique, 45*(Spring), 150–184.

Cooke, M. (2007). The Muslimwoman. *Contemporary Islam, 1*, 139–154.

Cooke, M. (2008). Religion, gender and the Muslim woman. *Journal of Feminist Studies in Religion, 24*(1), 91–119.

Copland, I. (2006). Christianity as an arm of empire: The ambiguous case of India under the company, C. 1813–1858. *The Historical Journal, 49*(4), 1025–1054.

Coppock, V., & McGovern, M. (2014). Dangerous minds? De-Constructing counterterrorism discourse, radicalisation and the "psychological vulnerability" of Muslim children and young people in Britain. *Children and Society, 28*, 242–256.

Cossins, D. (2018). Discriminating algorithms: 5 times AI showed prejudice. *New Scientist*. https://www.newscientist.com/article/2166207-discriminating-algorithms-5-times-ai-showed-prejudice/

Coutu, J. (2006). *Persuasion and propaganda: Monuments and the eighteenth-century British Empire*. Montreal: McGill-Queen's University Press.

Coward, H. G. (2008). *The perfectibility of human nature in Eastern and Western thought*. Albany: State University of New York Press.

Cowell, A. (2006). Jack Straw ignites a debate over Muslim veil – Europe – International Herald Tribune. *New York Times*. https://www.nytimes.com/2006/10/06/world/europe/06iht-london.3061419.html

Croft, S., & Moore, C. (2010). The evolution of threat narratives in the age of terror: Understanding terrorist threats in Britain. *International Affairs, 86*(4), 821–835.

Cromer, E. B. (1908). The government of subject races. *Edinburg Review*, 1–27.

Cromer, E. B. (1915). *Modern Egypt*. New York: Macmillan.

Crosby, A. (1966). *Ecological imperialism: The biological expansion of Europe, 900–1900*. Cambridge: Cambridge University Press.

Crummell, A. (1995). *Civilization and Black progress: Selected writings of Alexander Crummell on the South*. Edited by J. R. Oldfield. Charlottesville: University Press of Virginia.

Curran, A. (2005). Imaginer l'Afrique au siècle des lumières. *Cromohs: Cyber Review of Modern Historiography, 10*, 1–14.

Curtis, A. (2016). *Hyper normalisation*. British Broadcasting Corporation.

Dabashi, H. (2009). *Post-orientalism: Knowledge and power in a time of terror*. New Jersey: Transaction Publishers.

Dabashi, H. (2015). *Can non-Europeans think?* London: Verso.

Dabashi, H. (2019). When it comes to Islamophobia, we need to name names. *Al Jazeera*. https://www.aljazeera.com/indepth/opinion/islamophobia-names-190329125123813.html

Dabashi, H. (Forthcoming). *Europe and its shadows: Coloniality after empire*. London: Pluto Press.

Dahlgreen, W. (2014). The British empire is "something to be proud of". *YouGov*. https://yougov.co.uk/topics/politics/articles-reports/2014/07/26/britain-proud-its-empire

Daily Mail. (1965, February 22). If this man didn't exist he'd have to be invented. *Daily Mail*.

Daily Sabah. (2017). Muslim women form human chain on Westminster Bridge in London as symbol of unity. https://www.dailysabah.com/europe/2017/03/27/muslim-women-form-human-chain-on-westminster-bridge-in-london-as-symbol-of-unity

Dallmayr, F. (1999). *Border crossings: Towards a comparative political theory*. Boulder, CO: Lexington Books.

Dallmayr, F. (2001). Conversation across boundaries: Political theory and global diversity. *Millennium, 30*(2), 331–347.

Dallmayr, F. (2004). Beyond monologue: For a comparative political theory. *Perspectives on Politics, 2*(2), 249–257.

Dalrymple, W. (2006). *The last Mughal: The fall of a dynasty, Delhi, 1857.* New York: Knopf.

Dalrymple, W. (2019). *The anarchy: The relentless rise of the East India company.* London: Bloomsbury Publishing.

Daniels, J. (2015). "My brain database doesn't see skin color": Color-blind racism in the technology industry and in theorizing the web. *American Behavioral Scientist, 59*(11), 1377–1393.

Darby, P. (1997). At the edge of international relations: Post-colonialism. In *Gender and dependency.* London: Pinter.

Darby, P. (2004). Pursuing the political: A postcolonial rethinking of relations international. *Millennium – Journal of International Studies, 33*(1), 1–32.

Darby, P., & Paolini, A. (1994). Bridging international relations and postcolonialism. *Alternatives: Global, Local, Political, 19*(3), 371–397.

Darwin, J. (2009). *The Empire project: The rise and fall of the British world-system, 1830–1970.* Cambridge: Cambridge University Press.

Daulatzai, S. (2012). *Black star, crescent moon: The Muslim international and Black freedom beyond America.* Minneapolis: University of Minnesota Press.

Davies, L. (2008). *Educating against extremism.* Trentham: Stoke-On-Trent.

Davies, T., Isakjee, A., & Dhesi, S. (2017). Violent inaction: The necropolitical experience of refugees in Europe. *Antipode, 49*, 1263–1284.

Davies, T. (2018). Toxic space and time: Slow violence, necropolitics, and petrochemical pollution. *Annals of the American Association of Geographers, 108*(6), 1537–1553.

Davis, A. (1984a). *Women, culture, and politics.* New York: Random House.

Davis, A. (1984b). *Women, race, & class.* New York: Vintage.

Davis, A. (1995). Reflections on the Black woman's role in the community of slaves. In Guy-Sheftalled (Ed.), *Words of fire: An anthology of African-American feminist thought.* New York: New Press.

Davis, A. (2002). From the convict lease system to the super-max prison. In J. James (Ed.), *States of confinement: Policing, detention, and prisons*, Revised and Updated (pp. 60–74). New York: Palgrave Macmillan.

Davis, D. (2011). House of commons debate, 5 December 2011, Vol. 537, Col. 93.

Davis, D. B. (1975). *The problem of slavery in the age of revolution.* Ithaca: Cornell University Press.

DCLG. (2007a). *Preventing violent extremism: Winning hearts and minds.* London: Author.

DCLG. (2007b). *Preventing violent extremism guidance note for government offices and local authorities in England.* London: Author.

DCLG. (2008). *Prevent pathfinder fund – Mapping of project activities 2007/08.* London: Author.

De Noronha, L. (2018a). The mobility of deservingness: Race, class and citizenship in the wake of the "Windrush Scandal." *The Disorder of Things.* https://thedisorderofthings.com/2018/07/03/the-mobility-of-deservingness-race-class-and-citizenship-in-the-wake-of-the-windrush-scandal/

De Noronha, L. (2018b). There is no such thing as a "left" case for borders. *Red Pepper*. https://www.redpepper.org.uk/there-is-no-such-thing-as-a-left-case-for-borders/

De Tocqueville, A. (1838). *Democracy in America*. New York: Adlard and Saunders.

De Tocqueville, A. (1988). *De la colonieen Algérie*. Brussels: Editions Complexe.

Dearden, L. (2018). "Letterbox" insults against Muslim women spike in wake of Boris Johnson comments. *Independent*. https://www.independent.co.uk/news/uk/home-news/boris-johnson-burqa-muslim-women-veil-attacks-islamophobia-letter-boxes-rise-a8488651.html

Debord, G. (1994). *The society of the spectacle*. New York: Zone Books.

Deleuze, G. (2003). *Deux régimes de fous: Textes et entretiens, 1975–1995*. Paris: Minuit.

Deleuze, G., & Guattari, F. (1983). *Anti-Oedipus: Capitalism and schizophrenia*. Translated by R. Hurley, M. Seem, & H. R. Lane. Minneapolis: University of Minnesota Press.

Department for Education. (2014). *Promoting fundamental British values as part of SMSC in schools*. London: Author

Department for Education. (2015a). *Keeping children safe in education: Statutory Guidance for schools and colleges*, London: Author.

Department for Education. (2015b). *The prevent duty*. London: Author.

Devji, F. (2005). *Landscapes of the Jihad: Militancy, morality, modernity*. London: C. Hurst & Co.

Devji, F. (2008). *The terrorist in search of humanity: Militant Islam and Global politics*. London: C. Hurst & Co.

Devji, F., & In Kazmi, Z. (2017). *Islam after liberalism*. Oxford: Oxford University Press.

DiAngelo, R. (2011). White fragility. *International Journal of Critical Pedagogy, 3*(3), 54–70.

DiAngelo, R. (2019). *White fragility: Why it's so hard for White people to talk about racism*. London: Penguin.

Diawara, M. (2009a). Édouard Gliassnt's world mentality: An introduction to *one world in relation*. https://documenta14.de/en/south/34_edouard_glissant_s_world-mentality_an_introduction_to_one_world_in_relation

Diawara, M. (2009b). *One world in relation*. Directed by French with English Subtitles, 48 Minutes. K'aYéléma Productions.

Diawara, M. (2018). Édouard Glissant's world mentality. *Nka*, November, *1*(42–43), 20–27.

Dickey, C. (2005). Women of Al-Qaeda. *Newsweek*. https://www.newsweek.com/women-al-qaeda-113757

Dickson, A. (2018). Ex-colonies to UK: Forget Brexit "empire 2.0". *Politico*. https://www.politico.eu/article/commonwealth-summit-wont-be-empire-2-0-for-brexit-uk/

Dikötter, F. (2008). The racialization of the globe: An interactive interpretation. *Ethnic and Racial Studies, 31*(8), 1478–1496.

Dilley, A. (2018). Why Brexit can't transform commonwealth trade. *The Conversation.* https://www.theguardian.com/news/2018/apr/10/commonwealth-uk-brexit-leaving-eu

Dillon, M. (2008). Security, race and war. In M. Dillon & A. W. Neal (Eds.), *Foucault on politics, security and war* (pp. 166–196). Basingstoke: Palgrave Macmillan.

Dillon, M., & Reid, J. (2009). *The liberal way of war: Killing to make life live.* London: Routledge.

Dirks, N. B. (1996). Foreword. In B. S. Cohn (Ed.), *Colonialism and its forms of knowledge.* Princeton, NJ: Princeton University Press.

Dirlik, A. (1994). The postcolonial aura: Third world criticism in the age of global capitalism. *Critical Inquiry, 20*(2), 328–356.

Dockter, W. (2015). *Churchill and the Islamic world: Orientalism, empire and diplomacy in the Middle East.* London: I. B. Tauris.

Dodd, V. (2019). Met disproportionately White for another 100 years – Police leaders. *Guardian.* https://www.theguardian.com/uk-news/2019/feb/19/met-police-disproportionately-white-for-another-100-years

Dorling, D., & Tomlinson, S. (2019). *Rule Britannia: Brexit and the end of empire.* London: Biteback Publishing.

Dornhof, S. (2009). Germany: Constructing a sociology of Islamist radicalisation. *Race & Class, 50*(4), 75–82.

Downing, J., & Dron, R. (2018). Grenfell Tower: How Twitter users fought off fake news to honour Muslim heroes. *The Conversation.* https://theconversation.com/grenfell-tower-how-twitter-users-fought-off-fake-news-to-honour-muslim-heroes-98059

Drescher, S. (1987). *Capitalism and antislavery.* Oxford and New York: Oxford University Press.

Du Bois, W. E. B. (1946). *The world and Africa: An inquiry into the part which Africa has played in world history.* New York: International Publishers.

Du Bois, W. E. B. (1990). *The souls of Black folk.* New York: Library of America.

Du Bois, W. E. B. (2007). *Black reconstruction in America: An essay toward a history of the part which Black folk played in the attempt to reconstruct democracy in America, 1860–1880.* New York: Oxford University Press.

Duara, P. (2015). *The crisis of global modernity.* Cambridge: Cambridge University Press.

Duffield, M. (2010). The liberal way of development and the development—security impasse: Exploring the global life-chance divide. *Security Dialogue, 41*(1), 53–76.

Duke, B. (2019). "Islamophobia" definition poses a threat to free speech in the UK. *The Free Thinker.* https://www.patheos.com/blogs/thefreethinker/2019/05/islamophobia-definition-poses-a-threat-to-free-speech-in-the-uk/

Dussel, E. (1993). Eurocentrism and modernity (Introduction to the Frankfurt Lectures). *Boundary 2, 20*(3), 65–76.

Dussel, E. (1995). *The invention of the Americas: Eclipse of "the other" and the myth of modernity.* New York: Continuum.

Dussel, E. (2000). Europe, modernity, and Eurocentrism. *Nepantla: Views From South, 1*(3), 465–478.

Dussel, E. (2002). *Posmodernidad y transmodernidad: diálogos con la filosofía de Gianni Vattimo*. Puebla, México: Universidad Iberoamericana/Instituto de Estudios Superiores de Occidente.

Dussel, E. D. (2012). Transmodernity and interculturality: An interpretation from the perspective of philosophy of liberation. *Transmodernity: Journal of Peripheral Cultural Production of the Luso-Hispanic World, 1*(3), 28–58.

Earle, C. (2015). Good Muslims, bad Muslims, and the nation: The "ground zero mosque" and the problem with tolerance. *Communication and Critical Cultural Studies, 12*(2), 121–138.

Eggert, J. P. (2016). Women fighters in the "Islamic state" and Al-Qaeda in Iraq: A comparative analysis. *Journal of International Peace and Organization* (Special Issue on the "Islamic State"), *90*(3–4), 363–380.

Eickelman, D., & Piscatori, J. (Eds.). (1990). *Muslim travellers: Pilgrimage, migration, and the religious imagination*. Berkeley: University of California Press.

Eisenstein, Z. (2004). *Against empire: Feminisms, racism and the West*. London: Zed Books.

Eisenstein, Z. (2007). *Sexual decoys: Gender, race and war in imperial democracy*. London: Zed Books.

Elahi, F., & Khan, O. (2017). *Islamophobia: Still a challenge for us all*. London: Runnymede. https://www.runnymedetrust.org/uploads/Islamophobia%20Report%202018%20FINAL.pdf

El Fadl, K. (2005). *The search for beauty in Islam: A conference of the books*. London: Rowman & Littlefield.

El Fadl, K. (2014). *Reasoning with god: Reclaiming Shari'ah in the modern age*. London: Rowman & Littlefield.

El Fadl, K. A. (2019). Usuli Institute Khutbah: "From bearing witness to becoming the opiate of the masses," 8.23.19. *Usuli Institute*. https://www.youtube.com/watch?v=qsS7l_vtgEM&t=863s

Eliav-Feldon, M. (2009). *The origins of racism in the West*. Cambridge: Cambridge University Press.

Elkins, C. (2004). *Imperial reckoning: The untold story of Britain's Gulag in Kenya*. New York: Henry Holt & Company.

Elkins, C. (2005). *Britain's Gulag: The brutal end of empire in Kenya*. London: Jonathan Cape.

Elkins, C. (2011). Alchemy of evidence: Mau Mau, the British empire, and the high court of justice. *The Journal of Imperial and Commonwealth History, 39*(5), 731–748.

Elkins, C. (2015). Looking beyond Mau Mau: Archiving violence in the era of decolonization. *The American Historical Review, 120*(June), 852–868.

El-Rouayheb, K. (2005). *Before homosexuality in the Arab-Islamic world, 1500–1800*. Chicago: University of Chicago Press.

Elshimi, M. (2015). Prevent 2011 and counter-radicalisation: What is de-radicalisation? In C. Baker-Beall, C. Heath-Kelly, & L. Jarvis (Eds.), *Counter-radicalisation: Critical perspectives*. Abingdon: Routledge.

Emejulu, A., & Bassel, L. (2015). Minority women, austerity and activism. *Race & Class, 57*(2), 86–95.

Emerson, R. G. (2019). *Necropolitics: Living death in Mexico*. London: Palgrave Macmillan.

Emilio, C. V. (2018). Special issue on female migration to ISIS. *International Annals of Criminology, 56*(1–2), 1–226.

Enayat, H. (1982). *Modern Islamic political thought*. Austin: University of Texas Press.

Ensor, J. (2019). Jihadi Jack: The OCD teenager who took a football to bed with him who grew up to be a terrorist. *The Telegraph*. https://www.telegraph.co.uk/news/2019/06/21/jihadi-jack-ocd-teenager-took-football-bed-grew-terrorist/

Epstein, C. (Ed.). (2017). *Against international relations norms: Postcolonial perspectives*. London: Routledge.

Erickson, A. (1959). Empire or anarchy: The Jamaica rebellion of 1865. *The Journal of Negro History, 44*(2), 99–122.

Esack, F. (2013). Redeeming Islam: Constructing the good Muslim subject in the contemporary study of religion. *Alternation Journal, 11*, 36–60.

Esack, F. (2001). What do men owe women? Islam & gender justice: Beyond simplistic apologia. http://www.oocities.org/faridesack/fewhatdomenowe.html

Esack, F. (2013). *On being a Muslim: Finding a religious path in the world today*. London: Oneworld.

Escobar, A. (1995). *Encountering development: The making and unmaking of the third world*. Princeton, NJ: Princeton University Press.

Esposito, J. (Ed.). (1995). *Oxford Encyclopedia of the modern Islamic world, S.V. far Al-kifāyah*. Oxford: Oxford University Press.

Euben, R. L. (2002). Contingent borders, syncretic perspectives: Globalization, political theory and Islamizing knowledge. *International Studies Review, 4*(1), 23–48.

Euben, R. L. (2004). Travelling theorists and translating practices. In S. K. White & J. D. Moon (Eds.), *What is political theory?* (pp. 145–173). London: Sage Publications.

Evans, B. (2010). Foucault's legacy: Security, war and violence in the 21st century. *Security Dialogue, 41*(4), 413–433.

Evans, B. (2011). The liberal war thesis: Introducing the ten key principles of twenty-first-century biopolitical warfare. *South Atlantic Quarterly, 110*(3), 747–756.

Evans, G. (2018). The unwelcome revival of "race science". *Guardian*. https://www.theguardian.com/news/2018/mar/02/the-unwelcome-revival-of-race-science

Evening Standard. (2006). Kelly condemns multiculturalism. https://www.standard.co.uk/testnewsheadlines/kelly-condemns-multiculturalism-7083995.html

Everett, J. A., Schellhaas, F. M., Earp, B. D., Ando, V., Memarzia, J., Parise, C. V., Fell, B., & Hewstone, M. (2015). Covered in stigma? The impact of differing levels of Islamic head covering on explicit and implicit biases toward Muslim women. *Journal of Applied Social Psychology, 45*, 90–104.

Eze, E. C. (1997). The color of reason: The idea of "race" in Kant's anthropology. In E. C. Eze (Ed.), *Postcolonial African philosophy: A critical reader* (pp. 103–131). Oxford: Blackwell.

Fabian, J. (1983). *Time and the other: How anthropology makes its object*. New York: Columbia University Press.

Fahey, J. (2011). Officers beat me, says Al Qaeda suspect. *Independent*. https://www.independent.co.uk/news/uk/crime/officers-beat-me-says-al-qaida-suspect-2279398.html

Famine Inquiry Commission. (1945). *Report on Bengal*. New Delhi: Manager of Publication, Government of India Press. https://archive.org/stream/in.ernet.dli.2015.206311/2015.206311.Famine-Inquiry#page/n3/mode/2up

Fanon, F. (1965). *A dying colonialism*. New York: Grove.

Fanon, F. (1967). *Black skin, White masks*. New York: Grove Press.

Fanon, F. (2001). *The wretched of the earth*. London: Penguin.

Fanon, F. (2011). Pourquoi nous employons la violence. In M. Bessone & A. Mbembe (Eds.), *Œuvres*. Paris: La Découverte.

Farris, S. (2018). The political economy of homonationalism. *Social Text*. https://socialtextjournal.org/periscope_article/the-political-economy-of-homonationalism/

Farris, S. R. (2012). Femonationalism and the "regular" army of labor called migrant women. *History of the Present, 2*(2) (Fall), 184–199.

Feimster, C. N. (2009). *Southern horrors: Women and the politics of rape and lynching*. Cambridge, MA: Harvard University Press.

Ferguson, J. (1990). *The anti-politics machine: "Development," depoliticization and bureaucratic power in Lesotho*. Cambridge: Cambridge University Press.

Ferguson, J. (2006). *Global shadows: Africa in the neoliberal world order*. Durham: Duke University Press.

Ferguson, J. (2010). The uses of neoliberalism. *Antipode, 41*(Supplement 1), 166–184.

Fessenden, T. (2008). Disappearances: Race, religion, and the progress narrative of US feminism. In J. R. Jakobsen & A. Pelligrini (Eds.), *Secularisms*. Durham, NC: Duke University Press.

Financial Times. (2018). A British illusion of commonwealth trade after Brexit. *Financial Times*. https://www.ft.com/content/2761fc62-42eb-11e8-93cf-67ac3a6482fd; https://theconversation.com/why-brexit-cant-transform-commonwealth-trade-94919

Flacks, S. (2018). Law, necropolitics and the stop and search of young people. *Theoretical Criminology*.

Floyd, S. A. (1995). *The power of Black music: Interpreting its history from Africa to the United States*. New York: Oxford University Press.

Foucault, M. (1973). *The order of things: An archaeology of the human sciences*. Edited by and Translated by R. D. Laing. New York: Random House.

Foucault, M. (1977). *Discipline and punish: The birth of the prison*. New York: Random House.

Foucault, M. (1979a). *The history of sexuality, Vol. 1: An introduction*. Translated by R. Hurley. London: Allen Lane.

Foucault, M. (1979b). What is an author? In J. V. Harari (Ed.), *Textual strategies: Perspectives in post-structuralist criticism*. Ithaca: Cornell University Press.

Foucault, M. (1980). *Power/knowledge: Selected interviews and other writings 1972–1977*. Edited by C. Gordon. New York: Pantheon Books.

Foucault, M. (1982). The subject and power. *Critical Inquiry, 8*(4), 777–795.

Foucault, M. (1994). Face aux gouvernements, les droits de l'homme. In *Dits et écrits*, Vol. 4. Paris: Gallimard.

Foucault, M. (2003). *"Society must be defended": Lectures at the Collège de France, 1975–1976*. Edited by M. Bertani & A. Fontana. New York: Picador.

Foucault, M. (2004a). *Securité, territoire, population. Cours au Collège de France, 1977–1978*. Paris: Seuil/Gallimard.

Foucault, M. (2004b). *Naissance de la biopolitique. Cours au Collège de France, 1978–1979*. Paris: Seuil/Gallimard.

Foucault, M., Sheridan, A., & Foucault, M. (1972). *The archaeology of knowledge*. New York: Pantheon Books.

Fouda, I. G. (2019). "Broken-hearted but not broken": Al Noor imam's Christchurch speech in full. *Guardian*. https://www.theguardian.com/world/2019/mar/22/broken-hearted-but-not-broken-al-noor-imams-christchurch-speech-in-full

Fournier-Fabre, É. (1921). *Le choc suprême; ou, La melée des races*. Paris: G. Ficker.

Francois-Cerrah, M. (2015). State-sanctioned prejudice is at the heart of David Cameron's approach to countering extremism. *New Statesman*. http://www.new-statesman.com/politics/2015/07/state-sanctioned-prejudice-heart-david-camerons-approach-countering-extremism

Franklin, M. J. (2011). *Orientalist Jones: Sir William Jones, poet, lawyer, and linguist, 1746–1794*. Oxford: Oxford University Press.

Free Babar, A. (2018). "Timeline" free Babar Ahmad campaign. https://freebabarahmad.com/timeline/

Freedland, J. (2019). To prevent another Christchurch we must confront the right's hate preachers. *Guardian*. https://www.theguardian.com/commentisfree/2019/mar/15/prevent-another-christchurch-confront-right-hate-preachers

Freud, S. (2001). Our attitude towards death. In *The standard edition of the complete psychological works of Sigmund Freud, volume XIV (1914–1916): On the history of the psycho-analytic movement, papers on metapsychology, and other works*. Translated by J. Strachey et al. London: Vintage.

Freud, S. (2004). *Mass psychology and other writings*. Translated by J. A. Underwood. London: Penguin.

Fuerst, I. M. (2017). *Indian Muslim minorities and the 1857 rebellion: Religion, rebels and Jihad*. London: I.B. Tauris & Co.

Fussey, P. (2013). Contested topologies of UK counterterrorist surveillance: The rise and fall of project champion. *Critical Studies on Terrorism, 6*(3), 351–370.

Fyfe, C. (1962). *A history of Sierra Leone*. Oxford: Oxford University Press.

Garner, S., & Selod, S. (2015). The racialization of Muslims: Empirical studies of Islamophobia. *Critical Sociology, 41*(1), 9–19.

Garvie, C., Bedoya, A., & Frankle, J. (2016). *The perpetual line-up: Unregulated police face recognition in America*. Georgetown Law: Center on Privacy & Technology. https://www.perpetuallineup.org/findings/racial-bias

Geertz, C. (1973). Religion as a cultural system. In *The interpretation of culture*. New York: Basic.

Gentleman, A. (2018). The children of Windrush: "I'm here legally, but they're asking me to prove I'm British". *Guardian.* https://www.theguardian.com/uk-news/2018/apr/15/why-the-children-of-windrush-demand-an-immigration-amnesty

Ghumkhor, S. (2019). The hypocrisy of New Zealand's "this is not us" claim. *Al Jazeera.* https://www.aljazeera.com/indepth/opinion/hypocrisy-zealand-claim-190319104526942.html

Gidher, D., & Wheeler, C. (2019). UK sisters who wed Isis fighters lose citizenship. *The Times.* https://www.thetimes.co.uk/edition/news/uk-sisters-who-wed-isis-fighters-lose-citizenship-36sz69fn9

Gilbert, M. (1975). *Winston Churchill, IV.* London: Pimlico.

Gilmore, R. W. (2007). *Golden Gulag: Prisons, surplus, crisis, and opposition in globalizing California.* Berkley: University of California Press.

Gilroy, P. (1987). *There ain't no Black in the union Jack.* London: Hutchinson.

Gilroy, P. (1993a). *The Black Atlantic: Modernity and double consciousness.* Cambridge, MA: Harvard University Press.

Gilroy, P. (1993b). The peculiarities of the Black English. In *Small acts.* London: Serpent's Tail.

Gilroy, P. P. (2000). *Between camps: Race, identity and nationalism at the end of the colour line.* London: Allen Lane.

Gilroy, P. (2003). Race is ordinary: Britain's post-colonial Melancholia. *Philosophia Africana, 6*(1), 31–45.

Gilroy, P. (2004a). *After empire: Melancholia or convivial culture.* London: Routledge.

Gilroy, P. (2004b). *Postcolonial Melancholia.* New York: Columbia University Press.

Gilroy, P. (2005). Multiculture, double consciousness and the "war on terror". *Patterns of Prejudice, 39*(4), 431–443.

Gilroy, P. (2010). *Darker than blue: On the moral economies of Black Atlantic culture.* London: The Belknap Press of Harvard University Press.

Githens-Mazer, J., & Lambert, R. (2010). Why conventional wisdom on radicalization fails: The persistence of a failed discourse. *International Affairs, 86*(4), 889–901.

Glissant, É. (1928–2011) (1997). *Poetics of relation.* Ann Arbor: University of Michigan Press.

Glissant, É., & Chamoiseau, P. (2009). *L'intraitablebeauté du monde: Adresse à Barack Obama.* Paris: Galaade.

Gobineau, A. (1983). Essai sur l'inégalité des races humaines. In *Œuvrescompletes.* Paris: Gallimard, 1, 623, 1146.

Goldberg, D., Jadhav, S., & Younis, T. (2016). "Prevent." What is pre-criminal space? *Bjpsych Bulletin, 41*(2), 208–211.

Goldberg, D. T. (2002). *The racial state.* Malden, MA: Blackwell Publishers.

Goldberg, D. T. (2015). *Are we all postracial yet?* London: Polity.

Goldberg, D. T. (2017). Violence. *HKW.* https://www.youtube.com/watch?v=FTA4aR8qBR4

Gole, N. (1996). *The forbidden modern: Civilization and veiling.* Ann Arbor: University of Michigan Press.

Goodman, L. E. (1992). Time in Islam. *Asian Philosophy, 2*(1), 3–19.

Goodman, L. E. (2003). *Ibn Tufayl's Hayy Ibn Yaqzān: A philosophical tale*. Chicago: University of Chicago Press.

Gopal, P. (2013). Speaking with difficulty: Feminism and antiracism in Britain after 9/11. *Feminist Studies, 39*(1), 98–118.

Gopal, P. (2019). *Insurgent empire: Anticolonial resistance and British dissent*. London: Verso.

Gordon, M. (2015). Colonial violence and holocaust studies. *Holocaust Studies, 21*(4), 272–291.

Gornall, J. (2017). The Grenfell disaster has highlighted Muslim contributions to community. *The National*. https://www.thenational.ae/opinion/the-grenfell-disaster-has-highlighted-muslim-contributions-to-community-1.92231

Greaves, R. (1996). India 1857: A mutiny or a war of independence? The Muslim perspective. *Islamic Studies, 35*(1), 25–44, 30.

Green, E. (2017). Muslim Americans are united by Trump—And divided by race. *The Atlantic*. https://www.theatlantic.com/politics/archive/2017/03/muslim-americans-race/519282/

Greenfield, P. (2019). Sajid Javid accused of "human fly-tipping" in Shamima Begum case. *Guardian*. https://www.theguardian.com/uk-news/2019/may/31/sajid-javid-accused-shamima-begum-case-syria

Grewal, I. (2005). *Transnational America: Feminisms, diasporas, neoliberalisms*. Durham, NC: Duke University Press.

Grewal, I. (2013). Outsourcing patriarchy: Feminist encounters, transnational mediations and the crime of "Honor killings." *International Feminist Journal of Politics, 15*(1), 1–19.

Grewal, Z. (2014). *Islam is a foreign country*. New York: New York University Press.

Grierson, J. (2018). Choice of new UK anti-extremism chief criticised as "alarming". *Guardian*. https://www.theguardian.com/politics/2018/jan/24/leading-muslim-campaigner-sara-khan-head-anti-extremism-drive

Grosfoguel, R. (2003). *Colonial subject*. Los Angeles: California University Press.

Grosfoguel, R. (2006). The long-durée entanglement between Islamophobia and racism in the modern/colonial capitalist/patriarchal world-system: An introduction. *Human Architecture: Journal of the Sociology of Self-Knowledge, 1*, 1–12.

Grosfoguel, R. (2012). The multiple faces of Islamophobia. *Islamophobia Studies Journal, 1*(1), 9–33.

Grovogui, S.-N. (1996). *Sovereigns, quasi sovereigns, and Africans: Race and self-determination in international law*. Minneapolis/London: University of Minnesota Press.

Grovogui, S. N. (2001a). Come to Africa: A hermeneutics of race in international theory. *Alternatives, 26*(4), 425–448.

Grovogui, S. N. (2001b). Sovereignty in Africa: Quasi-statehood and other myths in international theory. In K. C. Dunn & T. M. Shaw (Eds.), *Africa's challenge to international relations theory*. International Political Economy Series. London: Palgrave Macmillan.

Grovogui, S. N. (2003). Postcolonial criticism: International reality and modes of inquiry. In *Power, postcolonialism and international relations* (pp. 45–67). London: Routledge.

Grovogui, S. N. (2006). Mind, body, and gut! Elements of a postcolonial human rights discourse. In *Decolonizing international relations* (pp. 179–196). London: Rowman & Littlefield Publishers.

Grovogui, S. (2016). *Beyond Eurocentrism and anarchy: Memories of international order and institutions.* New York: Palgrave Macmillan.

Gruffydd Jones, B. (Ed.). (2006). *Decolonizing international relations.* London: Rowman & Littlefield Publishers.

Gržinić, M., & Tatlić, Š. (2014). *Necropolitics, racialization, and global capitalism: Historicization of biopolitics and forensics in politics, art, and life.* Lanham, MD: Lexington Books.

Guénif-Souilamas, N., & Macé, Éric. (2004). *Les Féministes et le garçonarabe.* Paris: Éditions de L'Aube.

Haddad, Y. Y., & Esposito, J. L. (Eds.). (1998). *Islam, gender, and social change.* New York: Oxford University Press.

Hafiz, M. (2018). Brexit, propaganda and empire. *Discover Society.* https://discover-society.org/2018/12/04/focus-brexit-propaganda-and-empire/

Hafiz, M. (2020). Smashing the Imperial Frame: Race, culture, (de)coloniality. *Theory, Culture & Society, 37*(1), 113–145.

Hahn, S. (2003). *A nation under our feet: Black political struggles in the rural South, from slavery to the great migration.* Cambridge, MA: Harvard University Press.

Hall, C. (1992). *White, male and middle class: Explorations in feminism and history.* London: Wiley.

Hall, C. (2000). The rule of difference: Gender, class and empire in the making of the 1832 Reform Act. In I. Blom, K. Hagemann & C. Hall (Eds.), *Gendered nations: Nationalisms and gender order in the long nineteenth century* (pp. 107–136). Oxford: Berg.

Hall, C. (2002). *Civilising subjects: Metropole and colony in the English imagination.* Chicago: The University of Chicago Press.

Hall, C. (2006). *At home with the empire: Metropolitan culture and the imperial world.* Cambridge: Cambridge University Press.

Hall, C. (2008). Making colonial subjects: Education in the age of empire. *History of Education, 37*(6), 773–787.

Hall, C. (2010). *Defining the Victorian nation: Class, race, gender and the British Reform Act of 1867.* Cambridge: Cambridge University Press.

Hall, C. (2012). *Macaulay and son: Architects of imperial Britain.* New Haven, CT: Yale University Press.

Hall, S. (1978). Racism and reaction. In *Five views on multi-racial Britain: Talks on race relations broadcast by BBC TV.* London: Commission for Racial Equality.

Hall, S. (1980). Race, articulation and societies structured in dominance. In H. A. Baker, M. Diawara & R. H. Lindeborg (Eds.), *Reprinted 1996 in Black British cultural studies: A reader.* Chicago, IL: University of Chicago Press.

Hall, S. (1988). *The hard road to renewal.* London: Verso.

Hall, S. (1991). Old and new identities, old and new ethnicities. In A. King (Ed.), *Culture, globalisation and the world system*. Basingstoke: Macmillan.

Hall, S. (1996). When was the postcolonial? Thinking at the limit. In I. Chambers & L. Curti (Eds.), *The postcolonial question*. London: Routledge.

Hall, S. ([1991] 1997). The local and the global. In A. McClintock, A. Mufti, & E. Shohat (Eds.), *Dangerous liaisons: Gender, nation, and postcolonial perspectives*. Minneapolis: University of Minnesota Press.

Hall, S. (2000a). Frontlines/backyards. In K. Owusu (Ed.), *Black British culture and society*. London: Routledge.

Hall, S. (2000b). The multicultural question. In B. Hesse (Ed.), *Un/settled multiculturalisms*. London: Zed Press.

Hall, S. G. (2009). *A faithful account of the race: African American historical writing in nineteenth-century America*. Chapel Hill: University of North Carolina Press.

Hall, S.-M., McIntosh, K., Neitzert, E., Pottinger, L., Sandhu, K., Stephenson, M.-A., Reed, H., & Taylor, L. (2017). Intersecting inequalities: The impact of austerity on Black and minority ethnic women in the UK. London: Runnymede.

Hallaq, W. (2009a). *An introduction to Islamic law*. Cambridge: Cambridge University Press.

Hallaq, W. (2009b). *Shari'a: Theory, practice, transformations*. Cambridge: Cambridge University Press.

Hallaq, W. (2013). *The impossible state: Islam, politics and modernity's moral predicament*. New York: Columbia University Press.

Hallaq, W. (2014). Beyond secularism and Islamism. *VIDC*. https://www.youtube.com/watch?v=WFAqQiIVsF8&t=5518s

Hallaq, W. (2017). Seventeen theses on history. In L. Stone & J. Bahbak Mohaghegh (Eds.), *Manifestos for world thought*. Lanham, MD: Rowman and Littlefield.

Hallaq, W. (2018). *Restating orientalism: A critique of modern knowledge*. New York: Columbia University Press.

Halliday, J., Gani, A., & Dodd, V. (2015). UK police launch hunt for London schoolgirls feared to have fled to Syria. *Guardian*. https://www.theguardian.com/world/2015/feb/20/fears-london-schoolgirls-isis-syria

Halper, J. (2015). *War against the people: Israel, Palestinians and global pacification*. London: Pluto Press.

Hamami, R., & Reiker, M. (1988). Feminist orientalism and orientalist Marxism. *New Left Review, 170*(July–August), 93–106.

Haraway, D. (1988). Situated knowledges: The science question in feminism and the privilege of partial perspective. *Feminist Studies, 14*(3), 575–599.

Harding, S. (1993). Rethinking standpoint epistemology: What is strong objectivity? In L. Alcoff & E. Potter (Eds.), *Feminist epistemologies*. London: Routledge.

Haritaworn, J., Kunstman, A., & Posocco, S. (Eds.). (2014). *Queer necropolitics*. Abingdon/Oxon: Routledge.

Harris, C. (1993). Whiteness as property. *Harvard Law Review, 106*(8), 1707–1791.

Harrison, F. (1995). The persistent power of "race" in the cultural and political economy of racism. *Annual Review of Anthropology, 24*, 47–74.

Hartman, S. V. (1997). *Scenes of subjection: Terror, slavery, and self-making in nineteenth-century America.* Oxford: Oxford University Press.

Hartog, F. (2015). *Regimes of historicity: Presentism and experiences of time.* Translated by S. Brown. New York: Columbia University Press.

Hartsock, N. (2004). The feminist standpoint: Developing the ground for a specifically feminist historical materialism. In S. Harding & M. B. Hintikka (Eds.), *The feminist standpoint theory reader: Intellectual and political controversies.* New York: Routledge.

Hashmi, S. (1998). Islamic ethics in international society. In D. Mapel & T. Nardin (Eds.), *International society: Diverse ethical perspectives* (pp. 215–236). Princeton, NJ: Princeton University Press.

Heath-Kelly, C. (2012). Reinventing prevention or exposing the gap? False positives in UK terrorism governance and the quest for pre-emption. *Critical Studies on Terrorism, 5*(1), 69–87.

Heath-Kelly, C. (2013). Counter-terrorism and the counter-factual: Producing the "radicalisation" discourse and the UK prevent strategy. *The British Journal of Politics & International Relations, 15*, 394–415.

Heath-Kelly, C. (2017). The geography of pre-criminal space: Epidemiological imaginations of radicalisation risk in the UK prevent strategy, 2007–2017. *Critical Studies on Terrorism, 10*(2), 297–319.

Hegel, G. W. F. (1957). *Philosophy of right.* Oxford: The Clarendon Press, Sections 246 and 248.

Hegel, G. W. F. (1969). *Encyklopadie der philosophischen Wissenschaften: im Grundrisse.* Edited by F. Nicolin & O. Poggler. Hamburg: F. Meiner.

Hellyer, H. A. (2019). The Islamophobia that led to the Christchurch shooting must be confronted. *Guardian.* https://www.theguardian.com/commentisfree/2019/mar/15/islamophobia-christchurch-shooting-anti-muslim-bigotry-new-zealand

Heng, G. (2011). The invention of race in the European middle ages I: Race studies, modernity, and the middle ages. *Literature Compass, 8*, 315–331.

Heng, G. (2018). *The invention of race in the European middle ages.* Cambridge: Cambridge University Press.

Hersi, F. (2019). On being Somali: Not black enough, not Muslim enough. *Amaliah.* https://www.amaliah.com/post/21386/there-is-no-racism-in-islam-but-there-is-racism-in-the-muslim-community-being-somali

Hesse, B. (2004). Im/plausible deniability: Racism's conceptual double bind. *Social Identities, 10*(1), 9–29.

Hesse, B., & Sayyid, S. (2006). The postcolonial political and the immigrant imaginary. In N. Ali, V. S. Kalra, & S. Sayyid (Eds.), *A postcolonial people; South Asians in Britain.* London: Hurst.

Heuman, G. (1865 [1991]). Prologue to the Morant Bay rebellion in Jamaica. *New West Indian Guide/Nieuwe West-Indische Gids, 65*(3/4), 107–127.

Hewitt, R. (2005). *White Backlash and the politics of multiculturalism.* Cambridge: Cambridge University Press.

Hickman, M., Thomas, L., Nickels, H., & Silvestri, S. (2012). Social cohesion and the notion of communities: A study of the experiences and impact of being suspect for Irish communities and Muslim communities in Britain. *Critical Studies on Terrorism, 5*, 89–106.

Hidayatullah, A. (2002). Islamic feminism: What's in a name? *Al-Ahram Weekly Online*, no. 569(January 17–23, 2002). http://weekly.ahram.org.eg/2002/569/cul.htm

Hidayatullah, A. (2005). Between secular and Islamic feminism: Reflections on the Middle East and beyond. *Journal of Middle East Women's Studies, 1*(1) (January 2005), 6–28.

Hidayatullah, A. A. (2014). *Feminist edges of the Qur'an*. Oxford: Oxford University Press.

Hillyard, P. (2000). *Suspect community; Graham Ellison and Jim Smyth*. The Crowned Harp: Policing Northern Ireland, London: Pluto Press.

Hindess, B. (2005). Citizenship and empire. In T. B. Hansen & F. Stepputat (Eds.), *Sovereign bodies, citizens, migrants and states in the postcolonial world*. Princeton, NJ: Princeton University Press.

Hinnebusch, R. (2013). The politics of identity in Middle East international relations. In L. Fawcett (Ed.), *International relations of the middle east* (3rd ed., pp. 148–166). Oxford: Oxford University Press.

Hirsch, A. (2018). The scramble for Africa has moved on, but Britain hasn't. *Guardian*. https://www.theguardian.com/commentisfree/2018/sep/04/africa-britain-trade-theresa-may-brexit

HM Government. (1981). British Nationality Act 1981. http://www.legislation.gov.uk/ukpga/1981/61

HM Government. (2000). *Terrorism act 2000*. London: Home Office.

HM Government. (2006). *Countering international terrorism: The United Kingdom's strategy*. Norwich: HMSO.

HM Government. (2010). Securing Britain in an age of uncertainty. In *The national security strategy*. London: Author.

HM Government. (2012). *Channel: Vulnerability assessment frameworks*. London: Author.

HM Government. (2013). *Tackling extremism in the UK: Report from the Prime Minister's task force on tackling radicalisation and extremism*. London: Author.

HM Government. (2015a). *Channel duty guidance: Protecting vulnerable people from being drawn into terrorism*. London: Author.

HM Government. (2015b). *Counter-terrorism and security act 2015*. London: Author.

HM Government. (2015c). *Counter-terrorism and security bill: Explanatory notes*. London: Author.

HM Government. (2015d). *Working together to safeguard children*. London: Author.

HM Government. (2016). Building a stronger Britain together. https://www.gov.uk/guidance/building-a-stronger-britain-together

Hobbs, T. (2017). Checking in with Saffiyah Khan, the woman who faced down the EDL. *VICE*. https://www.vice.com/en_uk/article/z49jn8/checking-in-with-saffiyah-khan-the-woman-who-faced-down-the-edl

Hobson, J. M. (2007). Is critical theory always for the White West and for Western imperialism? Beyond Westphilian towards a post-racist critical IR. *Review of International Studies, 33*(S1), 91–116.

Hobson, J. M. (2012). *The Eurocentric conception of world politics: Western international theory, 1760–2010*. Cambridge: Cambridge University Press.

Hodgson, M. (1974). *The venture of Islam: Conscience and history in world civilization, volumes 1–3*. Chicago: University of Chicago Press.

Hoffman, B. (2009). A counterterrorism strategy for the Obama administration. *Terrorism and Political Violence, 21*(3), 359–377.

Holland, M., & Knutsford, V. (1900). *Life and letters of Zachary Macaulay*. London: Edward Arnold.

Hollinger, D. (1995). *Postethnic America: Beyond multiculturalism*. New York: Basic Books.

Home Affairs Committee. (2007). *Select committee on home affairs – Second report 2006–07*. London: House of Commons.

Home Affairs Committee. (2019a). The Macpherson report: Twenty years on. https://www.parliamentlive.tv/Event/Index/cd010bb3-558c-4575-9a23-ec4a5070a3cb

Home Affairs Committee. (2019b). The Macpherson report: Twenty years on inquiry. https://www.parliament.uk/business/committees/committees-a-z/commons-select/home-affairs-committee/inquiries/parliament-2017/macpherson-report-twenty-years-on-inquiry-17-19/

Home Office. (2011). *Prevent*. London: Home Office.

Homerin, E. T. (2005) Soul. In *Encyclopaedia of the Qur'ān, general editor: Jane Dammen McAuliffe*. Washington DC: Georgetown University.

hooks, bell. (1981). *Ain't I a woman: Black women and feminism*. Boston: South End Press.

hooks, bell. (1984). *Feminist theory: From margin to center*. Boston: South End Press.

Hooper, S. (2015). UK teachers see thin line between spy and protector. *Al Jazeera Online*. http://www.aljazeera.com/indepth/features/2015/04/uk-teachers-thin-line-spy-protector-150412075115174.html

Hooper, S. (2015). Stifling freedom of expression in UK schools. *Al Jazeera Online*. http://www.aljazeera.com/indepth/features/2015/07/stifling-freedom-expression-uk-schools-150721080612049.html

Hooper, S. (2016). Exclusive: UK "grassroots" anti-extremism campaign produced by home office. *Middle East Eye*. https://www.middleeasteye.net/news/exclusive-uk-grassroots-anti-extremism-campaign-produced-home-office

Hope, C. (2014). Sajid Javid: The millionaire bus conductor's son with a portrait of Margaret Thatcher on his wall. *The Telegraph*. https://www.telegraph.co.uk/news/politics/10755497/Sajid-Javid-the-millionaire-bus-conductors-son-with-a-portrait-of-Margaret-Thatcher-on-his-wall.html

Horton, H. (2017). Grenfell tower fire: Muslims awake for Ramadan among heroes who helped save lives. *The Telegraph*. https://www.telegraph.co.uk/news/2017/06/14/local-heroes-saved-lives-helped-residents-grenfell-tower-fire/

House of Commons Home Affairs Committee. (2009). *Project contest: The government's counter-terrorism strategy: Ninth report of session 2009–09*. London: The Stationary Office Limited.

Howell, A. (2014). The global politics of medicine: Beyond global health, against securitisation theory. *Review of International Studies, 40*(5), 961–987.

Howell, A. (2015). Resilience, war, and austerity: The ethics of military human enhancement and the politics of data. *Security Dialogue, 46*(1), 15–31.

Howell, A. (2018). Forget "militarization": Race, disability, and the martial politics of the police and of the university. *International Feminist Journal of Politics, 20*(2), 117–136.

Howell, A., & Richter-Montpetit, M. (2018). Racism in Foucauldian security studies: Biopolitics, liberal war, and the whitewashing of colonial and racial violence. *International Political Sociology, 13*(1), 2–19.

Hugo of St. Victor. (1961). *Didascalicon*. Translated by J. Taylor. New York: Columbia University Press.

Hunt, M. R. (2007). Women in Ottoman and Western European law courts: Were Western European women really the luckiest women in the world? In J. E. Hartman & A. Seeff (Eds.), *Structures and subjectivities: Attending to early modern women*. Dover: University of Delaware Press.

Huq, A. Z. (2010). Modeling terrorist radicalization. *Duke Forum for Law & Social Change, 2*, 39–69.

Husain, S. (2006). *Voices of resistance: Muslim women on war, faith and sexuality*. Emeryvill, CA: Seal.

Husband, C., & Alam, Y. (2011). *Social cohesion and counter-terrorism: A policy contradiction?* Bristol: Policy Press.

Hymas, C. (2019). Sajid Javid's decision to strip Shamima Begum of her citizenship questioned by one of UK's most senior judges. *The Telegraph*. https://www.telegraph.co.uk/news/2019/06/09/sajid-javids-decision-strip-shamima-begum-citizenship-questioned/

IMDb. (2018). Storyline. https://www.imdb.com/title/tt7493974/?ref_=nv_sr_1?ref_=nv_sr_1

Inayatullah, N., & Blaney, D. L. (2004). *International relations and the problem of difference*. New York: Routledge.

Inayatullah, N., & Riley, R. L. (2006). *Interrogating imperialism: Conversations on gender, race, and war*. New York: Palgrave Macmillan.

Inspire. (2014). Making a Stand Campaign, Inspire Website.

Institute of Race Relations. (2010). Evidence to the UK parliamentary select committee inquiry on pre-venting violent extremism. *Race and Class, 51*, 73–80.

Ipsos MORI. (2016). Perils of perception. https://www.ipsos.com/ipsos-mori/en-uk/perceptions-are-not-reality-what-world-gets-wrong

Islamic Human Rights Commission. (2009). Stunning victory for Babar Ahmad. *IHRC*. https://www.ihrc.org.uk/news/articles/4416-stunning-victory-for-babar-ahmad/

Islamic Human Rights Commission. (2018). Houria Bouteldja on "Whites, Jews and us: Toward a politics of revolutionary love". *IHRC*. https://www.ihrc.org.uk

/activities/event-reports/18514-houria-bouteldja-on-whites-jews-and-us-toward-a
-politics-of-revolutionary-love/

ITV News. (2019). Shamima Begum interview: The moment IS bride learns she's lost UK citizenship. *ITV News Online.* https://www.youtube.com/watch?v =CMFTjKgAWfg

Jabri, V. (2006). War, security and the liberal state. *Security Dialogue, 37*(1), 47–64.

Jabri, V. (2007a). *War and the transformation of global politics.* New York: Palgrave Macmillan.

Jabri, V. (2007b). Michel Foucault's analytics of war: The social, the international, and the racial. *International Political Sociology, 1*(1), 67–81.

Jabri, V. (2013). *The postcolonial subject: Claiming politics/governing others in late modernity.* London: Routledge.

Jabri, V. (2014). Disarming norms: Postcolonial agency and the constitution of the international. *International Theory, 6*(2), 372–390.

Jack, I. (2018). Britain sees the commonwealth as its trading empire. It is sadly deluded. *Guardian.* https://www.theguardian.com/commentisfree/2018/apr/07/ britain-commonwealth-trading-empire-brexit-eu-trade

Jackson, L. (2017). *Islamophobia in Britain: The making of a Muslim enemy.* Palgrave Macmillan UK.

Jackson, S. (2014). *Islam and the problem of Black suffering.* Oxford: Oxford University Press.

Jacquemond, R. (2009). Translation policies in the Arab world: Representations, discourse, and realities. *Translator, 15*(1), 15–35.

Jad, I. (2005). Between religion and secularism: Islamist women of Hamas. In F. Nouraie-Simone (Ed.), *On shifting ground: Muslim women in the global era.* New York: Feminist.

Jahangir, A. (2008). *Report of the special rapporteur on freedom of religion or belief: Mission to the United Kingdom.* United Nations.

Jalal al-'Azm, S. (2014). Orientalism and orientalism in reverse. *Khamsin: Journal of Revolutionary Socialists of the Middle East* 8, Politics of Religion in the Middle East. https://libcom.org/library/orientalism-orientalism-reverse-sadik-jalal-al-%E2 %80%99azm

James, J. (1996). *Resisting state violence: Radicalism, gender, and race in US culture.* Minneapolis: University of Minnesota Press.

James, J. (Ed.). (1998). *The Angela Y. Davis reader.* Malden, MA: Blackwell.

James, J. (Ed.). (2000). *States of confinement: Policing, detention and prisons.* New York: St. Martin's Press.

James, J. (Ed.). (2007). *Warfare in the American homeland: Policing and prison in a penal democracy.* Durham, NC: Duke University Press.

Jayawardena, K. (1986). *Feminism and nationalism in the third world.* London: Zed Books.

Jehring, A. (2017). Brummie Saffiyah Khan who SMILED at EDL protesters says: "I wasn't scared in slightest". *Birmingham Mail.* https://www.birminghammail.co.uk/ news/midlands-news/brummie-saffiyah-khan-who-smiled-12871182; https://www

.theguardian.com/world/video/2017/apr/10/saffiyah-khan-the-woman-who-defied
-the-edl-speaks-out-video

Jeory, T. (2016). UK entering "unchartered territory" of Islamophobia after Brexit vote. *Independent*. https://www.independent.co.uk/news/uk/home-news/brexit-muslim
-racism-hate-crime-islamophobia-eu-referendum-leave-latest-a7106326.html

Jessop, B. (1990). *State theory: Putting the capitalist state in its place*. London: Penn State Press.

Jessop, B. (2006). From micro-powers to governmentality: Foucault's work on statehood, state formation, statecraft and state power. *Political Geography, 26*(1), 34–40.

John, G. (2014). After Trojan horse: OFSTED on the gallop? http://www.gusjohn
.com/2014/11/after-trojan-horse-ofsted-on-the-gallop/

John, T., & Cotovio, V. (2019). Woke news platform aimed at young Muslims is actually a secret UK counter-terror program. *CNN World*. https://edition.cnn.com/2019
/08/16/uk/woke-counter-terrorism-facebook-intl-gbr/index.html

Johnson, B. (2018). Denmark has got it wrong. Yes, the Burka is oppressive and ridiculous – But that's still no reason to ban it. *The Telegraph*. https://www
.telegraph.co.uk/news/2018/08/05/denmark-has-got-wrong-yes-burka-oppressive
-ridiculous-still/

Johnson, B. (2019). Wishing everyone celebrating the joyous festival of Eid al-Adha a very peaceful and prosperous time – PM. *10 Downing Street*. https://twitter.com
/10DowningStreet/status/1160476648896114689

Johnson, D. (2007). Mapping the meme: A geographical approach to materialist rhetorical criticism. *Communication & Critical/Cultural Studies, 4*(1), 27–50.

Jolly, S. (2010). Birmingham's spy-cam scheme has had its cover blown. *Guardian*. https://www.theguardian.com/commentisfree/libertycentral/2010/jun/23/birming-
ham-spy-cam-scheme

Jones, O. (2014). Britain is going backwards on violence against women. *The Guardian*. https://www.theguardian.com/commentisfree/2014/mar/30/britain-vio-
lence-against-women-domestic-abuse-funding-cuts

Jones, O., & Bailey, S. (2019). Owen Jones meets Shaun Bailey: "Do you stand by your degrading comments about women and minorities?" *Owen Jones*. https://
www.youtube.com/watch?v=XSVwQ5LcMLo

Jung, H. (Ed.). (2002). *Comparative political culture in the age of globalization: An introductory anthology*. Boulder, CO: Lexington Books.

Kamola, I. (2017). A time for anticolonial theory. *Contemporary Political Theory, 18*(Suppl 2), 67–74.

Kamouni, S., & Fox, A. (2017). Muslim women gather to form human chain on Westminster Bridge in honour of victims killed in London terror attack. *Mirror Online*. https://www.mirror.co.uk/news/uk-news/women-gather-form-human
-chain-10105637

Kandiyoti, D. (Ed.). (1991). *Women, Islam, and the state*. Philadelphia: Temple University Press.

Kane, O. O. (2016). *Beyond Timbuktu: An intellectual history of Muslim West Africa*. Cambridge: Harvard University Press.

Kanji, A. (2019). Denationalisation: A punishment reserved for Muslims. *Al Jazeera*. https://www.aljazeera.com/indepth/opinion/denationalisation-punishment -reserved-muslims-190109164026878.html

Kapoor, N. (2017). *Deport, deprive, extradite: 21st century state extremism*. London: Verso.

Kapoor, N. (2019). Citizenship deprivation at the nexus of race, gender and geopolitics. *Verso Blog*. https://www.versobooks.com/blogs/4250-citizenship-deprivation -at-the-nexus-of-race-gender-and-geopolitics

Kapoor, N., & Narkowicz, K. (2019). Unmaking citizens: Passport removals, preemptive policing and the reimagining of colonial governmentalities. *Ethnic and Racial Studies, 42*(16), 45–62.

Karban, K. (2015). The impact of austerity on Bradford. Or, poverty, inequality and mental well-being: The Double-Whammy effect. *University of Bradford*. https://www.bradford.ac.uk/news/archive/2015/the-impact-of-austerity-on-bradford.php

Karim, J. A. (2006). To be Black, female, and Muslim: A candid conversation about race in the American Ummah. *Journal of Muslim Minority Affairs, 26*(2), 225–233.

Karmi, G. (1996). Women, Islam and patriarchalism. In Mai Yamani (Ed.), *Feminism and Islam: Legal and literary perspectives*. New York: New York University Press.

Kaufmann, E. (2018). *Whiteshift: Populism, immigration and the future of White majorities*. London: Allen Lane.

Kaviraj, S. (1995). The reversal of orientalism: Bhudev Mukhopadhyay and the project of indigenist social theory. In V. Dalmia & H. von Stietencron (Eds.), *Representing Hinduism: The construction of religious traditions and national identity* (pp. 253–279). New Delhi: Sage.

Kaviraj, S. (2010). *The Imaginary Institution of India*. New York: Columbia University Press, 254–290.

Kayaoglu, T. (2010). Westphalian Eurocentrism in international relations theory. *International Studies Review, 12*(2), 193–217.

Kazi, N. (2018). *Islamophobia, race, and global politics*. London: Rowman and Littlefield.

Keay, J. (1993). *The honourable company: A history of the English East India company*. London: HarperCollins Publishers.

Kellard, K., Mitchell, L., & Godfrey, D. (2008). *Preventing violent extremism pathfinder fund: Mapping of project activities 2007/08*. London: CLG.

Kennedy, G., & Tuck, C. (2014). *British propaganda and wars of empire: Influencing friend and foe, 1900–2010*. Oxford: Oxford University Press.

Khaleeli, H. (2015). "You worry they could take your kids": Is the prevent strategy demonising Muslim schoolchildren? *Guardian*. http://www.theguardian.com/uk -news/2015/sep/23/prevent-counter-terrorism-strategy-schools-demonising-muslim-children

Khalili, L. (2012). *Time in the shadows: Confinement in counterinsurgencies*. Stanford, CA: Stanford University Press.

Khalili, L. (2017). After Brexit: Reckoning with Britain's racism and xenophobia. *Poem, 5*(2–3), 253–265.

Khan, A. (2018). A portrait of Othello as a Black Muslim tragic hero. *Al Jazeera.* https://www.aljazeera.com/indepth/features/portrait-othello-black-muslim-tragic -hero-181019213737799.html

Khan, K. (2009). *Preventing violent extremism & prevent: A response from the Muslim community.* London: An-Nisa Society.

Khan, M. (2019). *It's not about the Burqa: Muslim women on faith, feminism, sexuality and race.* London: Picador.

Khatibi, A. (1983). *Maghreb Pluriel.* Paris: Denoel.

Khiabany, G., & Williamson, M. (2015). Free speech and the market state: Race, media and democracy in new liberal times. *European Journal of Communication, 30*(6), 571–586.

Khomani, N. (2015). Idris Elba says he's still smiling after comments by James Bond author. *Guardian.* https://www.theguardian.com/film/2015/sep/03/idris-elba-still -smiling-comments-james-bond-author-anthony-horowitz

King, D. (1995). Multiple jeopardy, multiple consciousness: The context of a Black feminist ideology. In Guy-Sheftalled (Ed.), *Words of fire: An anthology of African-American feminist thought.* New York: New Press.

Klein, N. (2007). *The shock doctrine: The rise of disaster capitalism.* New York: Metropolitan Books.

Knightley, P., & Simpson, C. (1969). *The secret lives of Lawrence of Arabia.* New York: McGraw-Hill.

Knobel, M., & Lankshear, C. (2007). *A new literacies sampler.* New York, NY: New York University Press.

Knutsford, V. (1900). *Life and letters of Zachary Macaulay.* E. Arnold.

Kohn, M., & McBride, K. D. (2011). *Political theories of decolonization: Postcolonialism and the problem of foundations.* Oxford: Oxford University Press.

Kolsky, E. (2005). Codification and the rule of colonial difference: Criminal procedure in British India. *Law and History Review, 23*(3), 631–683.

Koskenniemi, M., Rech, W., & Jiménez, F. M. (2017). *International law and empire: Historical exploration.* Oxford: Oxford University Press.

Kracauer, S. (1995). *History: The last things before the last.* Princeton: Markus Wiener.

Krishna, S. (2001). Race, amnesia, and the education of international relations. *Alternatives: Global, Local, Political, 26*(4), 401–424.

Kugle, S. A. (2001). Framed, blamed and renamed: The recasting of Islamic jurisprudence in colonial South India. *Modern Asian Studies, 35*(2), 257–313.

Kuhn, A., & Wolpe, A. M. (Eds.). (1978). *Feminism and materialism: Women and modes of production.* London: Routledge and Kegan Paul.

Kumar, D. (2012). *Islamophobia and the politics of empire.* Chicago: Haymarket Books.

Kundnani, A. (2009). *Spooked: How not to prevent violent extremism.* London: Institute of Race Relations.

Kundnani, A. (2012). Radicalisation: The journey of a concept. *Race and Class, 54,* 3–25.

Kundnani, A. (2014). *The Muslims are coming!: Islamophobia, extremism, and the domestic war on terror.* London: Verso.

Labat, J.-B. (1728). *Nouvelle relation de l'Afrique occidentale* (Vol. 1). Paris: G. Cavalier.

Lacan, J. (1991). *The seminar of Jacques Lacan, book I: Freud's papers on technique, 1953–1954.* Translated by J. Forrester. New York: Norton.

Lambert, R., & Spalek, B. (2008). Muslim communities, counter-terrorism and counter-radicalisation: A critically reflective approach to engagement. *International Journal of Law, Crime and Justice, 36*(4), 257–270.

Lamming, G. (1956). The Negro writer and his world. *Presence Africaine,* 8–10, 318–325.

Lamming, G. (1962). After a decade. *West Indian Gazette,* February.

Landau, J. M. (1990). *The politics of Pan-Islam: Ideology and organization.* Oxford: Clarendon Press.

Lang, P., Jones, G. M., & Schieffelin, B. B. (2009). Talking text and talking back: "My BFF Jill" from boob tube to YouTube. *Journal of Computer Mediated Communication, 14*(4), 1050–1079.

Lankina, T., & Getachew, L. (2012). Mission or empire?: The impact of Christian missionaries on India's democratic development. *LSE.* https://blogs.lse.ac.uk/southasia/2012/09/07/mission-or-empire/

Laqueur, W. (1999). *The new terrorism: Fanaticism and the arms of mass destruction.* New York: Oxford University Press.

Larson, G., & Deutsch, E. (Eds.). (1988). *Interpreting across boundaries: New essays in comparative philosophy.* Princeton, NJ: Princeton University Press.

Lattas, A. (1987). Savagery and civilisation: Towards a genealogy of racism in Australian society. *Social Analysis, 21,* 39–58.

Lauren, R. S., & Maras, M.-H. (2019). Women's radicalization to religious terrorism: An examination of ISIS cases in the United States. *Studies in Conflict & Terrorism, 42*(1–2), 88–119.

Lean, N. (2017). *The Islamophobia industry. How the right manufactures hatred of Muslims.* London: Pluto Press.

Lentin, A., & Titley, G. (2011). *The crises of multiculturalism: Racism in a neoliberal age.* New York: Zed Books.

Leroy-Beaulieu, P. (1908). *De la colonisation chez les peuplesmodernes.* Paris: F. Alcan.

Levin, D. M. (Ed.). (1993). *Modernity and the hegemony of vision.* Berkeley: University of California Press.

Lévy-Bruhl, L. (1910). *Les fonctionsmentales dans les sociétésinférieures.* Paris: F. Alcan.

Lévy-Bruhl, L. (1922). *La mentalité primitive.* Paris: Presses Universitaires de France.

Lévy-Bruhl, L. (1928). *L'âme primitive.* Paris: Presses Universitaires de France.

Lewis, B. (1990). The roots of Muslim rage. *The Atlantic Monthly* 266, September.

Lewis, I. (1844). *Conversation: Ida Lewis and James Baldwin* (pp. 83–92). Baldwin: Conversations.

Lewis, R. B. (1844). *Light and truth; collected from the Bible and ancient and modern history.* Boston: Franklin Classics Trade Press.

Lidher, S. (2018). British citizenship and the Windrush generation. *Runnymede.* https://www.runnymedetrust.org/blog/british-citizenship-and-the-windrush-generation

Ling, L. H. M. (2002). *Postcolonial international relations: Conquest and desire between Asia and the West.* Basingstoke, UK: Palgrave.

Ling, L. H. M. (2014a). Decolonizing the international: Towards multiple emotional worlds. *International Theory, 6*(3), 579–583.

Ling, L. H. M. (2014b). *The Dao of world politics: Towards a post-Westphalian, worldist international relations.* London: Routledge.

Ling, L. (Forthcoming). *A worldly world order: Epistemic compassion for international relations.* Oxford: Oxford University Press.

Locke, A. (1968). The Negro spirituals. In *The new Negro: An interpretation.* New York: Arno.

Long, D., & Schmidt, B. (Eds.). (2005). *Imperialism and internationalism in the discipline of international relations.* Albany, NY: State University of New York Press.

Lorde, A. (2007). The master's tools will never dismantle the master's house. In *Sister outsider.* New York: Ten Speed Press.

Losurdo, D. (2004). *Hegel and the freedom of the moderns.* Durham: Duke University Press.

Losurdo, D. (2011). *Liberalism: A counter-history.* Translated by G. Elliott. New York: Verso.

Losurdo, D. (2015). *War and revolution: Rethinking the twentieth century.* London: Verso.

Losurdo, D. (2018). *Class struggle: A political and philosophical history.* London: Palgrave Macmillan.

Love, E. (2017). *Islamophobia and racism in America.* New York: New York University Press.

Lowe, L. (2015). *The intimacies of four continents.* Durham: Duke University Press.

Lowndes, V., & Madziva, R. (2016). When I look at this van, it's not only a van: Symbolic objects in the policing of migration. *Critical Social Policy, 36*(4), 672–692.

Lugard, F. D. (1980). *The dual mandate in British Tropical Africa.* London: W. Blackwood and Sons.

Lugones, M. (2007). Heterosexualism and the colonial/modern gender system. *Hypatia, 22*(1), 186–209.

Lugones, M. (2010). Toward a decolonial feminism. *Hypatia, 25*(4), 742–759.

MacInnes, C. (1961). Britain's mixed half-million. *Africa South in Exile, 5*(2), 107–115.

MacKenzie, J. M. (Ed.). (1984). *Propaganda and empire: The manipulation of British public opinion 1880–1960.* Manchester: Manchester University Press.

MacKenzie, J. M. (1986). *Imperialism and popular culture*. Manchester, UK: Manchester University Press.

MacKenzie, J. (1999). The popular culture of empire in Britain. In W. R. Louis & J. M. Brown (Eds.), *The Oxford history of the British empire*. Oxford: Oxford University Press.

Magra, I. (2019). Why are milkshakes being thrown at right-wing politicians like Nigel Farage? *New York Times*. https://www.nytimes.com/2019/05/21/world/europe/milkshake-nigel-farage.html

Mahbubani, K. (2001). *Can Asians think? Understanding the divide between East and West*. Hanover, NH: Steerforth Press.

Mahfouz, S. (2017). *The things I would tell you: British Muslim women write*. London: Saqi.

Mahmood, S. (2005). *Politics of piety: The Islamic revival and the feminist subject*. Princeton, NJ: Princeton University Press.

Mahmood, S. (2006). Secularism, hermeneutics, and empire: The politics of Islamic reformation. *Public Culture, 18*(2), 323–347.

Mahmood, S. (2009). Feminism, democracy, and empire: Islam and the war on terror. In H. Herzog & A. Braude (Eds.), *Gendering religion and politics: Untangling modernities* (pp. 193–215). Basingstoke: Palgrave.

Mahmood, S. (2016). *Religious difference in a secular age: A minority report*. Princeton: Princeton University Press.

Mair, L. P. (1936). *Native policies in Africa*. London: Routledge and Kegan Paul.

Maira, S. (2009). *Missing: Youth, citizenship, and empire after 9/11*. Durham, NC: Duke University Press.

Maira, S. (2016). *The 9/11 generation: Youth, rights, and solidarity in the war on terror*. New York: New York University Press.

Makdisi, G. (1965). *Arabic and Islamic studies in honor of Hamilton A. R. Gibb*. Leiden: Brill.

Maldonado-Torres, N. (2007). On the coloniality of being. *Cultural Studies, 21*(2–3), 240–270.

Maldonado-Torres, N. (2008). *Against war: Views from the underside of modernity*. Durham: Duke University Press.

Maldonado-Torres, N. (2010). On the coloniality of being: Contributions to the development of a concept. In W. Mignolo and A. Escobar (Eds.), *Globalization and the decolonial option*. London: Routledge.

Malik, K. (2018). White identity is meaningless. Real dignity is found in shared hopes. *Guardian*. https://www.theguardian.com/commentisfree/2018/oct/21/white-identity-is-meaningless-dignity-is-found-in-shared-hopes

Malik, M. (2008). Complex equality: Muslim women and the "headscarf". *Droit et société, 68*(1), 127–152. https://www.cairn.info/revue-droit-et-societe1-2008-1-page-127.htm

Mamani, F. H. ([2010] 2015). *Vivir Bien/BuenVivir: Filosofía, políticas, estrategias y experiencias de los pueblos ancestrales* (6th ed., pp. 115–168). La Paz: Instituto International de Integración.

Mamdani, M. (2004). *Good Muslim, bad Muslim: America, the cold war, and the roots of terror*. New York: Pantheon/Random House.

Mandaville, P. (2002). Reading the state from elsewhere: Towards an anthropology of the post-national. *Review of International Studies, 28*, 199–207.

Manhire, T. (2019). Mark Zuckerberg, four days on, your silence on Christchurch is deafening. *Guardian*. https://www.theguardian.com/commentisfree/2019/mar/20/mark-zuckerberg-four-days-on-your-silence-on-christchurch-is-deafening

Mante, V., & Stinus Kristensen, M. (2018). Critique of Black reason. *Ethnic and Racial Studies, 41*(13), 2405–2406.

Manzoor-Khan, S. (2015). Intersectional, radical, unpalatable and abrasive. https://thebrownhijabi.com/2015/08/31/intersectional-radical-unpalatable-and-abrasive-that-is-the-feminism-im-about/

Manzoor-Khan, S. (2017). The last word festival 2017 – Poetry slam final – Suhaiymah Manzoor-Khan. *Roundhouse*. https://www.youtube.com/watch?v=G9Sz2BQdMF8&t=7s

Manzoor-Khan, S. (2019). Notes on Shamima. *The Brown Hijabi*. https://thebrown-hijabi.com/2019/02/18/notes-on-shamima/

Manzoor-Khan, S. (2019). Statement of explanation for withdrawal from bradford literature festival 2019 – Suhaiymah Manzoor-Khan. https://twitter.com/thebrown-hijabi/status/1141327385901617152

Manzoor-Khan, S., & Mir, S. (2019). Does Bradford festival's counter-extremism funding warrant a boycott? *Guardian*. https://www.theguardian.com/commentis-free/2019/jun/24/bradford-literary-festival-counter-extremism-funding-boycott

Martin, T. (2014). Governing an unknowable future: The politics of Britain's prevent policy. *Critical Studies on Terrorism, 7*(1), 62–78.

Massad, J. (2002). Re-orienting desire: The gay international and the Arab world. *Public Culture*, Spring.

Massad, J. (2015). *Islam in liberalism*. Chicago and London: University of Chicago Press.

Massoumi, N., Mills, T., & Miller, D. (Eds.). (2017). *What is Islamophobia: Racism, social movements and the state*. London: Pluto Press.

Matamoros-Fernández, A. (2017). Platformed racism: The mediation and circulation of an Australian race-based controversy on Twitter, Facebook and YouTube. *Information, Communication & Society, 20*(6), 930–946.

Matin, K. (2013). Redeeming the universal: Postcolonialism and the inner life of Eurocentrism. *European Journal of International Relations, 19*(2), 353–377.

Mauleon, E. (2018). Black twice: Policing Black Muslim identities. *UCLA Law Review, 1326*, 1326–1390.

Mavelli, L. (2013). Between normalisation and exception: The securitisation of Islam and the construction of the secular subject. *Millennium: Journal of International Studies, 41*(2), 159–181.

Maxwell, K. (2019). Sorry Cressida Dick, but as a Black former detective I know just how racist the met still is. *Independent*. https://www.independent.co.uk/voices/met-police-cressida-dick-no-longer-institutionally-racist-racism-black-offi-cer-a9001176.html

Mayblin, L. (2017). *Asylum after empire: Colonial legacies in the politics of asylum seeking*. London: Rowman and Littlefield International.

Mayblin, L. Kazemi, & Wake, M. (2019). Necropolitics and the slow violence of the everyday: Asylum Seeker welfare in the postcolonial present. *Sociology, 54*(1), 107–123.

Mbembe, A. (2016). Society of enmity. *Radical Philosophy, 200,* 23–35.

Mbembe, A. (2017). *Critique of Black reason*. Durham: Duke University Press.

McCulloch, J., & Pickering, S. (2009). Pre-crime and counter-terrorism: Imagining future crime in the "war on terror". *The British Journal of Criminology, 49*(5), 628–645.

McCulloch, J., & Wilson, D. (2016). *Pre-crime: Pre-emption, precaution and the future*. Abingdon: Routledge.

McGuire, K., Casanova, S., & Davis, C. (2016). "I'm a Black female who happens to be Muslim": Multiple marginalities of an immigrant Black Muslim woman on a predominantly White campus. *The Journal of Negro Education, 85*(3), 316–329.

McIntosh, P. (1989). *White privilege: Unpacking the invisible knapsack. Peace and freedom, July/August, 10–12*. Philadelphia, PA: Women's International League for Peace and Freedom.

McIntosh, P. (2015). Extending the knapsack: Using the White privilege analysis to examine conferred advantage and disadvantage. *Women & Therapy, 38*(3–4), 232–245.

McWhorter, L. (2004). Sex, race, and biopower: A Foucauldian genealogy. *Hypatia, 19,* 38–62.

McWhorter, L. (2009). *Racism and sexual oppression in Anglo-America: A genealogy*. Bloomington: Indiana University Press.

MEE Staff. (2018). Anger over Sara Khan appointment to lead UK counter-extremism commission. https://www.middleeasteye.net/fr/news/sara-khan-counter-extremism -commissioner-2047397586

Meer, N. (2013). Racialization and religion: Race, culture and difference in the study of Islamophobia and Antisemitism. *Ethnic and Racial Studies, 36*(3), 385–398.

Meer, N., Dwyer, C., & Modood, T. (2010). Embodying nationhood? Conceptions of British national identity, citizenship, and gender in the "veil affair." *The Sociological Review, 58*(1), 84–111.

Meer, N., & Modood, T. (2009). Refutations of racism in the "Muslim question." *Patterns of Prejudice, 43*(3–4), 335–354.

Mehta, U. S. (1999). *Liberalism and empire: A study in nineteenth-century British liberal thought*. Chicago: University of Chicago Press.

Mejcher, H. (1976). *Imperial quest for oil: Iraq 1910–1928*. London: Ithaca Press.

Mellino, M. (2011). Frantz Fanon, un classique pour le présent. *Il Manifesto,* May 19.

Mellino, M. (2013). The *Langue* of the damned: Fanon and the remnants of Europe. *South Atlantic Quarterly, 112*(1), 79–89.

Memmi, A. (1991). *The colonizer and the colonized*. Boston: Beacon Press.

Menski, W. (2003). *Hindu law: Beyond tradition and modernity*. Oxford: Oxford University Press.

Mercurio, J. (2018). Writer Jed Mercurio introduces "bodyguard". *BBC Writers Room*. https://www.bbc.co.uk/blogs/writersroom/entries/f5c09a37-a04d-4238-b4b3-0ba8f23a9a5d

Merleau-Ponty, M. (1964). *Le visible et l'invisible*. Paris: Gallimard.

Merleau-Ponty, M. (2013). *Phenomenology of perception*. Paris: Gallimard.

Mernissi, F. (1987). *The fundamentalist obsession with women: A current articulation of class conflict in modern Muslim societies*. Lahore, Pakistan: Simorgh/Women's Resource and Publication Centre.

Mernissi, F. (1991). *The veil and the male elite: A feminist interpretation of women's rights in Islam*. Translated by M. Jo Lakeland. Reading, MA: Addison-Wesley.

Metcalf, T. R. (1994). *Ideologies of the Raj, New Cambridge history of India, vol. III.4*. Cambridge: Cambridge University Press.

Middle East Eye. (2017). Muslim women form human chain along Westminster bridge after London attack. https://www.middleeasteye.net/news/muslim-women-form-human-chain-along-westminster-bridge-after-london-attack

Mignolo, W. (2000a). *Local histories/global designs: Coloniality, subaltern knowledges, and border thinking*. Princeton, NJ: Princeton University Press.

Mignolo, W. (2000b). Coloniality at large: Time and the colonial difference. In E. Larreta (Ed.), *Time in the making and possible futures* (pp. 237–272). Rio de Janeiro: unesCo.

Mignolo, W. (2009). Epistemic disobedience, independent thoughts and decolonial freedom. *Theory, Culture and Society, 26*(7/8), 1–23.

Mignolo, W. (2011a). *The darker side of Western modernity: Global futures, decolonial options*. Durham, NC: Duke University Press.

Mignolo, W. (2011b). Epistemic disobedience and the decolonial option: A manifesto. *Transmodernity: Journal of Peripheral Cultural Production of the Luso-Hispanic World, 1*(2), 44–66.

Mignolo, W., & Walsh, C. (2018). *On decoloniality: Concepts, analytics, praxis*. Durham, NC: Duke University Press.

Mignolo, W. D. (2002). The enduring enchantment (Or the epistemic privilege of modernity and where to go from here). *South Atlantic Quarterly, 101*(4), 928–954.

Mignolo, W. D. (2007a). Delinking: The rhetoric of modernity, the logic of coloniality and the grammar of decolniality. *Cultural Studies, 21*(2–3), 449–514.

Mignolo, W. D. (2007b). The decolonial option and the meaning of identity in politics. *Anales Nueva Epoca (Instituto Iberoamericano Universidad de Goteborg), 9/10*, 43–72.

Mignolo, W. D. (2012). *Local histories/global designs: Coloniality, subaltern knowledges, and border thinking*. Princeton: Princeton University Press.

Mignolo, W. D. (2015). Global coloniality and the world disorder. *World Public Forum*, November 2015. http://wpfdc.org/images/2016_blog/W.Mignolo_Decoloniality_after_Decolonization_ Dewesternization_after_the_Cold_War.pdf

Mills, C. W. (1994). Revisionist ontologies: Theorizing White supremacy. *Social and Economic Studies, 43*(3), 105–134.

Mills, C. W. (1997). *The racial contract*. Ithaca, NY: Cornell University Press.

Mills, P. (2009). Mosques and minarets. *New Humanist, 124*(3), 16.

Milstein, A. (2019). Islamophobia – The 21st century weapon to silence our freedom of speech. *JPost*. https://www.jpost.com/Opinion/Islamophobia-the-21st-century-weapon-to-silence-our-freedom-of-speech-588988

Millstein, S. (2017). Who is Saffiyah Khan? Her reaction to an EDL protester is captivating. *Bustle*. https://www.bustle.com/p/who-is-saffiyah-khan-her-reaction-to-edl-protester-is-captivating-50072

Milton, G. (2013). Winston Churchill's shocking use of chemical weapons. *Guardian*. https://www.theguardian.com/world/shortcuts/2013/sep/01/winston-churchill-shocking-use-chemical-weapons

Mishra, P. (2015). Bland fanatics. *London Review of Books, 37*(23), 37–40.

Mitchell, J. (1974). *Psychoanalysis and feminism*. New York: Pantheon Books.

Mitchell, R. P. (1969). *The society of the Muslim brothers*. Oxford: Oxford University Press.

Mittelman, J. H., & Pasha, M. K. (1997). *Out from underdevelopment revisited: Changing global structures and the remaking of the third world*. London: Macmillan.

Moallem, M. (2005). Am I a Muslim woman? Nationalist reactions and postcolonial transgressions. In Afzal-Khan (Ed.), *Shattering the stereotypes: Muslim women speak out*. Northampton, MA: Olive Branch Press.

Moallem, M. (2008). Muslim women and the politics of representation. *Journal of Feminist Studies in Religion, 24*(1), 106–110.

Moghaddam, F. (2005). The staircase to terrorism a psychological exploration. *American Psychological Association, 60*, 161–168.

Mohanty, C. T. (1988). Under Western eyes: Feminist scholarship and colonial discourses. *Feminist Review, 1*(30), 61–88.

Mohanty, C., Talpade, R., & Ann Torres, L. (Eds.). (1991). *Third world women and the politics of feminism*. Bloomington: Indiana University Press.

Mohdin, A. (2018). Racism in Britain: How we revealed the shocking impact of unconscious bias. *Guardian*. https://www.theguardian.com/membership/2019/jan/26/racism-in-britain-how-we-revealed-the-shocking-impact-of-unconscious-bias

Montagu, A. (1972). *Statement on race* (3rd ed.). Oxford: Oxford University Press.

Mooney, J. M. (1900). *Historical sketch of the Cherokee*. Chicago: Aldine Transaction.

Moore, C. (2006). My straw poll: Extremists must be seen for what they are. *The Telegraph*. https://www.telegraph.co.uk/comment/personal-view/3632947/My-Straw-poll-extremists-must-be-seen-for-what-they-are.html

Moraga, C., & Anzaldúa, G. (1981). *This bridge called my back: Writings by radical women of color*. Watertown, MA: Persephone Press.

Morris, R. C. (2002). Theses on the question of war: History, media, terror. *Social Text, 20*(3) (Fall), 72.

Morrison, T. (1975). A humanist view. *Black Studies Center Public Dialogue*. https://soundcloud.com/portland-state-library/portland-state-black-studies-1

Morrison, T. (1993). *Playing in the dark. Whiteness and the literary imagination.* New York: Vintage Books.

Morsi, Y. (2017). *Radical skin, moderate masks: De-radicalising the Muslim & racism in post-racial societies.* London: Rowman and Littlefield International.

Morsi, Y. (2018). The "free speech" of the unfree. *Continuum: Journal of Media & Cultural Studies, 32*(4), 474–486.

Moses, A. D. (2017). Empire, resistance, and security: International law and the transformative occupation of Palestine. *Humanity: An International Journal of Human Rights, Humanitarianism, and Development, 8*(2) (Summer), 379–408.

Moses, D. (Ed.). (2008). *Empire, colony, genocide: Conquest, occupation, and subaltern resistance in world history.* New York: Berghahn.

Mossman, J. (1965). *Race, hate, sex, and colour: A conversation with James Baldwin and Colin MacInnes* (pp. 46–58). Baldwin: Conversations.

Mubarak, A., & Walid, D. (2017). *Centering Black narrative: Black Muslim nobles among the early Pious Muslims.* Illinois: Itrah Press Publishing.

Mukerjee, M. (2010). *Churchill's secret war: The British Empire and the ravaging of India during World War II.* New York: Basic Books.

Mukhopadhyay, C. C., & Moses, Y. T. (1997). Reestablishing "race" in anthropological discourse. *American Anthropologist, 99,* 517–533.

Muppidi, H. (1999). Postcoloniality and the production of international insecurity: The persistent puzzle of US-Indian relations. In J. Weldes (Ed.), *Cultures of insecurity: States, communities, and the production of danger* (pp. 119–146). Minneapolis: University of Minnesota Press.

Muppidi, H. (2001). State identity and interstate practices: The limits of democratic peace in South Asia. In T. Barkawi & M. Laffey (Eds.), *Democracy, liberalism, and war: Rethinking the democratic peace debate* (pp. 45–66). Boulder, CO: Lynne Rienner.

Muret, M. (1925). *Le crépuscule des nations blanches.* Paris: Payot.

Murphy, F. (2011). Babar Ahmad's principled stand shames the IPCC. *Guardian.* https://www.theguardian.com/commentisfree/2011/jun/05/babar-ahmad-metropolitan-police-ipcc

Mythen, G., Walklate, S., & Khan, F. (2013). Why should we have to prove we're alright?: Counter-terrorism, risk and partial securities. *Sociology, 47*(2), 383–398.

Naber, N. (2006). The rules of forced engagement: Race, gender, and the culture of fear among Arab immigrants in San Francisco Post-9/11. *Cultural Dynamics, 18*(3), 235–267.

Nadesan, M. H. (2010). *Governmentality, biopower, and everyday life.* London: Routledge.

Nagl, J. A. (2005). *Learning to eat soup with a knife: Counterinsurgency lessons from Malaya and Vietnam.* Chicago: University of Chicago Press.

Nakamura, L., & Chow-White, P. A. (Eds.). (2012). *Race after the internet.* New York: Routledge.

Nandy, A. (1983). *Preface to the intimate enemy: Loss and recovery of self under colonialism.* Delhi: Oxford University Press.

Nazeer, T. (2018). Memo to bodyguard writers: Muslim women are more than victims or terrorists. *Guardian.* https://www.theguardian.com/commentisfree/2018/sep/24/bodyguard-muslim-islamophobic-attacks-muslim-terrorist-stereotype

Ndlovu-Gatsheni, S. J. (2013a). *Coloniality of power in postcolonial Africa: Myths of decolonization.* Oxford: African Books Collective.

Ndlovu-Gatsheni, S. J. (2013b). *Empire, global coloniality and African subjectivity.* New York: Berghahn Books.

Neal, A. N. (2008). Goodbye war on terror? In *Foucault on politics, security and war* (pp. 43–64). London: Palgrave Macmillan.

Neuman, S. (1998). *International relations theory and the third world.* London: Palgrave.

Neumann, I. (1999). *Uses of the other: "The east" in European identity formation.* Minneapolis: Minnesota Press.

Neumann, P. (2008). Perspectives on radicalisation and political violence. Papers From the First International Conference on Radicalisation and Political Violence. London: International Centre for the Study of Radicalisation and Political Violence.

Nietzsche, F. (1935). *The will to power.* London: Penguin, 3, 484.

Nieuwenhuis, M. (2014). The terror in the air. *openDemocracy.* https://www.opendemocracy.net/en/terror-in-air/

Noble, S. U. (2018). *Algorithms of oppression: How search engines reinforce racism.* New York: New York University Press.

Nouraie-Simone, F. (2005). *On shifting ground: Muslim women in the global era.* New York: Feminist.

Nuttall, S., & Mbembe, A. (2015). Secrecy's software. *Current Anthropology, 56*(12), 318–324.

Okafor, K. (2019). Thread. https://twitter.com/kelechnekoff/status/1149226175581032448

Okin, S. M. (1999). *Is multiculturalism bad for women?* Princeton, NJ: Princeton University Press.

Olusoga, D. (2017). Empire 2.0 is dangerous nostalgia for something that never existed. *Guardian.* https://www.theguardian.com/commentisfree/2017/mar/19/empire-20-is-dangerous-nostalgia-for-something-that-never-existed

Omi, W., & Winant, H. (1994). *Racial formation in the United States* (2nd ed.). New York, NY: Routledge.

Omissi, D. (1990). *Air power and colonial control: The Royal Air Force, 1919–1939.* Manchester: Manchester University Press.

Ophir, A., Givoni, M., & Ḥanafi, S. (2009). *The power of inclusive exclusion: Anatomy of Israeli rule in the occupied Palestinian territories.* New York: Zone Books.

Oreskes, N. (2007). The scientific consensus on climate change: How do we know we are not wrong? In J. F. C. DiMento & P. Doughman (Eds.), *Climate change: What it means for us, our children, and our grandchildren.* Cambridge, MA: MIT Press.

Orwell, G. (1945). *Notes on nationalism*. London: Penguin.

O'Toole, F. (2018). The paranoid fantasy behind Brexit. *Guardian*. https://www.theguardian.com/politics/2018/nov/16/brexit-paranoid-fantasy-fintan-otoole

O'Toole, T., Meer, N., DeHanas, D. N., Jones, S. H., & Modood, T. (2016). Governing through prevent? Regulation and contested practice in state–Muslim engagement. *Sociology, 50*(1), 160–177.

Owen, R. (2005). *Lord Cromer: Victorian imperialist, Edwardian Proconsul*. Oxford: Oxford University Press.

PA Media. (2019). Isis suspect Jack Letts stripped of British citizenship – Report. *Guardian*. https://www.theguardian.com/uk-news/2019/aug/17/isis-suspect-jack-letts-stripped-british-citizenship

Pantazis, C., & Pemberton, S. (2009). From the "old" to the "new" suspect community: Examining the impacts of recent UK counter-terrorist legislation. *British Journal of Criminology, 49*, 646–666.

Pappe, I. (2014). *The idea of Israel: A history of power and knowledge*. London: Verso.

Parasram, A., & Tilley, L. (2018). Global environmental harm, internal frontiers, and indigenous protective ontologies. In O. Rutazibwa & R. Shilliam (Eds.), *Routledge handbook of postcolonial politics*. Oxon: Routledge.

Parel, A., & Keith, R. (Eds.). (1992). *Comparative political philosophy – Studies under the Upas Tree*. London: Sage.

Parenti, C. (2003). *The soft cage: Surveillance in America from slavery to the war on terror*. New York: Basic Books.

Pascale, C. M. (2010). Epistemology and the politics of knowledge. *The Sociological Review, 58*(2 Suppl), 154–165.

Pasha, M. K. (1998). *Colonial political economy*. Oxford: Oxford University Press.

Patel, F. (2011). *Rethinking radicalization*. New York: Brennan Center for Justice at New York University School of Law.

Patnaik, U. (2017a). Revisiting the drain, or transfers from India to Britain in the context of global diffusion of capitalism. In B. B. Chaudhuri, S. Chakrabarti, & U. Patnaik (Eds.), *Agrarian and other histories: Essays for Binay Bhushan Chaudhuri*. New Delhi: Tulika Books.

Patnaik, U., & Patnaik, P. (2017b). *A theory of imperialism*. New York: Columbia University Press.

Pennington, J. W. (1841). *Text book of the origin and history of the colored people*. Hartford, CT: L. Skinner.

Pérez, E. (1999). *The decolonial imaginary: Writing Chicanas into history*. Bloomington: Indiana University Press.

Perraudin, F. (2017). Photo of Saffiyah Khan defying EDL protester in Birmingham goes viral. *Guardian*. https://www.theguardian.com/uk-news/2017/apr/09/birmingham-woman-standing-in-defiance-of-edl-protester-goes-viral

Perraudin, F., Amrani, I., & Heywood, M. (2017). Saffiyah Khan meets woman she defended at EDL demo. *Guardian*. https://www.theguardian.com/uk-news/2017/apr/11/saffiyah-khan-meets-woman-she-defended-at-edl-demo

Perraudin, F., & Dodd, V. (2019). Isis Briton Shamima Begum pleads to return to UK after giving birth. *Guardian*. https://www.theguardian.com/uk-news/2019/feb/17/shamima-begum-who-fled-uk-to-join-isis-has-given-birth-say-family

Perry, K. H. (2012). "Little rock" in Britain: Jim Crow's transatlantic topographies. *Journal of British Studies, 51*(1), 155–177.

Persaud, R. B., & Walker, R. B. J. (2001). Apertura: Race in international relations. *Alternatives, 26*(4), 373–376.

Perugini, N., & Gordon, N. (2015). *The human right to dominate*. Oxford: Oxford University Press.

Phillips, M. (2018). Islamophobia is a fiction to shut down debate. *The Times*. https://www.thetimes.co.uk/article/islamophobia-is-a-fiction-to-shut-down-debate-wwtzggnc7

Piscatori, J. (2003). Order, justice and global Islam. In R. Foot, J. L. Gaddis, & A. Hurrell (Eds.), *Order and justice in international relations* (pp. 262–286). New York: Oxford University Press.

Politowski, B. (2016). Terrorism in Great Britain: The statistics. *House of Commons Briefing Paper*, No. 7613, 9 June 2016.

Poynting, S. (2016). Entitled to be a radical? Counter-terrorism and travesty of human rights in the case of Babar Ahmad. *State Crime Journal, 5*(2), 204–219.

Pragna P. (2002). Back to the future: Avoiding Déjà Vu in resisting racism. In F. Anthias & C. Lloyd (Eds.), *Rethinking anti-racisms: From theory to practice* (pp. 128–148). London: Routledge.

Puar, J. K. (2007). *Terrorist assemblages: Homonationalism in queer times*. Durham: Duke University Press.

Puar, J. K. (2013). Rethinking homonationalism. *International Journal of Middle East Studies, 45*(2), 336–339.

Puar, J. K. (2015). Homonationalism as assemblage: Viral travels, affective sexualities. *Revista Lusófona de Estudos Culturais, 3*(1), 319–337.

Puar, J. K. (2017). *The right to maim: Debility, capacity, disability*. Durham, NC: Duke University Press.

Pybus, C. (2006). *Epic Journies of freedom: Runaway slaves of the American revolution and their global quest for liberty*. Boston: Beacon.

Pybus, C. (2007). A less favourable specimen: The abolitionist response to self-emancipated slaves in Sierra Leone. *Parliamentary History Supplement* (pp. 98–113).

Quijano, A. (2000). Coloniality of power, Eurocentrism, and Latin America. *Nepantla: Views from South, 1*(3), 533–534.

Quijano, A. (2007). Coloniality and modernity/rationality. *Cultural Studies, 21*(2), 168–178.

Quinn, B. (2017). How Churchill helped to shape the Middle East we know today. *Guardian*. https://www.theguardian.com/uk-news/2017/apr/22/winston-churchill-imperial-war-museum-middle-east-legacy

Qureshi, A. (2019a). My schedule 7 stop: Power and coercion presented as "choice" and a "friendly chat". https://5pillarsuk.com/2019/07/31/my-schedule-7-stop-power-and-coercion-presented-as-choice-and-a-friendly-chat/

Qureshi, A. (2019b). The excellent investigation by @IanCobain into the way RICU and the home office have been directly responsible for messaging for a "woke" Muslim project requires further lines of inquiry. https://twitter.com/AsimCP/status /1162388047062798336

Raab, D. (2011). House of commons debate, 5 December 2011, Vol. 537, Col. 82.

Rahman, F. (2002). *Islam*. Chicago: University of Chicago Press.

Rana, J. A. (2016). The racial infrastructure of the terror-industrial complex. *Social Text, 34*(4), 111–138.

Rashid, N. (2016). *Veiled threats: Representing "the Muslim women" in UK public policy discourses*. Bristol: Policy Press.

Ratcliffe, R. (2016). JK Rowling tells of anger at attacks on casting of Black Hermione. *Guardian*. https://www.theguardian.com/stage/2016/jun/05/harry-pot-ter-jk--rowling-black-hermione

Rawlinson, K. (2018). Windrush: 11 people wrongly deported from UK have died – Javid. *Guardian*. https://www.theguardian.com/uk-news/2018/nov/12/windrush -11-people-wrongly-deported-from-uk-have-died-sajid-javid

Reid, J. (2006). Life struggles war, discipline, and biopolitics in the thought of Michel Foucault. *Social Text, 24*(1.86), 127–152.

Reinhart, K. A. Ethics and the Qur'ān. In Jane Dammen McAuliffe (Ed.), *Encyclopaedia of the Qur'ān*. Washington, DC: Georgetown University.

Reuters. (2019). Boris Johnson: I compared Muslim women to letterboxes to "defend their right to wear Burqas". *Guardian*. https://www.theguardian.com/politics/video /2019/jul/06/boris-johnson-i-compared-muslim-women-to-letterboxes-to-defend -their-right-to-wear-burqas-video

Rhodes Must Fall Oxford. (2018). *Rhodes must fall: The struggle to decolonise the racist heart of empire*. London: Zed Books.

Richardson, M., & Fijałkowski, K. (1996). *Refusal of the shadow: Surrealism and the Caribbean*. London: Verso.

Richmond, M., & Charnley, A. (2018). Race, class and borders base. https://www .basepublication.org/?p=665

Richter-Montpetit, M. (2007). Empire, desire and violence: A queer transnational feminist reading of the prisoner "abuse" in Abu Ghraib and the question of "gender equality." *International Feminist Journal of Politics, 9*(1), 38–59.

Richter-Montpetit, M. (2014). Beyond the erotics of orientalism: Lawfare, torture and the racial–sexual grammars of legitimate suffering. *Security Dialogue, 45*(1), 43–62.

Rijke, A., & Minke, C. (2019). Inside checkpoint 300: Checkpoint regimes as spatial political technologies in the occupied Palestinian territories. *Antipode, 51*(3), 968–988.

Rippingale, J. (2018). The toll of burying Grenfell's dead: London's Muslim undertakers. *Al Jazeera*. https://www.aljazeera.com/indepth/features/toll-burying-gren-fell-dead-180926072155075.html

Robbins, B. (1994). Secularism, elitism, progress, and other transgressions: On Edward Said's "voyage in". *Social Text, 40*, 25–37.

Robertson, G. (2010). Cameron and Clegg must now do their moral duty and save Gary McKinnon. *Daily Mail*, 27 May 2010. https://www.dailymail.co.uk/debate/article-1281208/Cameron-Clegg-moral-duty--save-Gary-McKinnon.html

Robinson, F. (1999). The British Empire and the Muslim world. In J. Brown (Ed.), *The Oxford history of the British empire, volume IV: The twentieth century*. Oxford: Oxford University Press.

Rodger, J. (2017). Muslim women form human chain on Westminster Bridge after London terror attack. *Birmingham Live*. https://www.birminghammail.co.uk/news/midlands-news/muslim-women-form-human-chain-12801580

Rodney, W. (1972). *How Europe underdeveloped Africa*. London: Bogle-L'Ouverture Publications.

Rodrìguez, D. (2006). (Non) scenes of captivity: The common sense of punishment and death. *Radical History Review, 96*, 9–32.

Rodríguez, D. (2007). Forced passages: Imprisoned radical intellectuals and the U.S. prison regime. In J. James (Ed.), *Warfare in the American homeland: Policing and prison in a penal democracy* (pp. 35–57). Durham, NC: Duke University Press.

Roediger, D. R. (1999). *The wages of whiteness: Race and the making of the American working class*. London: Verso.

Rottenberg, C. (2014). The rise of neoliberal feminism. *Cultural Studies, 28*(3), 418–437.

Roy, A. (2003). *Confronting empire*. Porto Alegre: World Social Forum.

Roy, A. (2005). *An ordinary person's guide to Empire*. London: HarperCollins UK.

Runnymede Trust. (1997). *Islamophobia: A challenge for us all*. London: Runnymede Trust.

Runnymede Trust. (2017). Islamophobia—20 years on, still a challenge for us all. Retrieved February 15, 2018. https://www.runnymedetrust.org/blog/islamophobia-20-years-on-still-a-challenge-for-us-all

Sabaratnam, M. (2011). IR in dialogue . . . But can we change the subjects? A typology of decolonising strategies for the study of world politics. *Millennium—Journal of International Studies, 39*(3), 781–803.

Sabaratnam, M. (2013). Avatars of Eurocentrism in the critique of the liberal peace. *Security Dialogue, 44*(3), 259–278.

Sabaratnam, M. (2017). *Decolonising intervention: International statebuilding in Mozambique*. London: Rowman & Littlefield International.

Sabbagh, D. (2019). Detention of Muslims at UK ports and airports "structural Islamophobia". https://www.theguardian.com/news/2019/aug/20/detention-of-muslims-at-uk-ports-and-airports-structural-islamophobia

Sabir, R. (2017). Blurred lines and false dichotomies: Integrating counterinsurgency into the UK's domestic "war on terror." *Critical Social Policy, 37*(2), 202–224.

Saeed, T. (2018). *Islamophobia and securitization: Religion, ethnicity and the female voice*. Basingstoke: Palgrave Macmillan.

Safi, M. (2019). Churchill's policies contributed to 1943 Bengal famine – study. *Guardian*. https://www.theguardian.com/world/2019/mar/29/winston-churchill-policies-contributed-to-1943-bengal-famine-study

Sageman, M. (2004). *Understanding terror networks.* Philadelphia: University of Pennsylvania Press.

Sageman, M. (2008a). *Leaderless Jihad: Terror networks in the twenty first century.* Philadelphia: University of Pennsylvania Press.

Sageman, M. (2008b). The next generation of terror. *Foreign Policy, 165,* 37–42.

Said, E. W. (1981). *Covering Islam: How the media and the experts determine how we see the rest of the world.* New York: Vintage.

Said, E. W. (1993). *Culture and imperialism.* London: Vintage.

Said, E. W. (2000). *Out of place: A memoir.* New York: Granta Books.

Said, E. W. (2003). *Orientalism.* London: Penguin.

Saini, A. (2017). *Inferior: How science got women wrong and the new research that's rewriting the story.* London: Fourth Estate Books.

Saini, A. (2019). *Superior: The return of race science.* London: Fourth Estate Books.

Sajed, A. (2013). *Postcolonial encounters in international relations: The politics of transgression in the Maghreb.* London: Routledge.

Saleem, K. (2018). How should anti-Black racism in the Muslim community be tackled? *The Muslim Vibe.* https://themuslimvibe.com/social-issues/how-should-anti-black-racism-in-the-muslim-community-be-tackled

Salem, S. (2018). White innocence as a feminist discourse: Race, empire and gender in performances of "shock" in contemporary politics. *Working Paper.* https://www.academia.edu/37735749/White_Innocence_as_a_Feminist_Discourse_Race_empire_and_gender_in_performances_of_shock_in_contemporary_politics

Sardar, Z., & Davies, M. W. (2010). Freeze framing Muslims: Hollywood and the slideshow of Western imagination. *Interventions, 12*(2), 239–250.

Sargent, L. (Ed.). (1981). *Women and revolution: A discussion of the unhappy marriage of Marxism and feminism.* Boston: South End Press.

Sartre, J.-P. (1995). *Anti-Semite and Jew: An exploration of the etiology of hate.* New York: Shocken.

Sato, S. (2017). "Operation legacy": Britain's destruction and concealment of colonial records worldwide. *The Journal of Imperial and Commonwealth History, 45*(4), 697–719.

Savage, D. W. (1997). Missionaries and the development of a colonial ideology of female education in India. *Gender & History, 9,* 201–221.

Sayyid, S. (2014a). A measure of Islamophobia. *Islamophobia Studies Journal, 2*(1), 10–25.

Sayyid, S. (2014b). *Recalling the caliphate, decolonization and world order.* London: C. Hurst & Co.

Sayyid, S. (2018). Islamophobia conference 2017: Salman Sayyid on the contradictions of Islamophobia. *IHRCtv.* https://www.youtube.com/watch?v=BeP3u094ln4

Sayyid, S., & Vakil, A. K. (2010). *Thinking through Islamophobia: Global perspectives.* Columbia: Columbia University Press.

Scahill, J. (2007). *Blackwater: The rise of the world's most powerful mercenary army.* New York: Nation Books.

Schama, S. (2005). *Rough crossings: Britain, the slaves and the American revolution.* London: BBC Books.

Scheler, M. (1980). *Problems of a sociology of knowledge*. London: Routledge.

Scheverien, A. (2018). For mosque at heart of Grenfell tragedy, a bittersweet anniversary. *New York Times*. https://www.nytimes.com/2018/06/14/world/europe/mosque-grenfell-ramadan.html

Schmidt, B. (1998). *The political discourse of anarchy*. Albany, NY: SUNY Press.

Schmitt, C. (2000). *The crisis of parliamentary democracy*. Translated by E. Kennedy. Cambridge, MA: MIT Press.

Schmitt, C. (2003). *The Nomos of the earth in the international law of the Jus Publicum Europaeum*. Translated by G. L. Ulmen. New York: Telos.

Schmitt, C. (2007). *The concept of the political*. Translated by G. Schwab. Chicago: University of Chicago Press.

Schultz, J. (2018). Why the dream of empire 2.0 is still "cobblers". *Guardian*. https://www.theguardian.com/world/2018/feb/11/ties-that-still-bind-the-enduring-tendrils-of-empire

Schwarz, B. (2003). Claudia Jones and the West Indian gazette reflections on the emergence of post-colonial Britain. *Twentieth Century British History, 14*(3), 264–285.

Schwarz, B. (2011). *Memories of empire trilogy*. New York: Oxford University Press.

Schwarz, S., & Macaulay, Z. (1768–1838 [2000]). *Zachary Macaulay and the Development of the Sierra Leone Company, 1793–4*. Leipzig: Institutfür Afrikanistik, Universität Leipzig.

Scott, D. (1999). *Refashioning futures: Criticism after postcoloniality*. Princeton, NJ: Princeton University Press.

Scott, J. C. (1985). *Weapons of the weak: Everyday forms of peasant resistance*. New Haven: Yale University Press.

Scott, J. C. (1990). *Domination and the arts of resistance: Hidden transcripts*. New Haven: Yale University Press.

Scott, J. C. (1998). *Seeing like a state: How certain schemes to improve the human condition have failed*. New Haven: Yale University Press.

Scott, J. W. (2009). *The politics of the veil*. Princeton, NJ: Princeton University Press.

Sederberg, P. (2003). Global terrorism: Problems of challenge and response. In C. W. Kegley (Ed.), *The control of the new global terrorism* (pp. 267–284). New York, NY: Pearson.

Sedgwick, M. (2010). The concept of radicalisation as a source of confusion. *Terrorism and Political Violence, 22*(4), 479–494.

Segre, I., & Wolfe, R. (2018). A native with a pale face. *Los Angeles Review of Books*. https://lareviewofbooks.org/article/a-native-with-a-pale-face/#!

Seguino, S., Ashtiany, S., & Negra, D. (2015). Inequality matters: Austerity policies, gender and race. *LSE Public Lectures and Events*. http://www.lse.ac.uk/lse-player?id=3078; https://www.plutobooks.com/blog/women-of-colours-anti-austerity-activism/

Sengoopta, C. (2003). *Imprint of the Raj: How fingerprinting was born in colonial India*. London: Macmillan.

Seth, S. (2009). Historical sociology and postcolonial theory: Two strategies for challenging Eurocentrism. *International Political Sociology, 3*(3), 334–338.

Seth, S. (2011). Postcolonial theory and the critique of international relations. *Millennium, 40*(1), 167–183.

Seth, S. (2013a). *Postcolonial theory and international relations: A critical introduction.* London: Routledge.

Seth, S. (2013b). "Once was blind but now can see": Modernity and the social sciences. *International Political Sociology, 7*, 136–151.

Seth, S. (2016). Is thinking with "modernity" Eurocentric? *Cultural Sociology, 10*(3), 385–398.

Sexton, J. (2018). The world love Jam. *The Immanent Frame.* https://tif.ssrc.org/2018/06/20/the-world-love-jam/

Shafir, G. (1996). Zionism and colonialism: A comparative approach. In M. N. Barnett (Ed.), *Israel in comparative perspective.* New York: State University of New York Press.

Shaikh, S. (2003). Transforming feminisms: Islam, women and gender justice. In O. Safi (Ed.), *Progressive Muslims: On justice, gender and pluralism.* Oxford: Oneworld.

Shani, G. (2007). "Provincializing" critical theory: Islam, Sikhism and international relations theory. *Cambridge Review of International Affairs, 20*(3), 417–433.

Shani, G. (2008). Toward a post-Western IR: The Umma, Khalsa Panth, and critical international relations theory. *International Studies Review, 10*(4), 722–734.

Sharma, M. (2012). *Green and saffron: Hindu nationalism and Indian environmental politics.* Ranikhet: Permanent Black.

Sharpe, C. (2016). *In the wake: On blackness and being.* Durham: Duke University Press.

Shaw, M. (2018). Going native: Populist academics normalise the anti-immigrant right. *Politics.* https://www.politics.co.uk/comment-analysis/2018/10/31/going-native-populist-academics-normalise-the-anti-immigrant

Sherwood, H. (2016). Incidents of anti-Muslim abuse up by 326% in 2015, says tell MAMA. *Guardian.* https://www.theguardian.com/society/2016/jun/29/incidents-of-anti-muslim-abuse-up-by-326-in-2015-says-tell-mama

Shifman, L. (2013). Memes in a digital world: Reconciling with a conceptual troublemaker. *Journal of Computer-Mediated Communication, 18*, 362–377.

Shifman, L. (2014). The cultural logic of photo-based meme genres. *Journal of Visual Culture, 13*(3), 340–358.

Shiling, X. (2008). Theory of "returning to the original" and "recovering nature" in Chinese philosophy. *Frontiers of Philosophy in China, 3*(4), 502–519.

Shilliam, R. (2006). What about Marcus Garvey? Race and the transformation of sovereignty debate. *Review of International Studies, 32*, 379–400.

Shilliam, R. (2008). What the Haitian revolution might tell us about development, security, and the politics of race. *Comparative Studies in Society and History, 50*(3), 778–808.

Shilliam, R. (2009a). Hegel's revolution of philosophy. In *German thought and international relations. Palgrave studies in international relations series.* London: Palgrave Macmillan.

Shilliam, R. (2009b). The Atlantic as a vector of uneven and combined development. *Cambridge Review of International Affairs, 22*(1), 69–88.

Shilliam, R. (Ed.). (2011a). *International relations and Non-Western thought: Imperialism, colonialism and investigations of global modernity.* London: Routledge.

Shilliam, R. (2011b). The perilous but unavoidable terrain of the non-West. In R. Shilliam (Ed.), *International relations and Non-Western thought: Imperialism, colonialism and investigations of global modernity* (pp. 12–26). London: Routledge.

Shilliam, R. (2015). *The Black pacific: Anti-colonial struggles and oceanic connections.* London: Bloomsbury Academic.

Shilliam, R. (2018). *Race and the undeserving poor.* Newcastle Upon Tyne: Agenda Publishing.

Shiva, V. (1997). *Biopiracy: The plunder of nature and knowledge.* New Delhi: Natraj.

Shohat, E., & Stam, R. (1994). *Unthinking Eurocentrism: Multiculturalism and the media.* London: Routledge.

Sian, K., Law, I., & Sayyid, S. (2013). *Racism, governance and public policy: Beyond human rights.* Abingdon: Routledge.

Siddique, H. (2018). Flatshare bias: Room-seekers with Muslim name get fewer replies. *Guardian.* https://www.theguardian.com/uk-news/2018/dec/03/flatshare-bias-room-seekers-with-muslim-name-get-fewer-replies

Silva, D. F. (2007). *Toward a global idea of race.* Minneapolis: University of Minnesota Press.

Simmons, D. (2007). *The narcissism of Empire: Loss, rage, and revenge in Thomas De Quincey, Robert Louis Stevenson, Arthur Conan Doyle, Rudyard Kipling, and Isak Dinesen.* Brighton: Sussex Academic Press.

Simpson, A. W. Brian. (2004). *Human rights and the end of empire.* Oxford: Oxford University Press.

Singh, H. (2019). We must be free to criticise Islam. *Spiked.* https://www.spiked-online.com/2019/01/04/we-must-be-free-to-criticise-islam/

Sivanandan, A. (2008). *Catching history on the wing.* London: Pluto Books.

Sivanandan, A. (2008). The Speech by the IRR's Director, A. Sivanandan, at the IRR's Fiftieth Celebration Conference on 1 November 2008. *Institute of Race Relations.* http://www.irr.org.uk/news/catching-history-on-the-wing/

Slack, J., & Seamark, M. (2010, May 31). An affront to British justice: Gary McKinnon extradition CAN Be stopped, says Lib Dem QC. *Mail Online.* https://www.dailymail.co.uk/news/article-1282765/Gary-McKinnon-extradition-stopped-says-LibDem-QC-Lord-Carlile.html

Slahi, M. O. (2015). *Les Carnets de Guantanamo.* Paris: Michel Lafon.

Slesinger, I. (2018). A cartography of the unknowable: Technology, territory and subterranean agencies in Israel's management of the Gaza tunnels. *Geopolitics, 25*(1), 17–42.

Smedley, A. (2007). *Race in North America: Origin and evolution of a worldview* (3rd ed.). Boulder: Westview Press.

Smith, L. T. (1999). *Decolonizing methodologies: Research and indigenous peoples*. New York: Zed Books.

Smith, N. (1984). *Uneven development: Nature, capital, and the production of space*. Oxford: Blackwell.

Smith, W. C. (1980). The true meaning of scripture: An empirical historian's non-reductionist interpretation of the Qur'an. *International Journal of Middle East Studies, 11*(4), 487–505.

Snowden, K. (2016). Muslim boy's "terrorist house" spelling error leads to Lancashire police investigation. *Huff Post*. http://m.huffpost.com/uk/entry/9025336

Socialist Worker. (2017). Anger as labour council in Bradford plans huge "ideological" cuts to children's services. https://socialistworker.co.uk/art/45735/Anger +as+Labour+council+in+Bradford+plans+huge+ideological+cuts+to+childrens +services

Solomos, J. (1993). *Race and racism in Britain*. Macmillan International Higher Education.

Sophie-Abbas, M. (2018). The detrimental effects of current counter-extremism measures on British Muslim families. *LSE*. https://blogs.lse.ac.uk/politicsandpolicy/ the-detrimental-effects-of-current-counter-extremism-measures-on-british-muslim -families/

Soroush, A. (2000). Tolerance and governance: A discourse on religion and democracy. In M. Sadri & A. Sadri (Eds.), *Reason, freedom and democracy in Islam: Essential writings of Abdolkarim Soroush* (pp. 156–170). Oxford: Oxford University Press.

Spivak, G. C. (1988). Can the subaltern speak? In C. Nelson & L. Grossberg (Eds.), *Marxism and the interpretation of culture*. Chicago: University of Illinois Press.

Spivak, G. C. (1992). Acting bits/identity talk. *Critical Inquiry, 18*(4) (Summer 1992), 770–803.

Spivak, G. C. (1993). The politics of translation. In *Outside in the teaching machine* (pp. 200–225). New York: Routledge.

Stampnitzky, L. (2013). *Disciplining terror: How experts invented "terrorism"*. Cambridge: Cambridge University Press.

Stanard, M. (2009). Interwar pro-empire propaganda and European colonial culture: Toward a comparative research agenda. *Journal of Contemporary History, 44*(1), 27–48.

Steinberg. (2007). *Race relations: A critique*. Stanford: Stanford University Press.

Stepan, N. (1986). Race and gender: The role of analogy in science. *Isis, 77*(2), 261–277.

Stern, P. J. (2007). Politics and ideology in the early East India company-state: The case of St Helena, 1673–1709. *The Journal of Imperial and Commonwealth History, 35*(1), 1–23.

Stern, P. J. (2012). *The company-state: Corporate sovereignty and the early modern foundations of the British empire in India*. Oxford: Oxford University Press.

Stewart, M. W. (1988). Productions of Mrs. Maria W. Stewart, 1835. In S. E. Houtchins (Ed.), *Spiritual narratives* (pp. 51–56). Oxford: Oxford University Press.

Stoler, A. L., & Cooper, F. (2014). Between metropole and colony: Rethinking a research agenda. In *Tensions of empire: Colonial cultures in a Bourgeois world.* Berkeley: University of California Press.

Stoler, A. L., & Cooper, F. (Eds.). (1997). *Tensions of empire: Colonial cultures in a Bourgeois world.* Berkeley: University of California Press.

Strawson, J. (1995). Islamic law and English texts. *Law and Critique, 6*(1), 21–38.

Sukarieh, M. (2012). The hope crusades: Culturalism and reform in the Arab World. *Political and Legal Anthropology Review, 35*(1) (May), 115–134.

Sulayman, A. (1987). *Towards an Islamic theory of international relations: New directions for Islamic methodology and thought.* Herndon, VA: International Institute for Islamic Thought.

Sullins, J. (2018). Information technology and moral values. *Stanford Encyclopedia of Philosophy.* https://plato.stanford.edu/entries/it-moral-values/

Sullivan, S., & Tuana, N. (Eds.). (2007). *Race and epistemologies of ignorance.* Albany: State University of New York.

Sullivan, W. F. (2006). Comparing religions, legally. *Washington and Lee Law Review, 63*(1), 913.

SuperSisters. (2019). Status. *Facebook Page.* https://www.facebook.com/SuperSistersMag/posts/shamima-begum-was-one-of-four-young-british-women-who-fled-to-syria-to-join-isis/2027181044248956/

SuperSisters. About. https://www.supersisters.co.uk/about/

SupGaleano. (2015). The crack in the wall. First Note on Zapatista Method, May 3rd 2015. http://enlacezapatista.ezln.org.mx/2015/05/10/the-crack-in-the-wall-first-note-on-zapatista-method/

Tailor, N. (2019). This week saw police attack migrants in Paris while the met police say their institutional racism is over. *gal-dem.* https://gal-dem.com/this-week-saw-police-attack-migrants-in-paris-while-the-met-police-say-their-institutional-racism-is-over/

Tanis, F., Ericka, D., Mills, L., & Richter-Montpetit, M. (2018). Sexualized violence and torture in the afterlife of slavery: An interview with Farah Tanis and Ericka Dixon of Black women's blueprint. *International Feminist Journal of Politics, 20*(3), 446–461.

Tatchell, P. (2019). Free speech is under threat over Islamophobia. *The Times.* https://www.thetimes.co.uk/article/free-speech-is-under-threat-over-islamophobia-85r6h8czr

Taussig, M. (1997). *The magic of the state.* New York: Routledge.

Taussig, M. (1999). *Defacement.* Stanford: Stanford University Press.

Tawil-Souri, H. (2012). Digital occupation: Gaza's high-tech enclosure. *Journal of Palestine Studies, 41*(2), 27–43.

Taylor, D. (2019). Revealed: Five men killed in past year after being deported from UK to Jamaica. *Guardian.* https://www.theguardian.com/uk-news/2019/may/09/revealed-five-men-killed-since-being-deported-uk-jamaica-home-office

Taylor, I. (2009). Myths of the White working class. *Socialist Review, 336.* http://socialistreview.org.uk/336/myths-white-working-class

Taylor, M. (2006). Take off the veil, says straw - To immediate anger from Muslims. *Guardian*. https://www.theguardian.com/politics/2006/oct/06/immigrationpolicy .labour

Tell MAMA. (2016). *The geography of anti-Muslim hatred. Tell MAMA annual report 2015*. London: Faith Matters. https://tellmamauk.org/geography-anti-mus-lim-hatred-2015-tell-mama-annual-report/

Tell MAMA. (2018). Pensioners loudly echo Boris Johnson's Niqab comments in doctor's surgery. https://tellmamauk.org/pensioners-loudly-echo-boris-johnsons -niqab-comments-in-doctors-surgery/

Tharoor, S. (2017). *Inglorious empire: What the British did to India*. London: C. Hurst & Co.

The Office for Standards in Education, Children's Services and Skills (Ofsted). (2015). The common inspection framework: Education, skills and early years, Manchester.

Thomas, P. (2011). *Youth, multiculturalism and community cohesion*. Basingstoke: Palgrave Macmillan.

Thomas, P. (2012). *Responding to the threat of violent extremism – Failing to pre-vent*. London: Bloomsbury Academic.

Thomas, P., & Sanderson, P. (2013). Crossing the line? White young people and com-munity cohesion. *Critical Social Policy, 33*, 160–180.

Thomas, P. (2016). Youth, terrorism and education: Britain's prevent programme. *International Journal of Lifelong Education, 35*(2), 171–187.

Thompson, D. (2013). Through, against and beyond the racial state: The transnational stratum of race. *Cambridge Review of International Affairs, 26*(1), 133–151.

Thorsen, K. (1989). James Baldwin: The price of the ticket. https://www.kanopy.com /product/james-baldwin-price-ticket

Tickner, A. B. (2003). Hearing Latin American voices in international relations stud-ies. *International Studies Perspectives, 4*(4), 325–350.

Tickner, A. B. (2013). Core, periphery and (neo)imperialist international relations. *European Journal of International Relations, 19*(3), 627–646.

Tickner, A. B., & Wæver, O. (Eds.). (2009). *International relations scholarship around the world*. New York: Routledge.

Tilley, L. (2018a). Populist academics, colonial demography, and far-right discursive ecologies. *Discover Society*. https://discoversociety.org/2018/12/04/populist-aca-demics-colonial-demography-and-far-right-discursive-ecologies/

Tilley, L. (2018b). Recasting and re-racialising the "third world" in "emerging mar-ket" terms: Understanding market emergence in historical colonial perspective. *Discover Society*. https://discoversociety.org/2018/09/04/recasting-and-re-racialis-ing-the-third-world-in-emerging-market-terms-understanding-market-emergence -in-historical-colonial-perspective/

Tilley, L., Kumar, A., & Cowan, T. (2017). Enclosures and discontents: Primitive accumulation and resistance under global capital. *City: Analysis of Urban Trends, Culture, Theory, Policy, Action, 21*(3–4), 420–427.

Tilley, L., & Shilliam, R. (2018). Raced markets: An introduction. *New Political Economy, 23*(5), 534–543.

Tingyang, Z. (2009). A political world philosophy in terms of all-under-heaven (Tianxia). *Diogenes, 56*(5), 5–18.

Tolley, C. (1997). *Domestic biography: The legacy of evangelicalism in four nineteenth-century families*. Oxford: Clarendon.

Tomlinson, S. (1981). *Educational subnormality: A study in decision-making*. London: Routledge and Kegan Paul.

Tomlinson, S. (1989). The origins of the ethnocentric curriculum. In G. K. Verma (Eds.), *Education for all: A landmark for pluralism* (pp. 26–41). London: Falmer.

Tomlinson, S. (2014). *The politics of race, class and special education; the selected works of Sally Tomlinson*. London: Routledge.

Tomlinson, S. (2019). Inequality, Brexit and the end of empire. *LSE Public Lectures and Events*. http://www.lse.ac.uk/Events/2019/03/20190329t1830vOT/inequality

Topping, A. (2017). Women link hands on Westminster Bridge to remember victims. *Guardian*. https://www.theguardian.com/uk-news/2017/mar/26/women-westminster-bridge-london-womens-march-solidarity-attack-victims

Travis, A. (2013). "Go home" vans resulted in 11 people leaving Britain, says report. *Guardian*. https://www.theguardian.com/uk-news/2013/oct/31/go-home-vans-11-leave-britain

Travis, A. (2015, December 10). UK terror arrest at record level after increase in female suspects. *Guardian*.

Trevelyan, G. O. (1881). *The life and letters of Lord Macaulay*. London: Longman, Green.

Trevor-Roper, H. R. (1965). *The rise of Christian Europe*. New York: Harcourt, Brace & World.

Turner, B. (1984). Orientalism and the problem of civil society in Islam. In A. Hussain, R. Olson, & J. Qureshi (Eds.), *Orientalism, Islam, and Islamists*. Brattleboro, VT: Amana Books.

Tyrer, D. (2013). *The politics of Islamophobia: Race, power and fantasy*. London: Pluto.

Ucko, D. H. (2009). *The new counterinsurgency era: Transforming the U.S. military for modern wars*. Washington, DC: Georgetown University Press.

UNESCO Statement on Race UNESCO. (1950). The race question. http://unesdoc.unesco.org/images/0012/001282/128291eo.pdf

Valluvan, S. (2019). *The clamour of nationalism: Race and nation in twenty-first-century Britain*. Manchester: Manchester University Press.

Van der Veer, R. (2003). Primitive mentality reconsidered. *Culture & Psychology, 9*(2), 179–184.

Vargas, J. C., & Alves, J. A. (2013). Geographies of death: An intersectional analysis of police lethality and the racialized regimes of citizenship in São Paulo. In P. Amar (Ed.), *New racial missions of policing: International perspectives on evolving law-enforcement politics* (pp. 37–62). London: Routledge.

Vázquez, R. (2012). Towards a decolonial critique of modernity: BuenVivir, relationality and the task of listening. In R. Fornet-Betancourt (Ed.), *Capital, poverty, development: Denktraditionenim Dialog: StudienzurBefreiung und Interkultalitat 33* (pp. 241–252). Wissenschaftsverlag Mainz, Germany: Achen.

Vekaik, R. (2016). The trials of Babar Ahmad: From Jihad in Bosnia to a US prison via met brutality. *Guardian*. https://www.theguardian.com/uk-news/2016/mar/12/babar-ahmad-jihad-bosnia-us-police-interview

Versi, M., Aly, R., & Bano, A. (2016). Was Muslims like us a helpful portrayal of Islam in the UK? *Guardian*. https://www.theguardian.com/commentisfree/2016/dec/14/panel-muslims-like-us-islam

Vial, T. (2016). *Modern religion, modern race*. New York: Oxford University Press.

Violence Policy Center. (2018). More than 1,800 women murdered by men in one year, new study finds. *VPC*. http://vpc.org/press/more-than-1800-women-murdered-by-men-in-one-year-new-study-finds/

Virdee, S., & McGeever, B. (2018). Racism, crisis, Brexit. *Ethnic and Racial Studies, 41*(10), 1802–1819.

Vitalis, R. (2000). The graceful and generous liberal gesture: Making racism invisible in American international relations. *Millennium, 29*(2), 331–356.

Vitalis, R. (2005). Birth of a discipline. In D. Long & B. C. Schmidt (Eds.), *Imperialism and internationalism in the discipline of international relations* (pp. 159–182). New York: State University of New York Press.

Vitalis, R. (2008). From international relations – Back when "international relations meant race relations" – to area studies, ISA Annual Convention (San Francisco).

Vitalis, R. (2010). The Noble American science of imperial relations and its laws of race development. *Comparative Studies in Society and History, 52*(4), 909–938.

Vitalis, R. (Forthcoming). *The end of empire in international relations*.

Von Knop, K. (2007). The female Jihad: Al Qaeda's women. *Studies in Conflict & Terrorism, 30*(5), 397–414.

Vucetic, S. (2011). A racialized peace? How Britain and the US made their relationship special. *Foreign Policy Analysis, 7*(4), 403–421.

Wadiwel, D. (2017). Disability and torture: Exception, epistemology and "Black sites." *Continuum, 31*(3), 388–399.

Wadud, A. (2006). *Inside the gender Jihad: Women's reform in Islam*. Oxford: Oneworld.

Waghorn, D. (2019). Jihadi Jack: "Free me so i can fight against Islamic radicalisation." *Sky News*. https://news.sky.com/story/jihadi-jack-free-me-so-i-can-fight-against-islamic-radicalisation-11789744

Wagner, K. A. (2018). Savage warfare: Violence and the rule of colonial difference in early British counterinsurgency. *History Workshop Journal, 85*, 217–237.

Walker, A. (2019). Nigel Farage shelters on campaign bus to avoid milkshake attack. *Guardian*. https://www.theguardian.com/politics/2019/may/22/nigel-farage-shelters-on-campaign-bus-to-avoid-milkshake-attack

Walker, D. (1830). *David Walker's appeal, in four articles; together with a preamble, to the coloured citizens of the world, but in particular, and very expressly, to those of the United States of America*. Boston.

Walker, J. St. G. (1976). *The Black loyalists: The search for a promised land in Nova Scotia and Sierra Leone*. London: Longman.

Walker, K. (2018). Inquiry launches into history of eugenics at UCL. https://www.ucl.ac.uk/news/2018/dec/inquiry-launches-history-eugenics-ucl

Walker, P. (2019). Sajid Javid: Difficult to strip Shamima Begum of UK citizenship. *Guardian.* https://www.theguardian.com/uk-news/2019/feb/27/sajid-javid-difficult-to-strip-shamima-begum-of-uk-citizenship

Walker, R. B. J. (Ed.). (2006). Special section: Theorizing the liberty-security relation: Sovereignty, liberalism and exceptionalism. *Security Dialogue, 37*(1), 7–82.

Wallace, H. (2013). The UK national DNA database: Balancing crime detection, human rights and privacy. *EMBO Reports,* July 2006, s26–s30; *Home Office, National DNA Database Strategy Board Annual Report 2012–13.* London: Home Office.

Wallerstein, I. (1970). Frantz Fanon: Reason and violence. *Berkeley Journal of Sociology, 15*, 222–231.

Wallerstein, I. (1995). *After liberalism.* New York: New Press.

Walsh, C. (2014). Pedagogical notes from the decolonial cracks. *e-misférica, 11*(1). http://archive.hemisphericinstitute.org/hemi/en/emisferica-111-decolonial-gesture/walsh

Ward, S. (Ed.). (2001). *British culture and the end of empire.* Manchester: Manchester University Press.

Wasty, B. (2018). Why we're concerned about Sara Khan, the new anti-extremism chief. *Guardian.* https://www.theguardian.com/commentisfree/2018/jan/25/concerned-sara-khan-anti-extremism-british-muslims

Waters, R. (2013). "Britain is no longer White": James Baldwin as a witness to postcolonial Britain. *African American Review, 46*(4), 715–730.

Waterson, J. (2018). Bodyguard creator wanted twist to "completely alter dynamic". *Guardian.* https://www.theguardian.com/tv-and-radio/2018/sep/11/bodyguard-creator-jed-mercurio-bbc-twist-completely-alter-dynamic

Watson, H. (2001). Theorizing the racialization of global politics and the Caribbean experience. *Alternatives, 26*(4), 449–483.

Weizman, E. (2017). *Hollow land: Israel's architecture of occupation.* London: Verso.

Wekker, G. (2016). *White innocence: Paradoxes of colonialism and race.* Durham: Duke University Press.

Wheeler, K. R. (2020). Black Islam syllabus. https://docs.google.com/document/d/1avhgPrW30AFjegzV9X5aPqkZUA3uGd0-BZr9_zhArtQ/edit

Wheeler, K. R. (Forthcoming). *Fashioning Black Islam: Race, gender and belonging in the Ummah.*

White, R. (2017). Walter Benjamin: "The storyteller" and the possibility of wisdom. *The Journal of Aesthetic Education, 51*(1), 1–15.

White, S. (2002). Thinking race, thinking development. *Third World Quarterly, 23*(3), 407–419.

Whitehead, C. (1999). The contribution of the Christian missions to British colonial education. *Paedagogica Historica, 35*(Suppl 1), 321–337.

Wiktorowicz, Q. (2005). *Radical Islam rising: Muslim extremism in the West.* Oxford: Rowman & Littlefield.

Wilderson, F. B., III. (2010). *Red, White & Black: Cinema and the structure of U.S. antagonisms.* Durham, NC: Duke University Press.

Williams, P. (1997). *The genealogy of race, Reith lectures.* BBC Radio 4.

Wilson, E. G. (1976). *The loyal Blacks.* Ontario: Capricorn Books.

Winant, H. (2001). *The world is a Ghetto: Race and democracy since World War II.* New York, NY: Basic Books.

Wing, A. K. (2000). *Global critical race feminism: An international reader.* New York, NY: New York University Press.

Wiredu, K. (1992). Formulating modern thoughts in African languages: Some theoretical considerations. In V. Y. Mudimbe (Ed.), *The surreptitious speech: Presence Africaine and the politics of otherness, 1947–1987* (pp. 301–332). Chicago: University of Chicago Press.

Wiredu, K. (1998). Toward decolonizing African philosophy and religion. *African Studies Quarterly: The Online Journal of African Studies, 1*(4), 17–46.

Wolf, E. R. (1982). *Europe and the people without history.* Berkeley: University of California Press.

Wolfe, M. (2019). Obsession with White working class fuels inequality in North, study warns. *Guardian.* https://www.theguardian.com/uk-news/2019/aug/15/white-working-class-fuels-inequality-north

Wolfe, P. (2006). Settler colonialism and the elimination of the native. *Journal of Genocide Research, 8*(4), 387–409.

Wolin, S. (2016). *Politics and vision: Continuity and innovation in Western political thought.* New Jersey: Princeton University Press.

Wollstonecraft, M. (1996). *A vindication of the rights of woman.* New York: Dover.

Wood, L. (2016). *Islamic legal revival: Reception of European law and transformations in Islamic legal thought in Egypt, 1875–1952.* Oxford: Oxford University Press.

Wright, R. (2018). Windrush scandal spreads to other commonwealth countries. *Financial Times.* https://www.ft.com/content/ddbdf02e-47c8-11e8-8ee8-cae73aab7ccb

Wynter, S. (2001). Towards the sociogenic principle: Fanon, the puzzle of conscious experience, and what it is like to be "Black". In M. F. Duran-Cogan & A. Gómez-Moriana (Eds.), *National identities and socio-political changes in Latin America* (pp. 30–66). New York: Routledge.

Wynter, S. (2003). Unsettling the coloniality of being/power/truth/freedom: Towards the human, after man, its overrepresentation. An Argument. *New Centennial Review, 3*(3), 257–337.

Yacine. (2007). cartoon. *Agenda Intercultural* 256 (October 2007).

Young, J. D. (1999). *The world of C. L. R. James: His unfragmented vision.* Glasgow: Clydeside.

Younge, G. (2019a). Our glorious past is what we remember. The brutality behind it we've forgotten. *Guardian.* https://www.theguardian.com/commentisfree/2019/may/31/glorious-past-remember-brutality-forgotten

Younge, G. (2019b). Shocked by the rise of the right? then you weren't paying attention. *Guardian.* https://www.theguardian.com/commentisfree/2019/may/24/country-racist-elections-liberals-anti-racism-movement

Younis, T. (2019). Counter-radicalization: A critical look into a racist new industry. *Yaqeen Institute.* https://yaqeeninstitute.org/tarekyounis/counter-radicalization-a-critical-look-into-a-racist-new-industry/#.XYC5KJNKg1I

Yusuf, K. (2006). *A counter-productive extradition policy – The effect of the Babar Ahmad case in radicalising Muslims in Britain.* London: Free Babar Ahmad Campaign.

Yuval-Davis, N. (1992). Fundamentalism, multiculturalism and women in Britain. In J. Donald & A. Rattansi (Eds.), *Race, culture, difference.* London: Sage.

Zakaria, R. (2015). Women and Islamic militancy. *Dissent, 62*(1), Winter.

Zeynep, G. C. (2017). Decolonising international relations? *Third World Quarterly, 38*(1), 1–15.

Zine, J. (2008). Lost in translation: Writing back from the margins. *Journal of Feminist Studies of Religion, 24*(1), 110–116.

Zonana, J. (1993). The Sultan and the slave: Feminist orientalism and the structure of Jane Eyre. *Signs, 18*(3), 592–617.

Zuboff, S. (2018). *The age of surveillance capitalism: The fight for a human future at the new frontier of power.* London: Profile Books.

Index